IMPORTANT:

HERE IS YOUR REGISTRATION CODE TO ACCESS YOUR PREMIUM McGRAW-HILL ONLINE RESOURCES.

For key premium online resources you need THIS CODE to gain access. Once the code is entered, you will be able to use the Web resources for the length of your course.

If your course is using **WebCT** or **Blackboard**, you'll be able to use this code to access the McGraw-Hill content within your instructor's online course.

Access is provided if you have purchased a new book. If the registration code is missing from this book, the registration screen on our Website, and within your WebCT or Blackboard course, will tell you how to obtain your new code.

Registering for McGraw-Hill Online Resources

To gain access to your McGraw-Hill web resources simply follow the steps below:

1. USE YOUR WEB BROWSER TO GO TO: **www.mhhe.com/lattimore1**
2. CLICK ON **FIRST TIME USER**.
3. ENTER THE REGISTRATION CODE* PRINTED ON THE TEAR-OFF BOOKMARK ON THE RIGHT.
4. AFTER YOU HAVE ENTERED YOUR REGISTRATION CODE, CLICK **REGISTER**.
5. FOLLOW THE INSTRUCTIONS TO SET-UP YOUR PERSONAL UserID AND PASSWORD.
6. WRITE YOUR UserID AND PASSWORD DOWN FOR FUTURE REFERENCE. KEEP IT IN A SAFE PLACE.

TO GAIN ACCESS to the McGraw-Hill content in your instructor's **WebCT** or **Blackboard** course simply log in to the course with the UserID and Password provided by your instructor. Enter the registration code exactly as it appears in the box to the right when prompted by the system. You will only need to use the code the first time you click on McGraw-Hill content.

Thank you, and welcome to your McGraw-Hill online resources!

* YOUR REGISTRATION CODE CAN BE USED ONLY ONCE TO ESTABLISH ACCESS. IT IS NOT TRANSFERABLE.

0-07-293319-4 T/A LATTIMORE: PUBLIC RELATIONS

MCGRAW-HILL

ONLINE RESOURCES

REGISTRATION CODE

3NM9-SAHV-0763-HJA1-OVYN

Higher Education

Public Relations
The Profession and the Practice

Public Relations

The Profession and the Practice

DAN LATTIMORE,
OTIS BASKIN,
SUZETTE T. HEIMAN,
ELIZABETH L. TOTH,
JAMES K. VAN LEUVEN

Boston Burr Ridge, IL Dubuque, IA Madison, WI New York
San Francisco St. Louis Bangkok Bogotá Caracas Kuala Lumpur
Lisbon London Madrid Mexico City Milan Montreal New Delhi
Santiago Seoul Singapore Sydney Taipei Toronto

The McGraw·Hill Companies

PUBLIC RELATIONS: THE PROFESSION AND THE PRACTICE
Published by McGraw-Hill, a business unit of The McGraw-Hill Companies, Inc., 1221 Avenue of the Americas, New York, NY, 10020.

This book is printed on acid-free paper.

1 2 3 4 5 6 7 8 9 0 WCK/WCK 0 9 8 7 6 5 4 3

ISBN 0-07-242402-8

Publisher: *Phillip A. Butcher*
Sponsoring editor: *Phillip A. Butcher*
Developmental editor: *Jennie Katsaros*
Senior marketing manager: *Daniel M. Loch*
Lead media producer: *Erin Marean*
Project manager: *Ruth Smith*
Production supervisor: *Janean Utley*
Freelance design coordinator: *Gino Cieslik*
Supplement producer: *Kathleen Boylan*
Photo research coordinator: *Alexandra Ambrose*
Art editor: *Emma Ghiselli*
Photo research: *PoYee Oster*
Permissions: *Marty Granahan*
Cover and interior design: *Kay Fulton*
Cover photos: Top left—©Bob Daemmrich/Stock Boston, Top right and bottom—©Corbis
Typeface: *10/12 Minion*
Compositor: *Prographics*
Printer: *Quebecor World Versailles Inc.*

Library of Congress Cataloging-in-Publication Data
Public relations: the profession and the practice / Dan Lattimore . . . [et al.].
p. cm.
Rev. ed. of: Public relations / Otis Baskin, Craig Aronoff, Dan Lattimore. 4th ed. c1997.
Includes index.
ISBN 0-07-242402-8 (softcover : alk. paper)
1. Public relations. 2. Public relations—United States. I. Lattimore, Dan. II. Baskin, Otis W. Public relations.
HM1221.P82 2004
659.2—dc21

2003052650

www.mhhe.com

Brief Contents

Contents

PART TWO The Process 89

Preface

Public relations as a *profession* is changing rapidly. The *practice* of public relations has undergone almost revolutionary changes in the past few years thanks to Internet-driven technology. This major information source provides for the first time a way for organizations to communicate directly and instantly with a variety of its audiences, oftentimes without using traditional mass media. Globalization of worldwide markets and organizational restructuring are two more powerful influences on the practice of public relations.

These critical changes in globalization, technology, and organizational structure lend increasing importance to the management function of public relations. Practitioners are no longer mere technicians who shape and transmit messages from their organizations. They are professionals who shape the relationships an organization has with its various constituencies. Public relations practitioners must possess the communications expertise and social sensitivity necessary to enable organizations to adapt to the changing environment.

Public relations practitioners must bring not only all of the traditional communications skills to their broadened role, but must now bring the ability to research and understand problems, to plan the public relations programs, to create effective messages, and to evaluate the effectiveness of these programs. The goals of this edition are to present and explain the fundamental tools of the public relations practice and provide an understanding of the emerging trends within the field.

APPROACH OF THE TEXT

A multi-disciplinary approach has characterized the text from its inception and is continued in this edition. We believe that by drawing on the experience of professionals from journalism, business, psychology, and communication we can present a comprehensive and inclusive overview of public relations. The education, research, and teaching experience of the authors in each of these disciplines addresses the needs of the students who will be practicing in diverse environments.

We have tried to maintain the easy-to-read, personal style throughout the text. To that end, we have kept the jargon to a minimum, and have provided definitions for all terms that are particular to the profession. In addition, we have attempted to give public relations students and practitioners the tools and knowledge they need in ways that reflect the reality of public relations. For example, mini-cases provide insight into real-time activities conducted by organizations. They are interspersed throughout and provide applications for the basic concepts being introduced. Public relations spotlights provide various kinds of helpful information such as tips for getting good photographs and how to clear publicity releases.

ORGANIZATION AND CONTENT

This edition has retained the four part organization of earlier editions: the profession, the process, the publics, and the practice. Part One describes the current public relations situation, its historical roots, theories, and ethics and legal concerns. Part Two examines the core issues of the process that underlies public relations while Part Three focuses on the publics that are the object of these efforts. Finally, Part Four summarizes the practice of public relations and looks at the emerging trends of the profession. We believe that this structure truly reflects the growth and development of public relations as an emerging profession.

There are several structural changes to this edition. Chapter One is virtually a new chapter. Not only does it provide an overview of the field, it also incorporates coverage of organizational decision making. We have combined the chapters on law and ethics (now Chapter Four) because the two are inextricably intertwined. The chapters on public affairs and government relations have also been folded together into Chapter Fourteen. Finally, there is a brand new chapter (Chapter Seventeen) on emerging issues.

Every chapter has been completely updated, while retaining the classic material. The content truly reflects the direction of public relations on the 21st century.

PEDAGOGY

- Each chapter opens with a preview that provides an overview of the chapter content.
- Mini-cases in each chapter allow students to "see" public relations in action.
- Spotlights in each chapter add material to enhance students' understanding of chapter concepts.
- Numerous figures and tables explain and clarify concepts under discussion.
- An integrating case study runs through each of the four chapters of Part Two to help pull together the process.
- Each chapter ends with a case study.
- Highlighted glossary terms appear throughout the text, in addition to a complete end of book glossary with definitions.

WHAT'S NEW IN EACH CHAPTER

Chapter One: The Nature of Public Relations

From the outset this completely revised chapter introduces the reader to the changing nature of public relations campaigns and the multiple demands constantly placed on the public relations practitioner. Management and leadership functions are distinguished. Discussion of Dilenschneider's elements of public discontent and a discussion of the public relations education role of developing future leaders is included.

Chapter Two: The History of Public Relations

Unlike other public relations texts, this book's history chapter gives more attention to public relations contributions from non-profits, social movements, and historical models of public relations. Included are Arthur Page's six principles of public relations, a profile of Pat Jackson, and conceptual traditions in public relations.

Chapter Three: A Theoretical Basis for Public Relations

New dimensions are added to the models of public relations to explain how theories are evolving to better explain the practice of public relations. There is also a discussion of Pat Jackson's lasting contributions to public relations and coverage of the monitoring of relationships.

Chapter Four: Law and Ethics

This chapter gives new emphasis to the developing legal consideration of the Internet. The new Code of Ethics of the Public Relations Society of America (PRSA) is included along with the Code of the International Association of Business Communicators.

Chapter Five: Research: Understanding Public Opinion

The research chapter begins the process section with the initial part of the case study that runs throughout the four chapters in this section. The research terms are explained in lay language with a spotlight. Usability research for web-based material is included along with a new look at Internet, library, and data bank resources.

Chapter Six: Strategic Planning for Public Relations Effectiveness

New in this chapter are elements for a single-use campaign plan detailed including a sample plan and budget.

Chapter Seven: Action and Communication

Internet writing guidelines are included for this edition along with more emphasis in two controlled tools: advertising and the World Wide Web.

Chapter Eight: Evaluating Public Relations Effectiveness

New in this chapter is an examination of Ketchum's extranet efforts, additional measurement strategies, and new evaluation software.

Chapter Nine: Media Relations

This chapter has shifted to an e-mail and webpage-based process, especially when dealing with the trade press and national and regional media. A new section on a crisis response statement is included.

Chapter Ten: Employee Communication

This chapter considers the new labor force of the 21st century and its influence on employee communication. Public relations practitioners will have an integral role in creating communications that seek employee support for organizational change.

Chapter Eleven: Community Relations

This chapter provides new information about two areas of increasing importance in community relations: cause-related marketing and community activism. Case studies provide tangible examples of how community relations can have a significant impact on a corporation's branding and reputation. In addition, there is a section on employee volunteerism.

Chapter Twelve: Consumer Relations and Marketing

This chapter provides guidelines that communicators can use when selecting appropriate marketing communications activities. New sections include guerilla tactics, branded news strategy, and trends in brand naming.

Chapter Thirteen: Financial Relations

New to this chapter is an examination of corporations that have been faced with financial reporting scandals with a spotlight on Enron and the public relations lessons learned from that situation.

Chapter Fourteen: Public Affairs: Relations with Government

This chapter combines discussions of the specialization of public relations focused on building relationships to influence and inform key groups about political activities. The chapter introduces information on the use of websites as a political tool and how public affairs is carried out in non-profit settings.

Chapter Fifteen: Public Relations in Nonprofit Organizations

This chapter provides a global perspective on non-profit work, going far beyond small, well-intentioned community-based programs and including a discussion of the challenges faced by nonprofits. The Lutheran Services of America case study discusses how this $7 billion network provides a full range of health and human services in more than three thousand communities.

Chapter Sixteen: Corporate Public Relations

A corporation's most important concern is its ability to maintain an environment conducive to doing business. This chapter discusses the crucial role that public relations plays in creating and developing a corporation's image and reputation with its key publics, particularly life after corporate scandals. Included are the ten characteristics of effective corporate communication and the role of the CEO in public relations. The BP case study introduces some of the issues and challenges faced by corporations when merging with other entities.

Chapter Seventeen: Emerging Trends in Public Relations

This brand new chapter prepares future practitioners for the most pressing globalization, technology, and corporate social responsibility changes in the field. The Napster case study shows how the Internet can be used as a public relations tool.

SUPPLEMENTS FOR STUDENTS AND INSTRUCTORS

Student CD-ROM

The CD-ROM that accompanies the text offers students a variety of resources and activities. They are integrated with the text through the use of CD icons in the text margins that notify students which CD tool to use. They include:

- *Video*—The video includes clips of 15 interviews with public relations practitioners from public relations firms such as Ketchum and Burson Marsteller.

- *Self-Quizzes*—Students can assess their comprehension of the chapter concepts by taking practice tests that provide feedback for each answer.
- *Audio Flash Cards*—Students can use these digital flash cards to hear how key terms are pronounced and to study for exams.

Instructor's Resource CD-ROM

This CD-ROM includes the following resources:

- *Test Bank*—available as a computerized test bank or as a basic Word document.
- *Instructor's Resource Manual*—provides chapter summaries and objectives, media resources, activities, and test questions.
- *PowerPoint Slides*—This set of slides, developed by Dan Lattimore, includes chapter outlines and video clips.

Video: Interviews with Public Relations Professionals

Fifteen original video interviews conducted by the book's authors are part of the student CD-ROM and are also available in VHS format. Instructors can use the clips as lecture launchers or discussion starters. A printed video manual provides a summary and discussion questions for each segment.

Online Learning Center

This website, at www.mhhe.com/lattimore, provides instructors with professional resources, PowerPoint slides, and downloadable supplements and provides students with additional interactive test questions and glossary crossword puzzles to help them master course concepts. Icons in the text direct students to relevant resources on this website.

PowerWeb

PowerWeb is a component of the *Online Learning Center* that brings the information on the Internet to a course. It features current articles, informative and timely world news, curriculum-based materials, research tools, and additional resources. This content, which is password protected, is offered free with new copies of the text.

PageOut: The Course Website Development Center

All online content for this text is supported by WebCT, eCollege.com, Blackboard, and other course management systems. McGraw-Hill's PageOut service is available to get you and your course up and running online in a matter of hours, at no cost. PageOut was designed for instructors just beginning to explore Web options. Even the novice computer user can create a course website with a template provided by McGraw-Hill (no programming knowledge necessary). To learn more about PageOut, ask your McGraw-Hill representative for details, or fill out the form at www.mhhe.com/pageout.

ACKNOWLEDGMENTS

Our thanks go to many people: colleagues with whom we have worked in public relations education, our public relations mentors, leading practitioners who have been willing for us to interview them, and public relations firms and organizations that have provided many of the materials and examples. They are too numerous to name, but they all have our gratitude.

The following academics reviewed our manuscript and helped us to make it as useful as possible for students and professors:

Michael E. Bishop
Baylor University

Garry Bolan
Towson University

Brigitta R. Brunner
Auburn University

Karen Buzzard
Southwest Missouri State University

Rebekah Bromley
University of Tennessee, Chattanooga

Coy Callison
Texas Tech University

Todd Chambers
Texas Tech University

Joseph L. Clark
University of Toledo

Scott Dickmeyer
University of Wisconsin, LaCrosse

Sallie Gaines
Loyola University, Chicago

Louella Benson-Garcia
Pepperdine University

Kirk Hallahan
Colorado State University

Margaret Fitch-Hauser
Auburn University

Rachel Holloway
Virginia Tech University

Linda Childers Hon
University of Florida

John M. King
East Tennessee State University

Maryl Neff
Ithaca College

Beatrice Pittock
Central Washington University

Doug Swanson
University of Wisconsin, La Crosse

Eileen Wirth
Creighton University

We are deeply appreciative to those who distilled from their professional or teaching experiences the cases and spotlights that appear in each chapter and on the CD-ROM. Our appreciation goes to our universities for their support, services, and resources. Finally, we give our sincere thanks to the professionals at McGraw-Hill Publishing, particularly our developmental editor, Jennie Katsaros, and our copy editor, Rosalind Sackoff, who worked so hard and long assisting us in putting the project together.

Dan Lattimore, *University of Memphis*
Otis Baskin, *Pepperdine University*
Suzette Heiman, *University of Missouri, Columbia*
Elizabeth Toth, *Syracuse University*
James Van Leuven, *University of Oregon*

About the Authors

Dan Lattimore is vice provost for extended programs, dean of University College, professor of journalism at the University of Memphis, and an accredited public relations practitioner. He is the author of five books and represents PRSA on the Accrediting Council for Education in Journalism and Mass Communication.

Otis Baskin is professor of management at the George L. Graziadio School of Business and Management at Pepperdine University where he served as dean from 1995-2001. Dr. Baskin has served as an adviser to management for public and private organizations around the world. He is a frequent speaker to industry and executive groups including The Conference Board, The Family Business Network (Europe) and the International Security Management Network. Dr. Baskin's scholarly achievements include six books, in addition to numerous articles, and published papers.

Suzette Heiman is director of planning and communication and an associate professor at the Missouri School of Journalism at the University of Missouri, Columbia. Her professional background includes experience in public relations and advertising for nonprofits and she serves as a consultant to industry.

Elizabeth L. Toth is the associate dean and chair of the public relations department, and full professor at the S. I. Newhouse School of Public Communications at Syracuse University. She edits *Journalism Studies,* an international mass communications journal. She's received for her research and teaching the PRSA Jackson Jackson and Wagner Behavioral Science prize, the Institute for Public Relations Pathfinder Award, and the PRSA Outstanding Educator Award.

Jim Van Leuven holds the endowed chair in public relations at the University of Oregon. As chair of journalism at Colorado State University he developed a communications management master's program for working public relations professionals in Denver. He coordinated PRSA's original body of knowledge study and has taught on business faculties at the National University of Singapore and Kuring-gai College, Sydney, Australia, as well as on journalism communications faculties at the University of Idaho, Washington State University, and Oregon State University.

Visual Preview

The Profession and the Practice: A Structure that Reflects the Growth and Development of Public Relations

Unique 4-part organization ensures that students will leave your course with a thorough understanding of public relations and a basis for successful practice today and in the future.

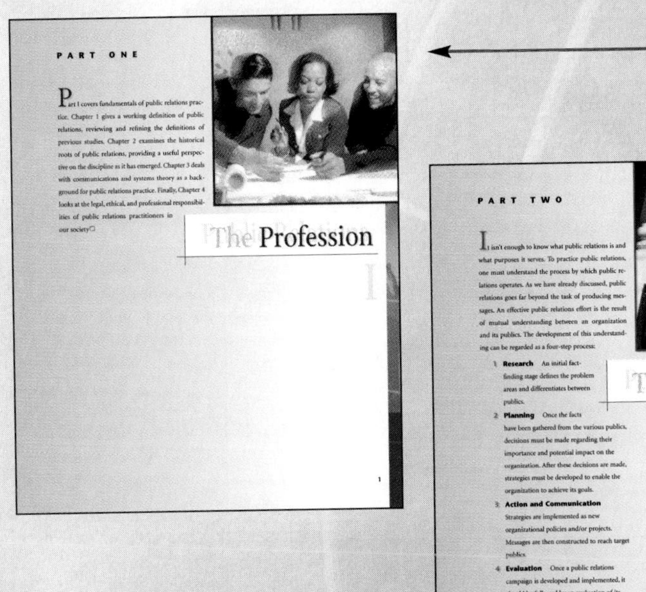

PART ONE

The Profession

I

Part I covers fundamentals of public relations practice. Chapter 1 gives a working definition of public relations, reviewing and refining the definitions of previous studies. Chapter 2 examines the historical roots of public relations, providing a useful perspective on the discipline as it has emerged. Chapter 3 deals with communications and systems theory as a background for public relations practice. Finally, Chapter 4 looks at the legal, ethical, and professional responsibilities of public relations practitioners in our society □

1

Part One *describes the current public relations climate, its history, theories, ethics and legal concerns.*

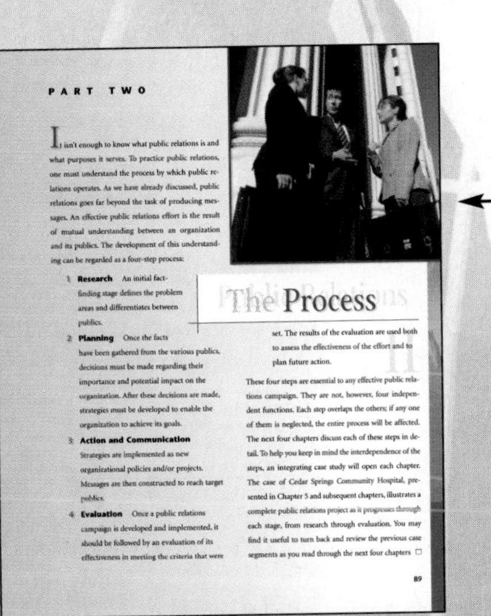

PART TWO

The Process

II

It isn't enough to know what public relations is and what purposes it serves. To practice public relations, one must understand the process by which public relations operates. As we have already discussed, public relations goes far beyond the task of producing messages. An effective public relations effort is the result of mutual understanding between an organization and its publics. The development of this understanding can be regarded as a four-step process:

1. **Research** An initial fact-finding stage defines the problem areas and differentiates between publics.
2. **Planning** Once the facts have been gathered from the various publics, decisions must be made regarding their importance and potential impact on the organization. After these decisions are made, strategies must be developed to enable the organization to achieve its goals.
3. **Action and Communication** Strategies are implemented as new organizational policies and/or projects. Messages are then constructed to reach target publics.
4. **Evaluation** Once a public relations campaign is developed and implemented, it should be followed by an evaluation of its effectiveness in meeting the criteria that were set. The results of the evaluation are used both to assess the effectiveness of the effort and to plan future action.

These four steps are essential to any effective public relations campaign. They are not, however, four independent functions. Each step overlaps the others; if any one of them is neglected, the entire process will be affected. The next four chapters discuss each of these steps in detail. To help you keep in mind the interdependence of the steps, an integrating case study will open each chapter. The case of Cedar Springs Community Hospital, presented in Chapter 5 and subsequent chapters, illustrates a complete public relations project as it progresses through each stage, from research through evaluation. You may find it useful to turn back and review the previous case segments as you read through the next four chapters □

89

Part Two *examines the core issues of the process that underlies public relations.*

PART THREE

The Publics

III

A public is a group of people with certain common characteristics. A public can be large—college students, Hispanics, blue-collar workers, or even all taxpayers. It can be small—the town council, the executive council for a university, newspaper editors, or even a three-person tax appeal board. Different organizations have different publics, often called stakeholders because they have a particular interest in that organization. The publics for the auto industry are different from those for the school board. Not-for-profit organizations have publics different from profit-seeking companies. Different levels of government organizations deal with different publics.

Part III describes five general types of publics that most public relations professionals face on a regular basis. Chapter 9 discusses the media, one of the most basic publics that practitioners deal with. Chapter 10 focuses on the organization's relationship with its employees, and Chapter 11 delves into the complex relationships between an organization and its community. Chapter 12 covers the importance of consumers to modern organizations. Finally, Chapter 13 discusses the impact of financial markets on public relations practice □

175

Part Three *focuses on the publics that are the object of the public relations efforts.*

PART FOUR

The Practice

IV

Public relations serves all types of organizations. Governmental organizations and agencies, nonprofit organizations, and corporations have embraced public relations and set it to work, recognizing it as a means of increasing organizational effectiveness in a complex and changing environment.

To operate effectively within these organizations, the public relations practitioners must be thoroughly aware of all we have discussed to this point: the process of communication, the role of public relations in organizational decision making, the four-step public relations process, and the primary publics of public relations. Practitioners must also recognize the problems and publics that are specific to public relations in each organizational type.

In this section, we look first at the practice of public relations in three distinct types of organizations: Chapter 14, government; Chapter 15, nonprofit organizations; and Chapter 16, corporations. We conclude in Chapter 17 with a realistic look at emerging trends in public relations □

299

Part Four *summarizes the practice of public relations and looks at the emerging trends of the profession.*

The Profession and the Practice: Tools and Knowledge that Reflect the Reality of Public Relations

***Mini-cases**—Appear throughout each chapter to allow students to "see" public relations in action. Some mini-cases are also on the CD-ROM and VHS videocassette.*

7.1 Mini•Case — The Pepsi Hoax

It began in Seattle when a TV station informed the local Pepsi franchise bottler that an 82-year-old Tacoma man had found a hypodermic needle in a can of Diet Pepsi. The report was broadcast that evening on the local news. It would be the nation's top story for the next 96 hours. Within hours another syringe turned up in a can in another locality. Soon news broadcasts from around the country had reports of people finding needles in Pepsi cans.[2] Eventually, more than 50 allegations were made in 23 states.[3]

Pepsi Cola set up a crisis management team at its corporate headquarters in Somers, New York. The team was led by Craig Weatherup, Pepsi president. Rebecca Madeira, Pepsi vice president for public affairs, directed the team's actions and coordinated the communications so the company could speak with one voice.

First, the Pepsi crisis team had to determine if the Pepsi bottlers were the problem. The crisis response plan had these key points:

- Put public safety first. Assess the problem through the public's eyes. Be clear that their needs and concerns come first.
- Find it. Fix it. Work around the clock with regulatory officials to investigate every aspect of the plant operation to identify and, if possible, correct the problem.
- Communicate quickly and frequently, using tools and timetables reporters use.
- Take responsibility for solving the crisis. Don't point fingers, assign blame, or pass the buck. Make your team accountable for a swift and sound resolution to the problem.[4]

Once Pepsi had gathered its facts and felt secure that this was not a problem caused by its bottlers, Pepsi took the offensive. President Weatherup said repeatedly through the media, "A can is the most tamper-proof packaging in food supply. We are 99.99 percent certain that this didn't happen in Pepsi plants."[5]

The crisis team decided to use VNRs to show consumers that Pepsi's canning process could not be tampered with. High-tech, high-speed equipment was shown filling Pepsi cans. Each can was turned upside down, cleaned with a powerful jet of air or water, inverted, filled and closed—all in less than one second! Video footage of the canning process was beamed by satellite to TV stations across the country. Within 48 hours the first video news release was seen by 296 million viewers, three times the number that usually watches the Super Bowl.

The company used the video to combat the visual images of the syringes that had been shown on network television constantly since the first instance in Seattle. Pepsi created three more VNRs within three days. By the end of the week, the president had appeared on a dozen network TV news shows and talk shows, and Pepsi spokespersons had conducted more than 2,000 interviews with newspapers, magazines, and TV and radio reporters. The strategy was to show the public that what was happening was really a hoax rather than a problem with Pepsi bottlers. The real turning point came with the third VNR. It showed a tape from an in-store surveillance camera that had filmed a shopper slipping a syringe into an open Diet Pepsi can while the cashier's back was turned. Pepsi could not release the tape though, until the next day when an arrest was made. After the third VNR ran, viewers were overwhelmingly supportive of Pepsi. The evaluation done indicated that Pepsi's response worked. Sales for the key July 4 period were not affected adversely, which was quite important.

Questions

1. Were the communication tools used by Pepsi to solve the problem the ones you would use today?
2. Evaluate the role of the VNRs.
3. Are they always effective?

required a change in organizational policy that could have been politically explosive. A policy change of this type could have alienated both the personnel manager and the department managers if not handled carefully. The public relations manager needed a good understanding of both communication and organizational dynamics to accomplish this objective. Such letters normally had been routed to the personnel department and then to the manager of the department involved. This meant that for a department to get any recognition, it would have to appear to "blow its own horn." Therefore, most letters of appreciation had been handled internally, without informing the rest of the organization. The private nature of this process worked against the new objective of improving employee perceptions by sharing patient feedback. Thus, the policy was changed so that the original letter was routed first to public relations where copies were made for the appropriate department manager and for human resources. Some were featured on the hospital website.

136

***Spotlights**—Provide various kinds of helpful information such as tips for getting good photographs and how to clear publicity releases.*

7.2 Spotlight — Internet Writing Guidelines

1. Don't build a site for your executives; they aren't the target audience. Know the characteristics of your target audience and write for them.
2. Establish and present a logical progression of the ideas.
3. Put blocks of no more than 75 words each on initial site pages. Longer text farther into the site is fine.
4. Don't use clever headlines, but structure your articles with several levels of headlines so a reader can complete a section and continue reading, or choose to move on.
5. Write 50 percent less at the beginning of an article. Most Internet users scan copy before deciding to spend time in depth to read an article.
6. Highlight key words through hypertext links, typeface variations, or color.
7. Use bulleted lists when the copy makes this possible. The computer screen is small, and people tend to glance at key elements quickly.
8. Use inverted pyramid style for most copy with the most important information first. Don't bury your key points.
9. Use one main idea per paragraph.
10. Keep your sentences short, but on the other hand, remember that the key to a good website is that you have provided the answers to the questions that the reader has, so you need to be thorough.

Source: Stephen Dembner, "Web Writer Pro: In Search of a Functional Model for Effective Text on the World Wide Web," unpublished master's thesis, University of Memphis, May 2000.

The preparation of a news release is different from the preparation of an advertising message, because news depends on a third party to select and deliver the message. This is the basic difference between controlled and uncontrolled media. **Controlled media,** including internal publications, direct mail, posters and advertising, allow the public relations practitioner to dictate what is published and how it is delivered to the primary audience. **Uncontrolled media,** for which someone else makes decisions about content, include newspapers, television, and radio.

Two controlled media have become especially important to public relations campaigns in the last few years: advertising and the World Wide Web.

The World Wide Web can be considered the first public relations mass medium because it allows managed communication to flow directly between organizations and mass audiences without the gate-keeping functions present in other mass media.[13] Writing for the Internet includes some special rules just for this particular medium. See spotlight 7.2.

The advent of this new medium as a communication tool for public relations has spurred increased interest in relationship building through the Internet. Although the potential is great, little is known about the impact of public relations principles as applied to website design. Preliminary studies suggest five guidelines for building relationships with publics using Internet technology:

1. Create a dialogic loop to allow and encourage publics to query the organization sponsoring the site. This includes the availability of an adequate and well-trained staff to handle responses.
2. Make the information useful to all publics who may use the site. Even a specialized website should have some general use information. Make information easy to get.
3. Focus on the generation of return visits through the use of interactive strategies. Forums, question-and-answer formats, and chats with experts or corporate officers tend to build visit frequency.
4. Develop an intuitive ease to the interface. The focus of websites should be on the organization, product, or information located there and not on the "bells and whistles" that make it possible. Websites with graphics that take too long to load may turn off some visitors.

144

Toxic Shock Syndrome

Case Study

At Denver's Children's Hospital, a new public relations director made a plea to doctors and staff members to let her know if anything happened that might be considered news. She briefly explained to them what "news" was. A few days later, a doctor sheepishly came to her with an item he thought might be newsworthy. "I think I've discovered a new disease; do you think that's newsworthy?" he asked the public relations director. After she told him it was newsworthy, he continued by saying, "I think I'm going to call it toxic shock syndrome." He wanted to announce it. She readily agreed but wanted to plan how to release the information so the hospital could get the maximum benefit from the exposure.

Children's Hospital in Denver is a major regional referral and research hospital for states in the west. It depends a great deal on its support from fund-raising efforts. If you were the public relations director, what would you do?

Source: Kyla Thompson, *Non Profit Public Relations,* interview by Dan Lattimore, videocassette, Colorado State University, 1986.

Questions

1. How would you announce the new disease?
2. How would you use the Internet to announce the new disease? Would you create a website? Assuming you did create a website, what would you include?
3. How would you handle the requests from more than 500 media calls you would receive in the few days after the announcement?
4. If you had just been named public relations director for the hospital when this occurred, how would you proceed to develop your media contacts to help the hospital?
5. How could you use the discovery of toxic shock syndrome in the years to come in your public relations efforts?

Key Terms

agenda	**news conferences**
B-roll	**news release**
crisis	**planned publicity**
crisis plan	**press conference**
extranet	**press kit**
Internet	**publicity**
intranet	**spontaneous publicity**
media kit	**third-party endorsement**
media relations	

Use the CD-ROM and Online Learning Center at www.mhhe.com/lattimore to further your understanding of the following terms

***Case Study**—Each chapter ends with a case study that invites students to apply that chapter's principles in a mock campaign. Each case provides a series of questions that encourage students to use what they've learned in designing the campaign.*

Public relations strategic planning provides organization to the public relations process. "Strategic planning is a process of assessing what you have and where you want to go."[1] The caliber and thoroughness of thinking preceding the execution of public relations activities will determine the value of the public relations operation. Understanding how to develop a public relations plan, then, is one of the main criteria that separates entry-level positions from top management in public relations.

Planning moves public relations from a reactive activity to a **proactive** process. Public relations practitioners, like most other managers, tend to be action oriented. The constant changes that take place both inside and outside any organization produce an endless procession of public relations problems. Too often, because of the number of pressing problems, managers find themselves responding only to exceptional situations. Such situations are usually negative in that they require the practitioner to intervene after a problem has already gotten out of control.

Although putting out fires is certainly part of the public relations function, it cannot be allowed to dominate all actions. If it does, the practitioner becomes a victim of circumstances, only able to react to the situation at hand. Perhaps the most frequent complaint of public relations practitioners is that other managers ask for their services only after the problem has become unmanageable. When damage to the organization's image has already been done, the public relations manager is often directed to "fix it." This may prove to be a no-win situation both for the organization and for the practitioner who must engage in usually fruitless remedial public relations.

For a long time, public relations practitioners have been advocating preventive public relations to avoid such problems. Part of this approach involves the type of fact-finding research we have already discussed in chapter 5. If practitioners detect potential problems before they erupt into damaging situations, they can give management early warning and advice. Sometimes even early detection cannot forestall some negative impact. When advanced warning is coupled with adequate planning, however, negative effects can be minimized and public relations management can provide well-designed, positive actions rather than hastily conceived reactions. As we continue our integrating case study begun in chapter 5, notice how the pitfalls of hasty reaction were avoided.

Integrating Case Study

Cedar Springs Community Hospital

Segment 2

You may remember that the physicians at Cedar Springs Hospital (chapter 5) were calling for immediate action to correct what they saw as a potentially life-threatening situation in patient care. Reaction to the problem as it appeared at the time would have generated a campaign to make employees more aware of the need for quality patient care and emphasize their responsibility for providing the best care possible. However, before taking action, the public relations director conducted some research to help him better understand the problem. The results were surprising and showed that the first action contemplated would have only made things worse. Employees already believed that the quality of patient care in the hospital was subpar and were frustrated because they felt they personally were doing a good job. In addition, research revealed that recently released patients rated the quality of care significantly better than the employees did.

***Integrating Case Study**—A continuous case study that runs throughout the four chapters in Part Two to help pull together and illustrate the process of public relations.*

***Chapter Opener**—Each chapter opens with a preview that provides an overview of the chapter content.*

***Key Terms**—Highlighted glossary terms appear at the end of each chapter with a link to send students to the Flash Cards on the CD-ROM and Online Learning Center for further review. In addition, they are listed in the end of book glossary with definitions.*

***End of Chapter References**—Include additional readings from PR books, professional journals* (Public Relations Strategist, Public Relations Review, Public Relations Quarterly), *magazines* (Business Week, Fortune magazine), *and Internet sources.*

***CD-Video Icons**—Appear at the end of each chapter to direct students to watch the appropriate video clip on the CD-ROM or visit the Online Learning Center.*

The Profession and the Practice: Pedagogy that Reflects a Solid Public Relations Text

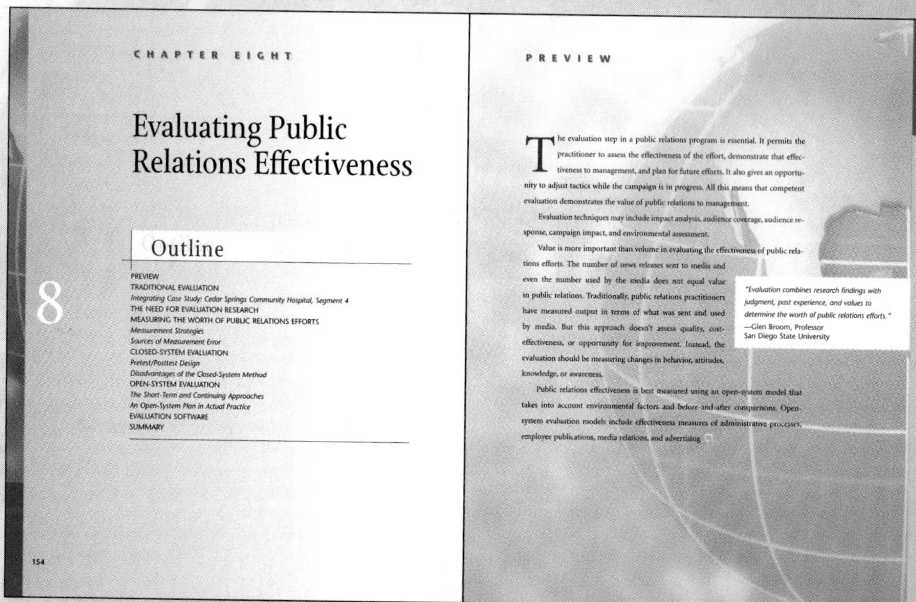

CHAPTER EIGHT

8

Evaluating Public Relations Effectiveness

Outline

PREVIEW
TRADITIONAL EVALUATION
Integrating Case Study: Cedar Springs Community Hospital, Segment 4
THE NEED FOR EVALUATION RESEARCH
MEASURING THE WORTH OF PUBLIC RELATIONS EFFORTS
Measurement Strategies
Sources of Measurement Error
CLOSED-SYSTEM EVALUATION
Pretest/Posttest Design
Disadvantages of the Closed-System Method
OPEN-SYSTEM EVALUATION
The Short-Term and Continuing Approaches
An Open-System Plan in Actual Practice
EVALUATION SOFTWARE
SUMMARY

154

PREVIEW

The evaluation step in a public relations program is essential. It permits the practitioner to assess the effectiveness of the effort, demonstrate that effectiveness to management, and plan for future efforts. It also gives an opportunity to adjust tactics while the campaign is in progress. All this means that competent evaluation demonstrates the value of public relations to management.

Evaluation techniques may include impact analysis, audience coverage, audience response, campaign impact, and environmental assessment.

Value is more important than volume in evaluating the effectiveness of public relations efforts. The number of news releases sent to media and even the number used by the media does not equal value in public relations. Traditionally, public relations practitioners have measured output in terms of what was sent and used by media. But this approach doesn't assess quality, cost-effectiveness, or opportunity for improvement. Instead, the evaluation should be measuring changes in behavior, attitudes, knowledge, or awareness.

"Evaluation combines research findings with judgment, past experience, and values to determine the worth of public relations efforts."
—Glen Broom, Professor
San Diego State University

Public relations effectiveness is best measured using an open-system model that takes into account environmental factors and before-and-after comparisons. Open-system evaluation models include effectiveness measures of administrative processes, employee publications, media relations, and advertising.

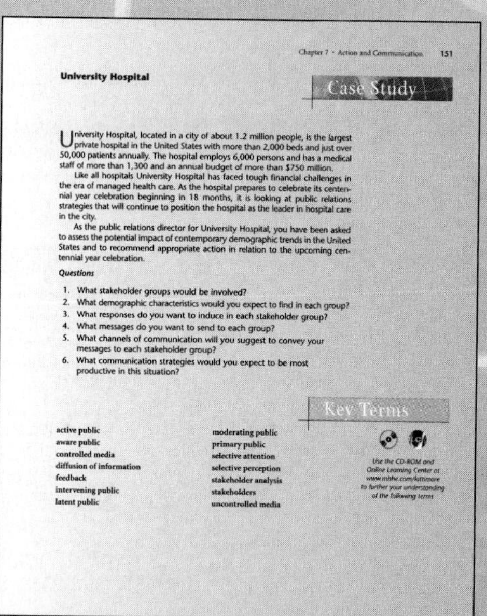

Chapter 7 · Action and Communication 151

University Hospital

Case Study

University Hospital, located in a city of about 1.2 million people, is the largest private hospital in the United States with more than 2,000 beds and just over 50,000 patients annually. The hospital employs 6,000 persons and has a medical staff of more than 1,300 and an annual budget of more than $750 million.

Like all hospitals University Hospital has faced tough financial challenges in the era of managed health care. As the hospital prepares to celebrate its centennial year celebration beginning in 18 months, it is looking at public relations strategies that will continue to position the hospital as the leader in hospital care in the city.

As the public relations director for University Hospital, you have been asked to assess the potential impact of contemporary demographic trends in the United States and to recommend appropriate action in relation to the upcoming centennial year celebration.

Questions

1. What stakeholder groups would be involved?
2. What demographic characteristics would you expect to find in each group?
3. What responses do you want to induce in each stakeholder group?
4. What messages do you want to send to each group?
5. What channels of communication will you suggest to convey your messages to each stakeholder group?
6. What communication strategies would you expect to be most productive in this situation?

Key Terms

active public
aware public
controlled media
diffusion of information
feedback
intervening public
latent public
moderating public
primary public
selective attention
selective perception
stakeholder analysis
stakeholders
uncontrolled media

Use the CD-ROM and Online Learning Center at www.mhhe.com/lattimore to further your understanding of the following terms

For self-testing and additional chapter resources, go to the student CD and the Online Learning Center at
www.mhhe.com/lattimore

The Profession and the Practice: Outstanding Tools that Reflect Technology Today
Student CD-ROM—Packaged for FREE with every new copy of the textbook, this CD-ROM provides several learning tools that help reinforce course concepts.

Video Clips—
Includes 4 case study interviews including Missing Children Case Study with Greg Wagner at D'Arcy Public Relations and 11 Public Relations practitioner interviews including Future Trends in Public Relations and advice to students by Cheryl Procter-Rogers at Home Box Office.

Quizzes—Practice quizzes with feedback help students reinforce their learning and comprehension.

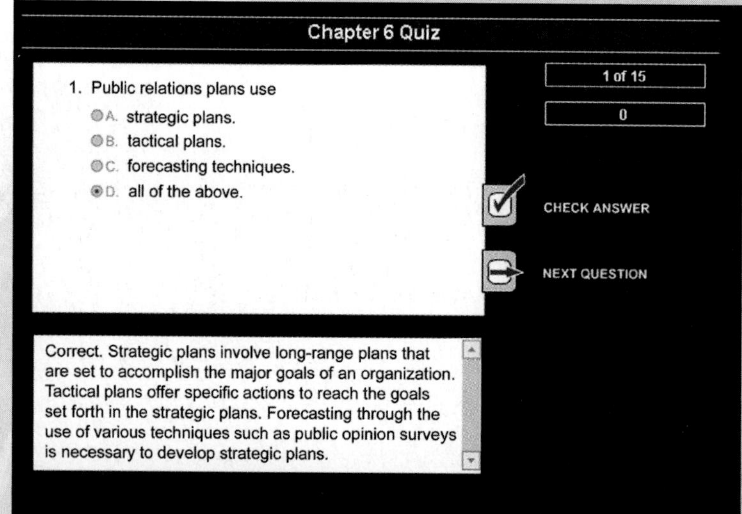

Flashcards—Interactive flashcards of key terms in each chapter allow students to practice vocabulary.

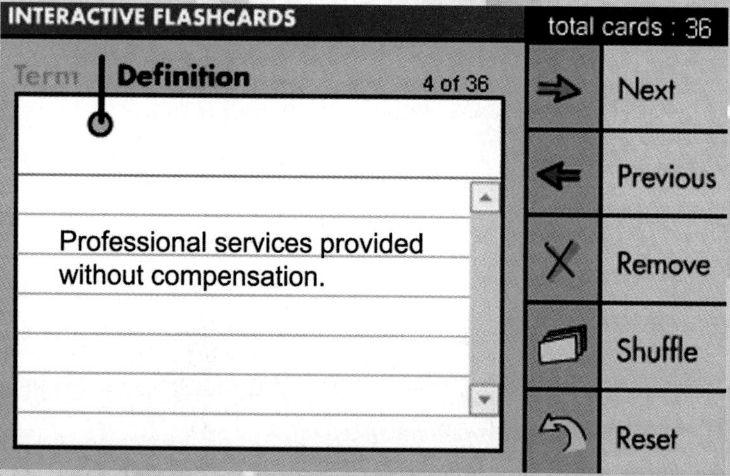

PowerPoint Tutorial—Presents the basic steps to creating and using PowerPoint effectively in presentations.

4 a **Use keywords for bullets.**

- Slides are visual notecards.
  - main ideas
  - not complete thoughts
  - full sentences only when quoting
- For every bullet try to eliminate:
  - articles (*a, an, the*)
  - pronouns that could be implied (*you, we*)
  - verbs that could be implied

If your PowerPoint presentation is meant to function ***by itself*** *(for example, as a tutorial like this one, or a display at a trade show) then it would be necessary to use full sentences to ensure audience comprehension.*

index

For self-testing and additional chapter resources, go to the student CD and the Online Learning Center at **www.mhhe.com/lattimore**

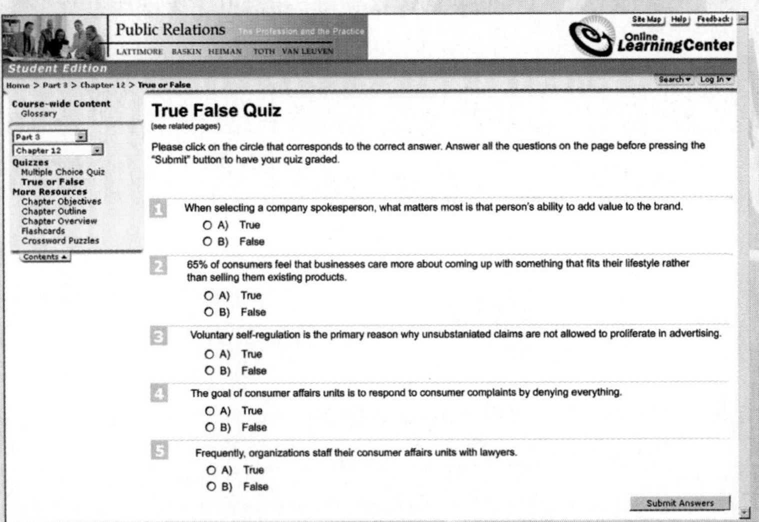

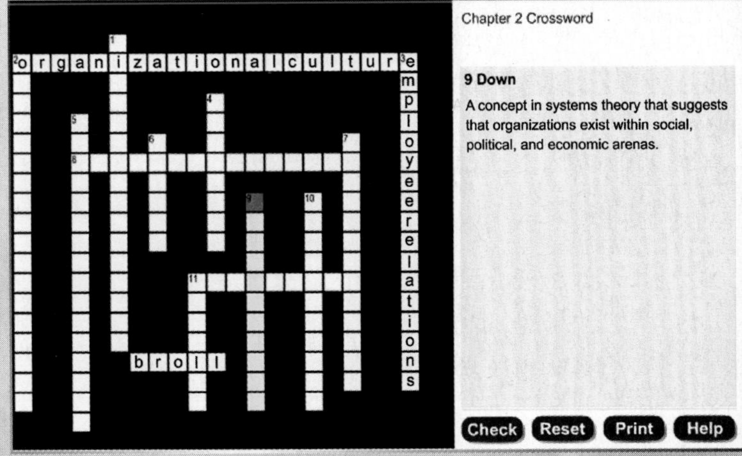

Online Learning Center—www.mhhe.com/lattimore—The Free Online Learning Center offers students and instructors a variety of resources and activities that support the content of the course. Icons in the text direct students to relevant website resources. These include interactive self-quizzes, vocabulary-enhancing crossword puzzles based on key terms, PowerPoint slides, and the Instructor's Resource Manual.

Public Relations

The Profession and the Practice

PART ONE

Part I covers fundamentals of public relations practice. Chapter 1 gives a working definition of public relations, reviewing and refining the definitions of previous studies. Chapter 2 examines the historical roots of public relations, providing a useful perspective on the discipline as it has emerged. Chapter 3 deals with communications and systems theory as a background for public relations practice. Finally, Chapter 4 looks at the legal, ethical, and professional responsibilities of public relations practitioners in our society□

Public Relations: The Profession

I

CHAPTER ONE

1

The Nature of Public Relations

Outline

PREVIEW

Public relations encompasses rapidly developing communication and management functions. The practitioner's work is filled with a wide range of media, creative, and strategic planning functions. This "professional breadth" is clearly reflected in the following paragraphs as Marissa, a young public relations professional, works through her daily assignments.

Marissa is feeling pretty good about her life and especially her job. She received her bachelor's degree two years ago with an emphasis in public relations. Then, following a paid summer internship, she competed successfully for a full-time account coordinator job at Waggener Edstrom, a Pacific Northwest public relations and strategic communication agency best known for its work on behalf of Microsoft. Now, almost two years later, she's just been appointed an account executive after having spent the last year as an assistant account exec.

Today is her first in the new job. She checks her e-mails and especially an overnight media tracking report to see what the media reported about her Microsoft product over the last 24 hours. She also looks to see what, if anything, has been said or written about her client's competitors. She summarizes the highlights and e-mails them to her clients and other members of her Microsoft product team.

After reviewing her schedule for the day, Marissa begins organizing artwork to accompany a new product launch announcement that's intended to run two months from now in the trade publication *WIRED*. She's been working with a *WIRED* reporter for several months so that the Microsoft announcement will be the lead article and featured on the cover. She gathers up the materials and takes them to an account team meeting where the members work on synchronizing the product announcement in *WIRED* with follow-up stories in other trade publications, consumer electronics magazines, and the financial press.

Lunch is spent advising a volunteer group of community library supporters who are trying to organize a summer reading program for latchkey children from low-income families. Marissa suggests local business sponsorships to help underwrite the program as well as a partnership arrangement with the city bus service to transport the children to and from the branch libraries.

When she returns to the office, a voice-mail is waiting from the *Seattle Times* technology reporter who wants to get a local angle on an Internet deregulation story coming from this morning's congressional hearings in Washington, D.C. Marissa locates a Microsoft executive who will answer the *Times* reporter's questions and explain the company's long-term deregulation positions.

It's now 3 P.M. and Marissa begins assembling research materials for a Microsoft brand manager who wants to know how public relations can support his marketing program that also includes advertising, corporate sponsorships, promotions, and sales materials.

Thus, in just the past six hours Marissa has clearly demonstrated what skillful public relations practitioners accomplish for their organizations and clients. In preparing the product launch announcement for the trade press, she showed how practitioners use communication strategically to gain a competitive edge in the marketplace among key audiences. By helping the library volunteers she demonstrated how public relations professionals think about building relationships or win-win situations with groups such as corporate sponsors. And finally, by thinking ahead, Marissa was able to connect the *Times* reporter with a smart company spokesperson who could explain how Microsoft was adapting to changing societal and business conditions, thereby enhancing the company's long-term reputation □

WHAT IS PUBLIC RELATIONS?

We'll examine other aspects of a job like Marissa's throughout this chapter and the entire book, but first let's define public relations and its key dimensions. The fact is that attempts to define public relations as a professional field and academic discipline are many and varied. The very nature of the profession and its constant adaptation to the needs of society make it at best a moving target for definition. Public relations is practiced in organizations that range from giant, multinational telecommunications companies to small human service agencies and fledgling social movement organizations. A public relations manager for a private university may devote most of her or his efforts to fund-raising and student recruitment. In contrast, the public relations staff of a large corporation may be responsible for the firm's relationships with customers, suppliers, investors, employees, and even foreign governments.

PRSA Official Statement on Public Relations

Spotlight 1.1

Public relations helps our complex, pluralistic society to reach decisions and function more effectively by contributing to mutual understanding among groups and institutions. It serves to bring the public and public policies into harmony.

Public relations serves a wide variety of institutions in society such as businesses, trade unions, government agencies, voluntary associations, foundations, hospitals, and educational religious institutions. To achieve their goals, these institutions must develop effective relationships with many different audiences or publics such as employees, members, customers, local communities, shareholders, and other institutions and with society at large.

The leadership of institutions needs to understand the attitudes and values of their publics in order to achieve institutional goals. The goals themselves are shaped by the external environment. The public relations practitioner acts as a counselor to management, and as a mediator, helping to translate private aims into reasonable, publicly acceptable policy and action. As a management function, public relations encompasses the following:

1. Anticipating, analyzing, and interpreting public opinion, attitudes, and issues which might impact, for good or ill, the operations and plans of the organization.
2. Counseling management at all levels in the organization with regard to policy decisions, courses of action, and communication, taking into account their public ramifications and the organization's social or citizenship responsibilities.
3. Researching, conducting, and evaluating, on a continuing basis, programs of action and communication to achieve informed public understanding necessary to the success of an organization's aims. These may include marketing, financial, fund-raising, employee, community or government relations, and other programs.
4. Planning and implementing the organization's efforts to influence or change public policy.
5. Setting objectives, planning, budgeting, recruiting and training staff, developing facilities—in short, managing the resources needed to perform all of the above.
6. Examples of the knowledge that may be required in the professional practice of public relations include communication arts, psychology, social psychology, sociology, political science, economics, and the principles of management and ethics. Technical knowledge and skills are required for opinion research, public issue analysis, media relations, direct mail, institutional advertising, publications, film/video productions, special events, speeches, and presentations.

In helping to define and implement policy, the public relations practitioner utilizes a variety of professional communications skills and plays an integrative role both within the organization and between the organization and the external environment.

Source: "Public Relations: An Overview" (New York: PRSA Foundation, 1991), pp. 4–5. Statement formally adopted by PRSA Assembly, November 6, 1982.

A Working Definition

Public relations practitioners help others establish and maintain effective relationships with third parties. Their work is usually performed in organizational environments like a public relations firm or an agency such as Marissa's, or as independent consultants or on the communication staffs of corporations, not-for-profit organizations, or government agencies. For the purposes of this book—and to establish a broad, realistic, and accurate description of the public relations function—we offer the following working definition:

> **Public relations** is a leadership and management function that helps achieve organizational objectives, define philosophy, and facilitate organizational change. Public relations practitioners communicate with all relevant internal and external publics to develop positive relationships and to create consistency between organizational goals and societal expectations. Public relations practitioners develop, execute, and evaluate organizational programs that promote the exchange of influence and understanding among an organization's constituent parts and publics.

We review the key dimensions of the definition on the following pages with further amplification given in spotlight 1.1, the official statement on public relations outlined by

1.2 Spotlight

Elements of Public Relations

- *Counseling.* Providing advice to the management of an organization concerning policies, relationships and communications; in effect, "what to do."
- *Research.* Determining attitudes and behaviors of publics and their causes in order to plan, implement, and measure activities to influence or change the attitudes and behavior.
- *Media Relations.* Developing an understanding of news media requirements and then providing reporters, editors, and television producers with story ideas and well-written releases and videos to publicize an organization's programs.
- *Publicity.* Disseminating planned messages through selected media without payment to further an organization's interest.
- *Employee/Member Relations.* Responding to concerns and informing and motivating an organization's employees or members, its retirees and their families.
- *Community Relations.* Continuing, planned and active participation with and within a community to maintain and enhance its environment to the benefit of both an organization and the community.
- *Public Affairs.* Developing effective involvement in public policy, and helping an organization adapt to public expectations. The public affairs term is also used by military services and some government agencies to describe the public relations activities.
- *Government Affairs.* Relating directly with legislature and regulatory agencies on behalf of an organization, usually as a central element of a public affairs program, often called "lobbying."
- *Issues Management.* Identifying and addressing issues of public concern in which an organization is, or should be, concerned.
- *Financial and Investor Relations.* Creating and maintaining investor confidence and building positive relationships with the financial community; also, sometimes known as Investor Relations or Shareholder Relations.
- *Industry or Trade Relations.* Relating with other firms in the industry of an organization and with trade associations.
- *Development/Fund-raising.* Demonstrating the need for and encouraging an organization's members, friends, supporters and others to voluntarily contribute to support it.
- *Minority Relations/Multicultural Affairs.* Relating with individuals and groups whose interests are often underrepresented in organizations, communities, and society.
- *Special Events.* Stimulating an interest in a person, product or organization by means of a focused "happening."
- *Marketing Communications.* Combination of activities designed to sell a product, service or idea, including advertising, collateral materials, publicity, corporate sponsorships and promotions, packaging, point-of-sale display, trade shows, special events, and relationship marketing.

Source: "Public Relations: An Overview," pp. 3–4.

the Public Relations Society of America (PRSA). PRSA is the oldest and largest professional association serving practitioners.

Public Relations Practitioners' Work

The public relations field continues to be one of the most dynamic in organizational life in America and throughout the world. That's because public relations practitioners bring such a diversity of skills and programmatic capabilities to their jobs as listed in spotlight 1.2.

DEVELOPING RELATIONSHIPS BASED ON TWO-WAY COMMUNICATION

Public relations work is all about developing effective relationships between organizations and groups who are important to them, including the media, customers, employees, investors, community leaders and members, activist groups, government agencies, and so on. Ideally, these relationships should benefit both parties just as you would expect from a relationship with another person. Lasting, win-win situations mean a great deal of give-and-take based on a mutual understanding of each other's interests. These general principles strike at the core of any interpersonal communication course, and their specific public relations applications have been explained and advanced over the years by public relations scholars James and Larissa Grunig. Effective two-way communication also implies doing well by doing good, as is exemplified with the following "Friends of Trees" case study.

HIV/AIDS prevention project uses Latino artists to prepare prevention posters for Latino communities.

INFLUENCING GROUPS, POLICIES, AND ISSUES

Much of the communicating that public relations practitioners do is both persuasive and purposive. That's why our earlier definition talks about promoting the exchange of influence among an organization's constituent parts and publics. Since the earliest times public relations has been seen as the planned effort to influence public opinion, generally through persuasive communication. Marketing communication campaigns, for example, utilize product publicity to introduce products. Social marketing programs are persuasion efforts designed to inform people and to change their behaviors regarding some public good. An example would be the HIV Alliance campaign promoting safe sex through neighborhood needle exchange programs. The public relations practitioner writes the message and selects the communication channel while the marketing specialists make sure that the messages and condoms are distributed at gay bars and other retail outlets.

THE PUBLICS IN PUBLIC RELATIONS

All definitions and discussions of public relations refer to *publics* and *public opinion.* How do people who study and practice public relations make use of these terms? To begin, groups that are almost always important to organizations are called **publics** and generally are defined in terms of their organizational relationships to us, including the media, employees, governmental officials, community leaders, and financial analysts, for example.

In other instances, publics are defined as categories of people who become important to our organization for one reason or another. In this sense, our link to them stems from the fact that our organization has purposely or even inadvertently created some consequence that serves to galvanize these people. Perhaps they are community members who resent our organization building a new office addition immediately adjacent to a wetlands area. Such a group can be defined as a public in the classic social science sense of how democracy supposedly works. That is, these community members become a public once they recognize an issue, understand its relevance to them, and then talk about it or even organize to do something about it.

1.1 Mini • Case

Friends of Trees

In 1989 a group of Portland, Oregon, residents formed *Friends of Trees,* a nonprofit organization with the simple goal of planting and caring for trees in urban areas to revitalize neighborhoods and to produce a healthier environment. They believed that trees and tree-lined streets make people proud of where they live, thereby potentially increasing neighborliness, civic pride, and community involvement. Tree-lined downtown areas and neighborhoods are thought to enhance tourism and increase property values.

Between 1989 and 1995 Friends of Trees members planted 3,000 trees and 30,000 seedlings in the Portland metropolitan area. This initial success gave Friends board members reason to hire the Metropolitan Group, a full-service public relations and social marketing agency to design and orchestrate a major five-year campaign involving more than 150,000 plantings. Their campaign, called *Seed the Future,* became an award-winning partnership program involving corporate, public, and foundation sectors as well as individual donors and homeowners.

For a relatively small nonprofit organization, Friends of Trees board members might well have been alarmed at the scope of the Metropolitan public relations plan. Its emphasis was on exacting behavioral outcomes matched with clear-cut strategies and tactics for reaching them as illustrated by the following campaign objectives:

1. Help create the urban forest canopy of the 21st century by planting trees along streets, in yards, and in parks and natural areas.
   a. Plant 13,000 trees along streets, 1,250 trees in yards, and 130,000 seedlings in parks and natural areas.
   b. Accomplish these plantings by forging partnerships with neighborhood associations, schools, church, youth groups, and other community organizations.
   c. Coordinate 150 planting projects in 50 neighborhoods, 20 schools, and in 25 parks and natural areas.
   d. Promote plantings in 1,000 yards.
   e. Involve 40,000 volunteers in these various projects
2. Improve the environment by sequestering carbon dioxide, conserving energy, and reducing stormwater runoff.
   a. Sequester approximately 66,000 metric tons of carbon dioxide at a cost per ton of approximately $35.
   b. Help 1,000 homeowners strategically select and site 1,250 trees for energy savings and stormwater retention.
   c. Plant trees in key watersheds to reduce and clear stormwater runoff.
3. Enhance economic growth and development by improving neighborhood and business district livability.
   a. Improve property values by creating greener, tree-lined streets and yards.
   b. Support Metro's 2040 plan and the City of Portland's growth management objectives by greening the city, thus maintaining urban livability in the face of increased development and denser housing.
   c. Create more attractive shopping centers and work areas in downtown Portland and other business districts.
4. Educate the public on the environmental, economic, and aesthetic value of urban trees through a multifaceted public awareness/advertising campaign.
   a. Conduct an education/advertising campaign via television, radio, newspaper, and billboard and bus signs resulting in more than 10 million impressions (put all this under strategy) per year through media sponsorship.
   b. Produce and distribute 100,000 brochures; 2,000 posters; 10,000 bumper stickers; and 5,000 T-shirts annually.
   c. Coordinate planting projects with at least 50 schools and youth groups.
   d. Conduct outreach and distribute information at fairs, festivals, conferences, and public meetings.

Most surprising was the extent to which these strategies were accomplished with little cash. Metropolitan's entire campaign was based on building and strengthening relationships between local businesses and the neighborhoods in which they operate. Business owners thus were encouraged to form partnerships with neighborhood associations and to jointly undertake tree-planting projects to build new relationships and strengthen existing ties with neighbors. Corporate and foundation donors provided the trees. Members of local Scout groups and other youth organizations would go door-to-door in targeted neighborhoods explaining the program and asking residents to participate by deciding where they would like new trees planted in their yards and along their parking strips. They were urged to compare their chosen sites with their neighbors' choices. Meanwhile, the neighborhood associations throughout the metropolitan area were recruiting and training volunteer tree-planters. When "planting Saturday" arrived, the sponsoring local business and its employees showed up with a catered breakfast for all the participants. Business sponsors also provided T-shirts commemorating the event as well as other logistical support. Tree-planting teams dispersed throughout the neighborhoods to plant the trees under the watchful eyes of property owners who, in turn, were asked to provide the watering and to do some of the cleanup.

In short, not only did the volunteers plant more than 150,000 trees at little expense, but corporate sponsors were rallied by the Metropolitan Group to cover the production costs of all collateral materials as well as certain agency charges. The success of the project gave local residents more confidence. Follow-up surveys indicated that they felt safer and more connected to their neighbors and neighborhood associations. Moreover, local residents recognized business sponsors as valued community leaders. Friends of Trees ended up with a volunteer base rivaling that of any environmental group or social movement organization in the metropolitan area.

We noted earlier that the Friends of Trees campaign was both a public relations and a social marketing program. **Social marketing** is a special form of public relations that generally involves changing attitudes and behaviors on behalf of a social cause whose work benefits society as a whole rather than the sponsoring organization. As a process, social marketing makes use of existing commercial outlets and community organizations to get its word out and to mobilize resources in addition to the traditional communication channels that public relations practitioners use.

Source: Interviews, The Metropolitan Group, Portland, Oregon, Summer 2001.

Alert public relations practitioners communicate with these groups very early in the process, perhaps even before they become organized activists or a social movement organization. Chances are, though, that these activists understand the processes by which the public begins to make up its mind on an issue once it gets publicized in local newspapers, on radio, and on television newscasts.

As the general citizenry learns about an issue, individuals begin to express opinions, talk with others about the issue, and to reconcile their opinions with more long-standing attitudes, values, and group affiliations. It's not surprising, therefore, that public relations practitioners know it's in their interests to monitor public opinion formation and change around many issues. Moreover, the study of public relations has always been aligned at least in part with knowledge about public opinion, attitude change processes, and social psychology. If public relations practitioners are to build and maintain an organization's reputation, they'll likely need to understand that public opinion formation is an evolving and contested process in which each of the major interests competes to frame the issue a particular way in the media. In addition, public relations practitioners influence public opinion by helping organizations attract and mobilize supporters.

USING COMMUNICATION SKILLS EFFECTIVELY

In many respects the heart of public relations work—at least for entry-level positions—is the ability to write, design, and produce materials for all media; public relations practitioners must also possess public speaking, group leadership, and event planning skills. Thus, a big share of day-to-day public relations work involves determining key messages and the best combination of communication channels for directing those messages to target audiences. The integrated public relations media model developed by Professor Kirk Hallahan and shown in table 1.1 illustrates the range of communication channels for which public relations students learn to write, design, and produce.

DISTINGUISHING PUBLIC RELATIONS FROM RELATED FIELDS

Because the words *public relations* are very general, it's not surprising that the work is not well understood by friends, parents, and the general public. Adding to the confusion is the fact that organizations label the function very differently; for example, the words *communication* and *corporate communication* are now more commonly used to label the public relations function in many corporate and nonprofit settings. Government agencies often use the terms *public information* or *public affairs* to delineate the public relations and communication functions even though the **public affairs** term generally refers to relations between organizations and

TABLE 1.1 An Integrated Public Relations Media Model

Characteristic	Public Media	Interactive Media	Controlled Media	Events/Groups	One-on-One
Key use	Build awareness	Respond to queries; exchange information	Promotion; provide detailed information	Motivate attendees; reinforce attitudes	Obtain commitments; resolve problems
Examples	Newspapers, magazines, radio, television	Phone based: automated response; audio text Computer-based: Internet, database, e-mail, listservs, newsgroups, chatrooms, bulletin boards, CD-ROMs	Brochures, newsletters, sponsored magazines, annual reports, books, direct mail, point of purchase displays, video, Web pages, e-mail	Speeches, trade shows, exhibits meetings/conferences, demonstrations, rallies, sponsorships, anniversaries, sweepstakes/contests, recognitions/awards	Personal visits, lobbying, personal letters, telephone calls, telemarketing/solicitation
Nature of communi-cations	Nonpersonal	Nonpersonal	Nonpersonal	Quasi-personal	Personal
Direction of communi-cations	One-way	Quasi-two-way	One-way	Quasi-two-way	Two-way
Technological sophistication	High	High	Moderate	Moderate	Low
Channel ownership	Media organizations	Common carrier or institution	Sponsor	Sponsor or other organization	None
Message chosen by	Third parties and producers	Receiver	Sponsor	Sponsor or joint organization	Producer and audience
Audience involvement	Low	High	Moderate	Moderate	High
Reach	High	Moderate-low	Moderate–low	Low	Low
Cost per impression	Extremely low	Low	Moderate	Moderate	High
Key challenges to effectiveness	Competition; media cutter	Availability, accessibility	Design, distribution	Attendance, atmosphere	Empowerment, personal dynamics

Source: Kirk Hallahan, *Strategic Media Planning: Toward a Public Relations Model* (Thousand Oaks, CA: Sage, 2001), pp. 461–70.

governments. Other terms include *corporate relations* and *marketing communication.* The labeling issue is further complicated by the fact that public relations practitioners are sometimes assigned to various departments throughout an organization rather than being housed together in a common public relations or communications department.

The terms *public relations* and *advertising* are often commingled as well. Advertising refers to paid space and time in the media, whereas public relations is more generally concerned with publicity or stories that run without charge in the news columns of the media. Paid ads and commercials run almost exclusively in major mass media, including television, newspapers, radio, and magazines.

A related area of terminological confusion regards *marketing* and *public relations.* Marketing is a sales and distribution function whose principal publics are the customers, the retailers, and distributors. In contrast, public relations practice involves many publics besides customers. In fact, sometimes the interests of these other publics collide with customer interests. Important public relations publics besides customers include the media, employees, community leaders, government regulators, investment analysts, activist groups, and more.

The distinction between *journalism* and *public relations* is envisioned two ways. Journalists do not represent the organizations about which they write, but public relations practitioners do, and this may influence the story's objectivity and the ways ideas are framed and facts are presented. Journalists are trained to write for one medium or possibly two in the case of newspapers and magazines. Public relations practitioners must master the basic writing, graphic design, and journalistic conventions of all mass media along with more specialized media whose content they control, such as direct mail, pamphlets, posters, newsletters, trade publications, and their website.

PUBLIC RELATIONS PROFESSIONALS AT WORK

Public relations departments range in size from more than 400 members in large corporations to one or two individuals in small organizations. The public relations function in large corporations is frequently headed by a vice president who helps develop overall policy as a member of top management. Large organizations also typically include various other public relations managers at both corporate and division levels, and they may employ a number of public relations specialists such as writers, researchers, and representatives to the media. In a small organization, however, one individual may handle all these responsibilities. Public relations counseling firms may contain specialists in a particular practice area, such as health care or financial services, as well as functional specialists for managing corporate culture change or coordinating content on the internal intranet.

This great diversity in the duties of public relations practitioners is illustrated by the following list of public relations functions published by PRSA in a booklet entitled *Careers in Public Relations:*

1. *Programming.* This involves analyzing problems and opportunities, defining goals and the publics (or groups of people whose support or understanding is needed), and recommending and planning activities. It may include budgeting and assignment of responsibilities to the appropriate people, including non-public-relations personnel. For example, an organization's president or executive director is often a key figure in public relations activities.
2. *Relationships.* Successful public relations people develop skill in gathering information from management, from colleagues in their organizations, and from external sources. They do this to strengthen their organization's ties to external groups including the media, community leaders, government policymakers and regulators, investors, financial analysts, educational institutions, activist groups,

and so on. The same holds for internal employee audiences and departments with which the public relations staff maintains daily contact, such as marketing, human resources, and the legal department.

3. *Writing and Editing.* Since the public relations worker is often trying to reach large groups of people, an important tool is the printed word. Examples of its use are found in reports, news releases, booklets, speeches, film scripts, trade magazine articles, product information and technical material, employee publications, newsletters, shareholder reports, and other management communications directed to both organizational personnel and external groups. A sound, clear style of writing that communicates effectively is a must for public relations work.

4. *Information.* Establishing systems for the dissemination of material to appropriate newspaper, broadcast, and general and trade publication editors and communicating with them to enlist their interest in publishing an organization's news and features are normal public relations activities. This requires knowledge of how newspapers and other media operate, the areas of specialization of publications, and the interests of individual editors. (Competition is keen for the attention of editors and broadcasters who have a limited amount of space and time at their disposal.)

   As one public relations practitioner puts it, "You have to get to the right editor of the right publication with the right story at the right time." Although ideas are accepted on the basis of newsworthiness and other readership values, an ability to develop relationships of mutual respect and cooperation with the news media can be useful to both the practitioners and the news people.

5. *Production.* Various publications, special reports, films, and multimedia programs are important ways of communicating. The public relations practitioner need not be an expert in art, layout, typography, and photography, but background knowledge of the techniques of preparation is needed for intelligent planning and supervision of their use.

6. *Special Events.* News conferences, convention exhibits and special showings, new facility and anniversary celebrations, contests and award programs, and tours and special meetings are only a few of the special events used to gain attention and acceptance of groups of people. They involve careful planning and coordination, attention to detail, preparation of special booklets, publicity, and reports.

7. *Speaking.* Public relations work often requires skill in face-to-face communication—finding appropriate platforms, preparing speeches for others, and delivering speeches. The person who can effectively address individuals and groups will enjoy an advantage over those whose facility of expression is limited to writing.

8. *Research and Evaluation.* All public relations work is underpinned by research—research on issues, organizations, publics, competition, opportunities, threats, and so on. Public relations practitioners spend considerable time incorporating their research findings into position statements, public relations plans, communication campaigns, media briefing materials, and so on. These factors are variously gathered through interviews, review of library materials, databases, websites, and informal conversations. Research may also involve the use of survey techniques and firms specializing in designing and conducting opinion research.

   Research findings influence a public relations program's objectives and strategies, which in turn form the basis for evaluating the planning, implementation, and effectiveness. More and more managers expect research and evaluation from their public relations advisers or staffs.

Public relations practitioners discuss campaign tactics.

THE MANAGEMENT AND LEADERSHIP FUNCTIONS OF PUBLIC RELATIONS

Public relations involves both leadership and management functions, and we distinguish between the two in this section. The discussion also addresses the roles that public relations practitioners and leaders play in advancing socially responsible behavior. And finally, we consider how public relations practitioners become involved with decision making in their organizations.

Business scholars often distinguish leadership from management by saying that leadership involves doing the right things and making the right choices, whereas management involves doing things right. As managers, public relations practitioners design and organize communication programs and campaigns. They're the communication experts for their organizations. Like leaders, communication managers are steeped in planning, but this is generally intermediate-range planning such as developing the communication for a multiyear marketing plan, determining the key messages for an organization's "cultural change" training program, or developing the content guidelines for the company webpages and its various intranet and extranet uses.

Traditionally, public relations professionals have been viewed more as communication managers than as organizational leaders. Leaders are the individuals charged with building and maintaining an organization's long-term reputation, helping to meet profit goals, advising organizations on how to act responsibly in the public interest, and reconciling strategic plans at the highest organizational levels with the interests and concerns of groups whose support is needed, whether those groups come from inside the organization, in the community, or even elsewhere in the world. Let's examine several dimensions of public relations leadership.

1.3 Spotlight

New Dimensions in Corporate Social Responsibility

By Robert L. Dilenschneider

You don't have to be a futurist to know that vast societal and worldwide changes, including the September 11, 2001, bombing of the World Trade Center, have tremendous impacts on public relations practice. Over the next 20 years we will have to continue to keep pace with the seemingly endless advances in communication technology that have already speeded up the delivery of messages. But the bigger challenge will be mustering the courage to insist that all organizations adopt a broader, more socially conscious view of their company's responsibilities to their employees, their customers, and the communities in which they operate.

Little attention was focused on corporate responsibility during the past 20 years as the revolution in information and communication technology, and the creation of huge worldwide conglomerates in the banking, investment, insurance, manufacturing, energy, entertainment, media and information industries, literally transformed the world into a global marketplace. Fortunately, these technological, economic, and political developments have revitalized democracy, reinvigorated capitalism, and generated immense global economic growth, particularly in the United States. And yet, these advances also suggest that large corporations have become so powerful that they no longer feel compelled to consider the public interests as they pursue their goals of maximizing profits.

Some of the elements of public discontent can be easily seen.

1. General prosperity is not being equally shared. It is widely perceived that, while the rich are getting richer, the middle class is working harder than ever to maintain its position and the poor are getting poorer.
2. The pain of the economic recovery has not been evenly shared. Most of the ruthless downsizing has fallen on the heads of the line workers, the clerks, or the middle managers, not the upper level of management.
3. CEOs are getting paid extraordinary salaries (as evidenced by the Enron downfall) while workers are asked to tighten their belts and suffer cuts in benefits. CEOs are generally raking in extraordinary amounts of money in salaries, bonuses, stock options, and perks.
4. Free trade is already under fire from workers and unions in the industrial nations. Multinational corporations are once again viewed with increasing suspicion in developing countries for fostering sweatshop wages and working conditions, for degrading the environment, and for shipping their profits back to corporate headquarters instead of investing them in host nations.

Unless public relations professionals and leaders address these problems in the next several years, we can expect huge societal problems. This effort will require a great deal of courage because the message concerns the growing discontent with business—and in most cases top management doesn't want to hear about it, and won't readily agree with it, or wants to avoid it. CEOs are pressured by Wall Street, and those waiting to be CEOs cannot afford to break ranks.

I am convinced that our biggest challenge in the next 20 years will be to convince corporate leaders that in order to preserve these economic gains, they need to restrain their pursuit of even larger profits by assuming greater responsibility for the lives their businesses affect.

So the job is on our shoulders to help those in charge of our organizations become leaders. Doing this requires more than rhetoric. It calls for original thinking and original ideas that respond to the following questions:

What can be done, for example, to show how corporations are loyal to the nations they operate in?

How can CEOs step out of isolation in the ivory tower and show compassion for average workers?

How do you muster the best minds in our country and elsewhere to develop ideas for peace and for addressing the burdened of the underclass in this country and around the world?

How do you get those who have made excess wealth in the past 20 years to recognize that they cannot take for their entire life and must start giving back and helping to solve some of society's ills?

How do you take some of the profit motive out of science and encourage those who have the capacity to develop products that can address serious illness?

How do you help CEOs address diversity in the workplace?

How do you help those CEOs who are fearful of stepping forward to overcome their anxieties?

How do you help the big egos—the big "I ams"— to put their personal power to work for good and not for intimidation or self-aggrandizement?

The list can go on and these are no easy tasks—for you or for those who expect to be leaders. But they must be addressed and the time is now.

Source: Robert L. Dilenschneider is chief executive of The Dilenschneider Group, the firm he founded in 1991. Mr. Dilenschneider formerly served as president and CEO of Hill & Knowlton, Inc., from 1986 to 1991.

Advancing Socially Responsible Behavior

Public relations leaders help keep organizations profitable and long-lasting through socially responsible behavior that serves the public interest as well as their own. Events like the Enron debacle, the September 11, 2001, World Trade Center terrorist attack, and regional conflicts throughout the world underscore how critical it is for businesses, governments, and nonprofit organizations to be viewed as credible and responsible in all places at all times. And yet the technology boom of the 1990s, together with overpaid executives at home and underpaid factory workers abroad, show that the public reputation and posture of many organizations are in serious jeopardy.

Against this backdrop, thoughtful observers today argue that institutions should assume more responsibility for the consequences of their actions. Insightful public relations practitioners recognize that socially responsive and responsible behavior helps prevent labor unrest and strikes, customer boycotts, environmental lawsuits, and random attacks by disaffected individuals and activist groups.

Veteran public relations practitioner and academic Rex Harlow makes much of the social responsibility theme, maintaining that the public relations practitioner defines and emphasizes the responsibility of management to serve in the public interest. Former Hill & Knowlton CEO Robert Dilenschneider takes an even stronger stand in spotlight 1.3, arguing that socially responsive behavior in this decade and from 2010 to 2020 will determine the extent to which globalization and the world economy will survive.

Public Relations Leaders and Decision Making

At this juncture it's important to ask what it is that gives public relations leaders and practitioners either the responsibility or the right to determine and influence socially responsive organizational behavior in the public interest. In truth, public relations leaders do not make all the decisions that lead to change within organizations, but because they constantly monitor and interact with all publics in the organization's environment, they often possess information that suggests a need for change or indicates the direction change should take. Public relations practitioners can discover a problem when it is still manageable, thus avoiding unnecessary crises. Indeed, the late Scott Cutlip, renowned public relations educator, believed that public relations practitioners' most important responsibility is to interpret the public opinion climate to management.

Public relations leaders can become articulate policy and strategic planning consultants for organizations based on their understanding of the interests of different publics. They acquire those skills by monitoring and interpreting multiple issues and the public opinion climates regarding them. With this knowledge public relations practitioners and leaders can assume special responsibilities for helping organizations establish philosophies, achieve objectives, adapt to changing environments, and successfully compete in today's markets. Public relations can make important contributions to forming an organization's ideas about itself—what it should do and what society wants and expects from it. Charles Steinberg described this aspect of public relations as the "structuring of company philosophy and carrying out that philosophy in practice so that what the institution says is not at variance with what it does."[1] In essence, then, public relations leaders spend a lot of time gauging the implications that social, political, and economic issues at home and abroad have on maintaining the organization's long-term reputation.

One reason we distinguish public relations leadership from managing an organization's communication functions is that the public's perceptions of business and organizational life are too far-reaching to be addressed solely by public relations professionals.

TABLE 1.2 Public Relations Agency Rankings by U.S. Revenues

Ranking in 2001	Agency Name	U.S. Revenues	Global Revenues	Staff Size
1	Weber Shandwick Worldwide	$283,084,398	$426,572,018	1,500
2	Fleishman-Hilliard	$263,345,095	$345,098,241	1,480
3	Hill & Knowlton	$190,931,000	$325,119,000	659
4	Ketchum	$161,425,000	$185,221,000	797
5	Edelman PR Worldwide	$152,365,810	$223,708,535	1,073
6	Burson-Marsteller	$150,417,000	$259,112,000	730
7	Porter Novelli	$116,764,000	$179,294,000	733
8	Ogilvy PR Worldwide	$ 94,904,500	$145,949,285	526
9	CCI Group/APCO Worldwide	$ 85,434,598	$151,081,645	621
10	Golin/Harris International	$ 81,897,283	$113,247,644	389

Source: "*PR Week*'s Annual Rankings: The Definitive Performance Guide to PR Agencies." *PR Week,* 2002.

Indeed, public relations is increasingly the responsibility of executives as well as the province of public relations staffers. We see the need to reinvent the "good" in business and organizational life as government agencies at all levels retrench in the face of new fiscal limitations. Hospitals struggle with regulations, rising costs, new technologies, and changing customer demands. Arts organizations seek new sources of funds as Congress plans to reduce or withdraw government support. Businesses deal with global competition, economic conditions, and a skeptical public. Successful leaders in all organizations incorporate public relations savvy and perspectives into their work.

Chief executive officers of major corporations are well aware that public relations contributes to decision making. Sir Gordon White, who as chairman of Hanson Industries made a career of buying companies and eliminating their corporate staffs, had a staff of only 12, but it included a public relations officer.

To blend public relations goals with organizational goals, public relations information must be part and parcel of the organizational decision-making process and must include intelligence regarding likely reaction and response by relevant publics. Moreover, the commitment and understanding that come through participating in organizational decision making are invaluable assets when communicating decisions to the organization's publics. Perhaps the most important task of public relations is to ensure the public relations-mindedness of management officials so that public relations considerations are in the mainstream of managerial decision making.

SCOPE OF THE PUBLIC RELATIONS INDUSTRY

Because the global reach of public relations practice is changing so quickly, it's hard to know exactly how many public relations practitioners there are around the world, but the best guess is that there are more than 200,000 public relations practitioners in the

United States where the field is most developed. In fact, U.S. organizations spent almost $10 billion annually on public relations by the year 2000. Worldwide, the public relations industry in Europe, including the Commonwealth of Independent States and former Soviet-bloc countries, is roughly one-third the size of the U.S. industry. Next comes Asia and especially Japan, China, Hong Kong, Korea, Singapore, and Malaysia. The field is growing rapidly in Latin America and somewhat in those African economies where market economies are growing the fastest.

Calculating the dollar value of public relations work around the world is difficult. Table 1.2 shows the volume of U.S. and global work billed by major public relations agencies at the end of 2001. What's not available in those figures, though, is a country-by-country breakout of the global figures. In large part, that's because the accounting standards for client organizations and their multinational public relations agencies may not assign or distribute the public relations expenditures to the locations to which the work was directed.

Within the United States, it's estimated that roughly one-third of all public relations practitioners work for agencies. Some of those agencies focus on public relations, but others combine public relations with marketing communication or advertising. Another third work for corporations, including consumer goods such as consumer electronics, manufacturing, financial, and investment businesses; insurance firms; industrial firms; and the entertainment and media industries. Trade associations, educational institutions, and foundations employ about one-seventh of the practitioners and health care about one-tenth. Municipal, county, state, and federal government agencies account for about 5 percent as do social welfare, charitable, and religious associations.

A PROFILE OF PUBLIC RELATIONS PRACTITIONERS

More than at any time in the past, today's public relations practitioner is better educated, better paid, and more prepared to take on a range of strategic planning and communication functions for organizations of all kinds. The following subsections describe the principal findings from a year 2000 large-scale U.S. and Canadian study of the profession.[3] The study was conducted by the two largest professional associations in public relations—the Public Relations Society of America (PRSA) and the International Association of Business Communicators (IABC).

Education

Two-thirds (65%) of public relations practitioners are college and university graduates with bachelor's degrees, and almost half say their degree programs focused on public relations.

More striking perhaps is that 30 percent, or almost a third, had master's degrees as of 1999, up from 27 percent two years earlier. Of those, close to half the master's degrees were in communications, public relations, or journalism or related media fields. Another 40 percent were master of business administration (MBA) degrees. The remaining 10 to 15 percent came from a range of related graduate majors. And surprisingly, an additional 2 percent of those surveyed held doctorate or PhD degrees.

Just under one-fourth (24%) of communicators surveyed have also passed national accreditation exams administered either by the IABC or the PRSA. We'll talk more about accreditation and graduate study in subsequent chapters.[4]

Salaries

Survey results showed that the average public relations practitioner with 13 years of experience earned a base salary of $69,000. As well, half of those earned annual cash bonuses that averaged $10,000.

Salaries varied a great deal depending on where the respondents worked. Public relations consultants were paid $110,000 annually with bonuses averaging $20,000, whereas survey respondents working in other organizations averaged $63,000 with cash bonuses of $9,000 for those in corporate settings.[5]

Age and Gender

The average age for those PRSA and IABC members surveyed was 39. It's important to note that the average age of practitioners has been dropping annually for at least the past decade.

More than 7 in 10 of the practitioners (71%) were female. In fact, the female/male ratio has nearly reversed itself in the last 25 or 30 years. Even so, men continue to hold proportionately more of the top managerial public relations posts, primarily because they have spent a greater number of years in the field. Salary differences between males and females is but one of the gender issues to be considered later.[6]

Summary

Although there are many useful definitions for public relations, we stress that public relations is a management and relationship-building function based on effective two-way communication with publics or those affected by organizations. The duties of public relations practitioners involve a wide range of writing and planning skills. At advanced levels public relations managers and leaders design and execute communication campaigns, contribute to organizational strategic planning and decision making, and assume responsibility for maintaining the organization's long-term reputation.

For self-testing and additional chapter resources, go to the student CD and the Online Learning Center at **www.mhhe.com/lattimore**

To learn more about the public relations profession watch the interview with John Puluszek, Clip #13 on the book's CD-ROM.

"Doing" Public Relations

By Nancy M. Somerick
School of Communication
University of Akron

You have applied for a public relations position with a $30.2 million savings and loan association, a conservative financial institution that has been in existence for over 50 years. The organization has never employed a public relations person before. Now that its assets have risen above $10 million, however, the president of the institution feels it is time to hire someone to "do the PR."

During an interview, the president admits he is not sure what public relations is, but he is fairly sure he wants the person he hires to plan promotions and stage events that will attract new customers, write stories that will get free space and time in the local media, and start an employee publication. The president also states that he is open to suggestions about the position and asks you to explain how you would establish a professional, effective public relations program if you were hired.

Questions

1. Do the responsibilities outlined by the president indicate that he understands how the public relations function can be utilized most effectively? Use the overview given in this chapter to list and discuss some areas of public relations the president has not mentioned that could benefit his company.
2. What would you tell the president about your plans for establishing an effective public relations program for the financial institution? Briefly discuss how the functions of public relations as discussed in this chapter could be a part of your response to the president. Relate your plans to the definition of public relations.

Key Terms

public affairs
public relations
publics
social marketing

Use the CD-ROM and Online Learning Center at www.mhhe.com/lattimore to further your understanding of the following terms

Notes

1. Charles S. Steinberg, *The Creation of Consent: Public Relations in Practice* (New York: Hastings House, 1975), p. 9.
2. Thomas Moore, "Goodbye Corporate Stuff," *Fortune* (21 December 1987), p. 68.
3. *Profile 2000—A Survey of the Profession,* International Association of Business Communicators and Public Relations Society of America, 2001, p. A22.
4. Ibid., p. A5.
5. Ibid.
6. Ibid., p. A20.

CHAPTER TWO

The History of Public Relations

2

Outline

PREVIEW
RHETORICIAN AND PRESS AGENT TRADITION
American Antecedents to Public Relations
Public Relations in a Young Nation
P.T. Barnum and Press Agentry
The Downside of Press Agentry
JOURNALISTIC AND PUBLICITY TRADITION
Early Public Relations Consultants
Not-for-Profit Organizations and Social Movements
Early Corporate Communications Departments
Early Government Public Relations
THE PERSUASIVE COMMUNICATION CAMPAIGN TRADITION
The Creel Committee
Edward Bernays
RELATIONSHIP-BUILDING AND TWO-WAY COMMUNICATION TRADITION
Arthur Page
The Depression and World War II
Post–World War II
Professionalization of the Field
New Stakeholder Groups
THE GLOBAL INFORMATION SOCIETY
The Internet
Global Communication Demands
Proliferating Communication Channels
SUMMARY

PREVIEW

Public relations is an outgrowth of three factors: the power of public opinion, continuous competition among institutions for public support, and the development of media through which the public can readily be reached.

From a historical standpoint, the work of public relations is considered here in terms of the following four somewhat overlapping sets of dominant practices and traditions:

Rhetorician and Press Agent Tradition
Journalistic Publicity Tradition
Persuasive Communication Campaign Tradition
Relationship-Building and Two-Way Communication Tradition

Rhetoricians and press agents have operated since early times. Their approach, largely spoken and based on boastful claims, predominated until the late 1800s when a journalistic and publicity tradition was made possible with the growth of newspapers to serve a rising American middle-class market. The persuasive communication campaign tradition that emerged after World War I was based in large part on the success of wartime mass mobilization and behavioral science persuasion efforts. And finally, a relationship-building or two-way communication tradition, grounded in theories of interpersonal and organizational communication, reflects the larger scope of communication responsibilities undertaken by today's practitioners.

Taken together, these traditions should be seen as orienting frameworks around which public relations work gets done rather than as models of ideal professional practice. The pattern in which they evolved probably owes most to the growth of mass media and specialized channels of communication as well as to larger economic, political, social, and cultural forces in society. Thus, these four traditions do not reflect any sort of linear movement from unprofessional or illegitimate practice to more fully professional and ethical work. We believe that this framework applies equally well to corporations, social movements, firms or agencies, not-for-profit organizations, government agencies, and even community groups.

Public relations has generally moved from an overriding focus on using media publicity for influencing public opinion to a broader management perspective based on using communication strategically for many purposes □

RHETORICIAN AND PRESS AGENT TRADITION

The forerunner to modern-day public relations practice can be found in the work of **rhetoricians, press agents,** and other promoters. Since early times speechmakers, called rhetoricians, provided such communication services as speechwriting, speaking on clients' behalf, training for difficult questions, and persuasion skills.

For example, by Plato's day, ca. 27 to 346 B.C., rhetoric as a distinct discipline was well established in Greece. The foremost rhetorician was Gorgias of Leontinium in Sicily (ca. 483 to 375 B.C.) who believed that the rhetorician's job was to foster persuasive skills more than it was to determine if arguments and claims were true or false, according to Helio Fred Garcia.[1] Garcia also noted that even in classical Athens, public opinion determined matters both large and small, from important public works projects such as building city walls to the appointment of generals and other high officeholders to settling matters of criminal justice.[2]

Persuasive skills have been used to influence the public and public opinion for hundreds of years. Artifacts of what can be construed as public relations materials survive from ancient India, Mesopotamia, Greece, and Rome. The Crusades, the exploits of Lady Godiva, the actions of Martin Luther, and the adventures of the conquistadores seeking El Dorado have all been explained as examples of ancient public relations activities. The creation in the 17th century of the Congregatio de Propaganda (the congregation for propagating the faith) by the Roman Catholic Church is often pointed to as a keystone in the development of public relations. The action brought us the term *propaganda* but was not a significant development in a church that exists to propagate the faith.

American Antecedents to Public Relations

Numerous examples of public-relations-like activities were identifiable in the early days of American settlement as each of the colonies used publicity techniques to attract settlers. Harvard College initiated the first systematic U.S. fund-raising campaign in 1641. The campaign was supported by the first fund-raising brochure, entitled *New England's First Fruits.* In 1758, King's College (now Columbia University) issued the first press release—to announce graduation exercises.

Publicity techniques were even more prevalent at the time of the American Revolution and all subsequent conflicts or situations when power has been threatened or when public support is needed. Indeed, public relations has prospered most in times of extreme pressure or crisis. Such were the circumstances preceding the American Revolutionary War, when Samuel Adams initiated what can be called a public relations campaign. Adams was to the communication dimension of the Revolutionary War what George Washington was to the military dimension. Adams recognized the value of using symbols like the Liberty Tree that were easily identifiable and aroused emotions.

Boston Tea Party staged by Samuel Adams.

Adams also used slogans that are still remembered, like "taxation without representation is tyranny." Because he got his side of the story to a receptive public first, shots fired into a group of rowdies became known as "the Boston Massacre." Adams directed a sustained-saturation public relations campaign using all available media. He staged the Boston Tea Party to influence public opinion. In the Sons of Liberty and Committees of Correspondence, he provided the organizational structure to implement the actions made possible by his public relations campaign.[3]

Public Relations in a Young Nation

In the infancy of the United States, public relations was practiced primarily in the political sphere. The publication and dissemination of the Federalist Papers, which led to the ratification of the U.S. Constitution, has been called "history's finest public relations job."[4]

Early in his presidency, Andrew Jackson appointed Amos Kendall, a member of the famous Kitchen Cabinet, to serve as the candidate's pollster, counselor, ghostwriter, and publicist. Although he did not hold the title, Kendall effectively served as the first presidential press secretary and congressional liaison. Jackson, who did not express himself terribly well, used Kendall as a specialist to convey his ideas to Congress and the American people through the newspapers of the day. Newspapers, for the first time, were beginning to reach a rising middle class as a result of urbanization and advances in public education and literacy rates. Still, communication was primarily face-to-face because a majority of Americans lived on farms or in small communities.

Publicity drove the settlement of the American western frontier, the biggest issue of the time. From Daniel Boone to Davy Crockett to Buffalo Bill, skillful and sometimes exaggerated promotion was the way to move easterners to the west. Even Jesse James got into the act when he issued a news release about one of his particularly daring train robberies. Business leaders, too, became aware of publicity's virtues. When Burlington Railroad initiated its 1858 publicity campaign, Charles Russell Lowell stated, "We must blow as loud a trumpet as the merits of our position warrants."[5]

P.T. Barnum and Press Agentry

Phineas T. Barnum has always been considered the master of press agentry, a promoter with endless imagination. Barnum promoted the midget General Tom Thumb; Jenny Lind, the "Swedish Nightingale"; Jumbo, the elephant; and Joice Heath, a 161-year-old woman (it was claimed, although an autopsy report after her death put her age at 70–80). Barnum used publicity to make money, pure and simple.

When P. T. Barnum died, the *London Times* fondly called him a "harmless deceiver." As long as press agentry is used to promote circuses, entertainment, and professional sports, its negative potential is limited. Its use in business and politics, however, is more threatening.

The Downside of Press Agentry

In the quest to gain media and public attention, press agentry can become increasingly outrageous, exploitive, and manipulative. Moreover, the manipulative attempt to gain the attention of the public through the media has an even darker side.

In 1878, French sociologist Paul Brousse described what he called the **"propaganda of the deed."** The term refers to a provocative act committed to draw attention toward an idea or grievance in order to get publicity. For European anarchists in the late 19th and early 20th centuries, propaganda of the deed meant bombing, murder, and assassination. European sociologists feared that press agents and rhetoricians could incite mob rule, thereby making governments and societies less stable.

JOURNALISTIC AND PUBLICITY TRADITION

Societal conditions surrounding the 19th-century American Industrial Revolution paved the way for a new dominant model of public relations practice. The Industrial Revolution hit America with full force during the last quarter of the 19th century. The nation's population doubled as immigrants rushed to the land of opportunity. New products and new patterns of life rapidly emerged. The enforced rhythm of the factory, the stress of urban life, and the vast distinction between the bosses and the workers were new and not always pleasant realities of American life. In fact, social harmony generally was breaking down as evidenced by rising conflict and confrontation.

Businesses were racking up enormous profits but were losing public support in the process. Workers began to organize themselves into unions, and they perceived their interests in many cases as directly opposed to those of business owners. Business was at once highly successful and increasingly besieged. Historian Merle Curti wrote that corporations gradually began to realize the importance of combating hostility and to court public favor. The expert in the field of public relations was an inevitable phenomenon in view of the need for the services he or she could provide.[6]

In short, industrialization altered the structure of society and gave rise to conditions requiring public relations expertise. By the early 1900s, business was forced to submit to more and more governmental regulations and encountered increasingly hostile criticism from the press. Corporations recognized that deception, manipulation, and self-serving half-truths were inappropriate responses to challenges raised by media and government. As a result, public relations became a specialized function broadly accepted in major corporations in order to counter hostility by courting public support.

Not surprisingly, the term *public relations* came into use at this time; its earliest appearance was probably in Dorman B. Eaton's 1882 address to the graduating class of the

Yale Law School. The concept, as noted, was not new, but the coining of the term suggested a new level of importance and consciousness. As historian Marc Bloch has commented, "The advent of a name is a great event even when the object named is not new, for the act of naming signifies conscious awareness."[7]

Early Public Relations Consultants

Former journalists began to find it possible to make a living in the public relations business. In 1900, George V. S. Michaelis established the Publicity Bureau in Boston. His job, as he saw it, was to gather factual information about his clients for distribution to newspapers. By 1906, his major clients were the nation's railroads. The railroads engaged the Publicity Bureau to head off adverse regulations being promoted by Theodore Roosevelt. The agency used fact-finding publicity and personal contact to push its clients' position, but it kept secret its connection with the railroad. The Publicity Bureau staff increased dramatically, with offices set up in New York, Chicago, Washington, D.C., St. Louis, and Topeka and with agents in California, South Dakota, and elsewhere.

President Theodore Roosevelt, who saw the presidency as "a bully pulpit," proved to be more than a match for the Publicity Bureau. The first president to make extensive use of press conferences and interviews, Roosevelt was said to rule the country from the newspapers' front pages. The passage of the Hepburn Act extended government control over the railroad industry and represented a clear victory for the Roosevelt administration.

The father of public relations and the man most credited with nurturing the fledgling public relations profession was Ivy Ledbetter Lee, son of a Georgia preacher. Lee was a reporter who, early on, saw better prospects in the publicity arena. After working in New York's 1903 mayoral campaign and for the Democratic National Committee, Lee joined George Parker, another newspaper veteran, to form the nation's third publicity agency in 1904.

Two years later, coal operators George F. Baer and Associates hired the partnership to represent their interests during a strike in the anthracite mines. John Mitchell, leader of the labor forces, was quite open and conversant with the press, which treated him and his cause with considerable sympathy. The tight-lipped Baer would not even talk to the president of the United States.

Lee took the assignment and persuaded Baer to open up. Then he promptly issued a Declaration of Principles to all newspaper city editors. The sentiments expressed in this document clearly indicated that public relations had entered its second stage.

As Eric Goldman observed, "The public was no longer to be ignored, in the traditional manner of business, nor fooled, in the continuing manner of the press agent."[8] Lee declared that the public was to be informed. The declaration read:

> This is not a secret press bureau. All our work is done in the open. We aim to supply news. This is not an advertising agency; if you think any of our matter ought properly to go to your business office, do not use it. Our matter is accurate. Further details on any subject treated will be supplied promptly, and any editor will be assisted most cheerfully in verifying directly any statement of fact. . . . In brief, our plan is, frankly and openly, on behalf of business concerns and public institutions, to supply to the press and public of the United States prompt and accurate information concerning subjects which it is of value and interest to the public to know about.[9]

In short, then, Lee's idea was to tell the truth about his client's organization's actions. He believed that if telling the truth damaged the organization, it should correct the problem so that the truth could be told without fear. That said, Lee's railroad clients did not react well to this treatise. Public relations historian Ray Hiebert wrote: "Many an old-timer with the railrord was dismayed when, almost immediately, Lee began revolutionizing things, putting into effect his theories about absolute frankness with the press."[10]

Lee's publicity arsenal was not limited to news releases. In helping stave off railroad freight regulations, Lee published leaflets, folders, and bulletins for customers; company news for employees; and other material for important decision makers including congressmen, state legislators, mayors and city councilmen, economists, bankers, college presidents, writers, and clergymen.[11]

Lee realized that a corporation could not hope to influence the public unless its publicity was supported by good works. Performance determines publicity. To achieve necessary and positive consistency between words and actions, Lee urged his clients in business and industry to align their senses and their policies with the public interest. The public, Lee thought, was made up of rational human beings who, if they are given complete and accurate information, would make the right decisions. As a result, he said that his job was interpreting the Pennsylvania Railroad to the public and interpreting the public to the Pennsylvania Railroad. In short, Lee saw himself as a mediator bridging the concerns of business and the public's interests.

Then, in 1914 Lee was hired to remake the image of John D. Rockefeller, the owner of Standard Oil of New Jersey. Nine thousand coal miners went on strike in southern Colorado in September 1913. The Rockefellers were the principal stockholders in the largest company involved, the Colorado Fuel and Iron Company. In April 1914, an accidental shot resulted in a battle in which several miners, two women, and 11 children were killed. The Rockefellers were blamed and, "the Rockefeller name was being denounced from one end of the country to another." Lee advised the younger Rockefeller to practice a policy of openness. After the strike, Lee advised Rockefeller to visit the mining camps to observe conditions firsthand.

Lee died in disgrace, the victim of his own public relations policies. In the early 1930s Lee advised the Interessen Gemeinschaft Farben Industrie, more commonly known as I. G. Farben, or the German Dye Trust. Eventually the Nazis took over and the company asked Lee for advice on how to improve German–American relations. He told the company to be open and honest. Shortly before his death, Lee's connections with the Germans were investigated by the House Special Committee on Un-American Activities. Headlines screamed that "Lee Exposed as Hitler Press Agent," and his name was blackened throughout the United States.

Other early publicity offices were established by William Wolf Smith in Washington, D.C., in 1902; Hamilton Wright, San Francisco, 1908; Pendleton Dudley, New York's Wall Street district, 1909; Rex Harlow, Oklahoma City, 1912; and Fred Lewis and William Seabrook, Atlanta, 1912.

Not-for-Profit Organizations and Social Movements

Not-for-profit organizations, including colleges, churches, charitable causes, and health and welfare agencies, began to use publicity extensively in the early 20th century. In 1899 Anson Phelps Stokes converted Yale University's Office of the Secretary into an effective alumni and public relations office. Harvard president Charles W. Eliot, who spoke as early as 1869 on the need to influence public opinion toward advancement of learning, was among the Publicity Bureau's first clients in 1900. The University of Pennsylvania and the University of Wisconsin set up publicity bureaus in 1904. By 1917, the Association of American College News Bureaus was formed.

Public Relations for Social Change: Clara Barton and the American Red Cross

Spotlight 2.1

By Kimberley Mangun

Clara Barton's four-year crusade to organize and promote the American Red Cross consisted of three different stages: a problem-definition phase, the development of communication strategies to attract press coverage and create legitimacy, and the elaboration of politically feasible solutions. Even though she had no formal training in public relations, Barton's choice of strategies can be considered an early example of advocacy public relations for a nonprofit organization. She used pamphlets, public speaking, newspapers, and letters—forms of communication popular in the late 19th century—to draw attention to the need for an American Red Cross.

Her initial task was to overcome America's ignorance of the International Red Cross, which had been formed in Geneva, Switzerland, in 1864. She did this by issuing a small pamphlet, *The Red Cross of the Geneva Convention: What It Is,* in 1878. Addressed to the "People of the United States, Senators and Representatives in Congress," Barton informed citizens and lawmakers alike of the international organization's origin, goals, and principles. Then, she succinctly defined the problem: Even if the United States never again fought a war, the country was subject to natural disasters such as insects and drought, as well as the spread of illnesses like yellow fever. The best way to handle all crises, she told her readers, was to establish an organization that could distribute necessary supplies quickly.[13]

Although Barton clearly explained the need for an American Red Cross, lawmakers still were not immediately convinced of its importance. During the next several years, she met with President Hayes, President Garfield, their secretaries of state, and numerous other legislators to iterate the need for an American Red Cross. Finally, in 1881, Barton met with James G. Blaine, Garfield's secretary of state. He assured her that he would cooperate fully with her efforts to encourage the Senate to sign the Geneva Convention, as 31 other nations already had done. Although Garfield's assassination stalled ratification of the treaty for another year, Barton took advantage of the lawmakers' support and launched the second phase of her public relations campaign: the development of communication strategies designed to attract press coverage and legitimacy.

Her goal was to make the name and emblem of the Red Cross as familiar in America as it was in the rest of the world. Although she noted that the public had become familiar with the name through her efforts to obtain approval of the treaty, she needed to focus her campaign on educating people about the organization and its mission. She did this by publishing additional pamphlets such as *A Sketch of the History of the Red Cross,* which was initially released in 1881 and then reissued with added material in 1883 after the adoption of the international treaty.

In addition, she understood that press coverage was vital to the organization's efforts to carry out its relief efforts. Barton's effectiveness as an advocacy communicator is evident in the amount of press coverage she generated: More than 500 periodicals and newspapers published notices about the publication of her Red Cross pamphlet. Also, Barton made sure to contact the Associated Press and some of the leading newspapers every time the newly formed American Red Cross responded to a natural disaster. The simple message "Everything is needed; everything is welcome" inspired a flood of donations and enabled the Red Cross to raise and distribute an estimated $2 million worth of relief and rehabilitation supplies during Barton's leadership.[14] As well, she acknowledged that the Red Cross was indebted to the "American newspaper press, and perhaps to the *New York Herald* more than to any other newspaper" for its "timely aid and noble furtherance of [the organization's] objects and aims."[15] Certainly, this publicity added to the legitimacy of the organization and helped it with future appeals for contributions.

To further the second stage of her public relations campaign, Barton relied on a fairly consistent set of activities that reflect those now considered typical of advocacy communicators. Frequently, advocacy groups use celebrity spokespersons as well as symbols and drama to successfully draw attention to their cause. The American Red Cross had Clara Barton, who was already well known for her private relief efforts during the Civil War. Newspapers had made her into a national figure; this status as a celebrity enabled her to gain access to presidents and their staff to promote the Red Cross.

A second tactic commonly utilized by advocacy groups involves the use of cultural and social symbols. Barton ensured that the Red Cross flag was displayed prominently at every disaster. In addition, Barton made sure that the distinctive brassard was sewed on the sleeves of all volunteers and medical personnel. The arm band helped to immediately identify the workers as representatives of the Red Cross. Because of its humanitarian significance, the distinctive cross has become the most stringently protected international symbol in the world.

Furthermore, Barton herself became an interesting symbol of the organization's humanitarian efforts. As a woman, she became a symbol of caring, no doubt enhanced by the various nicknames she earned during the Civil War, including "Angel of Mercy" and "The Florence Nightingale of America." Conversely, as head of the Red Cross, Barton held an official, prestigious position—a unique situation given the absence of women's rights in the 1800s. She used this power to bring attention to the Red Cross. For example, she began to wear the numerous medals and decorations she had been awarded. These symbols of power and authority—many of them awarded by European heads of state—helped to elevate the American Red Cross to a level of influence it might not have had otherwise. As one biographer has noted, the medals "gave to the Red Cross a definition in the mind of America."[16]

Barton had accomplished two of the three stages of her public relations campaign. All that remained was the offering of politically feasible solutions. In 1881, when Barton obtained the go-ahead to organize the American Association of the National Red Cross, she knew that its success depended on the creation of chapters in other states. However, the relationship between the local societies and the national organization often was unclear. Lacking congressional recognition and a common charter, the organization had become a loose association of chapters.[17]

Finally, in 1900, Congress granted the relief society its first federal charter and established it as the agency to carry out the purposes of the Geneva Convention in the United States. Due to Barton's successful public relations campaign, the Red Cross had grown from a grassroots relief agency to a nationwide organization with thousands of volunteers.

Clara Barton's efforts to organize and promote the American Red Cross were successful for two reasons. First, she believed in the importance of a permanent, organized relief organization to assist during times of war and peace. Her strong feelings for this cause were critical, because "a social condition gets to be recognized as such largely because it has been backed by someone, i.e., pushed or pulled to the media's attention by an advocacy group."[18]

And second, Barton combined communication tactics with symbolism to positively influence media content and public consciousness. Even though she had no formal training in public relations, her choice of strategies reflect those now considered typical of advocacy communicators who work to "bring about changes in laws, customs or the behavior of individual voters and consumers."[19] Clearly, Clara Barton deserves to be recognized as a pioneer in the field of nonprofit public relations.

In 1905, the Washington, D.C., YMCA sought $350,000 for a new building. For the first time, a full-time publicist was engaged in a fund-raising drive. By 1908, the Red Cross and the National Tuberculosis Association were making extensive use of publicity agents. The New York Orphan Asylum was paying a publicity man $75 per month.

Churches and church groups were quick to recognize the value of an organized publicity effort. New York City's Trinity Episcopal Church was one of Pendleton Dudley's first clients in 1909. The Seventh-Day Adventist Church established its publicity office in 1912. George Parker, Ivy Lee's old partner, was appointed to handle publicity for the Protestant Episcopal Church in 1913.

Though largely neglected in histories of public relations, the social movements of the day adopted the same public relations techniques that were used by other not-for-profit organizations, according to public relations scholar Karen Miller. Moreover, she notes that public relations texts give virtually no attention to the women who headed such movements, including Clara Barton, Margaret Sanger, Susan B. Anthony, Ida B. Wells, and Elizabeth Cody Stanton. Each of these women used public relations techniques of the day most effectively to inform the public about controversial issues despite the fact that their work is generally considered to be outside the business frame of the field.[12] Spotlight 2.1 draws special attention to Clara Barton's founding of the American Red Cross.

Early Corporate Communications Departments

As early as 1883, AT&T leader Theodore Vail expressed concern about the company's relationship with the public and the public's conflicts with the company. He built support from the middle class for AT&T programs by implementing cut-rate phone bills, friendly greetings from the telephone operator, employee morale programs, and paid advertising. In 1907 he hired James Drummond Ellsworth for AT&T's public relations. Ellsworth promoted efficient operation and consideration of customers' needs, a systematic method for answering complaints, and acceptance of governmental regulation as the price for operating a privately owned natural monopoly.

By 1888 the Mutual Life Insurance Company employed Charles J. Smith to manage a "species of literary bureau." A year later, George Westinghouse, head of Westinghouse Electric, established the first corporate communications department. Samuel Insull, an associate of George Westinghouse, rose to head the Chicago Edison Company, an electric utility. In 1903 he began to publish *The Electric City*, a magazine aimed at gaining the understanding and goodwill of the community. He pioneered films for public relations purposes in 1909, and in 1912 he introduced bill stuffers, messages to customers in their monthly statements.

Among the greatest of industrial publicity users was Henry Ford. One commentator suggests, "He may have been an even greater publicist than mechanic." The Ford Company pioneered use of several public relations tools. The employee periodical *Ford Times* was begun in 1908 and continues today. In 1914, a corporate film department was established. Ford also surveyed 1,000 customers to gain insights into their attitudes and concerns.

Astute corporate communicators began recognizing that well-informed employees could serve as ambassadors of corporate goodwill. In fact, George Michaelis, who had founded the Publicity Bureau in Boston, advised George Westinghouse in 1914 to pay more attention to internal "human relations." Thus, employees became recognized as a significant public and an appropriately important audience for public relations efforts. By 1925, more than half of all manufacturing companies were publishing employee magazines.

Early Government Public Relations

The greatest public relations effort in history, up to its time, was the one mounted in support of the U.S. effort in World War I. The military had utilized publicity for several years; the Marine Corps established a publicity bureau in Chicago in 1907. Never before had such a massive, multifaceted, coordinated program been mounted. Moreover, though often used by big business in a defensive fashion, public relations took the offensive when it came to war.

THE PERSUASIVE COMMUNICATION CAMPAIGN TRADITION

In many respects, the beginnings of the persuasive campaign tradition are imbedded in the U.S. World War I publicity and propaganda program.

The Creel Committee

Woodrow Wilson set up a Committee on Public Information in 1917, and newspaperman George Creel was asked to run it. With a staff of journalists, scholars, artists, and others skilled at manipulating words and symbols, Creel mobilized the home front with a comprehensive propaganda bureau that utilized all media, including film and photography.

Creel did not just work out of a central office; he decentralized the organization and the effort. Every industry had a special group of publicity workers tending to their particular contributions to the war effort. Political scientist Harold D. Lasswell was involved in the Creel organization. Looking back to assess the situation, Lasswell concluded, "Propaganda is one of the most powerful instrumentalities in the modern world."[20]

Although the methods used by Creel's committee were fairly standard tools of the public information model, the Creel committee achieved great success because it made use, without knowing it, of psychological principles of mass persuasion. Committee members constructed messages that appealed to what people believe and wanted to hear. Clearly, the Creel committee demonstrated the power of mass persuasion and social influence at a national level.

The success prompted thoughtful Americans to give more concerted attention to the nature of public opinion and the role of the public in society. Educational philosopher John Dewey and his supporters believed that wartime propaganda and postwar societal focus on business development signaled that the citizenry was losing interest in civic life. In contrast, well-spoken political commentator Walter Lippmann professed that American society had grown too complex for the average citizen to understand. The government, he thought, should be influenced and run by experts who could interpret the public will in light of national needs and concerns. The Lippmann interpretation prompted professional persuaders like Edward Bernays to emphasize that the function of public relations was to change images and influence public perception of issues.

Given pro-business attitudes of the 1920s and 1930s, it's little wonder that Lippmann's ideas swamped Dewey's. Critical scholar Margaret Duffy notes that Lippmann's ideas were "grafted" by Edward Bernays, the focal practitioner of the persuasive communication campaign tradition.[21]

Edward Bernays

The leading proponent of persuasion was clearly Edward Bernays, the nephew of psychoanalyst Sigmond Freud. Bernays grew up with dinner-table social science discussions prior to joining Creel's public information committee. After World War I he became a science writer, and then a theater promoter where he combined his journalistic and persuasion interests.

Bernays understood that publics could be persuaded if the message supported their values and interests. In many ways, the thrust of his philosophy is made clear in his first book, *Crystallizing Public Opinion.* At the time, he saw public relations as being more or less synonymous with propaganda, which he defined as "the conscious and intelligent manipulation of the organized habits and opinions of the masses."[22]

Throughout his career Bernays described public relations as the science of creating circumstances, mounting events that are calculated to stand out as newsworthy, yet at the same time do not appear to be staged. Staged "media events" were clearly a defining characteristic of the agency that Bernays started in 1919 with Doris Fleischman, his future wife and partner. Bernays's most well-known event was "Lights Golden Jubilee." Underwritten in 1929 by General Electric and the National Electric Light Association, the jubilee media event recognized the 50-year anniversary of Thomas Edison's invention of the electric lightbulb. Bernays cast the celebration as a premier testimony to the genius of American business and entrepreneurial spirit. It was staged as a massive display of lighting in Dearborn, Michigan, and at other locations around the world. Prior to the event Bernays orchestrated tremendous press coverage and magazine features, salutatory proclamations and endorsements from mayors, governors, and other statesmen throughout the United States and western Europe. The real newsworthiness, however, came on the day of the event when the assembled dignitaries on the Dearborn platform included President Herbert Hoover, J. P. Morgan, John D. Rockefeller, Jr., Orville Wright, Madame Curie, and *New York Times* publisher Adolph Ochs.

RELATIONSHIP-BUILDING AND TWO-WAY COMMUNICATION TRADITION

While Bernays was championing the persuasive campaign approach to public relations, a very different perspective was being set forth by Arthur Page, a successful businessman, public servant, writer, and editor.

Arthur Page

Arthur Page was approached with an offer to become vice president of AT&T, succeeding the pioneer public relations specialist James D. Ellsworth. Page agreed to accept the position only on the condition that he would not be restricted to publicity in the traditional sense. He demanded and received a voice in company policy and insisted that the company's performance be the determinant of its public reputation. Page maintained that

> all business in a democratic country begins with public permission and exists by public approval. If that be true, it follows that business should be cheerfully willing to tell the public what its policies are, what it is doing, and what it hopes to do. This seems practically a duty.[23]

Page viewed public relations as a broad-based management function that transcended both the journalistic publicity and persuasive communication campaign traditions. Under Page's leadership, however, the company recognized that winning public confidence required not merely ad hoc attempts to answer criticism. Rather, a continuous and planned program of positive public relations using institutional advertising, the usual stream of information flowing through press releases, and other methods were needed. Bypassing the conventional print media, the company went directly to the public, establishing, for instance, a film program to be shown to schools and civic groups.

AT&T sought to maintain direct contact with as many of its clients as possible. The company made a total commitment to customer service. Moreover, money was deposited into a number of different banks, legal business was given to attorneys throughout the country, and contracts for supplies and insurance were made with many local agencies. AT&T paid fees for employees to join outside organizations, knowing that through their presence the company would be constantly represented in many forums. Finally, the company sought to have as many people as possible own its stock. Today, AT&T and the successor companies that were created by divestiture in 1984 are the most widely held of all securities.

What truly set Page apart and established him as a pioneer was his insistence that the publicity department act as an interpreter of the public to the company, drawing on a systematic and accurate diagnosis of public opinion. Page wanted data, not hunches. Under his direction, the AT&T publicity department (as it was still called) kept close check on company policies, assessing their impact on the public. Thus, Page caused the company "to act all the time from the public point of view, even when that seems in conflict with the operating point of view."[24]

Page insisted that his staff practice six principles of public relations:

1. *Tell the Truth.* Let the public know what's happening and provide an accurate picture of the company's character, ideals, and practices.
2. *Prove It with Action.* Public perception of an organization is determined 90 percent by doing and 10 percent by talking.
3. *Listen to the Customer.* To serve the company well, understand what the public wants and needs. Keep top decision makers and other employees informed about company products, policies, and practices.

2.2 Spotlight

Public Relations Pioneers

Samuel Adams. Most active prior to and during the American Revolution, Adams organized the Sons of Liberty, used the Liberty Tree symbol, minted slogans like "taxation without representation is tyranny," staged the Boston Tea Party, named the Boston Massacre, and mounted a sustained propaganda campaign.

Amos Kendall. During the 1820s and 1830s, Kendall served candidate and President Andrew Jackson as public relations counselor, pollster, and speechwriter. He spearheaded the successful campaign against the Bank of the United States.

Matthew St. Claire Clarke. As publicist for the Bank of the United States in the 1830s, Clarke saturated the press with releases, reports, and pamphlets in the most extensive, albiet unsuccessful, public relations campaign to that date.

P. T. Barnum. A consummate showman during the middle and late 1800s, Barnum originated many methods for attracting public attention. He didn't let truth interfere with his publicity and press agentry techniques. Although he contributed positively to our understanding of the power of publicity, his lack of honesty led to a legacy of mistrust of publicity efforts that exists sometimes even today.

George Michaelis. Organizer of the nation's first publicity firm, the Publicity Bureau in Boston in 1900, Michaelis used fact-finding publicity and personal contact to saturate the nation's press.

Ivy Lee. Often called the father of modern public relations, Lee believed the public should be informed. He recognized that good words had to be supported by positive actions on the part of individuals and organizations. His emphasis on public relations as a management function put public relations on the right track with corporate America.

George Creel. As head of the Committee on Public Information during World War I, Creel used public relations techniques to sell liberty bonds, build the Red Cross, and promote food conservation and other war-related activities. In so doing, he proved the power of public relations and trained a host of the 20th century's most influential practitioners.

Edward Bernays. An intellectual leader in the field, Bernays coined the phrase "public relations counsel," wrote *Crystallizing Public Opinion* (the first book on public relations), and taught the first college-level public relations course at New York University in 1923. Bernays emphasized the social science contribution to public relations and was a leading advocate for public relations professionalism through practitioner licensing or credentialing. He remained an active counselor, writer, and speaker until his death in 1995 at age 103.

Arthur Page. When offered a vice presidency at AT&T, Page insisted he have a voice in shaping corporate policy. He maintained that business in a democratic country depends on public permission and approval.

John Hill. Along with Don Knowlton, John Hill opened a public relations agency in Cleveland, Ohio, in 1927. When John Hill moved to New York a few years later to open Hill & Knowlton, Knowlton was not part of the agency. The New York–based agency, though, continued to bear both their names. It became the largest public relations agency in the world and continues to rank in the top grouping. John Hill had major steel and tobacco accounts in his counseling career. His agency was sold to J. Walter Thompson in 1980 for $28 million. In 1987, it was sold to the English-based WPP Group for $85 million.

Doris Fleischman Bernays. Doris Fleischman Bernays was Edward Bernays's counselor partner from their marriage in 1922 until retirement in 1952. She counseled corporations, government agencies, and presidents along with her husband. She struggled for equality, not with her husband, but with the attitudes of American business that often paid less attention to the advice given by a woman public relations practitioner.

Carl Byoir. Carl Byoir, like Edward Bernays, was another member of George Creel's Committee on Public Information in World War I. After the war he founded Carl Byoir and Associates in 1930 to promote tourism to Cuba. He was known for his use of third-party endorsements, use of newspaper advertising as a public relations tool, and development of lobbying in legislative battles for clients such as A&P, Libby-Owens-Ford, and Eastern Railroads.

Rex Harlow. Harlow was a leading public relations educator. He began teaching a public relations course at Stanford in 1939 and may have been the first full-time professor of public relations. He also founded the American Council on Public Relations in 1939. The council eventually merged with the National Association of Public Relations Councils to form the Public Relations Society of America in 1947. In 1944 Harlow founded the *Public Relations Journal* and in 1952 founded *Social Science Reporter.*

Patrick Jackson. Highly regarded public relations counselor Patrick Jackson served the profession with distinction for more than 30 years until his death in 2001. He published the trade newsletter *pr reporter,* where he reported on current research affecting public relations practice with an emphasis on applying communication and behavioral science research findings. He also served as president of the Public Relations Society of America.

4. *Manage for Tomorrow.* Anticipate public relations and eliminate practices that create difficulties. Generate goodwill.
5. *Conduct Public Relations as if the Whole Company Depends on It.* Corporate relations is a management function. No corporate strategy should be implemented without considering its impact on the public. The public relations professional is a policymaker capable of handling a wide range of corporate communications activities.
6. *Remain Calm, Patient, and Good-Humored.* Lay the groundwork for public relations miracles with consistent, calm, and reasoned attention to information and contacts. When a crisis arises, remember that cool heads communicate best.

Public relations historian Karen Miller Russell believes that Page may come closest among early practitioners of representing the sense of the relationship-building and two-way communication tradition. This shows up, says Miller, in Page's continual quest for government-industry accommodation. He led the effort with Columbia University social scientist Paul Lazarsfeld to conduct regularly scheduled research with customers, employees, and other key publics to assess AT&T's standing among those groups. In turn, he used that feedback both to encourage organizational change and to fine-tune messages regarding the company's identity. (See spotlight 2.2 for a brief biographical sketch of leading public relations pioneers.)

The Depression and World War II

Although corporate and agency public relations practice grew handily as part of the 1920s business boom, it was the Great Depression of the 1930s and the personal leadership of President Franklin Roosevelt that further transformed the practice. With help from public relations practitioners like Carl Byoir, Roosevelt built public support and changed public opinion toward his New Deal recovery programs with weekly radio broadcasts and numerous other techniques, including those described in mini-case 2.1 featuring counselor Carl Byoir.

Roosevelt's presidency was highlighted both by the Great Depression and World War II. In June 1942, with America fully engaged in worldwide war, the Office of War Information (OWI) was established. Similar to Creel's effort in World War I, a massive public relations effort was mounted to rally the home front. Elmer Davis directed the program. The goals of the OWI included selling war bonds; rationing food, clothing, and gasoline; planting victory gardens; and recruiting military personnel. Other issues promoted were factory productivity and efficiency.

Post–World War II

The period following World War II represented a high point in professional growth and development of public relations practice. Many leading practitioners from the 1950s to the 1980s were among the nearly 75,000 Americans who had the "ultimate public relations internship" learning public relations practice during wartime while working for the OWI.

Several important communication agencies still active today trace their beginnings to OWI. These include the Voice of America, the American Advertising Council, and the United States Information Agency, which sponsors scholarly and cultural exchanges. Many OWI veterans applied their wartime skills to initiate public information and public relations programs for government agencies, nonprofit organizations, schools, colleges, and hospitals.

2.1 Mini•Case

Carl Byoir and FDR

Franklin Roosevelt became ill with polio in 1921 while vacationing a few months after his defeat as vice president on the James Cox Democratic ticket of 1920. Roosevelt narrowly escaped death from the polio and fought the crippling effects of the disease for the rest of his life.

In 1926, Roosevelt bought a rundown spa in Warm Springs, Georgia, from friend and philanthropist George Peabody. The spa—with 1,200 acres, hotel, and cottages—was in poor shape, but the curative powers of the hot mineral springs held promise for many polio victims.

When Roosevelt was elected governor of New York in 1928, he realized he wouldn't have time to oversee the rehabilitation effort at Warm Springs, so he asked his law partner, Basil O'Conner, to lead the effort. O'Conner formed the Warm Springs Foundation to raise money for the refurbishing of the health resort. However, the stock market crash in 1929 made fundraising difficult.

When Roosevelt became president in 1932, the foundation was nearly bankrupt. However, one of the foundation fund-raisers, Keith Morgan, hired a public relations counselor, Carl Byoir, to do the job. Byoir had founded his own public relations agency in 1930 to promote tourism to Cuba. Byoir's fundraising idea for the Warm Springs Foundation was to create a special event to raise the money. That event turned out to be birthday balls around the country to celebrate President Roosevelt's birthday on January 30, 1934.

Byoir sent letters to newspaper editors around the country asking them to nominate a birthday ball director for their area. If an editor didn't respond, he went to either the Democratic Party chairman in the area or to the Roosevelt-appointed postmaster to ask them to do the ball. Media were besieged with information about the balls. National syndicated columnist and broadcaster Walter Winchell presented an appeal that was so good it would be used for years for both birthday balls and the March of Dimes. Radio personalities tried to outdo each other in promoting the balls. In the end, 6,000 balls were held in 3,600 communities and more than $1 million was raised for the foundation.

The next two years the event was changed to split the proceeds, with 70 percent going to local communities and 30 percent to a newly created national polio research commission.

Carl Byoir led the first three birthday balls. He left after the third because he became disillusioned with President Roosevelt when FDR "packed" the Supreme Court in 1937.

But out of Byoir's effort not only came the birthday balls, but also the March of Dimes, the National Foundation for Infantile Paralysis, and finally victory over polio. Carl Byoir had elevated fund-raising to a new level through his public relations efforts and had given new insight into techniques that public relations practitioners continue to use today.

Source: Scott M. Cutlip, *The Unseen Power* (Hillsdale, NJ: Erlbaum, 1994), pp. 553–63.

Fundraising events such as this WalkAmerica for March of Dimes use public relations tools to make them successful events.

And yet the hallmark of postwar public relations growth took place in the private sector, in corporations and agencies. A consumer economy made use of both public relations and advertising to market products. Agencies came into full being, providing media relations and media contact capabilities not always available on the corporate side. The need for these skills was driven in part by the explosive growth of media outlets not available before the war—including FM radio, general magazines, suburban community newspapers, and trade and professional association publications. Their services expanded from a base of counseling and media relations to include public affairs or government relations, financial and investor relations, crisis communication, and media relations training for executives.

On the organizational or client side, new services areas were added to complement the existing areas of publicity/media relations, employee publications, community relations, and audiovisual services. Chief among these was a new public affairs component to develop relationships with governmental offices in the legislative and executive branches of government. Initially, governmental affairs, or public affairs, built on community relations practices but soon came into its own, oftentimes as a result of new federal Great Society programs begun in the 1960s and 1970s. Civil rights, environmental, urban development, and similar programs all mandated citizen involvement or public participation assessments to determine how various **stakeholders** and established publics were affected by changes in land use, zoning, and community development activities.

The new mandated citizen involvement and public participation programs exemplified the growing relationship-building and two-way communication tradition. The two-way tradition involved building long-term relationships with publics and important stakeholders for organizations to recognize. Programs were geared not toward persuasion but rather toward mutual understanding, compromise, and creating win-win situations for organizations and their affected publics and stakeholders. In many respects this approach had already been adopted across regulated industries such as public utilities, cable television business, and others for which license renewals and rate increases were contingent on government approval. In turn, that approval was contingent on the licensee demonstrating community support by showing that the needs of various publics had been addressed in the renewal application.

Professionalization of the Field

More important, perhaps, were the concerted measures taken to establish public relations as a defined, respectable, and accepted field of professional practice. In fact, the 40-year period from 1960 to 2000 is perhaps best characterized as the professional-development-building era in public relations. In 1947 Boston University established the first school of public relations. Two years later, 100 colleges and universities offered classes in the subject.

Perhaps more than anything else, the 50-year period between the end of World War II and the Internet explosion was characterized by professionalizing the practice. Two major national professional associations were formed from mergers of smaller groups. The largest, the Public Relations Society of America, began in 1948 and now maintains a membership of 20,000, including more than 110 local chapters as well as university student organizations under the name of the Public Relations Student Society of America. In 1954 the PRSA developed the first code of ethics for the profession. The society set up a grievance board for code enforcement in 1962, a program of voluntary accreditation in 1964, and a rewritten ethics code in 2000.

In 1970 the International Association of Business Communicators was formed by the merger of the International Council of Industrial Editors and the Association of Industrial Editors. The IABC has been at the forefront in underwriting research studies examining the current state and future of the public relations profession. Both PRSA and IABC now administer professional continuing education programs for their members and an accreditation program. Practitioners who pass both oral and written accreditation exams are deemed accredited and allowed to place the initials APR or ABC after their names on their business cards. PRSA uses APR (Accredited Public Relations); IABC uses ABC (Accredited Business Communicator).

In addition to PRSA and IABC, today more than a dozen national public relations organizations are based in the United States, not to mention those whose membership is largely outside the United States. They're listed here to indicate the range of professionally organized specialties within public relations:

Religious Public Relations Council, founded in 1929.

National School Public Relations Association, founded in 1935.

Public Relations Society of America, founded in 1948. Includes 20,000 members, not counting members of the affiliated Public Relations Student Society of America.

Agricultural Relations Council, founded in 1953.

International Public Relations Association, founded in 1955.

National Society of Fund-Raising Executives, founded in 1960.

National Investor Relations Institute, founded in 1969.

International Association of Business Communicators, founded in 1970 and now with 13,000 members.

Council for the Advancement and Support of Education (CASE), founded in 1975.

National Association of Government Communicators, founded in 1976.

Issue Management Council, founded in 1982.

The Arthur Page Society, founded in 1983.

Society of Healthcare Strategy and Marketing Development, founded in 1996 and subsuming previous hospital and health care public relations associations.

Association of Counseling Firms, founded in 1999.

Professional and specialized public relations organizations also started professional magazines and newsletters such as the *Public Relations Journal,* and *Communication World,* which were followed by other private newsletters and trade magazines such as the *Ragan Report, PR News, PR Tactics, PR Week, pr reporter,* and *Public Relations Quarterly.* Taken together, these professional publications form a distinctive literature aimed at those practitioners.

Public relations texts were published once college-level courses were offered, first as a concentration within the journalism or mass communication major and later within speech communication or integrated communication. Then came the academic journals where university professors published research findings or developed new theoretical traditions to explain the practice of public relations. The principal journals were *Public Relations Review, Public Relations Research and Education, Public Relations Research Annual,* and the *Journal of Public Relations Research.* A public relations literature or body of knowledge was developing separately from related fields such as advertising,

Spotlight 2.3

1920s. Systematic understanding of the importance and nature of public opinion emerged both in terms of polling and scientific measurement but also as a social organizing process around issues.

1950s. Persuasion and social influence principles, and especially those set forth with the Yale Communication Program, provided the strategies for establishing, maintaining, and changing opinions and attitudes.

1960s. The diffusion of innovations research tradition served as a conceptual framework for public relations practitioners, health communicators, and Peace Corps officials on how to combine interpersonal and media communication to change behaviors. Most recently, the diffusion framework has been used to illustrate the use of marketing communication elements including publicity, advertising, sales promotion, and direct selling.

1970s. Situational theory of publics was put forth. While public relations practitioners use a range of audience segmentation techniques, J. Grunig's situational theory explains which publics will become most active regarding specific issues.

Relational communication, with its roots in interpersonal communication, set forth by Rogers and Millar, accounts for conditions prompting and inhibiting relational development.

1960s–1990s. Social psychological foundations underpinning public relations practice flourished alongside specific public relations theories. Many of these theories are used to study cognitive or knowledge change and information processing in public relations and health communication. These include attitude/action consistency, expectancy value theory, co-orientation, theory of reasoned action, framing theory, social cognitive theory, and game theory.

1970s–2000. Normative influences on the practice of public relations have underpinned important research on practitioner roles, feminization of the field, and other gender-related effects.

1980s–2000. J. Grunig's four models of public relations based on one-way/two-way and balanced/unbalanced communication have prompted the greatest amount of recent research and theory development in public relations.

Social and organizational structural influences on the growth and nature of public relations work, including research on public relations in different industry categories, structurally determined cross-cultural impacts on the practice, and encroachment on the public relations functions by related areas, became evident.

1990s–2000. Critical theory approaches emerged. Scholars in this tradition believe that the practice and study of public relations from a business and organizational standpoint mask power differences in society and ignore nonmainstream groups, including social movements and third-party candidates.

journalism, public opinion, and interpersonal communication. Those conceptual underpinnings were grounded in theory and are outlined chronologically in spotlight 2.3.

Taken together, these new professional magazines, texts, and research publications all reinforced the growing consensus that public relations work could be organized in terms of a four-step process—research, planning, communication and action (implementation), and evaluation. As time went on, the field gained even more respect as program plans expanded to include measurable objectives and follow-up evaluation measures to assess the impact, the cost, and ways to improve future campaigns and programs.

New Stakeholder Groups

In the late 1960s and the 1970s, democratically inspired social movements used effective public relations techniques to oppose business interests. With little money or staff, environmental group members, for example, became proficient at staging tree huggings, road blockages, and other events whose conflict themes were almost guaranteed to generate television footage. They effectively used not only alternative and specialized media, but also journalistic conventions as well, sometimes at the expense of losing their hard edge, according to sociologists Todd Gitlin and Charlotte Ryan.[25]

Societal concerns during the late 1960s and 1970s prompted businesses and their public relations agencies to place new emphasis on governmental and community relations, issue tracking, issue management, and strategic planning. This was especially the case with regulated business such as utilities and telecommunication firms whose rate structures, franchises, and licensing requirements placed a premium on effective relationship building among key constituencies.

THE GLOBAL INFORMATION SOCIETY

Another more or less distinct phase in public relations history emerged around 1990 and was characterized by (1) the uses of the Internet and other new communication technologies and (2) the growth of public relations agencies, which occurred oftentimes either by merging with larger public relations agencies or with advertising agencies, or by forming alliances with other firms in regional cities.

The 1990s were also characterized by the growth of specialty practices in public relations. Investor relations, though begun 20 years earlier, came into its own as technology companies sought venture capital, became stock-held corporations through initial public offerings, and later merged with other public corporations. Thus, keeping stockholders informed and attracting new investors became a central, rather than peripheral, public relations function.

By 1990 leading firms had aligned their corporate giving with ongoing community relations programs. As well, their global reach throughout the 1990s led to more focus on corporate social responsibility generally rather than corporate giving in a narrow sense. Issues management and environmental scanning functions became more systematic owing to computer databases and tracking systems in which organizations could join chat groups and listservs.

The opening of new markets on a global scale led to systems of global strategic design with local implementation and a noticeably heavier emphasis given to intercultural issues or differences in the ways companies could offer themselves and their products in different cultures and regions of the world.

At home, a much greater degree of specialization began occurring at agencies as they sought to develop more subject matter competence in key industrial niches, including technology, health care, financial and investor institutions, and international practice.

Another milestone was reached when it became known that more and more public relations practitioners were seeking master's degrees either to become more specialized within the field of public relations or as a way of taking on more general management responsibilities.

The 1990s was a time of explosive growth for public relations and corporate communication stemming in large part from (1) growth and use of the Internet, (2) global communication demands, and (3) proliferating communication channels.

The Internet

It's little wonder that the Internet changed the nature of public relations work. In its early days, seven people every second logged on for the first time. Public relations Internet expert Don Middleberg forecasted 350 million Internet users by 2002, and he wasn't far off. He predicts 1 billion users by the end of the decade with most of the new users coming from outside the United States.[26] To put the impact of the Internet in perspective, those who study media adoption note that it took radio 30 years to reach an audience of 50 million and TV took 13 years—the Internet took just 4 years. By 2000, e-mail had become the preferred medium for reaching reporters with whom an organization had already developed relationships.

Before the Internet, the thrust of media relations work was "pushing" information from the organization to the desks of media reports, producers, and editors via news releases, news tips, and press kits. That all changed because the Web gives the reporter the opportunity to pull and parse needed company information from the website and all of its links without ever going through the public relations or media relations office. Dot-com journalists believe they have deadlines every second. As media relations expert Carole Howard notes, "The media day has turned into the media hour and now the media minute or second."[27] The key point here is that the Internet is a very different and more powerful media relations tool than almost any over the preceding 50 years.

In short, the Internet has changed the way reporters work just as much as it's changed the way public relations practitioners work. Most reporters check websites while writing their stories, especially broad-based pieces. This requires organizations to update their websites regularly and to make all the media "pages" and links readily accessible so that reporters who cover an organization come to consider its website a current, useful, and trusted source.

Global Communication Demands

Just as Internet websites and e-mail functions have reshaped public relations practice, so too have the creation of new consumer and financial markets around the world. Competition for worldwide markets speeds product introduction times. As a result, trade magazine editors and financial reports clamor for updated information almost by the hour. Gone, then, are the days when publicity releases could be planned and scheduled weeks and months in advance.

The new worldwide public relations environment means working simultaneously with the media across various cultures, nations, and regions. Under these conditions, public relations practitioners are forced to be better versed in intercultural communication practices and to understand differences in the ways media reporters and editors are approached or contacted in different cultures.

In Japan, for example, contact with the media is made through "press clubs" maintained separately by each industry or at government press rooms maintained by each government minister. Press club secretaries decide whether to issue press releases, call press conferences, or do nothing. The press club seal of endorsement—especially regarding press conferences—markedly increases newspaper coverage.

Proliferating Communication Channels

The proliferation of media channels—especially cable channels and new magazine titles—continues in response to individual and media desires for more specialized information tailored to the various reading and viewing interests of investors, customers, employees, donors, and so on. For public relations practitioners this means matching the qualities of traditional and **online** media to the information needs of their target audiences. Ray Kotcher, senior partner and CEO of Ketchum, explains how channel proliferation affects media relations work: "At the moment we are being asked to deal on a more strategic level (make this a new development) because of this incredible momentum in the media, messaging and information that's out there. Think about it. We only had one NBC network 15 years ago. Now we have CNBC, MSNBC, and I don't know how many NBC's on line."[28]

Summary

For self-testing and additional chapter resources, go to the student CD and the Online Learning Center at **www.mhhe.com/lattimore**

The scope of public relations work today clearly is nothing like it was in early times or even during the jump-start period following World War I. Even so, the pattern of development can be seen in the four orienting traditions: the rhetorician and press agent tradition, the journalistic publicity tradition, the persuasive communication campaign tradition, and finally, a relationship-building and two-way communication tradition. We close with a quote from veteran public relations educator and historian Scott M. Cutlip who wrote in *The Unseen Power*, "The essentiality of public relations as a management function that Ivy Lee envisaged in the early 1900s becomes clearer each passing day as our global society becomes even more dependent on effective communication and on an interdependent, competitive world."[29]

To learn more about the public relations history watch the interview with Harold Burson, Clip #5, on the book's CD-ROM.

Wreck on the Pennsylvania Railroad, 1906

By Craig E. Aronoff
Kennesaw State College
Marietta, Georgia

Severe railroad regulations passed in 1903 and 1906 caused Alexander J. Cassatt, president of the Pennsylvania Railroad, to seek the counsel of Ivy Ledbetter Lee concerning how to deal better with the press and the public. Lee went right to work. He believed in absolute frankness with the press. Veteran railroad men were distressed at Lee's behavior. They were convinced that revealing facts about accidents would frighten customers.

A golden opportunity for Lee to put his ideas into practice soon arose. A train wrecked on the Pennsylvania Railroad main line near the town of Gap, Pennsylvania. As was its time-honored practice, the company sought to suppress all news of the accident.

When Ivy Lee learned of the situation, he took control. He contacted reporters, inviting them to come to the accident scene at company expense. He provided facilities to help them in their work. He gave out information for which the journalists had not considered asking.

The railroad's executives were appalled at Lee's actions. His policies were seen as unnecessary and destructive. How could the propagation of such bad news do anything but harm the railroad's freight and passenger business?

At about the time of the wreck on the Pennsylvania, another train accident struck the rival New York Central. Sticking with its traditional policy, the Central sought to avoid the press and restrict information flow concerning the situation. Confronted with the Central's behavior, and having tasted Lee's approach to public relations, the press was furious with the New York line. Columns and editorials poured forth chastising the Central and praising the Pennsylvania. Lee's efforts resulted in positive publicity, increased credibility, comparative advantages over the Central, and good, constructive press coverage and relations. Lee critics were silenced.

Earl Newsom, himself a public relations giant, looked back at this accident nearly 60 years later and said:

> This whole activity of which you and I are a part can probably be said to have its beginning when Ivy Lee persuaded the directors of the Pennsylvania Railroad that the press should be given all the facts on all railway accidents—even though the facts might place the blame on the railroad itself.*

When Ivy Lee died in 1934, among the many dignitaries at his funeral were the presidents of both the Pennsylvania and the New York Central railroads.

Questions

1. Were Lee's actions in response to the railroad accident consistent with practice today? Explain.
2. Had the New York Central accident not occurred, what do you think would have happened to Ivy Lee and his relationship with the Pennsylvania Railroad? Do you think the course of public relations development would have been affected?
3. In certain totalitarian states, news of accidents and disasters is often largely suppressed. What do you consider their reasons to be for retaining a posture given up by American public relations practice more than eighty years ago?

*Earl Newsom, *"Business Does Not Function by Divine Right," Public Relations Journal* (January 1963): 4.

Source: Material for this case was gathered from Ray Hiebert's *Courtier to the Crowd* (Ames, IA: Iowa State University Press, 1966), 55–61, and Eric Goldman's *Two-Way Street* (Boston: Bellman Publishing, 1948), 8.

Key Terms

Use the CD-ROM and Online Learning Center at www.mhhe.com/lattimore to further your understanding of the following terms

online
press agents
propaganda of the deed
rhetoricians
stakeholder

Notes

1. Helio Fred Garcia, "Really-Old-School Public Relations," *Public Relations Strategist* (Summer 1998), p. 18.
2. Ibid., pp. 16–18.
3. Philip Davidson, *Propaganda and the American Revolution, 1763–1783* (Chapel Hill: University of North Carolina Press, 1941), p. 3.
4. Allan Nevins, *The Constitution Makers and the Public, 1785–1790* (New York: Foundation for Public Relations Research and Education, 1962), p. 10.
5. Richard Overton, *Burlington West* (Cambridge, MA: Harvard University Press, 1941), pp. 158–59.
6. Merle Curti, *The Growth of American Thought.* 3rd ed. (New York: Harper & Row, 1964), p. 634.
7. Marc Bloch, *The Historian's Craft* (New York: Knopf, 1953), p. 168.
8. Eric F. Goldman, *Two-Way Street* (Boston: Bellman Publishing, 1948), p. 21.
9. Quoted in Sherman Morse, "An Awakening on Wall Street," *American Magazine* 62 (September 1906), p. 460.
10. Ray E. Hiebert, *Courtier to the Crowd: The Story of Ivy Lee and the Development of Public Relations* (Ames: Iowa State University Press, 1966), p. 57.
11. Ibid., p. 65.
12. Karen S. Miller, "U.S. Public Relations History: Knowledge and Limitations," *Communication Yearbook* 23 (2000), pp. 381–420.
13. Blanche Colton Williams, *Clara Barton: Daughter of Destiny* (Philadelphia, PA: J. B. Lippincott, 1941), p. 447.
14. Charles Hurd, *A Compact History of the American Red Cross* (New York: Hawthorn Books, 1959), p. 63.
15. Clara Barton, *The Red Cross* (Washington, DC: American National Red Cross, 1898), p. 89.
16. Williams, vol. 2, p. 257.
17. Hurd, p. 57.
18. Charles T. Salmon, "God Understands When the Cause Is Noble," *Gannett Center Journal* (Spring 1990), p. 24.
19. Ibid.
20. Harold D. Lasswell, *Propaganda Techniques in the World War* (New York: Knopf, 1927), p. 220.
21. Margaret E. Duffy, "There's No Two-Way Symmetric About It: A Postmodern Examination of Public Relations Textbooks," *Critical Studies in Media Communication* 17, no. 3 (September 2000), pp. 294–313.
22. Stuart Ewan, *A Social History of Spin* (New York: Basic Books, 1996), p. 34.
23. George Griswold, Jr., "How AT&T Public Relations Policies Developed," *Public Relations Quarterly* 12 (Fall 1967), p. 13.
24. Allan R. Raucher, *Public Relations and Business, 1900–1929* (Baltimore: Johns Hopkins University Press, 1968), pp. 80–81.
25. Todd Gitlin, *The Whole World Is Watching: Mass Media in the Making and Unmaking of the New Left* (Berkeley: University of California Press, 1980) and Charlotte Ryan, *Media Strategies for Grassroots Organizing* (Boston, MA: South End Press, 1991).
26. Don Middleberg and Steven Ross, "The Middleberg/Ross Media Survey: Change and Its Impact on Communication," Eighth Annual National Survey, 2002.
27. Carole Howard, "Technologies and Tabloids: How the New Media World Is Changing Our Jobs," *Public Relations Quarterly* 45 (Spring 2000), p. 9.
28. Ray Kotcher, "Roundtable: Future Perfect? Agency Leaders Reflect on the 1990s and Beyond," *Public Relations Strategist* 8 (Summer 2001), p. 11.
29. Scott M. Cutlip, *The Unseen Power: Public Relations. A History* (Hillsdale, NJ: Erlbaum, 1994), p. 761.

CHAPTER THREE

A Theoretical Basis for Public Relations

3

Outline

PREVIEW
THEORIES OF RELATIONSHIPS
Systems Theory
Situational Theory
Approaches to Conflict Resolution
THEORIES OF COGNITION AND BEHAVIOR
Action Assembly Theory
Social Exchange Theory
Diffusion Theory
Social Learning Theory
Elaborated Likelihood Model
THEORIES OF MASS COMMUNICATION
Uses and Gratifications Theory
Agenda Setting Theory
PUBLIC RELATIONS ROLES
MODELS OF PUBLIC RELATIONS
SUMMARY

PREVIEW

Why have a chapter on theory in a beginning public relations principles textbook? Whereas most textbooks describe the state of public relations, its history, its practices, and its processes, we believe that it is also important to provide some context about how and why public relations is practiced as it is. More important, theory helps us make the practice of public relations more effective for organizations and society.

Theories are used to explain or predict the way things work or happen. They present an understanding of the relationship between various actions and events. As a public relations practitioner, you will need to build a set of theories to use and refine as you apply professional skill to the test of doing public relations.

There is no single theory to guide you. This chapter looks at several theories, which are categorized in three areas: relationships, cognition and behavior, and communication.

Another way to build an understanding of public relations is by using typologies and models. This chapter discusses a typology of roles: practitioners as managers and as technicians. Models of public relations show the interaction of two key concepts of public relations: communication and research. We provide a look at the four original models of public relations and how they have been tested and improved since their inception, and we note more recent models □

What would happen if we used a website to reach our publics? Why did our audience agree to donate money? Questions like these should sound familiar to anyone working in public relations. Public relations practitioners evaluate why a plan worked or didn't work so that they can adjust their strategies for future efforts.

Some of the questions we ask as practitioners are routine and some are not so routine. When someone knows answers to routine questions, we say that person has "common sense." When someone can correctly answer the nonroutine, we say that person is astute or experienced. But, to answer either type of question, a person needs to understand the relationships between actions and events.

A **theory** is a prediction of how events and actions are related. For example, *pr reporter* described as a failure a federally funded message campaign to keep kids off drugs.[1] Research showed that kids who reported seeing the ads were using marijuana even more than those who had not seen the ads. What caused this waste of $180 million a year? One expert said, "Scaring kids doesn't work. When people try pot for the first time, they wonder what the big deal is. Then, they don't believe the other stuff. The ads are not realistic."[2] This opinion reflects a great deal of theory on the use of fear appeals. Fear appeals theory predicts that there will be little change with an overreliance on fear appeals that threaten physical harm. More persuasive are balanced arguments with incentives for changing behavior.[3] We call this prediction a theory.

We have theories about many actions and events in public relations. Some theories serve us well because we test them regularly and observe the same relationships over time. For example, thank-you notes to express appreciation will almost always lead to an improved relationship between an organization and its customers, clients, employees, and so on. Other theories are dynamic and evolving and need more testing and refinement so that they will have better predictive value.

This chapter is about explaining and predicting the ways that public relations works or doesn't work. Theories make a difference in whether our choices are informed or not. Read some of former PRSA president Pat Jackson's lasting theories for public relations in spotlight 3.1. As a public relations manager, you should have knowledge of different theoretical models so that you can make the right decisions for your public relations plans and programs. Your value to your employer or client will be directly related to how well you use theory in your work.

No single theory covers all you need to know in public relations or any other discipline; therefore, it is valuable to look at theories by grouping them according to how they are used. We start with theories of relationships. Then, we discuss theories of cognition and behavior; that is, theories about how people take in information and what moves them to act. Next, we consider theories of mass communication. Finally, we look at ways to describe what public relations people do and how organizations approach public relations.

THEORIES OF RELATIONSHIPS

Both systems theory and situational theory are considered *theories of relationships.* We'll look at each theory here.

Systems Theory

Systems theory is useful in public relations because it gives us a way to think about relationships. Generally, systems theory looks at organizations as made up of interrelated parts, adapting and adjusting to changes in the political, economic, and social

Pat Jackson's Lasting Contribution to Public Relations

Spotlight 3.1

- Any profession exists only by public consent. Public relations provides an overriding social benefit when people have a voice.
- Harmony is an outcome of public relations practiced over a long time.
- Harmonious relationships—not just relations—fortified with trust require coauthorship.
- Remind managers that their communication role is to transmit not only information but emotions and intuition.
- The most important effect is to change behavior.
- Public relations practitioners' chief role is to serve as catalysts.

Source: From *pr reporter,* 2 April 2001, pp. 1–2.

Pat Jackson

environments in which they operate. Organizations have recognizable boundaries, within which there must be a communication structure that guides the parts of the organization to achieve organizational goals. The leaders of the organization create and maintain these internal structures.

Grunig, Grunig, and Dozier state that the systems perspective emphasizes the interdependence of organizations with their environments, both internal and external to the organization.[4] According to the systems perspective, organizations depend on resources from their environments, such as "raw materials, a source of employees, and clients or customers for the services or products they produce. The environment needs the organization for its products and services."[5] Organizations with "open systems" use public relations people to bring back information on how productive their relationships are with clients, customers, and other stakeholders. Organizations with "closed systems" do not seek new information but operate on past history or the preferences of the decision makers.

Organizations are part of a greater environment made up of many systems. We'll use as an example a hypothetical organization—United PRworks. This organization is depicted as an oval in the center of figure 3.1. Moving out from the organization, you can see that it has an environment—the area between the large circle and our organization. In that environment we see most of the groups we considered in chapter 1—customers, media, the community, financial institutions, and the government. These groups are called **stakeholders,** because "they and the organization have consequences on each other"[6]—they create problems and opportunities for each other. Whether organizations acknowledge it or not, they have relationships with each of these groups. The only decision is whether organizations will manage these relationships or let them happen.

We can use systems theory not only to examine relationships with our external stakeholders, but also to look at the internal functions and stakeholders of our organizations. Organizations structure their employees by specific jobs and functions. Many different departments, such as accounting, legal, and public relations, make up the managerial function. The production function of an organization might include skilled and unskilled employees who actually make the product or provide the service to customers. All of these different employees are interdependent on one another. Again, the only decision is whether organizations will manage employee relationships or let them happen.

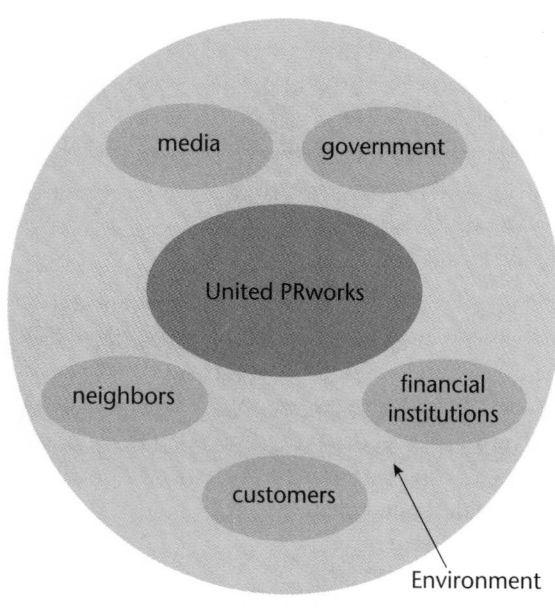

FIGURE 3.1 Systems model of an organization and its environment.

For example, the Roman Catholic church is a multinational, multilingual, multistructured organization; but the Roman Catholic church has no mechanism for managing its vast employee relationships. Critics of its continued support for priests accused of abusing children have said that the pope should just set a "zero tolerance" policy for all of the church to follow. But his role is not the same as that of a CEO. He has moral power, but not total power over the organizational functions. Power to train, employ, and discipline priests resides with local parish officials, who must adapt and adjust to their respective countries. These countries have different laws about child abuse issues. The Catholic church has neither one clear internal voice nor the internal communication mechanism to make decisions quickly that all of its employees can support and carry out.[7]

The monitoring of relationships is a major one for public relations people. Through systems theory, we think of public relations people as **boundary spanners,** straddling the edge of an organization—both looking inside and outside of an organization. Public relations practitioners are the go-betweens, explaining the organization to its stakeholders and interpreting the environment to the organization. Public relations people advise the **dominant coalition,**[8] the primary decision makers of the organization, about problems and opportunities in the environment and help these decision makers respond to these changes.

The environment imposes constraints on organizations. For example, customers can boycott an organization's products. The courts can make a business pay damages to people who are injured by its products. Banks can choose not to lend an organization money. Because we use systems theory, we can identify an organization's stakeholders and by spanning organizational boundaries, we can anticipate each side's communication needs.

If decision makers keep their systems open, they allow for the two-way flow of resources and information between the organization and its environment. They use that information for adapting to the environment, or they may use the incoming information to try to control the environment. That is a much more difficult but not impossible task. For example, British Petroleum provided a "peer assist" program through a technical infrastructure that encouraged offshore drillers in the Gulf of Mexico to share knowledge with operators on a drilling platform in the North Sea.[9]

Using the concepts of organizations and environments we can begin to create theoretical statements about relationships with stakeholders. For example, we might say: The more turbulent the environment, the more flexible the public relations department needs to be because the stakeholders that could have positive or negative consequences for the organization are constantly changing. Organizations that remain closed to new information from the environment are less likely to build effective relationships with key publics. If organizations have closed systems, it may take a crisis for an organization to accept environmental changes.

Situational Theory

Grunig and Repper[10] agreed that it was a good start to use the concept of stakeholders as a way of describing relationships. However, they concluded that not all people in stakeholder groups would be equally likely to communicate with the organization. They felt that public relations people could more effectively manage communications by identifying specific publics within stakeholder groups. These **publics** were subgroups that were more or less active in their communication behavior. An example of a stakeholder public would be active voters within the broader group of all registered voters. Candidates for political office focus their communication efforts on those voters who can be counted on to go to polls on election day. Grunig and Hunt proposed what they call a situational theory of publics to give us more specific information about their communication needs.[11]

Grunig and Hunt theorized that publics range from those who *actively* seek and process information about an organization or an issue of interest and those publics that *passively* receive information. According to these researchers, three variables predict when publics will seek and process information about an issue: problem recognition, constraint recognition, and level of involvement. The key is that publics are situational. That is, as the situation, problem, opportunity, or issue changes, the publics, with which the organization must communicate, change.

Problem Recognition Publics facing an issue must first be aware of it and recognize its potential to affect them. For example, parents of school-age children will be more aware of subpar school facilities than taxpayers without children.

Constraint Recognition This variable describes how publics perceive obstacles that may stand in the way of a solution. If they believe they have a real shot at influencing an issue, they will tend to seek and process information on that issue. Think again about parents with school-age children. They have more access to school decision makers because they have more contact with school principals, teachers, and administrators than do taxpayers without children.

Level of Involvement This variable refers to how much an individual cares about an issue. Those who care a lot would likely be active communicators on an issue. Those who care little would likely be more passive in seeking and processing information. We anticipate that the level of involvement would be much higher for those who saw firsthand substandard school facilities than those who had not.

Using these three variables, Grunig and Hunt described four responses that follow from being high or low in these dimensions. For example, those publics who have high problem recognition, low constraint recognition, and high involvement in an issue are much more likely to actively engage in communication about it.

Situational theory also helps explain why some groups are active on a single issue, others are active on many issues, and others are uniformly apathetic. The specific relationship is determined by the type of group (active, passive) and how an organization is linked with the issue. Public relations people can plan their communication strategies much more accurately if they know how actively their stakeholder publics will seek information.

Approaches to Conflict Resolution

If we begin with the notion that conflict is just one of many states a relationship can take, we will make a good start to understanding conflict and how to deal with it. All of us have a common sense understanding of conflict. It involves an individual or group actively opposing another owing to differences in values or goals.

Public relations professionals discuss campaign strategies.

Some people take the view that conflict is a phenomenon to be avoided. If you operate from this point of view, you must be alert to potential conflicts and attempt to handle them before they become unpleasant. Others see conflict as a natural stage that some relationships pass through and, therefore, it is something to be managed.

What we know about resolving conflict exists largely as a list of techniques and skills that negotiators have found useful. Fisher and Ury suggest the following four things to keep in mind when trying to resolve conflict:[12]

1. *Separate the People from the Problem.* Try to start from a position of respect for those with whom you disagree. Remember, it is the goals and values that you disagree with, not the person holding the position. The next three steps suggest ways to do this.
2. *Focus on Interests, not Positions.* It is normal for both sides to stake out positions and try to convince the other side of the wisdom in adopting their point of view. It is natural but not productive. Instead, try to move beyond positions to find out what the other side really wants. A position is just one expression of what someone wants. It may be possible to reach goals in a variety of ways. Until you explore the possibilities, you won't know.
3. *Invent Options for Mutual Gains.* You may know this as creative problem solving. The idea is to explore ways you can both meet your goals. Plan on generating lots of solutions before you reach an agreement. It sounds like an impossible task, but for many issues it just requires the will to move beyond the conflict in a way that respects the interests of both sides.
4. *Insist on Objective Criteria.* Seek early agreement on what a fair solution would look like. Is there a standard or index on which you could base a solution? Finding one makes evaluating solutions easier.

These guidelines are not expressed as formal theory, but those who use them regularly would likely agree that using this framework increases the chances of resolving a conflict early, results in higher-quality solutions, and preserves the integrity of the relationship between those involved in the conflict. That is theory any practitioner can understand.

THEORIES OF COGNITION AND BEHAVIOR

Public relations practitioners find it useful to think about effects—how products, services, and policies affect others. What we say and what we do are given meaning by others, and sometimes that meaning is not what we intended.

Typically, public relations people try to persuade their audiences to know something or to do something. Cognitive theories deal with the knowing, and behavioral theories cover the doing. There are many more approaches to thinking, behavior, and communication than are discussed here. It is a good idea for public relations students to take courses in general psychology, cognitive psychology, communication theory, and persuasion in order to learn more about human thought processes.

Action Assembly Theory

All behavior is logical to the person doing the behaving. If we accept this **action assembly theory,** then before we can understand behavior, we have to understand how people think. That sounds like an incredibly hard task, and at one level it is, but communication scholar John O. Greene believes thinking can be explained at an abstract level by three constructs: structures, content, and processes.[13]

> ***Cognitive structure*** defines the form of our thought. Some call this form a script, some call it a schema, others call it a frame. It's like a storyboard that defines how we expect a story to unfold. Over time we build up a set of expectations. These expectations affect what information we process and store.
>
> ***Content*** refers to the specific characters, details, and plot twists within the basic structure.
>
> ***Cognitive processes*** are the operations we use to take in, transform, and store information (the content).

That's all very abstract. How does it help us understand how people think? Let's look a little closer.

People are great observers. We see that certain actions result in predictable outcomes in similar situations. Over time we develop expectations about these relationships. In fact, the expectations become so strong that we may fail to notice when the details or outcomes vary from what we expect to see.

For example, if we are used to seeing clutter and useless information on bulletin boards, then our script says "don't bother to read bulletin boards because it is a waste of time." That script guides our behavior, and we ignore information on bulletin boards—even if the information could be useful. Consequently, if we want important information to reach our publics, we need to use messages and channels they perceive as important, such as face-to-face communication.

Another part of understanding cognitive structure concerns how content is stored in the mind. We don't record all that passes through our senses as if it were hooked to a flight data recorder. We abstract data, filtering information based on what we think is

3.1 Mini • Case

Action Assembly Theory in Action

Effectiveness of Info Mapping Shown in Humorous Treatment of *Atlanta Journal* Story on "Frenetic Lives"

What if every article in the *NY Times* or *WSJ* had a sidebar telling you how long it would take to read the article and bolding the content only? What if your newsletters ("e" and otherwise) did the same?

The *Atlanta Journal-Constitution,* in a three-part series on the hurried state of lives today, side-barred each story with "reading time" (60 seconds being the longest for bolded material only, 5 minutes 14 seconds for the full article—affectionately referred to as the "better version"). Skimming the article proved that you can glean key info much faster when the material is arranged for easy reading with bullets and bolding.

"So many organizations are shifting to e-newsletters—sometimes in place of traditional methods," says Robin Schell of Jackson Jackson & Wagner and frequent lecturer on info-mapping techniques. "But they sometime forget that *the info-mapping techniques for hard copy apply even more for the quick read of an e-mail newsletter.*"

Bulleted boxes at the end of each article in the *Atlanta Journal-Constitution*'s series give reference sources via the Web for more information on the article's subject. And as in most newspapers today, there is an e-mail address given to contact the reporter and offer feedback. How often do we remember that in our own communications?

Source: From *pr reporter,* 3 June 2002, p. 2.

important or useful. We determine this by checking to see if the new information is similar to information we labeled "important" in the past.

Have you noticed that when your instructor says, "There are seven . . ." everybody begins writing? Students know from experience that lists are typically important at test time. The key is to decide whether you want to tap into your public's existing memory structures to try to reinforce these structures or build entirely new ones. (See mini-case 3.1.)

When 7-Up decided to position itself as the "uncola," it was taking advantage of our preexisting beliefs about and responses to cola beverages. The uncola could be enjoyed in all the same settings as cola; it would just look and taste different.

Home Depot Corporation sponsored 2002 Olympic athletes by providing them jobs with steady wages and flexible hours so that it would be associated with the values and ideas of the Olympic Games. It achieved glowing television and print coverage by arranging media interviews and photo shoots with the employee-athletes. The media portrayed world-class athletes mixing paint and loading 2 × 4s in the aisles of Home Depot.[14] When the employee-athletes were victorious, Home Depot claimed proudly its role in getting the athlete to the medal platform.

Social Exchange Theory

Social exchange theory uses the economic metaphor of costs and benefits to predict behavior. It assumes that individuals and groups choose strategies based on perceived rewards and costs. This theory, developed by John Thibaut and Harold Kelley, applies to many fields of study, including interpersonal communication, public relations, and theories of organizations.[15]

Social exchange theory asserts that people factor in the consequences of their behavior before acting. In general, people want to keep their costs low and their rewards high. Get-rich-quick schemes have been using this principle for a long time.

But what does this have to do with public relations? Let's say we want people to respond to a survey. Remember, we want to keep costs to potential respondents low and perceived rewards high. What can we do to keep costs low?

Keep the instructions simple.

Keep the survey short.

If mailing is required, provide a post-paid return envelope.

If returning by fax, use an 800 number.

Avoid open-ended, complex, and personal questions.

Now, how can I increase the rewards for the respondent?

Make the survey interesting.

Emphasize that the person is being "consulted" for his or her thoughts and that her or his ideas are important.

Tell respondents how the results will be used—presumably to contribute to something worthwhile.

Offer an opportunity for a tangible reward, for example, a copy of the results or a chance to win something of value.

This same logic can be applied to more complex behavior by using a payoff matrix. Let's say our company, United PRworks, becomes aware of defects in a product that has already been shipped to customers. The defect may mean that the product will need repairs much sooner than a promised three-year guarantee. We can look at this situation as a set of possible decisions, with each decision having costs and rewards. In figure 3.2, the upper part of each cell contains perceived rewards and the lower part, possible costs. Some of the consequences, like recall costs, are certain. Others, like the possibility of lawsuits and negative publicity, have some probability associated with them.

If the head of United PRworks could see the decision this way, the company would recall the products and accept the short-term loss. The trouble is that human nature can blind us to the information in the cells associated with customers finding out about the defect. It would be human nature to ignore the problem, hoping it would go away. The public relations practitioner's job is to let the decision maker see a whole range of options along with the associated costs and rewards.

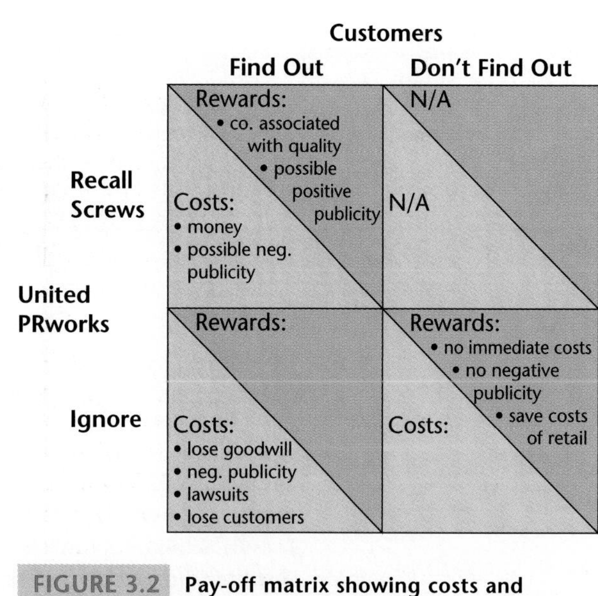

FIGURE 3.2 **Pay-off matrix showing costs and rewards involved in a recall decision.**

Diffusion Theory

Diffusion theory is another way to look at how people process and accept information. Diffusion theory says that people adopt an idea only after going through the following five discrete steps (or stages):

1. *Awareness.* The individual has to have been exposed to the idea.
2. *Interest.* The idea has to arouse the individual.
3. *Evaluation.* The individual must consider the idea as potentially useful.
4. *Trial.* The individual tries out the idea on others.

Schwab Marcom Campaign Creates "WINNING" Situation with Women

These days, with the bear often wreaking havoc on Wall Street, it can be a tough sell to persuade anyone to invest. But in 2000, Charles Schwab & Co. recognized an opportunity to expand its mindshare with a burgeoning demographic: female investors.

Women generally were more anxious than men about investing and were much more conservative when they did invest. According to Schwab's research, women lacked knowledge about Wall Street but were open to learning more. They tended to learn through seminars and women's investing clubs, however, versus the books, tapes, and websites men preferred.

Schwab set out to break down the perceived barriers for women with a program dubbed Women's Investing Now (WIN). The program would offer women motivation, expertise, and resources to help raise their financial acuity.

Schwab developed a comprehensive online resource for women featuring investing resources and information as well as forums, message boards, and other interactive features that allowed women to communicate with experts and with each other—fitting women's tendency to seek knowledge from "communities."

The company also leveraged the fact that, unlike many financial firms, approximately 40 of Schwab's employees are women. Thirty-six percent of the company's officers are women, and more than two-thirds of employees report to a woman.

Because the campaign was using the fact that its workforce was so heavily female, the company recognized the importance of starting its education initiative close to home. It used videos and other programs to encourage female employees to increase their knowledge of investment and become "money mentors" to other women.

In addition to the grassroots, inside-out approach used to bring Schwab employees in touch with other women, the PR team promoted local WIN seminars and other community functions where women could learn in a comfortable setting. Plus, they helped create, promote, and distribute Life Events brochures, designed to help women navigate emotionally and financially challenging situations like the death of a spouse or a divorce.

Media outreach also composed an important element of the campaign, including a major press conference to kick off the initiative and one-on-one interviews with Carrie Schwab-Pomerantz, vice president of consumer education and daughter of the company's founder and chairman. Media outreach also included a press kit, a press release on the launch of the WIN portal online, and promotions of the Life Event brochures.

Results included more than 254 million media impressions. Pomerantz was named one of four market movers by *Working Woman.* Best of all, more than 5,000 women participated in a WIN seminar or workshop and 25,000 Schwab employees were touched by the program.

Source: From *PR News,* www.prandmarketing.com.

5. *Adoption.* This represents final acceptance of the idea after having successfully passed through the four earlier stages.[16]

This theory is useful for explaining how we reach important decisions—not acts of impulse. We know from testing this model that mass media are important in the first two stages; personal contacts are important for the next two.

Let's take an example. United PRworks's annual family picnic is two weeks away. You are selling tickets at $1 per family as a way to plan how much food to order. You tell the boss at the morning staff meeting that ticket sales have been slow. If your boss is typical, she or he will say, "Make sure every employee gets a flyer."

Sending out more flyers virtually guarantees awareness, but you are still three steps away from getting people to decide to go (adoption). By knowing how people accept and process information, you plan systematically to move the employees through the remaining stages. You arouse interest in attending the picnic by sending individual invitations that tell employees how their families will enjoy the event. How about entertainment for the old and young? A special "snack" table for the kids, games and door prizes for adults and kids. Have your picnic organizers asked employees for their suggestions for how to make the event mesh with their interests? Free parking? Baby-sitting service? Get some "buzz" going by having the CEO talk about the picnic with employees. Finally, you will need lots of people at the shop level to talk about the picnic to their fellow workers. Then, they need to go sell the tickets. See mini-case 3.2 for an example of diffusion theory in action.

Social Learning Theory

So far, we have discussed theories that consider the receiver to be actively involved in information processing. **Social learning theory** attempts to explain and predict behavior by looking at another way individuals process information. This theory helps us understand that personal example and mass media can be important to acquiring new behaviors.

Social psychologist Albert Bandura says that we can learn new behaviors merely by observing others.[17] When we see behavior that interests us, we note whether that behavior seems to be rewarding the actor. These rewards can be external, as in praise, or internal, as in "it looks cool." Bandura says that we vicariously try out the behavior in our minds. If we agree that the behavior is potentially useful to us, it can lie dormant for long periods until we need it. The likelihood that a specific behavior will occur is determined by the expected consequences from performing that behavior. The more positive and rewarding the consequences, the more likely the behavior will occur.

Knowing this, public relations people shouldn't be surprised when employees model the inappropriate behavior of more experienced employees, particularly if that behavior is rewarded. If chronic complaining keeps someone from having to work a double shift or a weekend, you can bet others will copy or model this tactic. If a company promotes people who are cold and rigid, you can predict that those wanting to get ahead will model those behaviors.

Remember: You get the behavior you reward. Social learning theory explains one of the routes to this behavior.

Elaborated Likelihood Model

The notion of "routes" is central to a theory that describes two ways that people are influenced. Richard Petty and John Cacioppo describe the first route as the "central route"—the situation in which people actively think about an idea.[18] Relying on this route presumes people are interested in your message, have the time to attend to your arguments, and can evaluate your evidence with an open mind. This is how public relations people usually attempt to influence attitudes and behavior.

But what if the target group is not interested, is too busy, or just can't understand the issues? How do you proceed?

The **elaborated likelihood model** proposes a "peripheral route" in which people are influenced by such things as repetition, a highly credible spokesperson, or even tangible rewards. Advertising people frequently use this route when designing their messages. For example, candidates for local office can't engage all the voters in a discussion of the issues, so they take the peripheral route and blanket the town with yard signs. Message repetition provides familiarity with the candidate's name, and sign location suggests that many voters actively support that candidate. People who are not politically active don't have to think about the issues; they just vote for the obvious popular choice.

When long-distance phone companies claim they can save you money on plans that are not easily compared, it becomes difficult to make an informed decision. That's when the credibility of the spokesperson may be the deciding factor on which plan you select.

Other successful peripheral routes to changing behavior are found in the public relations efforts of weight-loss companies. They offer coupons and discounts to join their programs. They provide free counseling by phone if the weight management plan is too complicated. You are likely to receive free exercise videos and diaries and recognition for weight loss. Even though weight control prevents many health problems, this is not the central message that will help people with weight problems. It is direct but not usually persuasive.

THEORIES OF MASS COMMUNICATION

Two popular theories that apply especially to the mass media are uses and gratifications theory and agenda setting.

Uses and Gratifications Theory

It's important to remember that not everyone regularly reads the daily paper, watches the 6 o'clock news, or listens to talk radio. Papers, TV, and radio are called mass media, but each person chooses how and when to use mass media. Similarly, you shouldn't presume that employees uniformly read internal publications or view company videos. Even a note in every pay packet could go straight from the pay envelope into the wastebasket.

How do we explain this behavior? **Uses and gratifications theory** asserts that people are active users of media and selective in the media they use.[19] Researchers have found that people use media in the following ways:

As entertainment

To scan the environment for items important to them personally

As a diversion

As a substitute for personal relationships

As a check on personal identity and values

For public relations people this means that not everyone will see or hear the bad news about a company or product. It also means you can't count on people seeing or hearing the good news. Just because a message is available in some medium does not mean that people attend to it and remember it.

Public relations people should expect that messages in the mass media will be shaped, selected, and interpreted in multiple ways if these messages are seen or heard at all! For example, the American public never did understand why President Clinton's personal life should interfere with his presidency, even with hours of televised hearings and printed transcripts. Plenty of opinions were aired, even by Leno and *Saturday Night Live.* But American opinion never changed from a position of distaste for Clinton's morals and support for his presidency, despite the media.

Agenda Setting Theory

Bernard Cohen noted that although the media can't tell people what to think, they are stunningly successful in telling them what to think about.[20] This was an interesting idea but not widely accepted in 1963. About a decade later journalism scholars Maxwell McCombs and Donald Shaw demonstrated that Cohen was onto something.[21] During the 1968 presidential campaign, they followed public opinion and media reports of the key issues in Chapel Hill, North Carolina. They found that a strong positive relationship existed between what voters said was important and what media were reporting as important. Since the issues were evident in the media several weeks before they appeared in public opinion, McCombs and Shaw were reasonably sure that the media set the agenda and not the reverse. What was more amazing was that the voters were more likely to agree with the composite media agenda than with the position of the candidate they claimed they favored.

McCombs and Shaw do not say that simple agreement with the media changed voting behavior. What they demonstrated was that the media can set the agenda for what we talk and think about.

Theories Used in Public Relations

Spotlight 3.2

The 10 theories highlighted in the chapter are summarized as follows:

I. Theories of Relationships

1. Systems theory—evaluates relationships and structure as they relate to the whole.
2. Situational theory—maintains that situations define relationships.
3. Approaches to conflict resolution—include separating people from the problem; focusing on interests, not positions; inventing options for mutual gain; and insisting on objective criteria.

II. Theories of Cognition and Behavior

4. Action assembly theory—states that behavior is understood by understanding how people think.
5. Social exchange theory—predicts behavior of groups and individuals is based on perceived rewards and costs.
6. Diffusion theory—suggests that people adopt an important idea or innovation after going through five discrete steps: awareness, interest, evaluation, trail, and adoption.
7. Social learning theory—states that people use information processing to explain and predict behavior.
8. Elaborated likelihood model—suggests decision making is influenced through repetition, rewards, and credible spokespersons.

III. Theories of Mass Communication

9. Uses and gratification theory—states that people are active users of media and select media based on its gratification for them.
10. Agenda setting theory—suggests that media content that people read, see, and listen to set the agendas for society's discussion and interaction.

This talking and thinking can lead to information seeking and processing, following the situational theory of publics, but only if other conditions are met. That's an important point for public relations people to remember when their organization is taking a beating in the press. People may be talking about you, but it doesn't necessarily mean that strong opinions about your organization will be changed. You will need to do some research before you can draw such a conclusion.

Public relations people attempt to influence the media agenda by providing news items for public consumption. To accomplish this, they identify subjects that editors and news directors consider news, localize their messages, and help media representatives cover the story. (See spotlight 3.2 for a summary of the public relations theories.)

PUBLIC RELATIONS ROLES

Some of the most important theory building that has been developed in public relations is about the roles of practitioners in organizational life. Some of these roles are managerial; some are tied to marketing. There are communication demands from the human resources function. Even the legal department influences public relations activities when there is an organizational crisis. At issue is whether public relations people play the right roles to achieve organizational effectiveness.

Roles are the collection of daily activities that people do. Glen Broom and David Dozier have studied public relations roles for more than 20 years. Their role types have helped us learn about the power of the public relations function in the organization and how the activities of public relations people produce the right programs, influence strategic planning, and effect the short-range (bottom-line) and long-range (survival) goals of organizations.[22]

In research on public relations activities, two broad roles consistently emerge in public relations: the technician and the manager. The **technician role** represents the craft side of public relations: writing, editing, taking photos, handling communication production, running special events, and making telephone calls to the media. These activities focus on the implementation of the management's overall communication strategies. The **manager role** focuses on activities that help identify and solve public relations problems. Public relations managers advise senior managers about communication needs and are responsible for broad organizational results. Three types of public relations manager roles are as follows:

Expert prescriber: the person who operates as a consultant to define the problem, suggest options, and oversee implementation.

Communication facilitator: the person on the boundary between the organization and its environment who keeps two-way communication flowing.

Problem-solving facilitator: the person who partners with senior management to identify and solve problems.[23]

Public relations managers carry out all three roles. To perform these roles, much depends on the knowledge of the individual manager. If managers can deliver both manager and technical functions, they achieve higher status in organizational decision making. Public relations people cannot expect to achieve a "seat at the table" where they can influence how to achieve beneficial relationships with stakeholders unless they perform both roles; they especially must execute the manager role in such a way that top management will understand its value and demand it.[24]

MODELS OF PUBLIC RELATIONS

One of the most useful ways of thinking about public relations has been through the description of public relations **models** that identify the key concepts of public relations and how they are related to each other. In 1984 James E. Grunig and Todd Hunt proposed four models of public relations, based on two concepts: communication and research. Since that time Grunig and a team of scholars have proposed new models that have enriched our understanding of how public relations is practiced.

The original four models were press agentry, public information, the two-way asymmetrical model, and the two-way symmetrical model.[25] The first three models reflect a practice of public relations that attempts through persuasion to achieve the organization's goals. The fourth focuses on balanced self-interests rather than one-way persuasion.

Press agentry describes the model where information moves one way from the organization to its publics. It is, perhaps, the oldest form of public relations and is synonymous with promotions and publicity. Public relations people operating under this model are always looking for opportunities to get their organization's name favorably mentioned in the media. They do not conduct much research about their publics, beyond "counting the house." This model includes propaganda tactics such as use of celebrity names, and attention-gaining devices such as giveaways, parades, and grand openings.

Public information differs from press agentry because the intent is to inform rather than to press for promotion and publicity, but the communication is still essentially one way. Today this model represents public relations practices in government, educational institutions, and nonprofit organizations and even in some corporations. Practitioners operating under this model do very little research about their audiences beyond testing the clarity of their messages. They are "journalists-in-residence," who decide what information to tell in the public's interest.

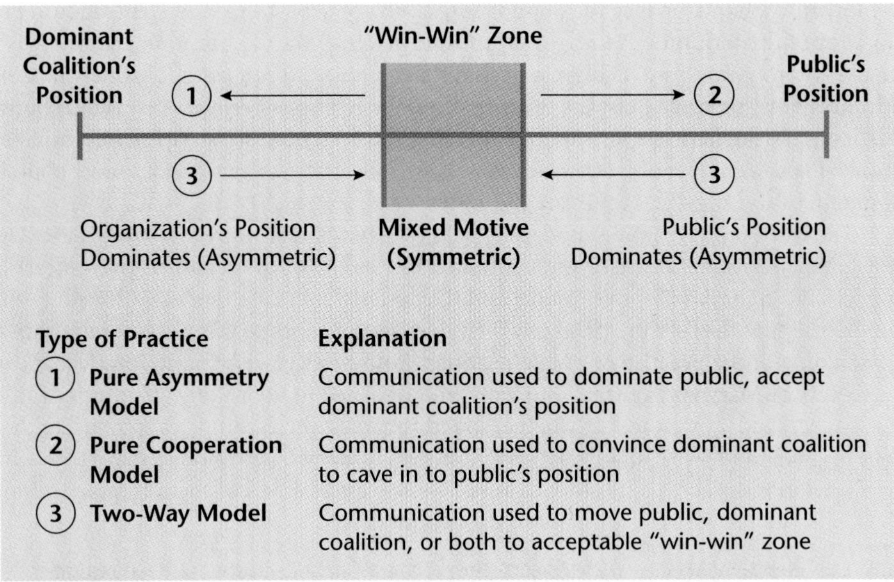

FIGURE 3.3 New Model of Symmetry and Two-Way Communication

The *two-way asymmetrical* model considers public relations to be scientific persuasion. This model employs social science research methods to increase the persuasiveness of messages. Public relations practitioners use surveys, interviews, and focus groups to measure public relationships so the organization can design public relations programs that will gain the support of key publics. Although feedback is built into the process, the organization is much more interested in having the publics adjust to the organization than the reverse.

The *two-way symmetrical* model depicts a public relations orientation in which organizations and their publics adjust to each other. It focuses on the use of social science research methods to achieve mutual understanding and two-way communication rather than one-way persuasion. In 2001 James E. Grunig created other names for the symmetrical model: mixed motives, collaborative advocacy, and cooperative antagonism. His intention was to present a model that "balanced self-interests with the interest of others in a give-and-take process that can waver between advocacy and collaboration."[26]

In 1995 David M. Dozier, Larissa A. Grunig, and James E. Grunig presented a new model of public relations that came from their research on excellence in public relations and communication management. They found in a study of 321 organizations in three countries that public relations people who exhibited the most effective or excellent public relations practices used the "new model of symmetry as two-way practice."[27] This depiction of public relations placed the organization and its publics on a continuum (see figure 3.3). Because in the best practice of public relations, public relations practitioners and their supervisors reported using both two-way symmetrical and two-way asymmetrical models, Dozier, Grunig, and Grunig reasoned that given each specific public relations situation, organizations *and* their publics would seek to persuade each other as much as possible. They are pictured at opposite ends of the continuum, either as a pure asymmetry model in which the dominant coalition tries to force a public into accepting the organization's position, or as a pure cooperation model in which the public uses communication to convince the dominant coalition to accept the public's position. The middle of the continuum is the "win-win" zone in which the organization and the public use communication to achieve a decision acceptable to both sides. This new model advances our thinking about the practice of public relations because it considers both parties in the public relations situation. Because the organization and its publics will be employing communication strategies as well, we have to be as savvy about our publics' communication strategies as we are our own.

The work on developing models of public relations that more effectively describe how public relations is carried out continued in 1996, with the report of two different models: the *cultural interpreter* model and the *personal influence* model. Although both models fall into the asymmetrical category, they give us more to think about in our understanding of the practice of public relations. Both models were found in research by University of Maryland graduate students who returned to their home countries of India, Greece, and Taiwan to test whether practitioners in these countries were using the four original models of public relations. Although these two new models may represent public relations practiced in other cultures, we see applications of them to practices in the United States. A brief summary of the two models follows:

> The cultural interpreter model: depicts the practice of public relations in organizations that do business in other countries, "where it needs someone who understands the language, culture, customs, and political system of the host country."
>
> The personal influence model: depicts a practice of public relations in which practitioners try to establish personal relationships with key individuals, "as contacts through favors can be sought."[28]

Summary

For self-testing and additional chapter resources, go to the student CD and the Online Learning Center at **www.mhhe.com/lattimore**

Theories of how public relations is practiced continue to develop. The original four models of public relations were a good starting point for describing the key activities that public relations people did: communication and research. They gave us a way of organizing our concepts by types of public relations practice. James E. Grunig proposed to move on from the models of public relations to more specific sets of measurable variables: symmetry and asymmetry; the extent of one-way versus two-way communication; the use of mediated and interpersonal forms of communication; and the extent to which public relations is practiced ethically.[29] These four dimensions give us even deeper and more sophisticated ways of thinking about public relations than did the original models. They help us predict more effectively what will and will not work in our practice of public relations.

Citizens to Stop the Coal Trains: Extension of Public Comment Period

Overview

Citizens to Stop the Coal Train (CSCT), a coalition of leaders who represent all facets of the Rochester, Minnesota, community, launched an aggressive grassroots campaign against a $1.4 billion coal train proposal proffered by the Dakota, Minnesota & Eastern Railroad (DM&E). If approved, the coal train proposal would be devastating to Rochester, resulting in a mile-long, open-car coal train rumbling through the heart of this bucolic downtown every 40 minutes,

365 days per year. Traffic delays at Rochester's railroad crossings would total nearly three hours per day.

More than 1.5 million national and international visitors come each year to Rochester, which has a population of approximately 80,000. The vast majority of these visitors come because of the world-renowned Mayo Clinic, which is the third largest private employer in Minnesota. Needless to say, Rochester's economy is heavily dependent on caring for these visitors, as well as their families, while they're in town.

Thirty-seven coal trains barreling through Rochester every day would endanger public safety, threaten economic vitality, and erode quality of life in this community, which is often near the top of national "Best Places to Live" rankings.

CSCT formed in July 2000 in anticipation of the Surface Transportation Board's (STB) release of its Draft Environmental Impact Statement (DEIS). One of CSCT's primary objectives was to persuade the federally appointed independent STB to expand the public comment period of the DEIS from the given 90 days to 180 days. An extension of this comment period would

- give experts in the legal and environmental fields adequate time to address problematic findings within the DEIS report and submit meaningful analysis to the STB;
- allow more time for CSCT to garner support from Rochester citizens and send personal letters to the STB;
- slow down the railroad's momentum for this project; and
- send a strong message to DM&E that Rochester is capable of thwarting its coal train project.

Research

We learned that the STB is an independent adjudicatory body, which enables this group of three appointed people to make decisions independent of any other federal office. However, the STB must consider all statements submitted during the public comment period for this coal train project, so we hoped we could sway the STB to grant an extension based on volume and quality of requests for an extension from citizens and their elected officials.

To help make CSCT's case to the Rochester public, we researched statistics about the railroad as well as Rochester's safety, economy, and quality of life. We discovered that the DM&E has the worst safety record of any in its class in the nation. We demonstrated how dependent Rochester's emergency response units to determine how congestion at railroad crossing would increase response times and threaten lives.

To better understand which statistics concerned Rochester citizens most, we interviewed citizens representing the groups we were attempting to mobilize—businesses, health care, schools, and senior citizens. We then incorporated these statistics into every news release, interview, and speaking opportunity, tailoring the statistics to the specific audience we were trying to reach.

Planning

We developed a comprehensive plan to increase our odds of securing an extension to the 90-day public comment period. Tactical elements of this plan included:

- Position the CSCT as a leader in advocacy for the city of Rochester and its citizens.
- Educate all Rochester citizens—not just those who live near the railroad tracks—about the dangers of the coal train proposal and how the coal trains would affect their lives every day.
- Gain media attention and coverage about the coal train issue and emphasize Rochester's concerns in clear, concise language. Add credibility by involving well-respected members of the community who represent affected sectors—business, health care, schools, and seniors.
- Bring Rochester's concerns about the coal train project to the attention of candidates and elected representatives at the local, state, and federal levels and persuade these representatives to submit their own statements and letters to the STB.
- Provide citizens modes of easy access in contacting the STB to voice their concerns. Drive traffic to the CSCT website and encourage mailing of response cards to the STB.

With objectives in place and budget set at $150,000 for project management, media relations, video and advertising production, event management and website creation, we set out to implement this aggressive plan within a short time frame—five months.

Execution

We gained momentum as each tactic within our program was executed. Some of our milestone efforts included:

- Holding a CSCT press conference the same day that the DEIS was released. The press conference drew more than 100 people and garnered numerous print and broadcast stories.
- Sending a CSCT delegation to Washington, D.C., to meet with key members of Congress. This trip prompted letters of support from Governor Ventura and Rep. Gutknecht for an extension to the public comment period.
- Producing a 10-minute video to capture the attention of local residents by showing how devastating the effects of coal trains would be for Rochester.
- Arranging dozens of speaking engagements across the Rochester community.
- Launching a local print and broadcast advertising campaign. This ad campaign was phased to target our key audiences—businesses, schools, heath care, and seniors. The print ads provided response cards that readers could fill out and sent to the STB, while broadcast ads drove traffic to the CSCT website.
- Developing a website to inform concerned citizens and provide them with the means to voice their own concerns to the STB.
- Promoting a public rally and town hall meeting. These events were a huge show of force, attracting hundreds of button-wearing, sign-carrying residents who supported our efforts.

Evaluation

On December 14, the STB announced that it was extending the public comment period by 60 days, and there's no doubt CSCT influenced that decision. Our four-month campaign resulted in front-page newspaper coverage of more than 300 citizens who turned out for the CSCT rally; 75,000 visitor sessions and more than 8,000 letters to the STB generated by www.stopthecoaltrain.com; many hundreds of response cards mailed from our advertising campaign; and letters of support from Congressional delegates following our Washington, D.C., tour.

Our campaign was recently featured in Ragan's Interactive Public Relations February 2001 issue. Here is an excerpt: "The extension is a significant win for us—one that'll give more time to fully review the 5,000 page document" that outlines the environmental impact of the train proposal, says John Wade, cochairman, Citizens to Stop the Coal Train.

Further, the time delay adds cost and aggravation for the Dakota, Minnesota & Eastern Railroad (DM&E), which proposed the rail line.

"As the process gets longer and more complex, the market changes, the economy changes and prices change. There could come a point when we're no longer able to afford the project," says Rick Daugherty, public affairs officer for DM&E. "The billion dollar question remains: How long will that be?"

Source: PRSA Silver Anvil Awards, 2001, Public Affairs section. Citizens to Stop the Coal Trains with Weber Shandwick Worldwide.

Questions

1. How could you use figure 3.2 to look at the costs and consequences to the DM&E Railroad's proposal?
2. How did the citizens use diffusion theory to get citizens to act?
3. How is the elaborated likelihood model illustrated in this case?
4. How did the citizens take advantage of agenda setting theory?

Use the CD-ROM and Online Learning Center at www.mhhe.com/lattimore to further your understanding of the following terms

action assembly theory
boundary spanners
dominant coalition
diffusion theory
elaborated likelihood model
manager role
models
publics
roles
situational theory
social exchange theory
social learning theory
systems theory
stakeholders
technician role
theory
uses and gratifications theory

Notes

1. "In Fighting the Drug War, Keep Kids' Behavior Focused on Positive Actions; Lessons Applicable for All," *pr reporter,* 3 June 2002, pp. 1–2.
2. Doug McVay, "In Fighting the Drug War, Keep Kids' Behavior Focused on Positive Actions: Lessons Applicable for All," *pr reporter,* 3 June 2002, p. 1.
3. Charles Atkin and Alicia Marshall, "Health Communication," in *An Integrated Approach to Communication Theory and Research,* ed. Michael B. Salwen and Don W. Stacks (Mahwah, NJ: Erlbaum, 1996), pp. 479–96.
4. Larissa A. Grunig, James E. Grunig, and David M. Dozier, *Excellence in Public Relations and Effective Organizations: A Study of Communication Management in Three Countries* (Mahwah, NJ: Erlbaum, 2002).
5. Ibid., p. 5.
6. J. E. Grunig and Fred C. Repper, "Strategic Management, Publics, and Issues," in *Excellence in Public Relations and Communication Management,* ed. J. E. Grunig (Hillsdale, NJ: Erlbaum, 1992), pp. 117–58.
7. "The Decentralized Network of the Catholic Church Underscores the Role in Leadership, Structure in Crisis," *pr reporter,* 8 April 2002, pp. 1–2.
8. David M. Dozier, Larissa A. Grunig, and J. E. Grunig, *The Manager's Guide to Public Relations and Communication Management* (Mahwah, NJ: Erlbaum, 1995), p. 15.
9. "How to Capitalize on Human Resources," *Purview,* no. 402, 27 May 2002, p. 1.
10. Grunig and Repper, pp. 117–58.
11. James E. Grunig and Todd Hunt, *Managing Public Relations* (New York: Holt, Rinehart & Winston, 1984).
12. Roger Fisher and William Ury, *Getting to Yes: Negotiating Agreement Without Giving In* (Boston: Houghton Mifflin, 1981).
13. John O. Greene, "A Cognitive Approach to Human Communication: An Action Assembly Theory," *Communication Monographs* 51 (1984), pp. 289–308.
14. "Orange to Gold: Home Depot's Olympic Sponsorship," *Homes Report,* 14 June 2002, www.holmesreport.com/holmestemp/story.cfm?edit_id=218@typeid=4.
15. John W. Thibaut and Harold H. Kelley, *The Social Psychology of Groups* (New York: Wiley, 1959).
16. Herbert F. Lionberger, *Adoption of New Ideas and Practices* (Ames: Iowa State University Press, 1960), p. 32.
17. Albert Bandura, *Social Learning Theory* (Englewood Cliffs, NJ: Prentice Hall, 1977).
18. Richard E. Petty and John T. Cacioppo, *Communication and Persuasion: Central and Peripheral Routes to Attitude Change* (New York: Springer-Verlag, 1986).
19. Elihu Katz, Jay G. Blumler, and Michael Gurevitch, "Utilization of Mass Communication by the Individual," in *The Uses of Mass Communications: Current Perspectives on Gratifications Research,* ed. J. G. Blumler, and E. Katz (Beverly Hills, CA: Sage, 1974), pp. 19–32.
20. Bernard C. Cohen, *The Press and Foreign Policy* (Princeton, NJ: Princeton University Press, 1963).
21. Donald E. Shaw and Maxwell E. McCombs, *The Emergence of American Political Issues: The Agenda Setting Function of the Press* (St. Paul, MN: West, 1977).
22. Dozier, Grunig, and Grunig.
23. Scott M. Cutlip, Allen H. Center, and Glen M. Broom, *Effective Public Relations* (Upper Saddle River, NJ: Prentice Hall, 2000), pp. 41–44.
24. Dozier, Grunig, and Grunig.
25. Grunig and Hunt.
26. James E. Grunig, "Two-Way Symmetrical Public Relations: Past, Present, Future," in *The Handbook of Public Relations,* ed. Robert L. Heath (Thousand Oaks, CA: Sage, 2000), p. 28.
27. Dozier, Grunig, and Grunig, p. 48.
28. James E. Grunig, Larissa A. Grunig, K. Sriramesh, Yi-Hui Huang, and Anastasia Lyra, "Models of Public Relations in an International Setting," *Journal of Public Relations Research* 7, no. 3 (1995), p. 183.
29. Grunig, p. 28.

CHAPTER FOUR

Law and Ethics

4

Outline

PREVIEW

This chapter introduces legal and ethical frameworks for the practice of public relations. **Law** is defined as "the rules of conduct established and enforced by authority in a society."[1] **Ethics** is "the criteria for determining what is right and wrong."[2]

Organizations carry out public relations in a legal environment that protects the free speech rights of individuals and organizations and puts limits on how communication activities are conducted. Public relations practitioners must know communication laws in order to counsel top managers on how to avoid illegal communication with such stakeholder groups as employees, labor unions, government officials, and activists.

Although communication activities are legal to carry out, they may be unethical. For example, under oath in a court of law, one must "tell the truth" defined by legal guidelines. But there are many "truths" in the court of public opinion. Critics accuse public relations people of "spinning" the truth. Public relations professionals are advocates for organizational points of view, but they also are held accountable for communications that are in the public interest. This chapter considers ethics from the standpoint of standards of social conduct, individual ethics, business ethics, standards of a developing profession, and codes of ethics ☐

THE LEGAL ENVIRONMENT

According to a survey of public relations practitioners, "Many public relations professionals may be placing themselves and their client organizations at risk of legal liability because they have little or no familiarity with important legal issues that affect public relations activities."[3] Thus, because public relations practitioners are increasingly vulnerable to legal liability, it is more important than ever that they be acquainted with key legal issues such as **First Amendment** rights and limits, libel, privacy, copyright contracts, **commercial speech,** and numerous federal, state, and local government **regulations.** Also, public relations practitioners work with organizational lawyers in the area of litigation. When an employer or client gets sued, public relations is involved in a court of law and the court of public opinion.

First Amendment Rights and Limits

One of the most strongly supported rights of U.S. citizens is the right to freedom of speech, which is guaranteed under the First Amendment to the Constitution:

> Congress shall make no law abridging the freedom of speech, or of the press; or the right of the people peaceably to assemble, and to petition the Government for a redress of grievances.

Court cases have clarified that organizations enjoy much the same freedom of speech as do individuals. In the 1964 Supreme Court case of *New York Times v. Sullivan,* nonprofit organizations for the first time received an endorsement to use advertisements to discuss matters of public interest. In the case, the *New York Times* carried a full-page ad entitled "Heed Their Rising Voices," which made claims that Alabama state college students had been harassed by police and other state authorities. The ad was paid for by a number of African American clergy. L. B. Sullivan, a Montgomery, Alabama, city commissioner claimed that the ad libeled him. But the Supreme Court ruled for the *New York Times,* because the speech

> communicated information, expressed opinion, recited grievances, protested, claimed abuses, and sought financial support on behalf of a movement whose existence and objectives are matters of the highest public interest and concern.[4]

First National Bank of Boston v. Bellotti involved a for-profit organization's right of political and social free speech. When the First National Bank of Boston wanted publicly to oppose and advertise against a Massachusetts personal income tax referendum, State Attorney General Francis Bellotti said a state law barred corporations from participation in referenda that did not affect the corporation directly. First National sued the state for violating its First Amendment right to speak. In 1978 the Supreme Court ruled in favor of the bank. Today, we see full-page and electronic forms of advertisements from both for-profit and nonprofit organizations freely entering the political and social debates of our society.

In a similar case in 1980, *Consolidated Edison Company of New York v. Public Service Commission of New York,* the court reaffirmed the utility's right to discuss public issues. Consolidated Edison had spoken out to its customers using brochures and flyers included with monthly billings. Justice Power reiterated from the *Bellotti* case: "The inherent worth of the speech in terms of its capacity for informing the public does not depend on the identity of the source."[5]

Mini • Case 4.1

Of Related Interest: Nike can be sued over its corporate policy statements, says the California Supreme Court in a 4-3 vote, according to an article in the May 3 issue of *The Recorder*—"Corporation PR Campaigns Lose Speech Protection" by Mike McKee.

The court ruled that companies can be sued for false advertising over policy statements made in public relations campaigns. Statements by the Oregon-based shoemaker denying allegations that some overseas factories are sweatshops were a form of commercial speech not protected by the First Amendment. "Because in the statements at issue here Nike was acting as a commercial speaker, because its intended audience was primarily the buyers of its products and because the statements consisted of factual representations about its own business operations, we conclude that the statements were commercial speech for purposes of applying state laws designed to prevent false advertising and other forms of commercial deception," wrote Justice Joyce Kennard. The court's ruling did not decide whether Nike's ads were false or misleading.

Nike appealed the ruling to the U.S. Supreme Court. The Supreme Court on June 26, 2003, dismissed the appeal and sent the case back to the California Supreme Court; however, five of the U.S. Supreme Court justices rejected the central argument that Nike's speech could be restricted as purely commercial.

Source: From *pr reporter,* 27 May 2002, p. 2. Also, press release from Nike, 26 June 2003.

The importance of commercial speech was made clear in yet another Supreme Court decision in 1976, *Virginia State Board of Pharmacy v. Virginia Citizens Consumer Council, Inc.* In this case, the Supreme Court extended First Amendment protection for truthful marketing of legal products and services. At issue was whether potential purchasers of prescription medicines had the right to know the price of prescription drugs, which at that time could vary as much as 600 percent from pharmacy to pharmacy.[6] The Supreme Court sided with the consumer's interest in the free flow of information rather than the pharmacist's claim that to discuss pricing was unprofessional conduct.

The Supreme Court decisions in these and other cases opened the door to issues-oriented advertising by corporations, associations, and special interest groups. The broadened interpretation of free speech protections resulted in increased corporate political activity through lobbying and political action committees (PACs).

Free speech is not without its limits. Most juries today interpret the First Amendment to mean that free speech should be balanced against other human values or rights. Those other rights—for example, the right to privacy, the right to a good reputation, or property rights—can restrict the right to free speech. Although free flow of commercial information is indispensable, public communications—news releases, company newsletters, speeches, and advertisements—are limited to the extent that they may slander or libel an individual, invade an individual's privacy, infringe on existing copyrights or trademarks, breach contracts, or violate regulatory requirements. These protections and limitations are now being extended to a new channel of communication—the Internet.

Defamation **Defamation** is speech defined as "the publication of material that would hold one up to hatred, ridicule, contempt or spite."[7] There are two types of defamation: libel and slander. **Libel** is published defamation, by written or printed words or in some other physical form. **Slander** is defamation by spoken words, gestures, or other transitory means.[8]

Public relations practitioners have to consider that "nearly every press release, news article, or advertisement holds the potential for a libel suit."[9] At risk as well are the products and services of clients that could be disparaged in a public way. Consider Oprah Winfrey's 1996 airing of a segment on mad cow disease that implied that the U.S. beef industry lacked protections for consumers. The program resulted in immediate financial losses to the industry even though the position expressed was not incorrect. In the subsequent lawsuit, the court eventually ruled in favor of Winfrey, stating that she had not defamed anyone. However, the free speech rights of corporations were questioned again in a California court ruling against Nike, as discussed in mini-case 4.1.

Public relations people have to concern themselves, too, with **product liability**. This refers to the "legal responsibility of companies to compensate individuals for injuries or damages resulting from defects in products that were purchased."[10] Facing negative publicity, McDonald's settled a product liability claim filed by a woman who spilled its coffee while attempting to drive and hold the coffee between her legs.

Libel law has two categories: criminal and civil. Although the Supreme Court has frequently overturned criminal convictions and they are rare today, individuals have been found guilty of **criminal libel** in cases of "breach of peace" or "inciting to riot."

More important to public relations practitioners is **civil libel**. For a statement to be libelous, it must contain certain elements. It must be published, it must be damaging, and it must identify the injured party. Negligence must be involved, and the statement must be defamatory. If the statement involves a public figure, another element becomes of paramount importance: It must involve **malice.**

Publication is considered to have occurred when the alleged defamation has been communicated to a third party. For example, it is "published" when the writer, the injured party, and one other person have seen or heard the remark.

Defamation deals with the words themselves or the implication behind the words. A person's reputation (not character) has been damaged by calling him or her a terrorist, a traitor, or a liar.

Damage has occurred if the remarks reflect poorly on one's reputation, impair one's ability to earn a living, or restrict one's social contacts.

Identification has occurred when readers or listeners are able to identify the person referred to, whether or not the person is specifically named.

Fault must be shown in order for the plaintiff to win a libel suit. If the wrong photograph is run with an article, if there is a typographical or mechanical error in the publication process, or if information is not carefully checked, the defendant may be found negligent.

Malice occurs when the plaintiff can prove that the defendant knew the published material was false or showed a reckless disregard for the truth. Only public figures must prove malice. Politicians, elected government officials, and CEOs of corporations are obvious public figures. So is entertainer Carol Burnett, who successfully sued *The National Enquirer* for $10 million for maliciously depicting her as a public drunk. She used her financial award to set up prizes for journalism ethics. While lawsuits are filed against media, any corporation, organization, or public relations practitioner can be guilty of defamation through written material or remarks made before any group of people.

Defenses Against Libel Charges There are three primary defenses against libel charges—truth, qualified privilege, and fair comment. The primary legal defense is the truth. A second legal defense is **privilege**. Privilege protects materials and remarks coming from official proceedings and actions of members in executive, legislative, and judicial branches of government. The third legal defense is **fair comment.** If communications involve matters of genuine public interest, expressing critical opinions is permissible. The information must be in the public interest and supported with factual material. Examples include movie, book, and restaurant criticism, but fair comment could apply to consumer products, services, or the work of charitable organizations. For the public relations person, all communications about employees, competitors, and

Legal issues are a constant concern for the public relations practitioner.

campaigns must be researched and controversial material pretested, and when there is concern, legal advice must be sought.

Rights of Privacy Defamation concerns broadly the publication of speech that is derogatory. But even complimentary information may break the law if it invades another's **privacy rights**. Public relations people disseminate many kinds of messages—about their own organizations, fellow employees, and participants in special events, customers, and students on a campus. None of these messages should be created without first thinking about protecting privacy.

There are generally four kinds of **invasion of privacy:** appropriation, publication of private information, intrusion, and false light. **Appropriation** is the use for monetary gain of a person's name, likeness, or picture without permission. **Publication of private information** concerns information that is true but not generally known by a large number of people. Health, employment, and student records are examples of private information for which permission must be granted before it can be shared. **Intrusion** concerns videotaping, bugging, or snooping into others' private affairs. It is illegal to secretly record others' voices or actions without informing a person that the recording is being done. **False light** concerns publication of truthful information that is exaggerated or used out of context.

The best defense against invasion of privacy charges is obtaining **written consent.** Standard consent forms should be used whenever individuals' likenesses or personal information are used in public relations materials (see figure 4.1).

The **Freedom of Information Act (FOIA),** passed in 1966 and amended in 1974, generally requires that all government records—documents, press releases, and publications—are open to the public. For example, U.S. Census data and Department of Labor reports are available to all citizens.

Adult Release

In consideration of my engagement as a model, and for other good and valuable consideration herein acknowledge or received, upon the terms hereafter stated, I hereby grant _______________, his legal representatives and assigns, those for whom _______________ is acting, and those acting with his authority and permission, the absolute right and permission to copyright and use, reuse and publish, and republish photographic portraits or pictures of me or in which I may be included, in whole or in part, or composite or distorted in character or form, without restriction as to changes or alteration, from time to time, in conjunction with my own or a fictitious name, or reproductions thereof in color or otherwise made through any media at his studios or elsewhere for art, advertising, trade or any other purpose whatsoever.

I also consent to the use of any printed matter in conjunction therewith.
I hereby waive any right that I may have to inspect or approve the finished product or products of the advertising copy or printed matter that may be used in connection therewith or the use to which it may be applied.

I hereby release, discharge and agree to save harmless _______________, his legal representatives or assigns, and all persons acting under his permission or authority or those for whom he is acting, from any liability by virtue of any blurring, distortion, alteration, optical illusion, or use in composite form, whether intentional or otherwise, that may occur or be produced in the taking of said picture or in any subsequent processing thereof, as well as any publication thereof even though it may subject me to ridicule, scandal, reproach, scorn and indignity.

I hereby warrant that I am of full age and have every right to contract in my own name in the above regard. I state further that I have read the above authorization, release and agreement, prior to its execution, and that I am fully familiar with the contents thereof.

Dated _______________

Signed _______________

(Address) _______________

____

(Witness) _______________

FIGURE 4.1 **This use of a standard release form can protect against possible charges of invasion of privacy.**

Government agencies must tell citizens what information is available to them and how they can obtain it. These agencies even have websites that include descriptions of types of information and direct links to this information over the Internet. Businesses use the FOIA to obtain government statistics and other research, such as environmental impact statements, and applications for government permits. Activist organizations keep track of laws and regulations under consideration by public bodies, of minutes of meetings, and proposed government plans for zoning and development changes.

Congress passed the **Sunshine Act,** which opened to the public some previously closed meetings of federal boards, commissions, and agencies, including the Securities and Exchange Commission and the Federal Trade Commission. Many state and local governments have similar statutes affecting their boards and commissions. For example, local officials may be prohibited from meeting as a group unless there is public notice of such a meeting.

Government Regulatory Agencies

Many federal government agencies have a watchdog role regarding business and organizational communication, such as the **Federal Trade Commission (FTC),** the **Food and Drug Administration (FDA),** the **Federal Communication Commission (FCC),** the **National Labor Relations Board (NLRB),** and the **Securities and Exchange Commission (SEC).** Regulatory complaints from any of these federal agencies may originate with the agency itself, or consumers, labor leaders, or competitors may bring them to the attention of the agency. Public relations personnel should anticipate how federal laws and regulations could be broken when an organization seeks to communicate with any number of consumer, employee, or competitor publics.

The Federal Trade Commission (FTC) The FTC governs all commercial advertising, and product or service news releases, typical media for marketing communications. Advertising and news releases are illegal if they deceive or mislead the public in any way. Likewise, promotional practices are illegal unless they are literally true. The FTC requires that unsubstantiated or false claims for products be omitted from future advertising, and some advertisers may also be required to run corrective ads.

Food and Drug Administration (FDA) The FDA regulates labeling, packaging, and sale of food, drugs, and cosmetics. The regulations govern both product safety and product advertising. Many product recalls and the prohibition of some drug products in the United States result from failure to meet FDA safety regulations or guidelines. The FDA is responsible for the nutritional labeling on many food products. Public relations people working on product introductions will have to be able to explain FDA regulations to many stakeholders, including customers and the media.

Federal Communication Commission (FCC) The FCC regulates broadcasting, television, and radio to ensure that licensees are operating in the public interest. Of concern to political public relations practitioners are Sections 315 and 317 of the Federal Communications Act. They monitor the content of political broadcasting so that all parties have an equal opportunity of being heard. A public relations practitioner for a political candidate should know the following in Section 315a:

> If any licensee shall permit any person who is a legally qualified candidate for any public office to use a broadcasting station, he shall afford equal opportunities to all other such candidates for that office in the use of such broadcasting station, provided that such licensee should have no power of censorship over the material broadcast under provisions of this section. No obligation is hereby imposed upon any licensee to allow the use of its station by any such candidate.[11]

Although Section 315 doesn't require stations to provide broadcast time, Section 312(a7) does. It requires stations to sell "reasonable amounts of time" to legally qualified candidates for federal office. Stations aren't held accountable for content, but candidates, their organizations, and their public relations people are accountable.

National Labor Relations Board (NLRB) The NLRB oversees the 1935 National Labor Relations Act, the primary law governing communications between unions and employers. The act deals with all aspects of union activities, including the right to join unions, to engage in collective bargaining, and to engage in union activities. The act protects also nonunion activities such as nonunion walkouts, working conditions, and employee discussions of compensation. All of these activities would require that managers and public relations people express company positions in ways that are not coercive or threatening to management-labor relationships.

Securities and Exchange Commission (SEC) The SEC enforces laws and regulations concerning the purchase of stocks of publicly owned corporations that are listed on any of the 13 largest U.S. stock exchanges or that have assets of $1 million and 500 stockholders. It enforces the **Securities and Exchange Act of 1934** and other regulations that require that corporations "act promptly to dispel unfounded rumors which result in unusual market activity or price variations."

The Securities and Exchange Act of 1933 requires the "full and fair disclosure of the character of securities . . . and to prevent frauds in the sale thereof." The Securities and Exchange Act of 1934 supplemented the previous year's legislation and was intended to "secure for issues publicly offered, adequate publicity for those facts necessary for an intelligent judgment of their value."

The SEC requires submission of three kinds of reports: annual reports **(Form 10-K)**, quarterly reports **(Form 10-Q)**, and current reports **(Form 8-K)**. Although the information in these reports is produced by accountants and lawyers, these publications have strategic public relations value because they are distributed to many audiences, including stockholders, financial analysts, and potential investors.

General Business Regulations

Public relations is a practice protected by the First Amendment and regulated as a function of organizations. But public relations is also a business activity, involved in creating and protecting organizational brands and reputations. Thus, public relations practitioners need to know general business regulations, such as **copyright** law, **trademark** law, contracts, and the laws of litigation. "Public relations practitioners must understand the extent to which the general laws of business also govern their field; but they and the media are subject to the normal laws of business, even though their expression may be protected by the First Amendment."[12]

Copyright Law Public relations practitioners must have legal consent to use another's creative expression or "intellectual property," such as graphic designs, music to use in videos, annual report and brochure copy, photographs, and other original artistic works fixed in any tangible form. Self-employed public relations consultants copyright their materials unless they contractually sign away that right to their clients.

Only when **fair use** is established can public relations practitioners produce or copy others' creative expression. The fair use provision of the Copyright Act allows use of others' materials with broad provisions addressing the following:

1. The purpose and character of the use, including whether such use is of a commercial nature or is for nonprofit educational purposes.

2. The nature of the copyrighted work is challenged.
3. The amount and substantiality of the portion used is verified with the copyright holder.
4. The effect of the use upon the potential market for or value of the copyrighted work is considered.

This means that in the preparation of communications, a portion of copyrighted material may be used without the author's permission

1. If it is not taken out of context.
2. If credit to the source is given.
3. If such usage does not materially affect the market for the copyrighted material.
4. If the work in which it is used is for scholastic, news, or research purposes.
5. If the material used does not exceed a certain percentage of the total work.

No percentage is given in the law; it depends on the work. One rule of thumb is: Don't use any music; use only a fraction of poetry; but you can use 100 to 200 words of a book or article.

Trademark Laws Trademark laws cover the names of businesses and business products. Just as patent laws often cover the products themselves, their names can be covered under trademarks. Organizations want exclusive rights to their brand or service names, logos, and symbols. It would be trademark infringement to market a product with a name strongly resembling or suggestive of an existing trademark or trade name.

Companies zealously protect their product brands against those who would try to use the brand without permission. They also guard against a brand name becoming generic for all of the products in its category, thus sacrificing its uniqueness and causing serious advertising and public relations problems. Think of such brands as Kleenex, Band-Aid, and Xerox that have lost their uniqueness because these trade names are used for all products in their categories.

Contracts Copyrighted and trademarked materials may be used if permission is given by the copyright or trademark holder. Permission for use can constitute a **contract,** a legal instrument that protects the rights of two or more parties.

Public relations practitioners often must use contracts. Independent public relations professionals need contracts between themselves and the firms or individuals they represent. Special events may require contracts with hotels, musical groups, caterers, and others. Practitioners contract with outside vendors, such as publishing or printing firms, mail distribution agencies, and electronic clipping services, to do production and research work.

For a contract to be binding, it must meet certain legal criteria. The essential elements of contracts include the following:

1. A genuine, legal offer
2. A legally effective acceptance
3. An agreement that includes an exchange of acts or promises, which is called "consideration."[13]

Some but not all contracts must be in writing. Courts often consider oral contracts binding if all legal tests have been met in the process. If obligations set out in a contract are not fulfilled, a possible breach of contract has occurred.

Legal Considerations Surrounding the Internet

The Internet has quickly entered the legal realm of our information society. Cyberspace is demanding new regulation in libel, copyright, and privacy. These are important issues to public relations people who have taken advantage of going directly to stakeholders with this immediate, compelling channel of communication.

Copyright and the Net Public relations practitioners are using the Internet and online services to send and find breaking news, feature stories, speeches, photos, and information about their agencies or organizations and to receive direct inquiries and feedback from stakeholders. Even though these resources are conveniently accessible, they are still copyright protected, and public relations people should not use materials without permission.[14] *Business Week* calls copyright violation on the Internet "highway robbery," claiming that infringement goes far beyond the copy machine violations. A digital copyright code was designed in 1995 to put a "cipher," or a code, identifying the owner into each copyrighted work on the Internet.[15]

Libel and the Net Though there is still debate in the courts about who is responsible for libel on the Internet, public relations practitioners would be held accountable for libel should they use the Net because the practitioner controls the messages sent to the public. Common carriers such as telephone companies, however, are not responsible because they don't control the statements. A New York court decided in 1995 that an Internet provider could be held responsible if it edited electronic messages posted by subscribers. The Long Island securities investment firm Stratton Oakmont Inc. sued Prodigy for $200 million because an anonymous user of Prodigy's "Money Talk" bulletin board falsely portrayed the company as criminals involved in fraud.[16] The court said that since Prodigy marketed itself as a family-oriented online service that screened new messages on its bulletin board, it was more like a publisher than like a common carrier.

Privacy and the Net Privacy is a "source of worry" for senders and receivers of Internet messages. Because Internet communication can be tracked, traced, and authors identified by authorities, hackers, and identity thieves, the public has a strong desire to have personal information protected as more and more of the world intrudes through e-mail and cyberspace. Organizations have varying policies on what types of information employees may exchange over the Net. E-mail addresses are being sold to vendors who want to use them for sales purposes. Public relations people have to weigh the gains and hazards of this channel of communication as a means of reaching stakeholders and maintaining relationships with them. See mini-case 4.2 as an example of the beginning of federal protection of Internet privacy.

Litigation Public Relations

Organizations must consider whether and how relationships with clients, employees, government, and the media would be affected should they find themselves in court. Accused of reputation-damaging activities, media interest could be constant enough that however the court case is resolved, the accused organization is found to be less credible and trustworthy by its constituents outside the courthouse. Dow Corning is being sued for billions of dollars by women who claim its silicone gel-filled breast implants caused them multiple ailments, pain, and suffering. This corporation found itself in litigation because of a CBS television show aired in 1990 in which Connie Chung interviewed

Financial Institutions Confuse Consumers About Their "Opt-Out" Right

Mini•Case 4.2

Financial institutions have until July 1 to inform customers of their right to remove their names from data-sharing programs. The Financial Modernizations Act of 1999 (also known as the Gramm-Leach-Bliley Act) extended the ability of banks, securities firms, and insurance companies to enter each other's businesses and to share information.

This law has consequently led to a flood of complaints by consumers and raised concerns by several privacy advocates and consumer groups. A 23-page position paper by EPIC, the Privacy Rights Clearing House, US PIRG, and Consumer Union points out that when combined, customer databases from giant entities contain "a vast amount of financial, medical and other sensitive information." Writing for *Wired Digital,* Joanna Glasner summarizes a variety of views and surveys on the subject.

"There's quite a bit of awareness that greater clarity is necessary for the consumer," states Susan Hart, a financial economist at the U.S. Treasury. An American Bankers Association survey found that 41 percent of people never even recalled getting an opt-out notice, some mistaking the forms for mere junk mail. A coalition of 37 state attorneys general is pushing the federal government to require that notices be couched in simpler language.

Source: From *pr reporter,* 20 May 2002, p. 4.

Senator Byron Dorgan, chair of the Senate Commerce Committee, points to a graph showing profits from Enron insider and restricted shareholder transactions during a hearing in 2001 investigating the collapse of the energy giant.

several women who claimed that their breast implants gave them autoimmune disease. Years later, Dow Corning was still spending thousands of dollars in time and money attempting in court to reach a bankruptcy reorganization and at the same time, seeking means through communication to keep its employees productive and its reputation credible so that it will keep its stockholders, customers, suppliers, and successful relationships with the community, government, and the media.[17]

THE ETHICAL ENVIRONMENT

Kant defined ethics as "a science that teaches, not how we are to achieve happiness, but how we are to become worthy of happiness."[18] What is legal is not always ethical and what is ethical is not always legal. Laws cover only so many situations in public relations. In many situations, public relations people have to make judgments about "the right thing to do" to build relationships between the organization and its publics. Public relations people must weigh the benefit versus the harm of their communication activities and/or have the moral resolve to say yes or no, because the long-term effects of a bad decision will offset a short-term gain.

Ethics is an area of concern for public relations for four reasons. First, practitioners are aware that, to some, public relations has a reputation for unethical behavior. Second, public relations is often the source of ethical statements from an organization and the repository of ethical and social policies for that organization. Third, practitioners have struggled to create suitable codes of ethics for themselves; and fourth, practitioners should act on behalf of their organizations as the ethical ombudsman for the publics they serve.

If public relations seeks to achieve professional status as a communication function that represents the public interest as well as the organization in business decision making, its practitioners must be held to higher standards.

Ethics as Standards of Social Conduct

Ethics is what is morally right or wrong in social conduct, usually as determined by standards of professions, organizations, and individuals. Ethical behavior is a major consideration that distinguishes the civilized from the uncivilized in society. Allen Center and Patrick Jackson argue that five factors regulate social conduct:

1. *Tradition.* Ways in which the situation has been viewed or handled in the past.
2. *Public Opinion.* Currently acceptable behavior according to the majority of one's peers.
3. *Law.* Behaviors that are permissible and those that are prohibited by legislation.
4. *Morality.* Generally, a spiritual or religious prohibition. Immorality is a charge usually leveled in issues on which religious teachings have concentrated.
5. *Ethics.* Standards set by the profession, an organization, or oneself, based on conscience—what is right or fair to others as well as to self?[19]

Individual Ethics

Ralph Waldo Emerson, the American philosopher, once said: "What you are stands over you the while, and thunders so that I cannot hear what you say." This same philosophy was evident in the work of Ivy Lee, one of the early pioneers of public relations. Lee considered the public relations *actions,* not words, more important. His 1906 Declaration of Principles was the forerunner of a **code of ethics** for public relations.

More important than ethical codes of public relations, though, is the nature of the individual, private ethics of the practitioner. When it comes right down to it, the practitioner must have a high personal standard of ethics that carries over into his or her own work. James E. Grunig, a leading proponent of public relations professionalism, argued that individual practitioners must have two basic guiding ethical principles:

1. They must have the will to be ethical, intending not to injure others, but rather to be honest and trustworthy.

2. They must make every effort to avoid actions that would have adverse consequences for others.[20]

At the heart of any discussion of ethics in public relations are some questions that are deeply troubling for the individual practitioner. For example, will she or he

1. Lie for a client or employer?
2. Engage in deception to collect information about another practitioner's clients?
3. Help conceal a hazardous condition or illegal act?
4. Present information that presents only part of the truth?
5. Offer something (gift, travel, or information) to reporters or legislators that may compromise their reporting?
6. Present true but misleading information in an interview or news conference that corrupts the channels of government?

Many public relations practitioners find themselves forced to respond to questions like these. By considering their ethical standards, practitioners can avoid difficult situations that may harm their individual reputations. Unfortunately, most ethical decisions are not black and white. When obligations to stakeholders collide over an ethical issue, the practitioner must decide whose claim is most important or entails the least harm to the fewest people. Thus, when the employer's policies are different from those of the profession or the dictates of individual conscience, which would take precedence?

Business Ethics

As controversial as the question of individual ethics is, so is the general issue of business ethics. It is relatively easy to agree in abstract terms that individual professionals have a duty to behave ethically. Unfortunately, translating abstract concepts into ethical standards for business practice in a competitive environment has not been so easy. Some practitioners have been fired arbitrarily for refusing to write news releases they felt would be false or misleading. One practitioner worked for a company that wanted him to prepare and distribute a release listing company clients before the clients had signed contracts for services. When he refused to prepare the release, this practitioner was fired and subsequently sued the company for unlawful dismissal, receiving almost $100,000 in an out-of-court settlement. Another public relations practitioner resigned after initially participating in several unethically questionable practices with a multinational fruit conglomerate. He charged the company with manipulation of press coverage as well as with political and military action involving a Latin American country in which the company was operating.

The increased attention of many organizations to ethical dimensions of operating can be traced back to the1968 Watergate investigation. President Richard Nixon resigned rather than face impeachment charges because of a bungled break-in at Democratic campaign headquarters and subsequent revelations of unethical campaign practices, cover-ups, and secret tapings of White House meetings.

Other indelible examples of ethical controversy that add to public skepticism of public relations include Firestone Tires, a corporation that has not yet admitted responsibility for the highway deaths linked to its tires. Coke maintains that its European distributions had no responsibility in the contamination of its product that led to schoolchildren reporting that they became ill from drinking Coke products, although Coke attempted to make amends by offering free Coke products. The American Red Cross faced negative public opinion twice after its efforts to form a September 11 liberty fund. First, the organization came under fire when it announced after 9/11 that it would hold back for future disasters donations that the American public had expected would go the victims of the World Trade Center and Pentagon attacks. Then, when it began to give out the money, it was criticized for being too generous.

When public relations practitioners participate in organizational decisions, they bear a heavy ethical responsibility—not only to themselves and their organizations but also to their profession and the public. They must weigh all these considerations when helping to make organizational decisions and communicate decisions once they are made.

Professional codes, corporate policy, and even law cannot ensure the ethical practice of any profession; only the application of sound personal values can guarantee ethical behavior. Nevertheless, professional codes, sound business policies, and appropriate legislation can serve as valuable guidelines for public relations practitioners who desire to maintain high ethical standards.

Establishing Standards for a Developing Profession

For any occupation to become a profession, it must meet four criteria: (1) expertise, (2) autonomy, (3) commitment, and (4) responsibility.[21] *Expertise* comprises the specialized knowledge and skill that are vital requirements for the profession to perform its function in society. *Autonomy* allows the practitioner to practice without outside interference. *Commitment,* the outcome of expertise, implies devotion to the pursuit of excellence without emphasis on the rewards of the profession. Finally, *responsibility* means the power conferred by expertise entails a trust relationship with the practitioner's stakeholder groups.

Though all four criteria are important, the last one, responsibility, is operationalized through codes of ethics, professional organizations, and licensure. Thus, to be considered fully professionalized, an occupation needs a well-developed and well-enforced code of ethics, active professional associations, and some means of controlling the practice. It is the licensure issue that continues to prevent public relations from being a fully professional occupation.

The PRSA Code

The ethics code of the Public Relations Society of America (PRSA) is the most detailed and comprehensive in the field of public relations, although it is strictly voluntary and not legally binding (see spotlight 4.1). When PRSA was founded in 1948, one of its actions was to develop a code of ethics so members would have some common behavioral guidelines, and managers would have a clear understanding of their standards. This code became the tool used to distinguish professionals in public relations from shady promoters and publicists who have been quick to appropriate the term *public relations* to describe their activities.

The most recent PRSA Code revisions, approved in 2000, changed dramatically how PRSA intended to think about and educate public relations professionals about ethics. First, the PRSA Code eliminated an emphasis on enforcement of standards based on members coming forward to lodge complaints or identify others in violation of the Code, although the PRSA board of directors retained the right to bar individuals from membership or expel individuals from the society. Second, the PRSA Code focused on universal values that inspire ethical behavior or performance. Third, the PRSA Code provided illustrations to help practitioners better practice important ethical and principled business objectives.

PRSA Code of Professional Standards for the Practice of Public Relations

Spotlight 4.1

A Message from the PRSA Board of Ethics and Professional Standards

Our Primary Obligation

The primary obligation of membership in the Public Relations Society of America is the ethical practice of Public Relations.

The PRSA Member Code of Ethics is the way each member of our Society can daily reaffirm a commitment to ethical professional activities and decisions.

- The Code sets forth the principles and standards that guide our decisions and actions.
- The Code solidly connects our values and our ideals to the work each of us does every day.
- The Code is about what we should do, and why we should do it.

The Code is also meant to be a living, growing body of knowledge, precedent, and experience. It should stimulate our thinking and encourage us to seek guidance and clarification when we have questions about principles, practices, and standards of conduct.

Every member's involvement in preserving and enhancing ethical standards is essential to building and maintaining the respect and credibility of our profession. Using our values, principles, standards of conduct, and commitment as a foundation, and continuing to work together on ethical issues, we ensure that the Public Relations Society of America fulfills its obligation to build and maintain the framework for public dialogue that deserves the public's trust and support.

Preamble

Public Relations Society of America Member Code of Ethics 2000

- Professional Values
- Principles of Conduct
- Commitment and Compliance

This Code applies to PRSA members. The Code is designed to be a useful guide for PRSA members as they carry out their ethical responsibilities. This document is designed to anticipate and accommodate, by precedent, ethical challenges that may arise. The scenarios outlined in the Code provision are actual examples of misconduct. More will be added as experience with the Code occurs.

The Public Relations Society of America (PRSA) is committed to ethical practices. The level of public trust PRSA members seek, as we serve the public good, means we have taken on a special obligation to operate ethically.

The value of member reputation depends upon the ethical conduct of everyone affiliated with the Public Relations Society of America. Each of us sets an example for each other—as well as other professionals—by our pursuit of excellence with powerful standards of performance, professionalism, and ethical conduct.

Emphasis on enforcement of the Code has been eliminated. But the PRSA Board of Directors retains the right to bar from membership or expel from the Society any individual who has been or is sanctioned by a government agency or convicted in a court of law of an action that is in violation of this Code.

Ethical practice is the most important obligation of a PRSA member. We view the Member Code of Ethics as a model for other professions, organizations, and professionals.

PRSA Member Statement of Professional Values

This statement presents the core values of PRSA members and, more broadly, of the public relations profession. These values provide the foundation for the Member Code of Ethics and set the industry standard for the professional practice of public relations. These values are the fundamental beliefs that guide our behaviors and decision-making process. We believe our professional values are vital to the integrity of the profession as a whole.

Advocacy

- We serve the public interest by acting as responsible advocates for those we represent.
- We provide a voice in the marketplace of ideas, facts, and viewpoints to aid informed public debate.

Honesty

- We adhere to the highest standards of accuracy and truth in advancing the interests of those we represent and in communicating with the public.

Expertise

- We acquire and responsibly use specialized knowledge and experience.
- We advance the profession through continued professional development, research, and education.
- We build mutual understanding, credibility, and relationships among a wide array of institutions and audiences.

Independence

- We provide objective counsel to those we represent.
- We are accountable for our actions.

Loyalty

- We are faithful to those we represent, while honoring our obligation to serve the public interest.

Fairness

- We deal fairly with clients, employers, competitors, peers, vendors, the media, and the general public.
- We respect all opinions and support the right of free expression.

PRSA Code Provisions

Free Flow of Information

Core Principle

Protecting and advancing the free flow of accurate and truthful information is essential to serving the public interest and contributing to informed decision making in a democratic society.

Intent

- To maintain the integrity of relationships with the media, government officials, and the public.
- To aid informed decision making.

Guidelines

A member shall:

- Preserve the integrity of the process of communication.
- Be honest and accurate in all communications.

- Act promptly to correct erroneous communications for which the practitioner is responsible.
- Preserve the free flow of unprejudiced information when giving or receiving gifts by ensuring that gifts are nominal, legal, and infrequent.

Examples of Improper Conduct Under This Provision:

- A member representing a ski manufacturer gives a pair of expensive racing skis to a sports magazine columnist, to influence the columnist to write favorable articles about the product.
- A member entertains a government official beyond legal limits and/or in violation of government reporting requirements.

Competition

Core Principle

Promoting healthy and fair competition among professionals preserves an ethical climate while fostering a robust business environment.

Intent

- To promote respect and fair competition among public relations professionals.
- To serve the public interest by providing the widest choice of practitioner options.

Guidelines

A member shall:

- Follow ethical hiring practices designed to respect free and open competition without deliberately undermining a competitor.
- Preserve intellectual property rights in the marketplace.

Examples of Improper Conduct Under This Provision:

- A member employed by a "client organization" shares helpful information with a counseling firm that is competing with others for the organization's business.
- A member spreads malicious and unfounded rumors about a competitor in order to alienate the competitor's clients and employees in a ploy to recruit people and business.

Disclosure of Information

Core Principle

Open communication fosters informed decision making in a democratic society.

Intent

- To build trust with the public by revealing all information needed for responsible decision making.

Guidelines

A member shall:

- Be honest and accurate in all communications.
- Act promptly to correct erroneous communications for which the member is responsible.
- Investigate the truthfulness and accuracy of information released on behalf of those represented.
- Reveal the sponsors for causes and interests represented.
- Disclose financial interest (such as stock ownership) in a client's organization.
- Avoid deceptive practices.

Examples of Improper Conduct Under This Provision:

- Front groups: A member implements "grass roots" campaigns or letter-writing campaigns to legislators on behalf of undisclosed interest groups.
- Lying by omission: A practitioner for a corporation knowingly fails to release financial information, giving a misleading impression of the corporation's performance.
- A member discovers inaccurate information disseminated via a website or media kit and does not correct the information.
- A member deceives the public by employing people to pose as volunteers to speak at public hearings and participate in "grass roots" campaigns.

Safeguarding Confidences

Core Principle

Client trust requires appropriate protection of confidential and private information.

Intent

- To protect the privacy rights of clients, organizations, and individuals by safeguarding confidential information.

Guidelines

A member shall:

- Safeguard the confidences and privacy rights of present, former, and prospective clients and employees.
- Protect privileged, confidential, or insider information gained from a client or organization.
- Immediately advise an appropriate authority if a member discovers that confidential information is being divulged by an employee of a client company or organization.

Examples of Improper Conduct Under This Provision:

- A member changes jobs, takes confidential information, and uses that information in the new position to the detriment of the former employer.
- A member intentionally leaks proprietary information to the detriment of some other party.

Conflicts of Interest

Core Principle

Avoiding real, potential or perceived conflicts of interest builds the trust of clients, employers, and the publics.

Intent

- To earn trust and mutual respect with clients or employers.
- To build trust with the public by avoiding or ending situations that put one's personal or professional interests in conflict with society's interests.

Guidelines

A member shall:

- Act in the best interests of the client or employer, even subordinating the member's personal interests.
- Avoid actions and circumstances that may appear to compromise good business judgment or create a conflict between personal and professional interests.
- Disclose promptly any existing or potential conflict of interest to affected clients or organizations.
- Encourage clients and customers to determine if a conflict exists after notifying all affected parties.

Examples of Improper Conduct Under This Provision:

- The member fails to disclose that he or she has a strong financial interest in a client's chief competitor.
- The member represents a "competitor company" or a "conflicting interest" without informing a prospective client.

Enhancing the Profession

Core Principle
Public relations professionals work constantly to strengthen the public's trust in the profession.

Intent

- To build respect and credibility with the public for the profession of public relations.
- To improve, adapt, and expand professional practices.

Guidelines
A member shall:

- Acknowledge that there is an obligation to protect and enhance the profession.
- Keep informed and educated about practices in the profession to ensure ethical conduct.
- Actively pursue personal professional development.
- Decline representation of clients or organizations that urge or require actions contrary to this Code.
- Accurately define what public relations activities can accomplish.
- Counsel subordinates in proper ethical decision making.
- Require that subordinates adhere to the ethical requirements of the Code.
- Report ethical violations, whether committed by PRSA members or not, to the appropriate authority.

Examples of Improper Conduct Under This Provision:

- A PRSA member declares publicly that a product the client sells is safe, without disclosing evidence to the contrary.
- A member initially assigns some questionable client work to a non-member practitioner to avoid the ethical obligation of PRSA membership.

The IABC Code

The International Association of Business Communicators (IABC), with approximately 19,000 members, also has a widely used code of ethics (see spotlight 4.2). This code differs from that of the PRSA in only a few ways. It seems to focus more on the worth of human beings in the many cultures of the world and to be sensitive to other cultural values and beliefs. It gives a more limited list of standards and does not try to spell out values that have led to the formally listed standards. Both codes are voluntary, but members are required to sign that they have read and are willing to abide by the codes.

The Question of Licensure

Some believe that codes of behavior are only part of what is needed to build professional status for the field of public relations. Controlled access is the hallmark of a recognized profession. Therefore, controlled access, through **licensure,** to the title of "certified public relations counsel" is viewed as the only way to separate the frauds and flacks from legitimate practitioners. Proponents such as Edward L. Bernays, who was instrumental in formulating the modern concept of public relations, believed that licensing could protect the profession and the public from incompetent and unscrupulous practitioners.

Those who would argue for licensure see it as the only effective method of enforcing professional standards, but efforts to impose such standards are highly controversial. Even if licensure were implemented, many practitioners would probably not be affected because they work in corporate departments. There would also have to be a compelling interest on the part of state governments to regulate the practice of public relations with a state agency.

Both PRSA and IABC offer accreditation programs for experienced practitioners who pass a comprehensive examination. These programs are the closest existing approximation to licensing procedures. However, less than half the memberships of both associations are accredited. Despite efforts by PRSA, few people outside the profession have any notion of the accreditation process and what it means.

4.2 Spotlight

IABC Code of Ethics for Professional Communicators

Preface

Because hundreds of thousands of business communicators worldwide engage in activities that affect the lives of millions of people, and because this power carries with it significant social responsibilities, the International Association of Business Communicators developed the Code of Ethics for Professional Communicators.

The Code is based on three different yet interrelated principles of professional communication that apply throughout the world.

These principles assume that just societies are governed by a profound respect for human rights and the rule of law; that ethics, the criteria for determining what is right and wrong, can be agreed upon by members of an organization; and, that understanding matters of taste requires sensitivity to cultural norms.

These principles are essential:

Professional communication is legal.

Professional communication is ethical.

Professional communication is in good taste.

Recognizing these principles, members of IABC will engage in communication that is not only legal but also ethical and sensitive to cultural values and beliefs; engage in truthful, accurate and fair communication that facilitates respect and mutual understanding; and, adhere to the following articles of the IABC Code of Ethics for Professional Communicators.

Because conditions in the world are constantly changing, members of IABC will work to improve their individual competence and to increase the body of knowledge in the field with research and education.

Articles

1. Professional communicators uphold the credibility and dignity of their profession by practicing honest, candid and timely communication and by fostering the free flow of essential information in accord with the public interest.
2. Professional communicators disseminate accurate information and promptly correct any erroneous communication for which they may be responsible.
3. Professional communicators understand and support the principles of free speech, freedom of assembly, and access to an open marketplace of ideas; and, act accordingly.
4. Professional communicators are sensitive to cultural values and beliefs and engage in fair and balanced communication activities that foster and encourage mutual understanding.
5. Professional communicators refrain from taking part in any undertaking which the communicator considers to be unethical.
6. Professional communicators obey laws and public policies governing their professional activities and are sensitive to the spirit of all laws and regulations and, should any law or public policy be violated, for whatever reason, act promptly to correct the situation.
7. Professional communicators give credit for unique expressions borrowed from others and identify the sources and purposes of all information disseminated to the public.
8. Professional communicators protect confidential information and, at the same time, comply with all legal requirements for the disclosure of information affecting the welfare of others.
9. Professional communicators do not use confidential information gained as a result of professional activities for personal benefit and do not represent conflicting or competing interests without written consent of those involved.
10. Professional communicators do not accept undisclosed gifts or payments for professional services from anyone other than a client or employer.
11. Professional communicators do not guarantee results that are beyond the power of the practitioner to deliver.
12. Professional communicators are honest not only with others but also, and most importantly, with themselves as individuals; for a professional communicator seeks the truth and speaks that truth first to the self.

Enforcement and Communication of the IABC Code for Professional Communicators

IABC fosters compliance with its Code by engaging in global communication campaigns rather than through negative sanctions. However, in keeping with the sixth article of the IABC Code, members of IABC who are found guilty by an appropriate governmental agency or judicial body of violating laws and public policies governing their professional activities may have their membership terminated by the IABC executive board following procedures set forth in the association's bylaws.

IABC encourages the widest possible communication about its Code.

The IABC Code of Ethics for Professional Communicators is published in several languages and is freely available to all: Permission is hereby granted to any individual or organization wishing to copy and incorporate all or part of the IABC Code into personal and corporate codes, with the understanding that appropriate credit be given to IABC in any publication of such codes.

The IABC Code is published in the association's annual directory, *The World Book of IABC Communicators*. The association's monthly magazine, *Communication World,* publishes periodic articles dealing with ethical issues. At least one session at the association's annual conference is devoted to ethics. The international headquarters of IABC, through its professional development activities, encourages and supports efforts by IABC student chapters, professional chapters, and districts/regions to conduct meetings and workshops devoted to the topic of ethics and the IABC Code. New and renewing members of IABC sign the following statement as part of their application: "I have reviewed and understand the IABC Code of Ethics for Professional Communicators."

As a service to communicators worldwide, inquiries about ethics and questions or comments about the IABC Code may be addressed to members of the IABC Ethics Committee. The IABC Ethics Committee is composed of at least three accredited members of IABC who serve staggered three-year terms. Other IABC members may serve on the committee with the approval of the IABC executive committee. The functions of the Ethics Committee are to assist with professional development activities dealing with ethics and to offer advice and assistance to individual communicators regarding specific ethical situations.

While discretion will be used in handling all inquiries about ethics, absolute confidentiality cannot be guaranteed. Those wishing more information about the IABC Code or specific advice about ethics are encouraged to contact IABC World Headquarters (One Hallidie Plaza, Suite 600, San Francisco, CA 94102 USA; phone, 415-544-4700; fax, 415-544-4747).

The issue of ethical practice in public relations is closely tied to efforts toward accreditation and licensure. By promoting professional responsibility and recognition, public relations organizations can encourage ethical behavior and awareness among its members.

For self-testing and additional chapter resources, go to the student CD and the Online Learning Center at **www.mhhe.com/lattimore**

To learn more about legal issues watch the interview with Julia Sutherland, Clip #8, on the book's CD-ROM.

Critical Incidents: The Practical Side of Ethics

By Donald B. McCammond, APR
Former Chairman Board of Ethics, PRSA

Sometimes, in everyday practice, situations arise where the proper thing, the ethical thing, even the legal thing to do is not always immediately clear. Following are several such situations.

1. A well-known athlete is charged with selling drugs and planning and carrying out, with others, the death of a young married couple. His attorney calls you, a close friend, to advise and assist him in handling the intense media interest in the case. During the period before the trial, you learn that the athlete was, in fact, a drug dealer and did participate in the murder. The lawyer tells you that the information is privileged. You decide to await the outcome of the trial. The lawyer is able to get his client acquitted. What should you do?
2. Your firm is one of six under consideration by a manufacturer planning to introduce a new service into your area. You are given confidential information as to the service and the plans of the company. You are aware that the company will face severe opposition from certain groups and politicians and that the job will entail overcoming this resistance. Your firm is turned down by the company, and the assignment is given

to the competitor. Can you disclose the information you have learned to the manufacturer's opposition in your area?

3. Your public relations firm publishes a newsletter directed to brokerage houses. A corporate executive asks your help in making his company better known among the brokerage community. A subsequent issue of the newsletter carries a highly optimistic forecast of the company but omits some information. Nothing in the story indicates the relationship between you and the company. Were you under any obligation to disclose this friendship? Should you print a retraction?
4. You are a corporate public relations director. Your employer tells you to set up a supposedly independent organization to introduce and promote the use of a new product made by your company. This new organization is to be financed secretly by your company and some of its suppliers. Is there anything wrong with establishing this organization?
5. A distributor of medicinal products arranges with your firm to put on a press conference for an independent British scientist who has tested the products and written favorably about them. You also arrange speaking engagements for the visiting scientist. After the press conference, you learn that the scientist was actually an employee of the research arm of the manufacturer of the products. What actions should you take?
6. A client asks you for help in a financial merger situation. You decline because the matter is outside your expertise and refer the company to a fellow practitioner who is knowledgeable in financial affairs. The fellow practitioner is so appreciative he sends you a check for $500. Can you accept the money without telling the client?
7. One of your clients calls you to assist in a takeover situation. You tell a friend who had originally helped you get the client. Several days later, your friend buys 5,000 shares in one of the companies involved in the takeover. You do not buy any yourself. The day after the merger announcement, your friend sells the shares, at a profit of $15 a share and a total profit of $75,000. Are you guilty of insider trading, even if you made no profit?
8. Your employer asks you to give a series of talks in communities served by your company regarding its new plant and the service it will provide. On a visit to the plant to acquaint yourself with its operation, you get clear evidence that it cannot fulfill the expectations outlined in the talk prepared by your company. Can you give the talks as originally prepared?

Questions

1. Which codes of ethics (either PRSA or IABC) apply to each incident description?
2. List the ethical questions involved in each.
3. Describe any legal questions raised by these incidents.

Key Terms

Use the CD-ROM and Online Learning Center at www.mhhe.com/lattimore to further your understanding of the following terms

appropriation
civil libel
code of ethics
contract
commercial speech
copyright
criminal libel
defamation
ethics
fair comment
fair use
false light
Federal Communication Commission (FCC)
Federal Trade Commission (FTC)
First Amendment
Food and Drug Administration (FDA)
Form 10-K, Form 10-Q, and Form 8-K
Freedom of Information Act (FOIA)
intrusion
invasion of privacy
law
libel
licensure
malice
National Labor Relations Board (NLRB)
privacy rights
privilege
product liability
publication of private information
regulation
Securities and Exchange Act of 1934
Securities and Exchange Commission (SEC)
slander
Sunshine Act
trademark
written consent

Notes

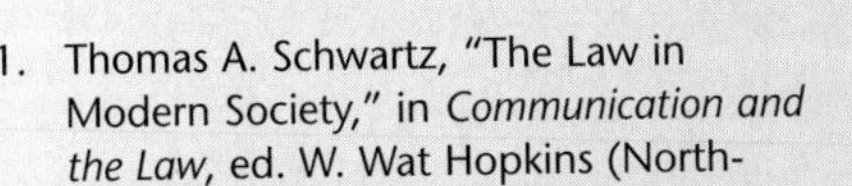

1. Thomas A. Schwartz, "The Law in Modern Society," in *Communication and the Law*, ed. W. Wat Hopkins (Northport, AL: Vision Press, 2001), p. 1.
2. Dean Williams, "Un-Spun." *Communication World*, April/May 2002, p. 26.
3. Kathy R. Fitzpatrick, "Public Relations and the Law: A Survey of Practitioners," *Public Relations Review* 22, no. 1 (1996), p. 1.
4. Roy L. Moore, Ronald T. Farrar, and Erik L. Collins, *Advertising and the Law* (Mahwah, NJ: Erlbaum, 1998), p. 50.
5. Ibid., p. 52.
6. Moore, Farrar, and Collins, p. 26.
7. Kyu Ho Youm, "Libel: the Plaintiff's Case," in *Communication and the Law*, ed. W. Wat Hopkins (Northport, Al: Vision Press, 2001), p. 88.
8. Ibid.
9. Moore, Farrar, and Collins, p. 189.
10. Moore, Farrar, and Collins, p. 174.
11. Section 315a, Federal Communications Act.
12. Greg Lisby, "Regulating the Practice of Public Relations," in *Communication and the Law*, ed. W. Wat Hopkins (Northport, AL: Vision Press, 2001), p. 167.
13. J. Edward Conrey, Gerald R. Ferrer, and Karla H. Fox, *The Legal Environment of Business* (Dubuque, IA: Wm. C. Brown, 1986), p. 197.
14. R. Penchina, "Venturing On-Line: Protecting You and Your Product in Cyperspace," *Editor and Publisher* 24 June 1995, p. 122.
15. "Halting Highway Robbery on the Internet," *Business Week*, 17 October 1994, p. 212.
16. P. H. Lewis, "Judge Allows Libel Lawsuit Against Prodigy to Proceed," *New York Times*, 24 May 1995, p. D4.

17. "Lessons from the Ultimate Crisis: Dow Corning in the Crucible," *The Strategist* 3, no. 1 (Spring 1997), pp. 6–12.

18. Larissa A. Grunig, "Toward a Philosophy of Public Relations," in *Rhetorical and Critical Approaches to Public Relations,* ed. Elizabeth L. Toth and Robert L. Heath (Hillsdale, NJ: Erlbaum, 1992), p. 79.

19. Allen Center and Patrick Jackson, *Public Relations Practices: Managerial Case Studies and Problems.* 5th ed. (Englewood Cliffs, NJ: Prentice-Hall, 1995), p. 476.

20. James E. Grunig and Todd Hunt, *Managing Public Relations* (New York: Holt, Rinehart & Winston, 1984), p. 72.

21. Dan Lattimore, "Professionalism and Performance: An Investigation of Colorado Daily Newsmen," Ph.D. dissertation, University of Wisconsin, 1972; and Blaine McKee, Oguz Nayman, and Dan Lattimore, "How PR People See Themselves," *Public Relations Journal* (November 1975), pp. 47–60.

PART TWO

The Process

It isn't enough to know what public relations is and what purposes it serves. To practice public relations, one must understand the process by which public relations operates. As we have already discussed, public relations goes far beyond the task of producing messages. An effective public relations effort is the result of mutual understanding between an organization and its publics. The development of this understanding can be regarded as a four-step process:

1 **Research** An initial fact-finding stage defines the problem areas and differentiates between publics.

2 **Planning** Once the facts have been gathered from the various publics, decisions must be made regarding their importance and potential impact on the organization. After these decisions are made, strategies must be developed to enable the organization to achieve its goals.

3 **Action and Communication** Strategies are implemented as new organizational policies and/or projects. Messages are then constructed to reach target publics.

4 **Evaluation** Once a public relations campaign is developed and implemented, it should be followed by an evaluation of its effectiveness in meeting the criteria that were set. The results of the evaluation are used both to assess the effectiveness of the effort and to plan future action.

These four steps are essential to any effective public relations campaign. They are not, however, four independent functions. Each step overlaps the others; if any one of them is neglected, the entire process will be affected. The next four chapters discuss each of these steps in detail. To help you keep in mind the interdependence of the steps, an integrating case study will open each chapter. The case of Cedar Springs Community Hospital, presented in Chapter 5 and subsequent chapters, illustrates a complete public relations project as it progresses through each stage, from research through evaluation. You may find it useful to turn back and review the previous case segments as you read through the next four chapters ☐

CHAPTER FIVE

Research: Understanding Public Opinion

5

Outline

PREVIEW

Research is an essential part of the public relations process. Information gained through careful research can be used to target audiences and their characteristics, to guide planning, to pretest messages, to evaluate results, and to guide follow-up efforts.

Effective research techniques for public relations practice include both scientific, or formal, research and informal, or non-scientific, research. The use of research data to evaluate current practice and forecast future events is well accepted in most organizations today. Public relations practitioners must be able to evaluate their efforts and demonstrate effectiveness.

Good public opinion research must be sensitive enough to identify publics as definable groups rather than as unrelated masses. Public relations audits, social audits, communication audits, and environmental monitoring are effective research methods for public relations planning and evaluation □

THE NEED FOR RESEARCH IN PUBLIC RELATIONS

Research is a vital function in the process of public relations. It provides the initial information necessary to plan public relations action and perform the important role of evaluating its effectiveness. Management demands hard facts, not intuition or guesswork. Public relations practitioners, like their colleagues in every area of management, must be able to demonstrate convincingly their ability to "add value" in producing a product or service. The economic realities of modern organizations make it necessary for public relations to incorporate data-gathering techniques into every phase of the process. One specific major use of public relations research is in **issues management.** The process of issues management, which has become a major part of public relations practice, must be informed at every stage by research data. The early identification of issues that may impact a client or organization is most thoroughly accomplished through research methods designed to scan the environment for potential issues. Analysis to determine which issues have the greatest possible impact requires various research methods designed to determine both the strength of opinion about an issue and its perceived centrality to the client or organization. Likewise, the selection of potential methods and actions available to the researcher and the evaluation of action implementation can be determined through well-planned research activities.

The Cedar Springs Hospital case study that follows shows how a public relations effort can utilize research in identifying and dealing with an organizational problem.

Integrating Case Study

Cedar Springs Community Hospital

Segment 1

Problem Identification

The Cedar Springs Community Hospital, Inc., was formed by the merger of competing hospitals. Two years later, a new management team was brought in to help resolve concerns about the ability of the newly formed hospital to serve the needs of its patients. Soon after the new administrator and his seven assistants assumed their duties, they began to hear reports of low employee morale and declining quality in patient care. Much of this input came from physicians who felt that the changes since the merger had produced an environment that was more routine and less personal. Many doctors felt that their relationships with other hospital employees had been undermined by the new organization's attempts to eliminate duplication and build a more efficient structure. In general, the growing consensus among the physicians was that the quality of patient care had significantly declined since the merger.

Secondary Research

Because physicians are a significant public for any hospital, their concerns received immediate attention from management. The physicians had suggested mounting a campaign to make employees more aware of their responsibility for providing quality patient care. However, the public relations director felt that more information was needed in the form of **secondary research** (research already done by someone else) before an effective communication campaign could be planned. He began to look into the background of the merger and the relationships between hospital employees and the medical staff.

A careful review of hospital records and local newspaper files, plus conversations with several longtime employees, revealed the complexity of the situation. Not only had the hospitals formerly been competitors, but they had also originally been founded by two very different religious groups and thus had developed two distinct constituencies. Although the religious affiliations of both hospitals had been discontinued long before the merger, an atmosphere of rivalry remained. This rivalry had been most obvious when the hospitals had attempted to outdo one another in terms of benefits for physicians.

Primary Research

One important public, physicians, clearly believed the quality of patient care was not acceptable. However, employees' and patients' views were not as easily defined. The public relations department devised a **primary research** plan (original research) to measure the opinions of each group. A random sample of hospital employees was asked to fill out a questionnaire about various aspects of patient care. Simultaneously, a telephone survey was conducted among recently released patients to gauge their opinions on the same issues. The results were surprising.

On a scale ranging from 1 (poor) to 10 (excellent), employees rated the hospital's performance a disappointing 6.6 overall. However, the survey of former patients produced an overall rating of 8.5. Other questions related to the quality of patient care also received significantly lower marks from the employees than from the patients.

Informal Research

To understand the reasons for the low ratings given by employees, a focus group was assembled to respond to the survey findings. This 10-member focus group was composed of six representatives from nursing services and two each from ancillary support and business services. They were interviewed as a group concerning their responses to the questionnaire. The interview revealed that while employees believed that the hospital in general delivered mediocre patient care, they felt that the care in their specific areas was significantly better than in the rest of the hospital and that they, personally, were slightly above average within their departments. These employees also indicated that their co-workers sensed something was wrong in the organization but were not sure what. This led to feelings of individual helplessness and produced a high level of stress and frustration.

In the Cedar Springs case, what originally seemed like a rather straightforward employee communication problem was identified as a complex situation involving three important publics: physicians, employees, and patients. Research showed the physicians' concerns to be overblown. Had the Cedar Springs management acted on the physicians' original recommendation without doing further research, the situation would have just gotten worse, increasing employee frustration and stress.

As you read about the different types of research methods public relations practitioners use, refer to this segment and notice how several of the techniques were applied. A quick comparison of the Cedar Springs case with the first step in figure 5.1 will reveal that each of the basic elements of research is present. The surprising nature of the findings in this case illustrates the need for public relations research.

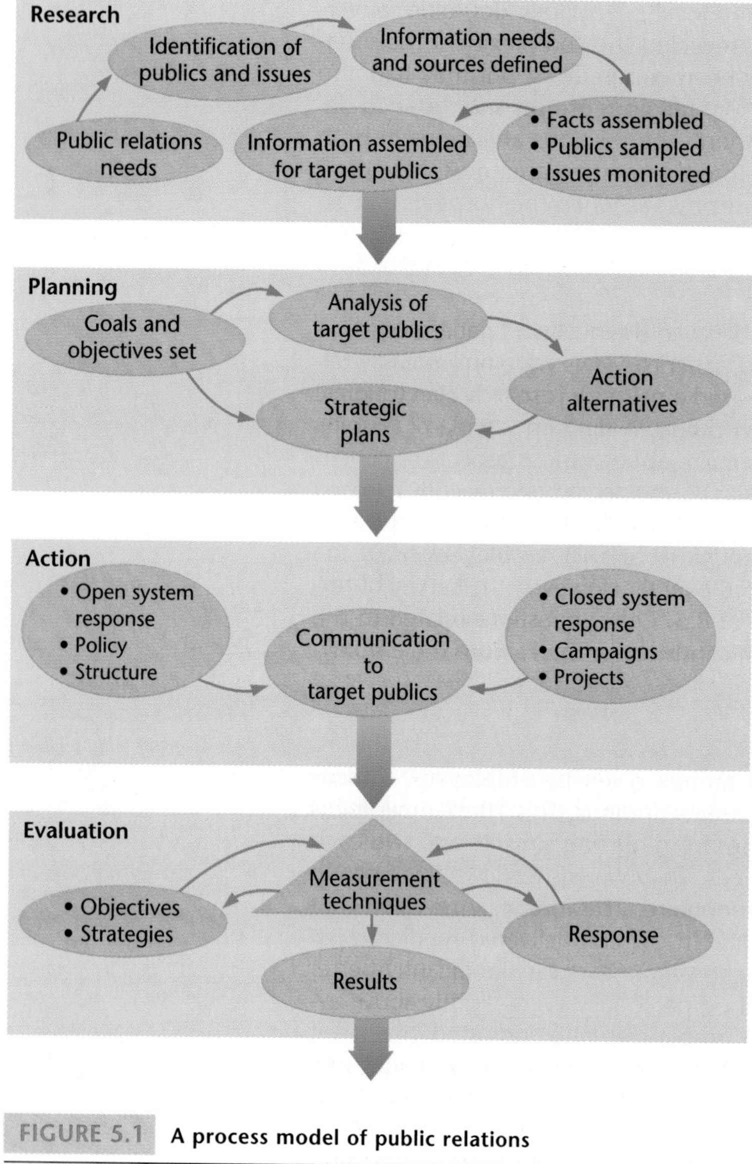

FIGURE 5.1 **A process model of public relations**

PROVING THE WORTH OF PUBLIC RELATIONS

Because public relations professionals have traditionally been doers rather than researchers, they often assume that others see the value of their function. That assumption places public relations necks squarely on budgetary chopping blocks. Even when economic conditions are not critical, public relations may be perceived as window dressing. Media, regulatory agencies, consumer groups, and many managers doubt that public relations has a useful purpose in American business. Typically, public relations professionals respond by claiming that they contribute to better understanding between publics and organizations, but they do not present tangible evidence of this contribution. When the Cobb County, Georgia, Chamber of Commerce went to the city council with a request for $100,000 to promote tourism, they took the council members out to dinner and made an appeal based on generalities. The council agreed to provide $10,000. Although the chamber was disappointed, communication chairman Dave Kaplan was circumspect. "We'll have to spend that $10,000 on something that gives us measurable results," he said. "Then we'll come back next year and show them what we can accomplish."

Public relations practitioners must speak with authority when asked to prove their value to business and society. This authority can only come through an ability to conduct research and apply the results to public relations campaigns. Public relations professionals must maintain good media relations, produce employee publications, release financial information, and conduct community relations programs. In addition, those who succeed must also be able to measure the effects of their programs, provide sound forecasts of future needs, and account for the resources they consume. Simply counting the number of column inches of print or the number of hits on the website is not enough.

An independent public relations counselor was seeking a new client. "What can you do for me?" asked the client.

"I can get you exposure," explained the public relations person. "I can get you speaking dates and get you in the newspaper."

"I can do that," said the person (who was rapidly becoming a less likely client). "What I need is someone to help me make money."

"That's marketing," said the public relations counselor. "I do public relations."

"You do nothing if you don't contribute to my bottom line," was the response. "All my expenditures make me money or they don't get made. No sale."

Informal Research Techniques

Research means gathering information. Research can range from looking up the names of editors of weekly newspapers in Nebraska to polling those people to discover their opinions about farm export policy. Research is not always scientific or highly structured. We begin this section by considering a few **informal,** or nonscientific, **research** methods and sources that practitioners use. Informal research is a method of gaining an in-depth understanding of an audience without the rigor of more formal, scientific research methods.

Record Keeping One of the most important skills necessary to the successful practice of public relations is the ability to keep comprehensive and accurate records. Practitioners are frequently asked to produce critical information at a moment's notice for use inside and outside their organizations. Thus, when an editor or manager calls for information, the public relations practitioner must produce the needed data within a relatively short time or suffer loss of credibility. By earning a reputation as a source of valuable information, the public relations practitioner can develop a network of internal and external information contacts.

Current technology allows for the organization and storage of large amounts of information in databases. This has raised expectations about the amount of information that can be provided in a very short time frame. Public relations practitioners must be comfortable using this technology and know where to find important information, particularly from within the organization. However, the GIGO principle still applies—Garbage In, Garbage Out. Those who create these databases need to think about what information will be needed, and in what form, when the information is created and stored in the first place.

Key Contacts Frequently, individuals who are **opinion leaders** in the community, industry, or organization act as **key contacts** for the public relations practitioner. Other people who possess special knowledge or who communicate frequently with significant publics are also good sources. For a community college, for example, key contacts would be significant business, political, student, and community leaders. Although these individuals can provide valuable information, they may not represent the majority opinion. Because they are leaders or individuals with special knowledge, they must be regarded as atypical of others in their group. Their special insight may give them a greater sensitivity to an issue than most people would have. Therefore, the practitioner must be careful not to overreact to feedback from these sources or plan major responses based solely on such information. Key contacts are best used to provide early warning about issues that may become significant.

Special Committees To help obtain necessary information, many public relations practitioners organize special committees. Internal and external committees of key communicators, decision makers, and opinion leaders can help identify issues before they become problems and suggest alternative courses of action. These advisory groups

Researchers observe a focus group. It is also being videotaped for future reference.

can be formed for a specified length of time, such as the duration of a campaign, or can be permanent boards that replace members periodically.

Focus Groups The most widely used technique for informal research is the focus group. As we saw in the Cedar Springs case, a focus group is a small number of people who share some demographic characteristic. Group members are interviewed, using open-ended questions to encourage interaction and probe the nature of their beliefs. A **focus group** is generally assembled only once, and the participants' responses are recorded on videotape or observed from behind a one-way mirror. This enables researchers to consider not only what is said, but also gestures, facial expressions, and other forms of nonverbal communication that may reveal depth of meaning. Although ethical and legal considerations require researchers to inform focus groups that they are being recorded or observed, experience shows that participants are seldom reluctant to discuss their feelings. Frequently, people selected for focus groups are glad someone is willing to listen to them. Sometimes the process of asking can be just as valuable as the information gained because the organization is perceived as being responsive to its publics.

Focus groups may be used as the only primary research tool. However, since you can't generalize the information to the larger group from which the focus group is drawn, it may not provide enough reliable information. Often, though, focus groups are used prior to survey research to help the researcher have enough information to ask appropriate questions in the survey questionnaire.

For example, Mountain Bell used several focus groups of women ages 18 to 35 before launching its "Let's Be Friends" campaign. Three 30-second commercials had been produced. Before they were aired they were shown to several focus groups. Two of the commercials were seen to be quite effective, but one was discarded even though the company had already spent thousands of dollars producing the spot. The campaign became one of the longest-running campaigns at Mountain Bell and later was picked up by other former AT&T companies.

In another example, Larissa A. Grunig reported on the use of focus groups to help plan a program for a county mental health department to reduce the stigma existing in the community regarding chronic mental illness. In addition to focus groups, a larger sample-size telephone survey of county residents was conducted. According to the departmental administrator, however, results of the phone survey provided fewer and more shallow responses for designing the subsequent communication campaign. Focus groups allowed researchers to discuss why residents felt the way they did while the survey did not.[1]

Thus, focus groups can also be used after a survey to probe some of the issues in more depth. For instance, prior to a campaign to increase student use of off-campus sites for taking classes, a university surveyed the students taking off-campus classes. One demographic that stood out was that 75 percent of all students taking classes off campus were female, compared with the roughly 52 percent female students overall at the university. To find out "why," several focus groups of female students were asked to talk about why they chose to take the off-campus classes. With few dissenting voices the females felt that the off-campus sites were safer than the main campus at night, so they were more willing to take a class off campus at night than on campus.

Casual Monitoring Many practitioners find it helpful to systematically screen material that regularly comes through their offices. Monitoring news reports in both print and broadcast media should be done to allow consideration of the quality and quantity of coverage. The Internet must also be monitored closely. The ease and speed with which any kind of information can spread, including rumors and untruths, means that constant attention should be paid to what is being said about the organization and its industry. This includes monitoring chatrooms, newsgroups, and activist organizations' websites.

Carefully tracking incoming mail, telephone calls, and sales reports can also provide valuable information. Like all information collected through informal research methods, however, these techniques have built-in biases because the data are not collected from representative samples of the target publics.

The Internet, Library, and Data Bank Sources The Internet has revolutionized how people search for information. Some kinds of data must still be sought in books or in proprietary databases that are only available in public or company libraries, but large amounts of information are easily available via the Internet. Most companies now maintain a website that provides information about their business. State and city governments, as well as the federal government, maintain exhaustive databases. The same is true of governments of many other countries. The use of a powerful search engine or directory such as Yahoo! can help locate information when the exact address is not known. Some data collections are especially helpful to know about and bookmark, however. For example, the Federal Reserve Bank of St. Louis has a very comprehensive collection of economic data for the United States (http://www.stls.frb.org/research/index.html). Or, the EDGAR database of documents filed with the SEC can provide background information on publicly owned businesses (http://www.sec.gov/edgar.html).

Public and private libraries are other sources of data that would be impossible for the practitioner to collect personally. Reference librarians are helpful in finding information, and many libraries now subscribe to computerized data retrieval networks that can obtain information from anywhere in the world, including data that are not available for free on the Internet. Census data and other types of public information are available at libraries that are designated as government depositories if you prefer researching hard copies instead of using a computer. In addition, a number of independent research organizations, such as the Survey Research Center at the University of Michigan, publish information that may be valuable to the public relations practitioner.

Media guides, trade and professional journals, and other reference books may prove useful in a public relations practitioner's personal library. Many valuable guides that are too large and expensive for personal libraries can be accessed at a public library. Further sources that should be noted and can be valuable in researching a future employer or competing organization include:

America's Corporate Families, The Billion Dollar Directory
Dun and Bradstreet Million Dollar Directory
Dun and Bradstreet Middle Market Directory
Hoover's Handbook of World Business
Moody's International Manual
D & B Principal International Businesses
Standard and Poors' Register of Corporations, Directors, and Executives
Thomas' Register of American Manufacturers
Fortune Magazine's "Directory of Largest Corporations" (also available online).
Fortune Magazine's "Annual Directory Issues"
Black Enterprise Magazine's "The Top 100"

Formal, Scientific Research Techniques

The growing importance of **formal,** or scientific, **research** in public relations has prompted several studies in recent years that attempt to assess preferred research techniques among professionals. In one such study, Walter K. Lindenmann sampled 253 practitioners, among them public relations executives from Fortune 500 companies, public relations agencies, nonprofit organizations, and academics. A summary of his findings is listed in table 5.1.[2]

As you read the next section, keep in mind that secondary sources like those mentioned in the table should be exhausted before a primary research effort is planned. Researchers should review the information available to make certain the questions to be asked have not already been answered by others.

TABLE 5.1 Research Techniques Respondents Claimed They Used Most Frequently

Literature searches/information retrieval	Sophisticated techniques (conjoint/factor analysis)
Publicity tracking	Psychographic analysis
Telephone/mail surveys with simple cross-tabs	Mall intercept/shopping center studies
Focus groups	Content analysis studies
PR/communications audits	Experimental designs
Secondary analysis studies	Unobtrusive measures (role-playing, observation participation)
Consumer inquiry analysis	Model building
Depth interviews with opinion leaders	
Readership/readability study	
Pre- and posttests (before and after polls)	

Memphis Image Survey Summary

Mini•Case 5.1

The Memphis PRSA research committee appointed to gather information concerning perceptions of Memphians to be used in developing its public relations plan presents this summary of its findings.

A mail survey was developed and implemented by committee members in May and June centering on several key topics including education, entertainment, race, health care, government, and other quality-of-life issues. A random sample of 1,900 was selected from the Shelby County phone directory. About 227 of the questionnaires were returned because of incorrect mailing addresses, but 305 usable questionnaires were completed and returned in the one-shot mail survey. The respondents were more likely to be white and more likely to not live in one of the more traditionally economically depressed areas of Memphis than is representative of the entire Shelby County area.

Key results include the following:

Overall: Almost 75 percent of those surveyed were proud to live in Memphis. The common wisdom in Memphis is that Memphians have an inferiority complex so this number was surprising. Also, about 92 percent surveyed like their neighborhoods and about 80 percent feel safe where they live. However, the respondents not liking the neighborhood where they lived also were the ones most likely not to be proud to live in Memphis. One thought by the committee was that perhaps the public relations plan should address strengthening and taking pride in individual neighborhoods rather than trying to promote Memphis as a whole.

More than half of the respondents do not feel safe downtown. This was not significantly different whether you lived in the suburbs or in midtown.

Riverfront development was thought by an overwhelming 85 percent to be a good means of attracting tourists and potential residents.

Racial Issues: Only about 30 percent of those surveyed felt that racial groups work well together in Memphis. However, 57 percent of African American population felt they worked well together compared to 27 percent for whites, indicating it was much more of an issue with the white community.

Arts, Health Care: About 90 percent felt that cultural arts make a city stronger and more attractive to newcomers. However, almost half didn't think there was enough variety in the cultural arts in Memphis and Shelby County. More than 80 percent think that the quality of health care in Memphis is good. Both are selling points and should be emphasized in selling Memphis.

Traffic: While 75 percent of the respondents felt that traffic in Memphis was much less congested than other large cities, 67 percent did not think it was as safe to drive here as other major cities.

Government: Only 23 percent of those responding felt city government was run efficiently compared to about half who think county government is efficient (still low). About 75 percent didn't trust elected officials, either city or county. So, while the city has a worse problem, it is clearly an issue that must be addressed with both levels.

Education: There was another split between city and county with city schools getting worse marks than county schools. However, neither was great. About 90 percent felt city schools were not excellent compared to about half answering the same for the county schools. This is a major issue that must be addressed if Memphis is to attract quality business and industry.

Questions

1. Given this data, what would you emphasize in the public relations campaign?
2. Was the sample adequate to determine citizens' perceptions of Memphis?
3. How might the return rate affect the results?
4. What would you do differently if you had been in charge of the survey?

Source: Dan Lattimore, Chair, Memphis Chapter of PRSA, Research Committee, October 2001.

Content Analysis **Content analysis** is a research method that allows the researcher to systematically code and thereby quantify the verbal content of written or transcribed messages. This technique provides a method of systematic observation, such as the analysis of news clippings. The content of chatrooms or newsgroups also can be analyzed for quantity and quality of coverage. Many organizations analyze the contents of the annual reports and other publications of their competitors to discover strategic plans.

Survey Research The practice of public relations employs all types of research processes, but the survey method is by far the most common. Cedar Springs Hospital used **survey research** to answer some critical questions. Laboratory and field experiments, and various types of simulations, can have a place (like pretesting a message) in a public relations research effort. However, surveys are the most effective way to assess the characteristics of publics in a form that allows the data to be used in planning and evaluating public relations efforts. Surveys should provide a means of separating publics rather than lumping them all together into one amorphous mass.

The term *survey,* as it is applied in public relations research, refers to careful, detailed sample examinations of the knowledge, perception, attitudes, and opinions of members of various publics. The general purpose of a survey is to obtain a better understanding of the reactions and preferences of a specific public or publics. For public relations efforts, we divide survey data into two types: demographic and opinion. Demographic data are those characteristics (age, sex, occupation, etc.) of the people responding to the survey that help a practitioner classify them into one or more publics. Opinion data are responses to those questions a practitioner raises concerning the attitudes and perceptions of certain publics about critical issues. See mini-case 5.1.

Experimental Research **Experimental research** is generally divided into two categories: laboratory and field experiments. Laboratory experiments take place in carefully controlled environments designed to minimize outside effects. Field experiments take place in real-world settings. The trade-off between field and laboratory experiments is essentially one of authenticity versus purity.

In a field experiment, the researcher sacrifices a great deal of control over the setting to obtain reactions in a real environment. In a laboratory setting, however, the researcher can control many outside stimuli that might contaminate the results of the study. For example, a public relations practitioner might decide to pretest a particular message by inviting people into a room to view the message in several forms and then measuring their reactions. A church foundation attempting to raise funds for a chaplain in a local cancer hospital used this method to test the graphics and photographs in its brochure to avoid negative effects before publication. When the U.S. government embarked on its first funded media campaign to reduce "risky" behaviors among young adolescents, it pretested the potential effectiveness of 30 different public service announcements (PSAs) by screening them for young people. In doing so, they found that some of the PSAs actually had the opposite effect than was intended.[3]

The laboratory setting ensured that the subjects' responses were based on the message being studied and not on other stimuli that might be in a normal environment. To test the effects of a message in a more authentic setting, a field experiment such as a test-market study could be arranged, using a specific group of young people in their normal environment.

Very little public relations research is done in a controlled, laboratory setting. Other than survey research, field experiments are the second most used scientific research method along with content analysis. Before the U.S. Department of Energy launched a major energy-saving campaign, it field-tested the program over a three-month winter period in six cities with one city as a control group (a city not given any of the campaign information like the other five cities). Each of the six cities had been surveyed with a random sample of residents prior to the campaign for awareness and use of energy-saving devices and techniques. Each was then surveyed after the three-month campaign. A small percentage increase in awareness and use occurred in the control city that was not subjected to the campaign. But a significant increase occurred in the other five cities. The difference between the control city's awareness and usage scores, then, was attributed to the public relations campaign efforts.[4]

Collecting Formal Research Data

We have described several methods of research. Next we look at ways to actually collect information.

Descriptive and Inferential Methods Formal research information can be obtained in a variety of ways that may be classified as either descriptive or inferential. **Descriptive data** are used to describe something, such as a particular group of people (a public). If the public relations practitioner in an organization asks the personnel department to prepare a demographic profile of its employees (average age, sex breakdown, years of education, experience level, etc.), he or she is requesting descriptive data. Such studies use averages, percentages, actual numbers, or other descriptive statistics to summarize the characteristics of a group or public.

Inferential data do more than describe a particular public. Inferential data describe (infer) the characteristics of people not included in the specific group from which the information was obtained. Through sampling, which we discuss later in this section, it is possible to select a relatively small number who represent a larger population. Using inferential statistics, a public relations practitioner can infer the characteristics of a very large public, such as a consumer group, from a relatively small but representative sample of that population.

Methods for Obtaining Information Whether research is classified as descriptive or inferential, survey or experimental, and regardless of the sampling technique employed, the three basic means for collecting public relations research data are **observations, interviews,** and **questionnaires.**

Observational techniques are easily misused in public relations research because of the informal nature of many observations used in **qualitative research** about publics. The personal observations of a practitioner are severely limited by his or her own perceptions, experiences, and sensitivity. These problems can lead to decisions based more on gut feeling than on reliable information. Personal observations are made more reliable by using structural techniques, because observers are trained within established rules to systematically observe and record data, but this is normally an expensive and complex process.

Interviews can be a successful way to get information from a public. Skilled interviewers can elicit information that individuals might not otherwise volunteer. Interviews may take place in person as well as over the telephone, and they are generally classified as structured or unstructured. Structured interviews use a schedule of questions with specific response choices ranging from yes/no to multiple choice. Unstructured interviews allow subjects to respond to open-ended questions however they wish. Although interviews are frequently employed, they have disadvantages. For example, the personality, dress, speech patterns or accents, and nonverbal cues of the interviewer may bias the response. To minimize such problems, it is necessary to use expertly trained interviewers, which are often costly.

Interviewers can use the open-ended personal interviews just described, or they may use a structured questionnaire. Personal interviews can be much more in-depth than a mail or phone interview. The phone interview must be short—usually 5 to 10 minutes in length—while the mail or web questionnaire should take no longer than 10 minutes to complete.

Questionnaires must be designed properly to gather data that is unbiased. That means questions must be simple and straightforward without being "loaded." Often

Researcher inputs data into computer.

questionnaires are designed using language that has emotionally charged words to influence the respondent in a certain way. Questions also must have only one answer per question.

Mail and web questionnaires are the most common form of data collection because they are stable in presentation and inexpensive to use. Once a questionnaire is printed or posted to a website, each respondent is asked the same questions in exactly the same way. Questionnaires are generally designed to measure one or more of the following: knowledge, attitudes, opinions, and demographic characteristics of the sample. But they may also measure intensity of those attitudes or opinions.

The decision about whether to use a mail or web questionnaire or a phone or personal interview to gather data for public relations research must take into account the study's budget, purpose, subjects, and a variety of other considerations. Questionnaires can be returned by mail or the Web and may be administered to either individuals or specific groups. They provide anonymity and present a uniform stimulus to all participants. However, the response rate may be low, and those who do respond may not be representative of the larger population. Web questionnaires have become quite popular to administer to groups with specific web access. However, the response rate is often similar to a mail questionnaire (low). On the other hand, personal or phone interviews are more flexible, get a higher percentage of responses in some situations, and can be used with relatively uneducated publics. They are also considerably more expensive to administer.

Sampling Methods A **sample** is a subset of a population or public. Public relations researchers use samples because in most instances, it is impractical to collect information from every person in the target public. There are numerous sampling techniques, but the best methods rely on the theory of probability to provide a miniature version of the target public. The theory of probability is the basis of all inferential statistics. The following sampling methods rely on the theory of probability to ensure that a sample is representative of the public from which it is drawn.

Simple random sampling is a technique that allows each member of a public an equal chance of being selected. If the sample is large enough and is selected totally at random, it will accurately reflect the characteristics of its public. For example, the Nielsen ratings use from 1,200 to 1,600 in a random sample to determine what households across the country are viewing each night.

Probably the most common example of simple random sampling is drawing a name from a hat. Assuming the names of all of the people in the target population are in the hat, and the slips of paper are mixed up adequately, each slip has an equal chance of being selected at the time of the drawing.

Systematic sampling uses a list, like a telephone directory or mailing list, to select a sample at random. Generally, a table of random numbers is used to find a starting point on the list and a selection interval. For example, a researcher might randomly pick the number 293006 from a table of random numbers. Using the first three digits, the researcher could start on page 293 of the telephone directory; then, using the last three digits, he or she could select every sixth name for the sample. This method is more practical than simple random sampling in most public relations research. However, finding complete lists may be difficult for some publics. Telephone books, for instance, will not include people who have unlisted numbers or who rely strictly on cell phones.

There are other less representative sampling techniques, but the pure random sampling is best to use when possible. With random sampling a smaller sample will give more significant results than determining your sample in any other way.

MEASURING PUBLIC OPINION

Most organizational goals and objectives dealing with public relations depend to some extent on the concept of **public opinion.** Therefore, often public relations research is used to sample public opinion. It is important to understand at the outset that an organization does not have a single indistinguishable public. The public relations practitioner who relies on so-called public opinion polls to provide insight into characteristics or opinions of his or her potential audience may be operating with erroneous data. Most polls of this type are not very useful from a public relations point of view, because they actually measure **mass opinion** rather than public opinion. Before using a survey, the practitioner should be aware of the difference between measuring mass opinion and measuring public opinion.

Mass Opinion

Mass opinion represents an average taken from a group with many different opinions. However, averages tend to blur the strength of some attitudes. When substantially different opinions are averaged together, the result may be very different from the original opinions stated. For example, if we conduct a poll asking people about the image of a particular organization, we might find that 60 percent of our sample gives it very high marks while 40 percent feel very negative. Looking at the average of these responses, we might deduce that the organization in question has a moderately positive image; however, this would hide the substantial amount of negative feelings that exist.

Our hypothetical survey has actually uncovered two publics—one that has a very positive image of the organization and another that has a very negative image. In fact, no one in our sample holds the moderately positive view the average implies. To respond properly, we should construct communication strategies for two groups of people with very strong but opposite opinions. Public relations must be concerned with the strength as well as the direction of public attitudes.

Many mass opinion polls are useful for little more than predicting political elections. They do not shed much light on the complexities of public opinion that an effective public relations program must address. However, if the results of the mass opinion poll are analyzed by different demographic characteristics of those polled, the result is more nearly a public opinion poll.

Public Opinion

Public opinion polls involve carefully targeted populations. The public relations professional must break the audience down into meaningful subgroups and design specific communication strategies for each segment. Public opinion sampling is not useful unless it reflects accurately the feelings of each significant audience group and provides some insight into why these opinions are held. For example, a political opinion poll that found that middle-class, white voters felt public school education was the key issue in the campaign because the school funding had been cut every year for the past 10 years might give the candidate enough information to develop more commercials geared to this issue. However, if he or she had just found that this group favored one candidate over another, it would not have provided the information needed.

Identifying Publics

John Dewey, in his 1927 book, *The Public and Its Problems,* defines a public as a group of people who

1. Face a similar indeterminate situation.
2. Recognize what is indeterminate in that situation.
3. Organize to do something about the problem.[5]

A public, then, is a group of people who share a common problem or goal and recognize their common interest. In the remainder of this chapter, we discuss specific methods for measuring public opinion and applying it effectively in public relations work. James Grunig proposed and tested three categories for the identification of publics based on Dewey's definition:

- **Latent public**—A group faces an indeterminate situation but does not recognize it as a problem.
- **Aware public**—The group recognizes a problem, that is, what is missing in the situation, and becomes aware.
- **Active public**—The group organizes to discuss and do something about the problem.[6]

Such categories group together people who are likely to behave in similar ways. This makes it possible for public relations practitioners to communicate with each group regarding its needs and concerns rather than attempting to communicate with a mythical "average" public. Researching public opinion in appropriate categories can help direct the public relations process. For example, it may be possible to classify the primary audience for a public relations campaign in one of the three categories listed above and develop specific messages for them. In the Cedar Springs case, physicians were an active public. However, if management had not taken care to determine the view of a latent public, the patients, costly errors could have been made.

Environmental Monitoring

Results of a survey by the Foundation for Public Relations Research and Education revealed that **environmental monitoring** is the fastest-growing category of public relations research.[7] Organizations today recognize themselves as dynamic, open systems that must react to changes in the environment, so keeping track of those changes is important.

Public relations practitioners can use formal systems for observing trends and changes in public opinion and other areas of the environment to guide many phases of organizational planning, including public relations. Issues management, discussed earlier, is one application of environmental monitoring. Another technique is scanning.

Environmental scanning is the monitoring, evaluating, and disseminating of information to key decision makers within an organization. It is an important tool for public relations because it can provide the initial link in the chain of perceptions and actions that permit an organization to adapt to its environment.

The advances in computer technology, particularly through the Internet, have made continuous scanning both more feasible and necessary. A recent study of the impact of Internet newsgroups on Intel's inability to manage the damage to its public image from a flawed Pentium chip demonstrates how quickly latent publics can become active.

The proliferation of newsgroups on the Internet has greatly increased the ability of single-issue publics to form. In the Intel case more than 130,000 people visited a newsgroup website in a matter of weeks, turning an obscure problem with a chip into a highly recognized problem in the minds of consumers. With the use of this technology rapidly expanding around the world, organizations need to have a regular presence in cyberspace to monitor all appearances of their corporate identity online.

The continuous scanning model supports the strategic planning effort of organizations. For example, the American Council of Life Insurance developed a Trend Analysis Program (TAP). TAP "seeks to identify the direction of major social and economic trends so that companies may plan for the years ahead with greater confidence."[8] The program operates as a cooperative effort, with over 100 life insurance executives monitoring the specialty press and other publications where emerging social and economic trends might first appear. Reports are issued whenever the data in a particular area are sufficient. For example, one report issued by TAP provided an in-depth survey of possible changes in American culture for the coming years.

SPECIAL PUBLIC RELATIONS RESEARCH TECHNIQUES

Special research techniques for public relations practitioners include the public relations audit, communication audit, and social audit.

The Public Relations Audit

The most frequently used mixed type of public relations research is the **audit.** The **public relations audit** is essentially a broad-scale study that examines the internal and external public relations of an organization. Many of the research techniques we have already discussed are used in public relations audits. Public relations audits provide information for planning future public relations efforts. Carl Byoir and Associates, one of the pioneers of public relations auditing, describes it as follows: "The Public Relations Audit, as the name implies, involves a comprehensive study of the public relations position of an organization: how it stands in the opinion of its various publics."[9] We can identify four general categories of audits in relation to organizations and their publics.

Relevant Publics An organization prepares a list of relevant publics. A list of the organization's relevant publics is made, describing each according to its function—stockholders, employees, customers, suppliers, and the like. Also included are publics that have no direct functional relationship but are nevertheless in a position to affect the organization, for example, consumer, environmental, community, and other social action groups. The procedure is basically one of audience identification to aid in planning public relations messages.

The Organization's Standing with Publics Each public's view of the organization is determined through various research methods, most commonly opinion studies and content analysis of newspapers, magazines, and other print media. Both of these research methods are discussed earlier in this chapter.

Issues of Concern to Publics Environmental monitoring techniques such as those already mentioned are used to construct an issues agenda for each of the organization's relevant publics. These data identify publics according to issues of interest and their stands on those issues. The findings are then compared with the organization's own policies. This is a vital step in planning public relations campaigns for various audiences.

Power of Publics Publics are rated according to the amount of economic and political (and therefore regulatory) influence they have. Interest groups and other activist organizations are evaluated according to the size of their membership, size of their constituency, budget size and source of income, staff size, and number of qualified specialists (lobbyists, attorneys, public relations professionals, etc.).

Public relations audits are regular components of many public relations programs. They provide input data for planning future public relations programs and help evaluate the effectiveness of previous efforts. Several public relations counseling firms offer audit services to their clients. Joyce F. Jones of the Ruder Finn Rotman Agency describes the audit process in four steps:[10]

1. *Finding Out What "We" Think.* Interviews with key management at the top and middle strata of an organization to determine company strengths and weaknesses, relevant publics, issues and topics to be explored.
2. *Finding Out What "They" Think.* Researching key publics to determine how closely their views match those of company management.
3. *Evaluating the Disparity Between the Two.* A public relations balance sheet of assets, liabilities, strengths, weaknesses, etc., is prepared based on an analysis of the differences found between steps 1 and 2.
4. *Recommending.* A comprehensive public relations program is planned to fill in the gap between steps 1 and 2 and to correct deficits of the balance sheet prepared in step 3.

Organizational Image Surveys

Attitude surveys that determine a public's perceptions of an organization help public relations managers obtain an overall view of the organization's image. Generally, such research seeks to measure: (1) familiarity of the public with the organization, its officers, products, policies, and other facets; (2) degrees of positive and negative perceptions; and (3) characteristics various publics attribute to the organization. Frequently, organizations use such surveys as planning tools to compare existing images with desired images. Once the differences are assessed, image goals can be set and strategic plans can be made to overcome the identified problems. For example, cities seeking to attract convention and tourist business periodically check their image as perceived by key groups, then use this data to evaluate their attraction techniques.

Although several organizations conduct their own image studies, many employ outside consultants or research organizations to supply them with data. Some major organizations that provide this type of data are Opinion Research Center, Inc.; Louis Harris and Associates; and Yankolovich, Skelly and White.[11]

Communication Audits

The **communication audit,** like the public relations audit, is applied in many different ways. An effective communication audit begins with a receiver-oriented, as opposed to

TABLE 5.2 Example of Second Section of Communication Audit: Assessing Specific Informational Needs and Media Preferences

Operations (NOTE: This category is just one of many possible topics that can be assessed): Operations information refers to information that is related to day-to-day operations, production, schedules, and use of resources.

How satisfied are you with the amount of information on operations that you receive?
(Please circle the number that best reflects your response.)

Very dissatisfied 1 2 3 4 5 Very satisfied

How understandable is the information on operations that you receive?
(Please circle the number that best reflects your response.)

Not at all understandable 1 2 3 4 5 Very understandable

In general, how would you prefer to receive information on operations?
(Please check your desired response.)

[ ] Through written materials
[ ] Through group meetings
[ ] Through one-on-one interactions
[ ] Verbally over the phone

The following section is designed to find out where you currently get information on operations and where you would prefer to get that information. Please check all of the boxes that apply and feel free to write in any sources of information that you currently use or ones that you would like to see used.

I currently get information on operations from:

[ ] The company newsletter
[ ] Weekly meetings
[ ] Weekly status reports
[ ] E-mail
[ ] Intranet
[ ] Supervisor updates
[ ] Other

I would prefer to get information on operations from:

[ ] The company newsletter
[ ] Weekly meetings
[ ] Weekly status reports
[ ] E-mail
[ ] Intranet
[ ] Supervisor updates
[ ] Other

Source: Dean Kazoleas and Alan Wright, "Improving Corporate and Organizational Communications, A New Look at Developing and Implementing the Communication Audit," in *Handbook of Public Relations,* ed. Robert L. Heath and Gabriel Vasquez (Thousand Oaks, CA: Sage, 2001), p. 477.

a sender-focused, model. These measures assess individual satisfaction with the amount of information employees or other publics receive on a topic relative to their needs, the understandability and usefulness of the information, and overall preferences for communication modes such as face-to-face or e-mail.

Generally, the communication audit attempts to monitor and evaluate the channels, messages, and communication climate of an organization. Sometimes audits are applied only to internal organizational communication systems; the same technique, however, can be used to evaluate external systems, too. Frequently, results of a communication audit reveal problems of distortion or lack of information See table 5.2 for a communication audit example.

Communication audits package several research methods for specific applications. The following research methods are used in appropriate combinations to audit organizational communication and investigate specific problem areas:

1. **Communication climate surveys**—These attitudinal measurements are designed to reveal how open and adequate publics perceive communication channels to be.
2. **Network analysis**—Generally done with the aid of a computer, this research method observes the frequency and importance of an interaction network,

based on the most frequent linkages. These patterns can be compared with official organizational charts and communication policies to determine disparities between theory and practice.

3. **Readership surveys**—These identify which articles or sections of publications are read most frequently. Although this method is strictly quantitative, it is an excellent way to determine the reading patterns of various publics.
4. **Content analysis**—This quantitative tool, discussed earlier, can analyze the content of all types of messages. It is frequently used to describe the amount of favorable and unfavorable news coverage an organization receives.
5. **Readability studies**—Several methods may be employed to assess how readily written messages are understood. Most of these methods are based on the number of syllables in the words and the length of the sentences used. These formulas will be discussed in more detail in chapter 8 when we discuss evaluation techniques. For now, we only note that they help determine the clarity of a written message and its appropriateness to the educational level of an audience.

Usability Research

The pervasive use of the Internet requires virtually every public relations effort to include the design of web-based materials. Because the nature of online messages is dramatically different from other visual images and printed text, they must be evaluated for usability in addition to other communication standards. A technique first applied to product and software development, usability research helps to assess both the objective and subjective responses of users to websites.

Social Audits

The concept of the **social audit** began in the early 1960s when businesses and other organizations were challenged to recognize their obligations to society. Social audits are generally attitude and opinion surveys that measure the perceptions of various publics about an organization's social responsiveness. This technique attempts to quantify the impact an organization has on its public in much the same way that a public relations audit does. However, social audits are generally confined only to issues of social responsibility.

Recent research has shown that organizations and their publics have professional, personal, and community relationships. Therefore, organizations need to be clear about the relationships they are attempting to manage with various publics. Professional relationships demand a businesslike service-oriented approach to a public, while personal relationships depend on a perception of trust. Community relationships require that an organization be seen as supportive and active in improving the social and economic interests of a public. Social auditing was common in the mid- to late 1970s. In recent years, social issues have been included in other types of research such as environmental scanning and public relations and communication audits. (See spotlight 5.1 for some of the terms used in this chapter.)

Research Terms in Lay Language

Spotlight 5.1

Many of the research terms used in this chapter may be unfamiliar to you. Although they are defined more thoroughly throughout the chapter and you may find the definitions in the glossary at the end of the book, it may be helpful to study these terms both before and after reading the chapter.

Secondary research is research from sources already produced, such as books, magazines, newspapers, published opinion polls, web articles, and other electronic records. You should read the existing research on your topic first so the name "secondary" research is perhaps misleading.

Primary research is original research. It is needed when secondary research cannot provide the answers to the questions.

Informal research is nonscientific research or information gathering. For example, it may include phone calls to the organization as well as letters, sales reports, and informal discussions with community leaders.

Formal research is scientific research. It is done to produce results that have a high degree of likelihood statistically that it will be accurate within a given range.

Focus groups focus or select from a certain characteristic(s) of your audience. From this select group, usually 8–12 people, a moderator asks open-ended questions to probe for the why or the in-depth answer to the question. Even though focus group research is considered informal research because the results from the group cannot be scientifically applied to the larger group or public it represents, this primary research tool has become one of the most popular of all research tools for the public relations practitioner.

Descriptive data are bits of information used to describe something such as a particular group of people. These data often include percentages, averages, or actual numbers to summarize the characteristics of a group or public.

Inferential data are the result of systematic sampling of a population and you can infer from the sample the characteristics of the larger group.

Sample is a subset of a population that is selected to give information from which the researcher can make inferences about the larger group. From that sample, if chosen properly, the researcher can provide a statistical degree of reliability that the sample is similar to the total population, depending on the sample size, questions asked, and type of sample.

Random sampling is a research gathering technique that selects a subset of the larger group with every member of the larger group having an equal chance of being selected. This type sampling gives you the best statistical chance of being accurate of any type sampling.

Stratified random sampling is simply random sampling within each strata or subgroup of the larger population. For instance, if you took 5 percent at random of all freshmen, then a 5 percent sample of sophomores, juniors, and seniors, you would have a different sample than a random sample of all undergraduate students. This type sample allows you to compare the different classifications (strata).

Summary

Research is an important part of any public relations effort. It supplies the initial inputs to guide strategy and message development and provides a method for predicting effectiveness and assessing results. Public relations professionals must be able to measure the effects of their work and make reasonable predictions about future success if they wish to influence managerial decisions in most organizations today.

Many public opinion surveys are not useful in public relations planning and evaluation because they tend to average responses so that the relative strengths of attitudes are disguised. Good public opinion research must be sensitive enough to segment publics according to the strengths of their opinions. Four basic categories of research in public relations are sufficiently sensitive: environmental monitoring, public relations audits, communication audits, and social audits.

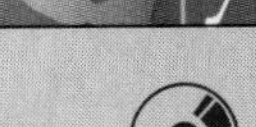

For self-testing and additional chapter resources, go to the student CD and the Online Learning Center at **www.mhhe.com/lattimore**

To learn more about public relations research watch the interview with Dr. Rick Fischer, Clip #15, on the book's CD-ROM

Case Study

University Blood Drive

Your university has been asked by the local nonprofit blood bank to prepare a public relations campaign for a universitywide blood drive next semester. The bloodmobile will be on campus for donations one week next semester. The university has asked your chapter of the Public Relations Student Society of America to do the campaign. You have been given the responsibility for conducting the research prior to the development of the campaign.

The person in charge has asked you to find out answers to questions like where would you find information on blood drives, blood banks, and blood donors? Who are your publics? How would you find out what they know about giving blood from experience, or what are their attitudes about donating blood? How would you find the most effective media to reach these publics? How would you decide what should your message be? What kinds of questions do you need to be asking in your research? Design a formal survey research plan to answer the questions, including who you would sample, how many participants you would need, and how you would administer the survey. Write the questions for the questionnaire.

Questions

1. Who are your target audiences?
2. What informal research would you use?
3. What sources would you use to find out the preliminary background information?
4. What formal, or systematic, research techniques would you need to use?
5. What kind of questions do you need to be asking?

Key Terms

Use the CD-ROM and Online Learning Center at www.mhhe.com/lattimore to further your understanding of the following terms

active public
audit
aware public
communication audit
communication climate survey
content analysis
descriptive data
environmental monitoring
environmental scanning
experimental research
focus group
formal research
inferential data
informal research
interviews
issues management
key contacts
latent public
mass opinion
observations
opinion leaders
primary research
public opinion
public relations audit

qualitative research
questionnaires
readability study
readership survey
sample
secondary research
simple random sampling
social audit
survey research
systematic samping

1. Larissa A. Grunig, "Using Focus Group Research in Public Relations," *Public Relations Review* XVI (Summer 1990), pp. 36–49.
2. Walter K. Lindenmann, "Research, Evaluation and Measurement: A National Perspective," *Public Relations Review* XVI (Summer 1990), p. 10.
3. "Avoiding the Boomerang: Testing the Relative Effectiveness of Anti-Drug Public Service Announcements before a National Campaign," *American Journal of Public Health* 92, no. 2 (February 2002), p. 238.
4. Nick Del Calzo, Del Calzo and Associates Public Relations, video interview with Dan Lattimore.
5. John Dewey, *The Public and Its Problems* (Chicago: Swallow, 1927).
6. James E. Grunig, "A New Measure of Public Opinions on Corporate Social Responsibility," *Academy of Management Journal* 22 (December 1979), pp. 740–41.
7. Otto Lerbinger, "Corporate Use of Research in Public Relations," *Public Relations Review* 3 (Winter 1977), p. 11.
8. Ibid., p. 15.
9. Ibid., p. 16.
10. Joyce F. Jones, "The Public Relations Audit: Its Purpose and Uses. R&F Papers," Number 3 (New York: Ruder Finn Rotman, Inc., 1975). Reprinted in *Public Relations Journal* 31 (July 1975), pp. 6–8.
11. Lerbinger, p. 12.

CHAPTER SIX

Strategic Planning for Public Relations Effectiveness

6

Outline

PREVIEW

Public relations effectiveness depends on planning. Understanding and developing the ability to implement an effective public relations plan is essential to progression from entry-level public relations practitioner to a top-level public relations manager. Tactical and strategic plans help public relations coordinate its efforts with those of other areas of the organization. Good planning is the best way to practice preventive rather than remedial public relations.

Strategic planning begins with a look to the future through various forecasting techniques, including examining public opinion surveys, initiating brainstorming sessions, and developing scenario construction. The planning process involves going through elements that provide a structure to the public relations program or campaign

"The strategist has to develop a management-oriented mindset, behaviors and attitudes."
—James Lukaszewski, APR, Fellow PRSA

Public relations strategic planning provides organization to the public relations process. "Strategic planning is a process of assessing what you have and where you want to go."[1] The caliber and thoroughness of thinking preceding the execution of public relations activities will determine the value of the public relations operation. Understanding how to develop a public relations plan, then, is one of the main criteria that separates entry-level positions from top management in public relations.

Planning moves public relations from a reactive activity to a **proactive** process. Public relations practitioners, like most other managers, tend to be action oriented. The constant changes that take place both inside and outside any organization produce an endless procession of public relations problems. Too often, because of the number of pressing problems, managers find themselves responding only to exceptional situations. Such situations are usually negative in that they require the practitioner to intervene after a problem has already gotten out of control.

Although putting out fires is certainly part of the public relations function, it cannot be allowed to dominate all actions. If it does, the practitioner becomes a victim of circumstances, only able to react to the situation at hand. Perhaps the most frequent complaint of public relations practitioners is that other managers ask for their services only after the problem has become unmanageable. When damage to the organization's image has already been done, the public relations manager is often directed to "fix it." This may prove to be a no-win situation both for the organization and for the practitioner who must engage in usually fruitless remedial public relations.

For a long time, public relations practitioners have been advocating preventive public relations to avoid such problems. Part of this approach involves the type of fact-finding research we have already discussed in chapter 5. If practitioners detect potential problems before they erupt into damaging situations, they can give management early warning and advice. Sometimes even early detection cannot forestall some negative impact. When advanced warning is coupled with adequate planning, however, negative effects can be minimized and public relations management can provide well-designed, positive actions rather than hastily conceived reactions. As we continue our integrating case study begun in chapter 5, notice how the pitfalls of hasty reaction were avoided.

Integrating Case Study

Cedar Springs Community Hospital

Segment 2

You may remember that the physicians at Cedar Springs Hospital (chapter 5) were calling for immediate action to correct what they saw as a potentially life-threatening situation in patient care. Reaction to the problem as it appeared at the time would have generated a campaign to make employees more aware of the need for quality patient care and emphasize their responsibility for providing the best care possible. However, before taking action, the public relations director conducted some research to help him better understand the problem. The results were surprising and showed that the first action contemplated would have only made things worse. Employees already believed that the quality of patient care in the hospital was subpar and were frustrated because they felt they personally were doing a good job. In addition, research revealed that recently released patients rated the quality of care significantly better than the employees did.

The sizable difference between the ratings of employees and patients pointed to a different problem than was originally suspected. The planning process based on this research redefined the issue from one of actual care to one of perceptions about care.

Objective: The objective that grew out of the research findings was to improve employee and physician views of overall hospital performance. Obviously, since both doctors and individual employees felt they were personally providing the best care they could and patients rated their performance high, the actual quality of care was good. However, their perception of poor performance was creating a morale problem for both doctors and employees.

Planning: Two basic strategies were devised to be implemented in a yearlong campaign. The first strategy was to continually reinforce employees' feelings of worth as members of the hospital's medical team through positive feedback from management. The second strategy was to help both physicians and employees more accurately judge the overall quality of care through increased feedback from patients.

Budget: A budget of $6,000 was developed to conduct additional surveys of recent patients and communicate the message of quality care through a variety of media. Communication channels would be selected to allow both internal and external audiences to get the message that hospital employees were a quality team. Policies were changed to allow any letters with positive comments from patients to be routed first to the departments involved before being filed.

IMPORTANCE OF PLANNING

In the Cedar Springs case, research and careful planning prevented the loss of time and employee confidence that would have resulted from reacting too quickly to the first symptoms of the problem. Only through continuous advance planning can public relations practitioners avoid having to react after the damage has been done. Even though many public relations managers feel they have no time to plan, the more time they spend planning based on adequate research, the less time they will need to spend putting out fires.

David M. Dozier summarized the significance of planning:

> The process of setting public relations goals and objectives in measurable form serves two purposes. First, the prudent and strategic selection of public relations goals and objectives linked to organizational survival and growth serves to justify the public relations program as a viable management activity. . . . Second, the specification of public relations goals and objectives in measurable form makes public relations accountable and makes program success or failure concrete and objective.[2]

Planning permits the development of integrated public relations efforts that support an organization's goals in a positive rather than a defensive manner. Planning provides the opportunity to involve management from other areas of the organization and to ensure their cooperation and support. When a manager from another department has input into the public relations plan, he or she is much more likely to support that effort.

Public relations efforts often fail because of communication breakdowns between practitioners and other managers within an organization. The cause of these breakdowns is frequently an imperfect alignment between the public relations planning process and planning done elsewhere in the organization. Misunderstandings can usually be prevented if public relations practitioners analyze the organizational management as carefully as they analyze any other audience.

Public relations departments must prepare messages that communicate their needs and potential contributions to other segments of the organization. Therefore, when planning, they must learn the terms and methods common to organizational management.

FUNDAMENTALS OF PUBLIC RELATIONS PLANNING

Planning is generally classified into two broad categories: strategic and tactical. **Strategic plans** are long-range plans, usually made at the upper levels of management, and they involve decisions concerning major goals of an organization, and policies for their implementation. Environmental scanning (chapter 5) has become a primary tool to identify and to prioritize the strategic issues upon which an organization's plans are ultimately founded.[3]

Tactical plans develop specific decisions about what will be done at every level of the organization to accomplish the strategic plans. Strategic planners typically deal with future events and must therefore rely on relatively uncertain data. The use of forecasting techniques to predict what effects economic and technical changes will have on an organization in the next five years is an example of strategic planning. Tactical planners, on the other hand, are more concerned with the day-to-day operation of an organization and its immediate future.

Public relations plans are both strategic and tactical. Decisions concerning the long-range future of an organization often take public relations into consideration. However, public relations staff members must develop tactical plans to implement and support strategic plans.

To begin the planning process, you will need to look to the future, or forecast. Planning always involves the future. Predicting barriers that may exist in the future is a much more difficult job than evaluating the existing situation, yet such predictions are necessary to determine the effects of future conditions on the programs being planned. The goal of attempting to look into the future is to better understand the environment in which your publics will be forming their opinions. Such efforts are designed to help identify and categorize stakeholder groups so that their attitudes, opinions, and behaviors can be assessed and predicted with some accuracy. In addition, these efforts can help to identify target audiences, understand audience lifestyles, and identify appeals that may be successful. Some of the techniques commonly used for such analyses are discussed next. They range from the complex and quantitative to the intuitive, but each has potential to contribute to the development of a successful plan.

Public opinion surveys forecast reaction to initiative or actions contemplated by politicians, government officials, and managers. Presidents, for example, often use public opinion surveys to determine whether or not to support a legislative issue, a nominee for a cabinet position, or a military action; President Bush looked closely at public opinion surveys in making decisions on the "War on Terrorism." Predictions should also be made concerning the effects of planned public relations activities on various publics and the corresponding effects public reaction will have on the programs being planned.

Often these judgments must be made by qualitative rather than quantitative means. Juries of executive opinion, sales force composites, and customer expectations are frequently employed.

Brainstorming is a group discussion technique used to generate large numbers of creative alternatives or new ideas. It has been used for some time by advertising agencies, public relations firms, and others who need to generate creative ideas. For example, often brainstorming is used to develop an appropriate theme for a public relations campaign. The basic rule of brainstorming is that no one is permitted to interject negative feedback or criticism into the discussion. As the group generates ideas, all are recorded to be critiqued later. No remark is considered too absurd or too simple, because it could produce the spark necessary for a truly creative idea. Brainstorming can be effective with a group that is comfortable functioning in a freewheeling atmosphere.

Scenario construction has been used by "think tanks," such as the Rand Corporation, to create very long range forecasts. A logical, hypothetical description of future events (scenario) is constructed to explore the dynamics of various alternatives. For example, if a large auto company wanted to choose one of several manufacturing plants to close, a scenario could be constructed for each case to detail possible effects on the environment, economic future of the community, availability of replacement jobs, and other positive and negative results.

With these, or other, approaches to examining the issues for the future of your organization the planning process with its various elements can begin.

ELEMENTS OF PLANNING

Strategic plans and tactical plans combined produce either **standing** or **single-use plans.** This hierarchy of plans is illustrated in figure 6.1. **Goals** refer to the basic direction in which an organization is heading. The purpose, mission, objectives, and strategies of an organization are all component parts of its goals. These terms are frequently used interchangeably; however, they may also be used in various combinations to indicate sublevels of planning. Since there are no universally accepted definitions for these terms, most organizations adopt their own very specific applications.[4]

In the next section, we discuss the elements that are characteristic of planning, especially related to public relations campaigns. Understanding this process, along with the specifics of planning, is important to the success of the public relations effort of an organization. However, it should be noted that this is not a step-by-step or linear process. Some of the planning elements must occur simultaneously, some are ongoing, and some may occur before others in certain situations.

Campaign Plans (Single Use)

Campaigns are a frequent output of public relations planning. Because campaigns are usually designed to accomplish unique objectives, they must be planned using nonroutine procedures. See spotlight 6.1. Some generally accepted elements for writing the campaign-planning document include the following.

1. Establishing Goals in Relation to the Mission Statement In the Cedar Springs case, patient care became the goal that unified physicians, administrators, and employees. Agreeing on a goal or a set of goals must be the first step in deciding what a public relations effort will need. Frequently, in a list of possible goals, two or more are

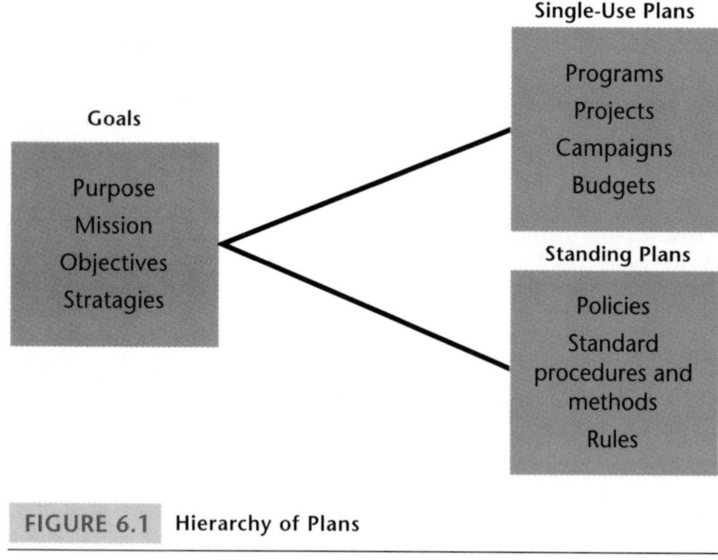

FIGURE 6.1 Hierarchy of Plans

mutually exclusive. When possible goals conflict, each must be evaluated to determine the long- and short-range effects of acceptance or rejection and is based on the organization's **mission statement.**

Resources often dictate the selection of goals. An organization may not be able (or willing) to devote the time, personnel, and capital necessary to accomplish some goals. Goals that are selected for the public relations function, however, must always relate to organizational purpose. When seeking approval for public relations goals, a manager will be more successful if he or she is able to relate them to the mission, goals, and objectives of the entire organization.

For example, Ben & Jerry's mission statement provides the basis for its public relations effort. It's a three-part statement:

Product Mission: To make, distribute, and sell the finest quality all-natural ice cream and related products in a wide variety of flavors made from Vermont products.

Economic Mission: To operate the company on a sound financial basis of profitable growth, increasing value for our shareholders, and creating career opportunities and financial rewards for our employees.

Social Mission: To operate the company in a way that actively recognizes the central role that business plays in the structure of society by initiating innovative ways to improve the quality of life of a broad community: local, national, or international.[5]

Major special events, such as this Centennial of Flight celebration at the Air & Space Museum, often require their own public relations plan. Usually, though, special events are only one strategy of a plan. This event honored the 100th anniversary of the Wright brothers' flight.

National Association of Insurance and Financial Advisers

Spotlight 6.1

Public Relations planning must be coordinated with, and supportive of, the mission and strategic plan of the organization it serves. The National Association of Insurance and Financial Advisers (NAIFA) and its communication partner BSMG Worldwide developed and implemented a multiyear communication campaign based upon the following:

GOAL—". . . to establish NAIFA as the association of choice in the financial services marketplace."

STRATEGY—"Working with our strong network of state and local associations, we wanted to energize current members and attract new ones. We wanted to position NAIFA as the only membership group offering programs across the full spectrum of financial services."

TACTICS—"NAIFA launched the positioning campaign with advertisements in five leading national trade publications and an effective direct-marketing campaign. NAIFA revved up the campaign in April, distributing a recruitment brochure to support the direct-marketing campaign and local recruitment efforts. The association then sent out a promotional CD-ROM, which NAIFA members received with the April issue of *Advisor Today*.

Since the disk's release, the positioning campaign has focused on more interactive communications.

Demonstrating its commitment to technology and on developing new benefits to help members grow their practices, NAIFA launched *eTIPS*. Distributed bimonthly by email to members who have registered their email addresses with NAIFA, *eTIPS* features sales, marketing and management advice from the top producers in the insurance and financial services industry."

Source: Jim Edwards, "The Positioning Campaign: Building on 'the Momentum,'" *Advisor Today* 96 (October 2001), p. 90.

Many of Ben & Jerry's environmental community relations efforts have been developed to implement the social mission statement particularly. These environmental community relations initiatives have contributed significantly to making the company known throughout the country as a socially responsible, environmentally friendly organization.

2. Determining the Present Situation In reality, it is impossible to separate planning from research because they occur almost simultaneously; thus, as a goal is considered, current data about the organization's environment must be collected and used to evaluate the likelihood that the goal can be reached. Information provided by the kind of fact-finding research discussed in chapter 5 is crucial at this point. Problem identification based on the available data should answer the following questions:

- Is this a relatively big or little problem?
- What are the larger areas of concern into which this problem may fit?
- Is this really a problem facing our publics?
- What background facts and issues from your client/organization research are relevant to this problem?
- If this is more than one problem, how should it be broken down?
- Does additional research need to be undertaken at this point to determine the extent of the problem?
- Is a public relations audit needed to understand the organization and its internal and external public relations opportunities?

Again, the Cedar Springs example demonstrates the importance of taking appropriate steps to get accurate information before a plan is begun. It is useless to set unrealistic goals or goals that have already been accomplished. Even after the goal has been firmly set, data about the current situation needs to be monitored. If the situation changes, it may be necessary to alter the goal or goals. Goals must be set with a good understanding of the current situation, the available resources, and what limitations must be placed on those goals.

3. Determining Threats and Opportunities to Reaching Goals After determining reasonable goals, a more careful investigation of the environment must take place to identify what will aid and what will hinder the attainment of goals. The resources of an organization (people, money, and equipment) are important aids for achieving any goal. On the other side of the coin, a deficiency of any of these elements is a barrier that must be overcome. Although money is frequently the first barrier to be considered, it is seldom severe enough to prevent the accomplishment of objectives. Many plans, like the one at Cedar Springs Hospital, can be carried out with relatively small budgets. Key questions to ask to define aids and barriers include: Do we have the *right individuals?* (rather than enough people) and Do we have *enough* money? (rather than how much money).

The structure and policies of an organization can also be either aids or barriers to reaching goals. For example, the goal of creating a sense of unity between labor and management could be severely hindered by policies that prohibit informal communication between the company and its union. Other barriers and aids are outside the organization—from government, competitors, consumer groups, and other special interest groups.

4. Researching and Selecting Your Target Audiences Based on preliminary research, the planning document should describe the primary target audiences, identify appeals and points of interest that will attract attention, define audience lifestyles, and determine the relative strength of each possible appeal. In selecting the audiences you must first identify and categorize your stakeholder groups. You may divide them into primary and secondary publics. You then may analyze each group determining which are the target audiences, or the stakeholders, you must reach if your public relations program is to be successful. Your research should also help you analyze and assess your target audiences' attitudes, opinions, and behaviors.

Audience analysis should include as thorough a description of the demographics and lifestyles of each audience as possible. It should also include identification of possible messages or other appeals that can be used to influence each audience. Once you've determined your target audiences, you can then begin to develop your objectives, strategies, and tactics to best reach those stakeholders.

Once you have identified the problems and opportunities, you must **prioritize** them. Seldom will you have the budget or the time to try to do everything at once. At this point you can develop a *problem statement* to reflect the research done to narrow the task to a manageable size. It should define the scope of the effort and recognize any special requirements of the organization, target audiences, and media. The planning document should tell how the purpose will be accomplished for the audience that has been identified. It should discuss specific tactics and alternatives, define expected outcomes, and specify communication media, activities, and channels to be used.

5. Developing a Theme for the Program or Campaign Not every public relations plan for a program or campaign has to have a theme, but often the theme has been the creative piece that has made a public relations campaign successful. An effective theme should do three things:

- Catch the essence of the plan or campaign
- Be short . . . around 3–5 words
- Be something that can endure over time

Phillips Petroleum Co. has had a long-lasting theme. It began in 1973 with the first major oil crisis when advertising to get consumers to buy more gas was not the appropriate thing to do. The company developed the theme: The Performance Company. That theme endures today. The emphasis of the company is on the many other aspects of the company beside the gasoline, for example, showing that the pipes used in much of the solar energy captured in homes and business for heat are developed with Phillips Petroleum products, or that the kidney dialysis machines use Phillips products for the filters. For three decades Phillips has used that theme to emphasize that it is a company that performs in many socially responsible ways and doesn't just sell gasoline.

6. Developing the Objectives for the Plan or Campaign Objectives should be the heart of the plan. They should focus on overcoming the priority problems or developing the key opportunities for the plan. Objectives for public relations plans should be written in infinitive form. Criteria for writing and selecting objectives include the following:

- Should be related to the overall goals of the organization
- Need to be improvement oriented
- Must be clearly defined
- Must be specific
- Should be measurable
- Need to be attainable

For example, if a community theater was relatively new to a growing town, was struggling financially because of low attendance and poor season ticket sales, and needed additional resources to produce the quality theater the community wanted, objectives for its fall public relations plan might be these:

- To increase awareness of the community theater by 25 percent within the local area
- To increase season ticket sales 10 percent
- To raise $25,000 in endowment for the theater
- To involve 25 new volunteers in working with the theater

7. Creating Strategies to Accomplish the Objectives Strategies may be the most difficult of the terms to define in the planning process. Strategies can refer to the type or emphasis of a message, the way we want to approach a task, or a variety of things. However, in this context a strategy is a way or ways you are going to accomplish your objectives.

For the community theater, some strategies to implement the first objective might include:

- Developing a media campaign to publicize the theater and its upcoming season
- Creating informational materials for the theater
- Preparing a special event, perhaps an open house with a concert from a relatively well-known music group

Volunteers examine a new theater brochure, one of the campaign's tactics.

Strategies, then, are used to define means for achieving objectives more precisely, are an intermediate step between objectives and tactics, and tend to group like tactics together.

8. Developing Tactics to Implement Strategies Tactics are the most specific, direct action that you can take in the plan. They are the most specific, concrete activity and should be related to the objectives and strategies. For the community theater, tactics for the second strategy (creating informational materials) might include these:

- To develop a brochure about the upcoming season to sell season subscriptions
- To develop a brochure to persuade residents to become volunteers at the theater
- To create posters for each play during the upcoming season
- To prepare programs for the performances
- To create a video about the theater to be used to promote the theater and its upcoming season.

9. Creating Evaluation Techniques To properly evaluate the plan, whether a campaign or a standing plan, procedures for the evaluation must be developed before implementation begins in order to have a benchmark with which to measure performance during and at the end of the program. The evaluation techniques used must evaluate each objective and should include formative as well as **summative evaluation** techniques. **Formative evaluation** (evaluation at various stages during the program) includes the monitoring necessary to make changes while the plan is still being implemented. On the other hand, summative evaluation provides the summary of what went right or wrong and why after the campaign had ended. See chapter 8 for detailed information on the evaluation process.

10. Developing a Budget Budgets are essential to any plan. Generally, they are designed to project costs through the duration of a campaign or other period of time. **Campaign** or **project budgets** are components of plans to accomplish specific public relations activities. They provide structure and discipline in terms of time and money costs. Budgeting for specific activities is a rather straightforward process. Public relations managers prepare budgets using a simple, three-step model. First, required resources such as people, time, material, and equipment must be listed. Next, the extent these resources will be used is estimated. Finally, the costs of the resources are determined. These are considered "zero-based" budgets since they are built by including all specific costs needed to accomplish the project. Other budgets may need to be developed, including functional budgets and administrative budgets, but the zero-based budget is typically the one used for campaigns.

When Pam Smith, a public relations staff member for our community theater example, set about producing a brochure to encourage community volunteers, she first had to develop a budget for the project. Table 6.1 shows her results. The left-hand column lists resources (step 1); the center column shows estimated quantities (step 2); and the right-hand column shows costs and how they are derived (step 3).

Project and campaign budgets are the building blocks for annual public relations departmental budgets and the basis for bids submitted by independent **public relations counselors.** In either case, budgets become instruments in the competition for organizational resources.

11. Working Out a Timetable A schedule of all activities for a public relations campaign should be developed. This is a process of "back-timing," or determining from what you want as a finished product how much time each step in the process will take. Various scheduling tools are available through computerized programs to provide assistance in detailing the exact time set for each of the tactics in the plan. Some organizations are small enough to use a simple calendar and denote the days needed for each activity, but whatever the means, it is essential that each individual activity or tactic be scheduled to know exactly when you need to begin in order to have it completed in time.

TABLE 6.1 Budget for Community Theater Brochure

Resources	Quantities	Costs
1. Pam's time (interview, write, integrate photos into copy, administer project)	56 hours	$1,234.00 (based on $64,000 yearly)
2. Photographer's time (freelance) (at $125 per hour)	10 hours	$1,250.00
3. Layout (graphics dept.)	8 pages	$ 500.00 (estimate, graphics)
4. Printer (outside contractor) with halftone (estimate, printer)	1,000 copies, 2 colors	$3,000.00
5. Distribution costs (mailing and handling)	Postage for 1,000 copies Mailing lists of 500 names	$ 380.00
		$6,364.00
	10% Contingency	646.00
	Total budgeted for brochures	$7,000.00

6.2 Spotlight

The Rhode Island Department of Health Campaign Plan to Encourage Breast Cancer Screening

Duration of Campaign: November to December (13 months)

Campaign Chronology

Fourth Quarter

- Press conference introduces Breast Cancer Screening Program
- Advertisements in one (1) statewide newspaper and three (3) regional newspapers
- Talk given to American Cancer Society volunteers
- Guest appearances on four (4) television programs and four (4) radio programs

First Quarter

- Advertisements in one (1) statewide newspaper and three (3) regional newspapers
- Newspaper article on mammography
- Talk given to American Cancer Society volunteers
- Guest appearances on three (3) talk-radio programs
- Mailing to all licensed MDs

Second Quarter

- Advertisements in one (1) statewide newspaper and three (3) regional newspapers
- Public service announcement distributed to all television stations
- Posters distributed to hospitals, radiologists, and hairdressers
- Pilot mail campaign to all eligible state employees

Third and Fourth Quarters

- Repeat messages as necessary
- Measure outcomes and evaluate campaign results with pre- and post-surveys
  - 60% of targeted women had heard of the program
  - 15% of women ages 40 and over received mammograms for the first time

Source: Vicki S. Freimuth, "Mass Media Strategies and Channels: A Review of the Use of Media in Breast and Cervical Cancers Screening Programs," *Wellness Perspectives* 11 (Winter 1995), p. 79.

For example, if you need to have a **video news release (VNR)** for your campaign, you will need to have the concept developed and approved, script written and approved, video shot, video edited, and the final production approved before distribution can begin. You need to schedule time for each step in the process. See spotlight 6.2 for an example of a timetable.

12. Assigning Personnel The plan must detail the human resources needed to accomplish the objectives. Thus, the plan must address which departmental personnel will be used for what activities and where the additional personnel will be found. Many times, the company's public relations agency is used for these additional personnel. Other times, freelance artists are hired, a research agency employed, or a video company contracted to provide the necessary expertise to complete the tactics required.

Although there is general agreement about the need for all the preceding steps in planning a campaign, some elements are often overlooked. A recent survey of 41 campaigns showed that 100 percent identified their target audiences, but only 63 percent specified a theme and only 62 percent documented outcomes.[6]

Management by Objectives

Once a situation has been described, aids and barriers considered, and forecasts completed, developing alternative courses of action should be relatively automatic. After listing as many alternatives as possible, the process begins, comparing alternatives in terms of costs and benefits.

The term **management by objectives (MBO),** an approach to planning that is detailed in spotlight 6.3, has become less popular in management jargon. However, the basic elements are still widely used to describe management plans. MBO is an administrative planning process characterized by setting both long- and short-range objectives and then developing plans to accomplish those goals. Frequently, the process spreads to

Public Relations by Objectives

Spotlight 6.3

Public relations often fails because managers do not understand what public relations people are saying and doing. This can be prevented if we talk in management's terms rather than trying to educate them in ours.

The Advantages of MBO

1. Communicates the way businesspeople think in terms of business problems and objectives.
2. Raises the importance of public relations in the corporate structure.
3. Presents a structure for implementing effective communications programs.
4. Helps keep the public relations practitioner on target in solving public relations problems.
5. Contributes to the public relations body of knowledge.

The Process

1. Get a fix on the business problem: Analyze the business problem using all available research techniques, then develop a clear, concise statement of what the problem is.
2. Translate the business problem into public relations objectives: This is the most difficult part of the process. The objectives should be stated in measurable terms.
3. Determine the audience(s): Identify to whom your message will be directed. There may be several audiences. Examples: print and broadcast media, company employees, customers, government officials.
4. Determine program elements: This includes exactly what vehicles will be used to effect the program. Examples: TV, news clips, news releases, institutional ads, speeches, and publicity events.
5. Determine budget: The ideal situation is to fit the budget to the need, using an objective and task approach.
6. Implement the program/campaign: Carry out the tactics of the campaign.
7. Evaluate the program: Utilize appropriate measuring instruments and techniques.

every level of an organization. Managers and their subordinates may begin the process by developing separate objectives and plans, then review each other's work and prepare a joint document as a final plan. This can occur at every level up the organization chart. Sometimes this flexible planning technique is called by other names. As we shall discuss in chapter 8, setting objectives prior to action is critical to the ability to demonstrate effectiveness in public relations efforts.

Standing Plans

Within all organizations, certain *programmable decisions* call for a standardized, consistent response. Standing plans provide routine responses to recurring situations. Once set, standing plans allow managers to make more efficient use of their planning time because they do not have to formulate a new plan for every similar situation. Before going further in our discussion, let us provide one note of caution: Overuse of standing plans may limit an organization's responsiveness to its environment, a critical issue for public relations. Nevertheless, standing plans do have a place in the public relations function. We discuss three types of standing plans: policies, procedures, and rules.

Policies **Policies** are generally established by an organization's top management as guidelines for decision making. Those who make policy usually seek to guide decision-making activities in ways consistent with organizational objectives. Other purposes include improving effectiveness or imposing the values of top management.

Sometimes policies originate informally at lower organizational levels as a pattern of decision making occurs over a long period of time. In such cases, top management merely formalizes what is already happening. In other situations, policy may be established either as a result of recommendations from lower-level managers or directly as a result of top management's observation that a problem exists.

6.1 Mini•Case

The Inevitable Tragedy: NASA's Emergency Planning

The space shuttle *Columbia,* on February 1, 2003, only 16 minutes from a scheduled landing at Kennedy Space Center in Florida, blew apart, spreading wreckage from Fort Worth across east Texas to Louisiana and killing all seven astronauts on board. NASA responded immediately with communication through all media, letting the world know that a disaster had occurred. While still searching for answers to the cause of the crash, NASA administrator Sean O'Keefe vowed that safety is still its top priority. President George W. Bush praised the space program in his message to the nation and to the families who suffered the loss.

But what was the public's response? A Gallup poll taken the day after the disaster showed 82 percent of the American public wants NASA to continue sending people into space. That was similar to the 80 percent wanting to continue the program after the *Challenger* had been lost. President Bush vowed, "America's space program will go on."

This time NASA was prepared, but years ago when the first space disaster occurred, it was not ready for a crisis situation.

There were no reporters or correspondents from any media on hand at Cape Kennedy when fire broke out in the command module of *Apollo-Saturn* 204, later known as *Apollo 1,* on January 27, 1967. The three-man crew, astronauts Virgil Grissom, Edward White, and Roger Chaffee, had entered the *Apollo* at 1 P.M. for the last simulated countdown test prior to launch. However, a series of problems quickly arose. Before launch two of the astronauts reported fire in the cockpit. Technicians were horrified to see flames inside the now smoke-filled *Apollo.* Despite the danger of explosion from the escape rocket, six technicians rushed to open *Apollo*'s hatch. By then, all three astronauts were dead from carbon monoxide asphyxia and thermal burns. They never even left the launch pad.

Although NASA knew within five minutes of the accident that all three astronauts were dead, the information was not released until two hours later. It was nearly midnight before UPI and AP received a NASA picture of two of the astronauts entering the capsule for the last time.

NASA claimed that withholding the facts and its issuance of misleading and wrong statements resulted from the lack of a plan for handling information in emergencies. As hard to believe as this may be, coming as it does from an agency with a public information staff of 300, there is undoubtedly some validity to the claim.

Since then NASA's information office has maintained that an emergency plan was in effect and followed at the time of the *Apollo 1* fire.[7] NASA states that it has contingency plans for each mission. Indeed, when a fire broke out on board *Apollo 13* three years later, many felt that NASA's handling of the crisis not only saved the lives of the three astronauts but so enhanced the image of the agency that it bolstered support for the entire manned space program.[8]

On January 28, 1986, tragedy again struck the nation's space program as millions of Americans and people all over the world witnessed via live television the explosion of the space shuttle *Challenger* shortly after liftoff. In their critiques of NASA's communication on the disaster, many professional observers and news reporters commented that little seemed to have been learned from earlier experiences. Although the flight controllers knew the fate of the *Challenger* crew almost instantly, speculation about their ability to survive the accident was allowed to continue for about an hour after the explosion while technicians "gathered data."

In its most recent tragedy, NASA once again was required to put an emergency communication plan into effect. NASA moved swiftly to provide information, especially in light of the fact that debris was scattered over large portions of Texas and Louisiana. Almost immediately the NASA website, http://www.nasa.gov, provided updated information, including video streams of press conferences. But as the investigation continued, questions were raised about the effectiveness of NASA's internal communication. After *Columbia*'s fatal descent, e-mails and reports surfaced that were written prior to the mission and contained warnings about the possibility of just such an explosion. Several panels will be looking at the tragedy. One has already been named, headed by retired Admiral Harold Gehman, but additionally it is probable that Congress will name its own investigation team. One area of investigation likely will be the internal communication efforts of the agency.

Sources: Dianne Calhoun, graduate student at the University of Memphis, gathered the case from Charles W. Petit, "A Star-Crossed Flight," *US News and World Report,* February 17, 2003, pp. 44–49; Thomas Hayden, "Landing in the NASA Hot Seat," *US News and World Report,* February 17, 2003, pp. 52–53; NASA's website; and James Skardon, "The Apollo Story: What the Watchdogs Missed," *Columbia Journalism Review* 6 (Fall 1967), pp. 13–14.

Outside organizations, such as governmental agencies, also set policies or at least influence them. Health and safety policies in most large organizations have changed considerably in recent years as a direct result of actions by government agencies.

Public relations departments, like all other subunits of organizations, must plan their daily operations to avoid conflict with policy. More important, public relations practitioners should be included in the strata of policymakers for any organization to ensure sensitivity to the interests of its publics. For example, policies that direct all contact with the press to go through the public relations department for approval and advice should be reviewed by the public relations staff.

Procedures Detailed guidelines for implementing policy decisions are called standard **procedures.** Standard procedures, or standard operating procedures, provide detailed instructions for performing a sequence of actions that occur regularly. Most public relations departments have standard procedures for news releases, internal publications, site tours, media interviews, and many other activities that are carried on from year to year. In addition, every organization needs a standard procedure for emergencies.

Emergencies, although infrequent, should be handled through set procedures because of the need to respond quickly and effectively. When a disaster happens, it is too late to begin a deliberate planning process that will consider every alternative before responding. See mini-case 6.1. Coordinated, deliberate, and effective response is vitally important. When an emergency situation exists, time becomes the key element in communication; plans must be made in advance so that reaction can be immediate.

Rules Whereas policies and standard procedures serve as guidelines for decision making, rules substitute for decisions. **Rules** are statements that specify the action to be taken in a particular situation. No latitude for application is provided other than the decision either to follow or not follow the rule. Rules may be necessary when certain procedures are crucial. For example, it is often wise to have a rule requiring that signed releases be obtained before photographs or other personal information are used in publicity releases.

Remember that the public relations plan is a message that must be communicated to an organization's executives. Whether or not that message is accepted depends on the effective execution of the planning process and how the plan is communicated to the decision makers who must understand and approve it.

Summary

Good public relations practice demands good planning. As exciting as they may sound, public relations actions that arise from spur-of-the-moment decisions usually produce short-term gains and long-term losses. Even emergency situations that cannot be predicted must have planned response systems. The process of planning is slow, complex, and frequently boring. However, in public relations, as in other managerial functions, careful planning increases the effectiveness and decreases the frequency of future actions. Adequate planning also establishes a system of goals that can be used to measure public relations success. This aspect of planning will be expanded in chapter 8.

Planning involves a look at the future. Several techniques for beginning the planning process include using existing public opinion surveys, scenario building, and brainstorming. Plans are both single-use (often public relations campaigns) and standing plans such as crisis plans.

For self-testing and additional chapter resources, go to the student CD and the Online Learning Center at **www.mhhe.com/lattimore**

To learn more about public relations planning watch the interview with Corey du Browa, Clip #2, on the book's CD-ROM.

Case Study

Cornados™—The World's First Stone-Ground Corn Fries

Situation

The J. R. Simplot Company (Simplot), one of the top three potato processors in the world, came to Ketchum in the fall of 1999 for help in developing a communications strategy to market a new product concept—french fries made from ground corn. The new product would launch to the restaurant industry in January 2001. Sales of potato products for Simplot had been relatively flat for several years and the company was looking for a new product to revitalize sales and profits. Code-named Project Orville, the project required extensive market research and communications counsel to direct the launch successfully.

Research

A series of focus groups were conducted with restaurant chefs and consumers—some in the Ketchum Food Center, others with outside research companies. The goal of the research was to determine how to position and package the new fry. Consumer panels indicated that the term *stone-ground corn* was essential to establishing appropriate expectations of the product. When consumers heard the term *corn fries* alone, they expected corn kernels in the fries. In addition, *stone-ground* made them feel that they were eating something healthy.

Chefs taught the company that the familiar fry shape offered both comfort and discomfort. The fry shape indicated how they would cook the product. But they had concerns on where it would fit on their menu. They did not want to cannibalize their extremely profitable fry sales by replacing traditional fries, so they thought it might work as an alternative side dish offering or as an appetizer. Success would depend on creating appealing menu ideas and effective merchandising tools for restaurateurs.

Planning

Ketchum was instrumental in the planning process. Working with "Team Orville," a group of Simplot sales and marketing personnel, Ketchum wrote the marketing plan and developed a project time line. Timing was tricky as the product first had to be introduced to the sales force and then launched into the marketplace with a bang.

Target Audiences

- Simplot sales chain and other internal audiences
- Restaurant chefs in casual/theme, family-style, college/university, business/industry, leisure/recreation and quick service restaurant segments
- Foodservice distributors
- Patrons of target restaurants

Program Objectives

1. To create brand awareness among restaurant chefs and foodservice distributors
2. To generate trial/purchase among restaurant chefs and patrons
3. To secure national distribution within three months of launching product

Communication Strategies

1. Develop a brand name and logo that resonates with restaurant patrons and chefs.
2. Communicate operator benefits via advertising, publicity, and sales collateral.
3. Offer coupons and other promotions to restaurant chefs.
4. Provide appetizing merchandising materials that communicate what the new product is.

Budget

Budget—$594,376

Execution

Brand Name and Logo. The first phase of the creative process was to develop a brand name and logo. Ketchum recommended that the brand name have an association with corn and that the words *stone-ground corn* be used in the descriptor to quickly illustrate what the product was. Hence, Simplot corn fries became Cornados™: Stone-Ground Corn Fries from Simplot.

Advertising, "Advertorials," and BRC Cards. Ketchum developed advertising next so that the remaining marketing, merchandising, and training materials could be developed from a single primary concept. Because french fries are associated with potatoes and Cornados are shaped like french fries, Ketchum recommended that Cornados be shown in a corn husk so that the reader could quickly understand that the product was made from corn. Cornados—The World's First Stone-Ground Corn Fries were launched with a heavy ad schedule in targeted trade publications in January 2001. Business reply cards were also inserted into select publications to generate sales inquiries. "Advertorials" demonstrated a wide variety of ideas for menus and promoting Cornados.

Sales Collateral, Merchandising, and Promotions. As a result of listening to what chefs asked for in the test market, recipe ideas and point-of-purchase merchandising materials were developed. Trial coupons encouraged first-time purchases. Menu mention programs encouraged permanent branded menu placement, and wait staff incentives stimulated sales of Cornados and created excitement with the wait staff. These programs and materials were described in a handy promotional kit that was sent to restaurant chefs and handed out at trade shows.

Sales Training. Cornados were launched to Simplot's sales and broker network at their national sales meeting in September 2000. Ketchum outlined a training program that included product demonstrations, marketing and merchandising programs, and pricing and packaging details.

Publicity. Cornados were introduced to key trade editors at the International Foodservice Editorial Council in November 2000. The editors were very interested in the product because it was so new and unique. Several feature placements resulted from this introduction. Additional press releases and photos generated further placements with national trade publications.

Evaluation

Objective #1—Create brand awareness among restaurant chefs and foodservice distributors.

- Cornados—The World's First Stone-Ground Corn Fry ad campaign reached chefs and distributors, generating 2,457,155 impressions, resulting in 1,648 responses via reader service cards.
- Advertising readerships scores were at or above issue averages in every instance.
- Inserts reached 265,734 restaurant chefs and generated 985 inquiries.
- The advertorials generated 309,130 impressions in foodservice publications.
- Foodservice publicity efforts resulted in 22 features/product placements in both chef and distributor publications, achieving nearly 2 million impressions.
- Features included recipes and articles highlighting "corn fries" as an interesting new menu item.

Objective #2—Generate trial/purchase among restaurant chefs and patrons.

- 6,406 free case trial coupons were redeemed (coupons could be duplicated by sales force, or; therefore total distribution is unknown).
- 1,149 dollar off coupons were redeemed (total distribution unknown, see above).
- 73 chefs took advantage of the menu allowance offer, adding Cornados to their menu as a permanent menu item.
- Over 750,000 point-of-purchase materials were distributed for use in restaurants. Coasters, table tents, and recipes booklets were the most requested items.

Objective #3—Secure national distribution within three months of launching product.

- By the end of February 2001, Simplot had secured distribution in all regions of the country and had shipped over 1 million pounds of product.

Questions

1. What theme would you suggest for this campaign?
2. How could the objectives be made stronger and easier to evaluate?
3. What additional tactics would you suggest for each strategy?

Source: PRSA Silver Anvil Awards, 2002, Integrated Communications Category.

Key Terms

Use the CD-ROM and Online Learning Center at www.mhhe.com/lattimore to further your understanding of the following terms

brainstorming
campaign budget
formative evaluation
goals
management by objectives (MBO)
mission statement
policies
prioritize
proactive
procedures
project budget
public opinion surveys
public relations counselor
rules
scenario construction
single-use plans
standing plans
strategic plans
summative evaluation
tactical plans
video news release (VNR)

Notes

1. Fran R. Matera and Ray J. Artigue, *Public Relations Campaigns and Techniques* (Boston: Allyn & Bacon, 2000), p. 103.
2. David M. Dozier, "Planning and Evaluation in PR Practice," *Public Relations Review* (Summer 1985), pp. 21–22.
3. Don Clare and Ron Nyham, "A Grand Scan Plan," *Association Management* 53 (January 2001), pp. 73–77.
4. L. J. Garrett and M. Silver, *Production Management Analysis* (New York: Harcourt Brace Jovanovich, 1966), pp. 364–65.
5. Ben & Jerry's plant in Waterbury, Vermont, June 4, 2002.
6. Sonja L. Myhre and June A. Flora, "HIV/AIDS Communication Campaigns: Progress and Prospects," *Journal of Health Communication,* April–June 2000 (Suppl.), p. 29.
7. James Kauffman, "Adding Fuel to the Fire: NASA's Crisis Communications Regarding Apollo 1," *Public Relations Review* 25 (Winter 1999), p. 421.
8. James Kauffman, "A Successful Failure: NASA's Crisis Communications Regarding Apollo 13," Public *Relations Review* 27 (Winter 2001), pp. 437–48.

CHAPTER SEVEN

Action and Communication

7

Outline

PREVIEW

The public relations actions required in modern organizations have expanded to include managerial decision making in virtually every aspect of operation. Socially responsible action on the part of the organization is necessary before the public relations practitioner implements the communication part of the process. Counsel for management to make those decisions is the key to effective implementation of communication efforts to follow. Once the organization has taken responsible "actions," the public relations staff may communicate within a target audience to induce desired behavioral outcomes.

Public relations practitioners often use five basic steps in the process of diffusing information to facilitate the adoption of new ideas by target publics. Critical paths lead an idea through the five basic steps: awareness, interest, evaluation, trials, and adoption. This process of diffusion must be planned and executed for each target public separately. Therefore, practitioners should plan actions appropriate to the needs and interests of each public. After channels of influence are identified for each public, appropriate public relations action can be initiated.

". . . the question will not be whether publics receive the message, but whether they act on it."
—Pat Jackson

Most public relations actions involve communication. Writing is the primary tool for constructing messages and is therefore a critical skill for practitioners. By applying the principles of effective writing, public relations messages can be developed for all audiences and media. Public relations action can be organized around three basic areas of planning: target audiences, channels of influence, and messages. These areas interact to provide a unique plan of action for every audience in every situation. Segment 3 of the integrating case study illustrates **action implementation** in the Cedar Springs Hospital Case □

PUBLIC RELATIONS IN ACTION

Early in the 20th century, Ivy Lee, one of the "founding fathers" of public relations, emphasized the importance of counseling management to take responsible action before beginning the communication process. The public relations practitioner, as part of the management team of an organization, must be involved in the decision-making process to ensure that management makes decisions to take positive action steps to resolve a problem or to create an opportunity. Once the organization has taken responsible actions, the public relations staff may communicate with a target audience to induce desired behavioral outcomes. For example, Standard Oil of California took immediate action to let the public know that it would spend whatever was necessary to clean up a massive oil spill in the San Francisco Bay after two of its tankers collided. The company followed up on its promise and cleaned up the bay. San Francisco papers editorialized that the "beaches had never been cleaner before."[1]

Traditionally, public relations action has included communication in some form, often a publicity release for print media. The world has changed, though, and so has the practice of public relations. Technology has impacted the types of media that practitioners must work with, requiring organizations to have a wider range of possible action alternatives from their public relations staffs. Today crisis situations, as well as many of the planned public relations programs, must make use of new technologies such as satellite transmissions of video news releases (VNRs), video interviews and other live news transmission on the Internet, and World Wide Web sites. PepsiCo, for example, used the VNR and video interviews as a major tool in combating a crisis of national scope when a claim was made that a foreign object was found in an unopened Diet Pepsi can in Tacoma, Washington. See mini-case 7.1.

Large organizations with access to modern technology are not the only ones that require a variety of response mechanisms. Cedar Springs Community Hospital took several action steps, none of them press releases. Although much of that action involved written communication, several important steps centered on managerial decision making.

Integrating Case Study

Cedar Springs Community Hospital

Segment 3

Action Implementation

In chapter 6, goals, objectives, and basic strategies were developed for solving the hospital's problem. Next, the public relations staff turned its attention to the execution of those plans. It was clear from the patient surveys that the hospital's primary goal of quality patient care was already being achieved. Therefore, strategies were developed to try to improve employee and physician perceptions of the hospital's performance.

The two basic strategies for which action steps needed to be developed were (1) reinforcement of employee feelings of worth as members of the medical team and (2) increase in feedback from patients. Several tactics were implemented to address these needs.

Employee Team

A theme was developed to increase all employees' awareness of their value as members of the medical team at Cedar Springs Hospital. The theme "Quality People, Quality Care" was communicated to employees, physicians, and other publics through six media:

1. Signs were painted over the entrances to all three main buildings.
2. Mailing panels were printed for all publications.
3. Birthday cards for employees were redesigned.
4. Special employee name badges were designed for those employees who had passed the 90-day probationary period, designating them as "Quality Providers."
5. T-shirts were printed with the theme and used as gifts for participating in the personnel department's annual Benefits Fair.
6. Employees who received honors had their photos put on the World Wide Web site of the hospital with a note about the honor. Doctors were also honored on the Web with special notes from patients.

Hospital management also wanted to make a very public statement about the quality of the employees and their work. Thus, an existing program, "Employee-of-the-Month," was revitalized. To give the recognition more visibility among patients, physicians, and the general public, a 24-inch display ad appeared in the local newspaper every month, featuring the honored employee, the "Quality People, Quality Care" theme, and a link to the hospital website with more information about the employee.

Patient Feedback

Three primary methods were used to increase feedback from patients to the hospital staff. First, the survey of recently released patients was repeated quarterly. Survey results were disseminated in various ways, such as using the hospital newsletter, table tents in the staff cafeteria, and e-mail. In addition, a contest was begun in which employees tried to guess the survey results before they were published. Second, positive letters from former patients were disseminated among the hospital employees. Third, a regular feature called "Worth Sharing" was begun in the monthly newsletter to highlight patient success stories. It was also placed on the hospital website.

Influencing Management Decisions

When it was first proposed that the new theme be placed over the entrances to the main buildings, many employees reacted negatively, believing that "advertising" was too commercial for a medical facility. An ad hoc committee of department managers investigated the complaints and made recommendations regarding use of the theme. The committee eventually recommended placing it above the entrances and sold the employees on the integrity of the idea. This group also suggested using the theme only on the nametags of employees who had passed the 90-day review period.

Management decision making was again the principal action leading to the wider distribution of letters of appreciation from patients. This relatively simple action

7.1 Mini•Case

The Pepsi Hoax

It began in Seattle when a TV station informed the local Pepsi franchise bottler that an 82-year-old Tacoma man had found a hypodermic needle in a can of Diet Pepsi. The report was broadcast that evening on the local news. It would be the nation's top story for the next 96 hours. Within hours another syringe turned up in a can in another locality. Soon news broadcasts from around the country had reports of people finding needles in Pepsi cans.[2] Eventually, more than 50 allegations were made in 23 states.[3]

Pepsi Cola set up a crisis management team at its corporate headquarters in Somers, New York. The team was led by Craig Weatherup, Pepsi president. Rebecca Madeira, Pepsi vice president for public affairs, directed the team's actions and coordinated the communications so the company could speak with one voice.

First, the Pepsi crisis team had to determine if the Pepsi bottlers were the problem. The crisis response plan had these key points:

- Put public safety first. Assess the problem through the public's eyes. Be clear that their needs and concerns come first.
- Find it. Fix it. Work around the clock with regulatory officials to investigate every aspect of the plant operation to identify and, if possible, correct the problem.
- Communicate quickly and frequently, using tools and timetables reporters use.
- Take responsibility for solving the crisis. Don't point fingers, assign blame, or pass the buck. Make your team accountable for a swift and sound resolution to the problem.[4]

Once Pepsi had gathered its facts and felt secure that this was not a problem caused by its bottlers, Pepsi took the offensive. President Weatherup said repeatedly through the media, "A can is the most tamper-proof packaging in food supply. We are 99.99 percent certain that this didn't happen in Pepsi plants."[5]

The crisis team decided to use VNRs to show consumers that Pepsi's canning process could not be tampered with. High-tech, high-speed equipment was shown filling Pepsi cans. Each can was turned upside down, cleaned with a powerful jet of air or water, inverted, filled and closed—all in less than one second! Video footage of the canning process was beamed by satellite to TV stations across the country. Within 48 hours the first video news release was seen by 296 million viewers, three times the number that usually watches the Super Bowl.

The company used the video to combat the visual images of the syringes that had been shown on network television constantly since the first instance in Seattle. Pepsi created three more VNRs within three days. By the end of the week, the president had appeared on a dozen network TV news shows and talk shows, and Pepsi spokespersons had conducted more than 2,000 interviews with newspapers, magazines, and TV and radio reporters. The strategy was to show the public that what was happening was really a hoax rather than a problem with Pepsi bottlers. The real turning point came with the third VNR. It showed a tape from an in-store surveillance camera that had filmed a shopper slipping a syringe into an open Diet Pepsi can while the cashier's back was turned. Pepsi could not release the tape though, until the next day when an arrest was made. After the third VNR ran, viewers were overwhelmingly supportive of Pepsi. The evaluation done indicated that Pepsi's response worked. Sales for the key July 4 period were not affected adversely, which was quite important.

Questions

1. Were the communication tools used by Pepsi to solve the problem the ones you would use today?
2. Evaluate the role of the VNRs.
3. Are they always effective?

required a change in organizational policy that could have been politically explosive. A policy change of this type could have alienated both the personnel manager and the department managers if not handled carefully. The public relations manager needed a good understanding of both communication and organizational dynamics to accomplish this objective. Such letters normally had been routed to the personnel department and then to the manager of the department involved. This meant that for a department to get any recognition, it would have to appear to "blow its own horn." Therefore, most letters of appreciation had been handled internally, without informing the rest of the organization. The private nature of this process worked against the new objective of improving employee perceptions by sharing patient feedback. Thus, the policy was changed so that the original letter was routed first to public relations where copies were made for the appropriate department manager and for human resources. Some were featured on the hospital website.

Diffusing Information

Although managerial decision making was one of the public relations actions used in the Cedar Springs case, the primary action process can be described as the **diffusion of information.** More often than not, the action implemented to accomplish a public relations plan can be explained as an attempt to spread information within a target audience.

Selecting a Target Audience The action process begins and ends with target audiences. Once each public is identified, its characteristics can be studied, and a *critical path* of influence can be planned for the issue in question.

When considering the individual characteristics of each target audience, it is helpful to categorize them as (1) primary, intervening, or moderating and (2) latent, aware, or active. A **primary public** is the group to which the action is ultimately directed. As we have shown, however, the critical path to this group frequently requires that other audiences be addressed. Individuals in **intervening publics** have direct contact with the primary audience and can pass messages along to them. All the channels of influence except personal experience may be intervening publics. **Moderating publics** are groups that share a common goal or guiding philosophy and can make an impact on the primary public. These groups usually have high credibility with the primary public in specific topic areas.[6] Only mass media and personal experience do not have the potential to be moderating publics.

As you will recall from our discussion in chapter 5, a **latent public** is not aware of a need to change or act. An **aware public** recognizes a need but is not prone to any action, such as accepting a new idea. An **active public** is aware and ready to do something. This classification system helps determine the extent to which a given public is ready and able to respond to any planned action.

Marchers attempt to make people aware of their issues.

The Diffusion Process *Diffusion* is a term used to describe *the way in which new ideas are adopted in a society.* Sociologists and communication researchers have long been fascinated by the paths that innovations follow as they make their way through a social system. Publics or target audiences are social systems that public relations practitioners seek to influence. Therefore, it is important that our knowledge about the diffusion of information be applied to the public relations process. (See chapter 3 where this theory is discussed.)

Critical Paths Those who study the diffusion process through which new products, ideas, and technologies spread have identified five steps that describe how people are influenced to change:[7]

1. *Awareness.* People become aware of the idea or practice, although their knowledge is limited. This awareness is often spread through the mass media.
2. *Interest.* People begin to develop an interest in the idea and seek more information about it. Again, the mass media are especially important in providing the information to large audiences in this step of the diffusion process.

3. *Evaluation.* People begin to mentally apply the idea to their individual situations. Simultaneously, they obtain more information and make a decision to try the new idea.
4. *Trials.* At this point, actual application begins, usually on a small scale. Potential adopters are primarily interested in the practice, techniques, and conditions necessary for application.
5. *Adoption.* Once the idea is proven worthwhile, it is adopted by the target audiences.

Channels of Influence Researchers have tracked innovations through the adoption process and concluded that they use five basic channels of influence:

1. *Mass Media.* Electronic and print media such as radio, television, newspapers, and magazines.
2. *Biased Intermediaries.* Individuals or groups that stand to benefit from another's adoption (such as salespersons).
3. *Unbiased Third Parties.* Consumer groups, government agencies, and other groups or individuals that have credibility.
4. *Significant Others.* Friends, relatives, and others who are admired by potential adopters.
5. *Personal Experience.* Actual use of the innovation.

In the early stages of awareness and interest, mass media are most effective. In the critical stages of evaluation and trial, however, emphasis shifts to the influence of significant others. Finally, at the point of adoption, personal experience becomes the primary channel. The secondary, or support path, begins with significant others, moving to unbiased third parties at the evaluation and trial stages and then back again to significant others at adoption.

Facilitating the Adoption Process

The public relations practitioner can apply the critical path approach by attempting to create awareness and interest through press releases and other media coverage. From the start of the campaign, the practitioner should plan to communicate with other publics that are significant to the target audience. When the initial goals of awareness and interest are reached, public relations actions should move away from the obvious to more subtle forms of communication through significant others and unbiased third parties. After the evaluation and trial stages are passed, success can be measured by the extent to which the target public accepts the new idea.

Pressure and Special Interest Groups Traditionally, a great deal of public relations practice has been based on a generally accepted *two-step flow of information theory.* This theory is built on the premise that certain people in our society are opinion leaders. Therefore, if those opinion leaders can be convinced to support a certain matter, they will influence others to support it also. For example, if ministers in your community strongly support a new senior center in town, as opinion leaders they are likely to have a great deal of influence on a number of their church members. The strategy, then, may be to use this two-step flow of information to convince the ministers that the senior center is good and to get them to encourage support from their membership.

Although the two-step flow theory contains a great deal of truth, both research and practice have shown that it is too simplistic. The theory allows for only two levels (leaders and followers) in any influence attempt. Further, it presumes a linear flow of information through a social system. From our discussion of systems theory and the diffusion process in chapter 3 it should be apparent that society is much more complex. Thus, some researchers now use a multistep flow theory to describe the process.

This multistep process is similar to the two-step flow, but instead of attempting to reach one target group who will in turn reach the ultimate audience, this theory suggests that the minister in our example might be only one opinion leader who might be used to influence other opinion leaders. He or she might influence several key church members who in turn might have more direct influence on others. Thus, the minister might influence the bankers, the doctors, the teachers, and the secretaries. In turn, these people would serve as opinion leaders for their small sphere of influence, ultimately reaching the larger target audience and convincing the community as a whole to support increased taxation for a new senior center.

When Mountain Bell decided to introduce Local Measured Service in the Phoenix area, the media devoted a great deal of coverage toward describing the advantages of the new system.[8] Because of the favorable publicity, the telephone company felt confident when the issue came up for approval by the Arizona Corporate Commission. When Mountain Bell representatives arrived at the hearing, however, they found senior citizens crowded into the chambers and other seniors picketing outside to protest the innovation. Obviously, one important public in the Phoenix area, senior citizens, had not adopted the idea. After its first request was turned down, the phone company began to work with senior citizen groups to win support from significant others and unbiased third parties. The proposal was approved without protest the next time it came before the commission. To secure the cooperation of various publics, Mountain Bell used an action strategy known as stakeholder analysis.

Stakeholder Analysis The concept of stakeholder management provides a more realistic framework for an organization to visualize its environment. **Stakeholder analysis** is a method for differentiating among publics. **Stakeholders** are those individuals who perceive themselves to have an interest in the actions of an organization. They may be customers, shareholders, employees, or just members of society. They generally express themselves through groups that share a common purpose, such as environmental or consumer causes.

Applying the stakeholder management approach to public relations practice allows actions to be organized around an entire system of stakeholder groups. The goal is maximum overall cooperation between the stakeholders and the organization's objectives. To accomplish this, strategies are designed to deal simultaneously with issues that affect multiple groups.

The stakeholder process does not fundamentally change public relations communication or other action processes. Instead, it organizes them for more efficient use. Stakeholder management can determine *who* should be the object of an action step, *what* that action should be, *what* results should be sought, and *how* each element will fit into the overall plan.

Traditionally, many public relations activities were managed through delivery systems like news bureaus, speakers' bureaus, and complaint departments. Because these focus on a single action, they have difficulty recognizing the differences among publics. In a stakeholder management system, however, action for each public is planned *separately.* The needs and interests of a given stakeholder group determine what actions are appropriate and how they should be implemented.

When Mountain Bell managers first attempted to begin Local Measured Service, they were trying to reach all consumers through the same action strategies. Further analysis led them to realize that the task required a more complex view of their publics. Stakeholders who needed to be considered in the Local Measured Service issue included:

1. *Internal Stakeholders.* Employees and shareholders.
2. *Residence Stakeholders.* Consumer advocates, the handicapped, minorities, low income segments, senior citizens, volunteer and service groups, educational organizations.
3. *Business Stakeholders.* Those dependent on telemarketing, small businesses, large businesses.
4. *Other Stakeholders.* Media, government, the Arizona Corporate Commission.[9]

Each stakeholder group was assigned to a project manager. These practitioners became familiar with the needs and interests of the groups assigned to them and worked with functional departments such as media relations, the speaker's bureau, internal publications, and others to target messages to their audiences.

Designing the Public Relations Matrix

After the appropriate channels of influence are determined and target audiences selected, messages are prepared within basic action categories. In a large organization, these functional areas, or subspecialties, within public relations are sometimes performed by different departments. Even if they are handled by one person, each action category must produce a distinct message. Frequently, different media are used as well. This creates a series of crossover or matrix relationships between target audiences and messages.

Table 7.1 illustrates the relationships between some of Mountain Bell's target audiences (stakeholders) and the action categories used to respond to the situation. In the case of Mountain Bell's response to the Local Measured Service protest, each target audience was assigned to a practitioner, while each action category was the responsibility of a functional department. For any message, at least two members of the public relations staff would be responsible for its design and implementation.

For example, a news release prepared by the press relations group could have been initiated by the residential or business consumer manager and closely reviewed by other managers for potential impact on media, employee, and government stakeholders. Un-

TABLE 7.1 Public Relations Matrix for Mountain Bell Target Audiences

	Media	Residential Customers	Employees	Business	Government
News Releases	Intervening	Primary	Moderating	Primary	Moderating
Speakers' Bureau	Intervening	Primary	Moderating	Primary	Moderating
Internal Publications			Primary		Moderating
External Publications	Primary	Primary	Moderating	Primary	Primary
Advocacy Advertising		Primary	Moderating	Primary	Moderating

Communication actions are on the left vertical axis and the publics are across the top horizontally.
Source: Reprinted through courtesy of Mountain Bell.

der this system, messages are prepared for primary audiences and checked for their desired effect on moderating and intervening audiences. This system allows functional specialists such as writers and editors to continue performing their tasks, while project managers assume the responsibility for making sure all messages received by their publics are prepared according to the public relations plan. A single manager can be responsible for supervising contacts with several publics in more than one project. These responsibilities change as projects are completed and new ones are added.

THE PRACTITIONER AS A COMMUNICATOR

We began this chapter by illustrating the variety of action steps possible from a single public relations plan. Although the actions that might be used are virtually limitless, one remains predominant. The ability to write effectively continues to be a primary skill demanded by those who employ public relations practitioners.[10]

Just as communication is the primary action step in a public relations plan, writing is the principal tool for constructing messages. Even messages that are primarily visual, like videotape or slide presentations, generally require well-written directions or a script. Webpages also rely on the effectiveness of the written word for maximum impact. Writing for the Internet often means using keywords to drive search engines. While the use of imbedded links and the compartmentalization of the screen into various messages bring different challenges, they must be met with clear, effective writing. Policies and other decisions are written as they are developed, transmitted, and preserved. Therefore, writing is a basic skill needed by all public relations professionals, regardless of the type or size of the organizations in which they work.

Principles of Effective Writing

Some people are born with an exceptional talent that cannot be explained or taught. The Ernest Hemingways of this world may not need to learn the principles of effective writing, but few of us are exceptionally gifted artists. Most people have to learn the craft of writing through study, practice, and hard work—that's the bad news.

The good news is that effective writing can be learned. People of average talent can learn to write effectively by practicing some basic principles. See spotlight 7.1.

Packaging Ideas The length of sentences in a written document is widely recognized as a key to its clarity. Many of the readability formulas use sentence length as their basis of measurement. Distinguished educator and journalist Harold Davis often tells the story of a journalist working with the American Press Institute in the late 1940s and early 1950s who helped firmly establish the link between clarity and length.

James H. Couey, Jr., of the *Birmingham News* helped conduct seminars for working journalists at Columbia University. Before a seminar began, he would ask each participant to send him a sample of his or her writing so he could test it. Couey repeated his test with dozens of articles. The results were always the same. A sentence is a package for ideas, and readers must struggle to get huge, bulky packages into their minds. By simply making the sentences shorter, he achieved large gains in understanding.

Couey continued to investigate the short sentence phenomenon and discovered some interesting facts:

7.1 Spotlight

Tips for Effective Writing

The following tips can help just about everyone effectively communicate technical and nontechnical information in letters, reports, news stories, booklets, and most other media that use the written word:

1. *Use short, simple words.* Prefer the simple to the complex. For example, write "use," not "utilize" in most situations.
2. *Use short, simple sentences and paragraphs.* Research shows the average sentence length should be 20 words or less.
3. *Write in the active, not the passive voice.* The exception to this rule is if you need to emphasize the receiver of the action.
4. *Avoid slang and jargon.* It makes copy more difficult for a mass audience to comprehend. For example, English is a second language for many, and they, as well as others, have considerable difficulty understanding slang and jargon.
5. *Use adjectives and adverbs sparingly.*
6. *Be brief;* for example, keep most news releases to one or two typewritten pages.
7. *Be specific.* Don't communicate in generalities, but be as concrete as possible.
8. *Cite reasons for your opinions.* Support your contentions with statistics, facts, and statements from impartial sources to provide credibility.

1. Short sentences usually contained only one idea each.
2. A story could contain both long and short sentences for variety, as long as the average was short.
3. The optimum average for most sentences seemed to be about 17 words.[11]

Pyramid Power Couey achieved tremendous gains in understanding by simply shortening sentences, but he never taught that sentence length was the only element in effective writing. Organization is another important skill that must be mastered.

Journalists often use the inverted pyramid style of writing (figure 7.1). This method organizes a story so the most important points are covered first. The inverted pyramid is equally useful for other types of informative writing. A message should begin by answering five questions: who, what, when, where, and why? These questions are answered in the first one or two paragraphs, called the *lead.* Journalists begin with the question that is most important to the message and proceed in descending order. Each successive paragraph contains details that are less important than the previous paragraph.

Public relations practitioners must master various writing styles. To be an effective communicator it is often necessary to blend seemingly disparate styles to serve multiple purposes for multiple audiences.[12] No matter the style, however, using the inverted pyramid offers several advantages. First, it puts the most important details near the beginning where readers who skim the message will be more likely to see them. Second, an editor may cut the story from the bottom up if necessary without losing important details. Third, a strong opening gets readers' attention and directs them into the rest of the message.

Media Selection

Various media and their audiences are discussed in detail in Part III, but it is appropriate at this point to outline a strategy for media selection. Although it is necessary to construct messages carefully so they communicate the desired meaning to an audience, it is equally important to choose the proper medium to carry them. For purposes of discussion, media may be classified as controlled or uncontrolled.

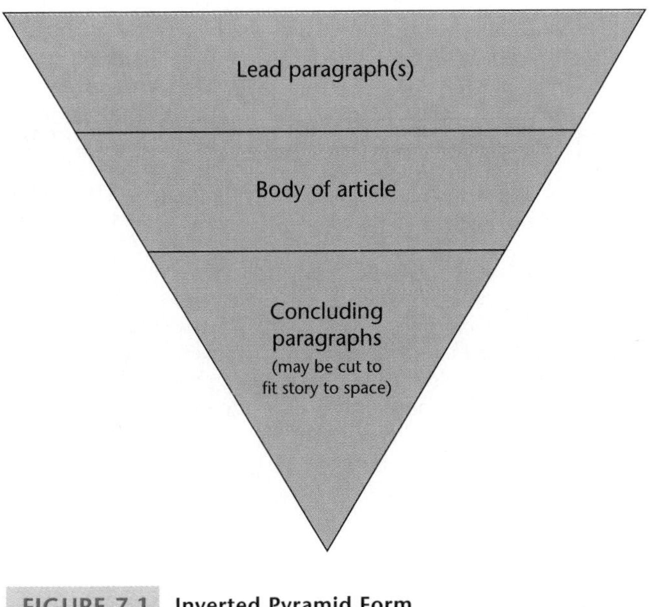

FIGURE 7.1 **Inverted Pyramid Form**

"Aspirin Called Aid Against 2d Heart Attack." Copyright © 1985 The New York Times Company. Reprinted by permission. Other headlines are representative of those which appeared in newspapers nationwide.

Using the news media to promote a product.

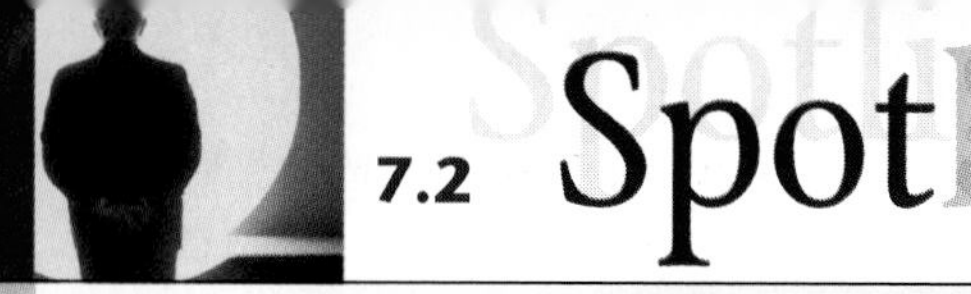

7.2 Spotlight

Internet Writing Guidelines

1. Don't build a site for your executives; they aren't the target audience. Know the characteristics of your target audience and write for them.
2. Establish and present a logical progression of the ideas.
3. Put blocks of no more than 75 words each on initial site pages. Longer text farther into the site is fine.
4. Don't use clever headlines, but structure your articles with several levels of headlines so a reader can complete a section and continue reading, or choose to move on.
5. Write 50 percent less at the beginning of an article. Most Internet users scan copy before deciding to spend time in depth to read an article.
6. Highlight key words through hypertext links, typeface variations, or color.
7. Use bulleted lists when the copy makes this possible. The computer screen is small, and people tend to glance at key elements quickly.
8. Use inverted pyramid style for most copy with the most important information first. Don't bury your key points.
9. Use one main idea per paragraph.
10. Keep your sentences short, but on the other hand, remember that the key to a good website is that you have provided the answers to the questions that the reader has, so you need to be thorough.

Source: Stephen Dembner, "Web Writer Pro: In Search of a Functional Model for Effective Text on the World Wide Web," unpublished master's thesis, University of Memphis, May 2000.

The preparation of a news release is different from the preparation of an advertising message, because news depends on a third party to select and deliver the message. This is the basic difference between controlled and uncontrolled media. **Controlled media,** including internal publications, direct mail, posters and advertising, allow the public relations practitioner to dictate what is published and how it is delivered to the primary audience. **Uncontrolled media,** for which someone else makes decisions about content, include newspapers, television, and radio.

Two controlled media have become especially important to public relations campaigns in the last few years: advertising and the World Wide Web.

The World Wide Web can be considered the first public relations mass medium because it allows managed communication to flow directly between organizations and mass audiences without the gate-keeping functions present in other mass media.[13] Writing for the Internet includes some special rules just for this particular medium. See spotlight 7.2.

The advent of this new medium as a communication tool for public relations has spurred increased interest in relationship building through the Internet. Although the potential is great, little is known about the impact of public relations principles as applied to website design. Preliminary studies suggest five guidelines for building relationships with publics using Internet technology:

1. Create a dialogic loop to allow and encourage publics to query the organization sponsoring the site. This includes the availability of an adequate and well-trained staff to handle responses.
2. Make the information useful to all publics who may use the site. Even a specialized website should have some general use information. Make information easy to get.
3. Focus on the generation of return visits through the use of interactive strategies. Forums, question-and-answer formats, and chats with experts or corporate officers tend to build visit frequency.
4. Develop an intuitive ease to the interface. The focus of websites should be on the organization, product, or information located there and not on the "bells and whistles" that make it possible. Websites with graphics that take too long to load may turn off some visitors.

5. The conservation of visitors should have priority over providing links to other sites. Too many links to other related sites too early in the design can take visitors away from your website before they have the chance to build a relationship.[14]

Increasingly the lines between public relations and advertising are blurred in an effort to communicate as effectively as possible. Public relations practitioners often use advertising as a campaign element to accomplish one or more of the following objectives:

1. Develop awareness of an organization
2. Tie a diverse product line together
3. Improve consumer relations
4. Improve the organization's image
5. Take a stand on a public issue[15]

The three basic considerations for media selection are the audiences, the timing, and the budget available.

Audiences Audiences must be the first consideration in any public relations effort (see chapter 5). It is necessary to identify the publics you are trying to reach and determine what will interest them. Uncontrolled media present a special problem to the public relations practitioner because publicity releases must be planned for two audiences. The primary audience, the public for whom the message is intended, is the most important; however, the editor or reporter who selects or rejects the release for publication or broadcast is the first hurdle. Thus, although the release is designed to communicate a particular message to the primary audience, it must first attract the journalistic attention of an editor.

After determining the target audience, it is next necessary to know which media are likely to be interested in particular types of information. By researching available media carefully, a public relations practitioner can become familiar with the types of stories they use and the audiences they attract. He or she may then select the best media for each release and package the information in a way that will attract the editor's attention. Chapter 9 discusses various strategies for media relations in greater detail.

Timing The timing necessary to reach an audience is the second important factor in media selection. Once the appropriate media are chosen, the time required to reach the primary audience is critical. Some publications have backlogs of material and may not be able to get a story out in time. Therefore, the question of when the primary audience receives the message may be just as important as whether or not it receives the message at all.

Budgets Budgets, the third important factor in media selection, are always limited, and frequently they, in turn, limit media selection. Usually the first decision that must be made is whether or not the message needs to be delivered by more than one medium. If a media mix is desirable, it may be necessary to consider cost when deciding which ones to use. Remember that while the costs of controlled media, such as advertising, are obvious, costs associated with uncontrolled media must also be counted.

Table 7.2 contrasts advantages and disadvantages of several different media. Considering these points with regard to audiences, time, and budget will help public relations practitioners select the media most appropriate to their messages.

TABLE 7.2 Principal Media: Advantages and Disadvantages

Medium	Advantages	Disadvantages
Television	1. Combines sight, sound, and motion attributes 2. Permits physical demonstration of product 3. Believability due to immediacy of message 4. High impact of message 5. Huge audiences 6. Good product identification 7. Popular medium	1. Message limited by restricted time segments 2. No possibility for consumer referral to message 3. Availabilities sometimes difficult to arrange 4. High time costs 5. Waste coverage 6. High production costs 7. Poor color transmission
Magazines	1. Selectivity of audience 2. Reaches more affluent consumers 3. Long closing dates 4. No immediacy of message 5. Pass-along readership 6. Good color reproduction	1. Often duplicate circulation 2. Usually cannot dominate in a local market 3. Offers prestige to an advertiser 4. Sometimes high production costs
Radio	1. Selectivity of geographical markets 2. Good saturation of local markets 3. Ease of changing advertising copy 4. Relatively low cost	1. Message limited by restricted time segments 2. No possibility for consumer referral to message 3. No visual appeal 4. Waste coverage
Newspapers	1. Selectivity of geographical markets 2. Ease of changing advertising copy 3. Reaches all income groups 4. Ease of scheduling advertisements 5. Relatively low cost 6. Good medium for manufacturer/dealer advertising	1. High cost for national coverage 2. Shortness of message life 3. Waste circulation 4. Differences of sizes and formats 5. Rate differentials between local and national markets 6. Poor color reproduction
Direct Mail	1. Extremely selective 2. Message can be very personalized 3. Little competition with other advertisements 4. Easy to measure effect of advertisements 5. Provides easy means for consumer action	1. Often has poor image 2. Can be quite expensive 3. Many restrictive postal regulations 4. Problems in maintaining mailing lists
Outdoor Posters (stationary panels)	1. Selectivity of geographical markets 2. High repetitive value 3. Large physical size 4. Relatively low cost 5. Good color reproduction	1. Often has poor image 2. Message must be short. 3. Waste circulation 4. National coverage is expensive 5. Few creative specialists
Point-of-Purchase Displays	1. Presents message at point of sale 2. Great flexibility for creativity 3. Ability to demonstrate product in use 4. Good color reproduction 5. Repetitive value	1. Dealer apathy in installation 2. Long production period 3. High unit cost 4. Shipping problems 5. Space problem
Transit Posters (on moving vehicles)	1. Selectivity of geographical markets 2. Captive audience 3. Very low cost 4. Good color reproduction 5. High repetitive value	1. Limited to a certain class of consumers 2. Waste circulation 3. Surroundings are disreputable 4. Few creative specialists

Medium	Advantages	Disadvantages
Movie Trailers	1. Selectivity of geographical markets 2. Captive audience 3. Large physical size 4. Good medium for manufacturer/ dealer advertising	1. Cannot be employed in all theaters 2. Waste circulation 3. High production costs 4. No possibility for consumer referral to message
Advertising Specialties	1. Unique presentation 2. High repetitive value 3. Has a "gift" quality 4. Relatively long life	1. Subject to fads 2. Message must be short 3. May have relatively high unit cost 4. Effectiveness difficult to measure
Pamphlets and Booklets	1. Offer detailed message at point of sale 2. Supplement a personal sales presentation 3. Offer to potential buyers a good referral means 4. Good color reproduction	1. Dealers often fail to use 2. May have a relatively high unit cost 3. Few creative specialists 4. Effectiveness difficult to measure

Source: Reprinted by permission of Publishing Horizons, Inc., from *Advertising Campaigns, Formulations and Tactics,* by Quera, pp. 71–74.

HOW TO BE HEARD

There are times when we not only want to be heard, but we need to be heard. Our message needs to be heard because our organizations may want to influence legislation, create goodwill among various publics, provide answers in times of crises, attract capable employees, increase sales, or raise money. There are many more reasons why we need to make sure our message is heard and acted upon, but these illustrate the variety of the reasons why organizations must communicate with target audiences.

How, though, can your message be heard and acted upon? In much like a funnel, the message must pass through four basic elements in which the audience may selectively decide to be involved with the communication or not. The four basic principles involved are as follows:

1. Attention
2. Understanding
3. Retention
4. Action

Each of the principles must be understood and used if you are to have your message really heard.[16]

Attention (Selective Attention)

Various publics, which an organization needs to communicate with, attend to only a few of the messages that they are bombarded with daily. This is called **selective attention.** For your message to be heard, it must first be attended to. It is necessary to analyze the stakeholders from the stakeholders' point of view. What will attract their attention? What do we know about them that will help build rapport with them? For example, though the issues may be the same, it may take different messages to reach legislators than it does to reach newspaper editors.

Selective attention is a communication concept often overlooked by those who would rather have a "low-key" approach to public relations. However, at times it is necessary to attract attention. On those occasions it may be helpful, even essential, to have a positive image. Like it or not, every group, organization, and individual has an image. Some images are good, some are not quite so good. But images are important to getting attention. Image building involves practically every part of your organization's activities and is often what is seen as "total communication." This is a first step.

Beyond image building, getting audiences to attend to your messages involves both the mechanics and content of your message. For example, the way you package your message to the chair of the Senate Subcommittee on Price Controls may determine whether or not your message is attended to. Some of the mechanical factors affecting attention to the message may include timing, setting, and authority. For instance, do you send out a news release about the importance of the independent petroleum marketers just after a price increase has gone into effect? Or would it be more effective to issue that release some months before the price increase? Do you send the release out single-spaced, 12 pages in length on both sides of hot pink paper (setting)? Do you use sources (authority) that only you know are experts in their disciplines?

Understanding (Selective Perception)

The content of the message not only determines whether or not a message is attended to, but it also determines to a great extent whether or not it is understood. Our experiences and our role in society (or frame of reference) shape the way we perceive things. But no one has had identical experiences. Each of us is unique. So each of us perceives things slightly differently. Result: Our unconscious assumption is that the world is as we see it. We tend to believe the way we see things is "correct" and that those who don't share our perceptions are "incorrect" or have "distorted views." (See figure 7.2.)

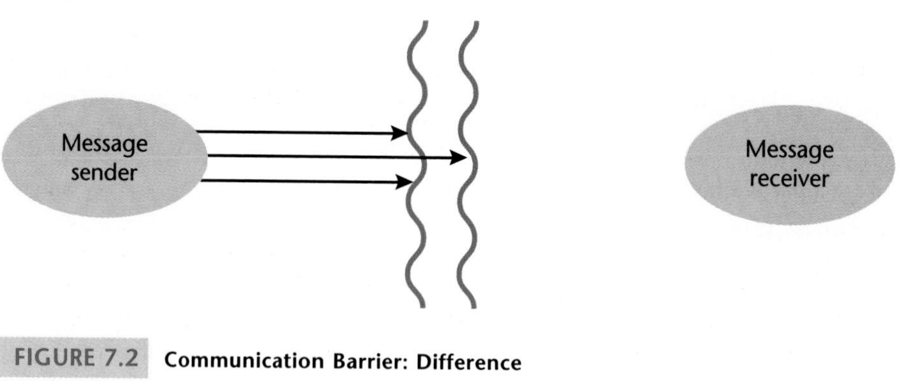

FIGURE 7.2 **Communication Barrier: Difference**

Thus, the major obstacles in communication are failure to acknowledge differences and the failure to successfully negotiate those differences in perceptions. Is your experience more "true" than the experience of others? From a communication viewpoint, the perceptions of each of us is "true" because they reflect what we know and what we are. If you had someone else's frame of reference, you might see things exactly as they do.

1. Though messages may be sent in figure 7.3, no communication occurs (hence, no understanding) because there is no shared experience.

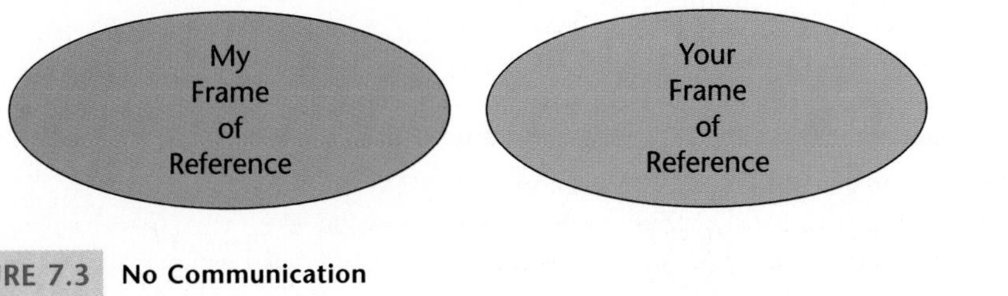

FIGURE 7.3 No Communication

2. Some understanding begins to occur in figure 7.4, however, because there is a common or shared frame of reference (shaded area).

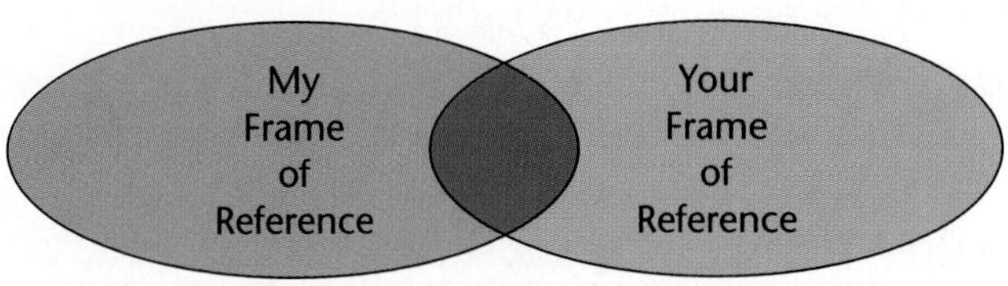

FIGURE 7.4 Communication Occurs in Shaded Area

How do we find common or shared frames of reference? We must find out what other people think and why they think that way. Why? So you can attack the problem—send the message in the context of your message receiver's frame of reference (his or her knowledge, social-cultural role, attitudes, communication skills, needs, wants), not yours. The reason you are communicating is that his or her frame of reference is different from yours. The objective is to understand your receiver's perceptions—not so you can change them or criticize them—but to broaden them so he or she has an understanding of your **selective perceptions** and thus has a better ability to support—or at least not to obstruct—the fulfilling of your objectives. For example, look at legislative issues from the view of the legislator and other groups seeking his or her support, not from your view. You find out these frames of references of your stakeholders through research, both formal and informal.

Retention and Action (Selective Retention and Action)

A message may be attended to and understood, but it still must be retained in order to be acted upon. Retention and the desire to act are increased if the message receiver can answer the following questions:

1. What's in it for me?
2. Is it compatible with my values, needs, and beliefs?

3. Is it easy to remember and do? (Divide complex issues into number of simple issues.)
4. Is it easy to try with little or no risk?
5. Can I observe the consequences of my actions?
6. Is my action positively reinforced by subsequent messages?

Even the most effective communicators don't successfully communicate all the time. Many factors of which we are unaware, or over which we have no control, may distort the messages. But by conscientiously applying the principles of communication, the percentage of success will increase.

Summary

For self-testing and additional chapter resources, go to the student CD and the Online Learning Center at **www.mhhe.com/lattimore**

The public relations practitioner as part of the management team of an organization must be involved in the decision-making process to ensure that the organization takes positive, socially responsible actions. These actions, then, become the source of much of the organization's communication.

Often the process used to implement a public relations plan can be seen as an attempt to spread, or diffuse, information throughout the organization's primary publics. The diffusion process is how new ideas are adopted in society. The critical paths through which new ideas, products, or technologies spread include: awareness, interest, evaluation, trial, and adoption. Mass media is key to the first two of these paths while personal contact may be more important in the last three paths.

The concept of stakeholder management provides a good framework to visualize an organization's environment and to differentiate among the stakeholders. The goal in stakeholder management is to develop maximum overall cooperation between stakeholders and the organization's objectives.

The public relations practitioner is the key communicator within an organization. Writing remains the primary tool of the communicator, but practitioners must master a variety of writing styles. While the inverted pyramid structure is especially important because it is used by most journalists, other styles, such as writing for the Internet, are also necessary.

Another important aspect of the communication process is media selection. The three basic considerations for media selection are the needs and desires of the audiences, the optimum timing for the message, and the budget available for the medium.

Finally, if you want your message to be heard, you need to make sure you get your audiences' attention, understanding, retention, and action. Unfortunately, to be heard a message must go through a "funnel" of selective attention, selective perception, selective retention, and selective action. Therefore, the message is often lost at various stages in the process unless steps are taken to improve the likelihood that the message will be heard.

The final step in the process of public relations, measuring the effects of these messages, will be discussed in the next chapter.

To learn more about public relations communication watch the interview with Steve Erickson, Clip #9, on the book's CD-ROM.

University Hospital

University Hospital, located in a city of about 1.2 million people, is the largest private hospital in the United States with more than 2,000 beds and just over 50,000 patients annually. The hospital employs 6,000 persons and has a medical staff of more than 1,300 and an annual budget of more than $750 million.

Like all hospitals University Hospital has faced tough financial challenges in the era of managed health care. As the hospital prepares to celebrate its centennial year celebration beginning in 18 months, it is looking at public relations strategies that will continue to position the hospital as the leader in hospital care in the city.

As the public relations director for University Hospital, you have been asked to assess the potential impact of contemporary demographic trends in the United States and to recommend appropriate action in relation to the upcoming centennial year celebration.

Questions

1. What stakeholder groups would be involved?
2. What demographic characteristics would you expect to find in each group?
3. What responses do you want to induce in each stakeholder group?
4. What messages do you want to send to each group?
5. What channels of communication will you suggest to convey your messages to each stakeholder group?
6. What communication strategies would you expect to be most productive in this situation?

Key Terms

Use the CD-ROM and Online Learning Center at www.mhhe.com/lattimore to further your understanding of the following terms

active public
aware public
controlled media
diffusion of information
feedback
intervening public
latent public
moderating public
primary public
selective attention
selective perception
stakeholder analysis
stakeholders
uncontrolled media

Notes

1. "Opinions of the Publics," New York: Public Relations Society of America, 16 mm film.
2. "The Pepsi Hoax: What Went Right?" Case study prepared by Pepsi Cola Public Affairs, Somers, NY, 1993.
3. Ray Stitle, Delta Beverage, in a speech for the Memphis Chapter of PRSA, September 13, 1995.
4. Ibid., p. 3.
5. Ibid.
6. Frank Walsh, *Public Relations Writer in a Computer Age* (Englewood Cliffs, NJ: Prentice-Hall, 1986), p. 10.
7. Herbert F. Lionberger, *Adoption of New Ideas and Practices* (Ames, IA: Iowa State University Press, 1960), p. 32.
8. *Mountain Bell Submission,* Public Relations Society of America Silver Anvil Awards Competition, 1983.
9. Ibid.
10. Burton St. John, "Whither P.R. Writing?" *Public Relations Tactics,* April 2002.
11. Craig E. Aronoff et al. *Getting Your Message Across* (St. Paul, MN: West, 1981), pp. 28–31.
12. Cynthia M. King, "The Write Stuff: Teaching the Introductory Public Relations Writing Course," *Public Relations Review* 27 (Winter 2001), pp. 27–46.
13. Candace White and Niranjan Raman, "The World Wide Web as a Public Relations Medium: The Use of Research, Planning and Evaluation in Web Site Development," *Public Relations Review* 25 (Winter 1999), p. 405.
14. Michael L. Kent and Maureen Taylor, "Building Dialogic Relationships Through the World Wide Web," *Public Relations Review* 24 (Fall 1998), pp. 326–31.
15. Suzanne Sparks FitzGerald, "Tips for Using Advertising in Public Relations," *Public Relations Quarterly* 46 (Fall 2001), pp. 43–45.
16. Dan Lattimore and Derry Eynon, "How to Be Heard," presentation for the Independent Petroleum Dealers Association, Vail, CO.

CHAPTER EIGHT

Evaluating Public Relations Effectiveness

8

Outline

PREVIEW

The evaluation step in a public relations program is essential. It permits the practitioner to assess the effectiveness of the effort, demonstrate that effectiveness to management, and plan for future efforts. It also gives an opportunity to adjust tactics while the campaign is in progress. All this means that competent evaluation demonstrates the value of public relations to management.

Evaluation techniques may include impact analysis, audience coverage, audience response, campaign impact, and environmental assessment.

Value is more important than volume in evaluating the effectiveness of public relations efforts. The number of news releases sent to media and even the number used by the media does not equal value in public relations. Traditionally, public relations practitioners have measured output in terms of what was sent and used by media. But this approach doesn't assess quality, cost-effectiveness, or opportunity for improvement. Instead, the evaluation should be measuring changes in behavior, attitudes, knowledge, or awareness.

"Evaluation combines research findings with judgment, past experience, and values to determine the worth of public relations efforts."
—Glen Broom, Professor
San Diego State University

Public relations effectiveness is best measured using an open-system model that takes into account environmental factors and before-and-after comparisons. Open-system evaluation models include effectiveness measures of administrative processes, employee publications, media relations, and advertising ☐

We have divided the process of public relations into four related functions: research, planning, action and communication, and evaluation. In reality, however, the methods discussed in chapter 5 and the material in this chapter are simply different applications of research function. For the sake of illustration and emphasis, we have separated the two chapters, but much of what we say here about evaluating public relations programs relates directly back to the research methods mentioned in chapter 5. Also, as noted earlier, the importance of the Internet and websites to effective public relations is widely accepted. However, early research seems to indicate that few, if any, practitioners use the basics of public relations research, planning, and evaluation of web management.[1]

TRADITIONAL EVALUATION

Most public relations efforts in the past have not been measured, or not been measured adequately, to provide answers to key questions such as the following: Why did the campaign work or fail? What were the most effective tactics? and What would have happened if we had made a change midway through the campaign? Public relations agencies and departments have often not been able to sell management or clients on the necessity of evaluation. One noted practitioner has argued that less than 5 percent of public relations programs have been effectively evaluated.[2]

Traditionally public relations evaluation has been used to measure output, including the number of press releases used, the hits on the website, and the number of video clips used. This is typically the implementation phase of a public relations effort. These implementation measures of output are necessary to provide input into the evaluation,

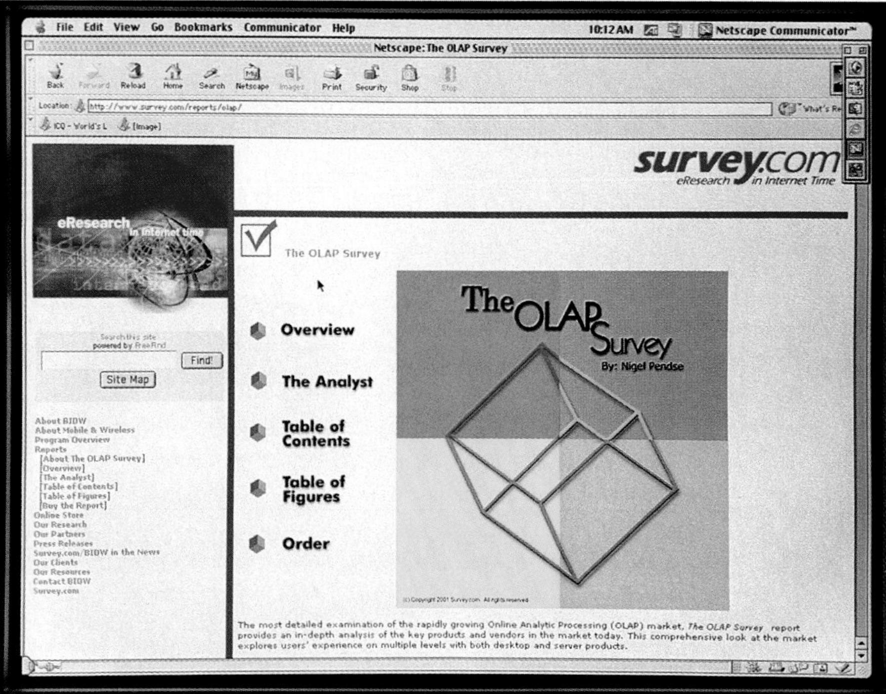

An Internet survey company is often used to create an online evaluation survey.

but they are not sufficient to provide the assessment of quality, cost-effectiveness, or opportunities for improvement. Instead, the practitioner should be measuring changes in behavior, attitudes, knowledge, and awareness.

There are at least three levels of evaluation of public relations efforts. These include preparation for the public relations program, implementation of the effort, and **impact analysis** of the program.

1. *Preparation.* Evaluating preparation may involve examining the adequacy of the background information that you gathered, the appropriateness of the message content and format, and the quality of the messages.
2. *Implementation.* Evaluating implementation involves measuring the number of messages sent (distribution), number of messages placed in the media, number of people receiving the message, and number of people who attend to the message.
3. *Impact.* When impact is evaluated, practitioners measure the number or percentage of the audience who learn the message content, who change their opinions, who change attitudes, and who behave in the desired fashion. They also may determine if the problem is solved or the goal is achieved.

To move toward a more successful evaluation effort all three levels must be examined, not just the traditional implementation measures.

THE NEED FOR EVALUATION RESEARCH

Although presented last, evaluation is not the final stage of the public relations process. In actual practice, **evaluation** is frequently the beginning of a new effort. The research function overlaps the planning, action, and evaluation functions. It is an interdependent process that, once set in motion, has no beginning or end.

To help explain how evaluation can be involved in virtually every phase of a program, figure 8.1 is divided into three evaluation segments:

1. *Implementation Checking.* The central question in this start-up assessment step is: To what degree is the target audience being reached? Regardless of how complete the planning process may have been, it will still be necessary to determine the difference between *planned* and *actual* implementation. Variations from the original plan must be analyzed and explained so that a decision can be made to either modify the plan or correct the discrepancies.
2. *In-Progress Monitoring.* Periodically during the program, actions undertaken should be reviewed, and if necessary, modified. This process is often called **formative evaluation.** These reviews can be planned for regular intervals to determine the effectiveness of the program in meeting its objectives. Any unanticipated results can be assessed and factored into the evaluation. The variance between actual and anticipated progress at each point can be examined for its effect on the overall outcome. Regular monitoring helps determine why some results differ significantly from the original plan and prevents unwelcome surprises.
3. *Outcome Evaluation.* The final step is to assess the program's end results. This process is called **summative evaluation.** Once again, objectives and results are compared to determine the variance. At this point, all prior evaluations become important for explaining the context in which the program was implemented and for interpreting the results. An evaluation report transmits this information, along with any suggestions for planning future efforts, to an appropriate decision maker.

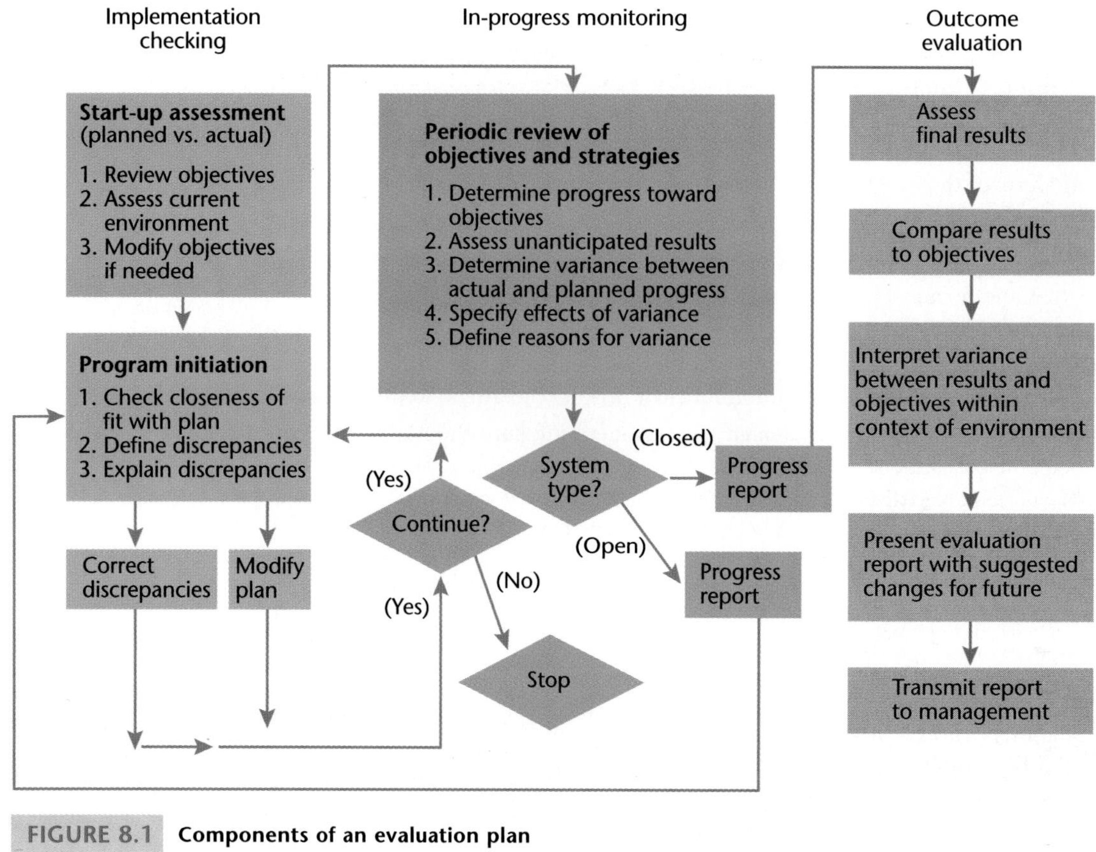

FIGURE 8.1 **Components of an evaluation plan**

Research in public relations should be continuous, constantly evaluating the process and its environment and providing new information to sustain it. Learning about the failures and successes of a public relations campaign provides information that can be used to plan more precisely for the next effort. Evaluation research is also valuable in assessing an existing campaign. This point is illustrated in the Cedar Springs Community Hospital Integrating Case Study. Research made a tremendous impact on the planning and action steps taken in the case. In this final episode, research helps determine the effectiveness of the total effort.

Integrating Case Study

Cedar Springs Community Hospital

Segment 4

Approximately one year after the program to improve the perceptions of employees regarding the quality of patient care began, follow-up research was conducted. This evaluation process began at the same point as the original research. Using the methodology of the initial employee survey, 300 names were once again chosen at random from the 1,226 employees. Each of the selected individuals received a questionnaire in the mail similar to the one used to begin the process.

Four key factors from the original survey had been selected as objectives for improvement during the preceding year. These same factors were measured again in the evaluation survey to determine how much progress had been made. The following comparisons were produced:

Factors	*Average Ratings: Start*	*Average Ratings: End*
1. Quality of care	6.6	7.0
2. Patients' understanding of procedures	5.7	6.2
3. Courtesy and respect shown to patients	7.4	7.8
4. Patient call lights answered <5 minutes	56%	82%

Obviously, a noticeable and positive shift in employee perceptions of the hospital's overall performance had taken place. In addition to the quantitative evidence, which showed gains in every category over the previous year, qualitative indicators also supported this conclusion. Another focus group demonstrated considerable improvement in employees' feelings about the quality of care available. This was reinforced through letters from employees and comments made during monthly employee group meetings.

Although employee perceptions did not rise to the same level as those of recently released patients in earlier surveys, the improvements were consistent and strong. Therefore, management concluded that a program to continue feedback to employees from patients would be an important part of future employee communication programs.

Another important reason evaluation research is a necessity for public relations programs is that it enhances organizational support. Public relations professionals must assume the same responsibility for effectiveness as their management colleagues do. Organizational resources are always limited, and competition for them is keen. Public relations managers must be able to demonstrate effectiveness in ways that can be measured against other competing functions, as Robert Marker, manager of press services for Armstrong Cork, reveals in mini-case 8.1.

MEASURING THE WORTH OF PUBLIC RELATIONS EFFORTS

Too many public relations programs have been eliminated or severely cut back because no "value" could be attached to them. The harsh realities of corporate existence make it necessary for public relations practitioners to demonstrate the worth of what they do. Particularly in difficult economic situations, every aspect of organizational activity is measured by its relative benefit to the firm. Public relations departments that cannot demonstrate their value to the organization will not be in a position to influence the policy decisions that affect their own fate.

8.1 Mini•Case

The Importance of Evaluation

I remember an occasion, some years ago, which started me thinking about the need for some kind of measurement device and internal reporting system to help explain the public relations function.

I was asked by a marketing executive at Armstrong to come to his office and inform him, as succinctly as possible, just what it was he was getting for what he was spending on public relations. It really didn't bother me at the time, because we had had these inquiries before, and I was pretty sure I could handle it. I came prepared with a considerable volume of newspaper clippings, magazine features, and case histories that we had produced in support of his product line that year.

I laid all this out in front of him. . . . After an appropriate interval, I pointed out that all this publicity—if strung end to end—would reach from his office located in the west wing of the building, clear across the center wing to the east wing, down the stairs, and out into the main lobby, and there'd still be enough left over to paper one and a half walls of his office. (That was a favored "measurement" device back in those days. We used to have our secretaries total the column inches, and then convert it all into linear feet of hallway space.) And then it came, the question no one had ever asked before: "But what's all this worth to us?"

I stammered for a moment and said something to the effect that I thought the material spoke for itself. After all, this was highly coveted editorial space we were talking about. . . . I said it would be difficult to attach a specific value to it.

He smiled. "My boy," he said, "I have to attach a value to everything in this operation. . . . Why don't you go back and write me a memo outlining clearly what this function does for us, and then we'll talk about your budget for next year."

Source: Robert K. Marker, "The Armstrong/PR Data Management System," *Public Relations Review* 3 (Winter 1977), pp. 51–52.

Measurement Strategies

The concept of measurement itself is not new to the practice of public relations. All public relations practitioners need to understand the following:

- Their relationship with media representatives
- The impact their messages have on publics they want to reach
- The number of people reached
- How many media use their messages
- What value their efforts have for the organization.[3]

The problem, as Robert Marker discovered, is that the rest of the business world has been using different standards. Marker's measurement system was quantifiable (linear feet of hallway), and it accurately reflected the effort that had been expended. When faced with the devastating question of "worth," however, the measurement strategy could not provide any data. Because the nature of public relations is intangible, assigning a value to its activities is difficult. Often the problem leads practitioners into the use of erroneous measures or measures incorrectly applied.

Like every aspect of public relations practice, evaluation needs careful planning. Ideally, the evaluation effort should be planned from the inception of the program. An evaluation attempt that is tacked on after a program is finished will produce incomplete and generally inappropriate data. When evaluation is part of the overall plan, each component can be constructed with an eye toward measuring its success later.

Measurement by Objectives The use of management by objectives (MBO), or any similar planning process, will help alleviate the measurement problem facing public relations. Although MBO is most frequently used for evaluating individual employees, its basic elements can also be applied to programs, projects, and work groups. The object is to prepare advance statements, usually during the planning phase, concerning legitimate expectations from a given effort. These must be mutually agreed on by all those involved before the action occurs. When the set time for evaluation arrives, objectives can be compared with accomplishments to assess the degree of success. The exact process used varies among organizations, but the basic MBO steps include:

1. *Work Group Involvement.* If more than one person will be working on the project, the entire group should be involved in setting the objectives. This is important so that no portion of the task is overlooked and each contributor feels committed to the effort.
2. *Manager-Subordinate Involvement.* Once the objectives of the group are established, each subordinate should work with the manager of the project to define a set of individual objectives. These keep the project moving by ensuring that everyone understands his or her role.
3. *Determination of Intermediate Objectives.* This step defines a series of objectives along the way toward the overall target. Setting intermediate objectives permits in-progress evaluation to be done more precisely and makes it possible to consider midcourse corrections before the project gets out of hand.
4. *Determination of Measures of Achievement.* The point when the effort will be considered complete should be specified either in terms of a time element or the achievement of a stated objective.
5. *Review, Evaluation, and Recycling.* Because no objective can be defined with absolute precision nor achieved perfectly, it is important to use information gained from each evaluation process to improve the planning for the next public relations effort.

Impact Analysis Measuring the impact or results of a public relations effort is always difficult and never totally objective. As we have discussed in this chapter, however, the more public relations practitioners can quantitatively measure the effects of their work, the better they will be able to plan future efforts and demonstrate their value to organizational decision makers. In this section, we offer four dimensions of measurement that can be applied to assess the impact of any public relations campaign, regardless of its size: *audience coverage, audience response, campaign impact,* and *environmental mediation.*

Audience Coverage Perhaps the first point that must be documented in evaluating any public relations effort is whether or not the intended audiences were reached. Other questions that should be answered in the initial phase are: To what extent was each target audience exposed to the various messages? Which unintended audiences also received the messages?

Two basic measures are used to help answer these questions. First, accurate records must be kept of what messages were prepared and where they were sent. Second, a system must be used to keep track of which releases were used and by whom. Although the first measure is the easiest to calculate, it is worthless without the second for comparison. Massive amounts of publicity have no value unless some of it actually reaches the intended audience. Therefore, some method must be devised to accurately measure the use of publicity and the coverage of events.

Essentially, such measurement can be accomplished if the practitioner and/or other staff members keep a careful check on target media and maintain clipping files. This, of course, is easier for print than for broadcast media, but some radio and television stations give periodic reports to public relations practitioners if requested. In addition, clipping services that monitor both print and broadcast media provide regular reports for a fee. Such a service must be selected carefully, based on the recommendations of other users concerning its accuracy.

The measurement of **audience coverage** involves more than just the ratio of releases sent compared with releases used. The practitioner must also be able to specify what audiences (both intended and unintended) were reached by which media. This type of data is available from *readership surveys* and audience rating information obtainable through media advertising sales departments. Audience profiles for each publication or broadcast station can be calculated with the amount of space or time used to yield a complete measure of audience coverage. Such data can be reported in terms of total column inches (for print media), airtime per audience (for broadcast media) for each release or event, or hits for a webpage. John Pavlik, John Vastyan, and Michael Maher used a readership survey at a medical center to determine that employees who were more integrated into the organization were more likely to read a company newsletter—the newsletter could then be designed to meet the needs of this public.[4] For more of a bottom line effect, however, many practitioners translate media time and space into dollar values based on prevailing advertising rates. Although it may be effective in illustrating a point to management, it has very little validity in determining what the effect was of that exposure on the intended audience.

Audience Response Once it is determined that a message has reached its intended audience, the practitioner must evaluate that audience's response. Frequently, this type of information can be obtained through various message pretesting methods like those discussed in this chapter and in chapter 5. Samples of each target audience are exposed to various messages before they are released. The resulting data help predict whether the message will cause a favorable or unfavorable reaction. It can also determine if the message attracts attention, arouses interest, or gains audience understanding. By applying good sampling techniques and questionnaire design (chapter 5), accurate predictions are possible, and problems can be corrected before messages are released. Some messages, however, such as spot news or stories written from releases, cannot be measured in advance because they are not controlled by the practitioner. Thus, it is necessary to measure audience response using the survey techniques discussed in chapter 5. Frequently, audience response can be predicted by tracking media treatment of stories in terms of favorable, neutral, and unfavorable tendencies, as we shall see later in this chapter.

Messages can also be pretested using *readability studies.* The basic premise of these tests is that written copy will be ineffective if it is too difficult to read. Most methods for measuring readability generate an index score that translates to an approximate educational level required for understanding the material. For example, *Time* and *Reader's Digest* are written at what is termed an 11th- or 12th-grade level. This indicates that their readers are primarily persons with at least a high school education. A great deal of controversy exists over which formula is the most accurate and what factors are necessary to compute readability. Readability tests may, however, be useful in public relations efforts to tailor writing styles toward target publications. The index score of a news release compared with the score of the publication for which it is intended should indicate whether or not the two are compatible.

Four standard readability instruments are described here:

1. The *Flesch Formula* produces both a reading ease score and a human interest score.[5]

2. The *Gunning Fog Index* measures reading ease only and is one of the simplest methods.[6]
3. The *Dale-Chall Formula* computes both sentence length and the number of infrequently used words.[7]
4. The *Cloze Procedure* is a technique designed to measure readability and comprehension of both spoken and visual messages.[8]

Remember that the simplest writing is not always the best. Meaning may be lost through oversimplification as easily as through complexity. Abstract or complex concepts cannot be adequately expressed in simple, short sentences using one- and two-syllable words. The important point is to match the written message to the publication and audience for which it is intended. This textbook, for example, was written for college students who are studying public relations, not for casual readers. Frequently, editors of internal publications for highly technical organizations must avoid talking down to their readers as much as they avoid "fog."

Campaign Impact In addition to considering audience response to individual messages, the practitioner must be concerned with the impact of the campaign as a whole. In this case, the whole is not equal to the sum of the parts. If a campaign is correctly researched and planned, its elements will interact to produce an effect that is much greater than the sum of the response to the individual messages. If the mix is not right, however, the elements of the campaign combined, no matter how individually excellent, may fall far short of the goal.

Therefore, it is important to measure the cumulative impact of a public relations campaign, keeping in mind the goals developed in the planning phase. This can be done only after the campaign has been in progress long enough to achieve some results. Effects are generally attitudinal, although they can also be behavioral. If one campaign goal is to maintain or increase favorable attitudes toward an organization among members of certain publics, research methods such as the organizational image surveys described in chapter 5 can be used to gauge success. Usually this calls for both pretests and posttests or for a series of surveys to track attitude trends. In addition, certain actions by members of a public can be measured, like complaints, inquiries about services, and requests for reprints.

Environmental Mediation Practitioners must realize that the public relations campaign is not the only influence on the attitudes and behaviors of their publics. Public relations campaigns exist in an environment of social processes that can have as much or more effect on the goals of the effort as the prepared messages do. Therefore, the measured results must be interpreted in light of various other forces in operation. Failure to reach a goal may not be failure at all when unforeseen negative conditions have arisen. Likewise, a striking success may not be entirely attributable to the public relations campaign when positive environmental forces were also present at the time. Therefore, techniques such as environmental monitoring and others discussed in chapter 5 should be used to evaluate the results of a campaign.

One method that can be used to check for environmental influences, even when the practitioner has a small budget and staff, is focus group interviewing. Focus groups are composed of individuals randomly selected from a public who meet to discuss the campaign. The group should be presented with the elements of the campaign and then directed through a discussion of its effects and the causes of those effects. A skillful interviewer will keep the discussion on the subject without disturbing candor or the free flow of ideas. Focus groups should be asked to discuss their reactions to the elements of the campaign and assess the campaign's overall effect. They can also help interpret data obtained in the campaign impact stage in relation to historical, social, and political events that may have had an effect.

These four stages of measurement can help a public relations practitioner more completely assess the results of a campaign and plan effective future efforts. These stages of measurement also provide the same kind of real-world data that managers in other areas of an organization use to support their activities.

Sources of Measurement Error

Some common mistakes in the measurement of public relations effectiveness include the following:

1. *Volume Is Not Equal to Results.* Too often, the working assumption is that if one press release is effective, three will be three times as effective. As Marker learned, a large stack or even a long chain of press clippings may be proof of effort. But results in terms of the effect of those clippings on the publics for which they were intended cannot be measured by volume. Even audience measurement devices designed to count the number of people exposed to a message do not show whether or not those exposed actually paid any attention or, if they did, what effect the message had on them.
2. *Estimate Is Not Measurement.* Relying on experience and intuition to gauge the effectiveness of public relations efforts is no longer acceptable as objective measurement. Experts know that appearances, even to the trained eye, can be deceiving. Guesswork has no place in a measurement system. It can be appealing and comfortable because it is easy to accomplish and flattering to the expert. However, when it comes to budget requests, managers like the one Marker encountered demand hard facts.
3. *Samples Must Be Representative.* Many wrong decisions about the future of a public relations campaign have been based on a few favorable comments that were either volunteered or collected unsystematically. Several dangers exist in doing this: Only those with positive (or negative) comments may volunteer them; some people, when asked, tend to give the response they think the interviewer wants to hear; or, the selection of interviewers may be unintentionally biased. Samples must be selected scientifically and systematically to avoid such errors.
4. *Effort Is Not Knowledge.* One of the most common public relations objectives is to increase the public's knowledge about a particular subject. Sometimes practitioners assume a direct relationship between the amount of effort they expend in communicating a message and the amount of knowledge a public acquires. This erroneous assumption leads to a problem similar to the volume error discussed earlier. The study of human learning suggests that after a certain level of knowledge is reached, the rate of learning slows in most people. Therefore, in spite of any communicator's best efforts, all publics will eventually reach a knowledge level at which very little additional learning occurs.
5. *Knowledge Is Not Favorable Attitude.* Communication is often assumed successful if the public gained knowledge of the subject of the message. Even when pretest and posttest results indicate an increase in knowledge, it cannot be assumed that more favorable attitudes have also resulted. A high degree of name recall or aware-

ness is not necessarily an indication that the public relations effort has been effective. Familiarity does not necessarily lead to positive opinion.

6. *Attitude Is Not Behavior.* Although positive public opinion may be a legitimate goal of public relations, it is incorrect to assume that favorable attitudes will result in desired behavior. When members of a particular public have favorable attitudes toward a client or organization, they will probably not consciously oppose that person or group. On the other hand, they still may not actively support the goals of the public relations campaign. Our discussion of latent, aware, and active publics in chapter 5 emphasized this point. Practitioners must be aware of the need to predict behavior, or at least potential behavior, when measuring public opinion.

CLOSED-SYSTEM EVALUATION

Mark P. McElreath describes two models of public relations research into which most measurement efforts can be categorized: open and closed evaluation systems.[9] A **closed-system evaluation** limits its scope to the messages and events planned for the campaign and their effects on the intended publics. This is the model of public relations evaluation most frequently used. The intent of the system is to test the messages and media of a public relations campaign before they are presented to the intended publics. This pretest strategy is designed to uncover miscalculations that may have gone unnoticed in the planning stage. The posttest evaluation is conducted after the campaign has been underway long enough to produce results. Posttest data can be compared with pretest results and campaign objectives to evaluate the effectiveness of the effort. These results also provide input for planning the next campaign.

Pretest/Posttest Design

The following factors are normally considered in the standard pretest and posttest evaluation design:

1. *Productions.* An accounting is conducted of every public relations tool used in the campaign (press releases, press kits, booklets, films, letters, etc.). The amount of material actually produced and the total cost of production yield important cost-effectiveness information. The amount of time and budget devoted to each segment of a public relations effort can be reassessed with this type of data.
2. *Distribution.* The evaluation design includes the channels through which the messages of the campaign are distributed. Clippings collected by professional services are often used to measure how many stories were actually printed. The number of radio and television stations that picked up the story can be important information. These kinds of data are perhaps most frequently used to evaluate public relations campaigns. Note that although these kinds of data provide a reasonable measure of the efficiency of the campaign, distribution data do not really address the issue of effectiveness.
3. *Interest.* Reader interest surveys determine what people read in various types of publications. A representative sample of the total potential reading audience is surveyed to obtain a quantitative measure of which items attract more interest. These are relatively good measures of what readers actually consume, but they do not measure comprehension or the effect of the message on the reader. Television and radio use similar survey methods to determine what programs and times people prefer.

4. *Reach.* Reader interest surveys not only provide information concerning whether or not a story was read, but also describe the people who read it. This information can be valuable because messages frequently reach publics other than those for whom they are intended. The efficiency of a message is the extent to which it actually reaches the intended audience. A reasonably accurate measure of which audiences are being reached by which messages is imperative to any evaluation effort. Television and radio ratings services provide information concerning the characteristics of audiences at various times of the day.
5. *Understanding.* Although it is important to determine whether the target audience is being reached, it is equally important to know whether or not the audience can understand the message. A public relations campaign cannot be considered successful if the public does not get the point. Frequently, readability tests are applied to printed messages to measure their reading ease. As we have already discussed, readability is measured according to sentence length and number of syllables in the words used. Much criticism has been directed at them, but they remain standard instruments for pretest evaluation.
6. *Attitudes.* Creating and maintaining positive attitudes or changing negative ones is a central purpose of all public relations activity. Therefore, measuring attitudes, or preferably attitude change, is a highly prized form of evaluation. Frequently a pretest/posttest measurement is conducted to determine the amount of change in the attitudes of target publics that can be attributed to the public relations campaign.

   Measuring attitudes is a sophisticated behavioral science technique that presents many opportunities for error. Few practitioners attempt major attitudinal studies without the help of professionals who specialize in this type of measurement. Several of the research techniques discussed in chapter 5 (e.g., the public relations audit) use some form of attitudinal measurement. Professional research organizations frequently provide attitudinal data for public relations evaluation. Many factors, ranging from the need for a scientifically selected sample to the construction of a questionnaire that will not bias results, make attitude measurement a difficult task for most practitioners.

Disadvantages of the Closed-System Method

Although closed-system evaluation is the model most widely used by public relations staffs, it has two major drawbacks. First, as we have already discussed, because a message was transmitted to the intended audience in an understandable form and that it produced favorable attitudes does not mean the campaign goals were reached. Second, the likelihood that desired results will occur, especially in terms of actual behavior changes, is influenced by a number of factors outside the elements of the campaign. If a public relations effort fails to achieve its goals, it may not mean that the elements or the plan of the effort were faulty. A number of environmental factors such as economic, political, and social change can nullify what might otherwise have been positive results.

Oil companies caught in the grasp of an embargo that caused rapidly rising prices, shortages, and long lines at the gas pumps experienced losses in favorable public opinion in spite of massive public relations efforts during the early 1970s. The effectiveness of their messages was eroded by events outside the control of any public relations campaign. Therefore, these events had to be considered in evaluating the public relations efforts. Even though losses rather than gains in positive public opinion were experienced, the campaigns may still have been effective. Without workable public relations plans already in place, the losses in favorable public opinion could have been even more devastating.

OPEN-SYSTEM EVALUATION

Although a pretest/posttest design may be appropriate for evaluating short-range projects, many public relations programs are too complex for simple before-and-after measures. Continuing or long-range programs, such as changes in organizational policy, require an evaluation method that can provide feedback throughout the process without waiting for end results. **Open-system evaluation** models attempt to incorporate factors outside the control of the public relations campaign when assessing its effectiveness.

The open-system model emphasizes the extent to which the public relations function is encompassed by numerous other aspects of an organization and its environment. Factors like unintended audiences and organizational administration and effectiveness are also included.

In chapter 5, we discussed the growing use of environmental monitoring and social audits as methods of gathering information. These same techniques provide valuable data for evaluating effectiveness in public relations campaigns. The effects of public relations efforts on various environmental factors can be one useful measure of results. In turn, the environmental data can help explain the effects of a campaign. Because most of these factors are outside the organization's control, they may operate as confounding variables in a closed-system evaluation. Economic conditions, for example, can have a significant effect on the attitudes of consumers toward an organization. Thus, results from a public relations effort that do not seem positive when considered alone might really be significant when the negative effects of certain economic conditions are considered.

Internal climate data are also useful for evaluating public relations campaigns. Public relations messages should be expected to have as much effect on the managers and employees of an organization as they do on other publics. In chapter 5, we suggested that organizations research their internal climate for public relations planning information, and this is also true for evaluation. Public relations practitioners should look inside and outside their organizations to measure the effects of their efforts. Just as with environmental factors, the internal climate of an organization can help explain the effect of a public relations effort. Union activities, management perceptions, and changes in company policy can all affect the results of a campaign.

Many of the factors included in the open-system evaluation model are difficult to measure accurately. Nevertheless, recognizing these factors is itself an important step toward evaluating public relations efforts. The value of the open-system method of evaluation is that it considers public relations in the broader spectrum of overall organizational effectiveness.

The Short-Term and Continuing Approaches

Both open- and closed-system models can be used in either short-term or continuing applications. When a public relations effort does not seek to establish a dialogue with an audience or receive feedback, a short-term approach to evaluation may be appropriate. Therefore, if the objective of an effort is simply to distribute news releases to media, a short-term approach to determine their usage could be sufficient.

However, for long-term, complex programs a more flexible approach to evaluation is needed. The continuing approach allows for an iterative loop that can take into account the effects that are being created by the program as it continues over time. Therefore, the program becomes self-correcting as it processes information about its impact

An employee asks a question of the Qwest CEO in Denver. Qwest is trying to return to its "roots" as a regional phone provider.

and redefines tactics and even strategies on a continuing basis.[10] This approach combined with an open-system model can allow public relations programs to evolve as environments change and publics change.

An Open-System Plan in Actual Practice

James F. Tirone, public relations director of American Telephone and Telegraph Company before its breakup, maintained that public relations is a managerial as well as a creative effort.[11] Tirone believed that public relations should meet the same tests of performance as other management functions. This belief is reflected in the classic measurement techniques developed by the Bell System to be uniformly applied in a wide variety of public relations situations. Although they are more than 20 years old, the following examples from the Bell System program still represent an excellent attempt to implement an open-system evaluation model in three areas: administrative processes, employee publications, and media relations.

Evaluating Administrative Processes To measure the effectiveness of public relations administrative processes, Tirone used information already available from standard organization sources to make some unique comparisons. By relating public relations budgets to these standard measurements in the industry, Tirone was able to show a "return" of public relations expenditures. Taking this comparison still further, Tirone demonstrated that when compared with the increase in the consumer price index (one way to measure inflation), the general public relations budgets fell significantly behind, while the advertising budget stayed even.

Evaluating Employee Publications The success of employee publications in the Bell System was measured against corporate objectives for them: to "reach all employees, create awareness, establish a reputation for reliability, be written so the material can be understood, and be readable at an educational level appropriate to the audience."

TABLE 8.1 **Top Recall by Employees of Company Newspaper Articles (Three Issues of the Publication)**

Subject Matter	Unaided Recall (%)
Employment office hiring (1)	56
Defending the company (3)	42
Pioneer circus (1)	40
Marketing/competition	36
Corporate planning seminar (3-week average)	6
Averaged recall	36

Source: James F. Tirone, "Measuring the Bell System's Public Relations," *Public Relations Review* 3 (Winter 1977), p. 29. Reprinted by permission.

TABLE 8.2 **Employee Publication Scoring**

Component	Score
Distribution	67%
Awareness	36%
Reliability (average)	34%
Very understandable	61%
Both sides/Excellent	12%
Source/Excellent	30%
Understanding (CPS only)	40%
Readability (CPS only)	16.5 years

Source: James F. Tirone, "Measuring the Bell System's Public Relations," *Public Relations Review* 3 (Winter 1977), p. 30. Reprinted by permission.

These objectives were translated into the following measurement criteria: "how effectively the publication was distributed within forty-eight hours, an average estimate of reader awareness of stories, a reliability index, understanding, and readability (as measured on the Gunning scale)." Table 8.1 reports the ability of a sample of employees to recall (without any help) certain stories that appeared in the company's weekly newspaper. Table 8.2 reports measures of all the components of publication efficiency as operationally defined.

Distribution. Percentage of issues delivered in 48-hour period.

Awareness. Average of recall data.

Reliability. Average response to three questions about the newspaper. Is it very understandable? Is it excellent at presenting both sides? and Is it an excellent source of information?

Understanding. Percentage of those recalling and comprehending the corporate planning seminar story.

Readability. The Gunning score for the corporate planning seminar story, which is roughly equal to the number of years of education required for comprehension.

TABLE 8.3 Newspaper Stories by Region, $N = 3{,}848$

	Favorable (%)	Unfavorable (%)	Neutral (%)	Totals (%)
Northeast	14	5	5	24
South	18	5	8	31
North Central	18	3	10	31
West	9	2	3	14
	59	15	26	100

Source: James F. Tirone, "Measuring the Bell System's Public Relations," *Public Relations Review* 3 (Winter 1977), p. 34. Reprinted by permission.

TABLE 8.4 Treatment by Media Services

	Favorable (%)	Unfavorable (%)	Neutral (%)	Totals (%)
AP	61	18	21	100
UPI	19	33	48	100
Syndicates	43	22	35	100

Source: James F. Tirone, "Measuring the Bell System's Public Relations," *Public Relations Review* 3 (Winter 1977), p. 34. Reprinted by permission.

Evaluating Media Relations Measuring the effectiveness of an organization's relationships with media representatives is a difficult task. Tirone reported three aspects of these relationships that can be measured to some degree: "the media's views of those relationships, the consequences which follow from news release output, and the activity of our (Bell System) media representative."[12] As a first step toward accomplishing these measurement objectives, Tirone proposed a nationwide survey of news media representatives to estimate their ratings of the quality and quantity of Bell System releases. He also instigated an analysis of the media to determine what was actually being said about Bell.

To begin the second phase of the process, Bell hired PR Data Systems, Inc., to code and computerize information collected from clippings and electronic media reports. Over a long period, this type of data could help measure both access to Bell spokespersons and the quality of their relationships with media representatives. Tables 8.3 and 8.4 report the percentage of favorable, unfavorable, and neutral stories according to region of the country and media service, respectively. From these data, certain discrepancies can be discovered that are useful in pinpointing problem areas and in planning future efforts.

EVALUATION SOFTWARE

As public relations practitioners have seen the necessity to begin to do more systematic evaluation, many have begun to use new technology to aid them in their efforts. Several new tools have been developed to help practitioners evaluate the effectiveness of their efforts. For example, Edelman Public Relations Worldwide reports that it has developed its own Edelman Media Analysis and Planning tool, which "doesn't just tell users where the story appeared—but also who exactly read it."[13]

PRTrack by TRAKWare, Inc., is a commercially available package designed to easily calculate what the program calls "media value" by computing the equivalent value of advertising in media. While these tools can be useful, they still provide "subjective numbers" that measure only output.[14] Outcome results require more sophisticated and multivariate approaches like those discussed in this chapter.

Summary

Frequently, evaluation is assumed to be the final step in the process of public relations; however, it is really best described as a new beginning. Measuring the effectiveness of a public relations effort frequently provides new direction and emphasis for an ongoing program. Even when the project being evaluated does not continue, the lessons learned concerning its effectiveness will be useful in numerous future activities. Knowledge gained through careful evaluation is an important payoff to any public relations effort. Evaluation of projects that are obvious failures can help prevent future mistakes. Careful measurements of successful efforts will help reproduce positive elements in future programs.

Public relations can no longer afford to ignore the question "But what's it all worth to us?" Practitioners must be ready to respond with appropriate methods, solid data, and accurate predictions.

For self-testing and additional chapter resources, go to the student CD and the Online Learning Center at **www.mhhe.com/lattimore**

To learn more about evaluation watch the interview with Dr. Rick Fischer, Clip #15, on the book's CD-ROM.

River City Symphony

Problem

The River City Symphony's board of directors decided to use the summer months to stimulate interest in the upcoming fall and winter concert series. They arranged for the symphony to present free open-air concerts in several area parks to give a "back-to-the-people" feeling to what had been considered a "highbrow" image.

Objectives

1. To change the image of the symphony to make ordinary people feel comfortable attending concerts
2. To sell 25% more season tickets
3. To increase annual fund-raising by $50,000

To accomplish its objectives, the symphony's board planned the following.

Strategies and Tactics

1. Prepare a Media Campaign
   a. News releases about the summer concerts
   b. PSAs for radio about the concert series
   c. PSA for TV; spot done by local university students
   d. Talk show interviews with symphony director and key members

2. Develop an Advertising Campaign
   a. Print ads for local newspapers
   b. Radio ads for local radio stations
   c. Cable TV ads
3. Encourage Volunteer Assistance
   a. AARP to provide ushering
   b. University music department to assist
   c. University art department to help with materials
4. Develop Informational Materials
   a. Summer series brochures
   b. Summer series posters
   c. Video: "Summer Symphony on Tour"

Questions

1. What benchmark data would you need?
2. What would you measure in the preparation stage? The implementation phase? The impact phase?
3. How would you prepare the evaluation section for the symphony's public relations plan?

Key Terms

Use the CD-ROM and Online Learning Center at www.mhhe.com/lattimore to further your understanding of the following terms

audience coverage
closed-system evaluation
evaluation
formative evaluation
impact analysis
open-system evaluation
summative evaluation

Notes

1. Candace White and Niranjan Raman, "The World Wide Web as a Public Relations Medium: The Use of Research, Planning and Evaluation in Web Site Development," *Public Relations Review* 25 (Winter 1999), pp. 405–19.
2. Pat Jackson, "Measurement and Evaluation," video interview, 1998.
3. Carole M. Howard and Wilma K. Mathews, "Measurement/Evaluation: How to Know If Your Program Is Working," in *On Deadline: Managing Media Relations* (Prospect Heights, IL: Waveland Press, 2000), p. 272.
4. John Pavlik, John Vastyan, and Michael F. Maher, "Using Readership Research to Study Employee Views," *Public Relations Review* (Summer 1990), pp. 50–60.
5. Rudolph Flesch, *How to Test Readability* (New York: Harper & Row, 1951).
6. Robert Gunning, *The Technique of Clear Writing* (New York: McGraw-Hill, 1968).

7. Edgar Dale and Jeanne Chall, "A Formula for Predicting Readability," *Educational Research Bulletin* 27 (January–February 1948).
8. Wilson Taylor, "Cloze Procedure: A New Tool for Measuring Readability," *Journalism Quarterly* 3 (Fall 1953), pp. 415–33; "Recent Developments in the Use of Cloze Procedure," *Journalism Quarterly* (Winter 1956).
9. Mark McElreath, "Public Relations Evaluative Research: Summary Statement," *Public Relations Review* 3 (Winter 1977), p. 133.
10. Tom Watson, "Integrating Planning and Evaluation, Evaluating the Public Relations Practice and Public Relations Programs," in *Public Relations Handbook,* ed. Robert L. Heath and Gabriel Vasquez (Thousand Oaks, CA: Sage, 2001), pp. 266–68.
11. James F. Tirone, "Measuring the Bell System's Public Relations," *Public Relations Review* 3 (Winter 1977), pp. 21–38.
12. Ibid., p. 31.
13. "Count Clips While You Make More," *PR Intelligence* 11 (January 1999), p. 4.
14. Howard and Mathews, p. 279.

PART THREE

The Publics

III

A public is a group of people with certain common characteristics. A public can be large—college students, Hispanics, blue-collar workers, or even all taxpayers. It can be small—the town council, the executive council for a university, newspaper editors, or even a three-person tax appeal board. Different organizations have different publics, often called stakeholders because they have a particular interest in that organization. The publics for the auto industry are different from those for the school board. Not-for-profit organizations have publics different from profit-seeking companies. Different levels of government organizations deal with different publics.

Part III describes five general types of publics that most public relations professionals face on a regular basis. Chapter 9 discusses the media, one of the most basic publics that practitioners deal with. Chapter 10 focuses on the organization's relationship with its employees, and Chapter 11 delves into the complex relationships between an organization and its community. Chapter 12 covers the importance of consumers to modern organizations. Finally, Chapter 13 discusses the impact of financial markets on public relations practice □

CHAPTER NINE

Media Relations

9

Outline

PREVIEW
THE ROLE OF MEDIA IN PUBLIC RELATIONS
The Internet
Newspapers
Newswires
Magazines
Radio
Television and Cable Television
Online News Services
THE RELATIONSHIP BETWEEN JOURNALISTS AND PR PRACTITIONERS
The Public Relations Practitioner's View of the Journalist
Mutual Dependence
Building Positive Relationships
WORKING WITH THE MEDIA
Preparing to Meet the Media
Preparation Strategies
Research and Planning in Media Relations
MEDIA RELATIONS IN PROGRAM ELEMENTS
Packaging News Releases
Distributing News Releases
Organizing Press or News Conferences
USES OF VIDEO
INTRANETS, EXTRANETS, AND WEBSITES
CRISIS COMMUNICATION
SUMMARY

P R E V I E W

Media relations work—or gaining support for your organization through the media—is a core component of public relations practice. In fact, the relative importance of media relations work increases because business demands instant communication on a worldwide basis. Journalists have mixed feelings toward public relations practitioners—suspecting them of manipulation while depending on them for information. Public relations practitioners view journalists as an audience, as a medium through which to reach the broader public, and as gatekeepers representing and responding to the public's need to know. This chapter outlines and illustrates the basic ingredients of a media relations program with additional attention given to crisis communication ☐

THE ROLE OF MEDIA IN PUBLIC RELATIONS

More than ever before, sophisticated **media relations** and publicity work form the backbone for public relations practice. In many respects developing and maintaining good relationships with the media continue to be hallmarks of the practice. Getting your organization's news and information printed or aired in the mass media has been the traditional means of gaining support for businesses, nonprofit organizations, and government agencies.

The media provide a relatively economical and effective method for communicating with large and dispersed publics. In this sense, the media serve as the gatekeeper or filter through which public relations practitioners reach the general public and other groups whose support they need. When the media publish or broadcast information supplied by organizations in news columns or within a news broadcast, that information seems to convey a sense of legitimacy that the organization may not get from paid advertising. This status or seal of approval that media coverage confers on an organization's news and information is called **third-party endorsement.**

Today, media relations work takes on added and somewhat different importance by reaching smaller, more defined target publics or audience segments through mass, specialized, and organization-controlled media. In large part, this new media relations environment is a result of the Internet and growing numbers of media outlets. By 2010, many believe that media relations work will be done almost exclusively online and that it will barely resemble what it was in 2000.

The Internet

The **Internet** turns every newsroom in the world into a round-the-clock operation. Writing in *PR Strategist,* Michael Lissauer describes the new media world from the vantage point of MSNBC and CNN. MSNBC.com draws five times the daily audience than its parent MSNBC cable TV news programming. CNN.com generates approximately 2.7 million unique visitors daily, compared with 450,000 and 545,000 viewers of its 5 P.M. and 11 P.M. cable news shows, respectively.[1]

Before the Internet, the thrust of media relations work was "pushing" information from the organization to the desks of media reporters, producers, and editors via news releases, news tips, and press kits. That's all changed, because the Internet lets the reporter pull and piece together company information from the corporate website without ever going through the public relations or media relations office of an organization or agency. Dot-com journalists believe they have deadlines every second. As media relations expert Carole Howard notes, "the media day has turned into the media hour and now the media minute or second."[2] The key point here is that the Internet is a very different and more powerful media relations tool than others.

In short, the Internet has changed the way reporters work just as much as it has changed the way public relations practitioners work. Reporters get their story leads and background information from the Internet. Beyond that, most reporters check the website while writing their stories, especially broad-based pieces. This calls for public relations practitioners to update their organizations' website regularly and to make all the media "pages" and links readily accessible so that reporters who cover an organization and industry come to consider it a current, useful, and trusted source.

As a result, organizations work diligently anticipating reporters' questions as a guide to what goes on the website and associated links. Typically, this includes basic company information such as history and background, product information, executive speeches, and news release files. Regular website updating is a must.

A journalist talks on the phone to a public relations contact.

Aside from the Internet, the number of media outlets proliferates weekly, adding new challenges to the media relations function.[3] This is especially the case with cable television channels and new magazine startups, including trade and professional publications. There seems to be no end to segmenting audiences into smaller niches. For the public relations practitioner this means there is an ever-pressing need to tailor messages to target audiences.

Before assessing these trends in more detail, let's picture the size of the U.S. media industry, not to mention media outlets on a worldwide basis. Our emphasis here is on the news media or what public relations practitioners call *uncontrolled media.* They're uncontrolled in the sense that public relations practitioners can send news and information to these media, but the media reporters and editors control if and how it will be used. In contrast, public relations practitioners do control the content and display of information in company publications and newsletters, e-mail, closed-circuit television, displays and exhibits, paid advertising, bulletin boards, billboards, brochures, flyers, posters and what goes on the website.

Newspapers

Newspapers remain the workhorses of the public information system. That is, newspaper reporters gather most of the daily news, especially the public affairs news or news about government, social change, and economic development. Newspapers are a primary means of reaching community publics. Although no longer the primary news medium for the majority, newspapers are still a powerful force in shaping the public agenda and influencing the outcome to date. And for individuals seeking political content, survey results show that they tend to turn to newspapers. In many respects, daily newspapers offer public relations practitioners the greatest opportunities because they have more space to fill and they offer the greatest range of special sections and specialized reporters assigned to such beats as environment, health, business, science, and so on.

The number of U.S. daily newspapers has been shrinking constantly since the 1950s. There were 1,772 daily papers in 1950, for example, and only 16 fewer or 1,756 in 1975. By 2001, there were 1,521 dailies, with losses owing to mergers and discontinued publications.[4] Average circulation of surviving dailies has increased, and adults who say they read newspapers spend an average of 28 minutes a day with their daily newspaper.

Weekly and semiweekly newspaper outlets have been holding fairly steady with 7,996 weeklies and semiweeklies published in 2001.[5] Weeklies include suburban, rural, urban neighborhood, alternative, immigrant, and ethnic papers. Combined circulation tops 70 million. These newspapers are still an effective, direct, and intimate means of reaching the people of suburbs, small towns, and rural areas who are often the source of grassroots opinion. Readers of weekly newspapers are loyal and read their papers thoroughly. A weekly newspaper arguably exerts a far greater impact on readers' opinions than does the typical daily.

Newswires

Daily newspapers and television stations get much of their news from one or more of the newswires. Associated Press is a cooperative whose subscribers include 1,600 family and weekly newspapers and 5,900 radio and television stations. Newspapers also subscribe to news services from the *New York Times, Washington Post, Los Angeles Times, Knight-Ridder,* and newspaper syndicates such as King Features, National Newspaper Syndicate, News America Syndicate, United Features Syndicate, and Newspaper Enterprises Syndicate. PR Newswire distributes news releases submitted by organizations to about 1,500 major media outlets in every area of the country. PR Newswire also helps media reporters by maintaining a news release library or files of past news releases it has distributed for its clients.

Magazines

Of the 22,000 regularly published magazines in the United States, nearly 12,000 are defined as general interest consumer publications and 10,000 as more specialized trade and industry publications.[6] Every possible hobby, interest, and occupation has its own magazine. Even so, magazine competition is so fierce that only 30 of the estimated 300 started each year actually survive.

Consumer magazines are best for production quality, placement of news near corresponding ads, reader services, and so on. Generally speaking, public relations practitioners do not make as much use of consumer magazines as they do of trade and professional publications. The "trades" reach those who work in particular industries or whose interests and information needs surpass those provided by mass media. As a result, trade magazine writers are very knowledgeable about their subject matters. Trade magazines are important, too, because they're read by leaders in each industry. Moreover, businesses often make their purchasing decisions based on trade magazine articles and product evaluations.

Radio

Radio is a growing medium with 12,428 stations being counted in 2001.[7] Of these, 4,735 broadcast on AM frequencies and 5,693 on FM. Noncommercial and public stations account for the remaining 2,000. There has been a marked shift in programming and listening patterns from AM to FM. By the 1990s three-fourths of the radio audience tuned to FM stations. Radio is a person-to-person medium that flourishes on conversation; hence, the popularity of talk shows.

Television and Cable Television

More than 1,500 television stations broadcast almost round the clock to almost every American household. Television continues to be a dominant force in children's lives, and the prime source of news and entertainment for most Americans. Television viewing habits are changing as the commercial networks now attract less than 60 percent of the viewing audience, compared with more than 90 percent in the early 1960s. The VCR has freed the viewer from being tied to program schedules as well. New transmission technology has expanded the channel-carrying capacity of cable networks, giving cable subscribers the choice of hundreds of program services and channels. From a media relations standpoint, television is usually best used for reaching large audiences on current news topics often involving the element of conflict. Television continues to be the principal medium for entertainment and product publicity.

About 74 percent of American homes are wired for cable, which translates into 240 million viewers.[8] Although most pay for only basic services, the sheer availability of up to 500 channels has already altered viewing patterns in many parts of the world. Beyond specialized and pay channels, cable operators offer subscribers Internet connections, ATM machine access, interactive health care, and local governmental services.

Online News Services

Major dot-com news sources include online pioneers like AOL and Yahoo!; myriad traditional media with an Internet presence like NBC-TV, CNN, *USA Today*, the *New York Times*, and the *Wall Street Journal*; and new online media players like The Street.com and CBS marketWatch.com. To date, public relations practitioners have found that online services reach select business, consumer, investor and professional audiences.

THE RELATIONSHIP BETWEEN JOURNALISTS AND PR PRACTITIONERS

A basic grasp of media relations work begins with understanding the relationship between journalists and public relations practitioners. Journalists who gather and organize information for the media tend to take their responsibilities to society and the story's subject matter very seriously. They conceive of themselves as the public's eyes and ears, being watchdogs over public institutions doing the public's business. They see their jobs as seeking the truth, putting it in perspective, and publishing it so that people can conduct their affairs knowledgeably.

To the journalist, a story is a transient element in the ongoing flow of information, whereas the public relations practitioner wants the story to make a lasting impression and to be seen in a positive light. The journalist is more interested in news reports that are accurate, fair, and balanced regardless of whether the organization is seen in a negative or positive light.

Yet for all the concerns organizations manifest about how their stories are covered, the media's power does not lie so much in their ability to slant material one way or another, but rather that editors, reporters, and producers choose to cover one topic over others. The fact that some news items get published, aired, and talked about while others do not is called the *agenda-setting function* of the press. Douglas Cater, special assistant to President Lyndon Johnson and author of *The Fourth Branch of Government*, put forth the agenda-setting idea this way:

> The essential power of the press is its capacity to choose what is news. Each day in Washington tens of thousands of words are uttered which are considered important by those who utter them. Tens of dozens of events occur which are considered newsworthy by those who have staged them. The press has the power to select—to decide which events go on page one or hit the prime-time TV news and which events get ignored.[9]

Reporters resent anything and anyone they perceive as standing between them and the facts. Anyone who seeks to keep a secret is regarded with deep suspicion. Organizations of all types invite media scrutiny when they conduct themselves in ways considered less than open.

Journalists collectively maintain that they not only have the responsibility to provide information to the public, but also to provide feedback from society at large to the administrators of public institutions. As society becomes more complex and institutions have greater impact on private lives, journalists hold that more thorough reporting and investigating provides necessary checks on possible business, governmental, and organizational excesses at the expense of the larger society.

Journalists sometimes have difficulty getting the information they need. They claim that highly placed news sources are generally overly insulated, secretive, and sensitive, recognizing neither the public's right to know nor the value of the media's role in exposing questionable practices. Another reason is that most reporters are relatively new to their job assignments that change as often as every 18 months. Public relations practitioners can and do provide them with issue background information so the reporters can learn how to ask and locate the right information and to trace the issue's history in a community.

Still, working journalists echo some of the complaints registered against them by the institutions they cover. Reporters recognize that they frequently have insufficient education and experience to adequately cover complex issues and institutions. They are frustrated by the lack of time, space, and staff and profit-making requirements needed to do their jobs thoroughly.

Even so, public relations practitioners and others who deal with journalists must remember that when reporters ask "nasty" questions, it is not necessarily because they are antagonistic or ignorant; they are just doing what good reporters are supposed to do.

The Public Relations Practitioner's View of the Journalist

From the public relations practitioner's perspective, the journalist is at once an audience, a medium through which to reach the larger public, and a gatekeeper representing and responding to the public's need to know. Practitioners know that they must facilitate the work of journalists if they expect their organizations to get covered.

Because of this dependency, practitioners' selection and presentation of information often conforms more to journalistic standards than to the desires of their superiors in their own organizations. In a sense, both the journalist and the practitioner, in dealing with each other, are caught between the demands of the organizations they represent and the demands of the opposite party. In short, the relationship between public relations practitioners and journalists is one of mutual dependency. Public relations practitioners, as boundary spanners, are often caught in the middle between journalistic and other institutions, trying to explain each to the other.

Mutual Dependence

Although journalists like to picture themselves as reluctant to use public relations information, economic considerations force them to do otherwise. A news staff capable of ferreting information from every significant organization in a city without the assistance of representatives for those organizations would be prohibitively expensive. Through the efforts of public relations practitioners, the media receive a constant flow of free information. Facts that journalists might not have acquired otherwise become available in packaged form. The reporter or editor, as we already noted, can then decide what is newsworthy. Indeed, numerous studies have placed public relations' contribution to total news coverage between 40 and 70 percent. In one sense, the public relations practitioner makes the journalist's job much easier, saving time and effort and providing information that might otherwise be unavailable.

There's another side to this issue as well. Media scholar Oscar Gandy and others criticize the process by which public relations practitioners subsidize media costs and reporters' time by providing news releases and other information to make reporters' jobs easier. The disservice, these critics say, is that many organizations, including social movements, nonprofits, and disadvantaged groups, lack the resources to provide these "subsidies." As a result, the media may perpetuate information inequalities in society, says Gandy.[10]

Building Positive Relationships

Although much may be said about the art and craft of preparing materials for media consumption, perhaps nothing is so important to successful publicity as the relationships established between public relations practitioners and journalists. When public relations practitioners take the time and make the effort to establish good personal relations with journalists, they are much more likely to attract positive news coverage for their organizations. Good public relations begins with good personal relations. As well, mutual dependency tends to increase when public relations practitioners deal with specialized reporters who cover their industry, when the issues are more complex, and when the reporter is given enough time and space to thoroughly cover the story.

Tips for Getting Along with Journalists As in all walks of life, it is good for public relations practitioners to get to know the people they work with. Sometimes the direct approach is effective. Call a journalist with whom you know you will be working. Introduce yourself. Suggest lunch or coffee. Another approach is to hand-deliver a news release to provide an opportunity for a brief introduction and meeting.

Other journalists may not want to be directly approached. With them, an indirect approach is required. Belonging to the local press club, attending meetings of the Society for Professional Journalists, or becoming involved in community activities in which journalists are also involved are ways of getting to know media counterparts. Indeed, journalists are often hired for publicity jobs not only for their writing skills but also for their network of media contacts. "Try to get to know the assignment editors. Encourage those people to come to your workplace. Good human interest stories can be developed from these types of visits."[11]

Former Clinton administration press secretary James L. Fetig, now director of national media relations at Lockheed, sums it up:

> It all comes down to relationships. I trust reporters I know and I don't trust reporters I don't know. Most of us have long-standing relationships with journalists that are based on mutual trust. My advice to PR professionals is to know the journalists who cover their industry well and develop mutual credibility. This is especially true . . . given 24-hour news channels and the Internet. PR professionals have to understand the 24-hour news cycle and, when talking to any reporter, lay down the ground rules with regard to the Internet.

> At one time I could talk to a magazine reporter early in the week and know that my comments would not appear on the newsstands until the end of the week. Speak to a magazine reporter today and it will likely be on the Internet tomorrow.[12]

Once relationships are established, protect and cherish them. Do not squander valuable relationships by using them for small favors or one-shot story placements. Do not ruin a relationship by expecting a reporter to always do what you want. Take no for an answer. Do not insult your relationship with inappropriate gifts because journalists, like other professionals, are sensitive to even the appearance of conflicts of interest.

Cultivate your relationships with journalistic colleagues by giving good service. Provide sufficient and timely information, stories, and pictures, when and how they are wanted. Be on call 24 hours a day to respond to reporters' needs and questions. Do not think that e-mail contact is an adequate substitute for one-on-one communication with journalists.

Nothing will destroy a relationship faster or more completely than an affront to the truth. Accuracy, integrity, openness, and completeness are the basis for trust bestowed by journalists. Once trust is broken, it can rarely be regained.

Finally, to ensure good relations with journalists, the practitioner should behave in a professional way. Live up to expectations. Don't play favorites among the media. Return phone calls promptly and with respect to deadlines. Don't beg for favors, special coverage, or removal of unfavorable publicity.

Lucy Caldwell in an article in *Government Communications* suggests:

> Once they (the media) trust that I actually return calls . . . the media will wait for me to confirm the information they have received from "sources" or scanners prior to releasing it themselves. It seems a simple enough task, but building these relationships requires time, patience and the right attitude.[13]

WORKING WITH THE MEDIA

With a basic understanding of the complex relationships between public relations practitioners and journalists, we can outline a few general principles for working with the media.

The best advice in dealing with the media is to give journalists what they need in the content, form, and language they want. For example, a public relations practitioner working with high-tech clients or start-up firms knows that reporters—especially those at trade and industry magazines—will want to verify the product claims with outside experts or analysts. Thus, the astute public relations practitioner will be prepared to give the magazine or financial reporter a list of experts and analysts to contact. This approach responds quickly and honestly to the media request. As well, public relations practitioners who work to establish a relationship of mutual trust with particular journalists can defuse many potentially antagonistic encounters.

Preparing to Meet the Media

Consider the following situations:

> You are the chief public relations official for a major company. A reporter calls your office at 9 A.M. She wants to see you for an interview at 11 A.M. She wants your company to respond to allegations made by a source that she is not at liberty to disclose. All she will say is that the charges deal with corporate finances and questionable conduct of certain corporate officials.

> As the public relations director of a major private university, you decide to hold a press conference to announce the initiation of an important fund-raising effort. A prominent alumnus has donated $5 million to kick off the campaign. You know that recent media coverage has criticized the university's budgetary problems, tuition hikes, and incursions into neighborhoods around the school that displaced poor people and eroded the community tax base.

> You are the community relations director of the local police force. A reporter calls to request a meeting with your chief about low police morale resulting from the city's inability to meet rank-and-file demands for pay raises. When you attempt to arrange an interview for the following afternoon, the chief berates you, saying: "It's your job to keep the press off my back. Why can't you handle the guy's questions?" You convince the chief that the reporter would not talk to you because he said he was tired of the chief hiding behind his "flack." You tell him departmental integrity and morale depend on his willingness to deal with the press. You promise to help him prepare. He reluctantly agrees to the interview.

In each of these cases, a meeting with the media represents a critical challenge to the organization. Some organizations see such challenges as problems to be overcome. It is more constructive, however, to view them as opportunities. Publicity cannot replace good works or effective action, but it can gain attention for issues, ideas, or products. It can spotlight an organization's personality, policies, or performance. It can make something or someone known.

Every media contact is an opportunity to get feedback, to tell your story, to create a positive response to your organization. Of course there are dangers, but what opportunity presents itself without risk? And what opportunity can be taken without preparation?

Preparation Strategies

Before anyone in an organization meets with the media, the first step is to develop the proper set of attitudes. Meeting the media is an opportunity, not a problem; therefore, defensiveness is not appropriate. There is no need to feel intimidated, especially if your objective is worthy. In the preceding university fund-raising campaign scenario, the purpose of the press conference must be kept firmly in mind. The public relations director should refuse, in a friendly way, to be dragged by reporters' questions into subjects other than the donation and campaign.

The attitude of an interviewee toward the journalist should be one of hospitality, cooperation, and openness. At the same time, the interviewee should realize that the reporter need not be the person in control. The interviewee should decide what needs to be said and say it—no matter what the reporter's questions may be. In other words, have your own **agenda** with the points you want to make no matter what the journalist may want. A positive mental attitude is essential. Once this attitude is established among everyone in an organization who may be called on to be interviewed, it becomes much easier and less traumatic to prepare for specific interviews. After the chief of police completes one interview successfully (from the previous example) the next will be more easily handled.

Before looking further at how individuals can interact successfully with the media, we discuss how organizations can publicize themselves effectively.

Research and Planning in Media Relations

The old saying "Success is when opportunity meets preparation" is never truer than when applied to publicity. As we showed in earlier chapters, preparation indicates research and planning. In media relations, research means knowing who you are dealing with and what they are interested in. Media relations specialists deal primarily with their own management and with the media, so they must understand both parties well.

After understanding the organization, the public relations practitioner must study the specific media with which he or she will work. Research in this area consists of finding out the interests and needs of the people affiliated with the various media outlets. Media guides can provide some of this information. Effective media relations specialists also maintain their own file systems, Rolodexes, computer programs, and charts to keep track of the personal qualities and preferences of the media people with whom they work.

Most organizational news and publicity is based on a media plan. Media plans describe the circumstances with which the organization is dealing, lay out goals or objectives, identify key audiences, and specify key messages and media channels. Company information is often considered to be **publicity,** a term that refers to the publication of news about an organization or person for which time or space was not purchased. The appeal of publicity is credibility. Because publicity appears in the news media in the form of a story rather than an advertisement, it receives what amounts to a third-party endorsement from the editor. Since the editor has judged the publicity material newsworthy, the public is not likely to perceive it as an advertisement. Publicity may, therefore, reach members of an organization's publics who would be suspicious of advertising.

Publicity can be divided into two categories: spontaneous and planned. A major accident, fire, explosion, strike, or any other unplanned event creates **spontaneous publicity.** When such an event occurs, news media will be eager to find out the causes, circumstances, and people involved. While spontaneous publicity is not necessarily negative, it should be handled through standing plans such as those for emergencies.

Planned publicity, on the other hand, does not originate from an emergency situation. It is the result of a conscious effort to attract attention to an issue, event, or organization. Time is available to plan the event and how it will be communicated to the news media. If a layoff, plant expansion, change in top personnel, new product, or some other potentially newsworthy event is contemplated, the method of announcing it is a major concern. How an event is perceived by an organization's publics can determine whether publicity is "good" or "bad."

MEDIA RELATIONS PROGRAM ELEMENTS

The method by which an event is communicated can determine its impact. Three direct ways of purposefully reaching the print media are through a release, a discussion (conversation, phone call, meeting, or interview), or a news conference. The broadcast media can be reached through the video news releases (VNRs), satellite interviews, or satellite media tours. Nonprofit organizations can also reach the electronic media with public service announcements (PSAs).

The most common type of publicity release is the **news release** (see figure 9.1). Any occurrence within the organization that may have local, regional, or national news value is an opportunity for publicity. Sometimes this news is not favorable to the organization. Even in these cases, however, a release is necessary. The news will always get out when something goes wrong. The role of the public relations practitioner is to be certain that the full story is told and that corrective actions are reported. Consider the following types of releases after having examined figure 9.1:

Business Features. An important form of publicity, and one highly prized by many organizations, is the feature article carried by professional, business, trade, or technical publications. Specialized periodicals that address a narrowly defined audience

Federal Express Corporation
Public Relations
2005 Corporate Avenue
First Floor
Memphis, TN 38132

U.S. Mail: PO Box 727
Memphis, TN 38194-1850

Telephone 901-395-3460

Contact: Federal Express
Sonja Whitemon
(901)395-3484

FOR IMMEDIATE RELEASE

FEDEX LAUNCHES NEW 8 A.M. DELIVERY SERVICE
Full range of services meets any customer need

MEMPHIS, TN (July 31, 1995) -- Federal Express Corporation today announced plans to launch a new service that will provide delivery by 8 a.m. to major metropolitan markets in the United States.

The new service, called FedEx First Overnight[SM], offers delivery by 8 a.m. from any U.S. ZIP code to more than 90 major markets, nearly 80 more markets than anyone in the industry.

The service, which will be available September 5, comes with two money-back guarantees: FedEx offers a money-back guarantee if the package is not delivered by 8 a.m. or if the status of the package cannot be reported within 30 minutes of inquiry. Customers around the nation will be able to request a package pick-up by calling 1-800-Go-FedEx. First Overnight rates are competitive with others in the industry.

FedEx has traditionally offered the most flexible delivery options in the industry. The company has long offered an early 9 a.m. hold service at no additional charge for customers who wanted to receive their packages at many of the company's nearly 2,000 locations around the world. This new service provides an early option for those who prefer to have their packages delivered.

"FedEx First Overnight offers our customers a complete range of services which meet every need. This new 8 a.m. delivery option allows customers to fit their delivery schedule to their own needs, whether it is for same-day, overnight or two-day delivery," said T. Michael Glenn, senior vice president, Worldwide Marketing, Customer Service and Corporate Communication for FedEx.

"Our research tells us that our customers will be excited about the opportunity to use FedEx for their most urgent shipments. For example, we deliver many repair parts for machinery to manufacturers who are depending on them to keep their production processes operating. We are pleased that we can now offer FedEx First Overnight and FedEx SameDay services to meet these urgent demands," said Glenn.

In addition to manufacturing industries, FedEx expects the 8 a.m. delivery service to appeal to other industries that ship highly time-sensitive packages, including the manufacturing, banking and entertainment industries.

Federal Express is the world's largest express transportation company, providing fast and reliable services for nearly 2.4 million items in over 200 countries each working day. The company employs more than 110,700 people and operates more than 500 aircraft, 35,000 vehicles and nearly 180,000 Powership® and FedEx Ship® automated systems in its integrated global network. Federal Express reported revenues of $9.4 billion for its fiscal year ended May 31, 1995, including $2.6 billion in revenues and more than $125 million in operating profit from international operations.

FIGURE 9.1 Sample news release

have increased dramatically in recent years, and these allow public relations practitioners to focus on a particular audience for maximum effectiveness. Some analysis of feature articles will provide an insight into the type and style of story editors prefer. Such publications tend to publish articles that define problems common to a particular profession or industry and describe an organization's attempts to deal with it. Unique uses of existing products, or products developed to meet old problems, are also frequent subjects. Public relations professionals often employ freelance writers who specialize in the particular field of the target publication. Most organizations have numerous other outlets for this type of publicity, including in-house technical reports, speeches discussing new technology or products, and papers prepared for professional societies. (See spotlight 9.1 for guidelines in clearing publicity releases.)

Consumer Service Features. Many newspapers and magazines, as well as some television stations, publish or broadcast material designed to assist consumers. Information about almost any consumer product or service can become a vehicle for both product and institutional publicity. Stories that provide consumer-oriented information concerning food, travel, fashion, child care, books, home management, and numerous other topics are in demand by many publications. Frequently, the recipes, food photographs, travel stories, and fashion news contained in special newspaper sections are provided by public relations practitioners representing various manufacturers and industry associations.

Financial Features. Most newspapers and television stations, and some magazines and radio stations, carry financial news and feature articles, and a growing number of publications specialize in that area. Such publicity can be an especially effective tool for shareholder relations because current and potential investors assign more credibility to information when an independent editor selects it for publication. Potential sources of financial publicity include: dividend announcements, mergers, profit reports, expansions, new product lines, major orders, changes in top personnel, research breakthroughs, and many other events that might be of interest to the financial community in general.

Product Features. Product publicity can frequently be newsworthy enough to be selected for use by news editors. Stories about products should be directed to periodicals, newspaper sections, and television and radio programs specializing in consumer product information. Editors and others who use this type of material are interested in information concerning the features, composition, performance, and application of products that will help consumers with their purchasing decisions. In addition to exploiting unique product features, the public relations practitioner can create newsworthy events to dramatize and illustrate product performance for media representatives.

Pictorial Features. The increasing popularity of photojournalism has made more newspapers and magazines receptive to newsworthy or unusual photographs that can communicate a message by themselves. Such photographs are often used with only a caption line and no accompanying story. Because these high-quality, unique photographs are difficult for assignment editors to plan, they provide an excellent opportunity for publicity. A public relations manager should always be alert for photographs that might be good enough for this purpose.

Many organizations employ staff photographers, and their work should be constantly examined for exceptionally good or unusual shots. Photographs taken

Clearing Publicity Releases

Spotlight 9.1

News releases and other publicity material are designed to create positive perceptions of your organization or client in the minds of target publics. Even the most experienced practitioner, however, cannot foresee all the potential consequences of any message. Thus, it is important to plan a system of checks for any message before it is released from your office. The following are some suggestions:

1. *Preparation stage* Preliminary approval of your first draft should be secured from the person(s) involved or in charge.

   A later draft should be sent to the top officer of the organization who is responsible for public relations activities.

   After any further revisions, the next draft should go to the legal department for review.

   In some cases, other managerial personnel should receive draft copies with an opportunity to comment before publication. This decision must be based on responsibilities and sensitivities in the organization.

2. *Distribution of final copy of release* An internal distribution list should be prepared for each release to target important internal publics. Those who should receive copies include:

   All personnel mentioned by name in a release;

   Editors of local and national internal publications;

   Everyone involved in the draft approval stage;

   Public relations and advertising firms associated with the organization; and all target media representatives.

for in-house publications, annual reports, or even advertising may present opportunities for publicity. Special events should always be planned with good publicity photographs in mind. Frequently, newspaper and television editors assign photographers to special events if they know in advance of a good possibility for getting an unusual or newsworthy photograph.

Publicity photographs should normally be printed on seven-by-nine-inch or eight-by-ten-inch paper, depending on the editor's preference. Print media prefer high-gloss photographs with a caption line attached, while television stations prefer slides instead of prints, but specifications should be determined in advance. Photographs for television should always be in color. Color photographs are sometimes used by newspapers and magazines, but black-and-white photos are standard. (See spotlight 9.2 for digital photography tips.)

Public service announcements. Nonprofit organizations are sometimes able to make use of another news release form called the public service announcement. PSAs are short spots that radio and television stations may feel obliged to run to demonstrate their "public interest" commitment at license renewal time. The public relations practitioner must work with the public service director at the broadcast station to determine the particular station's requirements for a PSA. Often the station will assist the organization in actually producing the PSA. TV stations in Denver, for example, allow an organization four TV spots a year. All TV stations in Denver contribute to the production work, which is done at one station. TV spots must conform to 10-, 20-, and 30-second time frames for commercial breaks. Radio PSA's usually are done with that time frame or an additional 60-second spot, but some radio stations prefer to have their disc jockeys read the announcement and don't require specific timed copy. One problem with PSAs, though, is that they may be played at any time of day or night. Your spot may air at 6 A.M. or 2 A.M. If you're lucky, it might air during prime time.

9.2 Spotlight

Ten Tips for Using Your Digital Camera

1. Digital cameras are quite different from film cameras so the first thing you should do is load fresh batteries, turn it on, and read the manual with the camera in your hands to thoroughly familiarize yourself with all its controls. Take a few pictures. *Never go on an assignment with a camera that you have not used before.*
2. Consider the camera's instruction book an essential piece of photographic equipment. Always carry it with you. You can accidentally push a button or combination of buttons even after using the camera for months and not be able to figure out what you have done. Or you can forget how to perform the simplest function because you haven't had to use it recently. At least keep the book nearby, in a briefcase or the glove compartment of your automobile.
3. Saving your images with a digital camera may be confusing. There are two main memory cards available at the consumer/prosumer level. They are Compact Flash and Smart Media. Compact Flash cards dominate the industry because they are available in larger sizes (up to 1 MB) and come as both type I and type II cards. The IBM Micro drives are type II cards. Generally speaking, Compact Flash is the professional's choice.
4. What file format should you save in, and what size? The better cameras ($500 and up as of this writing) will generally save as uncompressed TIFF and in JPEG with three different compression modes. Some will even save in what is called a RAW image file. The short answer here is to save in the highest quality JPEG mode. This will reduce the number of images on your card, but you should care about quality, not quantity. The solution to that problem is to buy a larger memory card. A 256 MB Compact Flash card can be purchased for about $100 and is well worth the expense. If you are going to reuse the images frequently, after downloading them to the hard drive, you should save the originals as TIFF files. The reason is that each time you resave them the quality deteriorates slightly. In other words, keep a master copy in TIFF format.
5. When shooting the picture you need to get close to your subject. Don't rely on trying to crop a smaller portion out of the center of image and then enlarging it. *It won't work.* You will be very dissatisfied with the results. Digital images deteriorate very quickly as they are enlarged. A general rule of thumb is that you can get away with a maximum 2X enlargement. That's it.
6. Digital enlargement is exactly what happens when you use digital zoom on your camera. The digital zoom simply crops in and enlarges a portion of the image. Digital zoom, therefore, is causing your image quality to deteriorate. Optical zoom, on the other hand, is enlarging the image through magnification. Just remember this about zoom: *Optical is good! Digital is to be avoided!*
7. Another shooting problem is that tiny little LCD panel on the back of the camera. Use it for reference. Do not rely on it for sharpness. Your eyes aren't that good. Shoot more pictures than you think you'll possibly ever need (many more in fact). You'll be very glad you did.
8. Digital does not handle high-contrast lighting well. When shooting portraits of people outdoors in bright sunlight, for example, it is a good idea to use flash to soften shadows. Unfortunately, some of the lower-priced digital cameras won't let you do that. Getting correct exposure is even more difficult than with film because the contrast ratio is so short. When the exposure is absolutely correct in digital, the results are beautiful. It does not happen as often as you would like, though, because digital does not have the latitude of film.
9. You need to worry about the camera's resolution. In simple terms the resolution is the number of pixels (picture elements) in the final image captured by the camera's image sensor. The manufacturer expresses these as horizontal and vertical numbers. For example a Nikon CoolPix 990 camera has a resolution of 2048 × 1536. These two numbers are multiplied to arrive at the number of approximately 3.1 million pixels (the total number of pixels in the final image). This is large enough to publish a 5 × 7 color photograph. The average camera today in the $700 to $1,000 price range is in the 4 to 5 million-pixel range. Be careful when purchasing a camera, though, because there is considerably more to it than just how many pixels there are on the CCD.
10. Finally, you really need knowledge of an image editor for output. The most widely used, of course, is Photoshop or Photoshop Elements, but they aren't the only ones. You need some method of working with your images because they are seldom ready for use directly out of the camera. You need to be able to remove the green cast caused by the fluorescent lights or to tweak the definition and perhaps crop away some unwanted areas on the fringe. If you are going to send your images to a conventional printer, you need to be able to convert them to CMYK as they will, in all likelihood, come from the camera in RGB mode. When you are using your photo for the Web (either taken with a digital camera or scanned photo into digital format), you will need to convert the file to either a GIF or a JPEG file. The GIF format takes less memory, but the JPEG will give you the highest quality.

Source: Art Terry, associate professor of journalism at the University of Memphis, and former photo layout editor for *National Geographic,* February 24, 2003.

Packaging News Releases

Packaging in the form of **media kits** can frequently increase the probability that information from a publicity release will actually be used by an editor. A media kit, sometimes called a **press kit,** includes a collection of publicity releases, fact sheets, brochures, photographs, or other information pieces enclosed in a cover or some other packaging device. But although attractive packaging can be helpful in gaining the attention of a busy editor whose desk is covered with competing releases, design is not the primary consideration in compiling a media kit. More important is that news releases, photographs, fact sheets, background information, and features are packaged in an organized and readable form to enable the editor to select the information he or she wishes to use. The strategy behind any media kit should be based on the realization that most major media will not use a release verbatim but will instead select information to be rewritten into a story unique to their publication. A media kit should be designed to help editors select the information they need.

Media kits do not need to be elaborate and costly. Releases can be packaged in simple but well-designed one- or two-color folders, as long as they are adaptable to a variety of media needs. The basic role of a press kit is to provide information to editors that would otherwise take many hours to research. Press kits can provide a service for the media by saving research time and identifying important information for consumers and others. The organization, of course, stands to gain favorable publicity. Today, many organizations distribute their media kits online from the corporate webpages (see mini-case 9.1). It's too early to forecast when these online versions will replace hard copy ones. For one thing, the hard copy media kits are often distributed to others besides media reporters.

Distributing News Releases

News releases today are more likely to arrive by e-mail than they are by fax, regular mail, or hand-carried delivery. In fact, most releases are now either faxed or sent by e-mail directly to the editor or person targeted by the release. Broadcast fax, which is the material sent by computer to all fax machines set up on your computer to receive the material, is being used more and more often by media relations departments.

Organizing Press or News Conferences

Once considered a basic component of media relations, the press conference today takes a backseat to Internet-distributed information and accompanying multimedia components. Except for rare occasions, there is little reason for reporters to take the time to attend an organization's press conference when they can get all of the information and multimedia support materials from the company website. Sometimes, they can even get "exclusives" off the website when the organization tailors one release as an exclusive business story, another as an exclusive personality feature, and a third as a technology story. In other cases the reporter uses answers to e-mailed questions as the basis for his or her story.

Let's assume that a press conference must be held. **Press conferences,** or **news conferences,** are structured opportunities to release news simultaneously to all media. They should be used only when the news is important and when interaction is required to promote understanding of complex or controversial topics. Do not call a news conference unless the event is extremely newsworthy and simply cannot be handled through releases or posting to the website, or unless there is someone very newsworthy to interview.

9.1 Mini•Case

Media Kit by Brunswick Bowling and Billiards Corporation

Brunswick Bowling and Billiard Corporation introduced its new bowling ball with glimmering works of art and an appeal to the individual tastes of potential customers. It introduced its Viz-A-Ball at a press conference in Los Angeles using Penn and Teller, "The Bad Boys of Magic," to unveil "The Art of Transformation" at a reception at the Museum of Contemporary Art in Los Angeles in the spring of 2001.

Brunswick promised to reinvent bowling's image and planned to reach a new consumer audience by forever changing the look and design of bowling balls. As part of its expanded distribution and marketing strategy, Brunswick launched a Viz-A-Ball website (www.viz-a-ball.com), which is an e-commerce initiative intended to reach a broad, global audience.

From favorite cartoon characters, sports heroes, and pop culture icons to corporate logos and rare collectible designs, Viz-A-Ball heralded a new direction for bowling and opened a new market opportunity for Brunswick. Brunswick was the first manufacturer in the bowling industry to launch a line of bowling balls through a dedicated, branded website.

The way public relations and marketing worked together in this integrated marketing communication strategy indicates a new direction for media relations. Using e-commerce tools as well as traditional media kits and media materials, Brunswick launched its new bowling line.

Source: Brunswick Bowling and Billiards Corp., Viz-A-Ball media kit, March 2001.

Brunswick used a variety of publiciy materials to promote its new line of bowling balls, Viz-A-Ball.

For those rare occasions when news conferences are appropriate, the following guidelines will help ensure success:

1. *Plan the Event Carefully.* Invite all representatives of all media that may have an interest far enough in advance for editors to plan to send reporters and photographers. Select an appropriate site close to the event being covered and convenient for major media (hotel, press club, airport, boardroom—never a public relations office). Check for enough electrical outlets and telephones. Time the conference to accommodate major media deadlines. Make certain you prepare enough handout material for everyone. Prepare any visuals that may be used so that they will photograph well from any place in the room. Prepare a poster of the organization's logo or name to go over the one on the speaker's stand if you use a rented facility.

Plan to phone major media the morning or afternoon before the conference as a reminder. Simple refreshments are generally a nice touch.

2. *Prepare Executives and Others to Be Interviewed.* Make certain they understand the topics that will be discussed. Help them anticipate and prepare for difficult or touchy questions. Advise them to be completely honest. If they don't know an answer, they should say so and offer to find out. If the answer to the question is considered proprietary information, they should state that it is not for public disclosure. Cultivate a pleasant, cooperative attitude among those who will be interviewed. If they are afraid of or resent the media, it will show. Advise them to avoid off-the-record comments.

   Recently, public relations practitioner Jan Harkness wrote that public relations practitioners should use the first training sessions as a stepping-stone. "Then, conduct more in-depth, one-on-one sessions for those who will serve as corporate spokespeople. Whenever possible, incorporate mock interviews into these sessions. During these interviews, think like a reporter. Ask questions to get to the heart of people and their motivations. Find out why your CEO chose his or her profession. Talk to the vice president about his or her move from human resources to information technology."[14]

3. *Coordinate the Meeting with Public Relations Practitioners Serving as Directors and Stage Managers.* Keep the meeting moving and interesting, but don't take over the jobs of the media representative. Try to keep relationships cordial and professional even in the heat of questioning. Never take obvious control of the meeting unless things get out of hand.

USES OF VIDEO

Video became a major method of delivering an organization's news to the broadcast media in the 1980s. Budget cuts in TV news operations coupled with new broadcast technology have both contributed to an increasing use of video technology by public relations practitioners in the 1990s. Video news releases (VNRs) have become the medium of choice in several major crises. For example, in the summer of 1993 when a Tacoma man touched off a panic by claiming to find a hypodermic needle in his Pepsi can, Pepsi-Cola used VNRs to show the nation that its cans could not be tampered with. A second VNR was produced showing a store surveillance camera catching a customer tampering with a can to perpetuate the hoax.

Despite the Internet, there are still four common uses of video:

1. *The video news release* is a short news package presenting the news item from the organization's viewpoint. The most popular VNR is about 90 seconds long but is accompanied by **B-roll** material (background video) with audio on separate channels. It is broadcast-quality videotape.
2. *Electronic media kits* are similar to the conventional media kit except they include VNRs, perhaps a longer version than normal giving more background material. They also include typical background print material such as still photos, new releases, brochures, background papers, fact sheets, or other pertinent information.
3. *Satellite press conferences* provide an opportunity for TV journalists to participate in question-and-answer sessions via satellite with an organization's representatives. Often the organization makes a presentation followed by the press conference. Some participants may be in studios with interactive uplink facilities, but some watch the satellite feed and phone-in questions.

9.3 Spotlight

Extranet Pays Off in Savings for Ketchum

Ketchum Inc., which spent the late 1990s touting its clients' e-business initiatives, is seeing an impressive return on investment from one of its own. The public relations giant introduced a client-focused extranet, MyKGN, in March 2000. Extranet, essentially a website specifically for clients, allows Ketchum employees to do research and deal with customers online. There are already 400 collaborative client sites within MyKGN, which the firm estimates saves 90 minutes a week in time per employee.

- Ketchum realized $2.8 million in cash flow and productivity benefits last year from MyKGN, according to Meta Group Inc., and the firm could realize up to $5.6 million by 2003.
- Employees can research a subject database with 5,000 documents, whereas research used to be done in piecemeal Internet searches.
- Ketchum is also using MyKGN as a customer relationship management tool to build collaborative sites for clients. Now clients can work with Ketchum employees in real time on such things as reviewing press releases and company logos.

Ketchum's extranet efforts and those of its rival, Hill & Knowlton Inc., which recently launched one of its own extranets, show that the technology is beginning to take root in public relations.

Source: B to B, Chicago: July 16, 2001; Philip B. Clark.

4. *Satellite media tours* provide individual interviews with the guest personality in a remote studio. Each interview is exclusive and some are carried live. Guests may appear on two or three dozen stations per day this way.[15]

INTRANETS, EXTRANETS, AND WEBSITES

No single technology application has changed media relations more than the Internet and the use of webpages, intranets, and extranets. The term **intranet** refers to computer-based systems for communicating with employees and other insiders while the term **extranet** refers to the same process for reaching such external audiences as investors, customers, community and governmental leaders, and so on (see spotlight 9.3). Media relations websites provide a dedicated location for all kinds of information of possible interest to the media. This includes for breaking news, pointing reporters to information sources, position statements, activity calendars, press release archives, speeches, government filings, and company and executive background material.

Almost all corporate, organizational, and even social movement websites include a link to the media relations department. The media relations webpages become the online newsroom for which Vocus software specialist Kay Bransford offers ten uses and tips:[16]

1. Link directly from your home page to the media relations site.
2. Post press releases simultaneously with distribution to the press.
3. Maintain a searchable database of press releases.
4. Offer online media kits.
5. Make it easy for reporters to reach you.
6. Include corporate and executive information.
7. Feature a searchable database of recent coverage.
8. Allow reporters to request news.
9. Provide additional tools and information.
10. List awards and recognition.

Experts advise that organizations with small media relations budgets use credible spokespeople, create strong graphic identities, skip press conferences, develop exclusive story angles for different media, and, generally, generate excitement for the media site.

One reason that Internet-based media strategies have become so popular is the availability and assistance of Internet media placement and tracking services. Media Link offers clients an electronic version of such traditional public relations services as VNR webcasting, and cybermedia tours, while NetCurrents measures traffic trends to correlate public relations efforts and the impact that they have on a site's success.

Beyond using the website to extend traditional media relations programs, public relations practitioners cultivate buzz online with postings to newsgroups, a working message board intentionally leading news to online outlets and newsletters. Media relations specialists know how to access newsgroups, respond to online inquiries, and to track what's being said online about your company and its competitors.

Media relations expert Carole Howard tells public relations practitioners to invest time experimenting and innovating on the Internet. "Establish home pages. Post your organization's message on bulletin boards. Host on-line forums. Promote your products to online reviewers. Stage on-line contests. Create on-line update centers in crisis situations. Put your organization's spokespeople in chat rooms to tell your story first-hand and answer questions live."[17]

CRISIS COMMUNICATION

Crisis communication can be viewed as a special application of media relations. That is, crisis communication involves using the media to preserve and strengthen an organization's long-term reputation whenever it's threatened. **Crisis** can be anticipated or even prevented when organizations build and maintain ongoing relationships with key stakeholders including employees, customers, government, and general and trade media. Regular two-way communication with these groups is the glue that translates into credibility and positive expectations should an unpredictable crisis hit. Thus, the more consistently an organization does what it tells its stakeholders it will do, the better its reputation.

For example, the Coca-Cola Company had to weigh the value of relationship building with the educational community against the cost of pursuing a marketing strategy involving exclusive arrangements in schools to ensure only its products would be sold on campus. Coca-Cola came down on the side of preserving its long-term reputation and franchise by concluding that it needed to support nonexclusive agreements in schools, allowing a range of beverages and brands to be available to students. As a result, there was no crisis with national education associations or parent-teacher groups to report because the soft drink company listened, assessed the facts, and made a decision.

After a tanker collision in the San Francisco Bay in the late 1960s, Standard Oil immediately spent whatever resources were necessary to clean up the mess. The rapid positive action led to newspaper editorials saying things like, "Beaches never were cleaner before." At the other extreme, Exxon paid a heavy price for not immediately facing up to the crisis prompted by the oil its tanker *Valdez* spilled off the Alaskan coast. Organizational credibility crises are often long-term issues more than they are responses to emergencies. This point is underscored in mini-case 9.2.

9.2 Mini•Case

Lessons from the California Energy Crisis

Americans depend on electricity to power their computers, appliances, and a multitude of other pieces of equipment. But what happens when there is no electricity?

California residents found out in late 2000 when the lights started flickering, and the power would surge off and on. Wholesale costs for electric utilities were exceeding their retail revenues, a situation caused by deregulation. Utilities, like many companies, must be able to pay their suppliers. Because there wasn't enough money to cover the bills, the utilities were forced to disrupt service to millions of businesses and homes.

Corporate communicators for the utilities faced a threefold challenge: informing consumers about the shortages and the need for conservation, emphasizing the severity and cause of the utilities' financial problems, and maintaining public support.

The challenge was exacerbated by public attitudes. Most Californians believed deregulation would lower their monthly bills, not raise them. And it was difficult to buy the story about declining energy supplies when no other states were experiencing similar problems. "We have been placed in the difficult position of trying to preach the solution—construction of new power plants and conservation—while people are calling us Satan," noted Mirant Energy Company communication director Chuck Griffin.

The electric utilities, their out-of-state owners, the California Public Utilities Commission, the Federal Energy Regulatory Commission, the California state legislature, the governor, the activist groups that blocked new plant construction, an increase in industrial energy use, and other factors were being blamed for the problem. But when the finger-pointing subsides, the California power crisis is an example of how a big business did not live up to society's expectations.

Source: *PR Week,* January 29, 2001.

Public relations practitioners deal with crisis communication by starting with a **crisis plan** that spells out how the entire organization will respond. When a crisis occurs, a written and rehearsed communication plan will speed up response time by having all the background information available and by having all crisis response duties preassigned. For example, chances are that almost all of the public relations staff will be working with the media and much of this will be providing up-to-the-minute online responses to the general media, the trade press, and financial writers. At least one public relations or human resource specialist will be providing employees with up-to-the-minute reports via e-mail over the intranet. With sufficient staffing, others will be assigned to provide website updates for customers and investors, but this will likely involve staff support from other departments.

Other more specific plan elements and guidelines include:

1. Putting the public interest first and especially the needs of all people directly concerned, including accident victims and their families and employees and their families. This means resolving the emergency and protecting the people affected until it is completely resolved.
2. Taking responsibility for correcting the situation. Seldom, if ever, should the organizational response to the media or affected stakeholders be "no comment."
3. Being as open as possible with all stakeholder groups, including governmental agencies, investors, employees and their families, victims and their families, customers, neighboring businesses, residences, and communities affected by the crisis.
4. Having a designated spokesperson whose job is to manage the accuracy and consistency of the messages coming from the organization.
5. Establishing a central media or information center although circumstances may require multiple centers that would include the corporate office, the crisis location, and the metropolitan area nearest the crisis location.

The Red Cross provides disaster relief for victims of a flood in California.

6. Responding to all media inquiries according to predetermined guidelines. Do respond to all media inquiries, but if you don't know the answer, say so. Then promise to get back as soon as possible with the answer. Do not release the names of dead or injured until relatives have been notified by appropriate police or public safety officials. Do not speculate.

As with real crises, rumors can have severe impacts on organizations. When faced with a rumor, a corporate communicator rarely has any statistical data available to guide decision making. There's little hard evidence to guide the practitioner in trying to figure out who is saying what, who is listening, the harshness of the comments, how long the rumors are likely to persist, and ultimately, if something should be done to counteract what is being spread. Although corporate public relations practitioners should expect rumors to circulate, it is important to address them. Corporations can face Securities and Exchange Commission actions if rumors are allowed to persist. This is because rumors can affect the company's stock price, and in some cases, the market in general.

The best defense is a good offense. Here are some practical ways to manage rumors:

1. Strive to increase and maintain trust and credibility.
2. Keep audiences regularly informed through a variety of communication channels.
3. Tailor each message to the audience receiving it so there's less likelihood of it being misunderstood.

4. Establish an ongoing rumor hotline and other two-way communication channels to seek questions and concerns from key publics. Use written communication to answer the questions posed.
5. Monitor possible effects of rumors so early intervention can be enacted if necessary.

The following example illustrates how important it is to be open and honest in managing rumors, recognizing that the truth will always surface at some point. Martha Stewart denied using insider information, an illegal activity, when selling one of her stock holdings in late 2001. She sold her 4,000 shares of ImClone System Inc. one day before the U.S. Food and Drug Administration rejected the biotech company's experimental cancer treatment, presumably on an inside tip supplied by the company's then CEO, Sam Waksal. Although Stewart repeatedly denied the controversial charges, new information suggested otherwise. By mid-2002, the price of her company's shares, Martha Stewart Living Omnimedia, fell to their lowest point since going public in late 1999. Beyond the insider trading allegations, the situation has many elements that make for juicy, gossipy rumors: Stewart's romantic links to Waksal; Waksal's arrest for conspiracy, securities fraud, and perjury involving an alleged insider trading scheme in ImClone shares; Stewart's statements that contradict those of her broker; the suspension of her stockbroker by Merrill Lynch; and close friends of Stewart's who suspiciously sold their holdings about the same time.

Summary

For self-testing and additional chapter resources, go to the student CD and the Online Learning Center at **www.mhhe.com/lattimore**

Media relations and publicity work are essential ingredients of public relations practice. In recent years the whole framework for media relations work has changed based on the growth and multiple uses of the Internet, global communication demands, and proliferating communication channels. The mass media offer an economical method for communicating with large and dispersed stakeholders while the specialized press and online newsrooms are more useful in reaching more narrowly defined audience segments and stakeholders, including customers, investors, employees, the business press, and so on.

The relationship between journalists and public relations practitioners is a difficult one. If practitioners understand the media and the reporter's role, however, positive relationships can be developed that are beneficial to all.

Specific techniques for communicating with the media include publicity releases, news kits, news conferences, video releases, and news posted to webpages. All of these approaches must be used judiciously—for publicity may backfire. Inappropriate publicity efforts can injure the relations that have been built over time with the media and the public. Electronic media have become especially important in the 1990s with VNRs, electronic media kits, satellite press conferences, and satellite media tours leading the way. Public service announcements provide a means for nonprofits to communicate through radio and television.

To learn more about media relations, watch the interview with Mark Shannon, Clips #4 and 7, on the book's CD-ROM.

Toxic Shock Syndrome

At Denver's Children's Hospital, a new public relations director made a plea to doctors and staff members to let her know if anything happened that might be considered news. She briefly explained to them what "news" was. A few days later, a doctor sheepishly came to her with an item he thought might be newsworthy. "I think I've discovered a new disease; do you think that's newsworthy?" he asked the public relations director. After she told him it was newsworthy, he continued by saying, "I think I'm going to call it toxic shock syndrome." He wanted to announce it. She readily agreed but wanted to plan how to release the information so the hospital could get the maximum benefit from the exposure.

Children's Hospital in Denver is a major regional referral and research hospital for states in the west. It depends a great deal on its support from fund-raising efforts. If you were the public relations director, what would you do?

Source: Kyla Thompson, *Non Profit Public Relations,* interview by Dan Lattimore, videocassette, Colorado State University, 1986.

Questions

1. How would you announce the new disease?
2. How would you use the Internet to announce the new disease? Would you create a website? Assuming you did create a website, what would you include?
3. How would you handle the requests from more than 500 media calls you would receive in the few days after the announcement?
4. If you had just been named public relations director for the hospital when this occurred, how would you proceed to develop your media contacts to help the hospital?
5. How could you use the discovery of toxic shock syndrome in the years to come in your public relations efforts?

Use the CD-ROM and Online Learning Center at www.mhhe.com/lattimore to further your understanding of the following terms

agenda
B-roll
crisis
crisis plan
extranet
Internet
intranet
media kit
media relations
news conference
news release
planned publicity
press conference
press kit
publicity
spontaneous publicity
third-party endorsement

Notes

1. Michael Lissauer, "Online Media Strategy: Reaching Dot-com Newsrooms," *Public Relations Strategist* (Fall 2000), p. 26.
2. Carole M. Howard, "Technology and Tabloids: How the New Media World Is Changing Our Jobs," *Public Relations Quarterly* (Spring 2000), p. 10.
3. "Future Perfect? Agency Leaders Reflect on the 1990's and Beyond," *Public Relations Strategist* (Summer 2001), p. 11.
4. Stanley J. Baron, *Introduction to Mass Communication: Media Literacy and Culture*—2001 Updated (Mountain view, CA: Mayfield, 2001), p. 103.
5. Ibid.
6. Ibid., p. 131.
7. Ibid., p. 192.
8. Ibid., p. 227.
9. Douglas Cater, *Press, Politics and Popular Government* (Washington, DC: American Enterprise Institute, 1972), pp. 83–84.
10. Baron, p. 228.
11. Cliff Webb quoted in Lucy Caldwell, "Maintaining Media Relations: One Perspective with Tips for Radio, Print and TV Personalities," *Government Communications* (July 1995), p. 16.
12. James L. Fetig, APR, in "Views on Media Relations From Both Sides of the Fence," Special Report, Public Relations, *PR Tactics* (December 1999). Online-1.
13. Caldwell, pp. 15–16.
14. Jan Sokoloff Harness, "Media Relations Training: Make It Work for You," *PR Tactics,* December 1999. Online-1.
15. Ibid., p. 165.
16. Kay Bransford, *Better Access, Better Information, Better News: The Ten Essential Elements of an Online Newsroom* (Lanham, MD: Vocus, 2001).
17. Howard, p. 11.

CHAPTER TEN

Employee Communication

10

Outline

PREVIEW

When organizations achieve effective employee communication, the results include more satisfied and productive employees, improved achievement of organizational goals, and improved customer, community, and investor relations.

Employees work in organizations with specific cultures. Effective employee communication depends on the establishment of a positive organizational culture, through clear communication policies, programs, and assistance with organizational change.

Employee communication will help employees become well informed about their organizations and encourage them to express their views to management

"The greatest continuing area of weakness in management practice is the human dimension. In good times or bad, there seems to be little real understanding of the relationships between managers, among employees, and interactions between the two. When there are problems, everyone acknowledges that the cause often is 'communications.' So now what?"

—Jim Lukaszewski[1]

Michael H. Mescon, a management professor and consultant, tells the story of an experience aboard a Delta Air Lines jet:

> I was just settling into my seat when I casually remarked to the fellow sitting next to me about the skyrocketing cost of airline tickets. The fellow didn't take my remark very casually. "Do you know why that ticket costs what it does?" he asked. "No," I said. "And I don't really care." "Well, you ought to care," he said. "Because what that ticket pays for is your safety, comfort and convenience." Well, by now I knew I was in for it. The guy told me what the carpet on the floor cost and why that particular kind of carpet had to be used. He explained the construction of the seat I was sitting in. He talked about support personnel on the ground for every plane in the air and, of course, he dealt with the costs of jet fuel. Finally, I stopped him. "I know the president and several of Delta's vice presidents," I said. "You must be one of the vice presidents I don't know." "No," the fellow said, "I work in the upholstery shop." "Well, how do you know so much about Delta's operations?" "The company keeps us informed."

When organizations commit themselves to effective communication with their employees, a number of important benefits result. Well-informed employees are usually satisfied employees. They are better, more productive workers who get more out of their work and do a better job for the organization. Employees will be the first spokespersons for their organization outside of work. Well-informed employees interacting with an organization's stakeholders will have significant positive influence on relations with customers, the community, investors, and the media, to name a few important groups. In a nutshell, when lines of communication are open between employers and employees, organizational goals are more likely to be achieved.

Achieving successful communication within an organization is no simple task. Amid the corporate changes of the last few years, including corporate takeovers and mergers, downsizing, scandals, cost cutting, and technological changes, organizations face challenges to keep good employees and to hire new ones.

Public relations practitioners look at plans for the employee website.

Employee Retention: It's the Employer Who's on Probation

Mini•Case 10.1

Remember ARCNET, the New Jersey engineering firm that gave each of its employees new BMWs as part of their benefits package (*pr reporter* 9/20/99)? Nice touch and it worked. But a new study from O'Connor Kenny Partners (Memphis) says employers need not be so dramatic in efforts to retain employees. "Before doling out bonuses and cars, an organization should first study the demographics of its workforce to determine how little it may take to keep employees on board," says director of communications Christine Luporter.

Luporter advises employers to take a look at their staffs and consider their true needs. She points to a case study of a midsized retailer with 2,000 stores. The retailer's workforce is 94 percent composed of female 20-something part-timers. Turnover rate is 1,170 percent, costing the retailer $1.3 million in a year. The company estimates it takes 30 days for an employee to decide to stay with the company. "It used to be employees were the ones on probation. Today it's the employees who look at the company to determine if they will stay." This new strategy was devised:

- Look at the demographics. "For 20-somethings, it's about friendships and relationships," the retailer's human resource vice president finds. "They want to feel they belong, fit in, and want to make friends at work."
- During this 30-day time period, managers were told to implement "critical care"—essentially, a buddy program with a twist. Each new employee is assigned a buddy with a list of skills to be learned and goals to be met within the first 30 days. If the new hire stays past the 30 days and meets the goals, the buddy receives the financial incentive.

This pilot program slowed turnover rate 20 percent last year. "The cost of that improvement is far less than a new fleet of cars," notes Luporter. "Essentially, employers should look at the root cause of the retention program. I'll bet they will find they can come up with a communications solution that is a lot cheaper than a new car or a huge bonus."

Source: *pr reporter,* January 31, 2000, p. 4.

When hiring new employees, given the following labor force projections for 2008, employers will have to throw out old thinking about what workers want and need on the job:

1. Women will account for 48 percent of the labor force.
2. The baby-boom cohort (ages 44 to 62) will show significant growth.
3. The Asian labor force will increase most rapidly.
4. The Hispanic labor force will be larger than the black labor force.
5. The youth labor force (ages 16 to 24) will grow more rapidly than the overall labor force.[2]

Each of these demographic groups will bring very different expectations to their places of work and will require different strategic thinking about their communication needs. Already, hiring and keeping productive employees means creating family-friendly policies, flexible scheduling, domestic partner benefits, sick days for dependent care, health club memberships, and time off for volunteer activities. See mini-case 10.1 as an example of how employee demographics mean different thinking about employee retention.

THE ROLE OF EMPLOYEE COMMUNICATION

Employee communication is a specialization of public relations concerned with "how public relations professionals in corporations, counseling firms, and nonprofit organizations help promote effective communication among employees and between line employees and top management."[3] Employee communication efforts begin before an employee is hired and carry on past the employee's departure from the organization. Thus, from recruitment to beyond separation, public relations has a major role to play in an employee's work experience.

Employee communication, also called **internal communication** or **employee relations,** creates and maintains internal systems of communication with organizations. Communication lines are two way, so that all employees participate freely in an exchange of information.

"Experts doubt that we'll ever return to the pre-boom era of 'company knows best.' In fact, as the economy continues to struggle, solid employee relations will play a key role in overall success," said Bernard Charland, senior vice president for Golin Harris, an international public relations firm.[4] To understand the process by which it is accomplished and the role of public relations in that process, we must first discuss the concept of organizational culture.

THE CONCEPT OF ORGANIZATIONAL CULTURE

Organizational culture refers to the character of an organization, "its history, its approach to decision making, its way of treating employees, and its way of dealing with the world outside."[5] Another definition describes organizational culture as "the sum total of shared values, symbols, meanings, beliefs, assumptions, and expectations that organize and integrate a group of people who work together."[6]

The groundbreaking study *Excellence in Public Relations and Communication Management* identified two types of organizational culture—authoritarian and participative. **Authoritarian cultures** feature centralized decision making with the CEO and a few high-level managers. Departments have different agendas, sometimes in conflict with each other. Employees do not perceive rewards for innovation, but for following orders. They believe that their supervisors are interested in them only as workers and not as people. Authoritarian cultures are closed and resistant to change from outside the organization.[7]

Organizations with **participative cultures** feature the common value of teamwork. Employees feel empowered to make decisions rather than to wait for orders from those in power. The departments work together "like a well-oiled machine."[8] Department goals match overall organizational goals. Workers feel valued as people, not just as employees. Participative organizational cultures are open to new ideas from inside and outside the organization.[9]

The primary responsibility for organizational culture belongs to management—the decision makers of the organization. Successful managers seek a workplace culture that supports the goals of the organization. For example, General Motor's management has acknowledged the influence on its productivity of the labor strife of the automotive industry in recent decades by attempting to change its culture. GM management is attempting to move away from employees as cogs to employees as "a potential resource."[10] "We want them (employees) developing an actionable plan about what they can do themselves to make GM a more successful company," according to GM's vice president of communication.[11]

Public relations professionals can make three contributions to a productive workplace culture: (1) they can strive to establish organizational communication policy based on a goal-oriented approach, (2) they can help in designing and implementing organizational change programs, and, most important, (3) they can provide expertise as employee communicators.

Establishing Communication Policy

An important factor in improving organizational culture is the establishment of communication policy. According to communication expert Norman Sigband, top management generally recognizes the need for and sincerely desires two-way communication.[12] The bottleneck in corporate communication is usually found in the middle of the corporate hierarchy. Breakdown in the communication process is most often at the first-line supervisor level.

Public relations managers can facilitate cultural change by convincing top management that communication, like finance, personnel, marketing, promotion, and almost every other area of organizational activity, should have established clearly stated policies. Unstated policies leave dangerous vacuums that rumor, confusion, and misinformation rapidly fill.

Communication policies must be goal oriented rather than event oriented. In other words, rather than addressing specific issues or topics, policies should help employees understand, contribute to, and identify with organizational objectives and problems. Successful communication policies should reflect management's desire to do the following:

1. Keep employees informed of organizational goals, objectives, and plans.
2. Inform employees of organizational activities, problems, and accomplishments or any subject they consider important.
3. Encourage employees to provide inputs, information, and feedback to management based on their experience, insights, feelings, creativity, and reason.
4. Level with employees about negative, sensitive, or controversial issues.
5. Encourage frequent, honest, job-related, two-way communication among managers and their subordinates.
6. Communicate important events and decisions as quickly as possible to all employees, especially before they learn from media. They must be told first.
7. Establish a culture where innovation and creativity are encouraged.
8. Urge every manager and supervisor to discuss with each subordinate the latter's progress and position in the firm.

Employees want information first from their immediate supervisors as shown in table 10.1. The last place they want to hear the company news is in the media.

TABLE 10.1 Worker's Preferred Information Sources

1. Immediate supervisor
2. Small group meetings
3. Top executive
4. Annual report to employees
5. Employee handbook/other booklets
6. Orientation program
7. Regular local employee publication
8. Regular general employee publication
9. Bulletin board
10. Upward communication programs
11. Mass meetings
12. Audiovisual programs
13. Unions
14. Grapevine
15. Mass media

Source: IABC Study, quoted in Allen Center and Patrick Jackson, *Public Relations Practices*, 5th ed. (Englewood Cliffs, NJ: Longman, 1995), p. 40.

Organizational Change

Employee communication expert Gary Grates believes that organizations of the future will be structured to accommodate change, and employee communication will have an integral role. This role should include forecasting and monitoring relationships with key audiences and planning flexible communication structures so that employees will understand and support new situations and organizational environments. Grates shared these lessons with the PRSA counselors:

1. Planning for communications replaces a communications plan.
2. Lead people through dialogue, discussion, dissent.
3. Think externally to legitimize internal actions.
4. Become conversant and knowledgeable about the goals and priorities of the organization.
5. Accept the fact that real change is about uncertainty.
6. Help management turn complex business initiatives into simple, easily understood concepts so employees can comprehend them and contribute to their successful implementation.
7. Understand what managers and employees understand.
8. Don't underestimate people's desire for relevant information.
9. Communications must be integrated into change by organizational leaders.
10. It is how you think, not what you do.
11. Become a teacher.
12. Define communication as information exchanged between and among human beings.[13]

Employee values have shifted. If employers want to count on a productive workforce in changing times, they have to understand why employees will work for an organization and the commitment they desire. (See mini-case 10.2.)

THE IMPORTANCE OF EMPLOYEE COMMUNICATION

Four realities of employee communication establish its importance for organizational success. First, employees want information about their companies and they crave communication, especially from their leaders. Second, there is a link between open communication and manager satisfaction with their roles. A study by the Institute of Excellence in Employee Management Communications reported that "more than 90 percent of managers who felt they had the ability to offer ideas and question management decisions were also highly satisfied and engaged in their jobs."[14] Third, effective two-way communication is key to addressing new business challenges because employees are more confident that they can help move their businesses forward.[15] Fourth, employee communications can be critical to maintaining good customer experiences. Employees convey the brand, according to Bill Margaritis, senior vice president of FedEx corporate communications:

> We like our employees to know what our brand attributes are, including the vision and values of the company. So, when we made some acquisitions and the new employees started wearing the FedEx uniform and selling the FedEx service, it was important that we made sure they understood the value of the culture and the value of the brand. We didn't want any gaps in what we promised and what we delivered.[16]

Employee Values Have Shifted; Learn Them and Win Over Your Workforce

Mini • Case 10.2

If reputation translates into bottom-line results, employees are huge stakeholders. Wirthlin Worldwide highlights the impact of shifting employee values and outlines what organizations can do to enhance commitment from this key public.

Wirthlin, which surveyed 1,012 adult American workers, found areas where values have changed and the leverage points provided by those changes.

What Makes Them Tick?

- Job satisfaction means pay and benefits to provide a better *balance of work and family life.*
- *Quality has become internalized,* driven by having the tools to the job—education, good communication within the organization, qualified managers. These lead to improved self-esteem and, ultimately, stronger organizational performance.
- Emphasis has shifted from jobs themselves to *gaining knowledge and involvement,* as jobs are no longer seen as for life.

Communication, Leadership, and Alignment

- *Aligning employees with the business plan* gets bottom-line results. This requires effective internal communication combined with effective leadership performance.
- Two-thirds of those surveyed say they understand the company's business plan and their role in achieving it, yet *fewer than half believe their manager translates the plan.*

Commitment Gap Widening

- Two-thirds feel very committed to employers; an additional 29 percent say they feel moderately committed (a significant change from 1998, when only 56 percent felt very committed).
- *Far fewer* (38%) feel commitment is returned by their employer. No change from 1998, but the gap has widened.
- *Managers who listen* and respond to employee feedback drive satisfaction with communication.
- *Other drivers:* (a) managers and employees working toward the same objectives; (b) providing employees with the info they need to contribute fully; (c) recognizing employees for their accomplishments; (d) offering opportunities for involvement; (e) honesty from management.

Wirthlin says employers should provide a thorough understanding of the workplace, both rationally and emotionally, providing a template upon which all strategies can be based. Once benchmark research has been completed, (1) provide employees with visible response to the data; (2) build ownership and commitment to act on strategic imperatives; (3) develop, share, and exchange effective practices; and (4) track change and refine strategy over time.

Source: *pr reporter,* June 4, 2001, pp. 3–4.

FedEx employee communication is spread worldwide and must make use of technology to keep them informed and to get their feedback.

10.3 Mini • Case

If Negative Talk Fuels Recession, Employers Can Help Avoid One by Using Internal Communications to Give the Facts

Precedent

Twenty years ago Coors Brewing Company found that a valuable win-win program an employer can offer workers is economic education. Through a series of courses and publications, employees got Economics 101 in a way that two objectives were achieved:

1. *Employees were better able to manage their personal finances,* thus making them more aware of job benefits but especially helping them concentrate on their work by alleviating financial worries.
2. *The company could gain understanding of its decisions and policies more readily* from a workforce that had a grasp of the economics of running a highly competitive business.

In an industry as hard fought as brewing, with a flat market and powerful domestic and import competitors, tough decisions must be made—regularly. Keeping the organizational family motivated even when things aren't rosy is vital to competing successfully. But if workers have unrealistic notions of how much profit or surplus an organization makes and what margins are, don't realize how waste and errors can be crippling, why financial markets must be served, and why customers must come first in any circumstance, the organization is at a huge competitive advantage.

Coors's program was extremely successful. Other employers asked to import it and eventually it was spun off as a profit center. Philips Petroleum had a similar program, as did others.

Recommendation

- *It's time to bring economic education back to the workplace.* A majority of today's workforce has never experienced a downturn. Despite higher education levels today, understanding of economic forces is not common. Yes, a campaign may cost money, or temporarily overshadow another effort, but with a nation riveted on the economic roller coaster, with lunchroom and water cooler conversations featuring it, management ignores this macro-societal influence at its peril. One can make a long list of ways it can debilitate the organization.

FDR was right: We have nothing to fear but fear itself. His speech and follow-up campaign on this theme were milestones in public relations history, and a major element in turning around the Great Depression.

A few public statements from CEOs, CFOs, and organizational economists giving a reasoned and balanced view wouldn't hurt, either.

Source: *pr reporter,* March 26, 2001, pp. 1–2.

Employee communication has become a distinctive specialization of public relations, involving ongoing programs of communication, communicating with labor unions in collective bargaining and strike situations, and explaining employee benefits. Employee communication has its own theories and practices, including controlled specialized media.

What Communication Programs Can Accomplish

When communication programs work, they are tremendously cost-effective. Sweetheart Plastics, for example, invested $7,000 in a communication program, hoping to increase productivity. The company realized a savings of $250,000 the first year and expects a ten-year savings of $2.5 million. Mini-case 10.3 cites another example.

Why Communication Programs Fail

When employee communication programs are ineffective, the costs are immeasurable. Inefficiency, waste, higher costs, low morale, absenteeism, strikes, turnover, and accidents are just some of the ways poor employee communication can adversely affect sales, profits, productivity, public image, and the individual employees.

Some reasons for ineffective communication are unclear corporate images, negative organizational culture, lack of employee communication policies, and lack of mutual trust and respect between employees and management. Employee communication too often attempts to "sell" management's line to employees. Interested only in getting their own messages accepted, managers neglect to listen to what employees will tell are their communication needs. Communication programs must have as their goal the building of mutually beneficial relationships.

Special Employee Communication Situations

One of the special employee situations involves communication with employees who are union members.

Unions in the Workforce Environment Unions are powerful organizations. They are active in the political arena. Sometimes in conjunction with business and sometimes in opposition to business, they exert a powerful influence on the government's role in the economy. Workers join unions to gain the power necessary to better pursue their needs and goals. Increased pay, shorter hours, and improved working conditions are common reasons for unionizing.

Many organizations attempt to use effective employee communications to ward off union efforts to organize their labor force. The threat of unionization, in effect, scares management into instituting communication policies and programs that should have existed in the first place. Unfortunately, the timing and motivation of efforts to establish the proper communication climate and facilitate upward communication have sometimes caused them to be perceived as antiunion techniques. Unionization of an organization's workforce places employee communication and public relations in a slightly different light, but basic practices of effective employee communication still hold.

Public Relations in Collective Bargaining When union representation has been established, management is required to bargain in good faith with its representatives. All matters relating to a previously established set of issues are resolved through a process known as **collective bargaining.** Harold Davey defines collective bargaining this way:

> A continuing institutional relationship between an employer . . . and a labor organization . . . concerned with the negotiation, administration, interpretation, and enforcement of written agreements covering joint understandings as to wages or salaries, rates of pay, hours of work and other conditions of employment.[17]

Davey's phrase "continuing institutional relationship" is an important one. The general public has a poor understanding of collective bargaining, associating the process with strikes, labor unrest, or protracted negotiations. In fact, these are exceptional circumstances. In 98 percent of negotiations, contracts are agreed on without resorting to strikes or lockouts.

Contract negotiations and strikes often draw intense public scrutiny. At such times, the public relations function becomes very important, and practitioners really earn their pay. Part of the challenge is the sensitive nature of the negotiations underway. Management and labor usually agree that public disclosure of the negotiating process would result in miscommunication at best and at the worst would lead to disruption and intransigence.

When negotiations are successfully concluded, the public relations spokesperson should tell the story of that success and explain the contract terms to the public. The contract and its impact on the local or national economy are matters of critical public interest and importance. Even after a strike, when the ending of conflict seems to be the main story, information concerning these factors has to be spelled out clearly in organizational and mass media.

Communicating Employee Benefits "Too often, we dismissed functions like internal communications or benefits communications as necessary but not too interesting. Well, get ready. Because of Enron, internal communication is about to take center stage,"[18] writes specialist Jody Buffington Aud. (See the end-of-chapter case study.)

Employee benefits are services an organization provides as part of employees' compensation. Benefits may include health and life insurance programs, sick leave, vacations, employer-paid social security, retirement programs, such as Enron's 405(k) plan, and a variety of other services ranging from day care to prepaid legal advice to physical fitness programs. Benefits attract and motivate employees and promote employee productivity.

In relation to employee benefits, managers often claim employees "just don't appreciate what they have." Often this lack of appreciation is the result of poor communication on the part of management, as the following episode illustrates:

> Workers at a corporation had just voted for union representation, and one of the strongest appeals the union offered was its benefits package. Management could not understand what had made the package so attractive to employees. "Those benefits offer no substantial improvements over the package we already had," complained one executive. Closer examination, however, revealed that the company had never prepared publications to explain its package. Employee meetings to discuss benefits were irregular, almost nonexistent. No employee handbook or guide had been published; no orientation program for new employees had been established. There is little doubt that when the employees cast their ballots for the union, they were not voting for better benefits, but for communication and a plan they understood.

Some organizations have become highly creative in benefits communication. United Technologies developed a 17-minute film/video featuring a popular comedian to discuss six benefit areas: retirement, health care, disability, life insurance, dental care, and savings plans. Bankers Land Company of Palm Beach Gardens, Florida, devised a game board to explain health benefits. Exxon Coal USA put together its 81-page *Guide to Your Employee Benefits* in the style of a magazine or annual report. Golin Harris used the theme "GH Lifeworks" to capture the idea of its employee benefits package.

The role of corporate communicators in dealing with employee benefits can be vitally significant. Public relations practitioners working in this area do not merely disseminate information about existing programs. Perhaps more important, they can serve as conduits for the expression of employees' needs and desires, and thus play a significant role in determining and evaluating benefit programs. Figure 10.1 is a model of the benefit communication process, demonstrating the various points at which corporate communicators can be useful.

THE MEDIA OF EMPLOYEE COMMUNICATION

In the first part of this chapter, we took a general approach to employee communication. We discussed a positive organizational culture supported by appropriate communication policies as prerequisites for effective employee communication. We also discussed employee communication under special circumstances and for special purposes.

This section is devoted to the technical aspects of employee communication media—how to get your message across. Internal media, video, and computers are means of reaching large numbers of employees on an ongoing basis. Personnel and resources devoted to these media have increased markedly in the past decade. This is the fastest growing aspect of the overall public relations effort. It is also the effort over which we have the most control. That's why **internal media** are often called "controlled media."

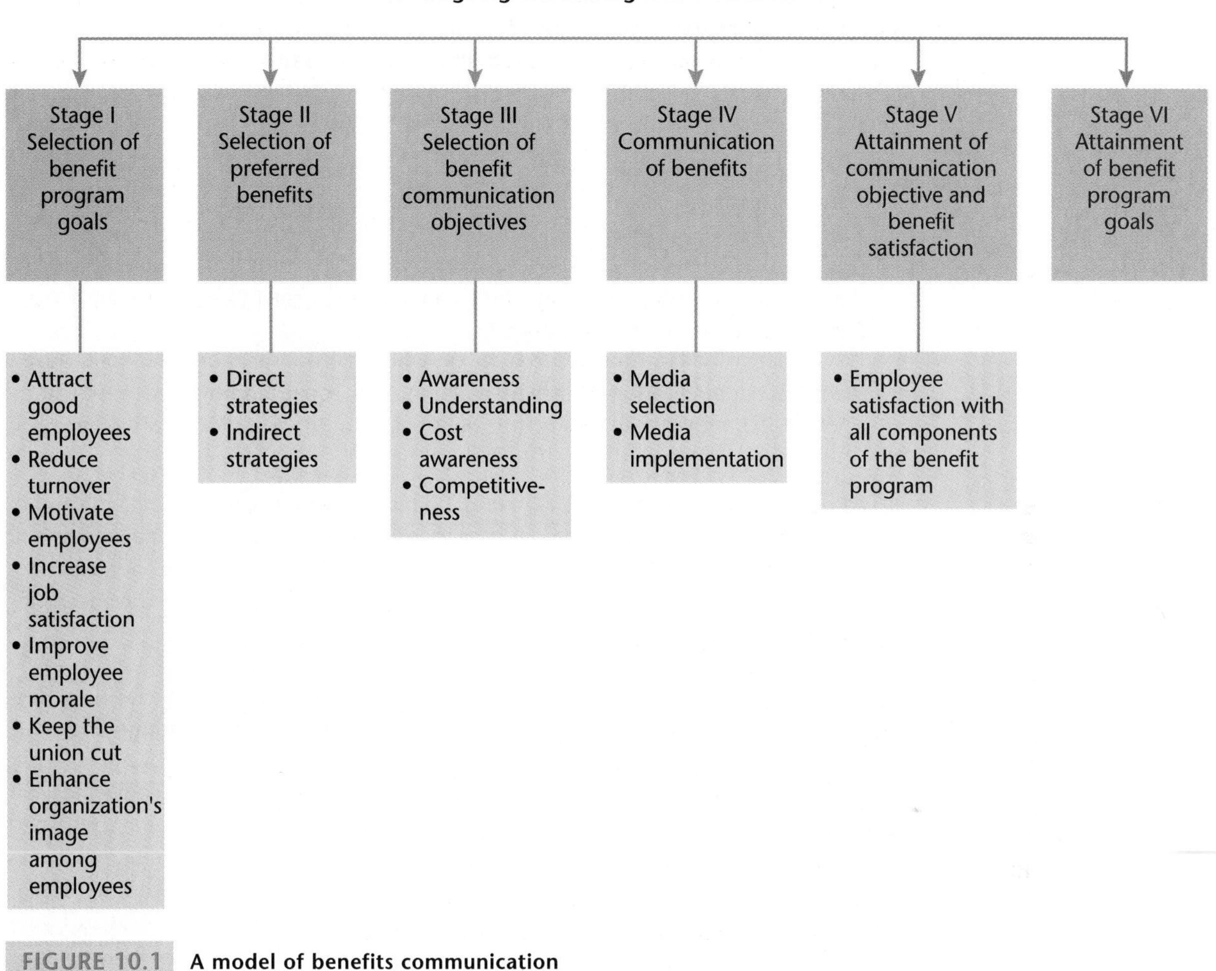

FIGURE 10.1 **A model of benefits communication**

Objectives of Internal Media

In a broad sense, the goal of internal media is the improvement of relationships between its employees and management. Setting policy and defining more specific objectives for such a medium is a complicated undertaking. Without specific guidelines, however, it is hard for an in-house medium to be successful, and it is even harder to measure its success.

As we have said, in-house media must fulfill the needs of both the organization and its employees. Employee audiences must see the information in the medium as useful and meaningful. Following are some broad topics that are frequently chosen by successful internal media:

1. *Employees' Understanding of Their Role in the Organization.* Internal media can stress the importance of each worker's job in meeting organizational goals. Information about the eventual use of products illustrates the importance of everyone's part in the process. Internal publications should support the idea that each employee is a representative for the organization.

2. *Clarification of Management Policies.* Consider the point of view of both management and employees. Employees must be accurately informed about business activities if management expects them to support its programs. Understanding can be helped by explaining policies and rules, which builds confidence in management, and combating rumors and misunderstandings.

3. *Employee Well-being and Safety.* This is explained through information on safety practices, rules, and procedures. Worker safety is always an appropriate area of concern for management and employees. In some organizations, this involves little more than ensuring that everyone knows the location of fire exits. In others, however, the success of the operation, and indeed the operation itself, may depend on adherence to safety procedures.

   There is a continuing need to explain benefits, vacations, holidays, taxes, workers' compensation, affirmative action, and equal employment opportunity policies. Employees can also be told about community issues and educational and training opportunities.

4. *Recognition of Employee Achievements.* This should occur both on the job and in the community, to encourage internal cooperation by helping management and employees become better acquainted with other members of the organization. Social activities can also be recognized but should not take precedence over job-related and community-service accomplishments.

An in-house medium can accomplish these objectives if it meets the needs of employees, says something that employees want to think about and talk about, and is attractive and easy to read.

What type of media does your organization need? An organization must decide what kinds of internal media will best meet its needs: a newsletter, a tabloid newspaper, a magazine, a home page, video news, an intranet, or some other format. Sometimes these needs change. Frequency of publication and methods of distribution should also be decided based on the preferences of the employee audiences. Most in-house publications are published monthly, but some appear quarterly or even weekly. The easiest, cheapest, and simplest method of distribution is to make them available for pickup around work areas. To get wider distribution, some organizations hand them directly to employees, use the in-house mail, or send them to employees' homes. All of these matters are interdependent. The format (size and shape) may limit the possibilities for distribution.

However, it is too easy to fall back on print media as the preferred choice. They are the most traditional forms used in organizations, but consider how best to communicate emergency information. It might be easy to send messages electronically to an established listserv, but what if there is no electricity? How about a cell phone chain? Our technology permits us to communicate rapidly—and we need to internally when a crisis occurs.

Other considerations in determining the number and kinds of media are budget and employee needs. Once a budget for the medium is established, information about employee needs must be gathered. Interviews and questionnaires can tell a great deal about content, frequency, and distribution needs. To help select a format, many companies ask employee panels to review sample media from other organizations. The panel can also evaluate data obtained in the interviews and questionnaires. The results of such planning efforts help determine which communication media to use and evaluate their effect.

Starting Internal Media

Producing an internal medium takes organization and coordination. It must appear at regularly scheduled intervals. Such consistency requires budget and staff. Putting out a medium on a shoestring may be worse than doing nothing at all. A medium, such as a website, that cannot be properly maintained creates negative attitudes by building expectations it cannot fulfill. Therefore, organizing the details of production is important to success.

What is news? The content of an internal medium varies from one organization to another. Remember, company information must satisfy the needs of its employees, not just those of management. Topics of most importance to employees in an IABC study are shown in order of importance in table 10.2. There is an increasing employee concern for job security, which is evident in the top item of importance, "organizational plans for the future." The wishes of workers are clear: They want to know where the organization is headed, what its plans are for getting there, and what that means to them.

Set and maintain strict policies about what will be published in-house. The following criteria can help evaluate a topic's newsworthiness:

1. *Timeliness.* Is the topic timely enough to interest most of the readers?
2. *Scope.* Does it affect enough people directly or indirectly?
3. *Noteworthiness.* Is something or someone important or well known involved?
4. *Human Interest.* Does it deal with things vital to the interests of the readers or those involved?

Objectivity is an important goal of internal media, but in-house media should have a more personal tone than public newspapers or magazines. They should reflect a sense of closeness and common interest that says to the reader, "We're all in this together." One

TABLE 10.2 Subjects of Interest to Employees

Rank	Subject	Scale (1–10)
1	Organizational plans for the future	8
2	Job advancement opportunities	7
3	Job-related "how-to" information	7
4	Productivity improvement	6
5	Personnel policies and practices	6
6	How we're doing vs. the competition	6
7	How my job fits into the organization	6
8	How external events affect my job	5
9	How profits are used	5
10	Financial results	4
11	Advertising and promotional plans	4
12	Operations outside of my department or division	4
13	Organizational stand on current issues	4
14	Personnel changes and promotions	4
15	Organizational community involvement	4
16	Human interest stories about other employees	2
17	Personal news (birthdays, anniversaries, etc.)	2

Source: IABC Study, quoted in Allen Center and Patrick Jackson, *Public Relations Practices,* 5th ed. (Englewood Cliffs, NJ: Longman, 1995), p. 39.

writer says an in-house publication "should look and read like . . . a letter from home . . . a pat on the back . . . a friendly handshake." Most important, the tone of in-house publications must never be condescending or frivolous.

Controlling Internal Media

Every medium should periodically evaluate its progress toward its objectives. Purpose, content, and frequency of publication should all be examined in terms of the needs of the target audience. The panel that originally identified the target audience can be used again to evaluate progress. Surveys and questionnaires also give useful information about how well a medium fulfills expectations. National magazines have found that even simple surveys can provide excellent insight into the interests of readers. To pretest the potential readership of planned articles, for example, a questionnaire can be prepared that lists various headlines and asks a sample of the intended audience which articles they would read. An editor can thus get feedback about the probable success of certain stories.

Occasional and Special Media

Most organizations prepare publications on miscellaneous topics at irregular intervals. Forms range from mimeographed one-sheet leaflets to books by professional writers. Responsibility for these often is with human resources personnel because of legal requirements, government regulations, or company policy. But in smaller organizations, public relations people may also become involved. These publications generally can be divided into three categories, according to purpose:

1. *Orientation literature* explains organizational policies to new members. It can help a new employee get off to a good start by setting forth the ground rules. Goals and objectives of the organization are often included to give a sense of where the company is going and the employee's role in achieving that objective.
2. *Reference material* is designed to be kept for future use. Because of the nature of these publications, it is unlikely that anyone will ever read them from cover to cover; therefore, they must give fast and easy answers. Because this information sometimes changes, publications should be designed so that supplements or other materials can be added later. Reference materials deal with subjects like benefits, insurance, and recreation programs.
3. *Position or special-topics publications* are put out only once. They deal with a specific subject or occasion the organization feels it should discuss. The free enterprise system, charitable and social commitments, history, awards, and scientific or technological developments are among the most frequently treated subjects. Occasional publications have more impact than regularly scheduled newsletters and give an organization the chance to convey a specific message. The same requirements of credibility and interest that apply to newsletters must be followed if special-topic publications are to state their message effectively.

Leaflets, Inserts, and Enclosures Inexpensive publications that may be read and thrown away are often printed on a single sheet that can be folded to produce any of several formats. Leaflets or handbills duplicated on a copying machine are inexpensive and fast to prepare. With a little more effort, single-sheet publications can be folded into brochures for information racks, in-house distribution, or direct mail. Many organizations use them as inserts in pay envelopes.

Booklets and Manuals Because of their expense, booklets and manuals are made to be read and saved for reference. Their greatest shortcoming is that they can be hard to read and use if not designed properly. Employee orientation manuals or insurance plan booklets need indexes, and their information can be more accessible if tabs or color-coded pages are supplied.

Booklets and manuals can be used successfully to do the following:

1. Orient new employees.
2. Write in jargon-free, nontechnical language.
3. Explain the safety regulations as they comply with Occupational Safety and Health Administration (OSHA) standards.
4. Explain the benefit plan and its value to the employee.
5. Explain company policies and their compliance with government regulations.
6. Explain the costs and benefits of the organization's insurance package.
7. Explain the company retirement plan and its requirements.
8. Give information helpful to the employee in his or her job.
9. Give information about social or community issues.
10. Explain organizational compliance with environmental standards.

Printed Speeches and Reprints Speeches and reprints are sometimes distributed as publications. When organization officials speak to professional, community, or other groups concerning topics of interest to employees, it may be useful to print them for distribution within the organization. Reprints of magazine articles of concern to the organization and its employees can be bought inexpensively. Magazine reprints have the advantage of outside credibility.

Message Displays A growing number of laws and regulations require that notices be posted where employees can see them, and many organizations find this a quick, inexpensive way to reach large numbers of people. Message displays include posters, kiosks, electronic and standard bulletin boards, information racks, and exhibits.

Bulletin Boards The bulletin board displays messages in regular locations with minimum effort and expense. The board remains a much-used and effective means of communication within organizations. Notices that have been mailed or given out to employees can also be posted as reminders. Details of announcements already made in meetings or in the house publication can be posted for those who wish more information. Further, bulletin boards are an appropriate location for information that the law requires to be posted.

To ensure credibility and readability, bulletin boards must be carefully planned and kept current. In electronic form through intranets, listservs, and special websites, they can provide time-sensitive information as well.

Posters and Billboards Like bulletin boards, posters and billboards offer fast, effective communication. They are most appropriately used to give emphasis to an idea and provide messages that can be grasped quickly. Posters and billboards should be placed in high-traffic areas where they can be easily seen by most employees.

Information Racks Information racks are designed to invite the reader to take the brochures or booklets displayed. Racks should provide information that cannot be handled in short messages, such as manuals, booklets, printed speeches, and reprints. Because the materials are selected by readers without pressure from management, interest is likely to be higher. The economic advantage to information racks is that only interested employees are likely to take material.

Information racks work best in areas where employees can look at the material in a leisurely way, such as cafeterias and lounges. Empty information racks suggest that management is uninterested, so regular maintenance is needed.

Exhibits and Displays Exhibits and displays rely primarily on visual messages. Their effectiveness is in showing a sample or model of what is being discussed. Many organizations recognize the value of exhibits and displays at industrial meetings or in sales-related contexts, but they are equally valuable in employee communication. Exhibits and displays can show how production facilities work, display products, honor those who receive awards, or depict the history of the organization.

Electronic Media New technology has led to at least three major electronic approaches to employee communication. Electronic-mail communication, through organizational intranets, computer home pages, and internal video are fast becoming the media of choice by employees alike.

E-mail. Because of its immediacy, ease of distribution, and virtually no added cost, electronic mail has become a major employee communication tool. It's even relatively inexpensive for organizations that are spread throughout the world and can maintain their own controlled intranets.

Home Pages. A fast-growing controlled media is the computer home page. With the graphic and sound capability coupled with the advantages of e-mail, this medium may soon replace the company newsletter as the employee communication tool of choice.

Internal Video. For the last 20 years larger companies, especially those spread over several distant locations, have turned to internal video to keep employees informed about the organization.

Summary

For self-testing and additional chapter resources, go to the student CD and the Online Learning Center at **www.mhhe.com/lattimore**

Employee communication is a large and complex aspect of public relations practice. Many different topics and issues confront practitioners working in this area. In this chapter, we discussed the importance of keeping employees informed, creating the proper organizational culture to facilitate proper communication, establishing communication policy, and building employee communication programs. We also considered the special issues of employer communication with a unionized workforce and communication of employee benefits. Finally, we detailed production of employee newsletters and other media. Armed with this knowledge and these tools, public relations practitioners can make great contributions to their organizations' success.

How Communications Helped Avert a Strike

When the Dow Chemical Company's Michigan Operations site began the three-month collective bargaining process with United Steelworkers of America (USWA) Local 12075 in December 2000, ongoing tensions and a contentious history made a work stoppage an extremely likely outcome. The company enlisted the help of its agencies and Ogilvy Public Relations Worldwide for employee communications and Ketchum for media and community relations and to develop and execute communications that would help bring about contract ratification.

The multiagency, multidisciplinary communications team worked together on site in Midland, Michigan, to develop communications that would reach not only the 1,525 bargained-for employees, but also all employees via different vehicles. The team also worked collaboratively on materials to help Dow articulate its position.

Ultimately, the comprehensive communications program greatly influenced the USWA Local 12075's decision to ratify the contract. In fact, union leadership went so far as to cite communications as the reason its membership voted against leadership's recommendations not to ratify.

Challenge/Opportunity

Dow sought to win concessions in the new contract to make the site more competitive through outsourcing and restructured job mobility, and both were sources of disagreement going into negotiations. The historically contentious relationship between the company and the union included a six-month, violent strike in 1974, and both sides feared a similar outcome. In addition, the confrontational attitude of local union leadership, coupled with dismissals and disciplinary actions taken against employees the previous summer for e-mail abuse, contributed to a growing environment of tension and uncertainty as the contract expiration date of February 12, 2001, approached and the threat of strike became very real.

The team faced the additional challenges posed by the company's and the union's agreement to a no-news blackout, as well as tight restrictions by the NLRA that governed the introduction of new communications vehicles to target employees.

Communications aimed to illustrate the positive impact of a potential contract settlement on Michigan Operations's drive to improve its productivity, efficiency, and safety and connect this impact to the larger goal of improved global competitiveness and long-term site growth.

Specifically, the communications objectives were to do the following:

- Use external and internal communications to help prevent a work stoppage.
- Create awareness and build support for the company's position and business direction.

- Foster improved labor-management relations through increased collaboration and communication.

Research

To help focus the communications strategy throughout negotiations and for the next five years, the team commissioned a survey of all site employees. The survey provided Michigan Operations leadership with specific feedback to help identify major issues and determine the most effective ways to reach employees. Key findings and observations included:

- Overall opinion of Dow and Michigan Operations was negative, primarily because of a perceived lack of concern for employees by the site management.
- The working environment, however, was perceived to be fairly positive, with a majority of employees indicating that they interacted well with their co-workers and felt positive about working as teams.
- Employees recognized that union leadership and management did not work well together.
- Employees understood that competitiveness was a key concern for the site.
- Employees were proud to work at Michigan Operations but did not believe that the site commanded the respect it deserved from the rest of the company.

Strategy

- Clearly and consistently articulate the company's position on issues and its commitment to reach contract agreement.
- Ensure that all employees understand the global competitive landscape in which the site operates and the steps necessary to keep the site competitive.
- Overcome employee distrust of and pessimism toward company leadership by frequent and honest discussion and communication.
- Consistently monitor employee, media, and community opinion to ensure that communications continually address audience needs, questions, and perceptions.

The primary audiences identified were bargained-for and salaried employees at the site. Other audiences included Michigan Operations site leadership (unit leaders to whom bargained-for and salaried employees reported), employee's families, local media, and community leaders.

Execution/Tactics

The integrated team developed a comprehensive communications plan (key messages, Q&A, talking points, advertisements, employee and community leader letters) to deal with multiple scenarios including strike, lockout, continuation of negotiations, or a tentative agreement. Specific tactics included the following:

- Developed a "Contract Decision" intranet site focused exclusively on contract discussions and used it to communicate information on the negotiation process to all employees. Updated the site on a regular basis during the final weeks of negotiations. This intranet site's main page received 23,978 hits during the negotiation process.

- Developed key messages, a fact sheet, a glossary of business terms, a site history, contingency plans, and Q&As.
- Created a white paper called "The Case for Change," which outlined the site's need to improve productivity, efficiency, and safety in order to compete and succeed. The site leadership used this document in employee presentations, media interviews, on the intranet, and in printed materials.
- Conducted training sessions for unit leaders and frontline supervisors to outline their responsibilities, share key messages and dos and don'ts, and describe procedures for handling employee questions.
- Created a template for use by the negotiating team to communicate the progress of contract talks on specific issues on a daily basis.
- Drafted backgrounders on key issues (such as job outsourcing and paid committeemen) that arose during the negotiations.
- Conducted media training for the site leader and chief spokesperson.
- Held meetings with the editorial staff of the local paper, the *Midland Daily News,* to state the site's position on the negotiations.
- Drafted letters describing the site's "last best offer" and Dow's "Case for Change" and mailed these letters to employees' homes and to community leaders.
- Created and placed an advertisement on the "Case for Change" and in the *Midland Daily News.*
- Created and placed an advertisement explaining the site's "last best offer" in the *Midland Daily News,* the *Saginaw News,* and the *Bay City Times.*
- Created a "dark" website to be activated only in the event of a work stoppage, detailing work policies and procedures pertaining to salaried employees.

Obstacles Overcome

- Union leadership's strong opposition to contract ratification.
- Agreement to a "no-news blackout."
- NLRA restrictions governing acceptable negotiations period communications.
- Strong community involvement and support for the union.

Evaluation/Measurement of Success

- Members of USWA Local 12075 voted to approve the labor contract on February 15, 2001, despite the fact the entire union bargaining team opposed ratification of the company's last and final offer.
- The union cited Michigan Operations's extensive employee communications efforts as a reason its members chose to vote to ratify the contract.
- Media relations efforts generated 21 print articles and 48 broadcast stories covering the negotiations.
- Union members approved the contract by a substantial margin, according to anecdotal information.

Source: *HolmesReport.*, Retrieved 16 September 2002, from http://www.holmesreport.com/holmestemp/story.

Questions

1. How would you describe the organizational culture as Dow and the union approached the contract expiration date? Authoritarian or participative?
2. What were the legal communication restrictions, based on the bargaining agreement?
3. What forms of internal communication were used to reach the primary audiences? Why do you think these types of internal media were used?
4. Did Dow's communications objectives in the case consider the shifts in employee values? If so, how? If not, why not?

Key Terms

Use the CD-ROM and Online Learning Center at www.mhhe.com/lattimore to further your understanding of the following terms

authoritarian cultures
collective bargaining
communication policies
employee benefits
employee communication
employee relations
internal communication
internal media
organizational culture
participative cultures

Notes

1. "Jim Lukaszewski's Strategy," A supplement of *pr reporter,* 11 October 2001, p. 1.
2. Howard N. Fullerton, Jr., "Labor Force Projections to 2008: Steady Growth and Changing Composition," *Monthly Labor Review* (November 1999), p. 1.
3. Employee Communications. www.prsa.org/empcom.
4. Bernard Charland, "Commentary: Employee Relations—Back to the Future?" Accessed at http://www.golinharris.com.
5. David M. Dozier, Larissa A. Grunig, and James E. Grunig, *The Manager's Guide to Excellence in Public Relations and Communication Management* (Mahwah, NJ: Erlbaum, 1995), p. 17.
6. K. Sriramesh, James E. Grunig, and Jody Buffington, "Corporate Culture and Public Relations." In *Excellence in Public Relations and Communication Management,* ed. James E. Grunig (Hillsdale, NJ: Erlbaum, 1992), p. 591.
7. Larissa A. Grunig, James E. Grunig, and David M. Dozier, *Excellent Public Relations and Effective Organizations: A Study of Communication Management in Three Countries* (Mahwah, NJ: Erlbaum, 2002), pp. 482–83.
8. Ibid.
9. Ibid., p. 482.
10. "Working with the Workers," *PR Week,* 1 July 2002, p. 15.
11. Ibid.
12. This discussion is based on Norman B. Sigband, "What's Happening to Employee Commitment?" *Personnel Journal* (February 1974), pp. 133–35.
13. Gary F. Grates, "Ten Tumultuous Years: Examining a Decade of Change (A Peek at the Future)." Retrieved 10 March 2002, from www.prsa_counselors.org.

14. "Managers Want to be More than a Channel of Communication," *Holmes Report.* Retrieved 18 July 2002, from www.holmesreport.com/holmestemp/story.
15. Ibid.
16. "Working with the Workers," p. 15.
17. Quoted in Donal P. Crane, *Personnel: The Management of Human Resources,* 2nd ed. (Belmont, CA: Wadsworth, 1979), p. 79.
18. Jody Buffington Aud, "What Internal Communicators Can Learn from Enron," *The Public Relations Strategist* (Spring 2002), vol. 9, p. 12.

CHAPTER ELEVEN

Community Relations

11

Outline

PREVIEW

An organization's community relations may be affected by such diverse factors as its recruitment methods, employee relations, waste disposal, energy use, design and maintenance of buildings and grounds, marketing and advertising strategies, and corporate philanthropy.

The quality of an organization's employees, the cooperativeness of citizens and governmental agencies, the patronage of community members, the ability to attract financial support, indeed, the success or failure of an organization may depend on the effectiveness of its community relations.

Community activism is increasing. Responsibility and accountability for business practices must be part of the overall mission and organizations must be prepared to deal with increased scrutiny by the media and its publics ☐

"Today, no matter how large, small, or important an institution may be, it can be undermined if its community relations are haphazard."
—Wilbur J. Peak

THE IMPORTANCE OF COMMUNITY RELATIONS

The headlines tell of global mergers and acquisitions, spin-offs, initial public offerings, and corporate earnings that are lower or higher than expected. Marketing, technology, resource acquisition, and management are increasingly international in scope, and the federal government is the most conspicuous aspect of many organizations' operating environments.

In this large-scale environment, concern for community seems almost small and old-fashioned. But appearances are deceiving. As the following two examples illustrate, citizens care deeply about what happens in their communities. It's where they live and work, raise their families, educate their children, and spend most of their time.

Some Orange County, California, residents and politicians wanted to convert a former Marine Corps air station into an international airport. Those in nearby suburbs opposed the proposal, dreading the inevitable noise, vibrations, and pollution concerns. A coalition of cities in the area proposed an alternative plan, one that would turn the air station real estate into districts for education, research and technology, arts and culture, sports and entertainment, and housing. The plan passed by a two-to-one margin, and the victory reshaped Orange County politics.[1]

Community groups protested when Walgreens announced it would reduce pharmacy hours in 30 Illinois stores, affecting many poor black and Hispanic families who live on Chicago's south and west sides. Cuts in the prescription-reimbursement rates for Medicaid recipients would make these stores unprofitable to operate, and the drugstore chain had been unable to work out an agreement with the state despite months of negotiation. The Reverend Jesse Jackson and community groups urged Walgreens to reconsider and added support to the company's case.[2] Walgreens solicited the support of the community on this issue, asking them to contact their state legislators and voice their opposition to the proposed Medicaid cuts. In late May 2001, the issue was resolved when the state agreed to restore half of the originally proposed cuts. This was enough to allow the Walgreens stores to continue operating as usual and to maintain their profitability.[3]

Countless other examples demonstrate how neighbors are banding together to improve their schools, security, and community services and how corporations and other organizations are reaching out to their communities. Back-to-the-city movements are repopulating many metropolitan areas; downtown businesses are reviving after years of

Old Defensive Approach	New Collaborative Approach
Fragmented	Integrated
Focus on managing relationships	Focus on building relationships
Emphasis on buffering the organization	Emphasis on opportunities
Company-driven	Shared control
Linked to short-term business goals	Based on corporate values
Idiosyncratic implementation dependent on interest and personal style of manager	Coherent approach driven by business goals, mission, values and stakeholder dialogue

FIGURE 11.1 **Characteristics of Corporate-Stakeholder Relations**
Source: Ann Svendsen, *The Stakeholder Strategy: Profiting from Collaborative Business Relationships* (San Francisco: Berrett-Koehler Publishers, 1998), p. 4.

inactivity; people are interested in family and community roots. As Detroit Mayor Kwame F. Kilpatrick noted, "If you don't have community pride, if you don't have a safe, clean city, you don't have a world-class city."[4]

The lesson for organizations is simple: Regional, national, and international concerns may preoccupy you, but don't forget the folks next door. In the past, constructive community relations programs were characterized by phrases like "corporate citizenship" or "good neighbor." Now the concept is one of selection, with communities and corporations choosing each other for mutually beneficial purposes.

Today's corporations must cooperate as well as compete to succeed. Figure 11.1 compares the old defensive approach to community relations with the new collaborative approach. An organization becomes part of the community, creating win-win solutions that result in a healthier bottom line and in benefits for stakeholders and for society as a whole. The key to any effective community relations program is positive, socially responsible *action* to help the community on the part of the organization.

AN INTERDEPENDENT RELATIONSHIP

Effective community relations depend on recognizing the interdependence of institutions with their communities. The cycle begins with people wanting to live in good communities and bringing their talents and skills to the local labor market. Corporations hire those employees who help the organization make a profit. A corporation then uses its resources to address needs and to make the community an even better place to live.

Ford Motor Company is just one example of this interdependence. The company's 2001 corporate citizenship report notes that the same employees who are the lifeblood of its organization are also the lifeblood of their communities. They live in the same communities in which the company operates, and many are investors in Ford. The car company's customers include employees, investors, business partners, and members of local communities and society more broadly. Ford considers this interdependence as an advantage: The steps they take to build deeper relationships with one stakeholder group may result in greater knowledge of another stakeholder group.[5]

All types of organizations practice community relations. Schools, churches, hospitals, museums, and groups like the Red Cross and the Boy Scouts depend on community relations the way businesses depend on marketing—as the primary means by which "customers" are attracted. Prisons, military bases, and universities must strive for community acceptance. Except for corporate philanthropy, however, the process of community relations is the same whether or not the organization seeks financial profit.

Every community has a vital stake in the economic health and prosperity of its institutions. Every organization has a vital stake in the health and prosperity of the community it inhabits. Quite naturally, therefore, organizations and their communities develop a mutual interest in each other's successful and effective operation. Spotlight 11.1 outlines the broad scope of Kodak's involvement in its headquarters community, Rochester, New York. At this level, the connection between institutional interest and public interest is most clear.

At the very least, organizations expect communities to provide adequate municipal services, fair taxation, good living conditions for employees, a good labor supply, and a reasonable degree of support for the plant and its products. In addition to employment, wages, and taxes, communities expect from their institutions an attractive appearance, support of community institutions, economic stability, and a focus for hometown pride.

11.1 Spotlight

Kodak and the Rochester Community: Support That Makes a Difference

Kodak volunteers gather worldwide to provide assistance to local communities and organizations by working on a wide range of projects.

Dollars for Doers

Kodak's support enables volunteers to nominate community organizations for $300, $500, or $750 grants to assist with special projects. Since 1989 Kodak has awarded, at the request of its employees, more than $625,000 to area not-for-profit organizations.

Scholarships

Kodak annually recognizes outstanding minority students who pursue careers in engineering, science, or business.

The Environment

Kodak initiated five-year worldwide environmental goals to address three strategic initiatives: reduce emissions further, conserve natural resources by reducing waste, and tighten its environmental management system. Cost is estimated at about $100 million.

Recycling

Kodak achieved its 250 millionth single-recycling rate for any consumer product in the United States.

Junior Achievement

Kodak employees volunteer in Rochester-area schools as tutors, mentors, and in enrichment programs.

Arts, Culture, and Sports

Kodak is a major contributor to Rochester museums and science centers, sports organizations, art galleries, and the philharmonic orchestra.

Local Grants and Contributions

Kodak is a generous supporter of the Rochester United Way, providing corporate grants of more than $2 million. Additional grants support other area organizations such as children's centers, women's foundations and area colleges and universities.

Sponsorships and Fund-Raisers

Kodak provides many forms of support to local organizations seeking to raise funds through luncheons, dinners, and special events, including financial support, manpower, and product and technical expertise.

Day of Caring

Thousands of Kodak volunteers have participated in this United Way–sponsored event to help organizations and individuals in efforts ranging from simple cleaning and basic repairs to major structural improvements.

Affordable Housing

Kodak continues to be a strong financial supporter for organizations that provide city home-ownership incentives and assistance to those who might otherwise never have the opportunity to purchase a home.

Source: Eastman Kodak.

Employees from People's Bank in New Haven, CT, spend a day volunteering to paint a low-income home.

Good community relations aids in securing what the organization needs from the community and in providing what the community expects. Moreover, it helps to protect organizational investments, increase sales of products and stock, improve the general operating climate, and reduce costs of dealing with government agencies. Positive community relations can affect worker productivity when organizations sponsor community health and education programs. Also, favorable community attitudes may influence worker attitudes toward the organization. The best community relations programs are those that flow naturally from the organization's resources.

THE COMMUNITY RELATIONS PROCESS

The clarity of the mutual interest of organizations and their communities, however, does not imply that community relations can be practiced without careful planning and execution. Effective community relations does not just happen, nor is it an inevitable by-product of a well-run, civic-minded organization. Like all aspects of public relations, successful community relations programs must be built into the structure and culture of an organization. Community relations is not based on pure altruism; it looks to the organization's self-interest. W. J. Peak offers the best definition of **community relations** we have seen:

> **Community relations,** as a public relations function, is an institution's planned, active, and continuing participation with and within a community to maintain and enhance its environment to the benefit of both the institution and the community.[6]

Good community relations is a mutually beneficial partnership, going far beyond, say, a generous financial donation to fund a civic project. Ideally an institution will garner its resources—the product and services the company provides, customer relations, recruitment, employee relations, production processes, marketing and advertising strategies, design of the organization's building and facilities—and use them to better the community and to shape the environment in which it exists. As Stanford University professor David P. Baron notes:

> For many companies, market success depends not just on their products and services, the efficiency of their organizations, their internal organization, and the organization of their supply chains, distribution channels and alliance networks. Success also depends on how effectively they deal with governments, interest groups, activists and the public. The forces these parties generate can foreclose entry into new markets, limit price increases and raise the costs of competing. They can also unlock markets, reduce regulation, handicap rivals and generate competitive advantage. These forces are manifested outside of markets but often work in conjunction with them.[7]

Arguably, community relations is an organizational attitude or state of mind, rather than any specific process or practice. Coca-Cola's Rob Baskin notes that building relationships in communities is "the best PR" and that it's "the kind of work that can never be abated."[8]

Determining Objectives

Companies are engaging their employees when planning and implementing their community relations activities. The needs of the local community and the concerns of their employees are the two most important criteria in determining which causes to support. These employees participate in the selected activities, bringing their social commitments to life and creating a team of ambassadors for the company in the community.[9]

General objectives, however, do not suffice. Companies should have a written strategic plan for community relations that defines management's view of its obligation to the community so that efforts can be coordinated and concentrated. Specific community relations objectives should be spelled out. Failure to do this kills too many community relations programs before they get started.

Knowing the Community

Community relations policies and objectives are not determined according to idealistic principles. They come about by assessing organizational needs, resources, and expertise on the one hand and community needs and expectations on the other. Before meaningful policies and objectives can be developed, the organization must know its community.

Although community relations usually stresses communication from the organization to the community, the success of such efforts rests on the communicator's knowledge of the audience. Each community defines its publics, and no two are exactly alike. Detroit, for example, has the largest Arab American population in the United States. Many technology workers who live in San Francisco are Asian, and one estimate notes that 80 percent of all first graders in Texas's public school system are Hispanic. But real knowledge of the community goes beyond the standard demographic, ethnic, historical, geographic and economic data. True understanding of the audience comes from listening and being involved.

A solid community relations program must be built on the answers to questions like these:

1. *How is the community structured?*
   Is the population homogeneous or heterogeneous?
   What are its formal and informal leadership structures?
   What are the prevailing value structures?
   How are its communication channels structured?
2. *What are the community's strengths and weaknesses?*
   What are the particular problems of the community?
   What is the local economic situation?
   What is the local political situation?
   What are the unique resources (human, cultural, natural) possessed by the community?
3. *What does the community know and feel about the organization?*
   Do its neighbors understand the organization's products, services, practices, and policies?
   What are the community's feelings about the organization?
   Do misunderstandings about the organization exist?
   What are the community's expectations regarding the organization's activities?

The answers to such questions are not necessarily easy to get. Moreover, answers change over time and thus require frequent monitoring. Good information can be acquired in several ways. The U.S. Census report contains a wealth of information about communities and the people who live there. Many organizations engage in survey research to determine community knowledge, attitudes, and perceptions. Professional polling organizations are often employed to provide such services. Close contact with community leaders is an extremely important source of information. Professional, civic, religious, or fraternal leaders; political officials; and media editors can generally be reached through membership in local organizations or through face-to-face meetings on a variety of subjects. Some organizations formalize such input by including community leaders on their task forces or committees that deal with important community issues.

Guidelines for Effective Community Relations Programs

Having established the means for ongoing community inputs, the following guidelines should be used to establish an effective community relations program:

1. Careful effort should be made to establish the objectives top management wishes to achieve. The organization may seek many objectives—reputation, experience with a potential future payoff, stability of environment, and so on—but whatever it seeks ought to be established in realistic and concrete terms.
2. Alternative strategies should be explored and choices made. If an organization wishes to improve housing conditions in a city in which it operates, for instance, possibilities for action range from partially funding research into new ways to build low-cost housing to actually building low-cost housing.
3. Impacts of community relations programs on the organization and the community should be anticipated. Offering training for jobs that will not exist when the training is concluded helps no one.
4. Attention should be paid to the likely total costs of a nonprofit action and to the volume of the organization's resources that may legitimately be allocated to community relations. It is not advantageous to either the organization or the community if the organization suddenly discovers a given program is costing too much and abruptly stops all community service.
5. Many managers have found that certain types of involvement in urban affairs require knowledge and understanding that go beyond the usual managerial and technical business talents. Political skills, deep understanding of community problems, and the ability to settle problems in an unfamiliar cultural setting are requisites for some activities. Special expertise may have to be acquired.[10]

Communicating with Communities

Community communication has no single audience. Corporations must be open to a variety of communication tactics if they are to reach important publics. One of the most significant ways to reach the community is through employee communication. For example, Home Depot employees usually live in the local community. These employees can share the company's messages with neighbors and friends at the high school football game, while shopping for groceries, when picking up children at school, while attending church, and at many other places.[11]

Other important communication channels consist of a community's opinion leaders: teachers, clergy, public officials, professionals and executives, bankers, union leaders, and ethnic and neighborhood leaders.

Local organizations are also important vehicles of communication in communities. Fraternal, civic, service, and social clubs; cultural, political, veterans, and religious organizations; and youth groups all provide platforms for institutional messages and ample opportunities for informal communication. Organizational managers should be encouraged to belong to such groups and should be available to make public speeches to them as well.

Channels of Communication

The communication channels through which audiences are reached may range from an informal chat over lunch at a Rotary or Kiwanis Club meeting to advertisements in local mass media such as newspapers, radio, and television. In-house publications, brochures, and annual reports can be easily shared with community leaders. Some organizations even create newsletters specifically for their neighbors.

A uniquely community-oriented method of organizational communication is the open house. Successful open houses provide small group tours of organizational facilities with knowledgeable guides. They include films, displays, and brochures, and usually provide product samples or mementos for participants to take home. The major message of such activities, of course, is the interdependence between the institution and the community.

In some cases, industrial or company tours become major tourist attractions. The General Motors Corvette assembly plant in Bowling Green, Kentucky, and the Callaway Golf plant in Carlsbad, California, are two examples. It may be necessary for organizations to limit, cancel, or restrict tours, however, because of staffing, industrial espionage concerns, world affairs, and many other reasons. Visitors at the Corvette plant are not allowed to take photographs. The city of San Jose, California, canceled tours of its water pollution control plant after the events of September 11, 2001, because the city was in an enhanced state of emergency readiness. The *Seattle Times* printing facility limits tours to its North Creek location, and an appointment is required.[12]

SPECIFIC FUNCTIONS OF COMMUNITY RELATIONS

Community relations managers would like to spend most of their time identifying and building relationships and networks with community leaders, organizations, and government officials (91%); developing and managing plans to meet community concerns, needs, and issues (85%); and developing and managing partnerships with organizations in the community (85%), according to the Center for Corporate Citizenship.[13] Although considerable time is spent on these activities, community relations managers also attend community relations meetings with colleagues, assist other departments with their community relations plans, assist with recognition ceremonies, speak before community groups, review requests for contributions, and conduct community events and programs.[14]

The average number of employees in a community relations department is about five, and the average number of employees per company is about 4,000, according to the Center for Corporate Citizenship.[15]

When an Organization Moves

Community relations is particularly critical when an organization moves into a new community or leaves an old one. Communities now ask questions before they accept new businesses, industries, or even nonprofit undertakings. Community response to an organization should be an important factor in the location decision.

Once the decision to move into a particular community is made, it is essential to provide local media with factual information on the timing of the move, the hiring of new employees, the opening of the plant, and other similar activities. The goal is to familiarize key groups with the organization and its products, activities, policies, and people, using all available media and methods.

The dependence of a community on its organizations is never clearer than when a plant or facility leaves town. When the Portsmouth Gaseous Diffusion Plant in Piketon, Ohio, closed, 2,000 workers were left without jobs. The economic impact strained the local economy as each of these workers made an average of $50,000 in salary and benefits a year.[16] The shutdown of Texas Instruments' Santa Cruz, California, plant left 600 workers feeling afraid and uncertain and city officials wondering how they would fund redevelopment activities such as downtown revitalization and street widening.[17] Beyond the economic implications, plant shutdowns may affect communities in many other ways, such as raising levels of psychological depression, alcoholism, drug abuse, marital stress, child abuse, and even suicide among former employees. A plant closing can have wide-ranging effects, and companies need to prepare appropriately if it becomes necessary to depart from a community.

Criteria for Community Relations Activities

In Philip Lesly's *Handbook of Public Relations* several criteria are suggested that organizations must apply to community relations activities. These criteria are presented here with a case example of how organizations have used each criterion to establish a community relations program.[18]

1. *Creating Something Needed That Did Not Exist Before.* Intel is harnessing spare processing power of personal computers to fight cancer. Based on the theory behind Napster, the Philanthropic Peer-to-Peer Program allows researchers to receive information from as many as 6 million people and could reduce the amount of time to develop new drugs from 12 years to as little as 5 years.[19]
2. *Eliminating Something That Is a Community Problem.* The Birmingham Summit, a national town meeting that focused on race relations, was sponsored by MSNBC and *Newsweek* magazine. Subtitled "The Challenge for America in the 21st Century," the two-day event featured an all-day conference and a panel discussion. It was the first such collaboration between two media giants.[20]
3. *Developing a Means of Self-Determination.* Kinko's uses its branches in the numerous communities it operates in as a way to heighten knowledge about environmental issues and to identify what can be done to improve and protect the community.
4. *Broadening Use of Something That Exists to Include "Havenots."* Hotelier Marriott provides day care for service-industry workers in Washington, DC, and Atlanta.
5. *Sharing Equipment, Facilities, and Professional Expertise.* McDonald's lets groups use its juice machine for parties, many banks let groups use their seminar rooms for meetings, and professional groups such as the American Bar Association provide free professional advice to the poor or elderly. Local CPA groups often provide free tax consulting to the elderly at tax time.
6. *Reconstituting, Repairing, and Dressing Up.* Whirlpool Corp. pledged an oven and a refrigerator for each of the new homes Habitat for Humanity hopes to build worldwide by 2005. The commitment is valued at $25 million.[21]
7. *Tutoring, Counseling, and Training.* Many corporations encourage their employees to teach classes and guest lecture in grades from kindergarten to college and to counsel start-up businesses in their area of expertise.
8. *Activating Others.* St. Jude Children's Research Hospital has worked with FedEx in Memphis to host the FedEx-St. Jude PGA Golf Tournament. In 2000 the event's volunteers raised approximately $1 million for cancer and other childhood illness research.

Typical community relations activities include open houses, speakers' bureaus, community service by employees on nonprofit boards of directors, and monetary support and volunteer support of community events. Community relations activities also include making facilities available, sponsoring social projects to attack major community problems, and creating employee volunteer programs. Publicity and promotion in all these community relations programs must be seen as tools in support of the actual programs, not substitutes for them.

Local Government and Political Action

Community relations goes beyond mere communication. It requires action by organizations in relation to community health and welfare, education, government, culture, recreation, and other areas.

Business/government relations is discussed in much greater depth in another chapter of this book, but community relations and governmental relations clearly overlap in local government and politics. In fact, the term *public affairs* is usually defined in public relations as two related activities—government relations and community relations.

As previously stated, local political officials can supply invaluable input to corporate community relations programs. Corporations have a great stake in effective local government since they are major taxpayers and users of municipal services. Part of the community relations effort, therefore, must be devoted to building solid relations with city officials, county commissions, and other agencies of local government. This is accomplished, in part, by making organizational expertise available to governments through loans of managerial personnel or through service on panels, commissions, or committees established by or for local government.

All institutions must mobilize on the local level those who recognize the importance of their contribution to the health and prosperity of the community and those who will speak out for policies in the best interests of their community and its institutions. The United Way Loaned Executive Program is one such example. Businesses lend key personnel to their local United Way during the fall fund-raising campaign. Through presentations and individual meetings at community-based businesses, these executives raise the awareness of and make a case for supporting United Way. Similarly, political experts now recognize that strength in Washington is derived from organized, localized grassroots support. In an era when virtually all members of Congress are looking out for their own districts and careers, local people making local demands and representing local interests are far more effective than Washington-based lobbyists. In this regard, community relations may be not only an end in itself but also an integral part of national efforts.

Corporate Philanthropy

Great controversy has raged over **corporate philanthropy** for many years. Only in the past 50 years has corporate charity been recognized as a legal use of stockholders' funds. Even after having established its legality, questions remain as to whether or not and to what extent the practice is appropriate and useful. Beyond these issues are questions of proper motivations, goals, and criteria for corporate giving.

Some maintain that corporate managers have no business giving away profits that rightly belong to stockholders. If stockholders wish to donate their money to what they consider good causes, that is their right—but corporate managers should not make such decisions for them. In fact, small stockholders and other individuals are responsible for 75–80 percent of all donations to charitable organizations in the United States.

By law, corporations are permitted to donate up to 10 percent of earnings to charitable organizations. Government tax incentives can serve as a powerful motivator for businesses to make charitable contributions. In practice, however, very few corporations give to the limit, perhaps because they feel that it is not in their interest or in the interests of their stockholders to do so. Overall, about 1 percent of corporate profits is actually given away. In the year 2000, total contributions from corporations totaled \$10.86 billion, up 11.1 percent from the previous year.[22] Figure 11.2 identifies the source of contributions.

Corporate giving can serve many corporate interests, including recruitment, sales, and employee morale, but it inevitably serves that interest called public relations. Consequently, corporate public relations personnel are almost always involved in, if not responsible for, charitable decisions.

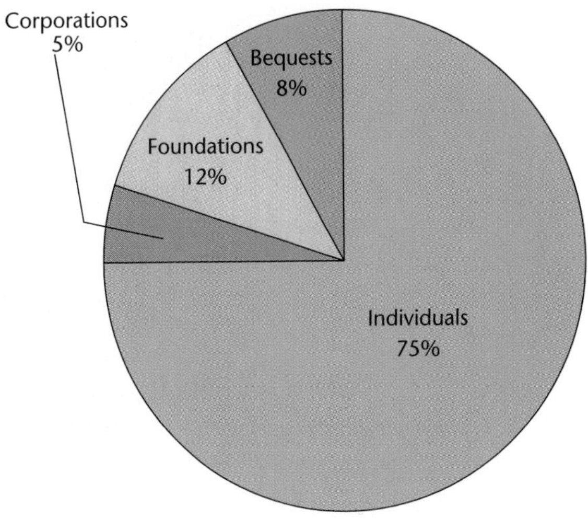

FIGURE 11.2 **2000 Philanthropic Contributions \$203.45 billion by source of contributions**
Source: AAFRC Trust for Philanthropy/Giving USA 2001.

Unfortunately, in some cases, corporate charitable decisions are still made capriciously and without adequate planning. In developing a coherent approach to corporate giving, several factors should be considered:

1. *Do no Harm.* Contributions should not be made to any cause that may be contrary to the best interests of the donor or the recipient.
2. *Communicate with the Recipient.* Effective grant-making requires a close partnership between donor and recipient.
3. *Target Contributions toward Specific Areas.* Gifts should achieve maximum impact on the community and maximum benefits for the donor. In this regard, donations should go to areas where individual corporations have unique expertise not available in the voluntary, nonprofit sector.
4. *Make Contributions According to Statements of Corporate Policy.* Fully developed policies of this nature should include the charitable aims and beliefs of the company, the criteria to be used in evaluating requests for funds, the kinds of organizations and causes that will and will not be supported, and the methods by which grants will be administered.
5. *Plan within the Budget.* Corporate giving should be tied to set percentages of net earnings.
6. *Inform all Persons Concerned.* Employees and the community at large should be fully aware of corporate activities.
7. *Do a Later Follow-Up.* The corporation does a valuable service by demanding of recipients high levels of performance and proper financial accounting.
8. *Remember That More Than Money May Be Needed.* An effective corporate contribution requires more than checkbook charity. Volunteer workers, managerial expertise, and corporate leadership are essential elements of an effective program.

Two trends in corporate giving hold the promise of making such philanthropic programs more effective. Rather than reacting to public issues and public pressures, more firms, particularly the larger ones, are taking greater initiative in channeling dollars and corporate talent into problem areas they deem significant and in which they wish to make an impact. Larry Ellison, founder and chief executive officer of Oracle, endowed the Ellison Medical Foundation, a philanthropic institution that provides vaccines to combat infectious diseases in the Third World. This center also funds research into finding cures for diseases of the elderly. Ellison rationalizes his commitment to funding research in the article, noting, "What do you think is cooler: being the richest guy on earth or helping find the cure for cancer?"[23]

A second trend in corporate giving is what might be called "venture philanthropy." Pierre Omidyar, the founder of Ebay, gives money to charities that follow solid business plans and can create income streams to support the nonprofit work. Omidyar also fosters a network of "social entrepreneurs," one example of which is New Profit Inc. This Boston nonprofit funds causes such as early reading and public health clinics by identifying the winning elements of successful programs. One example is an after-school program that keeps kids out of trouble by pairing them with volunteers from the working world.[24]

Many corporations match employee contributions to educational institutions, museums, orchestras, public TV, hospitals, and ballet, thus, in effect, permitting their contributions to reflect those of their employees. In these ways, employees can be the motivating force behind their companies' charitable donations. Beside cash contributions, corporate giving also includes sponsoring events, pro bono work, in-kind contributions, and cause-related marketing.

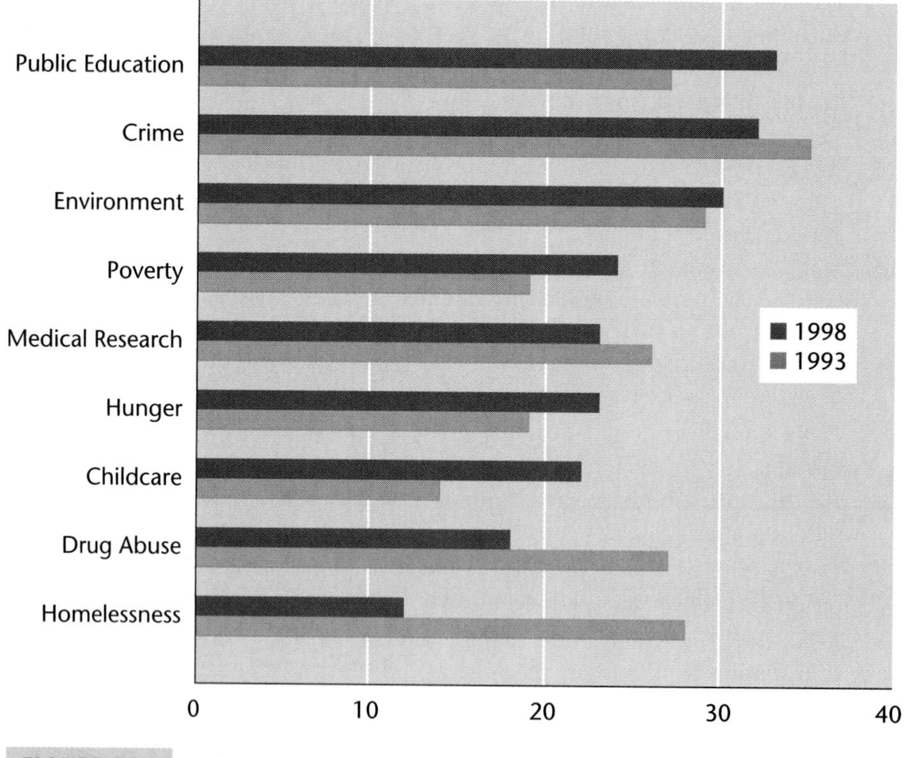

FIGURE 11.3 **Problems That Business Should Work the Hardest to Solve**
Source: Used with permission. 1999 Cone, Inc., and Roper Starch Worldwide Cause-Related Trends Report.

Fort Atkinson Schools: Reversing a Resounding "No" Vote on a School Referendum

Mini•Case 11.1

By Bill Nelson
Copy Chief and Special Projects Writer
Morgan & Myers

Situation Analysis and Research

Can an overwhelming defeat of a school referendum be transformed into victory a year later? That was the question facing the southern Wisconsin city of Fort Atkinson in the mid-1990s.

An initial school district referendum, on April 4, 1995, was decisively defeated—3,233 no votes to 1,486 yes votes. This meant that about two-thirds of the voters reacted negatively to the plan to construct a $23.1 million high school. A year later, the board of education wondered if a second referendum could possibly succeed. The school district decided to ask the citizenry to approve not only the previously defeated new high school, but also to endorse another referendum for additional athletic facilities and an enhanced auditorium. At a total of $27.1 million, this would be the largest referendum ever undertaken by the Fort Atkinson School District. The major challenge facing supporters, including largely pro bono help from Morgan & Myers, a communications consulting firm, was the goal of boosting the percentage of voters in support of the multiple-part proposal from 31 percent to better than 50 percent.

Research was conducted in two phases:

1. A qualitative approach allowing voters to record their views to identify key issues impacting the vote.
2. A 10-minute telephone survey of 450 selected voters to quantify the depth and breadth of feelings on the identified issues.

The research generated 4 broad and 19 specific directives, which gave direction to the board in shaping its approach to the second referendum. It also helped direct a grassroots communications effort involving 250 citizens. Key findings included:

- One major reason for the defeat was that the proposed school site was on low ground and tended to be spongy in times of heavy rain.
- Some 4,700 voters in the 1995 referendum were highly motivated to vote again, and at least 70 percent of them were open to considering the new proposal.
- About 500 parents of school-age children did not vote in the 1995 election, so they became a targeted group.

Audience

Voters of the Fort Atkinson School District, which includes the city of Fort Atkinson (population 12,000) and the surrounding rural area, include a substantial number of retirees who no longer have children in school.

Planning and Strategy

Based on the results of the research, the Fort Atkinson Board of Education made changes in its approach:

- The site would be altered. Higher ground across the street from the initially chosen site would be the new location, to better meet the community's criteria for the school.
- A close look would be taken at increasing the capacity of the existing high school. After concluding this was inappropriate, the board worked hard to communicate why.
- The school plan would be refined to carry the district 10 to 15 years into the future.
- A key message point was developed, showing that property taxes would go up less than 5 percent over what taxpayers had paid the previous year because of increased property tax relief from the state.

Execution/Tactics

A variety of campaign tactics was used, including:

- Morgan & Myers and a volunteer committee came up with a "Vote Yes for Kids" creative platform for the 1996 campaign.
- School officials spoke with civic leaders and at community organizational meetings as a way to educate the citizenry on the need for a new school.
- School information was disseminated through newspaper, radio, and cable television.
- The "Vote Yes" committee, which included teachers and community leaders, waged an advocacy campaign that:
  - Displayed "Vote Yes" yard signs throughout the district.
  - Mailed letters to voters and placed ads in the local newspaper.
  - Recruited 250-plus volunteers.
  - Conducted a "Brown Bag Button Campaign" in which the 250 each sought out 10 potential yes voters, presented them with a "Vote Yes" button, and phoned them on election day to remind them to go to the polls.

Measurement of Success

The referendum passed! The vote on the $24.6 million high school portion of the referendum was approved by 54 percent of the voters—2,354 to 1,903. And 52 percent of the voters supported the second question, providing $2.5 million to build an athletic field and swimming pool, and to equip the new high school's auditorium.

In the fall of 1998—a little more than two years after the referendum—the student body streamed through the school doors at the new westside location. Today, the attractive new school enhances the educational process and is considered a Fort Atkinson showpiece.

Education As figure 11.3 illustrates, public education is one of the issues Americans feel businesses should work the hardest to solve. This priority, along with crime and the quality of the environment, have remained constant over the last five years, shifting only by a small percentage.[25] Communities need good schools to keep their current businesses and to attract new companies that are looking to relocate. Mini-case 11.1 highlights how the Fort Atkinson, Wisconsin, community passed a referendum for a new multimillion-dollar high school.

It should come as no surprise that the largest portion of corporate philanthropy supports education. The Bill and Melinda Gates Foundation is the richest philanthropic organization in the world and disbursed $1 billion in 2000 for learning and health.[26] The Coca-Cola Company builds relationships with schools through its vending machines. The soft drink company provides a range of drinks, limits sales to certain times and locations, and uses noncommercial signage on the machines.[27]

Education, though, is an area in which corporate support calls for more than money. With school budgets stretched to the breaking point, donations of classroom and recreational materials are extremely important. Examples of contributions include pencils and pads, printing of high school newspapers, automobiles for driver training, and sophisticated computers and equipment for advanced research. Businesses can also provide plant tours for student field trips, speakers for classes and assemblies, internships for high school and college students, and managerial and financial expertise for school administrators. Bridges built between the corporation and the classroom are among the most important relationships in any community.

The JCPenney CAN DO Afterschool program aligned the company's core values with the number one issue of concern to millions of American families. Although the company had a 97-year history of giving back to the community, JCPenney customers didn't associate the company with a particular cause or identity. CAN DO Afterschool was created to help the nation's leading providers of after-school programs enhance curriculums, upgrade facilities, train staff and volunteers, and reach out to children across the country. As a result of the program, JCPenney forged new strategic partnerships with the government and other organizations, strengthened its relationships with its target audiences, built pride and enthusiasm among its employees, and maximized its resources.[28]

SBC Communications Inc. expressed its commitment to education, economic development, and Texas tradition by saving the Cotton Bowl. A Dallas New Year's Day football tradition since 1937, the Cotton Bowl Classic was experiencing record-low attendance, no title sponsor, and virtually no community activities. Southwestern Bell became the title sponsor of the sporting event in late 1996 and worked with Fleishman-Hillard to use public relations to increase local community interest and involvement in the Cotton Bowl Classic and to reinforce the company's brand position. Three years later the 1999 game was one of the fastest sellouts in Cotton Bowl history and Southwestern Bell has committed to title sponsor through 2006.[29]

Health and Human Services The self-interest of corporations in their philanthropic efforts is perhaps most obvious in the community health and welfare area. Classic examples of corporate community action are found in relation to health and welfare. Professors Keith Davis and Robert Blomstrom offer the following example:

> In the first decade of this century, Birmingham, Alabama, was menaced by serious health problems. Malaria, typhoid fever and other diseases were prevalent because of unsanitary community conditions. This city was the site of a United States Steel Subsidiary, Tennessee Coal and Iron Co., whose productivity was lowered by illness. Tennessee Coal and Iron organized a health department and hired a prominent specialist in the offending diseases from the Panama Canal Zone. In its first year of operation the health department spent $750,000 for draining swamps and improving sanitary facilities. This amount was 30 times the total health budget of the entire state of Alabama.[30]

Grassroots Community Relations Outreach Impacts People Where They Live

Mini•Case 11.2

When it comes to age-related macular degeneration (AMD), what you don't know might hurt you. AMD, the leading cause of blindness in people over 50, destroys central vision, leaving only peripheral vision intact. Yet 70 percent of Americans are unaware of AMD and its devastating effects. Like many other age-related eye diseases, early detection of AMD through regular eye exams is often the key to successful treatment.

Novartis Ophthalmics codeveloped a pioneering light-activated drug treatment for AMD called Visudyne (with QLT, Inc.). This therapy stops but does not reverse the progress of the disease. Novartis asked Ketchum to partner with them to raise public awareness for a relatively unknown disease and to build brand recognition and loyalty for Visudyne, all while motivating those over 50 to get regular eye exams. Ketchum ranks as one of the top 10 global public relations firms.

Research determined that two distinct strategic grassroots marketing initiatives would be the primary tactics to reach the target audience of adults 45–70+. For the first initiative, a community-focused traveling talk show called "Seeing Eye-to-Eye" visited senior centers and active adult communities. Its goal was educating audiences about AMD and the Visudyne treatment, while providing free AMD eye screenings. A high-energy host interacted with a local physician and AMD patient, helping to tailor each presentation for a particular community.

The second initiative was a traveling, interactive game show and educational exhibit designed to promote eye health and the benefits of maintaining healthy vision. A 28-foot truck housed the "Eye-Q Challenge," an electronic eye-health trivia game that offered participants the chance to "use their eyes to win a prize." The game delivered 10 minutes of education about eye health, while "challenging" onlookers to learn more through the exhibit's free-standing kiosks.

Media relations, collateral information on eye health, a website, and a toll-free hotline supported the grassroots initiatives.

From a public relations perspective, the Visudyne grassroots campaign was very successful, with thousands attending the shows, participating in the Eye-Q Challenge, and reading the educational material. More than 25 million media impressions with more than 100 placements were counted in the first eight weeks of the program alone. In a campaign that utilized a one-on-one approach, perhaps the real winners are the persons who screened positive for AMD and sought treatment to save their vision. It's a testimony to how community relations can impact people where they live.

Source: Ketchum, August 2001.

Health and human services continues to be a community relations priority, and the personal experiences of the executives can provide an impetus for giving. The then-girlfriend of Sidney Kimmel, the billionaire head of Jones Apparel Group, had a cancer scare, and later Kimmel watched as the young daughter of a longtime friend died of the disease. The result was several multimillion-dollar gifts to cancer centers that provide research and treatment under one roof.[31]

Other examples abound. Mini-case 11.2 discusses how the company Novartis Ophthalmics and the public relations firm Ketchum partnered in a grassroots approach to identify those with age-related macular degeneration. In another case, medical equipment manufacturer Agilent donated $1 million equipment featuring Agilent components to The Flying Hospital, an international nonprofit organization based in Virginia Beach, Virginia. The Flying Hospital is a fully equipped surgical hospital constructed inside an aircraft.[32] A celebrity golf tournament raises funds for pediatric eye cancer at the Children's Center for Cancer and Blood Diseases at Children's Hospital in Los Angeles.[33]

Urban Renewal Major problems have haunted our large cities since the 1960s, and most of them can be traced to poverty in one way or another. Minority groups are disproportionately represented. The inner areas are frequently centers of poverty, unemployment, pollution, and crime. In addition, civic functions such as sanitation, police and fire protection, and transportation are often inadequate. A project to reduce highway congestion in a highly populated area is discussed in mini-case 11.3.

11.3 Mini • Case

Lake County Transportation Improvement Project

The Lake County Transportation Improvement Project was a joint project of the Illinois Toll Highway Authority and the Illinois Department of Transportation. The goal was to develop a comprehensive plan to alleviate serious and steadily worsening highway congestion in northeastern Illinois.

Various groups had been vocal in opposition to the Lake County Transportation Improvement Project based on an incorrect assumption that the decision to build the extension already had been made and that the project's principal purpose was to mask this presumed fait accompli. And there were groups who were fundamentally against the project, including the Environmental Law and Policy Center, a Chicago-based advocacy group, elected officials with environmental platforms, and other environmental leaders with a stake in the situation.

The objective was to foster a public opinion climate fair to the Lake County Transportation Improvement Project by educating the public about the purpose of the project and increasing public involvement in developing the comprehensive plan.

Project officials asked Hill and Knowlton to assess the depth and breadth of public opposition with a baseline telephone survey and then convened focus groups, from which was learned that the opposition was open to learning more about the proposal. Based on this knowledge, a multifaceted strategy was developed to educate the public and opinion makers about the project.

Tactics used included the following:

- Two videos were shown to some 300–400 groups throughout the region
- Media training for each of the project spokespersons
- Speaking engagements for officials involved in the project
- Meetings with every legislator, mayor, and various other municipal officers in the region
- Editorial board meetings to explain the project
- Press releases disseminated about newsworthy events related to the project
- A series of public involvement meetings conducted by project officials for the residents of all counties in the project study area

The result is that the Lake County Transportation Improvement Project was able to proceed in an open manner, engendering public trust and awareness.

Source: Hill and Knowlton.

Many of the efforts to improve conditions for those who live in the inner cities have been conceived and initiated by concerned business leaders who feel their organizations have certain responsibilities to the society in which they exist. Notes philanthropist Ann Lurie, "I focus on organizations that have a proven ability to do well in their field—not to transform the mediocre but to help a few agencies improve their services." On this basis Lurie's foundation gave money to the Greater Chicago Food Depository, which supplies hot meals to the homeless.[34]

Business contributes to urban renewal in a variety of ways, including monetary donations for rebuilding and providing expertise and talent to address concerns. Beyond immediate problems, corporations are trying to equip residents with the knowledge and skills they need to improve their lives. Programs like the National Foundation for Teaching Entrepreneurship (NFTE) have helped more than 31,000 inner-city children, most of them African American, learn how to run a small enterprise; 36 percent have actually started their own business. Microsoft and Goldman Sachs contribute to NFTE's $6 million-a-year annual budget.[35]

Some programs are intended to address immediate needs. Mort Meyerson had just started his job as chief executive officer of Perot Systems when he realized that the company holiday party was going to cost $360,000. Shocked by the amount and seeing no return on the investment, Meyerson canceled the party. Instead he used the monies to buy toys, food, and clothes. Employees volunteered to personally deliver the items to needy folks in the inner-city of Dallas.[36]

The Arts The connection between community relations and arts patronage is very clear. "Successful businesses do more than simply pass through a community. We have a vested interest in living where the quality of life attracts the very best employees, customers, suppliers and government, academic and civic leaders. It is inconceivable that such a quality can exist where the arts are silent," notes A. Thomas Young, former executive vice president of Lockheed Martin Corporation.[37] Former Philip Morris chairman George Weissman made his company one of the nation's most generous arts patrons by observing, "More people go to museums than to ball games."

An engineer volunteers to help students after school.

Judith A. Jedlicka, president of the Business Committee for the Arts, defines the arts as "everything from A to Z—arboretums to zoos."[38] However it's defined, business continues to increase its commitment to arts activities. Overall financial support reached a record $1.16 billion in 1997, compared with $22 million in 1967.[39] Nonprofit arts organizations annually multiply this support to generate income for the arts, creating, on a national level, $37 billion for communities and accounting for 6 percent of the gross national product. More than 3.2 million Americans, or 2.7 percent, are employed in some aspect of the arts.[40]

Beyond the financial benefits, business-art partnerships create success stories in other areas such as economic development. When the retail stores in the once-thriving downtown area in Parkersburg, West Virginia, moved to the mall two decades ago, the downtown slowly transformed itself into a spotty collections of banks, government buildings, bars, and empty storefronts. Cultural and corporate organizations now are working together to revitalize the downtown area and to provide new business opportunities, one of which was the city's first Arts! Downtown Family Festival held in 1999.[41]

Commitment to the arts can sustain a business through tough times. Houston jeweler I. W. Marks feels that its support of the city's opera and symphony helped develop customer loyalty. It was this loyalty that helped the jeweler ride out the recession of the 1990s when many of its competitors closed their doors.[42]

Whether consciously or not, corporations routinely act as arts patrons whenever they engage the services of an architect. The community relations aspect of architectural decisions should not be overlooked. Cummins Engine has transformed Columbus, Indiana, into an oasis of architectural excellence by paying top architects to design new buildings and restore old ones in the town. Included are twelve schools, two churches, a fire station, a library, a golf course and clubhouse, newspaper and telephone company offices, a mental health clinic, city hall, and more.

To encourage participation by business in the arts, more than 160 top business leaders in the United States have established the Business Committee for the Arts. The committee assists companies of all sizes in their efforts to establish arts programs that can enhance a company's image, benefit employees, or provide tax breaks.

Typically art organizations approach corporations about sponsorships, and corporations usually have to make choices among the many options. But it can work the other way, with a corporation having a specific philanthropy in mind. Regardless of how the project is initiated, it's important that the gift support community needs.

For example, a man in Wisconsin gave a $100 million gift to build an arts center that no one wanted but him. Others thought the funds would be better spent elsewhere.[43] When reviewing the proposals, corporations are looking for compatibility between their goals and those of the arts organization. Some points to consider are the following:[44]

1. Why the corporation wants to invest
   - Network with others in the local community
   - Heighten awareness of the company and its products and services
   - Attract employees and increase job satisfaction
   - Enhance relationships with existing and future customers
   - Set the company apart from competitors
   - Increase the bottom line
2. Which arts organizations will reach present and future employees
3. Why type of partnership is desired
   - Donated services and products
   - Volunteer initiative
   - Marketing, advertising, and public relations tie-in
   - Financial assistance

The extent of corporate arts activities sometimes requires outside public relations counsel. Ruder Finn Public Relations established an innovative and revolutionary business and the arts consulting program when it opened its agency in 1948. Today, Ruder Finn advises corporations on cultural support programs. The firm develops and implements corporate public relations programming keyed to cultural activities. The organization assists in managing corporate-sponsored museum exhibitions, jazz festivals, corporate history books, an entertainment marketing CD-ROM game, performing arts presentations, symphony tours, and other arts-related activities.

Every company can make an important contribution to its local community by investing in the arts.

Cause-Related Marketing Cause-related marketing ties a company and its products to a cause. It's an area that has experienced huge growth in recent years because of its ability to sell products, enhance image, and motivate employees. Figure 11.4 illustrates how cause marketing has evolved from a short-term sales tool and a way to build customer loyalty to playing a major role in a company's branding and reputation

1984 Short-term sales	1990s Building customer loyalty	2000 Branding and reputation

FIGURE 11.4 **The Cause Marketing Spectrum**
Source: 1999 Cone/Roper Cause-Related Trends Report.

Employee Volunteerism: Addressing More Than One Objective

Spotlight 11.2

When American Express Company celebrated its 150th anniversary in 2000, the company took advantage of the occasion to focus commemorative plans on programs aimed at its employee base, in keeping with the company's efforts to instill pride among employees in the company's worldwide businesses. At the same time, there was an ongoing effort within the company to reinforce one of its six core values—that of being a good citizen in communities where employees live and work.

It was decided that both objectives could be addressed jointly by designing an initiative that came to be called "The 150th Anniversary Great Citizen Awards." Open to all 82,000 employees worldwide, the initiative would identify 150 employees who had exceptional records of service to their communities. The employees selected could be self-nominated or nominated by a colleague. Winners would receive a commemorative gift and would be able to designate a charitable organization to which the American Express Foundation would make a $1,500 grant.

The program was given high visibility throughout the company with the initial announcement coming jointly from the company's chairman and president, followed by promotional materials and news items disseminated throughout the company's worldwide workplaces. In all, there were nearly 1,200 nominees and the 150 winners—selected by a committee after review by 13 panels representing a cross section of employees from around the world—came from 32 countries, representing virtually every region of the world. Their inspiring stories included mentoring underprivileged children, walking and running thousands of miles to raise money to eradicate life-threatening diseases, building houses, and traveling to war-torn and underdeveloped countries to administer food and medicine.

Once the 150 Great Citizens were announced, local public relations activities resulted in media exposure in local communities. This provided the added benefit of raising pubic awareness of both employees' and American Express Company's involvement with community causes. Finally, the worldwide initiative addressed another of the company's ongoing objectives, that of reinforcing the message of American Express Company's growing global nature. With employees in Indonesia sharing the spotlight with employees from India, Brazil, Norway, the United States, and other countries, the Great Citizen Awards provided meaningful, real-life support to the message that the company's worldwide breadth was vast.

Employee volunteerism at American Express includes helping communities, instilling employee pride, and spreading the message that American Express is a good citizen as well as a growing global business.

efforts.[45] Today's consumers expect businesses to use their resources to address community concerns. When corporations contribute to the communities they serve, they make a powerful connection by sharing their customers' and employees' values. Cause-related marketing is *not* philanthropy.[46]

American Express is one of the leaders in cause-related marketing, supporting AIDS walks, Big Brothers/Big Sisters, American Red Cross, United Way, March of Dimes, Meals on Wheels, and Habitat for Humanity, among others. Spotlight 11.2 highlights American Express's employee volunteerism efforts. The W. K. Kellogg Foundation provided a $200,000 grant to Oral Health America, a Chicago-based nonprofit group, to raise awareness of dental-care deficiencies.[47] There are countless other examples.

The 2001 Best Practices in Corporate Communication report identifies three primary benefits for sponsors and corporations of cause-related marketing efforts.[48]

1. *Cause-Related Marketing Increases Sales.* Corporate citizenship is more effective than coupons, rebates, and discounting when it comes to attracting customers. Retailers from New York to Los Angeles attest to the power of partnering with a charity in boosting the bottom line.[49] According to the 1999 Cone/Roper study:
   - 78 percent of adults would be more likely to buy a product associated with a cause they care about.
   - 65 percent would change brands to help a cause.
   - 61 percent would switch retailers in support of a cause.
   - 54 percent would pay more for a product that backed a cause they cared about.[50]

2. *Cause-Related Marketing Enhances Image.* Supporting good causes can benefit corporations with an enhanced image as a good corporate citizen, a greater sense of integrity and dependability for its products, and more favorable media coverage as community needs are addressed.[51] LensCrafters has helped more than 1.3 million people worldwide through its Give the Gift of Sight program that helps needy people see more clearly.[52] Mervyn's California, a division of Target Corporation, has helped more than 2,000 women in 33 cities nationwide make the transition from welfare to the workforce by providing them with an appropriate outfit.
3. *Cause Marketing Benefits Properties and Sponsors.* Charities and other worthwhile causes on the receiving end typically enjoy more visibility that can lead to increased donations. The nonprofit that lends its name to a corporation can receive a rights fee or a cut of the purchase price of a product on top or in lieu of a rights fee.

In spite of the many benefits, cause-related marketing does have some downfalls. They include the following:[53]

- Nonprofits and corporations have different objectives. Alliances fail if the corporation is looking to mend its public image or if the nonprofit feels it is being used as the company's promotion agency.
- Size can bring about problems. Many nonprofits are small and entrepreneurial, the opposite of a large and well-established corporation. The decision-making and approval processes and accounting procedures of a global organization can seem slow and unwieldy when compared with a nonprofit office employing a handful of people.
- The public is finding it increasingly more difficult to distinguish between cause-related marketing and traditional philanthropy. Consumers may feel that they have already contributed by buying the product and the nonprofit suffers from reduced donations. And it's often hard for consumers to know how much money a corporation is actually giving to charity.

As with any other strategic initiative, a corporation should evaluate its cause-related marketing efforts from time to time to ensure the activities support the corporate mission and business objectives. For example, although Sprint has always supported initiatives in the communities where it has a presence, there was little continuity to what was being supported in different cities. In one city, Sprint would sponsor a walk or run for muscular dystrophy; in others, it might be participating in the local United Way, fundraising for breast cancer research, or building a playground. The company conducted consumer research to determine if it should continue community-specific programs or if it should be recognized for a universal cause. The result is that Sprint now focuses its community relations efforts on helping those with disabilities, one part of which is to enhance lives through wireless communication.

THE EMERGING CHALLENGE OF COMMUNITY ACTIVISM

Particular societal and community circumstances give rise to special challenges and opportunities for community relations efforts. Community activism is one such example.

Activism is intensifying in the 21st century. Organizations must be prepared to deal with the increased media scrutiny, potential disruptions to normal operations, and the fear and embarrassment that can occur with activist activity. Corporations are vulnerable to many different types of activists, including shareholders and disgruntled employees, on many different kinds of issues, such as human rights, environmental, health, biotechnology, and discrimination.

To be sure, organizations that are misusing, abusing, sidestepping, or violating laws and other commonly accepted practices should be held publicly accountable for their actions. But the kind of activism discussed in this section is more of a power struggle or a strong difference of opinion with an organization that is within compliance.

Problems with activism can arise in spite of an organization's best efforts to cooperate with its community. Community activists can exert undue pressure and unreasonable influence in attempting to raise public consciousness about issues and concerns that are more often based on emotion than scientific facts. These groups not only create opportunities to share their perspectives but also use national and local activities and problems to gain a voice.

In early 2000 telecommunication companies in many towns and cities experienced the wrath of community activists when they tried to construct towers to support the growing demand for wireless and digital communication. The result is that zoning requests were denied, health scares were initiated, and distrust of corporate entities was promoted. In turn, this upset customers who wanted better cell phone reception or who couldn't purchase additional phone numbers or other services due to lack of availability.

Activists use a variety of tactics, including e-mail, the Internet, signage, media interviews, lawsuits, and pickets, and they have been known to resort to violence, destruction, and terrorism. The attacks on the World Trade Center and the Pentagon in September 2001 that claimed thousands of innocent lives and disrupted many communities are the most extreme terrorist acts to have ever occurred in the United States. Much less severe, but no less frightening, is when an environmental group opposed to the expansion of the Vail, Colorado, ski area claimed responsibility for burning the resort's multimillion-dollar Two Elk Lodge.

Activists tend to use the same techniques when trying to gain media attention or gain supporters for their cause. Figure 11.5 identifies some of these predictable patterns of attack and how organizations can counterattack.

Companies should take a proactive stance when dealing with community activism and follow what practitioner David Schultz calls a "3-P" approach—planning, practice, and precision.[54] Phillips-Van Heusen Corporation's proactive stance helps the global garment manufacturer anticipate and avoid many problems. As one of the few American companies that has a vice president for human rights, it addresses on an ongoing basis issues such as wages, factory conditions, hours worked, and freedom from harassment and association for its employees. Like Phillips-Van Heusen's employees, its suppliers and vendors are expected to participate in human rights training and to adhere to the company's code of conduct.[55]

Yet even the most socially diligent companies can come under attack. The following are some of the ways that companies can handle situations involving community activists:[56]

- Identify what kind of protest groups you're dealing with. Some just want to damage the company, whereas others truly desire to effect mutually beneficial changes.
- Speak the truth and be open and accessible. Provide information.
- Keep your cool and don't become overly confrontational. Adopt a friendly tone.
- Know the strengths and weaknesses of your activist groups. Determine if they should become strategic partners.

Counteracting Predictable Patterns of Activists Attack	
Attack (They will . . .)	**Counterattack (You will . . .)**
1. Polarize the issue. No matter what, you're 120% wrong.	1. Point out the exaggeration; admit errors; outline action steps.
2. Build a base on the web; use e-mail lists; post to bulletin boards to create support for their cause.	2. Assess the actual damage; estimate potential damage; determine need for preemptive action.
3. Trivialize, emotionalize, insult, and humiliate; pick a web address like "companysucks.com."	3. Create a neat, clean, corporate-looking response site; contrast your legitimacy with their juvenile, trivial approach.
4. Anger, irritate, debilitate, violate trademarks, and misinterpret every response; force your hand by intentionally provoking a legal response to showcase their site.	4. Choose your battles carefully; respond calmly, deliberately, succinctly, competently, incrementally. Stay focused; use appropriate language for the medium and key themes.
5. Use ultimatums; bombard the company with "last chances" to correct allegations, charges and "testimony" before "going live" and staging demonstrations.	5. Respond carefully, positively, candidly, politely. If in the wrong, correct the problem. Point out errors; point out emotionalism; insist on independent, unbiased proof.
6. Register their site on research engines—in your corporate section, if possible.	6. Register your site in the same manner; when resolved, remove listings.
7. Post messages on electronic bulletin boards to promote their cause; promote their site; locate others suffering from the same problems; find disgruntled employees willing to help.	7. Monitor the Internet; assess actual impact. Discourage local employees from responding on your behalf; respond only if necessary. Have erroneous posts removed from search engines.
8. Work the news media; target specific journalists who cover your company or industry. The media never tire of finding ways to attack business.	8. Direct journalists to your response site. Point out the exaggeration; admit errors; outline action steps. Avoid whining.

FIGURE 11.5 **Counteracting Predictable Patterns of Activists Attack**

- Consider policy changes to neutralize or placate hostile organizations.
- Provide employees with the facts, to allay fears and to be ambassadors for the organization.
- Don't underestimate the power of an activist group to damage an organization.

Summary

Although community relations as an organizational activity is as diverse as the communities in which organizations operate, the key to effective community relations is positive, socially responsible action to help the community on the part of the organization. Depending on the organization, community relations may be carried out by an officially designated community relations staff, by a general public relations staff, or by various departments throughout the organization.

Many companies are focusing their philanthropy programs on issues in which they would like to make an impact. Cause-related marketing ties a company and its products to a cause. It can sell products, enhance image, and motivate employees.

Activists are demanding a larger voice in decisions made by institutions, highlighting an increasing need for community relations efforts.

For self-testing and additional chapter resources, go to the student CD and the Online Learning Center at **www.mhhe.com/lattimore**

A Civic/Corporate Partnership between the City of Detroit and Comerica—HUG Belle Isle: Help Uncover the Gem

By Gary D. Butkus
Director of Community Relations
Comerica, Detroit

Every year more than 8 million visitors enjoy Belle Isle, a 982-acre island park in the Detroit River. Although the park has been maintained by the city of Detroit, the high usage left the park areas somewhat trash-ridden, the shorelines murky, and some of the monuments and fountains in disrepair. Belle Isle, known as the "Jewel of Detroit," needed some polish.

The Detroit Recreation Department and Comerica Bank created a unique private/public partnership to help revitalize this historically significant park. Called "HUG Belle Isle—Help Uncover the Gem," this beautification day would take place on the first Saturday in May and, hopefully, become an annual event. Comerica, with its 150-year history in Detroit, felt a civic responsibility to spearhead this effort with the city. By bringing out volunteers from its own employee base as well as challenging other Detroit-based businesses to help out, Comerica took this project to a level that the city could not have alone.

Comerica began the process by providing a grant of $25,000 to offset the initial costs of the event such as mailings, food, volunteer items, and the like. The city of Detroit had not budgeted for a major project on the island, so the initial funding was critical. The Detroit Recreation Department also contacted other civic organizations and local businesses for volunteers and financial support of product donations. Comerica and the city of Detroit worked together on the media relations, promoting the event through their websites and sending press releases to all media outlets. On the day of the event, May 5, 2002, more than 1,500 volunteers showed up, of which 150 were Comerica employees. Thousands of bags of trash were collected, more than a dozen playground areas were painted and spruced up, and the park sparkled once again. In addition to the actual cleanup, new trash cans with the HUG Belle Isle logo were placed throughout the park. The project was considered a major success.

Questions

1. Why would Comerica want to partner on the city for such a project?
2. How could the city and the bank influence other community groups and local companies to participate?
3. How could the vision of HUG Belle Isle best be communicated to the general public?
4. What types of secondary projects could be generated from HUG Belle Isle?
5. How was the success of such a unique partnership measured?
6. Identify an area in your college or home community that needs to be restored or revitalized. What civic/corporate entities could work together on this? Develop a proposal to address this issue.

Key Terms

Use the CD-ROM and Online Learning Center at www.mhhe.com/lattimore to further your understanding of the following terms

community relations

corporate philanthropy

Notes

1. Al Hattal, "Orange County Counters Airport, *PRWeek,* 1 May 2000.
2. John Frank, "Walgreens Puts Image on Line to Rouse Community," *PRWeek,* 9 April 2001, p. 3.
3. Information provided by Michael Polzin, manager of media relations, Walgreens Co., 5 July 2002.
4. Kwame F. Kilpatrick, as quoted by Jodi Wilgoren, "Detroit Urban Renewal without the Renewal," *New York Times on the Web,* 7 July 2002.
5. "Connecting with Society," Ford Motor Company Corporate Citizenship Report, 2001, p. 28.
6. W. J. Peak, "Community Relations," in *Handbook of Public Relations,* 4th ed., ed. Philip Lesley (New York: AMACON, 1991), p. 117.
7. David P. Baron, "The Nonmarket Strategy System," *Sloan Management Review* (Fall 1995).
8. John Frank, "In-house PR Stretches Its Dollars in Slowdown," *PRWeek,* 19 March 2001, p. 13.
9. 2000 Cone/Roper Executive Study.
10. Adapted from Jules Cohen, "Is Business Meeting the Challenge of Urban Affairs?" *Harvard Business Review* (March–April 1970), pp. 81–82. Reprinted by permission of the *Harvard Business Review.* Copyright 1970 by the President and Fellows of Harvard College. All rights reserved.
11. Gloria Smith, "Doing Community Relations When You're the New Kid on the Block," *PRWeek,* 16 July 2000, p. 22.
12. "Printing Plant Tours," Seattle Times Co., 21 June 2000. http://www.seattletimes company.com/operations/tours.htm.

13. Platon Coutsoukis, assistant director of research, and Leslie Carbone, research analyst, "2001 Community Relations Index," Center for Corporate Citizenship at Boston College, pp. 8–9.
14. Ibid.
15. Ibid, p. 2.
16. Bob Dreitzler and Tom Sheehan, "Piketon Plant Is Latest to Fall in Struggling Region," *The Columbus Dispatch,* 23 June 2000, at http://www.dispatch.com.
17. Ken McLaughlin, "TI's Santa Cruz Employees Ponder Life After Plant Closing," *San Jose Mercury News,* 15 March 2001, at http://mercurynews.com.
18. Peak, "Community Relations," p. 130.
19. Associated Press, "Program Links Personal Computers to Fight Cancer," *Jefferson City News Tribune,* 12 May 2001, p. 7.
20. Craig McGuire, "Even News Media Like to Make News," *PRWeek,* 11 December 2000, p. 32.
21. Associated Press, "Habitat for Humanity Tries to Balance Corporate Influence, Volunteerism," *Jefferson City News Tribune,* 16 September 2001, p. 26.
22. AAFRC Press Release, "Total Giving Reaches $203.45 Billion As Charitable Contributions Increase 6.6 Percent in 2000," 23 May 2001.
23. Brent Schlender, "The Playboy Philanthropist," *Fortune,* 3 September 2001, pp. 163–66.
24. Quentin Hardy, "The Radical Philanthropist," *Forbes,* 1 May 2000, pp. 114–21.
25. "The Evolution of Cause Branding," 1999 Cone, Inc., and Roper Starch Worldwide Cause Related Trends Report.
26. Elizabeth Corcoran, "The World's Richest Donors," *Forbes,* 1 May 2000, pp. 116–17.
27. Julia Hood, "Coca-Cola Shows Class," *PRWeek,* 19 March 2001, p. 2.
28. JCPenney CAN DO Afterschool Case Study, Cone, Inc., 1999.
29. Fleishman-Hillard, 1999 PRSA Silver Anvil Entry, "SBC Saves the Cotton Bowl."
30. Keith Davis and Robert L. Blomstrom, *Business, Society, and Environment,* 2nd ed. (New York: McGraw-Hill, 1971), p. 277.
31. William P. Barrett, "I Don't Like Making Mistakes," *Forbes,* 11 October 1999, pp. 158–60.
32. www.forbes.com, 9 September 2001.
33. Heather Lindsey, "Golf Event Covered Despite No-Shows," *PRWeek,* 2 April 2001, p. 22.
34. Ann Lurie as quoted by Susan Adams, "Life After Death," *Forbes,* 20 September 1999, p. 166.
35. Tomas Kellner, "Rockfellers in the 'Hood," *Forbes,* 24 July 2000, pp. 180–82.
36. Geoffrey Colvin, "Think About This as You Don Your Tuxedo," *Fortune,* 18 December 2000, p. 74.
37. A. Thomas Young, former executive vice president of Lockheed Martin Corporation, as quoted in Best Practices in Event Marketing and Corporate Sponsorships, *2001 Best Practices in Corporate Communications,* p. 79.
38. Judith A. Jedlicka, Business-Arts Partnerships That Achieve Real Results, a speech posted at http://www.bcainc.org, 22 October 2001.
39. 1998 National Survey of Business Support to the Arts, http://www.bcainc.org, 22 October 2001.
40. "Why Business Invests in the Arts," Business Committee for the Arts, Inc., http:www.bcainc.org, 25 October 2001.
41. ArtsREACH: Strengthening Communities through the Arts, National Endowment for the Arts, http://arts.endow.gov, 25 October 2001.
42. Judith A. Jedlicka, Business-Arts Partnerships That Achieve Real Results, a speech posted at http://www.bcainc.org, 22 October 2001.
43. Dale DeGroff, Bill Downes, Rebecca Ascher-Walsh, and Joan Hoffman et al., "Reward Yourself," *Fortune,* 18 September 2000, p. 376.
44. Business Committee for the Arts, Inc.
45. "The Evolution of Cause Branding," 1999 Cone, Inc., and Roper Starch Worldwide Cause Related Trends Report.

46. "Cause-Related Marketing," Event Marketing and Sponsorship Report, *2001 Best Practices in Corporate Communication,* p. 93.

47. Steve Lilienthal, "Oral Health Group Kicks Off 10-Year PR Effort," *PRWeek,* 29 May 2000.

48. "Cause-Related Marketing," Event Marketing and Sponsorship Report, *2001 Best Practices in Corporate Communication,* p. 97.

49. Ann Zimmerman, "Promotional Ties to Charitable Causes Help Stores Lure Customers," *Wall Street Journal,* 4 December 2000.

50. "The Evolution of Cause Branding," 1999 Cone, Inc., and Roper Starch Worldwide Cause Related Trends Report.

51. Joseph J. Ptacek and Gina Salazar, "Enlightened Self-interest: Selling Business on the Benefits of Cause-Related Marketing," *Non-Profit World,* 7 July 1997.

52. "Doing Their Part," *Chain Store Age: The Newsmagazine for Retail Executives,* August 2000, p. 44.

53. "Cause-Related Marketing," Event Marketing and Sponsorship Report, *2001 Best Practices in Corporate Communication,* pp. 100–101.

54. David L. Schultz, "Strategic Survival in the Face of Community Activism," *Public Relations Strategist* 7, no. 2 (Spring 2001), pp. 37–38.

55. Elizabeth Howard, "Vice President for Human Rights," *Public Relations Strategist* 2, no. 7 (Spring 2001), pp. 23–26.

56. Douglas Quenqua, "When Activists Attack," *PRWeek,* 11 June 2001, p. 15.

CHAPTER TWELVE

Consumer Relations and Marketing

12

Outline

PREVIEW

Consumer relations and marketing are playing a more prominent role in public relations practice. No longer can retailers, manufacturers, and service providers simply respond to complaints from their customers. Sophisticated public relations techniques must be applied to understand the needs of consumers and solicit their comments. In addition, organizations must be prepared to respond to consumer action and other special interest groups who take notice of their products or services. Because of increased awareness and government interest, the consumer relations functions of many organizations has grown to command a substantial managerial role. More important, good consumer relations have demonstrated their value to the bottom-line productivity of many businesses. These changes have opened new opportunities for public relations practitioners in consumer-oriented organizations

> *"Public relations can help the organization take smart risks and avoid the bad ones."*
> —Judith Rich

TEAMING PUBLIC RELATIONS WITH MARKETING

Though it is wrong to view public relations as simply another method of product or service promotion, promotion is one of the most powerful ingredients in any organization's marketing mix. Public relations and marketing functions have some fundamental differences, but they share one significant goal. Both attempt to help an organization respond to a very significant public: the consumers of its products and services. Consider some of the ways that public relations is involved in this process.

Promoting the Value of Unseen Technology

Such was the case with the crash-reducing intelligent satellite system (ISS) on some upscale car models, which detects speed, motion, and steering angle and adjusts braking accordingly. A coalition of brake manufacturers formed the nonprofit ABS (antilock brake system) Education Alliance to teach drivers of cars equipped with ISS to not pump their antilock brakes in the event of an impending accident. The consumer education effort included **desk-side briefings** with automotive writers in major markets, presentations at traffic safety and driver education associations, and distribution of information and other materials through the Alliance's website, events, and other activities.[1]

Using Current Events to Reshape Attitudes

Arkansas Governor Mike Huckabee needed a place to live while the governor's mansion was being renovated. Champion Enterprises, a Michigan-based manufactured housing company, seized the opportunity to boost the image of its product beyond the low-class trailer stereotype by providing the housing. Champion created a clever banner for the luxury 2,131-square-foot home as it was moved to its position, noting, "My other home is the Governor's Mansion." Media tours of the governor's temporary home were conducted during a move-in event, and the governor's wife served as unofficial spokesperson, saying, "It's not hard to get us to move in, but it will be hard to get us to move out." Enterprise incorporated the governor's mobile-mansion publicity into its advertising, website, and other marketing materials.[2]

Increasing Awareness of the Product's Benefits

Rice Krispies wanted to snap, crackle, and pop to a greater extent with elementary-age children, so the cereal company created a nationwide contest challenging students in grades K–6 to create a sculpture using the Rice Krispies Treats recipe. The contest incorporated art, math, social studies, and teamwork elements so that it would appeal to educators. Flyers, a camera-ready story about the contest, a press release and photo of the previous year's winner, a radio alert, contest information on the website, a breakfast party at the winning school, and promotion of the winning sculptures were some of the public relations and promotional tactics used.[3]

These business-to-consumer examples and the business-to-business soy ink case in mini-case 12.1 illustrate a concept called by names such as **relationship marketing, integrated marketing communication,** or **integrated communication,** all used to describe a facet of how public relations and marketing can work together to build customer trust and loyalty while selling the product. **Public relations** focuses on the long-term goals of building positive relationships with consumers, suppliers, competitors, and other publics. Its primary goal is to "build and maintain a hospitable environ-

Soy Ink: Gaining a Bigger Market Share

Mini•Case 12.1

Off the Launching Pad

Soybean oil-based printing inks have been around since 1987, but their popularity didn't materialize overnight. They were developed by the Newspaper Association of America (NAA) after another shortage of imported oil threatened many industries dependent on petroleum-based chemicals and refined oil products. Printing inks traditionally have used a petroleum base. But soy ink, it was found, offers a compelling alternative. It delivers vibrant colors; comes from a plentiful, sustainable resource; reduces emissions causing air pollution; is cost-competitive with conventional petroleum-based commercial printing ink; and is more compatible with the recycling process. As a result, it represents a responsible environmental choice for manufacturers, printers, graphic designers, and print specifiers. Yet long-established traditions are not readily altered in the printing industry, so promoters knew the acceptance of and transition to soy ink would take time. In the mid-1990s, soy ink promotion needed a shot of adrenaline, and that's where Morgan & Myers entered the picture. The Iowa Soybean Association gave the midwestern-based communications counseling firm the challenge of increasing awareness of soy ink's benefits, then measuring its successes.

A "Soy Ink, America's Printing Plant" educational program was orchestrated, which positioned soy ink as the "first choice" ink. The goal was to convince printers and businesses to specify soy ink, and to show it proudly through use of the SoySeal on soy-ink-printed pieces.

Numerous steps were involved in executing the educational/awareness push.

- A "tool kit" was developed containing a video, brochure, and technical manual to inform target audience members of the benefits of requesting soy ink.
- A trade newsletter, "The Printing Plant," launched in 1995, was sent to graphic designers, print specifiers, the top 50 printing firms, and current SoySeal users.
- Educational luncheons were sponsored in cities with a substantial graphic designer market, a strong commercial printing and print specifier market, and stringent environmental regulations.
- Ads were placed in trade publications, and exhibits were established at printing and graphic industry trade shows.
- The 1995 campaign increased the number of SoySeal user agreements by 52 percent.
- Media coverage came in 12 trade journals, including one cover story. And eight state soybean boards, as well as the world's two largest ink manufacturers, opted to participate in the communications program.

Still Room for Growth

In little more than a decade, soy ink's U.S. market share had grown from zero to 20 percent. And there's considerable potential for more. The industry is taking dead aim at that goal.

Questions

1. Identify the audiences targeted in this business-to-business campaign.
2. How would you define the strategy used by the NAA? Are there other strategies you think might have been considered?
3. Identify the tactics used to reach the audiences. Are they different from those used in business-to-consumer campaigns? How?

Source: Bill Nelson, copy chief and special projects writer, Morgan & Myers/The Barkin Group.

ment for an organization."[4] Customers want to be served, not sold. Public relations can help an organization's corporate climate to be conducive to customer service. **Marketing,** on the other hand, is concerned with the quality, availability, and affordability of the product or service; it concentrates on selling. Its primary goal is to "build and maintain a market for an organization's products or services."[5]

Public relations and marketing are similar in that they do extensive research, identify target publics, and develop communication action plans. Robert J. Ristino, vice president of public relations for the Medical Center of Central Massachusetts, described the relationship of public relations to the marketing mix as it is illustrated in table 12.1. In this relationship, public relations provides support to the overall efforts to market goods or services. Because public relations is integrated completely into the marketing process, it is easy to understand why the distinction between the two functions is difficult for many to grasp.

Public relations addresses the following elements not associated with marketing:

- Internal publics such as employees, stockholders, and management
- Reputation, or image building

TABLE 12.1 Public Relations Support of the Marketing Mix

Product/Service	Distribution	Communication	Price
Informal research	Physical access	Educating the market	Strategy
Environmental surveillance	Time access	Advertising message and media	Image
Product life cycle	Informational and promotional access	Sales promotion	
Naming or branding			
Style and Packaging			

Source: Robert J. Ristino, "Public Relations Marketing: Applying Public Relations Techniques to the Marketing Mix," *Health Care Management Review* 14 (1989), p. 80.

- External publics (other than consumers) such as government and suppliers
- Crisis management
- Public opinion change and social issues
- Issues management

The Ford/Firestone tire crisis in 2000 is a key example of how quickly consumers respond to negative information about a product. The tread separated on some models of Firestone tires that were mounted as standard equipment on certain Ford vehicles, resulting in numerous injuries and fatalities. More than advertising and other traditional marketing tools are needed to restore customer confidence and sales in such situations. Firestone replaced millions of tires. Ford took the bold step of severing its more-than-century-old relationship with Firestone. This decision not only had business ramifications, but also personal ones. Likewise, product publicity can augment advertising efforts and make other marketing techniques more effective.

The positive relationships a company develops through public relations with its consumers and other publics are a means to an end: sales and profits that can be strengthened quarter after quarter, year after year. In many organizations the structure of departments and divisions blurs the relationships between public relations and marketing to the point that the two are almost always linked. Mergers of public relations firms and advertising agencies have further clouded this issue in the minds of many managers and others.

THE STARTING POINT

It's important to point out that consumer relations and marketing must be integrated into the overall communications planning process. One obvious reason for this is to ensure that a problem actually can be addressed by communicating. No amount of public relations activity can make up for an inadequate distribution system, a food that doesn't taste good, or a poorly designed product.

In a *New York Times* column, David Pogue talks about his research for a book he's writing on the backstage story of Palm, Handspring, and the palmtop craze. He noted that in the early days, Palm's vice president of marketing had a favorite saying: "Delight the customer." Pogue thought the saying not only sounded obvious, but hackneyed. No company sets out to disappoint the customer, he felt. Pogue's coauthor, who was one of the original Palm employees, responded by saying that that wasn't the point.

"In the technology industry, you'd be surprised how much 'Delight the customer' ISN'T the point. The alternative isn't 'Disappoint the customer,' but 'What can we do with this neat technology?' The customer doesn't even come up in the product designers' thoughts. . . . When you think of delighting the customer as a guiding light in making choices, it explains a lot why the Pilot ended up being a product people loved, and are so emotionally attached to."[6]

All companies have probably been guilty, to some degree, of overlooking, disregarding, or ignoring the needs of their customers. Inconvenient business hours or locations, hard-to-open containers, knobs that are too big or small, and product unavailability are just a few examples. The difference is that the smart, thriving companies constantly *listen* to their customers and act upon what they hear. These are the kinds of organizations that gain the most from their public relations and marketing activities.

APPLYING PUBLIC RELATIONS TECHNIQUES TO MARKETING

Imagination is the limit when it comes to applying public relations techniques to marketing. When Hewlett-Packard wanted to send out the message that it is a "total solutions provider" and an "innovative technology leader," the company felt that the Formula

Chick-fil-A used a collection of their "cows" to form a Cow Preservation Party to dramatize a "platform" of more chicken consumption.

12.2 Mini•Case

Restoring Profit through Nontraditional Solutions

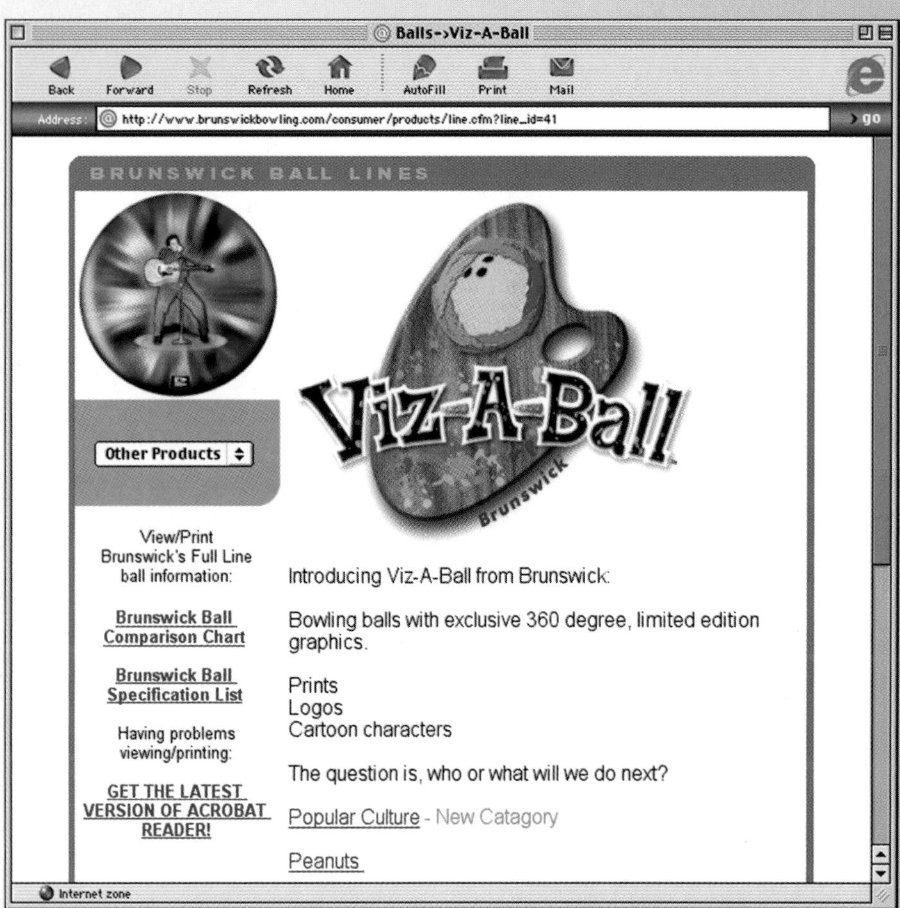

Brunswick's website promotes its new Viz-A-Ball line.

By David Lipson
Executive Vice President/
Creative Director
Ackerman McQueen, Dallas, TX

What's the world's most popular participation sport? Baseball? Golf? Tennis? Believe it or not, it's bowling—generating annual revenues of more than $4 billion.

The Bad News

Prior to 1998, traditional bowling leagues accounted for the majority of business from September to April, while summer league business was almost nonexistent. Each of the hundreds of Brunswick Recreation Centers (BRCs) was marketed individually with no unified theme, common purpose, or shared appearance.

League bowling income, which historically constituted about 80 percent of BRC revenue, had been steadily declining since the late 1980s. The number of league bowlers remained constant, but they bowled less often and spent less per visit than casual bowlers (who spend four times as much per visit).

Marketplace research indicated another year of substantial decline with:

- League renewals down 30 percent
- Open play (casual) bowling down 11 percent
- Kids' programs down 15 percent
- Perception that bowling centers are crowded with overweight smokers
- Perception that bowling isn't fun or "cool"

Serious business consequences loomed if these trends weren't corrected.

The Proposal

Brunswick asked the Oklahoma City–based agency Ackerman McQueen to propose a solution. After extensive research and concept development, the agency and client set out to consolidate BRC efforts with the intention to do the following:

1. *Reposition the experience.* Cater to the casual bowler by making an underutilized branded product, "Cosmic Bowling," available during prime time.

   Cosmic Bowling creates a nightclub environment with laser lights, fog, glowing pins and paints, themed music, DJs, dancing, contests, and prizes. This supports new bowling experiences that BRCs offer families and young adults.

2. *Reinvent the product.* Cater to the casual bowler with fun Viz-A-Ball designs with the promise, "We can put anything you want on a ball!"

   Viz-A-Ball transforms a plain black sphere into a vibrant, colorful work of art. Brunswick partnered with brands like Walt Disney, AOL Time Warner, Coca-Cola, Miller Brewing, the World Wrestling Federation, and others to offer bowlers Mickey Mouse, Winnie the Pooh, Marilyn Monroe, or a host of other figures on their bowling balls.

   A dedicated website was also launched solely for Viz-A-Ball—the first bowling ball manufacturer to do so—where customers can see the entire collection and purchase online. To drive customers to BRCs, Brunswick created exclusive Viz-A-Ball designs available only at retail locations.

3. *Redefine BRC as a national retail brand.* BRC staff were asked to think of themselves as unique cast members instead of league bowling center employees, catering to casual bowlers with a fun, customized bowling experience.

The Good News

As a result:

- League/open play revenue ratio shifted from 80/20 to 60/40.
- League populations migrated from focus on "serious" bowling to "fun" bowling.
- While league revenue remained flat, nonleague revenue went up, as did food sales, video games, parties, and club revenues.
- Ball sales went up 30 percent, shifting from "performance" balls to "fun" Viz-A-Balls.

The entire effort traded a portion of the less profitable league market for the more profitable casual market, transformed a collection of disparate centers into a centralized, unified marketing powerhouse, realized significant economies of scale, and shifted BRC from an operations-driven to a customer-driven marketing approach.

Questions

1. What research methods do you think might have been used to provide the data in this case?
2. What kind of public relations activities would you recommend to support the three points in the proposal?
3. What is the difference between an operations-driven approach and a customer-driven approach?

One motor sport racing at the Indianapolis Grand Prix provided the right kind of environment for this message.[7] Hasbro, maker of the Monopoly board game, had the public pick the first new game piece in 40 years and created a world championship as a way to keep up interest in the game.[8] Using a collection of pantomime-like cows (see photo), Chick-fil-A formed a political party called the Cow Preservation Party with a platform of promoting chicken consumption.[9] Mini-case 12.2 highlights how Brunswick Recreation Centers used a nontraditional approach to restore profitability.

Product and Service Design

Because public relations practitioners keep in constant touch with the various publics of an organization, they can provide valuable insight into consumer behavior issues. This type of informal research can be an important check on other data used in the design of products and services. The frequent monitoring of mass media, the use of social forecasting services, and other forms of environmental surveillance discussed in chapter 6 make public relations practitioners important sources of information in the marketing process.

All products and services have life cycles that must be a part of the marketing plan. The product life cycle starts with the development of new products and services, which are then introduced to a market. As industry sales increase during the market growth stage, so does competition. This often results in higher promotional costs and lower profits. The intense competitive environment of the third stage, that of market maturity, is usually marked with a decrease in sales and profits. The product life cycle begins to repeat itself during the final sales decline stage, as new products and services replace old ones.

12.1 Spotlight

Reviving a Beloved Icon and Creating New Interest in California Raisins

California Raisin Marketing Board developed new raisin characters to promote greater use of raisins by consumers.

Situation Analysis and Research

In the fall of 1999, the California Raisin Marketing Board (CRMB) decided the time was ripe to introduce a new Raisin character to promote its world-renowned product. The board charged Morgan & Myers with developing a high-profile public relations campaign that would attract national media attention. The firm's preliminary contact with the media indicated a high degree of interest in the character, and each contact seemed curious about how the new character would differ from the original Dancing Raisins. (Before their retirement in the late 1980s, the California Dancing Raisins had grown to be a popular American icon, dancing animatedly to Marvin Gaye's catchy hit, "Heard It Through the Grapevine.")

Marketing research indicated that although consumers continue to enjoy raisins, memory of the Dancing Raisins was fading. Raisin consumption was sluggish, too, despite its attributes as a chewy snack and tasty cooking ingredient. The timing was right for a revival crafted to encourage greater use of raisins.

Planning and Strategy

Morgan & Myers determined that only *one* raisin character would be introduced. The character would be a symbol for all that the product represents, including quality, exceptional taste, convenience, and good nutrition. Raisins are high in antioxidants, for instance, as well as being naturally sweet, fiber-rich, and fat- and cholesterol-free. The company worked with the CRMB staff to identify key traits that would help personify the next generation California Dancing Raisin. Their conclusion was that the character should be trimmer and fitter, a more active participant in life, and a vigorous promoter of good health.

For the kickoff, special events were arranged in 2000 in two major media markets—New York City and Los Angeles—using fitness guru Richard Simmons as spokesman accompanying the Dancing Raisin. In the Big Apple, a "Longest Grapevine Line" event was staged at Union Square Park, featuring the lively song and a large crowd following Simmons and the costumed Raisin, doing—you guessed it—"Grapevine" dance steps. In Los Angeles, a morning breakfast was conducted at Union Station, where the Dancing Raisin handed out raisin sample packs to commuters as well as flyers inviting recipients to attend a "Grapevine" workout at Universal Studios.

These New York and Los Angeles events allowed the firm to do the following:

- Reach consumers in a fun and entertaining way while at the same time promoting a significant health message
- Maximize media exposure by securing national print and broadcast coverage in the host cities
- Capitalize on the zany familiarity of Richard Simmons and his flair for communicating key messages

Measurement of Success

Richard Simmons and the California Raisin character proved to be impressive draws for the media in both cities. Launch events received coverage from top media, such as *Live with Regis & Kathie Lee,* the national Fox *News Now* program, the *Today Show* window, the *Tonight Show with Jay Leno,* Food Network, the *New York Times, Los Angeles*

Times, Entertainment Weekly, and Westwood One Radio. With all media combined, the events made nearly 40 million impressions.

Now, the word was out about the second generation of the Dancing Raisin, and U.S. consumers were reminded to think more about the health and nutritional benefits of these good-tasting dried grapes consumed in more than half of all American households.

Source: Bill Nelson, Copy Chief and Special Projects Writer, Morgan & Myers/The Barkin Group.

Public relations can help extend the life cycle of a product or service at several stages by developing events to support product introduction and sales and by generating positive news coverage of products and services. When a new product is launched, special events and publicity can help develop a positive reception. Schick Shave Shack, a mobile karaoke competition born from the idea of people singing and shaving in the shower, promoted the company's entire product line and attracted more than 100 million media impressions.[10] Publicity can help increase consumer awareness during the growth stage of a product. Tiger Woods has not only attracted more people of all ages and ethnicities to the sport of golf, but also has prompted increased coverage of products he endorses.[11] When a mature product has achieved almost universal name recognition, it often gets taken for granted and needs help in maintaining its visibility. For example, in spite of the high brand awareness that the Red Cross has developed in its 100+ years, public relations and other marketing activities are needed on an ongoing basis to maintain the nation's blood supply.[12] Spotlight 12.1 discusses the introduction of a new Dancing Raisin character a decade after this icon had been retired.

The public relations' information base regarding a wide range of publics, including but not limited to consumers, can be instrumental in naming, style, and packaging. Marketing texts are filled with examples of ill-chosen names that doomed or delayed the success of a perfectly good product. The Chevrolet Nova ("doesn't go" in Spanish) is one of the most famous of these legends. For that matter, should any restaurant have the word *unforgettable* in its name? In today's merger mania, brand names that profit from instant recognition are being lost as they are exchanged for initials or fused into new corporate identities. See figure 12.1 for trends in brand naming. Beyond the name, consumers view products and services as a bundle of utilities or collection of attributes that hold value. Packaging and style must add to that perception. Because of their skill in communication and understanding of publics, public relations practitioners can contribute to the selection of proper styling and packaging for products and services.

Distribution

Public relations people, and the information they provide, can assist marketing in making decisions about how and where a product or service will be offered to the consumer. Issues of logistics related to location and time availability must be thoroughly analyzed for target markets before a product or service is released.

Johnson & Johnson made a marketing decision to merge the sales forces for its German pharmacy and retail trades. German pharmacies did not carry feminine hygiene products before the merger. Pharmacies now carry J&J women's hygiene products o.b. tampons and Carefree protection shields, plus baby-care Penaten products. Nonpharmacy retail outlets sell the hand cream Neutrogena for the first time, a product only previously available in pharmacies. The integration saves customers money as products are less expensive in nonpharmacy stores. J&J promoted the new product distribution with

Changes in technology, science and other areas require new words to talk about things we previously never even imagined could exist. Here's what might be in store for brand names.

1. **Destination Branding**
   Names will reflect what the brand wishes to become and allow for expansion into other areas. A name like "Starbucks" can encompass any number of affordable gourmet food items, unlike Dunkin' Donuts.
2. **Speed Slows Down and Customization Becomes King**
   Names will be personalized with the prefix "my" or "I" or another personal reference. AskJeeves.com and itime.com are examples. Characters, such as G.I. Joe and Kool-Aid Man, have always been popular in children's marketing, and will probably become more prevalent in adult-targeted products.
3. **e-Nough Already**
   New letters might be used to designate the next generation of web-enabled products. For example, "p-books" might identify printed books and "e-books" for electronic books.
4. **Vive la Différence**
   With more and more ethnic groups gaining mainstream followings, names will reflect the blending of more than one culture. Language from ghettos, Latin America, American Indians, and Asian Americans and other groups will make its way into the general vernacular.
5. **New Combinations**
   There will need to be a whole new vocabulary to talk about new concepts in economics, politics and family structures. Some examples include BioCommerce, Globalopolies, Atmosfear, Egonomics and Stepfather-once-removed.
6. **Hooked on Phonetics**
   If consumers can't access your website because of spelling problems or a clever but difficult name, you're losing business. More phonetic spelling will help solve the problem. Anyone for hot dogs and "beenz"?
7. **Guiding Light**
   Smart chips will interconnect houses, cars, computers, and other systems and names will reflect the products that make use of this technology. Celestial, mythological, and even explorer names like the already-taken Polaris and Magellan will be used to label these products.
8. **Turn of a Phrase**
   Because it's hard to find a single word that hasn't already been used by some marketer, the use of phrases as names will probably increase.
9. **Nostalgia Naming**
   Technological backlash will lead to a desire for brands and names that evoke old-fashioned family values and simpler times such as Front Porch Lemonade.
10. **Ancient Revivals**
    As people try to cope in a chaotic and often seemingly immoral modern world, they will look to their roots, religion, and classical languages such as Latin and Hebrew for stability. Brand names will reflect something lasting and tangible to be a part of.

FIGURE 12.1 **Ten Predicted Trends for Brand Naming in the New Millennium**
Source: Adapted from Julie Cottineau, naming director, Interbrand, "Ten Predicted Trends for Brand Naming in the New Millennium." Reprinted with permission.

a combination of advertising and public relations activities, including television and cinema commercials, print ads, and event marketing.[13]

Banks learned that automated teller machines must be safe to use as well as near to their customers' homes and workplaces. Today, these machines are found in most supermarkets and convenience stores in addition to after hours at banks. Wireless technology addresses the desire of consumers to receive their e-mail, access the Web, and perform a host of other communication activities from anywhere in the world. Again, communication and promotion about product and service availability is important for success.

Communication

Today's marketers are finding they can't live by advertising alone. When Hertz Latin America experienced disappointing results with an advertising-only strategy, the vehicle rental company added public relations to its communication mix. Media relations efforts targeted business editors and columnists, hoping that such coverage would increase Hertz's travel and tourism accounts.[14]

Ziff Davis Media realized it couldn't count on reputation, advertising, or magazine covers alone to sell its publications. The company created a public relations department to help launch new titles and to highlight content in current ones such as *Expedia Travels* and *Family PC*.[15]

Arby's coordinated its biggest national public relations program with its first centralized advertising campaign to promote its new deli sandwiches. While the advertising reaches the fast-food public, the business-to-business public relations efforts are designed to help the franchisees implement promotions on the local level. Included in the Market Fresh PR guide are step-by-step instructions on how to reach out to local media, how to develop a media list, and how to create community outreach programs. Press release templates and media-ready folders for the restauranteurs to distribute to local reporters with food samples also were supplied.[16]

When *Pearl Harbor,* a movie about the 1941 Japanese attack that drew America into World War II, made its debut, the Walt Disney Corporation and U.S. Navy spent a reported $5 million on events in an effort to create box office buzz. Their efforts earned the front cover and extensive coverage in *Newsweek,* the major wire services, and entertainment television shows. The navy sent almost 40 navy reserve information officers to Hawaii to handle prerelease activities. The film screening for journalists was held on the outdoor flight deck of the USS *Stennis,* a working navy ship. The public relations endeavors paid off with to-die-for endorsements and being rated in polls as the summer's most anticipated movie.[17]

As you can see, public relations plays a natural role in supporting a variety of marketing activities. This makes it easy to overlook the critical role public relations can have in the company's larger environment of image and reputation management and handling whatever crises may occur.

Your CEO as the Marketing Spokesperson

The chief executive officer is usually the ideal spokesperson during a crisis. Does the same hold true for marketing activities? When the late Victor Kiam acquired Remington Product's shavers, the company was ailing. A positive bottom line one year later was the result of staff cuts, product line changes, and Kiam starring in Remington's aggressive television advertising campaign. "I liked it so much, I bought the company," confirmed Kiam's commitment to the brand in the ads.[18] David Oreck promotes the virtues of the eight-pound Oreck XL vacuum sweeper. The late Dave Thomas appeared in ads for his daughter's namesake restaurant, Wendy's. The spokesduo for Bush's Baked Beans, Jay Bush and his dog, Duke, credit the brand's great taste to a secret family recipe.

Bill Gates used television ads and personal appearances on talk shows to present Microsoft's side of the story in its antitrust battle with the U.S. Department of Justice. Lee Iacocca, former CEO of Chrysler, spoke to the American public about his personal pledge to quality when the company was experiencing credibility problems.

Merrie Spaeth, president of Spaeth Communications, Inc., Dallas, Texas, provides the following guidelines for using company CEOs in their own ads.[19]

1. The CEO who is an owner or part of the family who has owned the company for several generations can communicate a personal commitment to the brand.
2. The copy should sound like the CEO actually talks in real life.
3. Delivery skills are important but should not be the only criteria for determining if your CEO is suitable for the job. Message and audience also should be considered.
4. Charisma counts, as it lends credibility to the message. The listener or viewer needs to believe that the speaker believes what he's saying.
5. Reasons not to use your CEO include diction problems that probably can't be overcome or a top executive who doesn't look the part.

Although some CEOs enjoy being in the limelight and not having to pay for talent saves money, practitioners need to understand the strategy before selecting a CEO spokesperson over a celebrity endorser. For example, the accomplishments of major sports figures can influence buying decisions for athletic brands such as Nike, Reebok, and L.A. Gear in a manner that would be difficult for a CEO. Similarly, glamorous models and famous actresses build and refresh cosmetic brands. Movie, television, and rock stars can capture the attention of their fans as they try to increase awareness of a product or service. Britney Spears, for example, appeared in Pepsi commercials.

What matters in selecting a spokesperson, CEO, or celebrity is the ability of that individual to add value to the brand. Consumers' perception of the qualities of the spokesperson must match the messages that need to be communicated to the target audiences. Spokespersons must be able to transfer their values.

Guerrilla Tactics

Under normal circumstances it's hard for large and small companies alike to break through a cluttered and noisy communications marketplace. But when budgets are small, time is tight, the product isn't the category leader, or a host of other challenging factors exist, practitioners often turn to **guerrilla tactics.**

Guerrilla tactics are considered "under the line," which means that they aren't standard operating procedures. It's a way of using nontraditional communication vehicles to gain recognition and to get out information about a company's products or services. Many guerrilla tactics, like sidewalk art, Internet chatrooms, mass e-mail messages, and radio talk shows are available at low or no cost and can be targeted to specific publics. However, the practitioner gives up a good deal of control by using them, and there are many messages competing for attention. One study estimates that companies targeted consumers with more than 430 billion e-mail advertisements in 2002. By 2006, that number is expected to rise to 960 billion.[20]

The results of other guerrilla tactics can be hit-and-miss. As a result of increased television coverage of crime scenes, some funeral homes are now printing their names on their body bags. Trendy young people visit clubs and bars, initiating brand conversations with the question, "What are you drinking?"

EmployeeMatters is a virtual human resources department that handles payroll, benefits, and other personnel tasks for small and midsize technology companies. The company often uses major trade shows to reach high concentrations of their target audience. These shows are crowded, there's considerable competition for the attendees' attention, and it's hard to stand out as an exhibitor. Enter guerrilla marketing. EmployeeMatters hired actors to be a roving band of picketers, staging "strikes" against traditional business practices. The protesters wore T-shirts and held signs with messages such as "I QUIT managing employee administration" on the front, while the back said, "WE ACCEPT the opportunity to handle your employee administration." All signs and shirts identified the EmployeeMatters booth by number.[21]

Journalists report using rumors and hearsay on web chatrooms and online news groups as a basis for their news stories, often without verifying the information with an outside source. E-mails can expose thousands to a message in a matter of minutes. Sixty-five percent of customers who bought one of the first Palm organizers said that they had heard about the product from another person.[22] Seventy percent of Americans rely on the advice of others when selecting a new doctor.[23]

Of course, guerrilla tactics can boomerang if not done honestly. Sony Pictures created a phony movie critic, David Manning of the *Ridgefield Press,* who wrote glowing, highly enthusiastic reviews for several of the company's movies. When a *Newsweek* reporter challenged the reviewer's authenticity, Sony asked for absolution, saying, "It was a case of incredibly bad judgment. We're taking all the steps necessary to determine who's been responsible and will act appropriately." Ironically, the movies had already received excellent reviews by major, "live" critics.[24]

Integrating Disciplines

A multitude of communication tools (see figure 12.2) are at the disposal of the creative public relations practitioner to deploy singularly, in a multitiered effort, or to synthesize into new cross-discipline vehicles. Media relations, special events, trade shows, displays, and myriad other means can all become part of a carefully orchestrated plan to communicate with current and potential customers.

For many organizations, though, effective public relations also means communicating with other critically influential audiences like the media, investors, political groups, or policymakers.

Several factors explain why organizations have moved to the integrated approach. One is that corporate mergers, acquisitions, downsizing, and an increasing concern for the bottom line have caused management to look at ways to reduce expenses. A second factor is that public relations firms and advertising agencies are merging with and acquiring one another. This has created a natural tendency to consolidate functions that overlap between advertising, marketing, and public relations. Another explanation for integration is an increased emphasis on relationship marketing and one-to-one marketing, both of which require development of a good reputation, or image building, which is a public relations activity. A final motivation for integration is the importance of government public relations, an important function of public relations. Influencing laws and regulations at the local, state and federal levels often affect a firm's sales and marketing aspects.

A bold solution to this increasingly complex challenge is **branded news,** a new concept pioneered by the Oklahoma City–based Ackerman McQueen agency, which integrates objective newsgathering and reporting as a primary brand-building tool.

Branded news is live, Internet-based newscasting, narrowly focused on news about the product or service category of the organization that's providing the newscast. For

- Achievement Awards
- Advisory Boards
- Announcements
- Annual Reports
- Article Reprints
- Autograph Parties
- Backgrounders
- Biographies
- Brochures
- Celebrations
- Certificates
- Commemorative Events
- Conferences
- Contests/ Competitions
- Corporate Advertising
- Demonstrations
- Desk-side Visits
- Direct Mail
- Dramatizations
- Editorials
- E-mails
- Endorsements
- Exhibits/Displays
- Fact Sheets
- Flyers
- Gifts/Mementos
- Graphs and Charts
- Grassroots Campaigns
- Handbooks
- Identity Programs
- Instruction Manuals
- Intranet
- Junkets
- Letters
- Letter to Editors
- Media Advisories
- Media Lists
- Media Tours
- Meeting Planning
- Memorandums
- News Releases
- Newsletters
- Opinion/Editorial Pieces
- Open Houses
- Overhead Transparencies
- Pamphlets
- Parades
- Personal Contacts
- Photographs
- Pitch Letters
- Policy Statements
- Positions Papers
- Presentations
- Press Conferences
- Press Kits
- Proposals
- Publicity
- Public Service Announcements
- Research
- Schedule of Events
- Scholarships
- Scripts
- Slides
- Sponsorships
- Satellite Media Tours
- Speakers' Bureau
- Special Events
- Speechwriting
- Spokesperson Training
- Talk Show Appearances
- Telephone Messages
- Tip Sheets
- Training Aids
- Time Capsule Burial/Opening
- Videos
- Video News Releases
- Web

FIGURE 12.2 **Public Relations Tactics to Support Consumer Relations and Marketing Efforts**

example, one leading energy company sponsors a live 12-minute webcast every business hour, with veteran journalists covering timely, energy-related stories from news bureaus around the world. The Williams Energy case study at the end of this chapter provides a snapshot of branded news.

Like regular network and cable TV news programming, branded news is a live, objective, proprietary news product prepared and delivered by seasoned journalists. But unlike traditional news programming, branded news delivers content solely about a single product or service, packaged for a highly targeted audience—news they want and can't get anywhere else. Branded news can be very cost-efficient, compared with traditional public relations budgets that often tolerate significant inevitable waste.

The films on the BMW website are another example of integrating disciplines. Minimovies with major stars like Madonna and produced by well-known directors demonstrate the car's handling, aesthetics, and other features in an action-packed, engaging manner.[25] Traffic was generated to the site by having the stars appear on talk shows and through other media relations venues. Consumer information such as driving techniques and tips from an expert is included on the website.

CONSUMER RELATIONS BRIDGES THE CORPORATION AND THE CONSUMER

Consumer relations is the bridge between the consumer and the manufacturer. When unexpected shipping charges are added to a mail order, when the quality is poor, when a warranty is not honored, when local branches are unresponsive to requests for help, when products are not safe, when the advertising is misleading, when repairpeople don't fix the problem, when information is desired, when a multitude of things can and do go wrong, consumer relations is there to respond. And for good reason. What companies do and how they do it are under scrutiny like never before. Consumer relations helps a corporation cope and thrive under this analysis.

The Challenges of Consumer Relations

Nothing is perfect, of course. People have bad days. Products can be defective in spite of rigorous testing. As was noted earlier in this chapter, smart organizations constantly *listen* to their customers and act upon what they hear. When the Hedstrom Corporation, of Bedford, Pennsylvania, received reports about the seats on its backyard swings falling off, causing children to drop to the ground, it asked consumers to stop using the swings immediately and to detach them from the gym set. The company made a free repair kit available through a toll-free number.[26] The manner in which Hedstrom resolved this problem works well with the customer complaint process discussed later in this chapter.

At the same time, some consumers have not demonstrated common sense when using some products. One woman sued a fast-food company when she was burned after putting a hot cup of coffee between her legs while she was driving. Although parents should know better than to leave their infants alone in a baby bath seat in a filled tub, some want the product banned because some babies died when left alone in the seats. Consumers are often quick to blame others for their own lack of judgment or failure to follow directions. Unfortunately there's little a manufacturer can do when consumers choose to ignore safety guidelines, printed warnings, and other measures that spell out the safe use of a product or service.

Trust is at the heart of these issues, and there are no easy answers. What is for sure, though, is that these issues aren't new and they won't go away. Finger-pointing and not taking responsibility for one's actions isn't only a 21st century phenomenon. History provides abundant examples. Today's business environment requires both corporations and consumers to be much more diligent and proactive. Consumers demand a greater emphasis on product performance, quality, and safety than ever before. They're more aware of their rights and more responsible to political and legal initiatives to protect those rights.

Consumer relations is a direct reflection of a corporation's values about its business in general. The Palm example presented earlier in this chapter discussed how the company's desire to "delight the customer" drove the product from its development stage. August A. Busch III, president of Anheuser-Busch, has a saying: "Making friends is our business." A-B makes friends by encouraging responsible consumption of its products by adults of legal drinking age and by investing in communities through education, disaster relief, and environmental and numerous other areas.[27] This consumer relations viewpoint is nothing new. Thomas Carlyle is just one of many famous philosophers through the centuries to observe, "Thought is the parent of deed."

The bottom line is that consumer relations should be more than a toll-free hotline to the company. It's how an organization fulfills its promise to serve its key publics.

Know Your Consumer

Good consumer relations begins with an organization's knowledge of its key publics. It's hard to identify an area that isn't affected by this knowledge in some way, from the product itself and packaging to how the product is described and the selection of communication tactics. However, knowing your customer isn't always as easy as it first might seem. For example:

Your consumer might change traditional consumption patterns. Fast-food chains used to ignore the late-night eaters, those wanting a burger or pizza or other munchies between 10 P.M. and 5 A.M. No more. Denny's and Taco Bell restaurant chains say the late-night segment accounts for about one-fourth of their annual sales. Wendy's saw a significant 30 percent growth in purchases after 10 P.M. in 1999.[28]

Economic and social shifts might open up new audiences. Many states are recording an increase in their Hispanic, Asian, and other ethnicities populations. Reaching them might necessitate additional consumer research, marketing in languages other than English, adapting products, and using nontraditional communication vehicles. This trend affects global markets as well. By targeting distinct ethnicities in Brazil, manufacturers found 160 million new consumers who wanted to purchase clothes, cosmetics, soft drinks, toys, and a host of other personal and household products and services.[29]

Your brand may no longer resonate with your consumer. Nike's consumers started to switch to leather shoes from athletic shoes in 1997 and the company didn't produce this type of footwear. Competitors lured Nike's customers away with new products and aggressive marketing campaigns. Nike hopes the innovative technology in the recently introduced Shox will allow it to reestablish itself as a market leader.[30]

The preceding illustrations highlight that shifting demographics, converging technologies, and changes in customer expectations all reinforce the point that your consumer group isn't static and often isn't satisfied. Thus, consumer relations programs must be proactive to ensure that they are meeting the needs of those they serve. This might mean extending the hours of customer service phone lines, initiating new research projects, exploring alternative communication outlets, repositioning a brand, creating new packaging, and a host of other considerations.

PUBLIC RELATIONS AND CONSUMER AFFAIRS

In the past three decades, consumer affairs units have become fixtures in most organizations that have direct links to consumers. A variety of names describe this function: public affairs, customer relations, consumer relations, consumer advocate, or public relations. Whatever the title, these staff members usually work both inside and outside the organization. The staffing of consumer affairs units varies tremendously, with smaller organizations having only one consumer affairs specialist and larger ones having more than 100. Organizations frequently staff their consumer affairs units with employees who have enough prior experience in the company to handle complaints and investigate problems effectively.[31] Frequently, the staff is divided into groups responsible for certain functions, such as complaint handling, publications, consumer education, and the like.

The goal of consumer affairs is to improve the organization's relationships and communication with consumers by investigating consumer issues and conveying the results to management. Responsibilities of the consumer relations unit may include resolving customer complaints, disseminating consumer information, advising management on consumer opinion, and dealing with outside consumer advocate groups.

Frequently, the consumer relations unit is linked to the public relations department of an organization. This connection is natural, since consumers are one of the publics that public relations practitioners have traditionally served. The exact placement and design of consumer relations units vary, depending on the size and nature of the organization and the diversity of its products or services. One common characteristic does appear among the different approaches: The vast majority of consumer relations units report directly to top management. This provides the necessary autonomy to investigate issues and identify problems early with easy access to those who make policy decisions.

Consumer Information and Education

The major tenet of consumer advocacy is that consumers lack adequate information for making purchasing decisions. The complexity of the business system and the proliferation of products contribute to this difficulty, but many consumer problems result from product misuse or improper maintenance. A satisfied customer may tell another five to eight people, but dissatisfied and angry customers are taking their complaints to public forums like websites, talk shows, and other media outlets, in addition to telling 10 to 16 of their friends and acquaintances. Consumer relations units have responded to the need for fuller and clearer information by providing simplified warranties, clarified product use instructions, and educational programs to help consumers select the right products for their needs and use them properly.

Toll-free numbers, e-mail, and websites are among the ways that consumers can reach companies with their complaints, questions, and suggestions. What is important is that companies actually follow through and reply to customer complaints and inquiries. Some research suggests that corporations are failing miserably in responding to the feedback they have received or are not communicating to consumers the actions that have been taken to rectify the problems. As has been noted earlier, the kinds of organizations that gain the most from their marketing and consumer relations activities are those that constantly listen to their customers and act upon what they hear.

Consumers usually value a message more if it comes from the media than from company representatives. Recognizing that, managements work with their consumer and public relations staffs to schedule new product releases and major announcements for times when they will gain the most publicity possible. General Nutrition Centers rolled out its newest supplement, The Officially Licensed NASCAR® Kids Multi-Vitamin, for instance, at the Milwaukee Mile. The chewable vitamins come in three-dimensional race-car shapes, and the company included a free die-cast replica of the No. 36 GNC Live Well race car with purchase.[32]

When audiences are difficult to reach through traditional media, organizations must be extra creative. Spotlight 12.2 illustrates how Nokia created a campaign to encourage people to exercise polite cell phone manners.

Generally Satisfied, But Not Always Served

A 1999 Harris Interactive poll found most people believe that computer hardware and software companies, airlines, hospitals, car manufacturers, banks, telephone companies, and pharmaceutical companies generally are doing a good job in serving their customers and would do the right thing if they had a serious problem with one of their products or services. Although this is encouraging news, there are two other sides to the story. One is that this overall degree of satisfaction has been falling since 1997, from

12.2 Spotlight

Nokia Encourages Nation to Mind Their Mobile Manners

New issues of social etiquette were raised as the number of mobile phone users increased during the 1990s. Although wireless users enjoyed the freedom of being able to make and receive calls from just about anywhere, many of those within earshot at restaurants, in lines at the post office, at church, in meetings, and the like considered this behavior annoying, rude, and disruptive. Nokia, the world's largest mobile phone manufacturer, developed a cell phone courtesy campaign that reinforced the brand as a leader in all areas affecting mobile phones and educated consumers on effective communication without being disruptive to others while in public places.

The design of the campaign provided the company with an opportunity to showcase features and functions on any mobile phone that can be personalized to suit the environment, such as short text messaging, silent and vibrating alert, and caller ID and voicemail. Campaign tactics included the creation of a Cell Phone Courtesy Week in San Diego, selecting national food critic and etiquette expert Bill Boggs as the spokesperson, the development of a "Quiet Zone" logo for use in areas where courteous mobile phone use is requested, and an aggressive media relations effort that resulted in articles in *USA Today* and other major publications and a VNR airing on 118 television stations across the country as well as CNN fn and Bloomberg.

67 percent to 55 percent.[33] The other is that 65 percent of consumers feel that businesses care more about selling them products that already exist, rather than coming up with something that really fits consumers' lifestyle.[34]

Thus, the potential for problems often begins with the products and services themselves. Mass-produced products don't work and behave like those that are custom designed. This can be a breeding ground for consumer frustration and disappointment.

Unfair and Deceptive Practices

Damage to the buyer-seller relationship occurs when products and services are promoted using unfair or deceptive means. Although only a small percentage of goods do not live up to their advertising, enough consumers have had bad experiences with products in general to believe the worst and be suspicious of claims and promises.

Voluntary self-regulation is the primary reason why unsubstantiated claims are not allowed to proliferate in advertising. The National Advertising Division (NAD) and the Children's Advertising Review Unit, both part of the Council of Better Business Bureaus, are the investigative arms of the industry's program. Competitive challenges come from other advertisers and also from self-monitoring traditional and new media and consumers.

For example, a review board determined that AT&T had a reasonable basis to substantiate that its 1-800-CALL-ATT collect calling service "always cost less than MCI's 1-800-COLLECT."[35] A concerned consumer questioned whether M&M Mars's "NEW" Peanut Butter Twix bar could be described as "new" since it had been on the market before being discontinued in 1997. The panel found that the "new" version of Peanut Butter Twix was materially different from its earlier version and that the "new" claim was truthful and nonmisleading.[36] Unilever was asked to modify certain advertising claims for its Thermasilk line of shampoos and conditioners. While it was found that Thermasilk products help protect hair from damage caused by heat, there was inadequate evidence to support the claim that heat styling with the brand will make hair healthier.[37] The voluntary self-regulation system works. There is about a 96 percent compliance rate in the more than 3,750 cases reviewed since NAD's founding in 1971, with only about 4 percent referred to government agencies for further action.

Public relations practitioners need to be careful not to mislead or dupe the gatekeepers to the consumer: the media. When dot-coms were closing and agencies were handing out pink slips, *PRWeek* received a press release about a "Seattle Company Upsizing." It turned out the Internet and marketing firm in question had hired an art director. Future news releases from the company probably won't receive much attention.[38]

Handling Consumer Complaints

Although they are hard to quantify, probably the overwhelming majority of consumer inquiries and complaints are handled in a routine manner. The item is replaced or repaired, the purchase price is refunded, instructions are given, or whatever action is appropriate is taken. Companies of all sizes realize the critical importance of consumer relations and want to be responsive. Some companies like L.L. Bean, Lands' End, and Nordstrom have service reputations that are legendary in the retail business.

The more expensive the item, the more likely the consumer will complain, according to *Consumer Reports.* The Council of Better Business Bureaus provided complaint counseling and referral services to approximately 2.5 million persons in 1999, with about 14 percent of these inquiries resulting in a formal complaint being made to the company.[39] Automobiles receive almost twice as many complaints as the next highest category of household goods, which includes appliances, computers, electronics, and furniture. Major gripes include defective products, deceptive advertising, and manufacturers that don't honor warranties and refunds.[40]

To ensure fast and uniform processing of consumer complaints, many organizations have developed elaborate complaint control systems. Consumer affairs specialists generally hold the following views:

1. Consumer complaints should be solicited.
2. All complaints should be logged when received.
3. The complaining party should be notified at receipt as to how the problem will be handled.
4. Action to resolve the complaint should follow quickly.
5. Affected company personnel and departments should be notified promptly and their responses monitored.
6. Ongoing analyses of complaint patterns should be aimed at preventing future problems.

Don Peppers and Martha Rogers, in *The One to One Future,* suggest that we must learn to use customer dissatisfaction as an opportunity for collaboration. They argue that we should make complaining easier and try to resolve complaints in a collaborative fashion. The use of toll-free numbers for complaints is one measure that facilitates customer complaints. Communication through websites is another example. To hear more complaints, and thus establish relationship marketing on a one-to-one basis, the following steps should be taken:

1. Design your satisfaction questionnaire with the knowledge that its primary function is not research, but discovery of complaints.
2. Always ask your customer to identify himself or herself.
3. Be sure you do get back to a complaining customer. Don't simply ask a customer to contact you. If your first effort to make contact doesn't succeed, keep trying until you do make contact and make an effort to solve the problem together.

4. If you have a product that is sold in a store, encourage complaints by asking, on your package or inside it, for comments of any kind. Your package probably represents the only real customer-contact point available.
5. The economics of complaint handling will almost always work out to your benefit, as long as you pay attention to resolving one problem at a time, in a collaborative fashion, with each individual customer.[41]

Integrating "Click" with the "Brick"

A study conducted for the supermarket industry found that e-mail is replacing other methods of consumer relations communications, to account for approximately 20 percent in 2001. Consumers expect quick responses and automatic acknowledgment. Unfortunately, most supermarket websites offer basic information but limited interactive capabilities. So while consumers might be able to find out the hours of operation, they can't reorder their prescription. The industry sees "click-and-brick" integration as integral to their future success.[42]

The supermarket industry isn't alone. New technologies are changing how people shop, pay their bills, trade stocks, communicate with their families, and much, much more. What was dubbed as the "New Economy" several years ago is just the way business is conducted today.

FTD.com is one of many organizations that is trying to figure out how to integrate its Internet presence with its in-place distribution system, traditional consumer relations program, and other promotion efforts. The company accepted the then-conventional wisdom that Internet banner ads would draw traffic to its site, eliminating the need for expensive direct mail catalogs, and that flower sales could be increased through marketing partnerships with fast-food restaurants and gas companies. The anticipated results didn't happen. FTD.com had to modify its strategic plan, making necessary changes to ensure profitability.[43] With all of these changes, it's easy to see how the consumer can become confused, not knowing where and how to purchase goods, how to get information, what kind of quality controls are in place, and the like. Good consumer relations units anticipate the difficulties customers might face as a company realigns and refocuses its business practices and then puts systems in place to help prevent problems.

The Corporate Liaison

The consumer affairs role within corporations has become that of consumer spokesperson to management. Most consumer affairs specialists see it as part of their jobs to take an active role in decision making by speaking out for the consumer. They actively solicit consumer opinion and make management aware of the effects various decisions will have on consumers. The in-house ombudsman must balance the needs of the actual customers, the demands of consumer activists, and the goals of the organization. This role of liaison has always been the highest calling for public relations professionals.

Those who understand the purpose of public relations realize that the practitioner must do more than echo the company line. Public relations professionals should help senior managers stay in touch with their various publics. Doing so is especially critical in emergencies, when public relations professionals must serve as management's bridge to the media and the public.

Summary

Public relations and marketing can work together to build customer trust and loyalty while selling the product or service. The kinds of organizations that gain the most from their marketing and consumer relations activities are those that constantly listen to their customers and act upon what they hear.

A multitude of communication tools is available for marketing and consumer relations activities, to be used singularly, in a multitiered effort, or to synthesize into new cross-discipline vehicles.

An organization fulfills its promise to serve its key publics through trust. Consumer affairs improves an organization's relationship and communication with consumers by investigating and resolving consumer issues and concerns.

For self-testing and additional chapter resources, go to the student CD and the Online Learning Center at **www.mhhe.com/lattimore**

Case Study

Branded News

By Angus McQueen
Chairman/President/Chief Executive Officer
Ackerman McQueen, Oklahoma City

Imagine a news network where the lead story, the feature story, *every* story is about energy—energy prices, energy companies, energy technologies, energy policies.

This real-time network exists at www.EnergyNewsLive.com. (You can see a sample at http://www.ENLsample.com.) It's provided free to thousands of registered users by Williams Energy, a Fortune 500 company with a nearly 100-year history of finding, storing, trading, and transporting almost every form of energy.

Brands and News

Effective public relations means communicating not only with customers and prospects, but also with other influential audiences like the media, the financial community, political groups, regulators, and lawmakers. More than advertising, these audiences trust what's in the news about a brand.

That's why companies traditionally hire a public relations firm to pitch stories, sweet-talk editors, plaster newsrooms with press releases, and sponsor high-profile events. It's not uncommon to invest millions of dollars a year that way. And the competition for placement is stiff. Success in the media is often measured in the number and profile of news outlets that pick up a story, the impressions achieved, and the equivalent advertising value of those impressions.

The competition for attention is manifest in other significant ways, including the amount of time or space given to any topic, the tendency to tailor the story for a mass audience, and shallow treatment of the material.

Why not go into the news business yourself? This is the principle behind "Branded News," a bold concept pioneered by Oklahoma City–based agency Ackerman McQueen. Branded news is one part of Williams Energy's comprehensive media relations program. The in-house department sends out press releases, schedules interviews, meets with editorial boards, and conducts other activities to share information with key audiences through appropriate media outlets.

The Branded News Strategy

With the advent of broadband Internet technology, traditional news brands such as CNN, NBC, and other cable and news channels no longer have a monopoly on news delivery.

For energy influentials—energy buyers, traders, transporters, analysts, regulators, investors—no existing outlet offers an up-to-the-minute, full-time focus on energy news. Monthly trade publications, separate websites dealing with energy-related issues, annual meetings, and other similar activities can't provide timely and convenient information that the energy industry needs to stay current.

Besides, the trust once enjoyed by major news brands is suffering from a blurred distinction between news and commentary, a perception of media bias, and a widening values gap between the media and the general public. Most news outlets don't have editors and reporters who specialize in a particular industry.

Why shouldn't trusted brands, like Williams, fill this void? Who better to gather and package energy news than those who live it, understand it, and make it? Especially when no existing news outlet has the resources or financial incentive to do it.

Traditional news media are constrained by a profit motive. Branded news isn't. Their measure of success is revenue enrichment. Branded news's measure of success is brand enrichment. In Williams Energy's case, it means taking a clear position of leadership in the energy industry.

Branded News Is Born

Launched in October 2000, www.energynewslive.com (ENL) is the world's first and only real-time energy news network, featuring the following:

- Live, streaming video newscasts every business hour, with veteran journalists reporting from ENL news bureaus and energy trading floors around the world
- A proprietary weather modeling map, since energy prices are heavily influenced by weather
- A new, proprietary energy price index called the uE, or Universal Energy average, a composite indicator of aggregate energy pricing among all commodities
- A news experience as high quality as any network TV news experience

A Higher Standard

How can a company objectively report on its own industry? Simply put, a brand can't be enhanced by dishonest news. Audiences know what's legitimate news and what's not. Advertising masquerading as news would damage the brand.

That's why branded news, by definition, must not only meet but *exceed* traditional standards of objective journalism. Toward that end, Williams Energy doesn't employ, manage, or control the news-gathering team; they're a separate company. If there is bad news to report about Williams Energy, it's reported, just as it would be about any other company. Williams Energy has no control over the news-gathering process or coverage. Experienced anchors ensure that the integrity of the news process is maintained.

A Long-Term Relationship

Compared with traditional news outlets, ENL's audience is small. But they're all the audience Williams Energy needs. People not associated with the energy industry wouldn't be interested in the continual coverage of all things energy. That's why ENL eliminates almost all waste circulation and viewership by focusing solely on those interested in the subject. No sports scores or fashion reports here.

Since branded news requires viewers to register, important new data can be evaluated, like titles, companies, the depth and duration of access, and user feedback. Williams Energy can use this information to target specific messages to certain audience segments.

Branded News Tomorrow

With a fraction of traditional brand-building investment cost, Williams Energy enjoys a daily presence with energy influentials that it could never acquire through traditional public relations and advertising channels.

As American businesses harness the news delivery potential of the Internet, they, too, can cover their industry news for their audiences with more authority, expertise, and accuracy than anyone ever before.

In doing so, they'll add depth, dimension, and humanity to their brands, because people who are important to them can reach out and touch them every day. And that's the golden ring for good PR practitioners *and* good journalists.

Questions

1. What are the characteristics of traditional news and branded news? What are the advantages and disadvantages of each?
2. Select a company you're interested in. If you were to create a branded news site for them, what features would you include?
3. Assume you're the director of an automotive branded news site provided by Mercedes, whose CEO asks you not to run a story about a Mercedes recall. What do you do?
4. How do you rate the bias of today's national broadcast news media? Would you expect branded news to be generally more, or less, biased? Why or why not?

Key Terms

Use the CD-ROM and Online Learning Center at www.mhhe.com/lattimore to further your understanding of the following terms

branded news
consumer relations
desk-side briefings
guerrilla tactics
integrated communication
integrated marketing communication
marketing
public relations
relationship marketing

Notes

1. Sherri Deatherage Green, "Bad Press Prompts Education Initiative," *PRWeek,* 2 April 2001, p. 22.
2. Sherri Deatherage Green, "Champion Drives Messages Home," *PRWeek,* 26 March 2001, p. 36.
3. Heather Lindsey, "Rice Krispies Sculpt Contest a Real Treat," *PRWeek,* 9 April 2001, p. 22.
4. Glen M. Broom and Kerry Tucker, "An Essential Double Helix," *Public Relations Journal* (November 1989), pp. 40–41.
5. Ibid., p. 41.
6. David Pogue, "From the Desk of David Pogue: The Dumb and the Delightful," www.nyt.com, 7 June 2001.
7. David Rovella, "WSW Finds Formula to Tout PR Products," *PRWeek,* 9 April 2001, p. 22.
8. Thom Weidlich, "Monopoly: Entire World Is on Board," *PRWeek,* 2 April 2001, p. 22.
9. Kris Oser, "Cows Campaign in DC," *PRWeek,* 23 October 2000, p. 38.
10. Colin Nash, "A Shave and a Song," *PRWeek,* 16 October 2000, p. 24.
11. Hugh Clifton, "Sponsors Can't Get Enough of Tiger's Powerful Stroke," *PRWeek,* 23 April 2001, p. 14.
12. "The Red Cross Faces Disaster Undaunted," *PRWeek,* 13 November 2000, p. 10.
13. Dagmar Mussey, "J&J Increases German Ad Spending behind Key Brands," www.AdAge.com, 5 June 2001.
14. Robin Londner, "Hertz Adds PR to the Mix after Disappointing Latin America Results," *PRWeek,* 19 March 2001, p. 11.
15. Claire Atkinson, "Ziff Davis Creates Magazine PR Arm," *PRWeek,* 21 May 2001, p. 2.
16. Julia Hood, "New Deli Sandwiches Prompt Largest Arby's Marketing Push in Years," *PRWeek,* 30 April 2001, p. 5.
17. Robin Londner, "Film PR Blitz Leaves Nothing in Reserve," *PRWeek,* 21 May 2001, p. 2.
18. Laura Q. Hughes, "Never to Shave Again: Remington's Victor Kiam Dies," www.AdAge.com, 4 June 2001.
19. Merrie Spaeth, *Marketplace Communication* (New York: Mastermedia Limited, 1996), pp. 77–78.
20. Vanessa O'Connell, "E-mail, Online Advertisements Just Don't Click with Viewers," *Wall Street Journal,* 2 July 2002.
21. Thom Weidlich, "Two 'Strikes' and You're in Business," *PRWeek,* 5 February 2001, p. 20.
22. Emanuel Rosen, *The Anatomy of Buzz* (New York: Doubleday, 2000).
23. Ibid.
24. Associated Press, "High Praise from a Fictitious Reviewer," www.nyt.com, 3 June 2001.
25. Elvis Mitchell, "BMW Hopes That Its Mini-Movies Will Sell Cars," www.nyt.com, 26 June 2001.
26. Associated Press, "Backyard Gym Swings Recalled," *Jefferson City Post-Tribune,* 6 June 2001, p. 11.

27. "Making Friends. Making a Difference," Anheuser-Busch corporate brochure, 2001.
28. Suzanne Vranica, "Wendy's Feeds Off of Nighttime Cravings with Launch of New TV Ad Campaign," www.wsj.com, 13 June 2001.
29. Miriam Jordan, "Marketers Are Beginning to Target Blacks in Brazil as Consumer Group," www.wsj.com, 24 November 2000.
30. Judith Berck, "Has Nike Found the Springs Missing from Its Step?" www.nyt.com, 12 November 2000.
31. E. P. McGuire, *The Consumer Affairs Department: Organization and Functions, Report No. 609* (New York: The Conference Board, 1973).
32. "GNC Launches New Children's Multiple Vitamin; NASCAR Kids Multi Rolls Out During GNC Live Well Milwaukee Mile," www.individual.com, 29 June 2001.
33. Humphrey Taylor, "Public Sees Huge Difference Between Industries on 'Serving Their Consumers' and 'Doing the Right Thing,'" www.harris interactive.com, 28 April 1999.
34. 2000 Monitor
35. "National Advertising Review Board Panel Finds Advertising for 1-800-CALL-ATT Substantiated," www.bbb.org, 2 July 2001.
36. "M&M Mars, Inc. Substantiates Claims for 'New' Peanut Butter Twix," www.nadreview.org, 2 July 2001.
37. "Unilever & P&G Participates in Advertising Self-Regulatory Process," www.nadreview.org, 2 July 2001.
38. "Firm's Growth Nearly Slips by Undetected," *PRWeek,* 19 February 2001, p. 32.
39. "1999 Annual Complaint Summary," *Consumer Reports Online,* www.bbb.org, February 2001.
40. "Your Top Gripes," *Consumer Reports Online,* www.consumerreports.org, February 2001.
41. Don Peppers and Martha Rogers, *The One to One Future* (New York: Currency Doubleday, 1993), pp. 85–87.
42. "Supermarket, Consumers and the Web—It's Gonna Be Big!" *Store Equipment and Design* 9, no. 10 (October 2000), p. 3.
43. Calmetta Coleman, "Pruning Costs," www.wsj.com, 12 February 2001.

CHAPTER THIRTEEN

Financial Relations

13

Outline

PREVIEW

Effective financial public relations creates and maintains investor confidence. It builds positive relationships with the financial community by providing corporate information. Increased interest in investor relations following the Texas Gulf Sulphur case has greatly increased public relations involvement in the financial reporting of corporate information. With Enron's bankruptcy amid criminal charges against its accounting and financial advising firm, Arthur Andersen, the spotlight has again been placed on the need for accurate, current financial reporting.

Strong financial relations programs, characterized by responsiveness, openness, and regular communications, help lower the cost of capital for businesses. A key function of financial relations is to provide prompt disclosure of corporate news that is significant to the financial community.

> *"Today, investor relations is not only a job that entails communicating a company's strategic direction, it is a discipline that requires its own strategic design."*
>
> —Geraldine U. Foster, Senior Vice President
> Schering-Plough

Hostile takeover attempts through tender offers or management takeover through a proxy fight are two key financial public relations crises that may face management of a corporation. Public relations must become intimately involved in the battle for control when these crises occur.

Audiences for financial relations include individual stockholders, financial analysts, and the financial media. Major tools of financial relations to reach these key audiences include annual reports and annual stockholder meetings. But with many new technologies the company's financial reporting also includes use of cable or satellite television, placement on the Web, or discussions with key stakeholders through video conference calls.

Effective financial relations gives a business increased support for its management, higher stock prices, and greater ease in attracting new capital ☐

Two defining events have happened to highlight the essential function of financial relations in corporate America—one coming to the forefront in October 2001 and another a case settled by the U.S. Supreme Court in 1968. The Texas Gulf Sulphur case in 1968 underlined the essential nature of timely and full disclosure of information in avoiding "insider trading" charges against a publicly held company. The Enron situation, which may not be settled for some years, emphasized both to investors and to the business community the necessity of accurate financial accounting and of reporting that financial condition through a company's investor relations materials.

Ultimately the success of any organization depends on its ability to attract resources from its environment. Among the most important of these resources is capital—the money with which other resources can be purchased. Corporations raise money in a variety of ways, including selling stock, issuing bonds, and securing loans from financial institutions. In all cases, a company can attract capital only if investors have confidence in the business and its management. Without accurate, honest financial reporting the investing public cannot have this confidence. Investor relations has developed in the last 30 years as a specialized public relations function "to build and maintain relationships with financial audiences, primarily institutional investors, analysts, and individual stockholders."[1]

Bond ratings, interest rates, and stock prices are not just a matter of negotiation between a corporation's financial officers and its bankers or brokers. Such negotiations are preceded by and based on the business's current performance and future prospects. These facts must be persuasively communicated, and that is where public relations is essential.

GROWING INTEREST IN INVESTOR RELATIONS

Since 1968 when the Texas Gulf Sulphur case was decided by the Supreme Court, business has had an increased interest in improved investor relations. Company executives were fined and some served time in jail in the first major case of insider trading since the SEC had been formed in 1934. That case was a landmark decision that was the wake-up call to American corporations that the **Securities and Exchange Commission (SEC)** meant business with its insider trading and related disclosure of information rules.

Enron, and its connection with Arthur Andersen as its accounting and financial reporting firm, put financial reporting in the spotlight in 2001 (see spotlight 13.1). This spotlight has had a dual focus of a major public company filing bankruptcy and the inaccurate reporting of financial information that misled investors, analysts, and everyone else.

Other catalysts have vaulted investor relations into a multibillion-dollar-a-year operation. Among these factors have been a growing number of companies "going public" in the last three decades, high visibility of corporate mergers and acquisitions, efforts to stop hostile takeovers of companies, and much tougher requirements for disclosure by the SEC and the stock exchanges. In addition, the expanding importance of global financial markets and the growing understanding of need for expert public relations guidance in view of the court cases such as the Texas Gulf Sulphur case have increased management's interest in financial public relations.[2]

In the following sections of this chapter we examine the tasks of financial public relations, then look at disclosure of information and at the major issues facing the financial public relations practitioner. We also discuss the role of financial public relations practitioners, their audiences, and communication strategies including the annual meeting and the annual report.

Internal Public Relations Lessons Learned from Enron Inc.

Spotlight 13.1

The collapse of Enron, a leading energy company headquartered in Houston, Texas, sent shockwaves through the financial marketplace in late 2001 and early 2002. The congressional hearings, court cases, and other investigations may go on for years, but the immediate impact on financial reporting no doubt will be far-reaching. Included is the internal impact that it is likely to have for financial public relations practitioners.

Some of the internal public relations lessons learned from the debacle include these:

1. *Share the bad news as well as the good news.* Although not a new concept to public relations, sharing bad news as well as the good news is emphasized in this case because employees were heavily invested in the company through their retirement plan. The hardest time to convince a CEO to share bad news with employees is when things seem good and morale is high. But, to keep morale high, management needs to build long-term credibility by sharing the bad as well as the good with its employees before it becomes known outside, and especially before it is reported in the media.
2. *Treat all investors equally.* Often the largest number of investors comes from employees (although not usually the most total dollars). In Enron's case this especially was true because of the retirement funds being invested in Enron stock. SEC guidelines require disclosure of any information that would make a significant difference in the financial results of a publicly held company. Thus, employees who are stockholders should receive that same information. Investors must be given the potential downside as well as the upside of a company's performance whether they are external investors or employee investors.
3. *Give internal communication center stage.* Some of Enron's problems might have been mitigated with better communication; some will require new legislation. The question of how much investor information should go to employees will become an issue in the next several years. Congress is studying potential legislation to require certain disclosure to employees in regard to their stock. Another similar issue is that Enron employees were kept from selling their stock for a period of time when the stock was dropping in value rapidly. Today, these "lockdowns" are legal. Congress may change that, or at least it may require certain notice to employees about any such lockdowns. Companies must have good internal channels of communication to deal with these issues.
4. *Know the difference between motivating and misleading.* Enron's communication from its CEO was overly optimistic. A company should refrain from being misleading in its optimism. If you have knowledge something is wrong, it is misleading to say everything is great.

Source: Judy Buffington Aud, APR, "What Internal Communicators Can Learn from Enron," *Public Relations Strategist* 8, no. 2 (Spring 2002), pp. 11–12.

MAINTAINING INVESTOR CONFIDENCE

The first task of **financial public relations** is to create and maintain investor confidence, building positive relationships with the financial community through the dissemination of corporate information. Executives who fail to do this may be unable to attract capital investment. They may lose control over their organizations and even lose their jobs. Financial public relations is much easier to relate to the proverbial bottom line than are other kinds of public relations. Relative stock prices, bond ratings, and interest rates charged for loans are direct measures of confidence in a company. When confidence is high, stocks are worth more and bonds and borrowing cost less. When confidence is low, stock is worth less and higher interest is demanded by those who loan funds to the business. Most corporations consider their financial relations programs effective if they have been able to reduce the cost of funds or obtain the best cost of capital. (See mini-case 13.1.)

"The pace of communications and change in today's global marketplace, along with the thousands of institutions and millions of individuals around the world investing in equities has become increasingly complex, with thousands and thousands of investment alternatives,"[3] according to Mark Begor, executive vice president and chief financial

13.1 Mini • Case

U.S. Foodservice Launches NextDayGourmet.com

U.S. Foodservice, a $6.2 billion food distributor which distributes food and related products to restaurants and institutions throughout the country, decided to use the Internet to launch a dot-com, under the name NextDay-Gourmet.com, to grow its $580 million food equipment and supply business.

After extensively researching the competition, key customers, analysts, sales force, and market research of consumer attitudes, the company found two major things:

1. No competitor in the food service industry was involved at a high level in business-to-business e-commerce so the strategy was bold for the industry.
2. Communicating this industry-leading initiative to the investment community and to its sales force was essential to the company's long-term growth and success.

With an $850,000 budget, the company and its public relations agency, Imre & Associates, sought to achieve two major objectives:

1. Obtain favorable stock ratings among analysts and approval of the financial community for its initiative
2. Move 200 top customers to purchase the equipment and supplies on NextDayGourmet.com.

Among its many tactics to achieve these objectives were the "World's Largest Cyber Café" presented on Broad Street in front of the New York Stock Exchange (NYSE). The coverage on CNN brought international attention to the new company. They also used the "Stomp" group on stage using only NDG products in their performance; served coffee and muffins to 15,000 Wall Street employees on their way to work; had its chairman ring the opening bell on the NYSE; held a presentation for 120 analysts in the boardroom of the NYSE with a webcast for those unable to attend; held a reception on the floor of the NYSE after trading hours for analysts, customers, board members, and media; and held a town meeting with senior executives for the sales staff.

Following the launch of the company on November 9, 1999, analysts praised the move and gave it a "strong buy" rating. The company also had moved 268 of its top customers to use the new company for equipment and supply purchases by March 2000. Thus, the company met its objectives.

Questions

1. Once the customers moved to the new Internet company, what would the company need to do to build and maintain loyalty?
2. What objectives would you have for a follow-up campaign?

Source: PRSA Silver Anvil competition, 2000, investor relations category.

officer for NBC. He continued by noting that "communicating a clear, concise and meaningful message to those investors is critical."[4]

Characteristics of a Corporate Communications Strategy

Peter Anastas, financial analyst, suggests that a corporate communications strategy has three major characteristics: consistency, credibility, and clarity. Consistency needs to be not only in the style and culture of the annual report but also in what the company says it is going to do compared with what it actually does. Credibility is increased when the company uses a candid and straightforward approach to describe its operations with a minimum of hype and a maximum of information. Clarity needs to be the focus of the communication. The purpose should be to be understandable, not obtuse.[5]

Specific Objectives for Practitioners

The practice of financial public relations touches on diverse areas like finance, accounting, law, public affairs, community relations, marketing, and employee relations. Consequently, its list of objectives is a lengthy one. Practitioners are charged with doing the following:

Building interest in the company
Creating understanding of the company
Selling company products
Broadening the stockholder base by attracting new investors

Stabilizing stock prices
Winning stockholder approval for management
Increasing the company's prestige
Creating favorable attitudes in the financial community
Developing political sensitivities of stockholders for issues relating to the company
Improving employee relations
Building loyalty of stockholders

Arthur Roalman sums up the purpose and rationale for financial public relations:

> An individual is not likely to invest money . . . in a corporation's stocks, bonds, commercial paper, or other financial pledges unless he believes strongly that he understands fully what is likely to happen to that corporation in the future . . . most investors' willingness to invest in a corporation is influenced by their trust in its management. Trust isn't built overnight. It is the result of long-term actions by the corporation to provide factual financial information in proper perspective.[6]

Investor relations changed considerably in the last decade of the 20th century as it moved into the 21st century. It had been primarily a passive carrier of information delivered mostly to the financial community. Today it has become much more proactive. "Investor relations has moved from a primarily passive role to an active, indeed interactive, marketing function. In this evolving marketing role, investor relations serves as a link between the company and the investment community, responding to the needs of both."[7]

PROVIDING PUBLIC INFORMATION

Investors bet fortunes on what they believe to be true about a particular enterprise. Fraud and deception can part uninformed investors from their funds. These dangers have been reduced by government law and regulation, stock exchange policies, and the voluntary disclosures of corporate management. But, the recent cases with Enron and Xerox have illustrated the problems that can occur when these laws and regulations are ignored. For example, in April 2002 Xerox agreed to a $10 million settlement with the SEC after the commission filed suit against Xerox in connection with a four-year scheme to defraud investors.[8] The importance of corporate information to investor decisions, however, points out the second major function of financial public relations: prompt provision of public information required by law, regulation, and policy.

SEC Regulations

Many aspects of financial public relations are affected by laws and regulations. The Securities Act of 1933 was passed "to provide full and fair disclosure of the character of securities . . . and to prevent frauds in the sale thereof." The Securities Exchange Act of 1934 supplemented the act of the previous year and was intended "to secure for issues publicly offered, adequate publicity for those facts necessary for an intelligent judgment of their value." These and other SEC regulations apply to all companies listed on any of the 13 largest U.S. stock exchanges, or with assets of $1 million and at least 500 stockholders. Other regulations require that corporations "act promptly to dispel unfounded rumors which result in unusual market activity or price variations."

SEC regulations are copious and subject to frequent changes. It is therefore impractical to present them all here. The commission routinely requires submission of three kinds of reports: annual reports **(Form 10-K),** quarterly reports **(Form 10-Q),** and current reports **(Form 8-K).** Form 10-K asks for descriptions of a corporation's principal products and services; assessment of competitive conditions in its industry; the dollar amount of order backlog; source and availability of raw materials; all material patents, licenses, franchises, and concessions; and the estimated dollar amount spent on research.

All of the information required by Form 10-K must be accompanied by corporate financial statements prepared in accordance with SEC accounting rules and certified by an independent public accountant. Moreover, the entire form must be submitted to the commission no later than 90 days from the close of the fiscal year. Finally, 10-K must be available free of charge to anyone upon request.

The 10-Q quarterly report is much less detailed. It asks primarily for the corporations' summarized profit and loss statement, capitalization, and stockholder's equity at the end of the quarter, and sale of any unregistered securities.

In its effort to gather all relevant investment-related information on a continuous basis, the SEC also requires filing of Form 8-K, the current report. Filing this document is required when an unusual event of immediate interest to investors occurs. Examples would be the acquisition or sale of significant assets or changes in the amount of securities outstanding.

These documents are prepared largely by accountants and lawyers. They are described here, however, because public relations professionals should (1) recognize the extent to which SEC-regulated corporations must share information, (2) understand the kinds of information deemed significant by investors, (3) realize the extent of federal regulation in this aspect of business, and (4) avail themselves of the information contained in these forms.

In an effort to help restore investor confidence, the National Investor Relations Institute (NIRI) approved a 10-point program aimed at disclosure actions that would help the investor better understand what was in these reports. The first point of the 10 suggests that companies should use a two-tier system in information disclosure. The first tier would be a plain English summary, or executive summary, of information contained in these various required reports in order to help an investor better understand significant trends that would likely affect a company's performance. This summary, the NIRI suggests, should be placed on the company's website as well as in the annual report. The second tier would be the information required by the SEC and accounting requirements.[9]

Public relations should be involved in the preparation of the executive summary, as well as other parts of the reports. A 1998 SEC regulation requires that certain parts of disclosure documents must be written in plain English: "The cover page, summary, and risk factor sections of prospectuses must be clear, concise, and understandable, according to the new SEC regulations."[10] The SEC has prepared a handbook entitled *A Plain English Handbook: How to Create Clear SEC Disclosure Documents,* which is available online at the SEC website or can be obtained in hard copy from the commission.[11]

Stock Exchange Policies

Policies of various stock exchanges also influence the task of financial public relations. The New York Stock Exchange states, for example, that news on matters of corporate significance should be given national distribution.[12] What is significant is a matter of some debate. The American Stock Exchange considers the following kinds of news likely to require prompt disclosure and announcements:

(a) joint venture, merger or acquisition;

(b) the declaration or omission of dividends or the determination of earnings;

(c) a stock split or stock dividend;
(d) the acquisition or loss of a significant contract;
(e) a significant new product or discovery;
(f) a change in control or a significant change in management;
(g) a call of securities for redemption;
(h) the borrowing of a significant amount of funds;
(i) the public or private sale of a significant amount of additional securities;
(j) significant litigation;
(k) the purchase or sale of a significant asset;
(l) a significant change in capital investment plans;
(m) a significant labor dispute or disputes with contractors or suppliers;
(n) an event requiring the filing of a current report under the Securities Exchange Act;
(o) establishment of a program to make purchases of the company's own shares;
(p) a tender offer for another company's securities; and
(q) an event of technical default or default on interest and/or principal payments.[13]

To facilitate *timely* national disclosure, financial relations practitioners use several newswire networks and the World Wide Web. The Associated Press (AP) is the major general newswire service. Dow Jones and Reuters Economic Service specialize in business and financial news. PR News Wire and Business Wire charge a fee for their services but guarantee that corporate news is carried promptly. The key issue is that the disclosure of information must be made at the same time to all audiences.

The Disclosure Issue

One other SEC regulation of particular interest to the public relations practitioner is Rule 10B-5, which makes it unlawful "to make any untrue statement of a material fact or to omit to state a material fact . . . in connection with the purchase or sale of any security." In the landmark case *SEC v. Texas Gulf Sulphur Co.*, 401 F.2d 833 (2nd E.r. 1968), this regulation was applied to press releases.[14] In subsequent suits, public relations counsel has been named as a defendant when press releases and other materials "contained false and misleading statements and omitted to state material fact."[15]

Two later cases sharply focused on the disclosure issue, although financial relations officers were left in confusion by their outcomes. One involved the 1984 merger between food giants Nestlé and Carnation. The other involved Chrysler Corporation's struggle to survive in the early 1980s.

Nestlé was bidding secretly for Carnation. Rumors were flying, and Carnation stock rose nearly 50 percent before Nestlé announced the purchase for $83 per share. Throughout the negotiations, Carnation's spokesman refused to comment. A year after the merger, the SEC ruled that by saying no comment during negotiations, Carnation had been "materially false and misleading." Since the company no longer existed, however, the SEC took no action to back its ruling.

Chrysler was saved by an unissued press release. One day in early 1981, Chrysler was down to $8 million in liquid assets. Company lawyers held that Chrysler must issue a press release to disclose its near insolvency, but company officials risked being charged by the SEC rather than destroy what little confidence their creditors and customers had left. The release went unissued and the company survived—its potential insolvency made a moot point by its renewed financial health.

No simple formula provides guidance in disclosure situations. Although the Chrysler example is unusual, it shows that judgment must be used. Generally, however, disclosure is both required and desirable. "The bottom line: The moment you have information that will make a material difference in the outcome of your financial results, you should be preparing and disseminating a statement to disclose that information."[16]

CRISIS ISSUES IN FINANCIAL RELATIONS

Several issues may come up in the life of a corporation that are crises in its effort to survive. In the last decade we have seen mergers and acquisitions that have often been hostile takeovers. In an effort to thwart hostile takeover attempts, bitter proxy fights often have ensued. Win or lose, the company is often left with considerable debt and, if it can survive, may have to spin off some of its assets.

Eugene Miller, executive vice president of United States Gypsum Company, says "the most stressful and crucial element of investor relations is in forestalling and defending against efforts of outside interests to take over the company."[17]

Takeover attempts come in two fundamental forms: the proxy fight and the tender offer. Both attempt to persuade shareholders, but in different ways and perhaps for different reasons.

The Tender Offer

In a tender offer money is the key factor. The **tender offer** is an offer that is above the market price of the stock enough to entice the shareholder to sell despite his or her loyalty to the company or desire to keep the stock. For example, if the shareholder had bought stock at $20 per share and it was now selling for $25 on the stock exchange, the person might be given a tender offer of $35 per share to sell to whomever wanted to get control of the company. Because of the financial gain that the shareholder would make, this is a tough fight by management to keep control of the company.

The Proxy Fight

In a **proxy** fight, the two (or more) contestants striving for control of management (or an issue) seek to get the shareholders to let them cast their vote for them. Thus, shareholders are requested to give their "proxy," or absentee voting rights, to one side or the other. In this case, though, the shareholder does not sell his or her stock.

Public relations for the management of the company under siege in a proxy fight can do several things to defend itself. Primary, of course, is focusing on providing information to stockholders, the financial press, and investors about the present management's operation and strategic plans for the future compared with what the competing group is suggesting.[18]

Laura Johnston, investor relations specialist at Citigate Communications, suggests that public relations practitioners in the financial arena need to be prepared as soon as possible. If you know you are going to have a tough fight ahead in the next year, begin now to prepare. She suggests these four strategies in the preparation stage:

1. *Don't procrastinate.* Start planning your investor relations strategy early.
2. *Begin by managing your shareholder's expectations. . . .* Pave the way for the proposal by informing shareholders about management's general line of thinking on that particular issue well before a proxy statement is produced.
3. *Involve investor relations people in drafting the proxy statement.*
4. *Hire a proxy solicitor* who will get down in the trenches and fight for every vote.[19]

Once the fight is under way, you can take a number of tactics to help you win. You should use every means at your disposal to reach your shareholders. You may need to go online or set up a World Wide Web page. Use all the communication tools at your disposal. A key element is also to target your message to a few key ideas and repeat them throughout the proxy campaign. Your theme should be recognized quickly by your shareholders. Rally your past supporters and don't be afraid to use the endorsements of the media or other credible third party sources to your advantage.[20]

FINANCIAL RELATIONS PROFESSIONALS

Financial relations professionals must have a broad base of knowledge and skills to deal effectively with their many-faceted responsibilities. A survey of 300 senior financial relations officers in leading corporations showed that a broad financial background combined with marketing communication skills is considered the best preparation for the field.[21] The survey indicated that although financial and security analysts may go into financial relations, their lack of marketing and communication backgrounds often impedes their success. Knowledge of finance, marketing, law, and public relations skills are all important for those considering financial relations careers.

AUDIENCES FOR FINANCIAL RELATIONS

In addition to the SEC, those interested in a corporation's financial information include stock exchange firms, investment counselors, financial writers, brokers, dealers, mutual fund houses, investment banks, commercial banks, institutional buyers, employees, and both current and future stockholders. For the purposes of discussion, however, these categories can be lumped into three broad audiences: individual stockholders, financial analysts, and the financial press. Following is an examination of each group, their informational needs, the means by which they may be reached, and the best ways to secure positive relations with them.

Individual Stockholders

Some corporations consider their stockholders a vast untapped resource of potential customers and grassroots support on political and financial issues. Harrison T. Beardsley recommends that financial relations efforts, particularly of smaller companies, concentrate on stockholders rather than on financial analysts.[22]

As discussed previously, the SEC requires companies to keep their investors fully informed. Management has learned the hard way that uninterested stockholders may be quick to sell their shares to even the most unfriendly entity attempting takeover. Moreover, stockholders themselves have become more vocal and active—initiating proxy fights or raising financial, social, and ethical questions in relation to environmental issues, sex discrimination, corporate political activities at home and abroad, labor relations, and many other issues.

Most corporations now recognize that "a company's foremost responsibility is to communicate fully anything that can have a bearing on the owner's investment."[23] The extent and quality of their efforts vary widely, however. Informative annual and quarterly reports, dynamic web pages, and well-organized annual meetings with follow-up reports are the basic tools of stockholder relations.

Sound stockholder relations are built on three principles: (1) learn as much as possible about your stockholders, (2) treat them as you would your important customers, and (3) encourage investor interest from people who are predisposed toward your company. A basic principle of communication is "know your audience." Consequently, learning as much as possible about stockholders makes excellent sense from a communications perspective. The stockholder survey, which asks for demographic and attitudinal information, is a readily available tool, but too few actually use it.

Treating stockholders as important customers has a number of implications for financial relations officers. Communicating in readable, nontechnical language is a must. Welcoming new stockholders and writing to express regret when stockholders are lost is a good business practice. Prompt and appropriate response to stockholder correspondence or e-mails also helps maintain positive relations.

Sun Company follows a comprehensive stockholder relations plan. The company believes, "Shareholders are our business partners. It's helpful to us if management gets an insight on what they think of us." Each new Sun stockholder receives a welcoming note from the company's chairman. A very readable newsletter goes out with every dividend check. About 100 shareholders are selected at random six or eight times a year and invited to a dinner at which a top company executive speaks. Sun also maintains a toll-free telephone line to make corporate news available to stockholders and invites them to call collect to the shareholder relations department with questions or complaints.

Finally, just as a company should seek new customers among the most likely segments of the population, it should seek stockholders from those predisposed toward buying stock. Employees, suppliers, dealers, and members of communities where the corporation is located are the most likely prospects. They should receive annual reports and other materials that encourage investment.

Financial Analysts

Financial analysts include investment counselors, fund managers, brokers, dealers, and institutional buyers—in other words, the professionals in the investment business. Their basic function is to gather information concerning various companies, to develop expectations in terms of sales, profits, and a range of other operating and financial results, and to make judgments about how securities markets will evaluate these factors. They gather quantitative and qualitative information on companies, compare their findings to statistics from other companies, assess opportunities and risks, and then advise their clients. Corporate financial relations assists analysts by providing information and, in doing so, may positively influence expectations and judgments.

To maintain relations with financial analysts, the basic method is to identify the prospects, meet them, establish interest and understanding, and then maintain the relationship. All dealings with professional analysts should be characterized by responsiveness, openness, and regular communication, but care should be taken not to overcommunicate.

"Fluff and puff" will quickly sour an analyst's view of a corporation. When analysts become overenthusiastic based on what they have been told by a company's financial relations staff, and corporate performance fails to live up to their expectations, the results can be disastrous. When Toys "R" Us Inc. announced that its Christmas sales were up 17 percent, its stock dropped 20 percent. Based on discussions with the company, analysts had expected a sales gain of 30 percent and thus were disappointed.

The shoe manufacturer Nike Inc. lost half its value when it earned 88 cents per share rather than the anticipated $2. Rather than informing the financial community when it realized profits would be lower than expected, Nike management tried harder to live up to the inflated figures. The next year the company set aside more time for communicating with financial analysts.[24]

Analysts want to know the following: background; that is, the nature of the business, primary factors affecting the business, current operating conditions, and estimates of future outlooks. Analysts are also vitally interested in management forecasts, pricing data, capital expenditures, financial data, labor relations, research and development, and any other information that may materially influence the quality of an investment. Annual reports provide much of the needed information. A survey of institutional investors showed annual reports as the most useful and informative source of information within a company's financial relations program.[25] Annual reports are discussed in detail later in the chapter.

A primary way to reach financial analysts is through **investment conferences,** which are meetings that investment professionals attend specifically to hear company presentations or discuss corporate issues. These programs contain information on a company's performance and provide persuasive arguments for buying its stock. Although such presentations center on speeches by company executives, they usually provide slick publications and audiovisual support materials as well.

A more popular conference in recent years has been the **conference call,** rather than an actual meeting. In some cases it is a video conference and in others, a phone conference. The conference call has become a quarterly ritual for many companies. The call is held the day after the quarterly report comes out. The CEO and CFO sit in front of a speakerphone or video camera and brief analysts, financial reporters, and other members of the investment community on the meaning behind the numbers. These calls provide the same story and interpretation for all the interested audiences at one time. A recent NIRI survey reported 73 percent of the responding companies held quarterly conference calls.[26]

Relationships with financial analysts are not all one-way. Analysts can provide valuable information to companies as well. When communicating with financial analysts, first be prepared to listen. They can give significant feedback about a financial relations program in terms of its adequacy, credibility, and sufficiency of information. Perhaps even more important, this is an opportunity for the company to understand how the market perceives its strengths and weaknesses and the behavior of the business as a whole.

The Financial Press

The third major audience for financial relations is the **financial press.** "The financial press provides a foundation and backdrop for any corporation's financial communications program," says Hill and Knowlton executive Stan Sauerhaft. "It develops credibility and it can add impressive third-party endorsement."[27]

Financial public relations practitioners deal with media much as other public relations specialists do. The major difference lies in the specialized nature of the financial media. Major daily newspapers carry financial items of local, regional, or national interest. Weekly newspapers generally carry items of local interest. The business press includes the *Wall Street Journal, Forbes, Barron's, Business Week, Fortune,* and other national publications as well as various local business-oriented publications (for example, the *Business Chronicle* in Houston, Atlanta, Los Angeles, San Francisco, and other cities). These are primary outlets for financial news, but they are deluged with information, so their channels of communication should not be cluttered with trivia or fluff.

Do not overlook the financial columnists. They carry considerable influence and can offer unique perspectives on particular companies. Trade magazines, usually devoted to particular industries, occupations, or professions, are also important outlets. They may reach such likely prospects as suppliers and producers.

13.2 Spotlight

Bloomberg L.P.

Financial media companies have made a significant impact providing financial information to consumers through cable and satellite TV in recent years. One company, Bloomberg L.P., has become a major provider of financial news and information.

Bloomberg L.P. is an information services, news, and media company serving customers around the world. Headquartered in New York, it employs 8,000 people in over 100 offices worldwide.

Bloomberg has forged a unique position within the financial services industry providing an unparalleled combination of data, analytics, electronic trading, and straight-through processing tools in a single platform. By providing instantaneous access to real-time historical financial data—and the ability to act on it—Bloomberg transformed the securities business and leveled the playing field between buyers and sellers. Its clients include the world's central banks, investment institutions, commercial banks, government offices and agencies, corporations, and news organizations.

In addition to the Bloomberg Professional service, Bloomberg has grown to include global news, television, radio, Internet, and magazine and book publishing operations. Bloomberg News® was founded in 1990 as a financial newswire service and has grown to include 1,200 reporters in 85 bureaus worldwide.

Bloomberg Television®, a 24-hour business and financial news network, is produced and distributed globally in seven different languages. Bloomberg Radio℠ is syndicated through more than 700 affiliates worldwide and gives listeners up-to-the-minute business, national, and international news. Bloomberg's 24-hour flagship station is Bloomberg® WBBR 1130 in New York.

The company publishes four magazines in the United States for consumers and professionals. *Bloomberg Personal Finance®* is targeted to active individual investors; *Bloomberg Wealth Manager®* is published for money managers and advisers; *Bloomberg Markets™* is a business magazine for investment professionals and complements the Bloomberg Professional service. *On Investing* is a personal investment magazine produced exclusively for Charles Schwab's top-tier clients. Bloomberg also publishes, in conjunction with local partners, *Bloomberg Money™* in the United Kingdom and *Bloomberg® Investmenti* in Italy.

Bloomberg's website, Bloomberg.com℠, is among the top five most-visited sites in the United States for financial news and information.

Michael R. Bloomberg founded his online network in 1981. Prior to founding the company, Mr. Bloomberg was general partner at Salomon Brothers, where he headed equity trading, sales, and, later, systems development. Michael Bloomberg was elected mayor of New York City on November 6, 2001.

Bloomberg Television provides 24-hour business and financial news.

Cable television is now a major outlet for financial news. Several cable or satellite channels are devoted exclusively to business news. With additional stations made possible through direct satellite transmission to homes or through fiber optic cable systems this is likely to increase several fold. Certain local and network programs are devoted specifically to business. Bloomberg Television, Public Broadcasting's "Wall Street Week," Cable News Network's financial programs, and Associated Press Radio's "Business Barometer" are examples of such programs (see spotlight 13.2). Network or local major market news operations generally should be approached only if the information has news value that affects the community at large.

Finally, specialized financial media are extremely interested in company news. Market newsletters (often published by brokerage firms), investment advisory services, and statistical services (like Standard and Poor's, Value Line, or Moody's) frequently carry the greatest weight with potential investors.

COMMUNICATION STRATEGIES IN FINANCIAL RELATIONS

Strategies for communicating financial information, like those for implementing other plans (see chapter 6), must grow out of management's long-term view of the corporation. Communication strategy is a plan for getting from where you are to where you want to be. Thus, the perception of the company by its relevant publics should be compared with how it hopes to be perceived in the future.

The methods available for implementing strategy include personal meetings, financial literature (correspondence, quarterly and annual reports, dividend enclosures), financial news releases, and annual meetings. But with unprecedented advances in communication technology the mode of communicating these strategies also has been changing rapidly. Videoconference calls, e-mail, cable business news shows, and the World Wide Web all provide the potential to provide more timely, specific information. These new technologies also increase the possibility for interactive communication with key stakeholders such as financial analysts, investors, and company employees.[28]

Whatever a corporation's current status or ultimate objectives, its financial relations communication strategy must be characterized by responsiveness, regularity, and openness. Communication should never be evasive and must include bad news as well as good. "Telling employees bad news seems to be the hardest thing for senior management to do."[29] But this is essential to building credibility with your employees. Credibility is the key to a strong financial relations program.

Annual Meetings

Annual meetings are a kind of mandated ritual in which the actual owners of a business consider and vote on the effectiveness of management. In theory, stockholders have the power to do what they please (within the law) with their company. But in practice, issues are rarely discussed and even more rarely voted on because management collects proxies in advance to support its positions, appointments, and decisions.

Views on the annual meeting ritual are widely divergent. Whatever the case, the annual meeting presents certain opportunities and entails genuine risks; thus, careful planning and orchestration are essential. Most major public accounting firms publish guides for corporate executives facing annual meetings.

Besides trying to attract, inform, and involve the audience of stockholders, the annual meeting has other functions. It enables corporate management to reach all stockholders through pre- and postmeeting communication. It provides a showcase and a focus for corporate publicity. It permits personal contact between executives and stockholders through which actions can be explained, accomplishments recognized, and feedback offered. It is a marketing tool when products are displayed in their best light.

The annual meeting also is a safety valve by which stockholders can let off steam. The democratic nature of the annual meeting makes the company vulnerable, and organized dissent is possible from stockholders who have bought a few shares of stock just to gain a platform. Such individuals may intervene or disrupt—confronting management with embarrassing questions and drawing the attention of the news media. For example, Chrysler Corporation, the third-largest U.S. automaker, was confronted with the possibility of hostility at its 1995 annual meeting when Kirk Kerkorian, who held a large block of Chrysler stock, was unhappy with the performance of the stock. His concern led to actions by the Chrysler board to improve the stock price. G. A. Marken suggests doing the following to improve the chances for an effective, successful meeting:

- Ensure the CEO is well prepared for the presentation.
- Provide displays highlighting company products, services, and financial results.
- Invite the media and representatives from the financial community.
- Prepare an advance news release for the media to highlight the CEO's presentation at the meeting.
- Have handouts such as annual reports, product literature, CD-ROM, and videos available.
- Consider the meeting environment and amenities carefully (invitations, name badges, refreshments, tours, favors or specialty advertising gifts, etc.).
- Develop an executive summary or digest of the meeting, if it is particularly unusual or controversial.[30]

Commenting on such annual meetings, a former Atlanta newspaper business editor, Tom Walker, observed tongue-in-cheek that corporations should retain consulting sociologists, "especially during the annual meeting season when managements are forced to line up before their shareholders and give an account of themselves."[31] Financial relations actually plays the role that Walker would give to sociologists. By anticipating the concerns, issues, and even the mood of stockholders—based on continuous interaction—financial public relations should be able to prepare management for most situations that could arise. With careful planning, the positive potentials of annual meetings may even be realized.

Annual Reports

Annual reports are prepared not only to publish the required SEC information but also to perform a public relations and marketing function. Reports are usually released in March about six weeks prior to the company's annual meeting, which is often held in April or May. The trend in annual report preparation is for more CEOs to write their own letters to shareholders, to include the bad news up front, and to contract out the production of the annual report to consulting firms.

Annual reports come in a variety of shapes and styles. They are, on average, 44 pages long, according to Sid Cato, whose annual report newsletter office is in Kalamazoo, Michigan. Some reports, he says, "are spectacular, with glossy covers, creative art design, terrific color photographs and graphics, superior paper stock and easy to understand explanations of company performance."[32] Some reports are produced on CD-ROM and some on video; most are available on webpages, while others may be done as newspaper supplements. However, some companies only produce the 10-K report in black and white that is required by the SEC.

O'Charley's restaurant chain from Nashville, TN produces effective annual reports with excellent graphics, photos, and content.

Oscar Beveridge calls the annual report "unquestionably the single most important public document issued by a publicly held corporation."[33] Writing in *Fortune,* Herbert Meyer states: "Out of all the documents published by a Fortune 500 corporation, none involves so much fussing, so much anguish—and often so much pride of authorship—as the annual report to shareholders."[34] In short, the annual report can be considered the keystone of a company's financial relations program.

The Purpose of Annual Reports Fundamentally, the annual report fulfills the legal requirements of reporting to a company's stockholders. As such, it becomes the primary source of information about the company for current and potential stockholders, providing comprehensive information on the condition of the company and its progress (or lack thereof) during the previous year.

Some companies leave it at that. But nearly all major companies carry their annual reports considerably further, taking the opportunity to reinforce their credibility, establish their distinct identity, and build investor confidence, support, and allegiance. In this sense, the annual report becomes the company's calling card, a summary of what the company has done and what it stands for. By accident or by design, the report usually conveys much about the personality and quality of the corporation's management.

Some companies get further service from their annual reports by using them for marketing, public relations, and employee recruitment and orientation purposes. Most are on the World Wide Web for all the constituencies, from investors to reporters, that want to examine them. A report may also serve as an informational resource for financial advisers, a "backgrounder" for business editors, or even an educational tool for teachers, librarians, and students. General Motors uses its report to advertise its products. Goodyear produces a special edition for classroom use. Increasing numbers of companies produce special editions for employees to gain their loyalty and support, build morale by stressing their contributions, and improve their understanding of company operations.

Although accountants may decry verbal and pictorial embellishment of their ciphers, the communication opportunity presented by annual reports is too important to pass up. A few companies have toned down their documents, but annual reports are not likely to return to the minimum level of information required by the government.

Contents of Annual Reports The typical annual report consists of a cover; a president's letter; financial and nonfinancial highlights; a balance sheet and income statement; a description of the business (products and services); names and titles of corporate officers; names and affiliations of outside directors; location of plants, offices, and representatives; the address and telephone number of corporate headquarters; and reference to stock exchanges on which company stock is traded. The report may also include the company's history (particularly in anniversary issues), discussion of company policies, request for support of the company's stance on a political issue, results of stockholder surveys, and other reports or features. Figure 13.1 shows a sample of some annual reports.

Annual reports should always put corporate earnings in perspective and spell out prospects for the next year. They should answer these questions:

What is the major thrust of our company?
Where do we excel?
What are our weaknesses?
Why has the company performed as it has?
What are we doing about the future?

Financial highlights are a well-read aspect of annual reports. They generally include figures representing net sales, earnings before taxes, earnings after taxes, net earnings per common share, dividends per common share, stockholders' equity per common share, net working capital, ratio of current assets to current liabilities, number of common shares outstanding, and number of common stockholders. Other highlights include profit margin, percent return on stockholders' equity, long-term debt, and number of employees. Report designers are concerned not just with the numbers, but how they look. Financial data are most often integrated into the entire report and presented in interesting or unusual ways.

Herbert Rosenthal and Frank Pagani list eight elements of what they call "big league annual reports:"[35]

1. A meaningful or provocative pictorial cover
2. A well-designed format
3. Complete and understandable graphics
4. Unstilted photographs and artwork
5. Comprehensive text
6. Comparative figures
7. Tasteful presentation of products
8. Stylish printing

Annual reports come in a variety of styles.

Summary

Financial reporting has never been more important than it is today. This has been highlighted by the collapse of Enron and its lack of accurate financial information provided to the investing public and its employees.

Effective financial public relations is necessary to develop and maintain investor confidence. Relationships with the financial community are developed by strategically planning investor relations.

Well-planned financial relations programs help lower the cost of capital for businesses. To meet the legal guidelines of the SEC the company must provide prompt disclosure of corporate news that is significant to the financial community. But the corporation should go far beyond the minimum requirements. Good investor relations can help a company deal with hostile takeover attempts through tender offers or a proxy fight.

New technologies have provided an increasing array of tools for the financial public relations practitioner to communicate with its key audiences such as stockholders, financial analysts, and the financial media. Annual reports and annual stockholder meetings remain important investor relations functions, but additional tools including cable television, the Web, satellite interviews, and e-mail are becoming increasingly essential

For self-testing and additional chapter resources, go to the student CD and the Online Learning Center at **www.mhhe.com/lattimore**

to have an effective financial relations effort. This effort gives a business increased support for its management, higher stock prices, and greater ease in attracting new capital.

TurboBoosting Scios Inc.'s Reputation and Shareholder Value

Overview

A *Forbes* account of Scios, Inc., a biotech company, was not what the company management wanted to read. It depicted the 18-year-old company by calling it "the oldest biotech company in the world without an approved product." This came just before an FDA report that rejected the drug Natrecor, a product to combat heart failure, said it would need more research to show the drug was as good as intravenous nitroglycerin. With that announcement Scios stock dropped from $6 a share to $3.84 per share.

However, within a year and a half Scios was described by the *San Jose Mercury News* as being "like a phoenix that has risen from the ashes," as the stock had risen to $20 per share. Scios had been the beneficiary of a carefully executed and integrated communications program that focused on all key influencers in the health care, financial, and biotech industries.

Edelman Public Relations Worldwide, assisting Scios with a campaign entitled, "Project TurboBoost," used select news media, analyst sessions, and medical meetings as communication tactics to reach target audiences with strategic information on the restructuring of Scios and highly persuasive new Natrecor clinical trials that Scios thought would have positive results.

Goals

Three goals were set for the year 2000: (1) unlock the value of Scios's assets; (2) position the company as a capable player within the biotech industry; and (3) narrow the perception gap between what the company desired and what its target audiences perceived.

Strategies

Five basic communication strategies used were the following:

1. Re-launch Scios as a completely new company to new audiences.
2. Exploit business milestone achievement vigorously.
3. Plant first seeds of milestone achievement with key national media and stimulate broad-based support from other media.
4. Use third parties such as analysts and physician investigators to validate the Scios story.
5. Leverage value for all Scios pipeline activities and progress beyond Natrecor.

Tactics

Some of the tactics used to implement the strategies included the following:

1. Revising the company's investor audience presentation to portray a new, streamlined, focused company
2. Organizing more than 80 analyst and investor meetings
3. Leveraging scientific presentation to generate national publicity
4. Optimizing 11/15/00 American Heart Association–sponsored news conference that showcased the important data on Natrecor's role in heart failure therapy
5. Supporting Scios at prestigious biopharmaceutical investor meetings to the news media to increase Scios credibility
6. Issuing a video news release
7. Publicizing new key business partnerships for Scios
8. Publicizing new Natrecor application with FDA and all its research news, leading to major stories in publications such as *Investors Business Daily, BioWorld Today,* and *Genetic Engineering News* as well as numerous stories on Dow-Jones, Bloomberg, and Reuters.

Questions

1. What is the value of Scios's NASDAQ stock price today (NASDAQ: Scios)?
2. What would the value suggest about the long-term sustainability of the public relations effort by Edelman Worldwide?
3. Check the Scios Inc. web page at http://www.sciosinc.com to find out more information on Scios. Did the company get approval by the FDA for Natrecor? What effect, if any, do you think Project TurboBoost had on the FDA?
4. What evaluation techniques would you suggest for this campaign that was only measured in terms of increase of its stock price?
5. What public relations goals would you suggest at this point?

Source: PRSA Silver Anvil competition, 2001, Investor relations category.

Key Terms

Use the CD-ROM and Online Learning Center at www.mhhe.com/lattimore to further your understanding of the following terms

annual meetings
annual reports
conference call
financial analysts
financial press
financial public relations
Form 10-K
Form 10-Q
Form 8-K
investment conferences
proxy
tender offer
Securities and Exchange Commission (SEC)

Notes

1. Madeline Turnock, APR, "IR and PR Come Together," *Public Relations Strategist* 8, no. 2 (Spring 2002), pp. 13–14.
2. Eugene Miller, "Investor Relations," in *Lesly's Handbook of Public Relations and Communications,* 4th ed., ed. Philip Lesly (New York: AMACOM, 1991), pp. 164–65.
3. Richard Higgins, *Best Practices in Global Investor Relations* (Westport, CT: Quorum Books, 2000), p. xii.
4. Ibid.
5. Ibid., p. 15.
6. Arthur R. Roalman, ed., *Investor Relations Handbook* (New York: AMACOM, 1974), p. iii.
7. Higgins, p. 26.
8. "Xerox Settles SEC Enforcement Action Charging Company with Fraud," news release from SEC, 11 April 2002.
9. National Investor Relations Institute, "NIRI Ten Point Program to Help Restore Investor Confidence," NIRI Executive Alert press release, 9 April 2002, p. 1.
10. James B. Strenski, "The New SEC Regulations: Write in Plain English," *PR Tactics* (April 1998), p. 4.
11. Securities and Exchange Commission, *A Plain English Handbook: How To Create Clear SEC Disclosure Documents,* http://www.sec.gov/pdf/handbook.pdf, 9 June 2002.
12. NYSE Company Manual, 1 August 1977.
13. American Stock Exchange, "Part 4. Disclosure Policies" (last updated November 2000), http://www.amex.com/, 9 June 2002.
14. Henry Rockwell, "A Press Release Goes to Court," *Public Relations Journal* (October 1968).
15. G. Christman Hill, "Financial Public Relations Men Are Warned They're Liable for Clients' Puffery," *Wall Street Journal,* 16 March 1972, p. 30.
16. Jody Buffington Aud, "What Internal Communicators Can Learn from Enron," *Public Relations Strategist* 8, no. 2 (Spring 2002), p. 11.
17. Miller, p. 196.
18. Ibid.
19. Laura Johnston, "How to Succeed in a Close Proxy Vote," *Public Relations Quarterly* (Spring 1994), pp. 35–36.
20. Ibid.
21. "Investor Relations Pros Downplay PR Skills," *Communication World* (May 1983), p. 15.
22. Harrison T. Beardsley, "Problem-Solving in Corporate Financial Relations," *Public Relations Journal* (April 1978), p. 23.
23. Oscar M. Beveridge, *Financial Public Relations* (New York: McGraw-Hill, 1963), p. 68.
24. Stuart Weiss, "Hell Hath No Fury Like a Surprised Stock Analyst," *Business Week,* 21 January 1985, p. 98.
25. Holly Hutchins, "Annual Reports: Earning Surprising Respect from Institutional Investors," *Public Relations Review* (Winter 1994), p. 311.
26. Charles Nekvasil, "Getting the Most Out of Your Investor Relations Conference Calls," *PR Tactics* (August 1999), p. 10.
27. Stan Sauerhaft, "Won't Anybody Listen?" in Hill and Knowlton Executives, *Critical Issues in Public Relations* (Englewood Cliffs, NJ: Prentice-Hall, 1975), p. 37.
28. Higgins, p. 47.
29. Aud, p. 11.
30. G. A. Marken, "There's More to Being Public Than Being Listed," *Public Relations Quarterly* (Fall 1993), p. 44–45.
31. Tom Walker, "J. P. Stevens Fights Catholics' Proposal," *Atlanta Journal and Constitution,* 2 March 1980, p. 10.
32. Ibid.
33. Beveridge, p. 137.
34. Herbert E. Meyer, "Annual Reports Get an Editor in Washington," *Fortune,* 7 May 1979, p. 219.
35. Herbert C. Rosenthal and Frank Pagani, "Rating Your Annual Report," *Public Relations Journal* (August 1978), p. 12.

PART FOUR

The Practice

IV

Public relations serves all types of organizations. Governmental organizations and agencies, nonprofit organizations, and corporations have embraced public relations and set it to work, recognizing it as a means of increasing organizational effectiveness in a complex and changing environment.

To operate effectively within these organizations, the public relations practitioners must be thoroughly aware of all we have discussed to this point: the process of communication, the role of public relations in organizational decision making, the four-step public relations process, and the primary publics of public relations. Practitioners must also recognize the problems and publics that are specific to public relations in each organizational type.

In this section, we look first at the practice of public relations in three distinct types of organizations: Chapter 14, government; Chapter 15, nonprofit organizations; and Chapter 16, corporations. We conclude in Chapter 17 with a realistic look at emerging trends in public relations □

CHAPTER FOURTEEN

14

Public Affairs: Relations with Government

Outline

PREVIEW

Governmental activity at every level has tremendous daily impact—positive and negative—on every kind of organization in the United States. Public affairs units help organizations anticipate or respond to issues affecting their activities or environment, lobby public officials, build grassroots lobbying campaigns, and help shape public policy.

From the other side, government also has a public relations function. Governmental public relations plays a crucial role in keeping the public informed about issues, problems, and actions at all levels of government. Governmental public information officers seek citizen approval of government programs, help explain what citizens want from the government, strive to make government responsive to citizens' wishes, and attempt to understand and affect public opinion. Public relations operatives are pervasive in political campaigns, promoting both public understanding of candidates and candidates' understanding of publics □

"A popular government without popular information or the means of acquiring it is but a prologue to a farce, or a tragedy or perhaps both."
—James Madison, President

State revenues go down and universities suffer. A county budget passes, giving libraries and cultural centers a shot in the arm. A zoning hearing opens the way for a major new development. A tariff is enacted and an industry thrives. Changes in the federal tax code shift $100 billion in liabilities from wage earners to corporations. A local ordinance bans smoking in the workplace. The unwillingness of a local government to promote a bond issue makes a proposed museum seek another city in which to locate. A regulation is changed and a manufacturer goes out of business.

The list goes on and on. When organizations review the external forces that affect their operations, governmental bodies should be at the top of the list. Indeed, public opinion and media, employee, and community relations are considered important in part because of their potential influence on governmental action or inaction.

In this chapter we first examine the public affairs function of business and other organizations in their relationships with government at all levels. Then we look at the public affairs function from the point of view of governmental bodies with obligations to provide public information to many constituencies.

WHAT IS PUBLIC AFFAIRS?

Public affairs, a term sometimes used as a synonym for all of public relations, more often describes the aspect of public relations that deals with the political environment of organizations. Sometimes it is called *governmental relations.* Public affairs is related to issues management because through its relationship-building processes, it helps organizations anticipate or respond to issues affecting their activities. Public affairs efforts include seeking to shape public opinion and legislation, developing effective responses to matters of public concern, and helping the organization adapt to public expectations. Specifically, public affairs may be involved in monitoring public policy, providing political education for employees or other constituents, maintaining liaisons with various governmental units, and encouraging political participation. "Access to lawmakers and their staffs is without a doubt the most important aspect of public affairs work in Washington. Without access your message will not be heard."[1] As shown in figure 14.1, public affairs practitioners facilitate the two-way flow of information between an organization and its political environment.

Public affairs is a specialization of public relations that concerns building public policy relationships between organizations. To be successful, all organizations—businesses, nonprofits, and governments—must build governmental relationships and actively collaborate with those government contacts to influence public policies. The most prominent professional association of public affairs officers, the Public Affairs Council, defines public affairs as "used variously as a synonym for external affairs, government relations, and corporate communications. Most practitioners use public affairs as the name for the integrated department combining all, or virtually all, external noncommercial activities of the business world."[2]

Definitions of public affairs focus this specialization on the building of relationships in the public policy arena. John Paluszek, president of Ketchum public relations, defines public affairs as addressing public policy:

> Public affairs helps an organization develop and maintain quality relationships with the various groups of people ("publics") who can influence the future. Public affairs is the public relations practice that addresses public policy and the publics who influence such policy.[3]

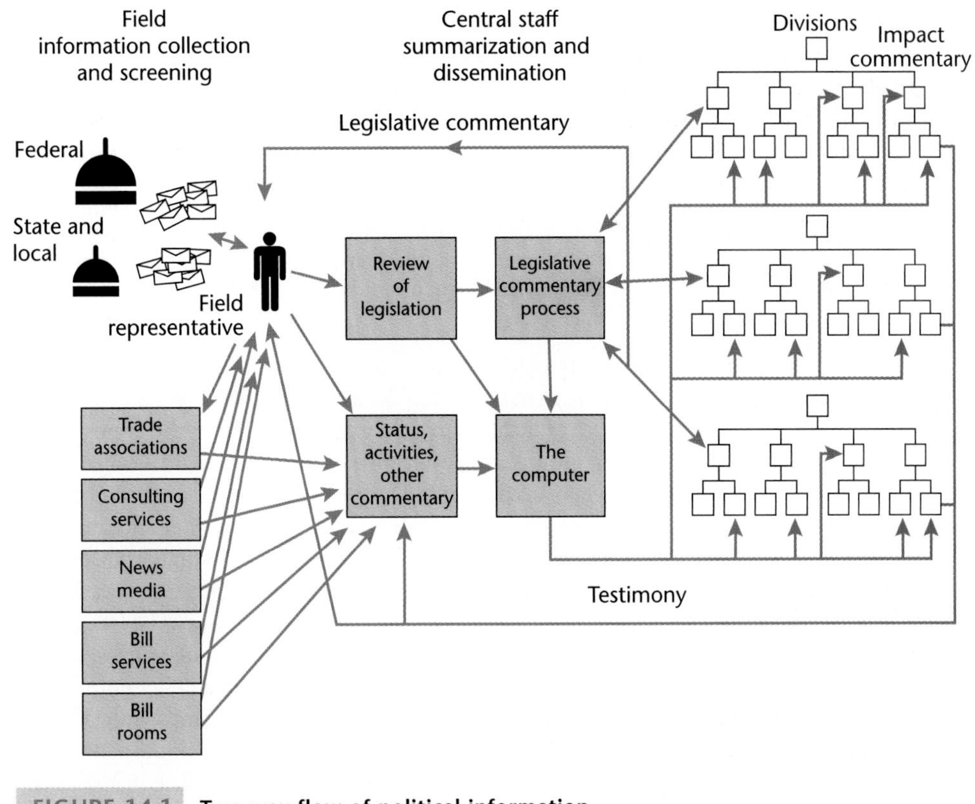

FIGURE 14.1 **Two-way flow of political information**

PUBLIC AFFAIRS FOR NOT-FOR-PROFIT ORGANIZATIONS

Unions, schools, hospitals, libraries, cultural organizations, foundations, businesses, and other organizations have both the problem and the opportunity of dealing with government. All want to improve communication with governmental agencies and employees, monitor and influence legislative and regulatory actions, encourage constituent participation, and expand the awareness and understanding of people in power.

These organizations realize that they can no longer even pretend to be above the political fray. Fundamentally, ours is a pluralistic society in which various interests compete in the political arena. Under these circumstances, nonprofit organizations recognize that their interests, indeed sometimes their survival, require political acumen and effort.

PUBLIC AFFAIRS IN BUSINESS

Because business practices public affairs most ardently and extensively, a deeper understanding of that function will give insight into how public affairs applies in all organizations. In relation to business and the economy, government now plays a variety of roles: stimulant, referee, rule maker, engineer, pursuer of social goals, defender, provider, customer, and controller. To be successful, business must be prepared to deal with government in any of these roles. That is the critical importance of governmental relations and why public affairs has become, in the last 20 years, a crucial dimension of public relations.

Government's enormous power and ability to take an active hand in business management are further pressures for corporate involvement. There are shifts in power from government to business, from business to activist groups, and back to government. Public affairs specialists assess and anticipate the possible interests that government will have on corporate activities. Sheila Tate, former George H. Bush press secretary, said:

> I recognized the shift in power 10 or 15 years ago when a merger was about to take place. All the two companies cared about was Wall Street. Then, at the end of the 1980s, and at the beginning of the 1990s, what happened was that Capitol Hill and the Department of Commerce, Justice and State became just as important and could derail a deal more quickly than Wall Street could.[4]

Not only does business have to detect shifts in public opinion and politics, it has to act quickly. At one time business merely reacted to the threat of government action, whether that action took the form of taxation, regulation, legislation, or the opposing efforts of labor, and public interest groups. However, corporate public affairs is called upon now to "run faster and jump higher," according to Doug Pinkham, head of the Public Affairs Council. Pinkham cites trends, such as the emergence of the Internet and other sophisticated communication tools that make business activities increasingly transparent. He cites the globalization of business, presenting such new public affairs issues as national differences in laws, customs, and political structures. See mini-case 14.1 as an example of proactive public affairs on the part of global chocolate manufacturers. Public affairs must also contend with public cynicism and mistrust of the business community.[5]

Business has realized the value of developing continuing relationships with government at all levels that permit early involvement in issues, policies, regulations, and legislation. Joseph Gleason, managing director of Manning, Selvage and Lee in Washington, says, "It's also important to develop relationships with policy-makers, many who know little about your client or organization prior to initial communication."[6] Advance notice can be a critical factor in political effectiveness. Moreover, early involvement makes provisions for crisis management less necessary when a critical bill comes to a vote later on.

The increasing importance of business public affairs and political activities has had substantial impact on management in general and public relations in particular. Because the issue is one of corporate control, top corporate leaders take an active role in public affairs efforts. Explains former congressman Donald G. Brotzman, past president of the Washington-based Rubber Manufacturers Association, "Involvement of top management is a most important principle. The chief executive officer and all top managers must be active participants. The direct and indirect influence of government action on business changes the kinds and mix of skills that one needs to succeed as a manager."[7] The effect on top management, he feels, is even more pronounced: "Top managers must now be as concerned about public policy as they are about anything else they do."[8]

PUBLIC AFFAIRS TASKS

Today no public relations program is complete unless it includes provisions for dealing with government. This job is, in part, a complex sequence of information acquisition, processing, and dissemination. Fact-finding and serving as a listening post may be the most important aspects of governmental relations.

After gathering information, governmental relations specialists weigh and evaluate its potential impact on the company or industry. Information is then disseminated to

Responsible Reaction to Highly Damaging Situation Gains Kudos for Chocolate Industry, Solves Problems

Mini•Case 14.1

Nike's and Kathie Lee's experiences with labor issues signaled for all organizations—global or otherwise—the need for (1) careful review of all aspects of the operation for potentially damaging activities, and (2) a more forthcoming response to identified problems. The world's chocolate industry has taken note of the latter as they deal with their own "slave" labor issue.

Two years ago, Kevin Bales, author of *Disposable People: New Slavery and the Global Economy,* and director of Free the Slaves (FTS)—the Washington, D.C., wing of the London-based Anti-Slavery International—brought a film crew into Africa. While there the crew found that 19 young men had escaped enslavement from a cocoa farm, and the report became part of their film. "The documentary was shown September 2000 in Great Britain. It launched a press inquiry—the industry had to respond."

"The chocolate industry was shocked by this," says Bales. As is often the response to bad news, there was denial, followed by confusion, anger, and despair. In England, execs from Nestlé, the British Cake, Chocolate, and Confectioners associations, and Cadbury and Roundtree candies met to decide what to do.

In the United States, the chocolate companies took the news very seriously and decided to take action. Their response was unprecedented. According to Bales, "Historically, companies would look at this and say, 'well this is happening in a foreign country, what can we do? If we don't buy from them, someone else will and we'll go out of business.' But the American chocolate industry didn't say that. They said, 'this is a serious matter. We have to do the right thing.'"

The Process of Responding

Despite the industry's good intentions, several months passed before a plan was put forth. "It is a *process,* not an event. It took quite of few months." Execs had to be made to understand that FTS wasn't attacking their industry, rather, "we were attacking *slavery* and asking them to join us, to look at this matter and see what their responsibilities are." Bales said it was imperative to get all of the companies "singing from the same song sheet." The following gave added impetus:

- *Legislation.* Senator Tom Harkin (D-Iowa) and Representative Eliot Engel (D-NY) wanted to put forward an amendment to a bill that, if passed, would have created chaos, says Bales. The amendment called for candy manufacturers to label products as free of child and slave labor. "This would have been impossible to achieve because there was no inspection system in place—it would have had a disastrous effect. But it helped everyone focus."
- *Stakeholders.* Chocolate Manufacturers Association, World Cocoa Foundation, Hersheys, M&M Mars, Nestlé, and other companies, as well as UN representative, government officials from the United States and the Ivory Coast, nongovernmental organizations, and other antislavery organization—all sat down to hammer out a protocol. "The protocol has some PR angles around it." The goal was to try to eradicate slavery on cocoa farms without administering a fatal shock to the industry. "They're doing a really good thing."

The industry is taking responsibility, notes Bales. It will spend millions to finance the following:

- *Independent research (industry funded but not controlled).* Research began last October to determine the extent of the problem. Research teams were dispatched to the fields, surveying farms to ensure that the crop is not picked by child slaves. "We should have results by month's end."
- *A charitable foundation.* This organization will work with child labor specialists and local advocacy groups on the Ivory Coast to improve labor practices and ensure compliance. "It will support other projects for the liberation of child laborers and all slaves."
- *An inspection and verification system.* "We have a model already in place—the rug mark which appears on hand woven rugs." Bales says an independent inspection guarantees that a rug with the mark was not woven by a child slave. He's not sure yet how this "mark" could be applied to cocoa.

"Now we can go to other industries that may fall prey to the same dilemma and help them before they have a pr problem," says Bales. "We will put the word out that we can help them with their problem before it becomes a crisis."

Source: *pr reporter,* 27 May 2002, pp. 1–2.

corporate decision makers, employees, stockholders, and the public. Indeed, public affairs has its greatest impact on an organization when it aids corporate planning. At the same time, government relations staffs convey information to legislators, regulators, congressional staffers, potential political allies, and the public.

Public relations is also sometimes called on to fight fire with fire on the governmental relations front. Investigation and publicity lack the force of law but are clearly among the weapons government uses to influence business. Leaks to the media by "high-level sources," visits to the sites of supposed infractions, staged public hearings, and the like may be used against business by government officials. Businesses' public

Anti–World Trade Organization protesters march in downtown Seattle.

affairs efforts must sometimes respond in kind. Their public relations specialists must compete with the public forums of government and the public relations operations of a variety of special interests. Honesty and forceful public communication is a crucial aspect of the government relations process.

UNDERSTANDING THE POLITICAL SYSTEM

To operate effectively, governmental relations professionals must thoroughly understand the United States's political process. In a general sense, political activities fall into three broad categories: electoral, legislative, and regulatory. Electoral activities involve the election of candidates favorable to an organization's interests and the development of plans for financially supporting selected political campaigns. Political action committees are the major vehicles for fund-raising efforts.

Legislative activities work to create or gain support for favorable legislation and build opposition against unfavorable activities. Lobbying is the major avenue for legislative activities.

The primary goal of regulatory activities from a public affairs point of view is to foster an understanding of the day-to-day problems of a particular organization or industry. Regulators are more difficult to lobby because they are rarely elected officials. Nonetheless, many public affairs efforts related to regulatory activity take a form quite similar to lobbying.

Electoral Activities

A few wealthy cattle ranchers, logging companies, and mining companies have used federal lands for tremendous gain while paying little to the government. Critics claim this usage has damaged the environment and cost the taxpaying public billions of dollars. When President Bill Clinton sent a bill to Congress in early 1993 to raise the rent for using federal lands, you would have thought it would easily pass. Not so. It was defeated soundly. Critics said this defeat was directly attributable to the $7million contributed to key congressmen by political action committees (PACs).[9]

Although political action is often thought of in electoral terms, most organizations actually place less emphasis on electing candidates than on working with the winner afterward. In 1974, however, the Federal Election Campaign Act legitimized the role of corporations and business-related groups in federal elections, greatly improving their position vis-à-vis labor and other special interests.[10] The law allowed the formation of business **political action committees (PACs).**

A PAC is a group of people who raise or spend at least $1,000 in connection with a federal election. The people belonging to a PAC usually have some common political concern, interest, or cause. To pool resources in support of favored candidates, PACs have been formed by unions, businesses, industry groups, church groups, professionals, and many others.

The objective of legislation allowing PACs was to reform campaign financing. Legal limits on and full disclosure of contributions are supposed to ensure fairness in the electoral process. However, numerous loopholes exist and have caused the concern that PACs may promote corruption or tip the political scales in favor of special interests. Some critics maintain that PACs are costly, time-consuming, and demeaning to candidates. Others say that since PACs multiply and therefore tend to neutralize one another, they should be abolished.

Supporters maintain that PACs are an example of citizens' rights to free speech, that they promote political awareness and involvement, and that they have brought campaign financing into the light. Table 14.1 shows the PACs that made the largest contributions to the 2000 election campaigns.

The money generated by corporate PACs goes to politicians of divergent views. The American Trucking Association PAC has given almost exclusively to incumbents regardless of party. Coca-Cola and Grumman PACs have favored Democratic incumbents. Ford and General Motors have tended to give to both incumbents and challengers. Amoco and Corning Glass Works have favored Republicans. "Overall, business-related PACs split their donations about equally between Democrats and Republicans with most of the money going to senior incumbents in both parties."[11]

TABLE 14.1 Largest PACs in 2000

1.	Realtors Political Action Committee	$3.42 million
2.	Association of Trial Lawyers of America Political Action Committee	$2.66 million
3.	American Federation of State County & Municipal Employees People, Qualified	$2.59 million
4.	Dealers Election Action Committee of the National Automobile Dealers Association (NADA)	$2.50 million
5.	Democrat Republication Independent Voter Education	$2.49 million
6.	International Brotherhood of Electrical Workers Committee on Political Education	$2.46 million
7.	Machinists Non-Partisan Political League	$2.18 million

Source: Federal Trade Commission.

Corporate PACs get their money from their employees or stockholders. Other PACs get funds from their members or constituencies. Thus, if a PAC is to be effective, it "must first educate its people and motivate them to participate."[12]

Some have charged that PACs attempt to "buy" political officials or unduly influence legislators in relation to pet issues. Senator Edward Kennedy has claimed that PACs "are doing their best to buy every senator, every representative, and every issue in sight."[13] Typically, PACs contribute to candidates whose philosophies are consistent with their own. One PAC official explained that his group has two tests for campaign contributions: Is the candidate someone we agree with, and is it someone in the area of government that relates to how we do business? Consequently, a senator on the banking committee gets contributions from bank PACs, and one on the agriculture committee receives funds from the Associated Milk Producers.

What PACs typically seek is access. That is why funds more often flow to incumbents. PACs are so eager to back winners, they often do so retroactively—making contributions after the election is over. Funds contributed after the election are called "hundred percent money," meaning none is wasted on losers. Many PACs switch sides after the votes are counted. When Senator Charles Hecht (R-Nevada) upset incumbent Howard Cannon, postelection contributions came from former opponents including the American Dental Association, the American Banking Association, and McDonald's Corporation. The National Association of Realtors kicked into Hecht's campaign chest after opposing him in the primary and the general election. In many cases, PAC funds are used to keep from making enemies.

Because a PAC contribution may be as much as $10,000 per election, the gift generally helps open the door to a legislator's office. Indeed, the most important outcome of electoral contributions is to obtain access to legislators and gain influence on legislative activities.

Legislative Activities

Most political decisions important to organizations are made long after elections are over. Consequently, business firms and other organizations concentrate their efforts on affecting legislation and regulation in relevant areas. These activities are known as **lobbying.**

Lobbying has been defined as "the practice of trying to influence governmental decisions, particularly legislative votes, by agents who serve interest groups."[14] Lobbying is an extensive and expensive activity. Although the term has acquired an unsavory connotation of graft and influence peddling, lobbying has long been recognized as a legitimate practice. James Madison, writing in 1788, held that an essential characteristic of a representative democracy is that the various interest groups in society are permitted to compete for the attention of government officials.

Today, lobbyists are likely to be very carefully selected professionals who have business acumen, a thorough grasp of sometimes highly technical information, and lots of political savvy. Henry Ford II sums up the new attitude: "The problem with 'lobbying' activities is not to conceal their existence, nor to apologize for them, but to make sure they are adequate, effective and impeccably correct in conduct."[15]

What do lobbyists do? Many things. They inform corporate executives about developments in legislation, report on the introduction and progress of specific bills, offer or arrange testimony to congressional committees, file statements, communicate with legislators, analyze policies and legislation, inform legislators about the potential effect of legislation, educate legislators about business and economics, help draft laws, publicize testimony, and develop strategy to support or oppose specific legislation.

Lobbyists dig out information from officials and records, then use it to inform corporate executives, persuade government officials, promote or oppose legislation or other governmental action, and obtain governmental cooperation. Lobbyists devote much time to creating contacts and programs that will improve communication with government, and to monitoring legislators' activities regarding statutes and laws.

Lobbyists involve themselves in the earliest stages of the legislative process. Recognizing that lobbying can only work while the legislator is still in the decision-making stage, lobbyists provide information before bills are drawn up. Their emphasis is on information and advocacy, not pressure. Lobbyists seek to define issues in terms of the legislators' constituencies and the public interest, providing briefly stated, neatly organized facts that answer questions. Often, they must communicate through a legislator's staff or assistants.

Facts must be presented in a truthful, straightforward, and helpful fashion. Honesty is essential because credibility is the lobbyist's most important asset. Lobbyists who have achieved credibility are relied on by senators, representatives, and their staffs. When such relationships are established, the lobbyist is in a position to suggest legislation, prepare speeches, line up witnesses for congressional hearings, and provide research and position papers. Under such circumstances, it is difficult to tell where legislator leaves off and lobbyist begins.

Perhaps even more important than establishing the order of the staff is establishing an order of issues. Legislative battles must be carefully chosen and related to the overall objectives of the corporation.

Politicking from the Grass Roots

In a democracy, the attempt to influence government occurs in the context of public opinion and requires dealing with an audience much broader than political officials. This broader audience is reached through **grassroots lobbying** and issue advertising. As we have mentioned in other chapters, businesses increasingly seek to organize employees, stockholders, community leaders, and others as potent weapons in the political arena. Washington lobbyists must demonstrate that their positions are those of the congressman's or congresswoman's constituents. To accomplish this, the constituents must be organized to make their voices heard.

According to *Business Week,* "The wedding of lobbying and PR makes sense . . . because of the increasing need to win public support for their causes."[16] Top lobbyist Charles E. Walker maintains, "Lobbying has come to require strong grass roots efforts. . . . I go to a congressman and he tells me 'You can sell me if you can sell my constituents.'"[17]

Different constituents can be mobilized to communicate in a variety of ways. The grassroots approach may consist of flooding Congress with mail or getting the right people to call their representatives. Grassroots lobbying means establishing an organization at the local level by which support can be activated when needed. The Associated General Contractors, for instance, maintain a legislative network among their 113 chapters across the country. At least one person in each chapter personally knows his or her senator or representative. On one occasion, this network was invaluable in defeating a labor law reform bill.

The American Bankers Association (ABA) asks legislators which bankers they want to hear from. Then the ABA asks those bankers to transmit the ABA's position on specific legislation. The ABA has 1,200 designated contact bankers, many of whom know members of Congress, have served as campaign treasurers, or have worked on campaigns.

Issue advertising (or **advocacy advertising**) is a way of taking an organization's position straight to the people, with the anticipation that they will support it politically.

This kind of advertising is not new. Organized labor, private voluntary groups, governmental agencies, and others have long used advertising to support their positions on public issues. Mobil Corporation is perhaps the nation's leading issue advertiser. Under its vice president of public affairs, Herbert Schmertz, Mobil pioneered corporate advocacy.

Regulatory Activities

In an era of governmental growth, government regulation is the area in which the most dramatic expansion has occurred. During the 1970s, the years of greatest growth in government regulations, 22 new regulatory agencies were created, including the powerful Environmental Protection Agency (EPA), the Consumer Product Safety Council (CPSC), and the Occupational Safety and Health Administration (OSHA). A total of 120 major regulatory laws were passed during the decade.

"We have become a government, not of laws passed by elected officials . . . but a government of regulation," claimed former Congressman Elliott H. Levitas (D-Ga.). "A Congress . . . will enact 500 laws during its two-year tenure. During that . . . time, the bureaucracies will issue 10,000 rules and regulations."[18]

Almost every facet of business activity is subject to the rules, standards, or other controls of one or more federal agencies that have the power to review, inspect, modify, or even reject the work of private industry.

State and Local Public Affairs

Traditionally, most attention has been paid to interaction with government at the federal level, but the relative importance of local and state governments has recently increased for organizations of many types. Although builders and developers have long sought to influence local zoning decisions, for example, the players in local and state government affairs are now more numerous and more intense.

Deregulation, federal budget cutbacks, and the Reagan administration's determination to return government to the people have forced state and local governments to pick up the slack. As a result, state officials are now dealing more extensively with environmental issues, labor legislation, bank deregulation, and international trade. Moreover, state and local funding in the areas of the arts, transportation programs, health care, education, and others has become more critical. Naturally, both profit-seeking and not-for-profit organizations have increasingly focused on the 50 state capitals, in addition to Washington, D.C.

Covering 50 cities is more difficult, complex, and expensive than merely focusing on Washington. "In a two-year period almost 250,000 bills are introduced in the various state legislatures. For a company with nationwide interests this volume appears to create an insurmountable obstacle."[19] To deal with this insurmountable obstacle some companies have established their own networks of private legislative information in all 50 state capitals. Others have monitored only those states where they have a major interest. Another approach has been to rely on the industry's association to do its surveillance and lobbying efforts for them. Often companies use a combination of all of these efforts.

When national organizations seek to influence local affairs, they must understand local politics and culture. A major New York corporation dealing with a tax problem in a southern state got an audience with the chairman of the state senate's tax writing committee. After an informative and persuasive 30-minute presentation, the senator asked, "Y'all aren't from around here, are you?"[20]

Staying on top of issues, tracking bills, knowing the right people, knowing which PACs to contribute to, cultivating the right media contacts, and all the other necessary lobbying activities may be approached in a variety of ways. Generally, goals and objectives, the scope of the effort, and key states must be identified. The corporation or association may then set up its own in-house operation, employ outside lobbyists or consultants on a retainer basis, or depend on industry or state business associations. The national interests, which prevailed, used a combination of in-house lobbyists and an industry association.

Internal Political Communication

We have already discussed PACs as a means of promoting employee and shareholder awareness and involvement. Beyond PAC activities, however, a public relations practitioner whose position requires monitoring government relations can also use in-house publications and other media to provide political instruction, increase employee awareness of political issues, and encourage employee political involvement.

Organizations stimulate employees' political awareness in a variety of ways. Bliss and Laughlin Industries of Oak Brook, Illinois, provides work sheets with employees' W-2 forms so employees can calculate how much of their wages have gone to taxes, what percentage of income goes to taxes, and how long each must work to support the cost of government. The employees have learned that their biggest expense is not shelter or food, but taxes.

Dow Chemical maintains an extensive public affairs program for employees. The program rests on four objectives:

1. Informing employees about national and local issues that potentially affect the firm
2. Making employees aware of governmental processes and legislative procedures
3. Encouraging employees to take part in the political process and giving specific examples of approaches they might use
4. Advising employees of the value of political contributions and providing the opportunity to do so through political action committees

Budd Company gives its managers a "discretionary bonus" of up to several thousand dollars based on evaluation in 11 categories, including "involvement in government affairs." Managers are judged on their ability to get their people involved in political campaigns, their willingness to write to government officials on issues affecting the company, and their ability to organize in-plant political education committees. All of these companies recognize that if business intends to remain a viable part of society, its leaders must encourage employee participation in the political process.

On the other side of public affairs efforts by nonprofits and businesses is the public information function of government itself. While the practitioners who deal with government are most likely to be called public affairs specialists, the governmental public affairs or public relations personnel are most likely to be called public information officers. In the remainder of the chapter we look at the task of the public information practitioner for government itself.

GOVERNMENTAL PUBLIC AFFAIRS

The framers of the U.S. Constitution believed that the American people were capable of governing themselves. To do so, however, citizens needed to be fully informed about issues and problems confronting them and actions taken by their government. Despite their belief, the founding fathers provided no specific means to disseminate information or any assurance that citizens would be kept informed. It was assumed that government would maintain open communications channels with the public and provide sufficient information to enable citizens to make intelligent decisions about its policies and activities.

To a certain extent, these ideals have been realized through a system that evolved in response to public needs. The mass media struggle to serve our right to know. In providing information to the public about governmental affairs, they draw on the public relations arm of government—local, state, and federal—that offers the media a constant flow of information.

Governmental public relations practitioners are often called **public information officers (PIOs),** suggesting that they simply transmit information in an objective and neutral fashion. In fact, they are no more neutral or objective than public relations professionals working in the private sector.

Because the success and stability of democratic governments are ultimately determined by continuous citizen approval, PIOs seek to ensure such approval. The democratic system implies that government will respond to the wishes of the governed, so PIOs work to determine those wishes, then strive to make government responsive to them. Because public opinion provides the climate in which public officials, agencies, and institutions succeed or fail, PIOs try to understand and affect public opinion. A multitude of institutional interests coexist in any society, so public relations practitioners both inside and outside government represent a similar variety of perspectives. As a consequence, much of the significant dialogue needed to ensure democracy's proper functioning is generated, molded, and enunciated by public relations practitioners.

In short, in government—as in any other organization—public relations is a management function that helps define objectives and philosophies while also helping the organization adapt to the demands of its constituencies and environments. Public relations practitioners, whether referred to as PIOs, **public affairs officers (PAOs),** press secretaries, or just plain administrative aides, still communicate with all relevant internal and external publics to make organizational goals and societal expectations consistent. Public information officers, like their counterparts in business and industry, develop, execute, and evaluate programs that promote the exchange of influence and understanding among an organization's constituent parts and publics.

Of course, because they work in a different context with different constraints and problems, government public relations specialists operate somewhat differently from their private sector counterparts. Public information officers face unique problems. Their mission and legitimacy are questioned more extensively. Their constituents are forced to provide financial support through taxation. Red tape, internal bureaucratic situations, and political pressures hinder their efforts. Career development opportunities are limited.

Background of Public Relations in American Government

In 1913 the U.S. Civil Service Commission announced an examination for a "Publicity Expert." On October 22 of that year, Congress passed the Gillett Amendment (38 U.S.C. 3107) that stated: "No money appropriated by any act shall be used for the compensation of any publicity expert unless specifically appropriated for that purpose."

Despite the law, the governmental public relations function continued. Most notable among government's early public relations endeavors was George Creel's World War I Committee on Public Information.

Public relations in the federal government came of age during the New Deal, when the creation of the so-called alphabet agencies "precipitated a flood tide of publicists

Pentagon spokeswoman Victoria Clarke along with Gen. Stanley McChrystall brief the media about the Iraqi situation.

into the channels of government."[21] The Office of War Information, created during World War II, gave further federal support to the profession. When the war was over, it became the United States Information Agency (USIA). During the late 1940s, public relations activity was increasingly evident in state and local government. By 1949 nearly every state had established a state-supported public relations program to attract both tourism and industry. Since 1970 at least 20 new federal regulatory agencies have been created. All of them have extensive public information programs.

Importance and Scope of Governmental Public Relations

Despite the limits placed on public relations activity by Congress, government publicity has always been necessary, if for no other reason than to tell citizens what services are available and how to use them. With the developing complexity of government has come a corresponding increase in publicity.[22]

Ron Levy, counselor to government communicators, argues that government needs to do a better job giving the public more information about what government literature is available, what services are available, and where to write for specific government information materials. He says government communicators also should give wider dissemination for speeches by government leaders.[23]

It is impossible to estimate the number of people involved or the money spent in governmental public relations. As William Gilbert states: "If you are in government, you are in public relations. . . . (There is a) public relations element in all the things . . . government . . . does."[24]

Governmental public information or relations became increasingly important after the terrorist attacks of September 11, 2001. Victoria Clarke, assistant secretary of defense for public affairs, has led the change from a public information service to working strategically to build alliances and relationships, seeking to engage not only the media but also religious leaders, education leaders, communities—a wider range of audiences. She stated:

> If you are going to do public affairs in the 21st century, you've got to do more than react to the 10,000 media hits every day. That's largely what I did. . . . That, in and of itself, is a high challenge. But, my challenge is to transform the public affairs department overall. . . . If you want support for a strong defense or a different defense, if you want support over the long haul, you're going to have to engage a wider range of audiences.[25]

Function of Governmental Public Relations

Governmental PIOs, like any other public relations practitioners, seek to achieve mutual understanding between their agencies and publics by following a strategic public relations process. They must gauge public opinion, plan and organize for public relations effectiveness, construct messages for internal and external audiences, and measure the effectiveness of the entire process.

Like all organizational boundary spanners, PIOs jointly serve two masters—their publics and their employers. On the one hand, they provide the public with complete, candid, continuous reporting of government information and accessible channels for citizen inputs. On the other hand, the late public relations educator Scott Cutlip maintained:

> The vast government information machine has as its primary purpose advancement of government's policies and personnel . . . the major objective is to gain support for the incumbent administration's policies and maintain its leaders in power.[26]

Hess found that press officers were trusted neither by the media nor by their own superiors. Because they are suspect in the eyes of their own political executives, according to Hess, "The career press officer is often the odd person out in the permanent bureaucracy."[27]

Public information officers serve neither master very well, as evidenced by millions of Americans viewing their "government as distant and unresponsive, if not hostile."[28] Both the public and the politicians might be better served if PIOs could provide more active input for governmental decision makers. In his seminal 1947 report, *Government and Mass Communication*, Zachariah Chafee, Jr., held that:

> Government information can play a vital role in the cause of good administration by exploring the impact of new social forces, discovering strains and tensions before they become acute, and encouraging a positive sense of unity and national direction.[29]

The most basic functions of governmental public relations are to help define and achieve government program goals, enhance the government's responsiveness and service, and provide the public with sufficient information to permit self-government. The goal of PIOs is to promote cooperation and confidence between citizens and their government. This, in turn, requires governmental accessibility, accountability, consistency, and integrity.

Practice of Governmental Public Relations

The practice of public relations in government is much like that in other institutions, but governmental PIOs do face some difficulties unique to their area. Because they are paid with public funds, their mission and legitimacy are questioned more than in private organizations. Gilbert points out that "the citizenry . . . regards government public information activities as wasteful of the taxpayers' money and essentially propagandistic."[30] This is why the Gillett Amendment has never been repealed and why governmental public relations practitioners ply their trade under euphemisms like "information officer," "public affairs officer," or "education officer."

Unlike the customers of corporations, the constituents of governmental entities are forced to support those entities financially through taxes. Thus, while government may be responsive to political forces, it is not directly responsive to market forces. "Government red tape" has become a sadly accurate cliché and a serious public relations problem.

David Brown points out other problems of PIOs: internal bureaucratic situations that hinder professional efforts, weak job standards, political pressure, and little career development or recognition. Moreover, he states, government public relations specialists are considered "after-the-fact operators, expected to put out fires started by others or to implement information about programs that we strongly feel will not stand the muster of the media."[31] Increases in the complexity of government policies, rules, and practices; the widening chasm between citizens and their government; and the escalation of demands made by citizens without understanding the political, legal, and financial constraints placed on government are additional difficulties PIOs face.

To deal with these problems, PIOs may adopt several strategies. First, they should strive to be generalists in both public relations and management skills while becoming expert in the language and discipline of particular fields within government (health, education, transportation, welfare, defense, etc.).

Second, PIOs should practice preventative maintenance, providing policy guidance before programs are approved. This requires them to enter government's management mainstream. Third, governmental PIOs must develop a service orientation—responding to a public composed of consumers of government services. Moreover, public relations should foster this perspective in all government employees, using established channels of internal communication.

Fourth, governmental PIOs should concentrate on inputs as much as outputs. As Rabin suggests, "The proverbial general audience . . . will be identified more and more as a consumer public."[32] This calls for getting direct feedback through citizen participation, surveys and questionnaires, and community meetings that will be used to adjust programs, messages, and media.

Finally, as the downfall of the Nixon administration so aptly demonstrated, great hazards confront governmental attempts to hide failures, ineptitude, or mistakes. Openness is essential to effective governmental public relations.

In the state of Washington many children were without health care services. The government stepped in with a program called, "Healthy Kids Now!" to provide these services and a public information campaign to get them covered. See mini-case 14.2.

Using the Internet

Using technology to communicate with the publics has become popular with government public relations because it is a relatively inexpensive two-way communication tool that can be used on low operating budgets prevalent in governmental public relations.

Government agency home pages often contain full-color photos or graphics and text that can be designed like a brochure or newsletter. They also provide an alternative to printing large documents. For example, census data can be downloaded from the U.S. Census Bureau's website immediately without having to order a publication, pay for it,

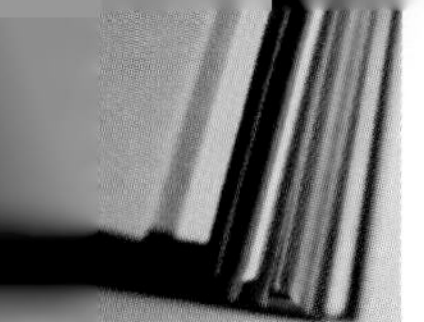

14.2 Mini•Case

Healthy Kids Now! Outreach Campaign for Children Without Health Insurance

Approximately 100,000 children in the state of Washington were without health insurance. These children often were without access to health care services. School was a problem for many because of time lost, inability to concentrate, and other problems that result from lack of health care. Some children were suffering lifelong impairment while others were actually dying for failing to have a life-threatening condition identified in time.

The Washington state legislature launched the Children's Health Insurance Program (CHIP) to provide low-cost health care coverage to children under 19 whose household income falls up to 250 percent of the federal poverty level, making many working families eligible. In order for these children to benefit from the legislation, families needed to learn about this new program and submit an application. Stigmas attached to government programs, myths about those who are enrolled in state medical programs, and a complex application system created barriers for families to apply.

To increase enrollment in all children's medical programs, the state hired DHC in partnership with HIP, a Spokane-based outreach project. To do this effectively, the state health department had to dispel myths about government programs, encourage collaboration among competing advocacy groups who normally did not work together, introduce private marketing tactics to resistant, budget-conscious government workers, and make boring government health insurance information and a complex application process appealing to consumers.

The "Healthy Kids Now!" campaign was designed using consumer, advocate, and national best practice research. At each step of the process, messages and concepts were tested with members of the target audience to ensure effectiveness. The strategies that were developed combined the best of grassroots outreach tactics with private sector advertising and marketing tactics.

The result has been a unique and successful marketing campaign—increasing enrollment in children's medical programs by 40,000 since the campaign's launch in February 2000 and, more important, ensuring children have good access to health care. The objectives and strategies of the campaign were the following.

Objectives

1. Create awareness about the availability of free and low-cost health insurance for uninsured Washington children.
2. Increase enrollment in state-sponsored children's medical programs.

Strategies

Basing the program content and implementation on key research findings the following strategies were developed:

1. De-emphasize the government nature of these programs to help break down enrollment barriers.
2. Redesign the existing complex DSHS-MAA children's medical benefits application to a shorter, more user-friendly application form.
3. Make the application process short and easy.
4. Gain input from key audiences through use of a voluntary advisory council composed of diverse advocates.
5. Rely on trusted local outreach workers to provide one-on-one interaction with consumers and support their efforts through a broad-based statewide marketing campaign.
6. Develop collateral and promotional materials that resemble commercial insurance programs to help remove stigma barriers.
7. Design and implement a multimedia PSA campaign to reach target audiences and support local efforts.
8. Utilize earned media coverage to put a face on the issue and dispel myths.
9. Assist families in applying for these programs by establishing and maintaining a toll-free hotline that helps to link families with resources in their local community.
10. Establish a consumer-friendly umbrella identity and brand for state-sponsored children's medical programs.

Evaluation

The Healthy Kids Now! campaign was extremely successful and resulted in continued funding for fiscal year 2001. Refinements continue to be made to the campaign based on research and ongoing assessment of strategies and tactics. Results to date are as follows:

1. Forty thousand more children have been enrolled in children's medical programs and now have access to health care.
2. Over 11,306 calls have been received by the hotline.

Source: PRSA Silver Anvil Award Winners 2001, http://www.prsa.org.

and wait weeks for it to arrive. Government websites range from the White House to local city and county ones such as one in Hennepin County, Minnesota. Almost all city governments from large to small cities have websites serving a public information function.

Websites can accomplish several objectives:

1. *Communicating with the Public.* With the Web you can bypass the media. The website can supplement your media relations efforts and may eventually replace much of the media effort.

2. *Communicating with Researchers, Activists, Specialists, and Journalists.* People will use your site for information they need.
3. *Distributing Large Volumes of Information.* The web user can pick and choose what he or she wants from the information provided. A good website, though, routes users to information that interests them.
4. *Publicizing Anything from a New Policy to an Upcoming Event.* A website is accessible all over the world, and it can be updated easily. You can also use other forms to invite the public to your website.
5. *Soliciting Public Comment.* The Web provides a two-way communication medium. You can build in an e-mail option with a click of the mouse.[33]

Public Relations and Political Campaigns

Government really cannot be discussed without recognizing its political context. While it provides many and diverse services to its constituents, government's policies are guided by politics. The political campaign is the most overt expression of politics. Public relations activity on behalf of political candidates is practically synonymous with the campaign itself.

Political campaigning is a nonstop industry, raising hundreds of millions of dollars from PACs and spending that money to attract votes. Public relations plays a critical role in both raising and spending those funds.

The public relations practitioner in the political campaign is not just a spokesperson to the media, but usually also a trusted adviser who helps formulate campaign strategy and positions on issues. Gaining votes first requires gaining funds, media exposure, and volunteers. Public relations practitioners work hard to attract all three. These resources must then be converted into political support. All of this activity is designed to get the candidate elected so that he or she can become a part of the governing process. Campaign press aides to successful candidates often become public information officers for the successful candidate.

Summary

The public affairs function of business and nonprofit organizations has increased in importance at the start of the new century. Whether it be corporations listed on the New York Stock Exchange or the American Red Cross, their employees, volunteers, and communities are demanding government intervention and leadership. Businesses and nonprofits seek to reach global markets and supporters, requiring increased knowledge of how to build relationships with different governmental laws, customs, and regulations.

From the government's perspective, public relations has become as critical to governmental organizations as it is to other institutions. Governmental activities depend on public opinion that is informed and involved in public policy. Citizens have still to understand the strategic role of governmental public affairs and information. Governmental public relations specialists can help to build support for its role by establishing their own professional practices and standards.

For self-testing and additional chapter resources, go to the student CD and the Online Learning Center at **www.mhhe.com/lattimore**

To learn more about public affairs watch the interviews with Ann Forristall and John Paluszek of Ketchum public relations, on Clips #11 and 13, on the book's CD-ROM.

Case Study

The Enron Scandal Impacts Every Aspect of PR—Part 2

The cozy relationship between Enron and the George W. Bush administration, and the fact that Enron was such a large campaign contributor (to both parties), is already bringing renewed pressure for campaign finance reform and is raising broader issues about the future of public affairs—with heightened public cynicism about the role of corporations in formulating public policy a likely outcome.

"Enron will cause politicians to more carefully scrutinize those who curry political favor," says Tom Goodwin, president of Step One Communications. "Politicians who assert that Enron didn't 'get' anything in exchange for its money are disingenuous. It did. It got to be left alone. The flow of cash anesthetized Washington to concerns that would have arisen had congressional and regulatory oversight responsibilities not lapsed so thoroughly."

The fact that campaign finance reform advocates were able to force a vote in the House "suggests that its day is near," says Goodwin. "Even if opponents succeed in delaying reform this spring, this issue continues an inexorable, steady trend upward. Do not be surprised if George W. Bush ultimately facilitates its enactment—much as 'only Nixon could have opened China.'"

But for now, at least, the administration is stonewalling, refusing to disclose details of its dealing with Enron, using executive privilege as a constitutional protection against self-incrimination. It is unlikely that the Enron scandal will significantly harm the president's sky-high approval ratings as long as he continues to wage his war on terrorism, but the administration's recalcitrance will undoubtedly drag scandal out longer and focus more attention on the kind of deals that get done behind closed doors by corporate lobbyists.

"I don't believe the Enron scandal signals the end of public affairs in our time," says Craig Martin, managing director of the Washington, D.C., office of Ruder Finn. "Enron isn't the first company to throw major dollars and resources at politicians, and it won't be the last. In this case, however, there are two converging influences that are likely to bring about a change in public affairs practices: first, an angry and increasingly empowered constituent base; and second, an ill-timed claim of executive privilege. Because of these factors, I think it will act as a catalyst for a change in emphasis and transparency within the profession."

If campaign finance reform measures are enacted, that could mean a windfall for public affairs practitioners, some observers suggest.

"Clearly the calls for increased transparency and stricter regulation will only grow louder," says Jody Powell, president of Weber Shandwick Worldwide's Powell Tate subsidiary. "The debate over specifics in these areas will involve a host of interests with a need for legal, government relations, and public affairs counsel." And if campaign finance reform is enacted and it does decrease the impact of cash contributions on the policy-making process, good public affairs counsel "will become even more valuable to those who wish to make their views known on matters that affect them."

"The future of public affairs lies in focusing on those very folks whose retirement savings went up in flames along with Enron," says Martin. "Specifically, grassroots mobilization and constituent-focused outreach will play an even more critical role in public affairs—advancing on pure government relations and traditional lobbying. Backroom discussions will continue to be a part of the public affairs mix, but will no longer be the focal point of the public affairs strategy. There will be a new sense of transparency in the conduct of public affairs, and thus a greater degree of public involvement.

"Messaging will need to change as well. The argument that 'what's good for General Motors is good for the country' won't work today, and will need to be expressed in more populist terms."

"The right to try to influence public policy is enshrined in our constitution," says Powell. "It is one of the more important rights we enjoy. We can and should be attentive to the need to correct abuses and inequities. The attempts of citizens to influence public policy, particularly through open public debate—read public affairs—it a pretty good definition of the democratic process."

Questions

1. How did the Enron scandal change the way public affairs is viewed?
2. How will PAOs have to change their roles?
3. Will government's PIOs have new roles as a result of the Enron scandal?

Key Terms

grassroots lobbying
issue advertising (advocacy advertising)
lobbying
political action committees (PACs)
public affairs
public information officers/public affairs officers (PIOs/PAOs)

Use the CD-ROM and Online Learning Center at www.mhhe.com/lattimore to further your understanding of the following terms

Notes

1. "Winning in Washington Takes Luck As Well As Skill," *Public Relations Journal* (February 1994), p. 6.
2. "Public affairs: Its Origin, Its Present, and Its Trends," Public Affairs Council. Accessed at http://www.pac.org/whatis/index.htm, 2001.
3. John L. Paluszek. "Editorial Note: Defining Terms." In *Practical Public Affairs in an Era of Change: A Communications Guide for Business, Government, and College,* ed. Lloyd B. Dennis (Lanham, MD: University Press of America), p. xvii.
4. Sheila Tate, as quoted in Elizabeth Howard, "Capital Gains: Public Relations Inside the Beltway," *The Strategist* (Summer 2002), p. 7.
5. Douglas G. Pinkham, "Corporate Public Affairs: Running Faster, Jumping Higher," *Public Affairs Quarterly* 43, no. 2 (Summer 1998), p. 33.
6. "Winning in Washington Takes Luck As Well As Skill," *Public Relations Journal* (February 1994), p. 6.
7. Starling, *Changing Environment of Business,* 2nd ed. (Boston: Kent, 1984), p. 96.
8. Ibid., p. 516.
9. Herbert Buchsbaum, "Money Talks, Lobbying in Congress," *Scholastic Update,* 5 November 1993, p. 10.

10. Edward M. Epstein, "An Irony of Electoral Reform," *Regulation* (May/June, 1979).
11. Ibid., p. 5.
12. Edie Fraser, *PACs: The Political Awakening of Business* (Washington, DC: Fraser & Associates, 1980), p. 2.
13. Ibid., p. 15.
14. Starling, p. 531.
15. "The Swarming Lobbyists," *Time,* 7 August 1978, p. 17.
16. Christine Dugas, "Now, Madison Avenue Runs Straight to Capitol Hill," *Business Week,* 4 August 1986, pp. 27–28.
17. Ibid., p. 28.
18. Elliot H. Levitas, "Bureaucracy Stifling America's Right to Self-Govern," *Atlanta Business Chronicle,* 9 June 1980, p. 4.
19. Richard A. Armstrong, "Working with State Government," in *Lesly's Handbook of Public Relations and Communication* (New York: AMACOM, 1991), p. 99.
20. *Parade* magazine, 9 November 1986, p. 8.
21. Wlliam H. Gilbert, ed., *Public Relations in Local Government* (Washington, DC: International City Management Association, 1975), p. 9.
22. Ibid., p. 8.
23. Ronald Levy, "New Realities in Government Communications," *Government Communication* (November 1995), pp. 8–9.
24. Ibid., p. 5.
25. Victoria Clarke, "Life at the Pentagon," *The Strategist* 8, no. 3 (Summer 2002), p. 23.
26. Scott Cutlip, "Public Relations in Government," p. 12.
27. Ibid.
28. Final Report of the 32nd American Assembly, Columbia University.
29. Zachariah Chafee, Jr., *Government and Mass Communication,* 2 vols. (Chicago: University of Chicago Press, 1947), chap. 2, p. 736.
30. Gilbert, p. 11.
31. D. H. Brown, "Information Officers and Reporters: Friends or Foes?" *Public Relations Review* (Summer 1976), p. 33.
32. K. H. Rabin, "Government PIOs," p. 23.
33. Cliff Majersik, "Deciding Whether to Build a World Wide Web Site," *Government Communications* (September 1995), pp. 7–8.

CHAPTER FIFTEEN

Public Relations in Nonprofit Organizations

15

Outline

PREVIEW

The scope of nonprofit organizations goes far beyond small, well-intentioned community-based programs. Today's nonprofits are business oriented and expect public relations to contribute to the bottom line. The lines between nonprofit, for-profit, and government are becoming increasingly blurred.

A variety of nonprofit sectors exist, each practicing public relations in a distinctive way. Membership recruitment and retention, influencing government, managing change, dealing with volunteers, and fund-raising are primary public relations activities in many of them.

Nonprofits face numerous public relations challenges. Gaining recognition in a crowded environment, competing for resources, and integrating technology are a few. Yet nonprofits have unique needs such as recruiting and retaining volunteers, balancing multiple bottom lines and publics, and building brand awareness.

"There is a tremendous opportunity for practitioners who think broadly and who welcome accountability. This is not an era for communications technicians."

—Frank J. Weaver, APR, Director of Public Affairs
Cleveland Clinic Foundation

Success factors in nonprofit public relations are similar to those in for-profits. They include a focus on mission, strong internal and external communication, active board participation, and simple messages ☐

FOR-PROFIT VERSUS NONPROFIT ORGANIZATIONS

It's not a simple task to define what a modern-day nonprofit organization actually is. For-profits are operating nonprofits, and nonprofits are operating for-profits. To make matters even more confusing, the government not only purchases services from both for-profits and nonprofits, but also provides some of the same services. Consider the following examples.

A front-page article in the September 15, 1996, issue of the *New York Times* announced a new playing field for nonprofits.[1] Two for-profit organizations were each preparing to bid for the management of $563 million in welfare operations in Texas. These state government contracts had traditionally been awarded to nonprofits. Although this particular bid was not awarded to the for-profits, one of them, Lockheed Martin IMS, has since been awarded more than 20 welfare-to-work contracts and provides the case management, skills training, and job placement assistance that U.S. government had contracted to nonprofits for years.[2]

The nonprofit Made in the USA Foundation is trying to save American manufacturing jobs by buying for-profit C. F. Hathaway, the nation's last major maker of domestically sewn men's dress shirts. The foundation hopes to expand the product line, open retail stores, and win government contracts that must give preference to U.S. manufacturers.[3]

A nonprofit organization that serves the Hispanic community created a for-profit culinary school and catering business. The money made in the for-profit venture funds the mission of the nonprofit, which is to help clients become self-sufficient in America. The school and business provide a way to help clients learn food preparation and business skills, become more proficient at speaking English, and then have work prospects. Similarly, a nonprofit domestic abuse shelter opened a for-profit catering company to develop business expertise and career opportunities for the women it serves.

Perhaps one of the easiest ways to differentiate between a **for-profit organization** and a **nonprofit organization** is by determining what happens to any monies that are not spent on overhead and operating expenses. In a for-profit organization, this money is called "profit," and it's distributed on a prorated basis to those who own the company. Thus, someone who owns 20 percent of the company will get more of the profit than someone who owns 1 percent. Examples of for-profit companies include large ones such as Microsoft, Starbucks, and McDonald's as well as many locally owned restaurants, tire centers, or appliance stores. In a nonprofit, the excess monies are called "surplus." Surplus funds are reinvested in the organization, to strengthen and expand the scope of the work.

Beyond dollars, the goals of for-profits and nonprofits are different. For-profits develop products and services that will make money for its owners, as a way of financially rewarding them for their investment in the company. A nonprofit organization focuses on fulfilling an educational or charitable mission, recognizing that all organizations must maintain positive bottom lines to exist. The terms *nonprofit* and *not-for-profit* can be used synonymously and interchangeably, the former a result of the American urge to truncate.

Some nonprofits would like to think that their mission-oriented agenda provides some flexibility in evaluating programs and overall effectiveness, allowing nonprofits to measure success in subjective and intangible ways. Yet some for-profits such as The Body Shop and Patagonia have successfully merged mission and profit. The reality is that today's nonprofits must go beyond warm, fuzzy stories to achieve their mission. Nonprofits that expect to thrive will be those that run well-managed, fiscally sound operations, deliver quality services, and are accountable to the publics they serve. Michael Ertel, manager of public relations for Quest, a nonprofit servicing the disabled in Florida, suggests that the implications for communicators is that "nonprofit is a tax code, not a way of doing public relations."[4]

THE NONPROFIT ENVIRONMENT

There are approximately 1.6 million nonprofits in the United States,[5] the largest of which is a nearly $7 billion dollar network.[6] This would place Lutheran Services in America in the 2001 Fortune 300 list, just behind Newell Rubbermaid and ahead of America Online.[7] By comparison, Compassion International, the 100th largest nonprofit organization, had revenues of $92 million.[8] See figure 15.1 for a list of the top 10 revenue-generating nonprofits. Nonprofits include hospitals, museums, research centers, homeless shelters, rehabilitation centers, symphony orchestras, and many other organizations in every community across the nation.

Because not all nonprofits are required to file with the U.S. Internal Revenue Service, it's difficult to grasp the true size and scope of the sector. By any measurement, however, it's huge. Large organizations with total expenses of $10 million or more in 1992 represented 4 percent of public charities, but they held half of all public support dollars and three-fourths of all expenses and assets.[9]

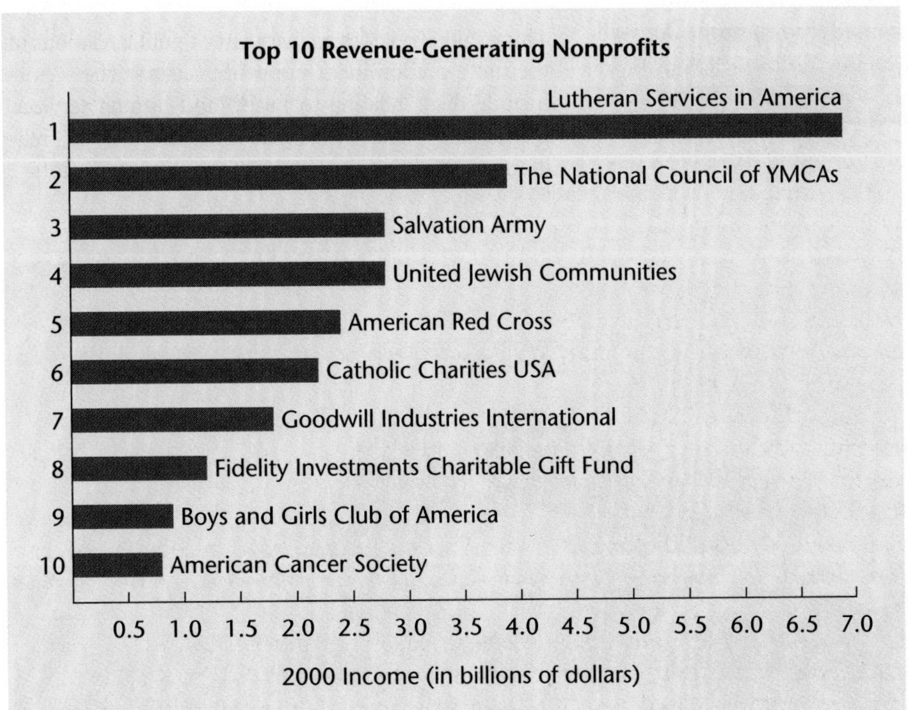

FIGURE 15.1 **Revenue-Generating Nonprofits**
Source: Matthew Sinclair, "Top 100 Revenues Zoom to $49 Billion," *NonProfit Times*, http://www.nptimes.com, November 1, 2000.

The human services area added the greatest number of nonprofits between 1989 and 1994, more than twice the number of any other type of nonprofit organization. The fastest rates of growth were among environmental/animal organizations, which grew by 56 percent, and educational organizations, which grew by 44 percent. The slowest rate of growth was among health organizations, which grew 20 percent, thought to be a reflection of an increase in for-profit competition and mergers and acquisitions.[10] Approximately 7 percent of Americans are employed by a nonprofit charitable, social welfare, and religious organization and revenues accounted for roughly 6 percent of the national income.[11]

Nonprofits have been on a public relations fast-learning curve in recent years, hiring practitioners and integrating the communication function into their strategic plans. The importance of job factor priorities across the nonprofit and for-profit sectors is strikingly similar, with practitioners citing access to technology, creative opportunity, and professional development opportunities as most essential. Many factors affect salaries, including the size and culture of the organization, geographical location, the area of the nonprofit's endeavor, and the qualifications and experience level of the candidate. Entry-level practitioners will earn in the $22,000 to $27,000 range, while the average salary for all job titles in nonprofit public relations work is $47,000. The range for practitioners who work for organizations with budgets greater than $20 million is $48,400 to $96,000. Overall, most practitioners are satisfied with their career, with 8 out of 10 saying they would choose a career in public relations if they had it to do all over again.[12]

THE PRACTICE OF NONPROFIT PUBLIC RELATIONS

This section provides an overview of public relations in the more predominant nonprofit sectors. The sectors include those relating to health and human services, membership associations, educational facilities, religious organizations, and other miscellaneous sectors.

Human services includes helping low-income families with affordable housing as Habitat for Humanity does.

Health and Human Services

Health and human services organizations are the most common kind of nonprofit. tionally, more than one in three public charities is a human services organizati Health constitutes 18 percent of all public charities, and nonprofits spend appı mately 63 percent of their revenues on health activities.[14] Understandably, areas dense populations have more nonprofits than less populated areas. For example, York will have two to three times as many charities as Idaho. The health and hu services sector is very broad, encompassing hundreds of areas, such as help for t with disabilities, food services, temporary shelters and permanent housing, disaster response services, pregnancy care, health care, adoption services, employment assistance, and child and adult day care.

A variety of challenges face the health and human services sector, including high demand, high cost, access, and ethics of criteria used to select those who receive services. Public relations is often called upon to provide positioning statements and to respond to critics. Many look to nonprofits to fill gaps and supplement services provided by government agencies and others. For example, a *Wall Street Journal* headline noted that "Rising Welfare Rolls Prompt States to Make Cuts to Job-Aid Programs."[15] The article notes that "services that help people make the transition from welfare to work—ranging from helping provide cars to substance-abuse treatment—are losing funding."[16] It's at times like this that nonprofits often see an increase in the number of persons seeking their services, creating many public relations opportunities. Generally health and human services topics of interest to the media tend to be seasonal and are often a reflection of the economy. Homelessness, for example, received major media coverage in the 1980s, but interest in this subject waned in the 1990s, perhaps due to a rising stock market and an abundance of jobs. Notes Steven Rabin, a former public relations practitioner and now assistant to the president of Kaiser Family Foundation, "Health and family get good coverage." He goes on to say, "Issues like poverty, race relations and some of the more thorny issues have a tougher uphill climb."[17]

Public relations audiences for health and human services nonprofits are often those who can do something to solve or alleviate the problem. This would put legislators and other government officials high on the list, as they can allocate monies or sponsor laws and public policies. And this group is particularly sensitive to constituents' suffering as might be shared through human interest stories. Poor families who can't afford to pay their electric bills in the winter, sick people who don't have money to buy their lifesaving prescriptions, foster children who have been placed in abusive households—all can make for compelling media drama.

Membership Associations

Membership associations are organizations that allow those with similar interests and goals to join together to address common needs, often in the areas of legislation, law, education, and training. There are thousands of different kinds of membership associations for lawyers, teachers, health care professionals, food producers, consumer safety personnel, and the like. Some well-known ones include the American Medical Association, Chambers of Commerce, and the AARP, formerly known as the American Association for Retired Persons. There are also associations for associations. The American Society of Association Executives represents the more than 25,000 members who lead trade, professional, and philanthropic associations. The National Council of Nonprofit Associations is a network of 38 state and regional associations of nonprofits representing more than 17,000 nonprofits in the United States.

At the heart of any successful membership association are relationships, and this is where public relations efforts often are focused. Practitioners are always looking for new and effective ways to build and maintain a sense of community, a task made increasingly difficult by the broad range of membership demographics and the pressures of time, schedules, technology, and proximity. To accomplish this, groups often use a combination of "old" technology such as newsletters, magazines, and brochures; "new" technology such as e-mail, websites, and chatrooms; and face-to-face communication at statewide and regional meetings. Beyond communications vehicles, operational decisions can affect relationships. The Missouri State Teachers Association, for example, has made a conscious decision not to have an automated voice attendant. The receptionist, who is considered the "manager of first impressions," greets and personally connects callers with the best person or department to meet their needs.

Associations might be called upon to comment on current events within the sector. For example, the Magazine Publishers of America was surprised to learn the U.S. Postal Service planned to raise the postal rate for periodicals an average of 15 percent, after being told to expect a single-digit hike. On behalf of its members, MPA worked to convince the USPS to stick to its original promise. A public relations campaign was created that included contact with reporters who cover politics and government, advertising, a luncheon with key influentials, and lobbying. The rate was reduced to 9.9 percent.[18]

Associations may respond publicly on behalf of all of their members to personal news involving one of their high-profile members. When Dave Thomas, the founder of Wendy's restaurants, died, the National Restaurant Association expressed sympathy and noted that Thomas's death was a loss that would be felt by the whole food service industry.

Associations receive an annual report card of sorts at membership renewal time as members decide if the organization is worth joining for another year. Public relations must communicate how the organization has met and will continue to meet the needs of its members.

Educational Institutions

Public schools, as well as higher education institutions, have found that public relations is increasingly important to them as they seek funds, deal with crises, or face many of the special situations revolving around education.

Elementary and Secondary Public Schools A quick glance at the headlines highlights the need for public relations in public elementary and secondary schools. School bond issues are being voted down, teachers and bus drivers are striking, students and teachers are being shot and killed, there's concern about curriculum and standardized test scores, teachers are in short supply, and teacher competency is questioned. School districts realize that part of their responsibility as publicly funded agencies is to keep taxpayers and other publics informed about their operations.

Any issue that affects public schools is likely to affect large segments of the community; even people without school-age children will have an interest in the school system because their taxes support it, and schools are a focus of civic pride and concern. Most people in our society feel it is their right to know and have a voice in what happens in the public schools. A mini-case in chapter 11, "Community Relations," discusses how the Fort Atkinson, Wisconsin, school district received voter approval to build a new high school.

Elementary and secondary schools have numerous, overlapping audiences. For example, a teacher might be a graduate of the school, be a taxpayer, and have children in the school. What this means from a public relations perspective is that publics form opinions based on information from a number of different perspectives. The most important internal audiences for elementary and secondary schools are teachers, students, parents, and district residents. Other key internal and external audiences for public schools include local school administrators and staff; alumni and school board members; local business and industry leaders; service and civic clubs; churches and religious organizations; athletic boosters; legislators; local, state, and federal government agencies; and teachers' organizations and unions.

Beyond education, schools are taking positive steps to address issues that today's young people face. For example, the Drug Abuse Resistance Education program reaches more than 60 percent of elementary children, and schools partner with local police departments to offer it. Pregnancy prevention programs are also typical. Girls Inc. in Washington County, Maryland, has offered two teen pregnancy programs through the Western Heights and Springfield middle schools since the late 1990s.[19]

When policies of elementary and secondary schools are questioned, public relations must respond. Almost all Arizona school districts follow the Arizona School Boards Association's zero-tolerance rule for any type of druglike substance, including vitamins and nutritional supplements, except when special provisions have been made.[20] When parents of students with drug-related offenses publicly challenge the policy, public relations must communicate the rationale and sustain continued support.

Higher Education From a public relations perspective, the culture of an institution of higher education is both a blessing and a curse. On the plus side, it's a great environment for creatives as scholars are developing new knowledge and processes, students are creating trends, and there's an openness to exploring new concepts and ideas. On the down side, there is no clear-cut hierarchy of power, but, rather, one that is diffused among a variety of internal groups such as administration, faculty, and students. Communicators often walk a tightrope in trying to explain, to internal audiences as well as to the external constituents of the campus departments, why some decisions were made.

Successful public relations practitioners in colleges and universities involve representatives from areas that will be affected by the issue or activity. The following list gives examples of which college or university departments might be involved in planning a campus event and what each might contribute.

- *Public relations:* Identify goals and purpose for the event; ensure appropriate university administration is present at the event; secure a master of ceremonies and suggest program content (including overseeing protocol); develop a schedule of related activities; draft speeches/write scripts.
- *News bureau:* Promote the event; respond to media inquiries.
- *Government affairs:* Identify legislators or other government officials who might need to be present; determine what information needs to be sent to them prior to the event; spot them at the event because they will probably need to be introduced.
- *Events staff:* Reserve rooms, plan menus, manage any catering and decorations, and handle RSVPs; accommodate the needs of visitors, from directions and parking to handling VIP guests and distributing materials.
- *Web editor:* Post the event on the institution's main site or create a special site for a major event.
- *Development and alumni relations:* Identify which segments of the alumni/friends audience should be included, how they should be contacted, and the role of alumni at the event; answer questions.

- *Special interests:* Depending on the scope of the event, various representatives from special interest or other campus groups might need to be involved to ensure the event is handled properly and if any representatives from those areas need to be involved in the program. Especially for major outdoor events, campus facilities staff will need to be involved to handle setup.
- *Campus police:* Ensure safety for all participants and to accommodate any special law enforcement needs.

Beyond educational issues, institutions of higher education need to be good citizens. Webster University in St. Louis wanted to create a new campus-zoning district and to install heating and air conditioning equipment, both of which raised the concerns of nearby residents. They cited the potential negative impact three chiller units might have on their property values. The community-at-large wondered about noise and odors. In a wise public relations move, the university tabled the measures to seek the input of the community before proceeding.[21]

Colleges and universities face employer-employee issues. Harvard University cut the wages of its more poorly paid workers at a time when its endowment was tripling and its undergraduate fees were rising 11 percent faster than inflation. The wages of its custodians, food-service workers, and guards dropped 10–15 percent because the school undercut pay by outsourcing these services. Students protested, a report was commissioned, and the university was admonished to raise wages immediately. Interestingly, the report also found that even though Harvard is a nonprofit, its situation was similar to that faced by for-profit employers.[22]

Religious Public Relations

Religious organizations generally must rely on public relations to promote their work because funds are usually not available for large-scale advertising efforts. On the local

Young people working with World Changers assist in building churches as mission activity learning to give their work and time as well as their money to the church.

National Service Project Raises Awareness for World Changers

Spotlight 15.1

When the Southern Baptist Convention decided to establish a national service project for high school students, it used the tenets of good public relations and media relations to get the job done and gain positive publicity.

Dubbed "World Changers," organizers brought 200 to 400 students to cities and towns across the United States to perform light renovation work to the homes of low-income people. To gain support and backing in each community, project organizers met with local leaders to outline their Good Samaritan plan.

Organizers pitched how the work done by students helps upgrade dilapidated housing and gains coverage by local media. Advance publicity for each project used examples of success stories of how people are assisted through World Changers. Once on-site, members of the media were encouraged to interview residents, project organizers, and city leaders.

What resulted was good public relations for all involved and the growth of World Changers from a pilot project numbering a little more than 100 participants to more than 23,000 participants in 24 states and two foreign countries in 2002.

Source: Tim Yarbrough, North American Mission Board, Southern Baptist Convention.

level, public relations helps congregations promote their worship services, Sunday and vacation Bible schools, music programs, and other activities. State, national, and international efforts often focus on denominational, evangelical, and larger social issues. United Methodists helped with flood recovery efforts in 2002 when South Texas was hit with 15 to 35 inches of rain in a seven-day period.[23] Jews, Presbyterians, Unitarians, and people from other denominations and belief systems are involved in literacy programs, hunger programs, after-school programs, and shelters for battered women, among others. Spotlight 15.1 highlights a Southern Baptist Convention national service project. Religious organizations receive 60.1 percent of all donations made by individuals.[24]

Given their nature, religious organizations often are held to standards higher than those for other organizations. Internal quarreling, wrongdoings of leaders and members, and other such scandals can threaten beliefs and destroy the foundations of the denomination's principles and values—the very opposite of what they want to accomplish. For example, some Catholic priests have been accused of and have admitted to being pedophiles. Some married ministers have committed adultery and sought divorces from their spouses. Religious conflicts can be corporate as well as individual in nature. Fundamentalists and moderates have battled over control of the Southern Baptist Convention, often in a manner typical of a malicious corporate takeover. The challenge for religious public relations is to separate the poor judgment and mistakes that its human leaders and members make from the divine meaning and purpose of faith.

Larger denominations have well-defined and well-organized communication functions. For example, the Church of Jesus Christ of Latter-Day Saints (Mormons) provides story packages, TV/video clips, radio sound bites, broadcast fillers, photos, news releases, facts, and background and contact information to the media.

Other Nonprofit Sectors

The multitude of other nonprofit sectors that actively engage in public relations are too numerous to provide detail in this chapter on each one. For example, some nonprofits promote economic development and tourism. The Irish Tourist Board developed an "Ireland Is Open for Business" public relations campaign to reassure tourists that the country was free of foot-and-mouth disease.[25] Historically, nonprofits like the Colonial Williamsburg Foundation attract the attention of tourists by generating a national dialogue about history education.[26] Others like the Montgomery Improvement Association

15.1 Mini•Case

Forty-Fifth Anniversary of the Montgomery Bus Boycott

When Rosa Parks was arrested for refusing to give up her seat and move to the back of the bus in 1955, little did the 42-year-old African American seamstress realize that the incident would spark a yearlong bus boycott that would galvanize America's civil rights movement and ultimately lead to the U.S. Supreme Court declaring that segregation on public buses was unconstitutional.

In December 2000, to celebrate the 45th anniversary of the Montgomery (Alabama) bus boycott, the Montgomery Improvement Association (MIA), with public relations support provided by Ketchum, chose to honor three key women instrumental in the boycott's success and the civil rights movement: Mrs. Rosa Parks, Mrs. Coretta Scott King, and Mrs. Juanita Abernathy. According to its bylaws, MIA continues to direct "a course of action in an effort to improve the status of all people who are deprived of any of the blessings of the society in which they live."

To prepare for the events, Ketchum conducted extensive research on the history of the civil rights movement, reviewed the 40th anniversary celebration activities, and met with civil rights leaders and organizations and other influentials to gain insight and input into the planning process.

The research highlighted the need to heighten the public's understanding of the historical significance of the Montgomery bus boycott and the significant leadership role women of the movement played, and the contributions of all city and state-elected officials and community leaders who assisted in this effort. To accomplish this, a weekend full of events remembering the boycott was planned by committees made up of prominent civil rights, political, and business leaders. Key audiences for the events included national media outlets, major news markets, the African American community, national and state policymakers, and business leaders across the nation.

Events included a 45th anniversary gala dinner hosted by the Alabama governor with remarks by Martin Luther King III and NAACP president Kweisi Mfume, a public policy forum held at Harvard University's John F. Kennedy School of Government's Institute of Politics, and a website that showcased the importance of the Montgomery bus boycott.

The results of the 45th Montgomery bus boycott anniversary events were significant. Media attention was extensive in national publications such as the *New York Times* and *Washington Post* and numerous regional papers. More than 1,000 individuals attended the celebration gala, packing the Montgomery Civic Center to capacity. Many dignitaries attended the events in Montgomery, and more than 200 letters were sent by members of the president's cabinet, members of Congress, mayors, and governors. The website experienced a tripling of hits in the first three months after being posted. The public policy forum at Harvard attracted a standing-room-only crowd.

The 45th anniversary of the Montgomery bus boycott reminded millions of Americans of the large steps that have been taken to further racial harmony and equality. And it is hoped that the successes of the 40th and 45th celebrations will serve as a foundation for the 50th anniversary of the Montgomery bus boycott in 2005.

focus on racial equality. Mini-case 15.1 highlights the 45th anniversary of the Montgomery bus boycott, one aspect of the civil rights movement that made seating segregation on buses illegal.

Nonprofit activist and environmental groups also use public relations. "Boardroom activism" is a guerrilla public relations technique in which activists become shareholders, infiltrate annual meetings, and present their demands in shareholder proposals.[27] As an activist organization, Mothers Against Drunk Driving used grassroots support to push for tougher alcohol laws and enforcement and related legislative issues. As a result, alcohol-related traffic deaths have dropped by 40 percent since the early 1980s and MADD has broadened its public relations efforts to include a proposed constitutional amendment on crime victims' rights and a federally funded anti-youth drinking advertising campaign.[28] Volvo partnered with the Caribbean Conservation Corporation to initiate a major educational and environmental campaign to conserve sea turtles.[29]

PUBLIC RELATIONS CHALLENGES FACED BY NONPROFITS

Like their for-profit counterparts, nonprofit organizations face a multitude of public relations challenges, all of which can affect their ability to survive and thrive. They include the following.

Gaining Recognition in a Crowded Environment

The sheer number of nonprofits makes for an extremely competitive environment. A 2001 Independent Sector report noted that the number of charities grew 74 percent between 1987 and 1998 to a total of 1.6 million organizations.[30] Nonprofits of all sizes are challenged to gain a significant share of voice and receive support and recognition for their work in such a crowded marketplace.

One valuable tool that nonprofits use to communicate is information technology. Websites, e-mail, and Internet access allow organizations to conduct research, to share information with key constituents, to raise funds, to network with affiliates, to attract employees and volunteers, to provide training, to sponsor 24/7 information services, and to enhance their overall ability to carry out their programs and mission.

Effective websites focus on audience needs. The search engine for the Habitat for Humanity International website allows visitors to access information in 11 languages. The site includes a special events calendar, the opportunity to sign up for house-building trips worldwide, stories about work completed and in progress, and much more.[31] The Cystic Fibrosis Foundation recognizes that many of its visitors will use their site for background information. Their website provides facts about the genetic disease that affects 1 out of every 31 Americans, information about research and clinical trials, and human interest stories about persons affected by cystic fibrosis. Those wishing to make a donation to this cause can do so online, and details about other fund-raising events and activities are included.[32]

Competing for Resources

Nonprofits compete with other nonprofits and for-profits for a variety of needs and resources, including good employees, conscientious volunteers, steady contributions, and proper recognition. Catherine Palmquist, executive director of the YWCA of Chester County, Pennsylvania, notes that one of her biggest challenges is finding people to hire. "Corporations are trying to hire people and they're paying these bizarre salaries, which we can't compete with," she explains.[33] Competition in all of these areas can be intensified in other ways, such as through job terminations, layoffs, a drop in the value of stocks, and plant closures. For example, when one of the largest employers in Rochester, New York, shut down and layoffs were occurring at other local businesses, the area's United Way fell $1.8 million short of its $38 million goal.[34] Also affected was the volunteer base as some needed to leave the community to find jobs.

Nonprofits always need volunteers to serve in numerous capacities, from serving on boards and fund-raising to working in the office and providing direct services to others.[35] Although Stan Hutton of http://www.nonprofit.com notes that "you haven't really been initiated into nonprofit work until you've done at least two bulk mailings,"[36] most of the more than 110 million people who volunteer[37] aren't content to stuff envelopes. They want to assist senior citizens, cheer up frightened children, work at homeless shelters, help put out fires, clean up roadways, read stories at the library, give tours at museums, serve in the Peace Corps, and help others in a myriad of other ways.

Communicating the need, benefits, and value of volunteerism is one of many tasks for public relations practitioners in nonprofit organizations. Although appeals can be made directly to individuals, many nonprofits are working with community-minded corporations who sponsor volunteer days.

One such company, Atlanta-based Turner Broadcasting System, Inc., hosted a Turner Volunteer Day in 2000, selecting volunteer projects most attractive to employees.

Sixteen hundred Turner Volunteers, from top-level executives to administrative staff, donned special T-shirts as they volunteered at more than 30 sites in five cities. Public relations efforts, with assistance from Ketchum public relations, included an internal campaign to build momentum, media relations before and after the day to tell the story and make employees proud, sponsorships and partnerships with other community members to provide transportation, food and beverages, and free live remotes and public services announcements. The event was a win-win for everyone. More than 50,000 people of the benefiting nonprofits were affected, employee participation exceeded expectations, and community and organizational leaders praised TBS's efforts. In addition, the company found a new way to retain a loyal employee base by linking itself with something it found within its employee community—a passion for volunteering.[38,39]

The overriding implication for public relations is clear: Ongoing communication is essential if a nonprofit is to attract its share of scarce resources.

Weathering Crises and Scandals

Nonprofits are treated like any other organization that experiences a crisis or scandal: They get media attention. But when a nonprofit finds itself in such a situation, the whole mission and future existence of the organization can be jeopardized.

When the Boy Scouts of America organization refused to hire gay men as scout leaders or to accept them as members, they were the subject of heated discussions about discrimination and whether or not the group should receive United Way funding. Some United Ways shifted these funds to other organizations that accept homosexuals and female members.[40] Such funding changes can eventually erode the financial foundation of an organization that had relied on United Way donations to offset operating costs.

The American Red Cross kept collecting blood it knew it didn't need after the 2001 attacks on the World Trade Center and ended up destroying 50,000 pints. A Red Cross spokesperson tried to defend the action by muttering, "We did our best guess and came within 5 percent of using it all."[41] Such actions can damage the reputation of an organization that depends on the goodwill and support of the nation's citizens.

The bankruptcy of energy giant Enron in early 2002 had serious ramifications for the accounting industry. In response, the 330,000-member-strong American Institute of Certified Public Accountants initiated a public relations campaign to help restore the public's faith in the auditing and accounting system.[42]

Nonprofits of all sizes need to think about how they would handle a potential emergency, an embarrassment, and some other urgent situations *before* they occur. A multitude of training organizations exist that can help nonprofits develop a strategic plan, which would include an assessment of their risks and vulnerabilities, when and how to call the media, how to develop message points, how to prepare for funding alternatives, and how to be specific about what to ask for.

Managing Multiple Publics

Nonprofits are accountable to numerous publics, including corporate and individual donors, board members, employees, volunteers, opinion makers, lawmakers, clients and customers, members, government funders and regulators, neighbors and citizens, foundations and grantees. These complex audiences have different public relations needs, and satisfying all of them isn't easy.

For example, board members of large nonprofits are often wealthy and influential corporate executives. As a group, they use their high-level management expertise to help address the nonprofit's bottom-line issues, and they help support the mission of the organization through substantial gifts. Getting the right composition of board members and satisfying information needs about operations and finances can be difficult.

Bill Lowman, the executive director of the Idyllwild School of Music and the Arts in Idyllwild, California, had such a problem. The school, one of only three residential schools in the country for performing arts, had serious financial problems in 1983, almost to the point of closing. Lowman sought counsel from the affluent weekend residents who had been coming to this mountain retreat for many years. And he did it in an untraditional way: Lowman appointed both spouses to the board instead of the common practice of just one. The result was fresh and frank input, and board meetings that resembled social activities, with dinners and concerts by the school's musicians. Today Idyllwild is a 70-building complex with 250 students from 33 states and 23 countries.[43]

Other audiences present equal challenges. Disagreements can erupt over priorities, where and how resources are allocated, ownership issues, different interpretations of the mission, and how results are to be interpreted and evaluated, to name just a few. Practitioners must try to balance these numerous perspectives.

Balancing Multiple Bottom Lines

Nonprofits often use an axiom to describe their bottom line: No margin, no mission. Without sufficient funds to operate the business, the organization is short-lived. Nonprofit public relations efforts go far beyond financial concerns. For example, their publics expect them to meet needs appropriate to the organization; to be a persuasive, unifying voice on key issues; to maintain an ever-readiness in their ability to offer support and services; and to comfort in times of crisis. The National Association of Broadcasters, for example, wanted to help the general public, policymakers, and television executives better understand the implications of switching from the current analog transmission system to a digital format by 2006. Their public relations campaign will create awareness through special events, media relations, advertising, and other appropriate tactics.[44] For organizations like the Christopher Reeve Paralysis Foundation, the only true measure of the organization's success will be effective treatments and a cure for paralysis caused by spinal cord injury.[45] Public relations for CRPF can raise public awareness, keep the issue current, and help increase funding for research.

Building a Brand and an Identity

When you consider the passion that most nonprofit workers have for their particular cause, it's obvious why most resources are allocated to mission-related projects and not public relations. Yet many nonprofits have realized that low name recognition, an obscure image, limited knowledge about their work, and a competitive nonprofit marketplace can significantly affect the amount of support and funding they receive. Strategic public relations is a necessity, not a luxury.

United Way organizations realized this firsthand when contributors were allowed to identify where they wanted their dollars to go. Those groups with little brand awareness began to lose funds while those who had invested in their brands maintained donor support.[46] Mini-case 15.2 discusses how the stale image of the 91-year-old United Way of Central Maryland was refreshed through a public relations campaign.

Although nonprofits who undertake branding and identity efforts are often criticized for spending money on such activities, impressive results quell the dissenters. A national branding effort by Volunteers of America allowed the organization to double the number of people served and increased the number of youth and senior volunteers.[47]

15.2 Mini • Case

Community Safety Net to the Rescue

The 91-year-old United Way of Central Maryland (UWCM) realized that its image had become generic and nonspecific. Although it was recognized as the largest philanthropic organization serving the region, donations represented 20–30 percent less than United Ways in cities of similar size. Many contributors were using the United Way as a "pass-through," meaning non–United Way agencies and causes were receiving their donations instead of member agencies. UWCM found itself on an uncomfortable plateau.

The solution? Weber Shandwick Worldwide, Baltimore, created an unprecedented pro bono public service campaign in 2000 to launch the "Community Safety Net" subbrand, grouping more than 250 programs and 74 health and human services agencies funded by UWCM under a single banner. The campaign would prove successful in capturing the hearts and dollars of donors for UWCM member agencies.

Research

Weber Shandwick used a variety of research methods to identify the best course of action for UWCM. These included the following:

- One-on-one and group interviews with United Way board members and staff
- Review of previous United Way campaign materials
- Review of focus group research
- Review of past campaign results, including trends for donor giving
- Review of other Community Safety Net branding campaigns by United Way organizations in other states
- Creative testing of Community Safety Net themes, headlines, and visuals
- Pre- and postcampaign telephone surveys of Central Maryland residents.

Objectives

Based on the research, Weber Shandwick identified four objectives:

1. To increase overall giving
2. To increase major gifts of more than $10,000, especially among women
3. To create consumer awareness for the Community Safety Net as a United Way brand
4. To match or exceed United Way's media budget of $500,000 with donated print space and airtime

Execution

A variety of tactical applications was used to communicate the Community Safety Net brand:

- Campaign video featuring stories of individuals in need
- Community Safety Net logo
- Multimedia public service campaign, which included television and radio spots, print advertising, billboards, bus and metro signage, web banner ads, enhanced website, and materials for the workplace where the bulk of United Way donations are given through payroll deductions

Results

By any measure, the Community Safety Net campaign was an over-whelming success, as illustrated by the following:

- The 2000 campaign exceeded its financial goal, raising $43.1 million, 5.1 percent more than in 1999. It had more first-time givers than ever before and drew the first $1 million gift in the history of UWCM.
- Three new members joined UWCM's Millennium Club, representing those who have given more than $100,000. There was a record 46 percent increase in those giving more than $10,000.
- The number of women giving more than $10,000 increased from 4 to 46, more than a tenfold increase.
- Awareness and recall of United Way as a "top charity" and "regional leader" increased.
- Pro bono media commitments exceeded $600,000 in donated print space and airtime.
- Some contributors cited the Community Safety Net campaign as the reason for their gift.

Summary

Any brand that intends to thrive and survive cannot grow old gracefully. Instead, its image must be carefully nurtured and cultivated year after year, guarding against campaigns that can easily become too bland, too general, and inconsistent in their executions. As the UWCM case demonstrates, public relations can create more differentiation and a more compelling positioning for aging brands.

Camp Fire Boys and Girls, a leading youth development organization, introduced a new name and identity in 2001: Camp Fire USA. The branding was considered essential to revitalizing and strengthening the identity central to the organization's mission of building caring, confident youth and future leaders. The new name positions the organization as innovative, progressive, and all-inclusive and relevant to a broader age group.[48] Figure 15.2 showcases the rebranding look.

Branding issues take on a new perspective as nonprofits join networks while maintaining their own identities. As noted earlier in this chapter, Lutheran Services in America (LSA) is the largest nonprofit in terms of revenue. Mini-case 15.3 outlines the pros and cons of LSA developing a brand identity.

A Nonprofit Evaluates the Challenges of Creating a Recognized National Identity

Mini•Case 15.3

Lutheran Services in America is a well-kept secret. What started out as local churches meeting the needs of their communities has grown to more than 280 individual social ministry organizations related to the two major Lutheran denominations in the United States. These individual organizations, together with the two denominations, comprise the network that is Lutheran Services in America (LSA). LSA provides a full range of health and human services, serving in more than 3,000 communities with collective operating budgets of over $7 billion in 2000, making it the largest nonprofit in terms of revenue.*

LSA's challenge is that few recognize who it is and what it does. Its member organizations and board members now believe the network must focus on developing a national branding identity as a way of strengthening its ability to meet community-based needs. Here are some of the challenges LSA faces as it begins this task:

- *Tremendous diversity.* Individual LSA organizations have very different local identities, use many different names, offer a wide variety of services, and vary greatly in size. Also, trying to describe an entity that involves multiple Lutheran church bodies can be confusing to those unfamiliar with the LSA network.
- *Cost.* Developing a national identity is expensive. Some may be critical of spending money on communications strategies and activities. New personnel may need to be hired and current staff may allocate more of their time to this project.
- *Elective participation in branding efforts.* LSA has no formal authority over member organizations, so it cannot require participation in a brand identity project. Member organizations will have to be persuaded that they can add value to their work by hooking onto this identity and being known as a part of the LSA system.
- *Initial "inward" focus.* The most important task in initiating this branding effort will be in establishing ongoing communication with member organizations and their boards, with the two denominations, and with others in the Lutheran community and beyond. Developing a consensus among this many individuals and organizations will be difficult.
- *Misunderstandings about messages.* LSA will need to consider how its clients might receive the new brand identity. The religious affiliation, for example, might confuse some, leading them to believe they are not eligible for services.
- *Potential negative impact on charitable giving.* When a system such as LSA is seen as large, those who don't understand its federated nature may believe that support isn't needed, resulting in a negative effect on philanthropy.
- *No corporate control.* LSA can provide guidelines, but it will have no control over how the identity might be expressed on the local, community level. Yet some level of branding consistency will have to be present in order to be of any value to member organizations.

As daunting as these challenges may be, LSA feels that it is time for member organizations to highlight their strong witness of faith in action and increasingly to claim their Lutheran identity as that becomes more valuable. A recognized national identity can allow LSA to expand its services and missions. It can enhance the sense of pride among staff, volunteers, Lutherans in the pew, and the clients who are served.

Questions

1. As public relations manager for LSA, how would you initiate work on the branding identity project?
2. Who are the key audiences for this branding effort?
3. Identify other organizations, both for-profit and nonprofit, which face or have faced similar identity problems. What lessons could LSA learn from them?

*These figures are from "Top 100 Revenues Zoom to $49 Billion," *NonProfit Times,* 1 November 2001.

FIGURE 15.2 New name and logo developed for Camp Fire Boys and Girls.

SUCCESS FACTORS FOR NONPROFIT PUBLIC RELATIONS

It's no mystery why some nonprofits are more successful at public relations than others. Those who see measurable results usually incorporate the following into their communication strategies and plans.

Focus on Mission

Like any organization, nonprofits need to revisit their mission statement from time to time to ensure they are fulfilling their purpose. It's easy to take advantage of new opportunities to grow and to dilute the focus on the original purpose and role. Nonprofits of all sizes are vulnerable to mission erosion, and it can happen even under the watchful eyes of board members and the public.

Scholars and activists demanded the resignation of the Smithsonian Institution's top administrator for commercializing what has been called "the nation's attic," a collection of more than 140 million artifacts. Critics said that corporate and private sponsorship of exhibits and zoo animals allowed outside interests to dictate the Smithsonian's mission, sacrificing integrity and independence. The Smithsonian comprises 16 museums and galleries, the National Zoo in Washington, and research facilities in the United States and abroad.[49]

Strong Internal Public Relations

Fleishman-Hillard executive Dan Barber[50] champions a philosophy that says that all great external public relations begins with great internal public relations. Accomplishing this task with a small staff is an entirely different task than for a national organization with thousands of employees and volunteers in chapters and affiliates around the country. Still, it's important to gain support from those associated with the organization, to add strength to external efforts.

Beyond newsletters, intranets, and other similar tactics, internal public relations can mean involving employees in communication planning efforts. Some test their emergency preparedness, allowing the public relations department to test and evaluate the accuracy and effectiveness of media contact lists, special crisis communications websites, other backup systems, and even ensuring that the batteries work in the flashlights. By participating in these scenarios, employees at all levels have a better understanding of what communication systems are in place.

External Public Relations That Unify

Public relations response to issues is usually conducted on an individual nonprofit-by-nonprofit basis; that is, each nonprofit generates communication from its perspective. Often more than one nonprofit is addressing the same issue, increasing the possibility of conflicting messages received by various publics.

During the national anthrax crisis in late 2001, Americans expressed disappointment over how the anthrax scare was handled. There was confusion as to how serious the threat actually was, how contamination could occur, how to safeguard businesses and households, and the like. Given the organization of the U.S. Department of Health and Human Services, it's easy to understand how conflicting messages were created. There are a dozen agencies under the HHS umbrella, most of which have their own, independent communications functions. More than 200 persons are employed in these departments, and HHS has hundreds of millions of dollars worth of contracts with private public relations firms. It's a system in which few checks and balances exist to ensure that a consistent, single message is delivered.[51]

When the public hears conflicting messages, organizations can lose credibility and trust. Practitioners are urged to look beyond their own agendas when developing message strategies, to better meet the information needs of the public.

Active Participation of Board Members

Board membership usually carries a price tag in that its members are expected to make a substantial financial gift. But their contributions can extend beyond money as the following example illustrates. Camp Fire Boys and Girls (now known as Camp Fire USA) and Fleishman-Hillard created a special annual one-day awareness campaign called the "Absolutely Incredible Kid Day." Adults are urged to write at least one letter filled with appreciation and love to a child, creating treasured memories that can last a lifetime. National board members helped secure celebrity participation, and they themselves were actively involved in the national call to action. Many celebrities, including former President Bill Clinton, wrote letters as a result.[52]

Fortune 500 companies generally encourage their employees to serve on boards of nonprofits, and some help train them for board leadership. American Express provides its managers with a toolkit created by the National Center for Nonprofit Boards. The materials include information about the role of the board, an overview of fund-raising activities, its role in strategic planning, and a question-answer book.

Simple Messages

Nonprofits that break through the clutter are those that focus on one idea. The best messages are those that support the program goals. When a constant barrage of highly publicized high-protein diets cast foods like bread, cereal, and pasta as "high-carbohydrate demons," sales and consumption for wheat and grain products dropped. The Wheat Foods Council, a nonprofit devoted to increasing awareness of dietary grains as an essential component to a healthy diet, developed a simple seal, "Grains: Harvest the Energy." The seal was placed on the packages of grain-food products in grocery stores and resulted in strong sales with higher margins for the retailers.[53]

Spotlight 15.2 on FAMILY MATTERS is an example of what message points look like. They organize the key points for the spokespersons and provide a rationale for making the case.

EVALUATING NONPROFIT PUBLIC RELATIONS

Nonprofits have the same bottom-line accountability as for-profits. As discussed earlier in this chapter, nonprofits manage budgets in the millions and even billions of dollars. Their corporate underwriters, government granters, and donors expect measurable results, those that go far beyond the "do good/feel good" variety. Both qualitative and quantitative research should be used to evaluate public relations results. Spotlight 15.3 outlines results from campaigns developed by the Ad Council for nonprofit organizations and other social issues.

The nonprofit Habitat for Humanity International worked with Delahaye Medialink to develop a comprehensive measurement process. A team of participants, including communication department heads, senior representatives from fund-raising and development, as well as individuals from other critical areas, was formed to determine how to develop a plan. One of the first issues to be addressed with the team was the fear of

15.2 Spotlight

Message Points for FAMILY MATTERS 1999

FAMILY MATTERS, an initiative of the Points of Light Foundation in 1999, was ready to spread the word about the benefits of family volunteering and position itself as *the* family volunteering resource. An annual nationwide call to action encouraging families to volunteer together was created. The following message points for national spokespersons provide the rationale for the topic of family volunteering, explain why FAMILY MATTERS is qualified to serve as a liaison between families and their communities, and include a call to action.

Message Points

Family volunteering works.

- It strengthens the family.
- It strengthens the community.
- It strengthens local business.
- It strengthens not-for-profits.

FAMILY MATTERS connects families and communities.

- FAMILY MATTERS, an initiative of the Points of Light Foundation, partnered with the Kellogg Foundation to research how nonprofit agencies nationwide were using family volunteering. We identified an opportunity to fill a need connecting families to their communities.
- After implementing and evaluating family volunteering programs in test markets, FAMILY MATTERS established successful models in 20 cities.
- FAMILY MATTERS sites facilitate family volunteers through linkages between neighborhoods, businesses, not-for-profit organizations, and state and local agencies. FAMILY MATTERS can also help individuals start FAMILY MATTERS clubs.
- FAMILY MATTERS's goal is to make family volunteering the norm in America.

Try it, you'll like it.

- There's a role for everyone during National Family Volunteer Day.

Source: The Points of Light Foundation and Fleishman-Hillard.

measurement and how poor results might reflect on individuals or units. Related to this was an assumption that much work can't be measured. It was important for the team to understand how they valued their work and how their work was valued as well as to consider how and if intangible factors such as feelings and emotions might be indicative of communication effectiveness.

The next step identified eight top effectiveness indicators, including a high percentage of renewals and a high degree of satisfaction with communications and with the program overall and the number of message impressions per month, message tone, and message content. Finally, it was determined how evaluation information could be collected in a timely, efficient manner. This would include assigning an advocate to each of the eight priorities, establishing benchmarks, identifying what's being measured, and determining the presentation format, audience, and frequency.

The end product of this planning is a media measurement device called "MediaScope." Early results are encouraging. This device allows Habitat employees to review all print coverage on a monthly basis and television on a daily basis, making available a valuable source of homeowner stories and testimonials for the work of Habitat departments.[54]

For all nonprofits, the importance of measuring how communication contributes to the bottom line will increase. The competitiveness of the marketplace demands a careful management of resources and results that indicate real effectiveness.

Ad Council Helps Nonprofits Make a Difference in Society

Spotlight 15.3

Can forest fires be fought on Madison Avenue?

Absolutely. Smokey Bear and countless other characters and slogans have addressed a significant number of public issues since 1942 through the work of the Ad Council.

Each year the Ad Council produces and distributes approximately 40 campaigns from the hundreds of requests for campaigns it receives from nonprofit organizations and government agencies. Topics typically include issue areas such as improving the quality of life for children, preventive health, education, community well-being, environmental preservation, and strengthening families.

The nation's top advertising agencies do the creative work **pro bono,** and leading corporate marketing executives lend their time and expertise. The media generously donate advertising time and space for the campaigns. In 2001, the media donated a record \$1.5 billion in ad value or media space and time.

The public service campaigns produce results. The following is a sample of how Ad Council campaigns have effected social change.

- Smokey Bear and his famous words of wisdom, "Only You Can Prevent Forest Fires," are recognized by 95 percent of adults and 77 percent of children. At the campaign's inception (1942), forest fires consumed more than 22 million acres per year. Today they consume less than 4 million acres per year.
- Since the introduction of the slogan "Friends Don't Let Friends Drive Drunk" America has experienced the lowest number of alcohol-related traffic fatalities, and 70 percent of Americans have tried to stop someone from driving drunk.
- The United Negro College Fund has raised more than \$1.7 billion since 1972, helping more than 300,000 minority students graduate from college.
- Seat belt usage has risen from 21 percent at the start of the "Buckle Up. Always. You Could Learn a Lot from a Dummy" campaign (1985) to 73 percent in 2001, saving an estimated 75,000 lives.
- Nearly 6,000 youths have been paired with a mentor as a direct result of the "Do Good. Mentor a Child" campaign.
- In the first full year of the Library of Congress's "Log On. Play Around. Learn Something" campaign (April 2000–March 2001), the number of hits to the America's Library website totaled 100 million.
- Awareness of child abuse and the need to prevent it has risen 80 percent in the past 20 years.

Source: Ad Council, http://www.adcouncil.org, 11 January 2002.

Summary

Public relations plays an essential role in helping nonprofit organizations gather support for its mission and in communicating with its key publics. Nonprofits face challenges unique to this sector. Public relations helps nonprofits balance multiple fickle publics and quantitative and qualitative bottom lines.

Public relations tactics in nonprofits include media relations activities, employee and volunteer communication, special events, and the Internet. Public relations is expected to deliver real bottom-line results to nonprofit ventures.

For self-testing and additional chapter resources, go to the student CD and the Online Learning Center at **www.mhhe.com/lattimore**

To learn more about nonprofit public relations watch the interview with Greg Wagner, Clip #3, on the book's CD-ROM.

Tulsa Race for the Cure

By Liz Taylor
Account Executive
Ackerman McQueen

The dream of a world without breast cancer is what motivates thousands of runners and walkers to participate in the annual Susan G. Komen Race for the Cure®. The first run was held in Dallas in 1982, and the event has grown to more than 100 cities throughout the United States. Tulsa, Oklahoma, held its fifth Race for the Cure® in 2001. The Tulsa office of the Ackerman McQueen agency volunteered to handle the public relations and other promotional activities for the race.

The Challenge

Perhaps the biggest challenge with an annual event is maintaining interest from year to year. Race organizers set a goal of 6,000 participants for the 2001 race, a 15 percent increase from the previous year. Ackerman McQueen would need to reach new participants to meet this significant increase. Having adequate resources to publicize the event was a second challenge. The agency would need to accomplish its goals using the airtime, space, and production services donated by Tulsa media outlets.

Research

Research questions focused on the *why* and the *who.* Why should the public care about Race for the Cure®? Three simple reasons answered this question:

1. Breast cancer affects more than the one out of every 11 women who will be diagnosed with the disease. Families, friends, co-workers, and many others provide support in a variety of ways.
2. All women can benefit from general information about breast health.
3. Research money is needed if the fight against breast cancer is to be won. The Race for the Cure® raises millions of dollars every year for research.

The who for this campaign would be a diverse group. The target market would include breast cancer survivors, women of all ages, families, volunteers, media, sponsors, and opinion leaders in this northeastern Oklahoma community.

Implementation

Ackerman McQueen determined that public relations, advertising, and the Internet would be the most effective tools to reach Tulsa residents about the Race for the Cure®. A local television station, the event's primary sponsor, donated their production services and airtime for commercials promoting the race. Similarly, the Tulsa newspaper contributed space for print ads. An outdoor advertising company stepped forward and provided space on several of their special events billboards that were strategically located to maximize exposure on Tulsa's busiest streets. The value of these combined donations was more than $150,000.

Key to the campaign was one of the honorary chairs of the race, Amber Valletta, an international supermodel, a Tulsa native, and the daughter of a survivor. Not only was her face instantly recognizable, but also she had a hometown connection and a personal story to boot. Amber became the face of the race, appearing in the television and print ads.

From a new media standpoint, the race was very lucky to have an outside volunteer willing to serve as webmaster, working closely with Ackerman McQueen to promote the race on the Internet. All pertinent race information was featured, in addition to biographies of the honorary co-chairs and news stories featured in the local media.

An aggressive media relations campaign supported all aspects of the campaign, including interviews with Amber and other race organizers, press releases, and providing informational material to editors and reporters.

Results

The race was a huge success by any measurement. More than 7,000 people participated in the Race for the Cure®, a 33 percent increase from the previous year. The event raised $362,000. Media provided extensive coverage of the race. Thousands showed up to support their family members and friends who participated in the race.

Until a cure for breast cancer is found, the race continues. Organizers set a 2002 participation goal of 10,000, with the hopes that when a cure is found, this is one race that will have run its course.

Questions

1. Events like the race have audiences beyond those identified in the case study. Create a comprehensive list of audiences that would be involved in the planning and execution of an event and what kind of communication would be appropriate for each group.
2. As the Tulsa Race for the Cure® continues to grow, what additional communication strategies would you recommend to reach key audiences?
3. Can the Race for the Cure® get too big? Identify the public relations advantages and pitfalls of growing an event like the race.
4. Develop a public relations plan for Tulsa's next Race for the Cure®.
5. Research the relationship between the Tulsa Race for the Cure® and its national sponsor, the Susan G. Komen Breast Cancer Foundation. (See http://www.komen.org.) What additional public relations opportunities might exist for future races?

Key Terms

Use the CD-ROM and Online Learning Center at www.mhhe.com/lattimore to further your understanding of the following terms

for-profit organization
nonprofit organization
pro bono

Notes

1. Nina Bernstein, "Giant Companies Entering Race to Run Welfare Programs," *New York Times,* 15 September 1996, p. 1.
2. William P. Ryan, "The New Landscape for Nonprofits," *Harvard Business Review* (January–February 1999), p. 127.
3. Associated Press, "Foundation Hopes to Keep 'Made in the USA' Label on Shirts," *Jefferson City News Tribune,* 4 August 2002, p. 30.
4. As quoted in article by Ana Vargas, "Doing PR for Fun and Nonprofit," *PRWeek,* 21 August 2000, p. 17.
5. "The Nonprofit Almanac IN BRIEF," published by the Independent Sector, 2001.
6. Mathew Sinclair, "Top 100 Revenues Zoom to $49 Billion," *NonProfit Times,* http://www.nptimes.com, 1 November 2001.
7. "The 500 Largest U.S. Corporations," *Fortune,* 16 April 2001, p. F11.
8. Sinclair, "Top 100 Revenues."
9. Carol J. DeVita, "Viewing Nonprofits Across the States," Charting Civil Society: A Series by the Center on Nonprofits and Philanthropy, Urban Institute (August 1997), no. 1.
10. Ibid.
11. "The Nonprofit Almanac IN BRIEF."
12. "PRSA/IABC Salary Survey 2000," http://www.prsa.org.
13. DeVita.
14. Ibid.
15. Russell Gold, "Rising Welfare Rolls Prompt States to Make Cuts to Job-Aid Programs," *Wall Street Journal,* http://www.interactive.wsj.com, 16 January 2002.
16. Ibid.
17. As quoted in article by David Ward, "When It Comes to Social Injustice, Drama Sells," *PRWeek,* 11 June 2001, p. 12.
18. Thom Weidlich, "MPA Gets USPS to Deliver Lower Rate," *PRWeek,* 4 December 2000, p. 38.
19. Scott Butki, "State Grant Will Aid Pregnancy Prevention Efforts," *Herald-Mail Online,* http://www.herald-mail.com, 4 January 2002.
20. Kristen Go, "No Drugs, Vitamins," *The Arizona Republic,* 12 December 2001.
21. Janet McNichols, "Webster University Will Wait for Public Input on Plans," *St. Louis Post-Dispatch,* 15 November 2001.
22. David Wessel, "Harvard Gets a Labor Lesson," *Wall Street Journal,* http://www.interactive.wsj.com, 20 December 2001.
23. United Methodist News Service, 11 July 2002.
24. "The Nonprofit Almanac IN BRIEF."
25. David Rovella, "Irish Tourist Board Springs into Action," *PRWeek,* 23 July 2001, p. 19.
26. Larry Dobrow, "History Revisted for Future's Sake," *PRWeek,* 15 October 2001, p. 19.
27. Douglas Quenqua, "When Activists Attack," *PRWeek,* 11 June 2001, p. 15.
28. Sherri Deatherage Green, "MADD's Efforts Continue to Drive into New

Territory," *PRWeek,* 21 January 2002, p. 8.

29. Eric Arnold, "Volvo Races to Aid the Environment," *PRWeek,* 21 January 2002, p. 19.
30. "Number of Charities Grows 74% in Just Over Decade," Independent Sector, http://www.independentsector.org, 18 July 2001.
31. Website for Habitat for Humanity International: http://www.habitat.org, accessed January 5, 2002.
32. Website for the Cystic Fibrosis Foundation: http://www.cff.org, accessed January 5, 2002.
33. As quoted by Gina Bernacci, "Nonprofits Weathering Economic Storm, Recession," *NonProfit Times,* http://www.nptimes.com, 15 December 2001.
34. David Cay Johnston, "United Way Is Reporting a 3.8% Increase in Donations," *New York Times,* 8 August 2001, Section C, p. 2.
35. Stan Hutton, "Volunteers: The Heart of Nonprofit Work, Typical Board Positions," http://www.nonprofit.about.com, 19 April 2001.
36. Stan Hutton, "Volunteers: The Heart of Nonprofit Work, Part 1: How Many Americans Volunteer Each Year?" *NonProfit Times,* http://www.nonprofit.about.com, 19 April 2001.
37. "The Nonprofit Almanac IN BRIEF."
38. Ketchum public relations.
39. Yusuf Davis, "1,100 TBS Volunteers Tackle Tasks; Employees, Families, Pals Devote Saturday to Projects Citywide; Turner: Volunteers Span the City," *Atlanta Journal and Constitution,* 14 September 2000, p. 1JD.
40. Julie R. Bailey, "United Ways Still Support Boy Scouts," *Columbus Dispatch,* 11 November 2000, p. 7.
41. Gilbert M. Gaul and Mary Pat Flaherty, "Red Cross Kept Asking for More; 5% of Blood Given After Attacks Was Discarded; Donor Backlash Feared," *Washington Post,* 16 December 2001, p. A34.
42. Julia Hood, "Accountancy Body Hopes to Rebuild Post-Enron Confidence with PR," *PRWeek,* 21 January 2002, p. 1.
43. Jaye Scholl, "In the Boardroom: No Fistfights, So Far: An Unconventional Board of Trustees Produces Surprising Results at Idyllwild Arts Academy," *Wall Street Journal,* http://www.interactive.wsj.com, 14 December 2001.
44. Dougles Quenqua, "NAB Seeks PR Firm to Educate Everyone about Switch to DTV," *PRWeek,* 23 July 2001, p. 2.
45. CRPF news release, "Quality of Life Programs Expands to Offer International Assistance," http://www.apacure.org, 16 January 2002.
46. Ana Vargas, "Doing PR for Fun and Nonprofit, *PRWeek,* 21 August 2000, p. 17.
47. Ibid.
48. Gregg K. Hibbeler, "Camp Fire Boys and Girls Introduces Bold New Brand: Leader in Youth Development Undergoes Identity Transformation to Camp Fire USA," Camp Fire USA news release, http://www.campfire.org, 25 June 2001.
49. Associated Press, "Scholars, Activists Want Top Administrator Fired for Commercialism of Smithsonian Institution," *Jefferson City News Tribune,* 17 January 2002, p. 10.
50. Telephone conversation with Dan Barber, partner and senior vice president, Fleishman-Hillard, Kansas City, 11 January 2002.
51. Douglas Quenqua, "HHS Makes Strides Toward Consolidated Messaging," *PRWeek,* 21 January 2002, p. 1.
52. Fleishman-Hillard public relations agency.
53. Fleishman-Hillard public relations agency.
54. Institute for Public Relations.

CHAPTER SIXTEEN

Corporate Public Relations

16

Outline

PREVIEW

Today's corporate environment is complex. New product introductions, mergers and acquisitions, layoffs, technological changes, and globalization create opportunities and challenges for corporations to communicate with their key publics. Corporations that succeed are proactive, have well-defined communication strategies linked to business objectives, and demonstrate concern for the world around them.

Business enhances its credibility when it practices honest performance, open communication, consistency between performance and communication, commitment to problem solving, and establishment of feasible expectations.

Corporate public relations faces many challenges in the 21st century, including public perceptions of business, consumer alienation, and misunderstanding about business profits. In addition, other key issues facing the corporate sector are globalization, technological change, and diversity

"Organizations that cannot understand the new era and navigate a path through the transition are vulnerable and will be bypassed."

—Don Tapscott and Art Caston
Paradigm Shift

OVERVIEW OF CORPORATE PUBLIC RELATIONS

Business has had to adapt to increasingly complex and dynamic environments such as new product introductions, mergers and acquisitions, layoffs, lawsuits, and new technology. Business leaders must manage relations with a variety of publics and balance their responses to many conflicting demands of these diverse publics.

Public relations helps corporations deal with this complex environment, and it's important these efforts support the organization's overall business mission and objectives. This is done in a number of ways, including helping corporations anticipate and adapt to societal demands and trends; positively impacting a company's image and reputation, resulting in a better operating environment; and smoothing and enhancing a company's operations, which can lead to an increase in sales.

A Corporation's Audiences

The groups and individuals that corporations communicate with vary from industry to industry. High-technology companies, for example, focus on different media, anticipate different crises, and deal with different issues than would an organization whose business is health care. While the terms *audiences, publics,* and *markets* are sometimes used interchangeably to identify those to be reached in a campaign, distinctions should be made among these words. **Target audiences** is a term used when the goal is to reach people with media. When the goal is to talk about communal issues, the term **target publics** is used. When communication is supporting the marketing function and is geared toward those who make buying and selling decisions, the term **target markets** is used.

For example, Southwestern Bell, a subsidiary of SBC Communications, a global telecommunications company, has many important audiences. A *partial* list is as follows:

- *Residential and Business Customers.* Southwestern Bell wants to update its end users about its products and services. Advertising and the media play important roles in communicating with this audience.
- *Municipalities.* Southwestern Bell provides telecommunications services to many cities and government operations, as well as pays taxes to municipalities for use of public rights-of-way. Thus, any information about disruptions or telephone outages, new services, or other changes must be communicated to the proper persons.
- *Employees.* Those who work for Southwestern Bell want to know information that could affect them in a positive or negative way.
- *Unions.* Many of Southwestern Bell's employees are members of the Communications Workers of America union. Consistent communication with this group is essential to ensure no disruption of telecommunications services.
- *State and Federal Government.* State and federal government organizations, such as public service commissions and the Federal Communications Commission, are responsible for enacting legislation that can directly impact Southwestern Bell's operations.[1]

Role of the CEO in Corporate Public Relations

As indicated in earlier chapters, public relations is practiced by all managers in business, not just those whose titles or job descriptions contain the term *public relations.* Effective corporate public relations, though, must begin with the chief executive officer. A Burson-Marsteller national study's respondents said that CEO reputation influences decisions to invest in a company (95 percent), believe a company is under pressure from the media (94 percent), recommend a company as a good alliance/merger partner (93 percent), and maintain confidence in a company when its share price is lagging (92 percent). Moreover, business influentials are more likely to recommend a company as a good place to work (88 percent) if the CEO is favorably regarded.[2]

About 60 percent of Fortune 700 CEOs have worked in one of four functions at some point in their career: finance, 22 percent; operations, 14 percent; marketing, 12 percent; and sales, 11 percent.[3] Thus, they may not have much familiarity with communications as a strategic tool and may not understand how it adds value to everyday operations. The organization's top leader must believe in the value of communication and make this function a priority by spending substantial portions of his or her energies and efforts on public relations–related matters.

Edward A. Blechschmidt, chairman, president, and CEO of Gentiva Health Services, a Melville, New York, provider of specialty pharmaceuticals and home health care services, said he wishes he had learned about handling corporate communications when he was the second in command. He noted that "the experience would have made him much more aggressive about creating user-friendly Internet communication with employees, shareholders, applicants and patients when he advanced to CEO."[4] Such communication builds and strengthens the relationships a corporation has with its publics as well as helps ensure the corporate public relations function has the resources it needs to do the job.

Boeing's chief executive officer is one who understands communication. The company's vice president of communications, Judith Muhlberg, considers herself "the luckiest girl in the world. I have a CEO who gets it." Muhlberg has a **seat at the table,** which means that she discusses issues and creates strategies with the company's other top executives, ensuring that communication concerns, rather than being overlooked, are integrated into critical business decisions. Boeing's public relations staff of more than 100 goes overboard in making information available to its employees, the media, the aerospace industry, and other relevant audiences.[5]

The positive result of having a CEO who values communication and relationships has a trickle-down effect throughout the organization. Employees have the information they need to make better decisions, better decisions lead to a higher performing organization, which in turn helps attract the best and brightest employees who have the skills and motivation to be successful in a competitive marketplace. Informed people outperform uninformed people, when all else is equal.

Public Relations Specialties

The demands placed on large corporations are great and diverse. Business organizations must fulfill a long list of responsibilities and still compete effectively in domestic and international markets.

The job of public relations in large corporations is ultimately to ensure that corporate power is maintained by responsible use and to help develop cooperative relationships between corporations and other societal institutions. To promote these goals successfully, public relations practitioners rely on a variety of specialties. We discuss these specialties as they relate to specific publics in Part III, "The Publics."

- *Media relations* is used to gain support and sympathy from print and broadcast outlets, to generate positive publicity, to tell its side of the story.
- *Employee relations* contributes to harmonious labor relations and helps attract and retain good employees. Effective employee communication can also stimulate

Toyota and Marlboro both were corporate sponsors of this Indy car race in Long Beach, CA. Corporations often sponsor major sporting events to promote their image or products.

worker creativity and input, boost attitudes and morale, improve product quality and customer service, and enhance productivity.

- *Community relations* supports sales, attracts employees, improves the quality of public services, provides support for business initiatives, and improves the quality of life for employees and executives.
- *Consumer relations* builds positive relations with customers, responds effectively to consumer complaints and problems, and supports sales and marketing efforts.
- *Financial relations* provides sound financial communication, allowing business to attract capital at the lowest possible cost. Other financial relations goals include ensuring that public firms' stock is appropriately valued, building knowledge and confidence in fund sources, and responding to investor questions or needs.
- *Public affairs* deals with business's interaction with government on various levels. Government relations have a direct impact on a business's flexibility and manageability. Regulation, taxation, labor law, and international trade policies are only a few ways in which governmental actions constrain business decision making and success.

In short, **corporate public relations** is a means by which businesses seek to improve their ability to do business. Effective corporate public relations smooths and enhances a company's operations as well as eases and increases its sales. It enables a business to better anticipate and adapt to societal demands and trends. It is the means in which businesses improve their operating environment.

Public Relations Activities

Corporate public relations deals with a variety of activities, issues, and events. Here's a brief glance at the activities and issues a corporate public relations department might be asked to deal with at any time.

- Hard Rock Café, a subsidiary of London-based The Rank Group PLC, announced to the media that it would offer live performances at its 55 company-owned restaurants. This represented the first of many new initiatives to reposition the brand beyond the core restaurant business. Hard Rock hotels, new merchandise, new menu items, and expanded restaurant hours are on the horizon.
- Ericsson, a Swedish telecommunications firm, sponsored an 11-day tennis tournament, called the Ericsson Open, to initiate its rebranding process. The company gave away free mobile phones to several hundred tennis professionals and sponsored a trivia contest for attendees. The phones were equipped with free interactive service, providing real-time game updates and scores. The company also created the Ericsson Open Hall of Fame.
- Six-and-a-half million tires manufactured by Bridgestone/Firestone for Ford Explorers were recalled when they were found to be the cause of countless accidents, some involving fatalities. Communication was poorly handled, leaving executives of both companies vulnerable to criticism on safety issues and suffering a huge loss of public confidence.
- Burger King franchise owners revolted against the company's owner, a British conglomerate. Some of the problems the fast-food chain faced were poor sales, weak advertising, undefined image, unstable management and a boycott by African Americans urging more minority-owned Burger Kings and increased advertising in minority media.
- Microsoft Corporation was the target of lawsuits alleging racial discrimination. Employees claimed they were given fewer stock options, were paid less, and were passed over for promotions. The software giant claimed to have a "zero tolerance policy" toward discrimination and to require that all managers receive diversity training.

This is but a mere snapshot of the world of corporate public relations. Businesses deal with and adapt to increasingly complex and dynamic situations, issues, and environments. They manage relations with a variety of publics and balance numerous complicated and pressing issues, including business ethics, equal opportunity, the quality-of-work life, consumerism, environmentalism, global commerce, and others.

The Role of the Corporate Communicator

The 21st-century corporate communicator must be proactive, anticipating issues and events so the corporation is prepared to deal with them. The 2000 Best Practices in Corporate Communications report cites the following areas that will be of greatest importance to the public relations practitioner:

- *Corporate image/reputation:* Understanding how the corporation is perceived by various corporate constituencies (surveying, polling, focus groups)
- *Strategy:* Gauging in advance how different decisions could potentially be perceived (strategic planning)
- *Message measurement:* Measuring the effectiveness of messages as they're communicated and then using this information for revising them (message measurement and adaptation based on feedback)
- Using these perceptions to develop *targeted messages* to distinct groups
- *Communication and message management:* Creating the capacity for reaching large, diverse constituencies with precision and speed, and managing communication messages through preemptive activities to influence news as it is reported[6]

The Role of Public Relations in Multinational Corporations

In the last decade U.S. companies have expanded rapidly into global markets. International trade, though, is much more complicated than trade within the United States, because different laws and cultural norms often cause considerable confusion. Conditions of competition are often quite different as well. Many barriers not found in American markets are found in international business.

Fortune magazine categorizes corporations into almost 50 industries, from the cutting-edge businesses of telecommunications, computer technology, and pharmaceuticals to the mature sectors of steel, chemicals, and autos. In figure 16.1, you will note that the top 10 of the 2001 Fortune Global 500 includes six American, two British, one Japanese, and one German corporation and represents five industry groups: motor vehicles and parts, general merchandising, petroleum refining, trading, and diversified financials. The 2002 Fortune 500 top 10 U.S. corporations, also shown in figure 16.1, make up a slightly more diversified group, representing six different industries: motor vehicles and parts, general merchandising, petroleum refining, computers, diversified financials, and tobacco.

The challenge of global public relations is to eliminate as many of the barriers to effective communication as possible. Thus, that communication must be able to transcend cultural as well as geographic barriers. Three major barriers that often confront business and public relations are differences in language, law, and culture. Other barriers in many countries include extremely bureaucratic governments, multiplicity of languages, and an underdeveloped mass media.

Public relations for multinational corporations is a complex area of practice requiring all the skills discussed elsewhere in this book plus extraordinary cross-cultural sensitivities.

The public relations function in multinational corporations has three distinct aspects. In one role, public relations practitioners represent multinational corporations at home, dealing with public opinion and governmental activities that relate both to specific corporations and to multinational enterprise as a whole. The second role of multinational public relations is to help bridge the communication gap that inevitably exists

2001 Largest Global Corporations

1. Wal-Mart Stores (U.S.) *General merchandising*
2. Exxon-Mobil (U.S.) *Petroleum refining*
3. General Motors (U.S.) *Motor vehicles and parts*
4. BP (Britain) *Petroleum refining*
5. Ford Motor (U.S.) *Motor vehicles and parts*
6. Enron (U.S.) *Petroleum refining*
7. DaimlerChrysler (Germany) *Motor vehicles and parts*
8. Royal Dutch/Shell Group (Britain/Netherlands) *Petroleum refining*
9. General Electric (U.S.) *Diversified financials*
10. Toyota Motor (Japan) *Motor vehicles and parts*

2001 Largest U.S. Corporations

1. Wal-Mart Stores *General merchandising*
2. Exxon-Mobil *Petroleum refining*
3. General Motors *Motor vehicles and parts*
4. Ford Motor *Motor vehicles and parts*
5. Enron *Petroleum refining*
6. General Electric *Diversified financials*
7. Citigroup *Diversified financials*
8. ChevronTexaco *Petroleum refining*
9. International Business Machines (IBM) *Computers*
10. Philip Morris *Tobacco*

FIGURE 16.1 **Top 10 Global and U.S. Corporations**
Source: Used with permission. *Fortune* magazine, 22 July 2002 and 15 April 2002.

between foreign operations and top management in the world headquarters. Finally, public relations must be conducted in the various host countries of the corporation.

John M. Reed concludes that public relations in the host country "has to have three legs upon which it is built: cultural savvy; language savvy; a savvy use of the tools of the craft. Forget one leg and the edifice topples. Use them in balance and success is assured."[7]

Corporations often use public relations agencies to handle the long list of communication responsibilities necessary to compete effectively in domestic and international markets. Strategically placed global agency offices ensure that the corporation has access to experts knowledgeable with the culture, language, government, media, and other important aspects of the country they're trying to operate in. Two major advantages that outside firms bring to a corporation are their unbiased perspective and their depth of experience in dealing with organizational issues.

The corporate public relations staff manages agencies and other outside consultants. Many times this is by function, such as media relations, employee relations, or government relations.

The Role of Public Relations in Smaller Corporations

The challenge to most small business owners and managers is finding time to devote to public relations. They not only must satisfy their customers, hire dependable employees, and pay their bills, but also must be a good community citizen, work with suppliers, and find ways to grow the company. Because they are responsible for all aspects of the business, small business owners and managers must focus first on the core business, the part that brings in the profits. Customers and sales come before public relations. This less-than-systematic approach means small businesses may not realize the consistent benefits that a planned public relations program could deliver.

Most small businesses have lean public relations staffs. This demands that its practitioners be generalists. For example, the corporate communicator might perform senior-level tasks like developing a strategic plan for a new plant opening and supervising employees and outside consultants, as well as overseeing junior-level tasks such as the employee newsletter and pitching story ideas to reporters. A practice analysis conducted by the Public Relations Society of America Universal Accreditation Board and Gary Siegel Organization found that corporate communicators spent most of their time on strategic planning, supervision, and doing the work.[8]

Skills Necessary for Success in Corporate Public Relations

To be successful in corporate public relations, a practitioner must have a broad range of skills and abilities and be able to apply them as the situation demands. Those new to public relations, such as recent college graduates, often start as **technicians.** Technicians develop and polish their writing, research, and other foundational public relations skills by finding information about the company's industry, writing press releases, coordinating production schedules, developing marketing communications materials, and assisting with special events. Technicians also begin to understand how senior practitioners diagnose communication problems and develop strategic plans.

As technicians assume greater managerial responsibilities, other qualities assume higher importance. Gerald C. Meyers, former American Motors chairman and chief executive officer, identifies five key attributes for senior corporate public relations professionals. First, this person must keep the boss informed and offer advice on appropriate actions. Being at the top of the organizational pyramid often isolates CEOs from others, notes one in that position. "It is very lonely being CEO because everyone you come in daily contact with is working for you," said Frank Newman, former chairman, president, and CEO of Eckerd, JC Penney's drugstore chain.[9]

Other critical qualities Meyers identifies for public relations professionals include being a sounding board to the CEO, providing early warning about potential problems, rethinking the value of conventional wisdom, and being objective and dependable.[10] These points are reinforced by John C. Knapp, president of Knapp Inc.: "PR serves clients best when it raises uncomfortable questions, introduces competing points of view and offers an unbiased interpretation of actions and implications."[11]

Corporate Public Relations Budgets

The corporate communication budget is usually a mere fraction of what the company may spend on advertising. Still, a number of factors impact the cost of communication, causing global corporate communication budgets to increase an average of 8 percent in 1999.[12] These include staffing new offices, penetrating new markets, increased competition, investing in technology, and dealing with inefficiencies in reporting structures.

Unlike consumer companies, business-to-business companies often combine their marketing efforts with public relations. A placement in the industry's premier trade publication, for example, can raise the image of the company as well as generate sales.

Tactics Used by Corporate Public Relations

Corporate public relations departments work with public relations agencies to develop comprehensive communication plans. Freelancers often supplement the corporate staff to execute the tactical aspects of the plan. Dallas-based Spaeth Communications recommends that communicators evaluate both the controlled and uncontrolled routes of communication when determining appropriate tactics. Notes Merrie Spaeth, president, "The first step in leveraging communication is to understand how a target constituency can receive conflicting messages."[13] Controlled routes are those that the corporation has editorial discretion over, such as its annual report, newsletters, advertising, Internet site, and marketing communication materials. The uncontrolled route, that which the practitioner is not able to control, represents the most powerful and credible vehicles for communicating; that is, the media and groups that influence the intended audiences.

Thus, communicators should consider **cross-disciplinary integration** and **tool integration** when determining the appropriate mix of controlled and uncontrolled tactics for the company's key audiences. Cross-disciplinary integration allows all messages communicated through advertising, media channels, or any other method to be consistent and constant. A communicator might use, for example, the disciplines of advertising and marketing communications in addition to public relations. Tool integration means that the communicator will use whatever means is available and appropriate to send a message to external and internal audiences. News releases, advertisements, e-mail, posters on bulletin boards, in-person meetings, newsletters, brochures, and the Internet and the company's intranet are all possibilities. See figure 12.2 in Chapter 12, "Consumer Relations and Marketing," for a larger list of tactics.

A first-ever study about corporate funding of publications found that the average amount that companies of all sizes spend annually on corporate publications is close to $800,000. Approximately 81 percent of this figure, or $631,865, is tagged for print publications, with 19 percent, or $168,135, earmarked for electronic publications. The study also found that the average salary of a professional working on corporate publications is $51,500.[14]

External Publiction Unifies Health Chain's Image

Mini•Case 16.1

Columbia One Source health magazine, a quarterly, was launched in January 1995 with two objectives in mind:

1. To improve publicly traded Columbia Healthcare's bottom line by retaining customers and attracting new ones.
2. To capitalize on acquisitions that had changed the small regional player into the nation's largest hospital chain. Decentralized Columbia needed a national image, but not at the expense of local decision making and marketing autonomy at its 342 hospitals.

Audiences

The primary audience of *One Source* was middle-aged women, the demographic profile proven responsible for making 80 percent of all health care decisions in America for themselves, their families, and their aging parents.

Media and Research

Internal databases and external purchased lists were used to select targeted recipients of *One Source.* A 1996 reader survey proved the intended audience was being reached. The average reader was a health-insured female in her early 40s with children who had been to the doctor at least once in the last year.

The reader survey also was used to better understand reader interests. Weight and high blood pressure were the biggest health concerns of readers. The average reader used a personal computer more than four hours a week. Tailoring content to match these needs resulted in increased readership, a prerequisite to generating inquiries. The average recipient spent 22.6 minutes reading the 32-page magazine. More than 93 percent of recipients wanted to continue receiving the magazine.

Results

Results related to the first objective included the following:

- A total of 950,000 consumer inquiries were generated by the first 12 issues. The single-issue high was 4.77 percent, or 140,000 inquiries.
- Individual issue results were used to learn about readers, and as a result, continually increase the inquiries per issue. The average number of inquiries for the last three issues was 95,000 against a per-issue average of 48,000 for the first three issues.
- A substantial amount of revenue resulted from the inquiries. Gross charges outpaced project costs by a 7:1 margin. More than 32 percent of the total charges came from new customers who hadn't used Columbia in the past three years. This tracking was made possible by an elaborate system that ties marketing and information systems together.

Results related to the second objective included the following:

- *One Source* was introduced to Columbia's 342 hospitals as an optional program in November 1995. They could produce their own publications internally, purchase noncorporate syndicated publications, not publish at all, or use *One Source.* Ninety-six percent of all Columbia hospitals used *One Source* and rated its quality in the upper 90th percentile. Hospitals found irresistible the lower prices resulting from pooled volume, coupled with higher quality and greater local customization options than they could have purchased elsewhere.

Summary

By satisfying local market needs and creating a product the markets could customize to fit their financial and communication parameters, Columbia gained a unified publishing effort and nationwide image-building tool circulated to nearly 4.8 million households each quarter.

Source: Chris McMurry, McMurry Publishing, Phoenix, AZ.

Mini-case 16.1 illustrates how a corporate publication can help a company improve its bottom line. All communication tools used are expected to play a strategic role in reaching audiences.

CORPORATE CREDIBILITY AND REPUTATION

If business and private enterprise are to exert positive influence on public attitudes toward business, they must be perceived as honest and responsible. As of this writing, the trust that many Americans have in corporations and the people who run them has been shaken. The WorldCom stockholders who watched in horror as their investments shrank to junk status had a hard time believing the company's new CEO, John Sidgmore, when he said, "We don't have a liquidity crisis, just the perception of a liquidity crisis."[15] Embattled Tyco CEO Dennis Kozlowski, in the midst of his much promoted, finally abandoned plan to break up the company, claimed, "There's absolutely no talk, no indication, no anything about any

16.1 Spotlight

Life After Corporate Scandals

The accounting and other business practices of more than two-dozen major companies, including WorldCom, Enron, Bristol-Myers, AOL Time Warner and Merck, made the headlines in 2002. Financial statements were altered to misrepresent and deceive investors. Top executive officers exhibited greed, arrogance, and a self-centered attitude. While the full extent of the corruption is not known as of this writing, there's no doubt these scandals have had a negative impact on corporate ethics and credibility. Eighty-two percent of Americans think tough new laws are needed to battle corporate corruption, according to a Harris poll.[1] The same poll noted that almost seven out of ten persons think corporate executives are less honest and trustworthy than 10 years ago.[2]

With 30 to 50 percent of a company's worth resting in its "intangible" assets,[3] public relations can have a direct and powerful impact on a corporation's overall valuation. Perhaps the place to start the process is with the top executive, a.k.a. the chief reputation officer. One study found that fewer than 10 percent of CEOs think reputation can influence stock prices.[4] Only 42 percent viewed corporate behavior as one the biggest threats to a company's reputation and only 6 percent of the executives thought there were formal measures for reputation beyond media coverage and word of mouth.[5]

Clearly senior management teams need to understand the importance of reputation and its impact on the bottom line. Building and maintaining vital relationships with key internal and external publics is about trust, integrity, and following through on promises made.

1. "Americans Want Stiff New Laws to Fight Corporate Corruption," *Wall Street Journal* (27 July 2002).
2. Ibid.
3. Douglas K. Spong, APR, "Predatory Threats and the Evolution of PR," *The Strategist* (Spring 2002), p. 40.
4. J. P. Donlon, "Guess Who's the Chief Reputation Officer?" *Chief Executive*, June 2002.
5. Ibid.

Former WorldCom Chief Financial Officer Scott Sullivan (center) is escorted to a court appearance. He was charged with one count of conspiracy to commit securities fraud, one count of securities fraud, and five counts of false filing with the SEC.

kind of change or leaving the company."[16] The so-called accounting "errors" of Enron and Arthur Andersen left thousands without jobs and retirement funds. The list of failing companies could go on: Merck, Kmart, Global Crossing, Rite-Aid, Warnaco, even Martha Stewart's empire. Spotlight 16.1 discusses the role of the chief executive officer in managing a company's reputation.

Today's marketplace is one of intense pressure—to grow, to reward stockholders, to create new jobs, to be exciting—quarter after quarter, year after year. These expectations demand that established companies constantly develop new business models in order to survive. The result is that old notions of the value of a reputation, of a brand, and of dependability are challenged and often sacrificed for short-term gain. "The most important thing is to educate them (the public) not only on where the industry is going, but what your company's role will be," says Lynn Kettleson of Clarke & Company, a public relations agency.[17]

One timeless truth is reinforced in this unsettling business environment: A corporation's best tool in achieving its business objectives and in establishing and reinforcing credibility is an excellent reputation. Fleishman-Hillard, one of the world's top public relations agencies, notes that "all the goals a corporation can set—higher stock multiple, stronger ability to attract and retain good employees, better margins, more attractive partners for mergers or acquisitions, more customers—benefit from a strong, well-managed reputation."[18]

Public relations helps a corporation build a world-class reputation. The positive relationships with key publics and the resultant mutual understanding on policies and issues can enhance a corporation's stature within its community and industry. There is a correlation between a good reputation and a healthy bottom line. However, as Ivy Lee, the "father of public relations," pointed out in the early years of the development of the discipline, it is actions, not words, that count. Reputations are earned by following through, by being trustworthy, by doing the right actions. Public relations helps counsel management to consider its publics in determining what is the correct course to take.

One study that illustrates this point is the annual *Fortune* magazine "The World's Most Admired Companies" report. Business executives and analysts who study corporations rank companies according to eight multifaceted attributes:

- Quality of management
- Quality of products and services
- Innovativeness
- Long-term investment value
- Financial soundness
- Employee talent
- Social responsibility
- Use of corporate assets

One of the chief responsibilities of corporate public relations is to work to enhance the company's image or reputation by taking positive action and then communicating that action. Figure 16.2 ranks the 10 most admired companies and notes a positive return on investment from 1996 to 2001, as reported by *Fortune* magazine. The top 10 most admired companies had a solid 25.5 percent rate of return compared with a 10.7 percent for the 10 largest corporations. You would have earned almost 15 percent more by investing on reputation alone. The formula for earning this kind of admiration is simple: A corporation needs to consistently deliver what it promises to deliver to its multiple audiences. When this is accomplished, reputation can positively impact the bottom line.[19]

The Challenge of Earning a Good Reputation

Confidence levels have been falling for most major American institutions since the early 1970s, as tracked by The Gallup Organization.[20] There are a variety of reasons for this.

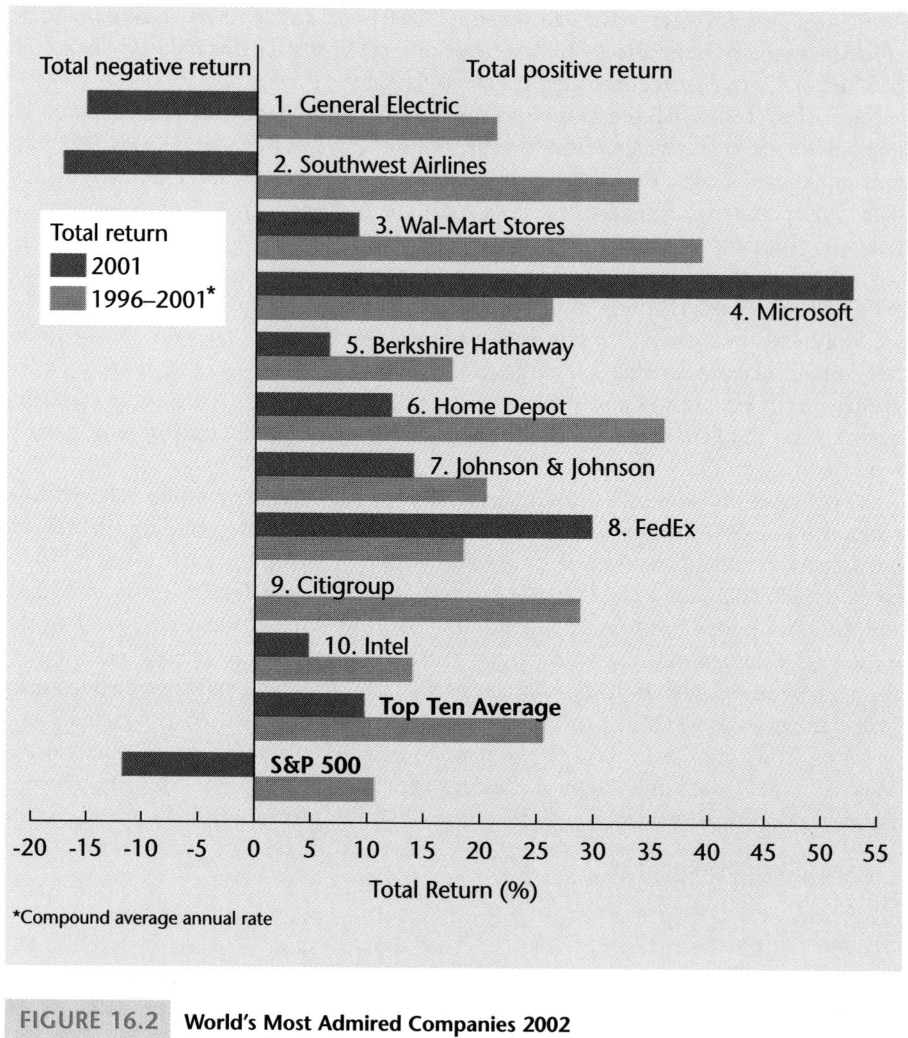

FIGURE 16.2 **World's Most Admired Companies 2002**
Source: Used with permission. *Fortune* magazine, 4 March 2002.

Big business can be seen as evading issues, disclaiming responsibility, exaggerating facts, or overpromising results. It's easy for the general public to feel that corporations are only looking out for themselves, supporting persuasion research that says disinterested parties are perceived as more credible than interested ones.

It could be argued that big business's problems began in the early 1930s, when President Hoover and American business promised "prosperity is right around the corner." When the promises proved false, the American public invited Franklin Roosevelt and the New Deal to change the face of American business, government, and society. In the ensuing years, American business made promises it could not keep, accepted credit for accomplishments that were not really its own, pushed costs and problems into a future that has now arrived, oversold and underdelivered, and kept score with a crooked measuring stick. Whether such mistakes and misdemeanors are intentional or not, and whether business is the perpetrator or the victim of these circumstances, is not the point. What matters is that public and consumer expectations have been pumped up in thousands of small ways—through corporate statements, advertising, marketing techniques, and public relations—and that those expectations have not been fulfilled. Such is the power of promises perceived to be broken.

Current Gallup poll data places the military at the top of the list of institutions Americans have the most trust in, although its confidence rating has fallen in the past decade from an all-time high of 85 percent during the Gulf War in March 1991 to 64 percent in November 2000. Big business is consistently near the bottom of the list, receiving a confidence rating of 29 percent in 2000. Honesty and ethical standards of business executives are considered very high or high by only 23 percent of respondents. Small business, on the other hand, led all rated in the poll when it was included in the list of institutions evaluated, receiving a 63 percent confidence rating in 1997.[21] Perhaps one simple explanation for the disparity is that the public expects more from big business than business can possibly provide. According to George A. Steiner, "Society expects business to help society improve the quality of life, and expectations are running ahead of reality."[22]

Hill & Knowlton executive William A. Durbin echoes Steiner's comment: "The single most critical problem facing today is . . . lost credibility."[23]

Restoring Credibility

Credibility once lost is difficult to regain. Nevertheless, a number of policies, if implemented and practiced by businesses individually and collectively, can substantially contribute to the reestablishment of public trust.

Openness and Honesty As a first step, business must tear down the walls. The notion that public relations can be used as a shield is passé. The idea that the corporate domain is impervious to the prying eyes and ears of consumers, competitors, the media, and the regulators is an illusion. Honesty is no longer just the best policy; it is the *only* policy when even painful truths cannot be securely and permanently hidden. Procter & Gamble's handling of Rely tampons, Johnson & Johnson's Tylenol response, and the Pepsi syringe hoax all show how businesses have become more open and forthcoming. Spotlight 16.2 discusses communication concerning an environmental project.

Complete candor and forthrightness is the only way to achieve credibility. This candor must be active rather than passive. It is not enough to say, "I will answer any question," when you know that your audience does not necessarily know what questions to ask. Instead, businesses must listen to their constituents (including employees, customers, regulators, and other stakeholders) and respond to their incompletely articulated questions and concerns.

American corporations, represented by their upper-level executives, must reach out into their communities directly and through the media on a regular and continuing basis, responding to public concerns and explaining the impacts and rationales for corporate actions and decisions. Chief executive officers recognize in most cases that they should play a leading role in public outreach. It is no longer uncommon for top executives to spend one-fourth to more than one-half of their time on externalities.

Openness, in this case, refers again to many publics. Employees need more information on the finances, economics, and policies of their employers. Members of communities in which businesses operate should be informed in advance of decisions and actions that may affect them. Corporations have already painfully learned that voluntary disclosures of corporate problems, mistakes, or wrongdoing hurt far less than the consequences of not being forthcoming.

16.2 Spotlight

Corporate Environmental Project

A major chemical company's clean-up of polychlorinated biphenyls (PCBs) at an industrial location had the potential to become another negative "corporate polluter" story. The Vandiver Group, Inc., St. Louis, was hired to communicate the cleanup project to the public.

The goal was to present the company's cleanup efforts in a constructive light and help the company build and maintain its relationship with the community.

The first step was to establish immediate and long-term objectives in order to develop a proactive communications program. The program included both reactive and proactive strategies and was assessed regularly during implementation.

One key goal was to keep citizens informed of actions the company was taking to investigate and clean up the area. Another goal was to present information on other charitable or community efforts being undertaken by the company, and how these efforts were helping create better communities. The communications program encouraged interaction among company officials from corporate headquarters, officials at the local plant, and key members of the community.

Some elements of the plan included:

- Town hall meetings
- Company-sponsored forums
- Direct mail
- Community newsletter
- Fact sheets/Q&A/brochures
- A community-information hotline staffed by a company representative working on the project
- Specific publicity through local media

This approach to environmental issues had the potential to become a model for other company projects, as adverse publicity could have negatively affected the company's bottom line.

Consistent Actions The second step in restoring the credibility of business is to remove the glaring contradictions of business behavior. What business says and what it does should correspond. Fast-food chains McDonald's, Burger King, and Wendy's ensure the animal products they purchase are produced in a humane manner by only buying from those who agree to meet certain standards and conditions such as unannounced inspections.[24] Not walking the talk leads to problems. Although BellSouth says it is committed to equal and respectful treatment of every employee, it was served with a class-action lawsuit charging racial discrimination against African Americans.[25]

Social Responsibility Third, if business is to be treated and trusted as a central force in American society, it must address issues perceived as crucial to society. Businesses must be visibly involved in public issues, making substantial commitments in time, energy, resources, and discipline toward solving problems of public importance.

In a sense, the focus of corporate concerns needs to be refined. As one former major corporate CEO put it: "Companies like ours are public institutions with several publics to account to—not just shareholders. This requires a different type of informational approach. Part of my job is to be a public figure and to take positions on public issues, not just company activities."[26]

Public Education Finally, business must strive to offer the public a better understanding of what it can do, what it cannot do, how it operates, and the constraints on its operations. Public expectations, must be brought into line with reality.

Renewed credibility must be built on a firm foundation of honest performance, open communication, and removal of inconsistencies between performance and communication. Business should reemphasize its commitments to problem solving in areas usually considered beyond its purview, and business should avoid creating or encouraging expectations that cannot be met. Restoring business credibility is, however, only a first step in the overall rehabilitation of public attitudes toward business.

CHALLENGES OF CORPORATE PUBLIC RELATIONS

Public attitudes toward business are developed neither by reading stories about business in the newspaper nor by listening to the pronouncements of executives in public forums. Most people develop their opinions as a result of their experiences as consumers, employees, or investors. Every interaction between buyer and seller or employee and employer has not only economic but also educational and political implications.

Polls have revealed the widespread belief that business lacks concern for the consumer. Harris found that 71 percent of the population feels business would do nothing to help the consumer if it might reduce its own profits—unless forced. A *New York Times* article noted how disgruntled customers are turning to the Internet to vent their frustrations with unresponsive companies. Although the complaints vary from serious to minor to furious, all share a common theme: that the people filing the complaints deserve better.[27]

It is really not necessary to go to the pollsters or the Internet to discover consumer dissatisfaction. Everyone has not one but several horror stories about their experiences as a customer, including battles with computers, insensitive salespeople, false and misleading advertising, abusive repair services, warranty problems, and so on. At the heart of all such difficulties is the consumer's perception that business is unconcerned and unresponsive. Business, on too many occasions, reinforces feelings of depersonalization and alienation—of being just a number. It is in this fertile ground of hostility and alienation that the roots of the consumer movement have grown.

Consumer Relations

Consumer relations is an essential component of corporate communication. The quality of the average individual's daily experiences with a company's products, services, employees, and other aspects should be outstanding, but that isn't always the case. The role of public relations in this effort is to advise top management of appropriate responses to alienated consumers and to work with management to ensure the problems aren't repeated. Consumer relations is discussed in detail in chapter 12.

Promoting Public Understanding

If we want the public to understand profits or private enterprise, we must see to it that communicators present information in terms the public can understand. Statistics must illuminate, not exaggerate. Here again, public relations practitioners should heed the basic tenets of their creed: Consider the audience, carefully word the communication, and be consistent. We cannot achieve public economic understanding by blocking it with statistics, generalities, technical language, or the like. Frequently, such communication does more harm than good.

One example is a newspaper headline that reported a major company's "Profits Up 273 Percent." During the next few days, other corporations' second-quarter earnings were reported in similar terms: an automaker's profits were up 313 percent; three chemical companies' profits were up 109 percent, 430 percent, and 947 percent, respectively. Various sources reported that all industries enjoyed average profit increases ranging from 31 to 36 percent. People who have business experience understand these figures and can immediately put them in perspective. Indeed, such statistics are designed to impress knowledgeable stockholders and investors. But these astronomically high figures also reach the general public who interpret them as big, even "obscene" profits.

An insurance company offered another example of inflammatory rhetoric, reporting "operating earnings . . . almost four times greater than . . . a year earlier." Consumers who do not understand the statistics that follow this claim consider their higher insurance premiums and conclude that they are being ripped off. With the help of a calculator, however, one can see that the company's margins rose from .92 percent to 2.57 percent. An informed emotional response changes from hostility to sympathy. But the company cannot assume that the ordinary consumer will understand such figures. As Disraeli said: There are lies, damn lies, and statistics.

Other major issues facing corporate public relations in the early part of the 21st century include globalization of business operations, with resulting globalization of public relations; unprecedented technological change; increased emphasis on diversity issues; and intensified crises and disasters.

Global Public Relations

Business has expanded rapidly into global markets in the last decade by lowered trade barriers; development of worldwide, almost instantaneous financial markets; and acquisition of many American businesses by foreign companies. Consequently, public relations, too, has become global. Major technological changes including the Internet, fax machines, and digital telephone relays have speeded globalization and have linked even the most remote parts of the world with business everywhere.

Technological Change

Emerging technologies are revolutionizing the way public relations people do business and communicate with their key publics. The Internet, intranet, chatrooms, websites, e-mails, and other computer-based tools as well as wireless technology provide numerous opportunities for disseminating information, giving and receiving feedback, purchasing goods and services, tapping into what consumers are thinking, providing access to corporate materials, updating consumers and employees, and more.

One example of technology's impact is the way that some corporate investor relations departments are reaching influential financial analysts and investors. Instead of using the media to report news about companies, the financial area is taking their messages directly to decision makers through webcasts. These television-like programs supplement traditional public relations and advertising tools and provide companies with editorial control over the broadcast content.[28]

What is important for public relations practitioners to understand about technology is that it represents the emergence of new channels of communication. Those who entered the public relations field in the 1960s and early 1970s probably used a manual typewriter and sent their copy to newspapers that used hot lead in its production process. Cordless has given way to wireless. These tools of the past seem like relics of a time much longer ago than 30 years. Although there's no limit of opinions on how technology will continue to shape our lives, there's no doubt that it will impact the practice of public relations.

Diversity

Diversity, or inclusion as it is sometimes referred to, encompasses the mix of race, age, gender, sexual orientation, religious beliefs, national origin, and disability. J. Donald Turk, APR, a public relations manager for Exxon Mobil Corporation, expresses his belief in the future: "There will be greater diversity of employees, customers, and constituencies." Turk has served as the chair of the Corporate Section of the Public Relations Society of America and anticipates that the global economy will be a place where "diversity will be characteristic of the work force and customer mix, as well as one in which diversity will be valued and even required to be a successful business."[29]

Diversity means different things in different countries. For example, almost one-fourth of Lucent Technologies's workforce is employed outside of the United States. Whereas Hispanic-, African- and Native American issues receive much attention in the United States, most non-Dutch employees in the Lucent Netherlands office are from North Africa, the Middle East, or Europe. Local employment laws and practices create difficulties in transferring training programs from one country to another.[30] Because of Lucent's commitment to global diversity, the company developed a New Realities Diversity Campaign. The essence of this program is captured in figure 16.3, comparing the old and new ways of doing business.

Global companies like Hilton Hotels Corporation operate hotels around the world. The HHC diversity mission statement emphasizes the importance of "developing and maintaining a workplace culture which reflects awareness and sensitivity to individual abilities and appreciation of ethnic, gender, racial, religious, and cultural differences."[31]

Lucent Technologies presents its stand on diversity in this poster.

Commitment to diversity affects how corporations do business. Bank of America, for example, commits 15 percent of its total procurement budget with business owned by minorities, women, and disabled individuals. The program, initiated in 1999, has already led to increases in revenue and cash flow and stronger market positions.

Business can perhaps borrow from former commerce secretary Ron Brown's seven tenets for planning to achieve diversity. At the U.S. Census Bureau the following guidelines are used to achieve a diverse workforce:

1. *Inclusion.* Valuing all employees regardless of race, gender, color, religious belief, national origin, age, disability, or sexual orientation.
2. *Opportunity.* Recruiting aggressively and developing career programs to ensure a diverse pool of qualified candidates for the job.
3. *Comprehensiveness.* Considering diversity in business affairs such as training, seminar procurement, grant processes, trade missions, regulatory matters, business liaison and every other program of the department.
4. *Accessibility.* Strengthening EEO complaint procedures to ensure fair and timely processing of complaints.
5. *Training.* Encouraging participation of senior managers in training on diversity policies and conflict resolution techniques.
6. *Management.* Adding diversity efforts as a factor to job performance evaluations of management personnel.
7. *Evaluation and Communication.* Establishing a diversity council to monitor, evaluate, and facilitate programs to implement diversity.[32]

Looking Back *(the way we used to do things)*	New Realities *(the way we do things now)*
People are identified as part of a group	People are treated as individuals or within their own self-defined cultural context
Actions limited to compliance with EO/AA mandates	Create and encourage a multicultural environment
Diversity as one of a series of periodic human resources programs	Diversity is seamlessly integrated in to the business (becomes the context for the way we do business)
Lucent Technologies employees are responsible for their own actions	Lucent Technologies employees (at all levels) are accountable for demonstrating diversity leadership and modeling behaviors
Place emphasis on policies and procedures (what to do and what not to do)	Place emphasis on tools and values
Risk avoidance	Maximize business performance through diversity and related initiatives

FIGURE 16.3 **Lucent Technologies New Realities** **Source:** Used with permission from Lucent Technologies.

Summary

For self-testing and additional chapter resources, go to the student CD and the Online Learning Center at **www.mhhe.com/lattimore**

This chapter explores the aspects of public relations practice that apply to corporations. Effective public relations must begin with the chief executive officer. The CEO who values communication has a trickle-down effect, enabling employees to make better decisions, which in turns helps to attract the best employees who apply their skills and talents in a competitive environment.

Effective corporate public relations has a positive impact on the bottom line. Customers want to do business with companies that have good reputations.

Global public relations, diversity, technological change, and crisis management are major issues facing corporate public relations practitioners. How they prepare to deal with these issues may well be the margin of success or failure in the next decade.

To learn more about corporate public relations watch the interview with Kathy Jeavons, Clip #10, on the student CD-ROM.

Taking BP Beyond

By Michael Fox
Ogilvy Public Relations
New York

Situation Analysis

Following the 1999 merger of British Petroleum and Amoco, the combined company proceeded to acquire the Atlantic Richfield Corporation (Arco) and Burmah Castrol and launch a unifying global branding initiative, renaming the company BP. The rebranding entailed the introduction of a new visual identity and a new brand positioning, designed to help BP transcend the oil sector, deliver top-line growth, and define the company as innovative, progressive, environmentally responsible, and performance-driven. BP set out to demonstrate to key opinion formers, business partners, and its 100,000 employees how it intended to go "beyond petroleum."

Objectives

- Define the new BP brand promise.
- Engage, enroll, and transform the organization around the new brand.
- Create awareness and generate openness toward the new brand among business partners and opinion formers.
- Launch the new brand.

Audience

The campaign was targeted at, in order, BP employees, its business partners, and opinion leaders.

Research

- Competitive research—identified best practice activities among top brands.
- Employee surveys—GGC conducted monthly to gauge perceptions of the existing company and needs/wants.
- Customer surveys—PS&B surveyed jobbers and dealers in the United States about the change in brand status.
- Fuel price analysis—Ogilvy PR monitored public opinion about this volatile issue prior to brand launch.

Planning

For six months, the Ogilvy PR BP team collaborated across practices, offices, and even companies to support the global rebranding and launch. The integrated team included Ogilvy PR's offices in New York, Chicago, DC, London, Singapore, Sydney, and Thailand and involved Ogilvy PR's Workplace Performance, Corporate Communications, Marketing and Public Affairs practices as well as Research, Information, and Creative Services. This 360-degree communications team worked in conjunction with Ogilvy & Mather, OgilvyOne, and Mindshare.

Strategy

The strategy was to position BP as a new type of energy company that confronts the difficult issues, such as the conflict between energy and environmental needs, and takes actions *beyond* what is expected of an oil company.

Execution/Tactics

Ogilvy PR developed an integrated communications plan designed to work with all BP business streams and to address a variety of internal and external audiences.

Internal Communication

- *Brand Story*—a presentation that outlined the "case for change" and a vision of the new BP.
- *Brand Speeches*—for executives to deliver consistent messages about the meaning and importance of "brand."
- *Brand Champions*—a network of internal leaders established across the company to help execute engagement tactics and get employee feedback.
- *Employee Engagement Toolkit*—developed for senior level leadership to cascade messages to their staff, which contained key messages, facilitation guides, Q&As, brand presentations, a CD-ROM, and interactive exercises.
- *On-line Message Board/Chatroom called* In Motion—Ogilvy PR promoted this site internally through contests and a campaign that asked, *Are You In Motion?* and distributed magnetic poetry, T-shirts, Hacky Sacks and notepads, all featuring the campaign slogan.
- *Launch Day Kits*—distributed globally to all major facilities via Brand Champions, included:
  - Posters and CD-ROMs with copies of launch advertising
  - Brand Book—overview of what the brand means for employees
  - Brand Film (created by O&M)
  - Pens, hats, premiums featuring the new company name and logo
- *CEO Satellite Broadcast*—on launch day, BP CEO Sir John Browne hosted a live satellite broadcast, which was taped and posted to the company intranet site.
- *Leadership E-mails*—on launch day e-mails were sent by the CEO and by local business unit leaders.
- *Launch Day Town Hall Meetings*—local offices held town hall meetings with staff to view the CEO satellite broadcast and the brand film. Town Hall facilitation guides developed by Ogilvy PR enabled executives to highlight key brand messages and address employee questions.
- *Launch Celebrations*—celebrations were held in BP locations throughout the world, including an IMAX theater presentation in Australia, a dragon dance/celebration in Thailand, and team-building exercises at the Cleveland Zoo. Celebrations built genuine excitement among BP staff and addressed the values and key messages that underlie the brand relaunch.

Business Partner Communication

BP's key business partners, particularly its retail partners, were instrumental to the success of the brand launch. Research was conducted to determine the issues of concern to this audience. To gain their support, an orchestrated outreach program began several months before the brand launch that provided them with information about the company's strategy for the future and the importance of branding. Working with O&M, a special video was created to underscore the key points of the retail strategy. Key messages were provided to retail account representatives to enable them to engage partners about the coming changes.

On the day before launch, Ogilvy PR and BP hosted the company's top partners at a warehouse in Atlanta that is home to a prototype of the new BP service station. A full-day tour and set of events closed with a four-star dinner and champagne toast to "the future." Key messages and Q&As were developed for employees at retail service stations to address customer questions or concerns.

Ogilvy PR helped further the introduction of BP's new brand with key partners by orchestrating a convention in San Francisco three weeks after the brand launch that introduced the new brand to 600 jobbers and dealers. The event featured three days of activities and a special video appearance by NFL commentator John Madden, which was coordinated by Ogilvy PR.

Media/Opinion Former Communication

For the media, the Ogilvy team produced press releases, press kits, and a VNR of the new BP Connect retail service station. Ogilvy PR managed a press tour of major media to the Atlanta warehouse prototype that included the *Wall Street Journal, Financial Times, New York Times, Bloomberg, Chicago Tribune, Washington Post,* and CNN. Follow-up media outreach helped deliver the new brand message to key opinion formers along with BP's launch day advertising.

Obstacles

BP faced numerous obstacles in the United States, where the name BP has very little presence. Record high gas prices consumed the nation's attention for much of the summer. The brand launch occurred just several weeks after the FTC announced an investigation into possible price gouging by oil companies. BP also faced the challenge of a foreign company taking over a popular American brand, a problem exacerbated by the fact that the company had promised a year earlier to maintain the Amoco name. The combination of four companies and the fact that BP has operations in more than 100 countries presented enormous logistical challenges.

Evaluation or Measurement of Success

Launch day media coverage included excellent placements in the *Wall Street Journal, WSJ Europe, Financial Times, Times of London, New York Times, Bloomberg, Chicago Tribune,* and the *Washington Post,* among 175 other great hits internationally in 20 countries spanning six continents and in the U.S. major markets. Major broadcast coverage was secured on CNN, CNNfn, and numerous national affiliates. Despite the fuel crisis, coverage focused on the company's new logo, the completion of the merger, and the company's retail business strategy. The new offering was presented in the context of the new brand and the effort to "go beyond."

The brand contributed to a strong outlook across the entire workforce with 90 percent saying the company was going in the right direction. In just one month following brand relaunch, 76 percent were favorable to the new brand,

80 percent were aware of the four brand values, and 77 percent believed it was credible for BP to go "beyond petroleum."

Response from BP's business partners in the United States far exceeded expectations with great support for the new brand and the company's retail strategy going forward.

Questions

1. Given the global nature of this re-branding effort, identify possible obstacles BP might have faced in launching the new brand. How might these challenges affect the communication efforts?
2. What questions do you think the employees might have had about the re-branding? Would the tactics that were used have addressed these questions? Why or why not?
3. Assume you are an entry-level employee at Ogilvy PR and have been assigned to help with the launch of the new BP brand. What kind of assignments do you think you'd be asked to do?

Key Terms

Use the CD-ROM and Online Learning Center at www.mhhe.com/lattimore to further your understanding of the following terms

corporate public relations
cross-disciplinary integration
seat at the table
target audiences
target markets
target publics
technicians
tool integration

Notes

1. Provided by SBC Corporate Communication Department.
2. Peter Himler and Melanie Driscoll, "CEOs Have Only Five Quarters to Prove Themselves According to New National Study of Business Influentials," Burson-Marsteller proprietary research, Building CEO Capital, www.CEOgo.com, 2001.
3. Tom Neff and Dayton Ogden, "Sixth Annual Route to the Top: Anatomy of a CEO," Chief Executive/Spencer Stuart (February 2001).
4. Edward A. Blechschmidt, quoted in Joann S. Lublin,"Pros Give Advice to Managers Making the Leap to Top Spot," *Wall Street Journal,* www.WSJ.com, February 6, 2001.
5. Judith Muhlberg, quoted in Tony Seideman, "Boeing Learns to Stop Worrying and Love PR," *PRWeek,* 26 June 1999, p. 16.
6. Executive Summary: Best Practices in Global Communications, 2000, Best Practices in Corporate Communications website: http://www.tpag.com, 6.
7. John M. Reed, "International Media Relations: Avoid Self-Binding," *Public Relations Quarterly* (Summer 1989), pp. 12–15.
8. Universal Accreditation Report, www.prsa.org, October 2000.
9. Lublin, "Pros Give Advice to Managers Making the Leap to Top Spot."

10. Mike Davis, "Most Desirable PR Traits Told at PRSA," *PRWeek,* 13 November 2000, p. 7.
11. John C. Knapp, "Thinkpiece: Public Relations Will Never Be Considered a True Profession Unless Pros Give Objective Advice," *PRWeek,* 26 June 2000, p. 15.
12. Ana Vargas, "Global Corporate Budgets Grow 8%," *PRWeek,* 26 June 2000, p. 4.
13. Merrie Spaeth, Spaeth Communications, Inc. http://www.spaethcommunications.com, 6 March 2001.
14. McMurry Publications Management survey report, http://www.pubmgmt.com, 6 March 2001.
15. Charles Haddad, "Saving WorldCom: An Impossible Dream?" *Business Week,* 13 May 2002, p. 49.
16. Forbes market newswire, 25 April 2002.
17. Lynn Kettleson, as quoted by Craig McGuire, "Switching on to PR," *PRWeek,* 16 October 2000, p. 21.
18. Fleishman-Hillard website: http://www.fleishmanhillard.com, 25 November 2000.
19. Matthew Boyle, "The Shiniest Reputations in Tarnished Times," *Fortune,* 4 March 2002, p. 72.
20. The Gallup Organization website: http://www.gallup.com.
21. Ibid.
22. G. A. Steiner, *Business and Society,* 2nd ed. (New York: Random House, 1975), p. 72.
23. Hill & Knowlton Executives, *Critical Issues,* p. 223.
24. Anita Chabria, "Safeway Talks to PETA and Turns Protest into Support," *PRWeek,* 27 May 2002, p. 2.
25. Kimberly Krautter, "BellSouth Reputation Hit by Racial Discrimination Class-Action Suit," *PRWeek,* 13 May 2002, p. 5.
26. William Agee, quoted in *Business Week,* 22 January 1979.
27. Hilary Appelman, "I Scream, You Scream: Consumers Vent Over the Net," http://www.nytimes.com, 4 March 2001.
28. David Ward, "Virtual Investor Relations: Using Webcasts to Bypass Journalists," *PRWeek,* 26 June 2000, p. 46.
29. J. Donald Turk, quoted in Susan Bovet, "Forecast 2001," *Public Relations Journal* (October 1995), p. 13.
30. Jan Neuteboom, "Reliving Diversity in a Multi-Local Company," *Profiles in Diversity Journal* (February 2001).
31. Dorothy Hayden-Watkins, "Diversity—The Right Thing," *Profiles in Diversity Journal* (February 2001).
32. Carol Shaw, "Achieving Diversity After Work Force Downsizing," *Government Communications* (November 1995), p. 18.

CHAPTER SEVENTEEN

Emerging Trends in Public Relations

17

Outline

PREVIEW
COMMUNICATION TECHNOLOGY IMPACTS—ESPECIALLY THE INTERNET
Implications for Media Relations
Implications for Investor Relations
Implications for Marketing Communication
Implications for Internal Communication
Implications for Activists and New Stakeholders
A Paradigm Shift Among Practitioners
PUBLIC RELATIONS AND GLOBAL MARKETS
THE CHANGING INSTITUTION OF PUBLIC RELATIONS
Rethinking Internal Communication
Changing Organizational Structures and Settings
EVOLVING PRACTITIONER ROLES
From External Counsel to Internal Communication Consultant
From One-Way Communication to Two-Way Communication and Interaction
From Marketing Support to Integrated Communication
From Program to Process
From Media Craftsperson to Communication Planner
From Short-Term Items to Long-Term Relationship Development
From Firefighters to Crisis Managers
From Manipulation to Understanding, Negotiation, and Compromise
From a Male- to a Female-Dominated Profession
From U.S. Profession to Global Profession
SUMMARY

P R E V I E W

The practice of public relations is continually being reshaped and that's especially the case today given the many uses for new communication technology, the impacts of **globalization,** and organizational restructuring. This chapter examines these societal-level trends and then considers how the nature of the public relations practice and the qualifications of practitioners are changing in response. And finally, the chapter concludes by overviewing 10 ongoing and long-term changes in the practice.

Much of what's considered to be "public relations" work today may not be recognizable as such by 2010 if the pace of Internet-driven technology changes, globalization of worldwide markets, and organizational restructuring continue at present rates. To estimate the significance of these changes, Grupp/PR Strategist notes that 95 percent of all information will be generated by machines, and only 5 percent by people communicating face-to-face in 2010.[1]

The relationship-building business that many see as public relations may soon look completely different, though the big reasons seem fairly clear-cut. First are the uses of new communication technologies and especially such Internet capabilities as speed, targeting, repetition, and consistency. Second, the massive building and restructuring of market economies around the world remind us that the nature of public relations work is often shaped by larger social, economic, political, and cultural changes. And third, the huge number of mergers and acquisitions brought on by the dot-com bulge and bust, the stock market plunge of 2001 and beyond, results in organizational restructuring that vastly increases the relative importance of a whole range of communication technology and training functions. Many of these new functions are not now managed by the public relations or communication department, but they soon will be.

To be sure, solid public relations accomplishment will always come from effective relationship-building grounded in principles of two-way, relatively balanced communication. What's different is that so much more of this will be mediated, rather than taking place face-to-face, in small groups or even in organizational meetings. Thus, for today's public relations students, these changes should prompt future practitioners to think carefully about their journalism and communication course selections, not to mention minors and double majors. That's because most students want graduation to be followed by an entry-level professional job rather than a glorified third or fourth internship

COMMUNICATION TECHNOLOGY IMPACTS—ESPECIALLY THE INTERNET

New communication technologies have always influenced public relations practice, but perhaps none so profoundly as the **Internet** and e-mail. Budgets have been reallocated to make optimal use of digital technology. An array of new practices capitalizes on Internet speed and currency to keep key constituencies aware of current developments. These include crisis management programs, multimedia campaigns, round-the-clock media relations programs, and partnerships and alliances with new and existing groups. The results show up in sales to new customers, in repeated sales to existing ones, and in lower operating costs because technology helped create a dialogue between organizations and activist groups.

First, let's consider the Internet—its rate of adoption, the way it has intensified the nature of relationship building with key constituencies, and how it has changed specific practice areas in public relations, including media relations and crisis communication, employee and internal communication, investor relations, marketing communication, and communication with activist groups in the community and throughout the world. Media relations expert Carole Howard notes that it took the Internet just four years to reach an audience of 50 million people compared with the 13 years it took television to reach the 50 million mark and the 30 years it took radio. Conservative forecasts suggest that as many as 550 million users are now surfing the Net.[2] That's close to 10 percent of the world's population. Carried further, seven people log onto the Internet for the first time every second. The fastest growth in Internet use is now outside the United States. One billion users are expected by 2010. Steve Lawrence of NEC Research Institute reported in the journal *Science* that the growth of Internet pages will increase 10 times by 2003, totaling 3.5 billion pages.[3]

What these adoption statistics don't show are the ways the Internet has fundamentally changed how journalists and businesses operate. Grasping this involves knowing a few basics. First, the Internet alters the way people get information from organizations. Communicating through the Internet means that people or members of an organization's constituencies are pulling information off the Net about the organization rather than the organization pushing information onto them as is the case with regular news release dissemination.

Second, communication is not just top-down and one-to-many. By making all appropriate information available on the website along with accompanying links means that customers, media reporters, investors, industry analysts, employees, government regulators, activists, and others can get whatever information they want and put it together in any order they want without going through the public relations practitioner.

In this sense, the Internet has noticeably displaced the "gatekeeping" functions previously provided both by editors and public relations practitioners.

In short, the Internet offers channel capabilities unequaled by other media. Some believe that being able to pull information from the Internet gives busy people better control of their time—they get their news when they want it and where they want it; thus, individuals are relying more heavily on the Internet as the news source versus traditional print or broadcast media outlets.

The Internet is considered a rich medium in that its interactive qualities give it many of the characteristics of interpersonal communication or the sense of actually being there in face-to-face conversation. Thus, **rich media** "touch" more of the senses, and their messages can be personalized enough to convey a sense of conversing with someone as if you were building a long-term relationship.

Because of fast, direct, and consistent contact with key constituencies, Internet technology advances almost every facet of public relations practice. Seen this way, the practice areas discussed in this section, although not representing the full scope of public relations work, nevertheless highlight common new uses of Internet technology for public relations. A discussion of Internet uses in public relations would be incomplete, however, without mention of common misuses. Unfortunately, the Internet generally and e-mail in particular are too often used for spamming or blitzing the immediate world with overly one-sided or near-useless information.

Besides Internet use, e-mail has become a mainstay for public relations practice, especially in media relations. A majority of reporters and editors prefer to get news releases by e-mail and even to contact their own story sources at least initially through e-mail. In fact, e-mail has replaced the fax as the principal source of company news releases. Digitally edited video is transmitted over satellite or through fiber optic cables laid by the telephone, telecom, and cable companies. Like other professionals, public relations practitioners make significant use of cell phones although it's too early to forecast all the ways that wireless communication technologies will be used in public relations.

Implications for Media Relations

Media relations work, more than other practice areas, has benefited from Internet technology and the **World Wide Web.** That's because journalists and other insiders have come to expect news and information to be announced seven days a week on a round-the-clock basis. What a switch from the days when news releases were fully developed and then sent by mail, fax, or courier. Thus, the Internet provides stiff competition for all traditional media because of its ability to transmit news virtually instantaneously. The old "news cycle" is obsolete. The media day has turned into the media hour and now into the media minute or second, says Carole Howard.[5] Internet technology has created access to and demand for immediate information and frequent updates. The upshot is that as many people now get their breaking news online as those who read it in the newspapers. Today, half of all print and broadcast media allow their websites to scoop their parent publications, networks, or stations.

The adoption of Internet technology by journalists and public relations practitioners has been benchmarked annually. Don Middleberg and Steven Ross have been cataloging the Internet's use patterns since 1994.

Here are a few highlights from the Middleberg/Ross 2000 study:[6]

1. Seventy-eight percent of reporters use the Internet to find news sources, up from 58 percent in 1996.

2. Seventy-three percent of journalists use the Internet for locating press releases, up from 26 percent in 1995.
3. Fifty-three percent of journalists use the Internet for receiving story pitches, up from 25 percent in 1996.
4. Ninety-two percent of journalists use the Internet to conduct research on assignments, up from 66 percent in 1995.
5. The percentage of journalists using a cell phone doubled between 2000 and 2002.

At least three new media relations benchmarks took hold between 2000 and 2002.[7] For the first time, journalists covering breaking stories said in 2000 that they are more likely to turn first to an organization's website than to a live source at the company or in the community. Also, for the first time in 2002, e-mail became journalists' preferred medium when working with new or unknown sources. Unfortunately, journalists have often resorted to taking information from chatrooms and usenets as secondary sources.

Perhaps the most common uses of the Internet by public relations practitioners involve story pitching and story development. The typical process would involve a public relations practitioner pitching a story idea via e-mail to a New York trade magazine editor. If they knew each other, they might phone. The trade magazine reporter assigned to this segment or beat would then scope out the information and story possibilities by viewing the organization's website. This is followed by another e-mail exchange or phone call to the practitioner asking for the names of others sources, including industry analysts and perhaps financial analysts. From this point on, the public relations practitioner is likely to be responding to specific information requests from the reporter.

Another common practice is for the public relations consultant to pitch particular stories to particular media based on knowing their editorial calendars or schedules of stories or themes for upcoming issues. Second only to story pitching and development is for media relations experts to use the Internet to track their media coverage and that of the competitors. As well, tracking services peruse chatrooms and discussion groups so they can report what the media and other influential citizens or groups are saying about an organization and its competitor organizations.

Implications for Investor Relations

Raising the necessary capital to develop markets worldwide, as well as 24-hour financial markets, has transformed investor relations into a markedly more integral public relations function over the course of the last decade. Online media are proving to be especially useful in investor relations because they connect the organization to the business and financial press, shareholders, and institutional investors.

Public relations practitioners, especially those in investor relations departments, focus on Internet audiences that matter most in building credibility and awareness—media, industry analysts, venture capitalists, individual investors, and the financial community, writes Middleberg.[8] He believes that the Internet helps explain why organizations put more money into public relations and communication programs prior to the dot-com bust and subsequent recession.

Implications for Marketing Communication

The Internet has undoubtedly done more than any other communication technology to strengthen relationships with customers through relationship marketing. In fact, Internet public relations expert Don Middleberg[9] maintains that public relations consistently

Bon Jovi performs during the promotion for NFL Kickoff Live from Times Square, a special event concert preceding the rare Thursday night opening pro football game between the San Francisco 49ers and the New York Giants at Giants Stadium.

plays a bigger role in branding products and companies than do any other communication tools, including advertising. That is, public relations is utilized to demonstrate market demand primarily through third-party endorsements from industry analysts and other experts. Moreover, public relations practitioners have become astute at building brand acceptance by attracting customers to the company website through contests and continuous information updates. Creating this online "buzz" may also involve working through message boards and postings to newsgroups.

Unlike other elements in the marketing communications process (advertising, sales promotions, corporate sponsorships, direct selling), website updating does not take months of planning and production and, therefore, becomes a principal tool for increasing market share. All of this promotes customer loyalty that translates into repeat purchases by existing customers, thereby cutting the number of advertising dollars that must be spent to attract new, replacement customers. It's little wonder then that companies build market share by being online first with a website geared to attracting new customers and keeping old ones.

Internet and e-mail technologies are used increasingly to maintain contact with existing customers through a process called **relationship marketing.** Relationship marketing is based on the premise that keeping an existing customer is less costly and more profitable than finding a new one. Unfortunately, the process routinely breaks down when companies fail to respond to their customers' e-mails in a timely way.

Implications for Internal Communication

Though less apparent, using the Internet to improve employee productivity and loyalty is making a major bottom-line contribution to organizational success. In fact, providing useful on-the-job information has become the source of about three-fourths of the value added in manufacturing, according to James Brian Quinn of Dartmouth's Amos Tuck School of Business Admnistration.[10]

Writing in *Communication World,* Richard Nemac describes this work as *knowledge management,* a set of processes that organizes knowledge and makes it easy to use, distribute, and share either from an individual workstation, by a "virtual team" of employees linked by a listserv, or with far-flung agency subsidiaries and branch operations.[11] We'll return to knowledge management practices later in this chapter.

Implications for Activists and New Stakeholders

Because of its ability to personalize messages, the Internet offers opportunities for relationship building or connecting people and organizations in ways not feasible with traditional media. Listservs, electronic bulletin boards, or usenet discussion groups are helping community groups, community leaders, and organizations understand one another's concerns and the common ground between them.

Public relations scholar Timothy Coombs has identified the Internet as a potential equalizer for activist organizations because now they can communicate directly with the organizations whose practices they oppose.[12] That's because the Internet is an affordable communication channel open to everyone, including groups and social movements that can't afford expensive public relations services. When organizations respond to queries and comments from activist groups, they begin to establish dialogue, to better understand each other's viewpoint, and to interact more in areas of common concern—all of which may lead to greater long-term interdependence, writes scholar Maureen Taylor.[13]

A Paradigm Shift Among Practitioners

All of these new Internet-based communication opportunities have led Dr. Donald Wright[14] to argue that the Internet represents a paradigmatic shift in corporate communications, opening the door to full two-way communication between a corporation and its publics. Therefore, it is incumbent upon corporate officers, he says, to develop policies supporting and effecting more interactive communication. To support this claim, Wright reports the following results from a study of senior-level public relations practitioners conducted for the Institute of Public Relations:[15]

> Seventy-nine percent of respondents said the Internet has already improved two-way communication between their company and its publics.
>
> Eighty-nine percent believe that the Internet (including intranets and extranets) will change how communications/public relations resources are deployed at their companies from now until the foreseeable future.
>
> Seventy-two percent of the surveyed communication policymakers believe that the Internet has forced their companies to consider broader social policy issues, including electronic privacy, security and commerce, and civil rights in cyberspace.
>
> Ninety-two percent said that their companies had developed guidelines for managing their organization's website development.

We should not close this discussion regarding the Internet's implications without first underscoring the need for some organizational unit not only to manage the website but also to enhance the organization's long-term reputation among its constituencies by ensuring that its key messages stand out among all the other website information. Because of their primary interest in reputation management, public relations practitioners may be best positioned to assume these responsibilities.

And finally, future public relations practitioners should be alerted to the fact that a joint IABC-PRSA study on the status and future of the profession conducted in 2000[16]

Music City: From Zero to Napster in 30 Days

Mini•Case 17.1

After Internet file-sharing company Napster announced its transition to a paid-subscription service, frustrated users tested other free networks such as Lime Wire, Gnutella, AIMster, and MusicCity. The crunch of new users forced MusicCity to develop a new software application called Morpheus that allowed users to trade digital files freely.

MusicCity asked KVO Public Relations (now Fleischman-Hillard) to help move at least 1,000 current users to Morpheus in 30 days before these users could switch to competing services. The agency's idea was to work directly with file sharers to request that they sign up their friends; more than 1 million people were encouraged to download and use Morpheus in less than a month.

But the bigger story was the type of Internet-based media relations approach that made this possible. MusicCity could not afford a large-scale media outreach plan, and its own team of 10 employees would be busy with development and operating issues. How to develop a media-based campaign "on the cheap" was a huge challenge.

Research and Planning

Initial research indicated that aggressive media relations such as extensive story pitching, press release distribution, and executive/founder exposure often resulted in coverage focusing on the company rather than the products' features. By studying Internet chatrooms, bulletin boards, relevant articles, and the reactions of file-sharing experts, KVO professionals discovered that Morpheus wasn't much different and certainly no better than competing services. Moreover, the client and the agency team worried that existing users would resent MusicCity's sudden switch to a proprietary service, that somehow it was selling out and would soon start charging as Napster had done. To counter these concerns, Fleischman-Hillard/KVO decided that the most feasible approach wouldn't be extensive media relations, but instead would be to approach users on a grassroots level, similar to Napster's beginnings. This approach would also help preserve MusicCity's independent or "indie" reputation, differentiating it from its overexposed competitors.

Objectives

With a total budget of only $20,000 and two months to execute the program, KVO set three campaign objectives for Morpheus:

1. Encourage at least 1,000 MusicCity users to download the Morpheus application. (Evaluation measure: download figures)
2. Preserve MusicCity's "indie" credibility and user-friendly brand. (Evaluation measure: user approval ratings)
3. Communicate with media economically. (Evaluation measure: substantial coverage of the product using a streamlined proactive effort.)

Strategy

Considering the objectives and limited budget, the agency advised MusicCity to reach out to users through the Internet: website, e-mail, instant messaging, and bulletin boards. The plan was to secure coverage in consumer technology and file-sharing publications while keeping a low profile in mainstream media to draw attention and intrigue from mainstream media who'd heard about Morpheus's high user interest.

With only two weeks for prelaunch activities, Fleischman-Hillard/KVO prepared all the copy, including material for the software application and the company's website as well as online marketing initiatives that included instant messages, e-mail messages, online bulletin board postings, and a frequently asked questions (FAQ) document for users. For media inquiries and outreach, they prepared agency spokespeople and MusicCity executives with mock interviews, media statements, and press releases. They filled a database with contact information on consumer technology and file-sharing media. Media inquiries were responded to with a combination of e-mail, phone, and Internet bulletin boards.

Once Morpheus launched, Fleischman-Hillard/KVO was flooded with phone calls and e-mails from users. Users appreciated the quick, meaningful customer support replies delivered through e-mail and acknowledged that Morpheus was a great alternative to Napster. These "converts" were then persuaded to spread the word to friends and asked that they rate Morpheus highly on Downloads.com where the application was available. Soon afterward the old users replied with tallies of new Morpheus converts, which in turn led to favorable ratings appearing in Downloads.com.

Agency staff studiously contacted consumer-technology and file-sharing publications regarding the launch and rapid growth of Morpheus. At this point, mainstream journalists noticed the Morpheus underground buzz on the Internet and then contacted Fleischman-Hillard for information. What followed were myriad articles announcing the launch. Thus, by highlighting the product's features and popularity first to niche publications, the mainstream media became enticed. And the product-centered articles preserved MusicCity's "indie" credibility. As a result, MusicCity appeared not only exotic, but also as an attractive subject among otherwise overly promotional start-ups clamoring for mainstream attention.

Consider the following results in light of the campaign objectives:

1. Approximately one month into the grassroots campaign, CNET's Downloads.com reported nearly 1 million downloads to Morpheus. As of January 25, 2002, Downloads.com had tallied more than 44 million downloads of the Morpheus application onto consumers' desktops.
2. Morpheus's approval rating jumped 50 percent at launch to 74 percent in 30 days. On January 25, 2002, the approval rating was at 92 percent.
3. Morpheus appeared in hundreds of articles, including coverage in mainstream and consumer-technology publications such as CNET, ZDNET, *New York Times, Wall Street Journal, Los Angeles Times, Industry Standard,* MTV, *Forbes,* Associated Press wire, *Fortune, Time, Webnoize, TEHVT, PC-World, San Francisco Chronicle,* Reuters news service, *Internet-com* file-sharing publications such as *Slyway.com,* and TV newscasts.

Lessons

Public relations can help organizations make big changes even with small budgets. Look what $20,000 accomplished here. The key was the strategy by which KVO received such substantial media coverage by directing the story first to the niche consumer technology and file-sharing publications. In turn, mainline media reporters picked up the story once their sources indicated the existence of a significant audience for file-sharing music services. The website, e-mail, chatrooms, and bulletin board channels were very useful as well. In addition, mainline journalists scored with their stories by illustrating the magnitude of the underground buzz among file sharers and the extent to which these users rely on Internet media largely unknown to the general public. And finally, the Fleischman-Hillard/KVO professionals incorporated a consumer response plan that followed up with e-mail contact to users who switched to Morpheus. E-mails acknowledged the importance of these users who doubtlessly contributed to their willingness to pass the word on to friends and virtual friends and to record their support through Downloads.com.

Source: Interview with Jeffrey Hardison, Fleischman-Hillard (formerly KVO Public Relations), Portland, Oregon.

reported that knowing technology uses offers the greatest opportunity for career advancement in public relations in coming years. See mini-case 17.1 for an example of a company that used the Internet strategically to accomplish its objectives.

PUBLIC RELATIONS AND GLOBAL MARKETS

The opening of worldwide markets throughout the latter part of the 20th century was a financial boon that redirected public relations practice and the structure of the industry. Consider, for instance, that 13 of the world's largest public relations agencies are now owned by advertising agencies. In turn, some of these already-big advertising/public relations firms are owned by or linked to other multinational conglomerates. The result is that these firms have sufficient resources to mount extensive public relations initiatives almost anywhere at any time. And that's exactly what's happening with 40–50% of annual revenue from leading U.S. advertising/public relations firms now coming from outside the United States.

Writing in *Communication World*, Brian Heiss and Edie Fraser reported that in world-class companies, the communication function leads in supporting the corporation in its globalization effort: "In the current era of globalization, corporations are faced with pressure to gain international market share and stockholders have made it increasingly important to keep global sales and stock prices high. The claims seem reflected in practice."[17]

Ray Kotcher, Ketchum's CEO, noted that in the mid-1990s the share of business at Ketchum on a worldwide basis was less than 25 percent. In 2001 the business that was shared across two or more geographies and/or practices was almost 50 percent.[18]

To meet these challenges and to elevate a corporation's global reputation, corporate communication teams need to be part of designing and implementing global strategy as described in the Starbucks case study (see mini-case 17.2). Doing public relations internationally involves infinitely more coordination and synchronization with foreign business partners, overseas local public relations firms, and a host of cultural norms and regulations not adhered to in the United States.

Heiss and Fraser have noted some of the ways in which public relations efforts are coordinated between headquarters and local subsidiaries on a global scale: "Globalization has increased the need for clear, consistent, and central corporate messages with adaptation at the local level. Companies must reach customers, potential customers, alliances, partners, employees, stakeholders, the investment community, distributors, media, government, trade and professional constituencies."[19] The trick seems to be for the multinational corporations to enhance their overall reputations and brand identities in ways that take advantage of local cultures, media availability, and political climates.

At the corporate level, the public relations function has three distinct aspects. In one role public relations practitioners represent multinational corporations at home, dealing with public opinion and governmental activities that relate both to specific corporations and to multinational enterprises as a whole. The second role of multinational public relations is to help bridge the communication gap that inevitably exists between foreign operations and top management in the world headquarters. Finally, public relations must be conducted in the corporation's various host countries. All this points to better internal communication.

Though public relations has been a critical component in the unfolding of the global economy, many practitioners are skeptical about the future. For example, will the big marketing/advertising/public relations conglomerates give disproportionate emphasis to customers at the expense of such other key constituencies as employees, local and national governments, and community and activist groups in the overseas communities where these firms are doing business for their corporate clients? Concerns of at least equal import arise at the societal level where thoughtful observers in other countries fear that economic globalization will lower their nations' and their citizens' economic viability by promoting consumer expectations that can't be met given substandard wages, cultural differences, and infrastructures that don't readily accommodate the global economy.

THE CHANGING INSTITUTION OF PUBLIC RELATIONS

At the outset of this chapter we asserted that public relations practice by 2010 would be very unlike what it has been. Already we have seen that new communication technologies speed up every dimension of the practice as well as encourage new and uncharted relationship building with established and emergent constituencies.

The capital that's been required to finance and shape the global economy into a more or less single market system places enormous pressures on short-term profits, on cutting planning cycles from years to months to weeks, not to mention the rush to adapt public relations procedures and practices to fit the cultural prerequisites of countries and regions of the world that businesses enter.

Taken together, these societal-level changes signal whole new formulations for public relations work. Today, public relations and corporate communications work is being integrated into broader communication processes to integrate organizations' operations as never before. By redefining themselves as communication experts and consultants—rather than more narrowly defined technical specialists in public relations—today's university communication and public relations majors will find themselves working within a more comprehensive public relations and communication management practice.

Try to imagine the extent of the long-range reputation management tasks facing organizations in light of the dot-com bulge and bust as well as the recent unscrupulous accounting practices to inflate stock prices. While all this was going on, most public relations practitioners—technically competent and highly motivated as they were—failed to understand and communicate the adverse effects of short-term profit taking on the protection and enhancement of the long-term reputation, the brands, and the franchise.

At least some of the blame might go to the mixed messages that people receive from organizations because content is added to their organizational intranets and extranets

17.2 Mini•Case — Starbucks Enters Global Markets

Specialty coffee company Starbucks is fast becoming as well known outside the United States as it is within. With more than 1,000 stores outside the United States, Starbucks's international business constitutes about 20 percent of total store units. The company opened its first international stores in 1996 in Japan. Today, Japan has the largest number of Starbucks's outlets outside the United States followed by the United Kingdom with about 300 stores. All told, Starbucks operates in 24 countries in Asia, Europe, and the Middle East.

The company's latest ventures are into Latin America, where Starbucks was scheduled to open 10 to 15 stores in Mexico by 2003 and a total of 900 stores across Latin America by 2005 with Mexico as the key location. Although Starbucks has plenty of room to grow in the United States judging from its 7 percent coffee market share, the company clearly is laying the groundwork for future growth once the U.S. business slows.

Rather than opening company-owned stores or subsidiary operations outside the United States, Starbucks locates business partners around the globe whose management philosophies and cultural sensitivities support Starbucks. And international public relations director Soon Beng Yeap gets in on the ground floor in selecting their overseas business partners.

"We want to know early on if partners help raise our reputation or will have problems. By sitting in on all discussions, I am able to ask questions and pose alternatives to our top executives. In terms of public relations, I am especially concerned with the prospective partner's issues, credibility, strength of his/her current brands, and financials. We need to know if their image is consistent with ours and what we want it to become. At the same time we're sizing up the prospective partner, we're learning more about all the cultural influences impinging on business, " Soon Beng says.

Once the partner is selected, public relations planning moves to overall launch plans, including media relations, internal or employee relations, community relations, corporate philanthropy, and dealing with activist organizations. Together with the business partner and perhaps a local agency, Starbucks's management considers all the cultural ramifications of the launch and seeks input on building community and media support and in attracting the most desirable local employees.

Starbucks does not advertise. Instead, it builds its brand image through effective media relations to gain the credibility that comes with third-party endorsement. Starbucks's credibility shoots up in the marketplace when reporter-written media coverage presents Starbucks favorably. This all comes about because Starbucks hosts elaborate media briefings months prior to a grand opening. A couple of months ahead of the scheduled opening, Starbucks invites top magazine and business editors from that region of the world to gather at Starbucks expense for a preview of the new store plans. When the reporters return home and write their stories, the published clips go into the press books that Starbucks distributes to local media just before the scheduled store opening. This process also works as a form of third-party endorsement in that the local media are induced to publicize the topics that have been covered by larger metropolitan, national, and global media.

Local public relations firms or agencies are selected to support on-site media relations and especially follow-up requests from reporters, to implement grand opening event plans, and to help initiate some of the community

Customers surf the Internet in Shinsei Bank in Tokyo where a Starbucks serves its vast array of coffees. Starbucks has built its brand image without costly advertising.

involvement activities. What's important, though, is that overall strategic planning remains either at corporate headquarters in Seattle or international division offices located in Amsterdam, Hong Kong, and Miami, Florida. By keeping public relations planning centralized, Starbucks hopes to build the brand image with message consistency and to be positioned to handle overall corporate reputation issues.

As corporate public relations director, Soon Beng Yeap also has input into employment issues because work norms vary from culture to culture. In Asia, for example, Starbucks employees wear name tags because uniforms and name tags are highly regarded both by employees and their families. Elsewhere, employee name tags might be seen as an invasion of privacy and tempting to potential stalkers. Public relations strategies are also employed to position Starbucks as the employer of choice by (1) producing a great working environment, (2), child care, (3) stock options, (4) dress down opportunities, (5) open access to executives, and (6) involvement in corporate-sponsored community service projects.

Starbucks's community relations programs are intended to reflect a corporate sense of social responsibility adjusted to varying laws and cultural and ethnicity issues. For instance, the community relations program begins with a community preopening to show the community that Starbucks wants its blessing and permission to operate there. Preopenings are set up as friends and family events with a guest list made up of community leaders, neighbors, and parents of employees.

In Asia, all first-day sales go to charity as selected by the employees. This simple gesture underscores giving back to the community. Because Starbucks's principal community relations program is the books for children literacy campaign, the company asks its international business partners if such a program would support community relations efforts there. The fact is that several U.S.-based community relations programs do not work abroad, including recycling, which is not seen as a respected or revered practice in many parts of the world.

This case study underscores several principles for conducting public relations work internationally. First, there's no single pattern governing how businesses expand globally; consequently, there's no single recipe for preparing international public relations programs. Second, the Starbucks case underscores the importance of understanding cultural differences and intercultural communication patterns and then refitting the public relations plan accordingly. And finally, the skillful use of media relations and third-party endorsement principles gives Starbucks sufficient high-level, free media coverage so that it has not yet had to use consumer advertising to implement its business model or to achieve desired profit levels.

Source: Interviews with Soon Beng Yeap, Starbucks corporate public relations director.

in such a haphazard manner. Rarely has a single unit been given responsibility for coordinating corporate Internet content so that the core themes and messages would dominate or at least be present most of the time. Instead, intranet and extranet sites became filled with submissions coming directly from the CEO's office, from the finance and legal offices, from marketing, from human resources, from various operating and production units, from public relations—not to mention the thousands of many and varied individual submissions.

Under these conditions, is it any wonder that users found it difficult to see the organization's big picture? To overcome the clutter and to highlight key messages, Jack Bergen, first president of the Council of Public Relations Firms, believes that intranet and extranet content control should reside in public relations and corporate communication, rather than either the information technology (IT) or human resources (HR) departments:

> The website is your company in cyberspace. You should control it. It helps you manage coalitions and it's the cheapest way of getting to a lot of people at one time. Use internal and external websites to develop communities of interest, building coalitions and establishing relationships with employees, customers, and other stakeholders.[20]

Rethinking Internal Communication

Loss of shareholder value and declining consumer confidence and organizational support have prompted many corporations, nonprofit organizations, and government agencies to reexamine their core communication processes and ways of doing things. In doing so, they can't help but note that increased employee productivity gains have boosted the bottom line. Using communication to increase productivity introduces whole new directions for the internal communication work taken on by public relations practitioners.

One such new direction, as noted earlier, is called knowledge management. **Knowledge management** is a collection of practices for getting products out the door faster by better ensuring that all employees have the right information they need at the right time. Knowledge management accounts for the ways an organization captures, stores, shares, and delivers information using appropriate software. Thus, as Kate Vitale has noted, knowledge management boosts the bottom line by creating smarter employees.[21] Knowledge management practices provide access to all who need it while simultaneously cutting information overload for those who don't. Behind these processes, then, are beliefs that employees come to feel more empowered and satisfied the more quickly they get the information they need.

To date, however, corporate communicators have not embraced knowledge management work, even though a recent IABC report[22] called it one of the three principal areas for organizational communication research. Ironically, corporate communicators are perhaps best trained and qualified to match the capabilities of different communication technologies with message types and desired outcomes.

Becoming a knowledge management consultant is only one such new internal communication role for public relations practitioners and communication managers. Another is to become a **change management expert,** someone who uses a wide range of communication skills to help change organizational cultures, to increase employee loyalty, and to assist the organization in adapting to intercultural conditions. For instance, the recent-year economic downturns have prompted companies to merge. When two or more previously separate organizations must now work together to accomplish the same goals, the skills of communication consultants become in real demand to build the new shared culture or dominant values and themes that must be communicated up, down, and across the organization.

Public relations professionals with some training in organizational communication are pivotal corporate change agents. They often begin with communication audits or diagnostic tools designed to assess the effectiveness of various internal communication processes. Audits uncover mismatches between information sought and information received, between channels used and channels preferred, satisfaction with the communication climate, and the most appropriate communication networks for different types of information.

Results from communication audits help public relations practitioners and communication managers to improve organizational effectiveness by incorporating new ideas more quickly and by being more responsive to changes in the overall environment(s) in which the organization operates. The need for this type of public relations expertise appears to be supported in findings from the 2002 Middleberg/Ross survey showing that 81 percent of respondents agreed that the ability to manage change would be the most fundamental component of business success in coming years.[23]

Changing Organizational Structures and Settings

The work and structure of public relations firms or agencies and corporate or organizational departments are changing relatively quickly as well and largely in response to technology, globalization, and the new publics whose interests have been previously shortsighted or overlooked.

One reason for the changes is that it is not altogether clear that existing public relations work captures a significant amount of the communication activity in organizations. In recent years, for example, corporations have willingly parceled out traditional public relations functions such that (1) the investor or financial relations component reports either through the financial or legal department, (2) the employee and newsletter work reports through the human resources department, which also takes on all sorts of communication training, (3) the product publicity and consumer relations work gets assigned to the marketing division, and (4) the public affairs and government relations work is directed to the legal department. Some believe that these varied reporting relationships represent encroachment on the public relations function, whereas others argue that such placement reflects the decentralized nature of communication work in organizations.

Another persistent and growing trend is for alternative work arrangements outside traditional firms and departments. This might include public relations specialists working as part of virtual teams on some sort of global project where the only contact with team members is through the Internet. Such work often requires dual reporting relationships, with the project supervisor being in charge until the work is completed, when the public relations practitioner again becomes more the direct responsibility of managers in her or his home department.

The 1980s and 1990s saw the rise of thousands of independent public relations and communication consultants who either work totally on their own or distribute some of their extra work to other independent consultants on a contract basis. Within the public relations field, independent consultants are now thought to represent the largest single job category or classification.

Within firms and agencies one clear trend is the move toward specialization by industry or by general practice areas such as health care or technology. Today, account coordinators and account managers are assigned to fewer clients and oftentimes within the same industry such as health care, technology, consumer goods, or financial services.

As well, the opening of global markets has brought about intensive consolidation of public relations agencies by advertising agencies. When public relations agencies are merged into advertising ones, the tendency is for relatively more of the work to be focused on product publicity or developing the public relations practices within an overall marketing framework.

Despite mergers and globalization impacts, very few of even the biggest public relations firms have or want the capacity to service their clients' needs in each of the world's cities and regions where the client does business. That's because many clients prefer the combination of having the overall public relations planning done by a single, multinational firm, but then parceling out much of the implementation work to local agencies who no doubt better understand the cultural traditions in their cities, the customary ways of working with local news media, and the community leaders whose support is often useful in mounting community and governmental relations efforts as well as in staging special events. The larger independent public relations firms or agencies respond to the need for localization by becoming partners or affiliates in networks of independent professionals located around the world. The largest of these are PRIO (Public Relations Organization International), Pinnacle Worldwide, IPREX (International Public Relations Exchange), and World Communication Group. Affiliating with networks of other independently owned firms provides opportunites to compete more effectively with multinational public relations and advertising conglomerates.

On the organizational or client side there's an ongoing examination of the mix of communication programs and activities undertaken in-house versus those assigned to firms or independent consultants and vendors. Typically, the communications or public relations department handles the core strategic planning functions in-house while subcontracting specific program planning, execution, and communication support services to firms and independents. In fact, during periods of economic recession corporate communicators are likely to bring more of the planning work back in-house, thereby casting the firm in more supportive and implementing roles.

In more healthy economic periods, though, what's left for the corporate communication department are media relations, managing issues and crises, and consulting with top management on long-term reputation management issues. Work that is typically outsourced includes routine media relations, some product publicity, events management, and selected community relations functions. A few corporations have adopted an in-house creative services model under which corporate communication specialists are assigned to various divisions or brands where they act like account executives for a firm or agency.

EVOLVING PRACTITIONER ROLES

Against this backdrop of new technology, global markets, and business responsibility issues, it's little wonder that practitioner roles are changing. We end this chapter by considering 10 evolving changes.

From External Counsel to Internal Communication Consultant

The field of public relations was established as a legitimate occupation and worthwhile field of study by a handful of ex-newspapermen and press agents in the early decades of the 20th century. These pioneers, for the most part, set up their own firms and frequently succeeded in building larger-than-life reputations for themselves as well as their clients. This external, independent counselor model of public relations practice quickly became the ideal.

The actual practice of public relations has evolved far beyond this original model. Although counseling firms have flourished, a new breed of practitioner has emerged, primarily within the structures of large, complex organizations. These practitioners are concerned with internal communication as well as external publicity.

Public relations specialists in organizations must understand the concerns and attitudes of customers, employees, investors, managers, special interest groups, and a vast array of publics. The job cannot stop with an understanding of these complex issues; public relations practitioners must be able to integrate their strategic planning skills into the organization's managerial decision-making process. Public relations practitioners of today and tomorrow must continue to exhibit high-quality communication skills to do the jobs for which they are hired. They must also understand both their role as managers affecting the actions of an organization and the importance of public relations input into the process.

Public relations is increasingly the responsibility of CEOs and top executives. Thus, part of the practitioner's job is to train and advise the organization's leaders on the appropriate uses of communication and in talking to the media.

From One-Way Communication to Two-Way Communication and Interaction

With its roots in rhetoric and persuasion, it's not surprising that campaign theory and concepts were initially designed as one-way publicity blitzes to create awareness and attitude change that might, in turn, influence behavior. Public relations theory development and conceptualization over the last quarter century, though, has focused on two-way communication that is more or less balanced between the organization and its key publics or constituencies.

The two-way symmetric, or balanced, communication formulation has been developed and tested over the past quarter century by James Grunig and colleagues at the University of Maryland.[24] Two-way communication processes involve infinitely broader and more comprehensive roles for public relations practice than one-way persuasion models ever did. Using two-way communication, practitioners now hope that their communication efforts will result in knowledge gain, understanding, and other high-order cognitive effects that are more likely to underpin longer-lasting relationships. Because two-way communication principles involve each group or side understanding the other's point of view, the process is more likely to lead to negotiation, compromise, and a host of win-win outcomes for all.

Two-way communication principles, unlike one-way principles, are best for maximizing the capabilities of e-mail and the Internet, including Listservs, chatrooms, electronic bulletin boards, and discussion groups. By promoting dialogue and conversation—rather than one-directional information flows—these new technologies help organizations create and continuously maintain ties to key publics.

From Marketing Support to Integrated Communication

Not very long ago, the primary justification for public relations was its effort to sell products. Public relations was seen as an adjunct to the sales effort, concerned primarily with product publicity, special events coordination, and getting free advertising.

For some time, though, the trend has been to move public relations work from a marketing adjunct role to the marketing communication mainstream. Public relations plays different marketing communication roles over the course of a product's life cycle. Prior to product launch, practitioners work with the trade press and through Internet sites to generate news stories and favorable product reviews that will be seen by major customers, distributors, wholesalers, and retailers. Closer to product launch they write product publicity features for publications and programs reaching target audiences. All of this product anticipation buildup happens before consumer advertising is launched.

From Program to Process

Traditionally, public relations has placed tremendous emphasis on programs and campaigns and other tangible outputs of public relations efforts, including news clips. In this sense, the job of the public relations practitioner has consisted of a progression of discrete tasks—media releases, publications, public service announcements, publicity campaigns, and the like. Such products and programs are still a time-consuming responsibility for public relations departments. They are the bulk of the expanding work of public relations agencies. One of the clearest observable trends in public relations, however, is the growing view that organizational communication is a continuous process, not just a succession of programs.

Although public relations practitioners will still develop and deliver specific products and programs, they will be increasingly involved in broader, less discrete responsibilities and more focused on multiple programs aimed at enhancing and preserving the long-term reputation. They will spend more time and effort developing communication objectives that are consistent with an organization's overall objectives. They will act as counselors to management and serve on teams with managers and other organizational specialists, working closely and cogently on a broad array of organizational programs. They will adopt a long-term, general perspective instead of specific short-term ones.

From Media Craftsperson to Communication Planner

Owing to the traditional emphasis on producing specific products and programs, public relations practitioners have been viewed as possessing a specific set of skills. Writing ability has always led the list, followed by speaking, interpersonal skills, and a potpourri of other abilities, including photography, graphic design, and the like. Over time, the skill base only gets broader and work more varied. Consider how much there is to know today about webpage design; expanded e-mail uses, including the intranet; and visual communication. And yet the greater the number of media and communication outlets, the greater the need for future practitioners to know how to use each medium most effectively and creatively. Knowing how to best use each of these skill sets or tactics is what makes public relations as much a thinking and planning process as it is a "doing" process.

From Short-Term Items to Long-Term Relationship Development

In times past, public relations practitioners sought to place items in the media and measured their effectiveness by their success. The current trend carries public relations away from that stage, through defending against negative publicity, and toward issues management.

Issues management is the identification of key issues confronting organizations and the management of organizational responses to them. This process involves early identification of potential controversies, development of organizational policy related to these issues, creation of programs to carry out policies, implementation of these programs, and communication with appropriate publics about these policies and programs and evaluation of the results.

The issues management process is an area in which public relations has its greatest potential in terms of contributions to managerial decision making. Organizations can avoid negative publicity and gain positive public notice by adapting in advance to environmental demands. In this way, they are able to reap benefits by being perceived as responsible leaders. Public relations practitioners must be prepared to identify and deal with issues that confront their organizations.

From Firefighters to Crisis Managers

Among the most fully established trends affecting public relations practitioners is the evolution of their role from being "firefighters" to "fire preventers." Effective public relations does not exist merely to clean up messes once they are made but seeks to avoid such dilemmas. Preventive public relations is a widely held ideal among practitioners. Public relations practitioners are moving into positions that allow them to more fully recognize areas of potential danger, to be equipped to deal with those dangers, and to possess sufficient power and influence to effect needed changes before potentials become realities. It is now standard practice for public relations practitioners to prepare and rehearse written crisis communication contingency. In fact, the crisis planning process gained steam in the months following the September 11, 2001, terrorist attack on New York's World Trade Center and the U.S. Pentagon in Washington, D.C.

From Manipulation to Understanding, Negotiation, and Compromise

Public relations was born as a manipulative art. Its intent was to achieve specific results in terms of customer response, election outcomes, media coverage, or public attitudes. Public relations' purpose was to communicate in such ways as to ensure the compliance of relevant publics' behavior and attitudes with an individual or organization's plans. The means, methods, and media of communication were determined by what it took to get the job done and little else. Stunts, sensationalism, and embellished, highly selective truth were the hallmarks of the trade.

Such crass manipulation made for short-term rather than long-term impact, thereby limiting the effectiveness of public relations. The fact is that public relations is still about persuasion and social influence. What's changed are the myriad sophisticated ways in which persuasive techniques are utilized today.

From a Male- to a Female-Dominated Profession

There were still more male than female public relations practitioners in 1983 when this book was first published. Today, however, female practitioners outnumber their male counterparts 71 percent to 29 percent. In recent years, female public relations graduates outnumber males almost 10 to 1. Even so, older males continue to hold a disproportionate number of senior and managerial level positions that carry higher salaries. Ongoing research attempts to understand gender-based differences in salary, rates of promotion, and leadership in the top public relations or communication corporate role.

From U.S. Profession to Global Profession

The last decade has seen worldwide expansion of public relations as a global function. Cultural, language, and legal differences make global public relations more difficult, but rapidly evolving communication technologies has made these barriers less of a factor. Marshall McLuhan's "global village" predicted almost 40 years ago has finally arrived. The future of public relations must take the global community into account in all its efforts.

In summary, the public relations profession is fast growing and fast changing in response to the Internet, the globalization of the economy, and the shrinking reputation of business. While still seen as a publicity and media relations function, public relations is becoming both more strategic in nature and also more broad based in its communication services. Beyond that, the future of public relations work seems to hinge on planning communication programs that serve an organization's business goals or overall strategic plan.

For self-testing and additional chapter resources, go to the student CD and the Online Learning Center at **www.mhhe.com/lattimore**

To learn more about emerging trends in public relations watch the interviews with Jeffrey Hardison, Clip #1; John Graham, Clip #6; Dawn Gilpin, Clip #12; and Cheryl Procter-Rogers, Clip #14, on the book's CD-ROM.

Public Relations Helps Latvia Establish Democracy

By Virginia Sullivan, APR
Arkansas State University
Jonesboro, Arkansas

In 1991 Latvia regained its independence from the U.S.S.R. and established a democratic government. The new government did not automatically declare all residents of Latvia as citizens, as some of the other new democracies had, because only one-third of the residents of Latvia were ethnic Latvians and nearly 25% of the rest of the residents were ethnic Russians. Strict citizenship laws were enacted to ensure the Latvians maintained governmental power and the government established the Latvian Naturalization Board in 1995. Due to distrust of the government, the LNB was initially regarded as a bureaucratic agency designed to prevent people from becoming citizens.

In 1998 the Latvian parliament passed a new, more lenient citizenship law and the LNB became proactive in improving its image as a helpful, friendly, and professional agency. With the assistance of a USAID funded program, the LNB launched a nationwide PR campaign to promote citizenship and the naturalization process in a sensitive, multicultural environment. One aspect of the campaign was a national student contest, which would solicit students from all ethnic backgrounds to participate in a four-tiered competition about Latvia's history, language, culture and specific topics on the naturalization process and social integration. The PR department of the LNB was in charge of setting up the program and worked with the LNB's branch offices to administer the competitions at the local, county, and district levels.

Throughout the year the PR department staged events such as the celebration of the 20,000th naturalized citizen, when the mayor of Riga and the head of the Naturalization Board presented special certificates to the country's newest citizen. By working with nongovernment organizations, the PR department mounted campaigns that ranged from naturalization brochures in Russian to several television productions in both Latvian and Russian featuring celebrities and university students. Other PR projects promoting the naturalization process included a contest for high school students to learn more about Latvia's history as well as citizenship and its process. These contests were held at local, regional, and national levels and received extensive media coverage.

With the aid of the USAID funds and a foreign PR consultant, the LNB promoted the student contest, "Toward a Civic Society," throughout the 1999–2000 school term. Schools with ethnic Russian students as well as Latvian and other ethnic nationalities provided teams for the competitions. As the teams proceeded from the city to district levels, the competitions were covered by one of the national TV networks, received extensive coverage in the local press, and pulled in family, school officials, and friends as spectators. The final competition was conducted near Riga with the head of the LNB on the panel of judges and the PR department in charge of writing the questions, grading the answers, and tallying the scores. While at each level the winning team was presented a prize, the grand prize for the final winners was a trip.

The result of the national campaign was an increased awareness of the naturalization process, more recognition of the LNB—both the headquarters in

Riga and the 14 branches throughout Latvia—and a doubling of the number of naturalized citizens during the year. In a content analysis of media coverage regarding Freedom House and the Naturalization Board, an independent agency found that more than 90 percent of the coverage was favorable and less than 5 percent was unfavorable. As the students learned more about citizenship and the naturalization process, so did their parents, siblings, other family members and friends. Because the heads of the LNB's branches were intimately involved in the student contest, often managing the contest and participating as judges, these members of the LNB improved the image of the LNB as a "friendly and professional" government agency.

Questions

1. How did a student contest improve the LNB's image? How could the LNB have better promoted the student contest? What other methods of publicity could the LNB have employed on a limited budget?
2. What are some other ways a community outreach program like this could improve the image of a government agency?
3. Was it wise to use the LNB's own branch heads to conduct the contest and to be judges? Could this have been perceived as a conflict of interest? What would have improved the integrity of the program?
4. How could more people have been reached to promote the naturalization process? How significant is local coverage of a program like the student contest?

Key Terms

change management expert
globalization
Internet
issues management
knowledge management
relationship marketing
rich media
World Wide Web

Use the CD-ROM and Online Learning Center at www.mhhe.com/lattimore to further your understanding of the following terms

Notes

1. Bob Grupp, "Public Relations Must Control the Web Site," *Public Relations Strategist* 5, no. 4 (Winter 2000), p. 34.
2. Carole Howard, "Technology and Tabloids: How the New Media World Is Changing Our Jobs," *Public Relations Quarterly* 45, no. 1 (Spring 2000), p. 9.
3. Steve Lawrence, "Access to Information on the Web," *Science* 280, no. 5357 (June 1998), p. 1815.
5. Howard, p. 9.
6. Don Middleberg and Steven Ross, "The Middleberg/Ross Media Survey: Change and Its Impact on Communications," Eighth Annual National Survey, 2002.
7. Ibid.

8. Don Middleberg, *Winning PR in the Wired World: Powerful Communications Strategies for the Noisy Digital Space* (New York: McGraw-Hill, 2001).
9. Ibid.
10. James B. Quinn, "Strategic Outsourcing: Leveraging Knowledge Capabilities," *Sloan Management Review* 40, no. 4 (Summer 1999), p. 9.
11. Richard Nemec, "What's New? Everything," *Communication World* 16, no. 7 (August/September 1999), pp. 21–24.
12. Timothy Coombs, *Ongoing Crisis Communication: Planning, Managing, and Responding* (Thousand Oaks, CA: Sage, 1999).
13. Maureen Taylor, Michael L. Kent, and William J. White, "How Activist Organizations Are Using the Internet to Build Relationships," *Public Relations Review* 27 (2001), p. 264.
14. Donald Wright, "Corporate Communications Policy Concerning the Internet: A Survey of the Nation's Senior-Level Corporate Public Relations Officers," Institute for Public Relations, 1998.
15. Ibid.
16. An IABC/PRSA Joint Survey of the Profession, "Profile 2000," *Communication World* (June/July, 2000).
17. Brian Heiss and Edie Fraser, "Is Your Company Ready to Go Global?" *Communication World* 17, no. 6 (August/September 2000), p. 29.
18. Ray Kotcher, "Roundtable: Future Perfect? Agency Leaders Reflect on the 1990s and Beyond," *Public Relations Strategist* 8, no. 3 (Summer 2001), p. 11.
19. Heiss and Fraser, pp. 29–30.
20. An interview with Jack Bergen.
21. Kate Vitale, "Knowledge Management: An Executive Summary for Busy Practitioners," *Journal of Communication Management* 3, no. 2 (November/December 1998), pp. 44–51.
22. IABC, "Think Tank Report," www.iabc.com, retrieved November 2002.
23. Middleberg/Ross survey.
24. James Grunig and Todd Hunt, *Managing Public Relations* (New York: Holt, Rinehart & Winston, 1984).

Glossary

A

action assembly theory Understanding a person's behavior by understanding how that person thinks.

action implementation Any attempt to spread information within a target audience as part of a public relations plan.

active public People who are aware of a problem and will organize to do something about it.

advocacy communication Communication techniques used by advocates of a political cause or public policy change.

agenda Items or ideas the public relations practitioner wants to get across in a media interview.

annual meetings Yearly meetings at which a corporation's stockholders have the opportunity to meet and vote on various issues related to company management.

annual reports Yearly reports to stockholders prepared by publicly held corporations, containing required financial performance information and other material designed to promote the organization.

appropriation Commercial use of an entity's picture, likeness, or name without permission.

audience coverage Whether and how well intended publics were reached, which messages reached them, and who else heard the messages.

audit An evaluation and inventory of an organizational system.

authoritarian cultures Centralized decisions made in organizations by top management.

aware public People who know about a problem but don't act on it.

B

boundary spanners Public relations people who look inside and outside of the organization to anticipate issues, problems, and opportunities.

B-roll Extra video footage often sent along with a video news release (VNR) for use by TV stations to prepare their own video stories about the topic on the video.

brainstorming A technique of group discussion used to generate large numbers of creative alternatives or new ideas.

brandstanding Corporate sponsorship of special events as a way of getting publicity and gaining goodwill.

branded news An independent electronic news outlet that uses a corporate-sponsored website as its vehicle for reporting in-depth news about one particular industry.

C

cause-related marketing Effort by corporations to let their customers give some of the proceeds of the sale or other transaction to particular nonprofit groups or causes.

change management expert Someone who assists an organization in adapting to various changes, especially in relation to change in culture.

civil libel Cases involving published, defamatory information showing negligence and identifying the injured party; the injured party seeks monetary damage under civil statutes.

closed-system evaluation A pre-/post-event assessment that considers only the controlled message elements.

code of ethics A formal set of rules governing proper behavior for a particular profession or group.

cognitive processes Operations we use to take in, transform, and store information.

cognitive structure A script, schema, or frame that defines how we expect a story to unfold.

collective bargaining A continuing institutional relationship between an employer and a labor organization concerned with the negotiation, administration, interpretation, and enforcement of contracts covering wages, working conditions, and other issues related to employment.

commercial speech Public communication by business organizations through advertising or public relations to achieve sales or other organizational goals.

communication audit Research to determine the flow of communication within an organization.

communication climate The degree of trust and openness that exists in the communication processes of an organization.

communication policies Final statements of organizational positions related to communication activities and behaviors and information sharing.

community relations A public relations function consisting of an institution's planned, active, and continuing participation with and within a community to maintain and enhance its environment to the benefit of both the institution and the community.

conference call (financial) Video or phone conference with the chief executive officer (CEO) and the chief financial officer (CFO) of a company and analysts, financial reporters, and other investment stakeholders. The call usually is scheduled the day following the release of a quarterly report to enable the CEO and CFO to explain the meaning behind the numbers to the financial stakeholders.

consumer relations The aspect of public relations that improves the organization's relationships and communication with consumers. This includes resolving customer complaints, disseminating consumer information, dealing with outside consumer advocacy groups, and advising management on consumer opinion.

content Refers to specific characters, details, and plot twists within the basic structure.

content analysis Systematic coding of messages into categories that can be statistically analyzed.

contract A legal instrument that protects the rights of two or more parties.

controlled media Those media that the public relations practitioner has actual control over, such as a company newsletter.

copyright Legal protection from unauthorized use of intellectual property fixed in any tangible medium of expression.

corporate philanthropy Recognition of corporate obligations and responsibilities to communities represented by monetary and other contributions to charitable organizations.

corporate public relations Public relations activities that are intended to build a sound relationship between the organization and its employees.

counseling firm A public relations or marketing company hired by another organization to help with campaigns or run an entire public relations function.

criminal libel Public defamatory communication causing breach of the peace or incitement to riot; the state, or the injured party through the government, seeks punishment under criminal statutes, which may result in fine, imprisonment, or both.

crisis A situation, issue, or event that attracts public scrutiny through mass media and disrupts an organization's working environment.

crisis plan A standing public relations action plan to deal with how to react to crisis situations that is instituted the moment a crisis occurs.

cross-disciplinary integration Messages from all media are consistent.

cyberspace A term used to refer to the place where online conversations and information exchange take place.

D

defamation Any communication that holds a person up to contempt, hatred, ridicule, or scorn.

descriptive data Data used to describe something, such as a particular group of people (a public).

desk-side briefings A visit made by a public relations practitioner to a member of the media to pitch a story idea, provide background information, and update the reporter on current activities.

diffusion of information The way in which information spreads through a public.

diffusion theory Theory that states people adapt an idea only after going through five stages: awareness, interest, evaluation, trial, and adoption.

dominant coalition People who have the power to direct their organizations.

E

elaborated likelihood model A cognitive processing model that explains whether people skim messages for relevant cues (peripheral processing) or read and think through the material (central processing).

employee benefits Aspects of employee compensation, often including health and life insurance, vacation and sick leave, pension programs, and other valuable considerations.

employee communication A special audience within an organization that management must communicate with in order to have good internal public relations.

employee relations Public relations activities that are intended to build a sound relationship between the organization and its employees.

environment A concept in systems theory that suggests that organizations exist within social, political, and economic arenas.

environmental mediation Other influences that affect a campaign and are outside the control of the public relations practitioner.

environmental monitoring Formal systems for observing trends and changes in public opinion that are used either once, periodically, or continuously.

environmental scanning The monitoring, evaluating, and disseminating of information to key decision makers within an organization.

ethics The criteria for determining what is right and wrong based on standards of conduct and morality.

evaluation An examination of the effectiveness of a public relations effort.

experimental research Scientific testing that usually includes a control group that isn't tested; test results from the group or groups tested can be measured against the control group to seek to determine the extent of difference.

extranet An Internet-based external communication system that organizations use as a link to the media and other outside stakeholder groups.

F

fair comment A defense against libel, the expression of opinion on matters of public interest.

fair use Permission to use creative expression of others without compensation; it is based on four criteria specified in the 1976 Copyright Law.

Federal Communications Commission (FCC) A regulatory body established in 1934 to regulate television and radio broadcasting.

Federal Trade Commission (FTC) That federal government regulatory body charged with ensuring fair dealing in relation to goods and services in terms of such things as truth in advertising; it governs all commercial advertising.

feedback Information received in response to actions or messages about those actions or messages.

financial analysts Investment counselors, fund managers, and others whose function is to gather information about various companies, develop expectations of the companies' performances, and make judgments about how securities markets will evaluate these factors.

financial press Media outlets devoted to coverage of business and financial information.

financial public relations The process of creating and maintaining investor confidence and building positive relationships with the financial community through the dissemination of corporate information.

First Amendment The initial section of the United States Bill of Rights that guarantees the freedoms of press, speech, assembly, and religion.

focus group A small group of people representative of a demographic or other characteristic of an organization's various publics who are called together, usually only once, to give advance reaction to a plan.

Food and Drug Administration (FDA) The agency that regulates labeling, packaging, and sale of food, drugs, and cosmetics.

formal research Scientific research or information gathering.

formative evaluation Monitoring of a program or campaign at various intervals as it progresses to determine what is working and what isn't and where changes need to be made.

Form 10-K, Form 10-Q, and Form 8-K Reports required by the Securities and Exchange Commission from publicly traded companies.

for-profit organization An organization in which any extra monies not spent on overhead and operating expense are distributed on a prorated basis to company owners.

Freedom of Information Act (FOIA) A law passed in 1966, and amended in 1974, requiring disclosure of certain categories of government information.

FTP File transfer protocol, the main means by which one retrieves files from the Internet.

G

gatekeeper An individual who is positioned within a communication network so as to control the messages flowing through communication channels.

globalization The process of developing worldwide markets and overall economic interdependence among the nations of the world.

goals Basic direction of an organization or other entity. Goals are generally considered to be the top priority within an organization because they provide a sense of direction.

grassroots lobbying Organizing local constituencies to influence government decision makers.

guerrilla tactics The concept of using nontraditional communication vehicles to gain visibility for a product or service. Sidewalk art, Internet chatrooms, and radio talk shows are some examples of guerrilla tactics.

H

home page A site on the Internet or World Wide Web where one can place data, including words, sound, and graphics, to be retrieved by Internet users.

I

impact analysis Measuring the results of a public relations effort to determine its effect on an organization's program.

inferential data Information that not only characterizes a particular group or situation but also allows researchers to draw conclusions about other groups or situations.

informal research Nonscientific research or information gathering.

information subsidy The savings in reporter time that media organizations are said to gain when they accept news releases and video materials from organizations.

integrated communication Coordinating public relations, marketing, and advertising to create and strengthen the relationship the organization has with a consumer while selling the product or service.

integrated marketing communication Another term used for coordination of public relations, marketing, and advertising to create and strengthen relationships the organization has with a consumer while selling the product or service.

internal media Channels of communication controlled by the organization and directed to audiences within the organization.

Internet A vast, interconnected computer network that allows computers anywhere in the world to communicate instantly with computers in another part of the country or the world.

interpersonal communication The exchange of messages between individuals through which needs, perceptions, and values are shared and by which mutual meanings and expectations are developed.

intervening public People who may make it more difficult for an organization to reach those it is aiming to influence or gain approval from.

interviews Gathering of information from a respondent; they may be obtained in person, on the phone, by mail, or on the Internet.

intranet An Internet-based internal communication system that organizations use as a link to employees and board members.

intrusion Surreptitious recording or observing of other people's private documents, possessions, activities, or communications.

invasion of privacy Four areas in which one entity may violate the privacy of another: appropriation, publication of private information, intrusion, or publication of false information.

investment conferences Meetings attended by investment professionals especially for the purpose of hearing company presentations.

issue advertising (advocacy advertising) Advertising designed to communicate an organization's stand on a particular issue and seeking to generate support for that position.

issues management The process of identifying issues that potentially impact organizations and managing organizational activities related to those issues.

K

key contacts People who either can influence the publics an organization is trying to reach or who have direct power to help the organization.

knowledge management The computer-based system designed to increase productivity by getting the right information to the right people at the right time.

L

latent public People who are not aware of an existing problem.

law The rules of conduct established and enforced by authority in society.

libel Published defamation by written or printed words or in some other physical form that is communicated to a third party.

licensure A formal certification process that indicates a person measures up to a set of professional standards and qualifications.

lobbying The practice of trying to influence governmental decisions, usually done by agents who serve interest groups.

M

malice A requirement of civil libel in cases involving public figures that states that the plaintiff must show the defendant's knowledge of the falsity of published material, or a reckless disregard for the truth.

management by objectives (MBO) A process that specifies that supervisors and employees will jointly set goals for employees; usually followed by a joint evaluation of the employee's progress after a set period of time.

marketing Business discipline concerned with building and maintaining a market for an organization's product or services. It focuses externally on selling and how quality, availability of a product, or service affect its ability to be sold in the marketplace.

mass opinion The consensus of the public at large.

media kits See *press kit.*

media relations Activities that are intended to build open channels of communication between an organization and the media, as a way of sharing news and features of potential interest to media audiences.

mission statement Defines the overall direction for an organization.

model A way of looking at something.

moderating publics Those people who could make it easier for an organization to get its message through to the public it really wants to reach.

N

National Labor Relations Board (NLRB) That federal government regulatory body charged with overseeing union activities and union/management relations. It governs communication between unions and employers.

network Two or more computers linked together.

news conferences Structured opportunities to release news simultaneously to multiple media with an opportunity for the media personnel to ask the subjects questions.

news release A news story prepared for the media by the organization.

newsroom An area set aside to provide information, services, and amenities to journalists covering a story.

nonprofit organization A group or company whose primary purpose is not to make a profit, regardless of whether it actually does so in a given year.

O

observations Data or information secured by observing; qualitative evidence as contrasted with experimental or scientific evidence.

off-the-record An agreement with an interviewer not to print information provided.

online A situation where two or more computers are "talking" to each other.

open-system evaluation An ongoing assessment of the effectiveness of public relations actions considering the impact of uncontrolled elements.

opinion leaders People who are instrumental in influencing other people's attitudes or actions.

organizational culture The values, symbols, meanings, beliefs, and ways of doing things that integrate a group of people who work together.

P

participative cultures Organizational environment in which employees are empowered to make decisions in the organization.

planned publicity Publicity that is the planned result of a conscious effort to attract attention to an issue, event, or organization.

policies Types of standing plans that serve as a guide for decision making and usually are set by top management.

political action committees (PACs) A group of people who raise or spend at least $1,000 in connection with a federal election.

press agents Individuals who use information as a manipulative tool, employing whatever means are available to achieve desired public opinion and action.

press kit A collection of publicity releases packaged to gain media attention; often called "media kit."

primary public The group of people an organization ultimately hopes to influence or gain approval from.

primary research The gathering of information that is not already available.

prioritize Put in order of most important to least important.

privacy rights Protection from unauthorized intrusion into a person's private life.

privilege A defense against libel; the allowance of what might otherwise be libelous because of the circumstances under which a statement was produced. A person has "qualified privilege" to report fairly and accurately a public meeting or record, even if it turns out to be untrue.

proactive Taking an action(s) to be on the offensive.

pro bono Professional services provided without compensation.

procedures Types of standing plans that consist of standard instructions for performing common tasks; procedures carry out an organization's policies.

product liability The principle that companies are responsible for any damage or disease that might be caused by the use of their products.

propaganda of the deed Provocative actions designed solely to gain attention for ideas or grievances.

proxy Absentee voting rights; in publicly held companies stockholders may give their "proxy" to someone else to vote based on their shares of stock.

public affairs That aspect of public relations dealing with the political or governmental environment of organizations.

public information/public affairs officers (PIOs/PAOs) Public relations practitioners working for the U.S. government or other institutions using those titles.

public opinion An attitudinal measure of the image a public holds concerning some person, object, or concept that is a collection of opinions within society.

public opinion surveys Surveys to measure the attitudes and opinions of specific audiences.

public participation programs or citizen involvement programs Government-mandated programs to assess the social impacts of proposed changes on affected individuals, groups, and organizations.

public relations A management function that helps define an organizational philosophy and direction by maintaining communication within a firm and with outside forces and by monitoring and helping a firm adapt to significant public opinion.

public relations audit A research process to determine what the image of an organization is both internally and externally.

public relations counselor One who works with both publics and organizations in the effort to create relationships of mutual benefit and support.

publicity Publication of news about an organization or person for which time or space was not purchased.

publics Groups of individuals tied together by a sense of common characteristics or responses.

Q

qualitative research A method of delving into audience opinion without relying on formal, rigorous, number-based research methods.

questionnaire List of questions used to gather information or to obtain a sample of opinion.

R

readability study An assessment of the difficulty an audience should have reading and comprehending a passage.

readership survey A study to determine the characteristics, preferences, and reading habits of an audience.

regulation A proposition underlying systems theory that maintains that the behavior of systems is constrained and shaped by interaction with other systems.

relationship marketing Another term related to integrated marketing. It focuses on building relationships with consumers through marketing, advertising, and public relations.

rich media Media channels that more closely resemble face-to-face communication because they allow for continual feedback and touch more of the senses by incorporating words, visuals, and sound.

roles The collection of daily activities that people do.

rules Statements that specify the action to be taken in a particular situation.

rumor An unconfirmed report, story, or statement that gets into general circulation.

S

sample A subset of a population or public.

scenario construction A forecasting tool that explores likely consequences of alternative courses of action in a hypothetical, logical future situation.

seat at the table The inclusion of the public relations head on the executive management team.

secondary research The gathering of available information from published sources.

Securities and Exchange Act of 1934 Requires adequate publicity for sale of stocks and full disclosure of any pertinent information when it becomes available; it set up the Securities and Exchange Commission to regulate financial markets.

Securities and Exchange Commission (SEC) Federal government regulatory body established by Congress in 1934 to oversee the trade of stocks and bonds and the operations of financial markets.

selective attention Attending to only a few messages.

selective perception Filters composed of needs, values, attitudes, expectations, and experiences through which individuals selectively process messages to derive meaning.

simple random sampling A technique that allows each member of a public an equal chance of being selected.

single-use plans Plans developed for use in one specific situation.

situational theory A principal technique for segmenting audiences in public relations based on their likelihood of communicating.

slander Oral defamation.

social audit Research to determine the social programs of an organization to determine its ability to be a socially responsible organization.

social exchange theory A theory that assumes individuals and groups choose strategies based on perceived rewards and costs.

social learning theory A theory that attempts to explain and predict behavior by looking at ways individuals process information.

spontaneous publicity Publicity accompanying unplanned events.

stakeholder analysis Method for characterizing publics according to their interest in an issue.

stakeholders Individuals or groups who perceive themselves as having an interest in the actions of an organization.

standing plans Plans for dealing with certain types of situations, particularly common situations and emergencies.

strategic plans Long-range plans concerning a group's major goals and ways of carrying them out. These plans usually are made by top management.

summative evaluation Measurement to determine the success or failure in reaching a program or campaign's objectives that is done at the completion of the program.

survey research A formal or scientific study usually accomplished through the use of a questionnaire administered to a sample of the audience being studied.

systems theory A theory that suggests how organizations are made up of interrelated parts and how they use these parts to adapt to the environment.

Sunshine Act A law requiring meetings of governmental boards, commissions, and agencies to be open to the public.

systematic sampling A technique that uses a list to select a sample at random.

T

tactical plans Short-range plans for accomplishing the steps that lead up to achievement of an organization's goals. These plans are carried out at every level of an organization and on an everyday basis.

target audience The primary group an organization is trying to influence.

target market Communication with key publics to support the marketing function.

target publics Key publics concerned with common issues.

technicians Public relations practitioners who perform the skills of writing, editing, or producing the public relations materials.

tender offer An offer above the market price of the company's stock that is high enough to entice shareholders to sell despite their loyalty to the company.

theory An explanation or belief about how something works.

third-party endorsements Testimonials or other support for an organization, person, or product by someone outside the organization to give validity to the message.

tool integration Communicator chooses from a mix of media to use the medium or media needed to reach internal and external audiences necessary for a particular campaign.

trademark A legally protected name, logo, or design registered to restrict its use to the owner.

U

uncontrolled media Those media whose actions are not under the public relations practitioner's control, such as community newspapers and radio stations.

universe A system providing the environment for ecosystems.

uses and gratifications theory A theory that asserts people are active and selective users of media.

V

variable Object or event that can be measured or manipulated.

Video News Release (VNR) A video package sent as a news story for use on television news broadcasts.

W

World Wide Web Another term for the Internet, or interconnected computer system.

written consent Defense against invasion of privacy and copyright violation when permission is given in writing.

Cre

Chapter 1

Page 1: © ThinkStock; **p. 7:** Created by Agustín BarónContrasida-aids.org; **p. 13:** © Fisher-Thatcher/Getty Images

Chapter 2

Page 23: © Bettmann/CORBIS; **p. 34:** © Rachel Epstein/Photo Edit

Chapter 3

Page 47: Photo courtesy of Stacey Smith; **p. 50:** © Thinkstock/Getty Images

Chapter 4

Page 71: © Phyllis Picardi/Stock Boston; **p. 77:** © Reuters NewMedia Inc./CORBIS

Chapter 5

Page 89: © ThinkStock; **p. 96:** © Spencer Grant/Stock Boston; **p. 102:** © Michael Newman/Photo Edit

Chapter 6

Page 118: © Alex Wong/Getty Images; **p. 122:**, Photo courtesy of Topeka Civic Theatre & Academy

Chapter 7

Page 137: © Jonathan Nourok/Getty Images

Chapter 8

Page 156: © Jonathan Nourok/Photo Edit; **p. 168:** AP/Wide World Photos

Chapter 9

Page: 175: © PhotoDisc/Getty Images; **p. 179:** © Spencer Grant/Stock Boston; **p. 193:** Used with permission by Brunswick Bowling & Billiards Corp.; **p. 197:** © Lou Dematteis/The Image Works

Chapter 10

Page 204: © PhotoDisc/Getty Images; **p. 209:** © Marty Katz/The Image Works

Chapter 11

Page 228: © Michael J. Doolittle/The Image Works; **p. 241:** © PhotoDisc/ Getty Images

Chapter 12

Page 257: Courtesy of Chick-fil-A; **p. 258:** Used with permission by Brunswick Bowling & Billiards Corp.; **p. 260:** Courtesy of California Raisin Marketing Board

Chapter 13

Page 290: © David Young-Wolff/Photo Edit; **p. 293:** Courtesy of O'Charley's; **p. 295:** Courtesy of O'Charley's, LTV and American Funds

Chapter 14

Page 299: © Photo Disc/Getty Images; **p. 306:** © AFP/CORBIS; **p. 313:** AP/Wide World Photos

Chapter 15

Pages 326, 330: Courtesy of North American Mission Board, SBC

Chapter 16

Page 350: © Jonathan Nourok/Photo Edit; **p. 356:** © Reuters NewMedia Inc./CORBIS; **p. 363:** Used by permission from Lucent Technologies Inc.

Chapter 17

Pages 375, 380: AP/Wide World Photos.

Index

A

B

C

D

E

F

G

H

I

J

K

L

M

N

O

Q

R

S

T